D0828407

A POET'S *Glossary*

Edward Hirsch

Houghton Mifflin Harcourt
Boston ❧ New York

For information about permission to reproduce selections from this book, write to Permissions, Houghton Mifflin Harcourt Publishing Company, 215 Park Avenue South, New York, New York 10003.

www.hmhco.com

Library of Congress Cataloging-in-Publication Data is available.
ISBN 978-0-15-101195-7

Book design by Greta Sibley

Printed in the United States of America
DOC 10 9 8 7 6 5

Credits appear on pages 708–709.

To Poetry

Don't desert me
just because I stayed up last night
watching *The Lost Weekend.*

I know I've spent too much time
praising your naked body to strangers
and gossiping about lovers you betrayed.

I've stalked you in foreign cities
and followed your far-flung movements,
pretending I could describe you.

Forgive me for getting jacked on coffee
and obsessing over your features
year after jittery year.

I'm sorry for handing you a line
and typing you on a screen,
but don't let me suffer in silence.

Does anyone still invoke the Muse,
string a wooden lyre for Apollo,
or try to saddle up Pegasus?

Winged horse, heavenly god or goddess,
indifferent entity, secret code, stored magic,
pleasance and half wonder, hell,

I have loved you my entire life
without even knowing what you are
or how — please help me — to find you.

Acknowledgments

My dear friend and colleague André Bernard first convinced me to write a glossary for *How to Read a Poem and Fall in Love with Poetry*. Everything here flows from that initial idea. He generously went over the manuscript of *A Poet's Glossary* letter by letter, and it is a much clearer book because of his editorial hand, his decisive pencil, which I welcomed. I owe a special debt of thanks to my friend and editor Andrea Schultz, who gently but stubbornly coaxed this book out of me, and has seen it through with her characteristic good will and clear judgment. Special thanks, too, to her exemplary team at Houghton Mifflin Harcourt, especially Naomi Gibbs, who cleared the permissions, and Anne McPeak, who copyedited the manuscript. I am also eager to acknowledge my exemplary agent, Liz Darhansoff. I had three excellent short-term assistants who were lent to me by the MFA program at Hunter College, Sue Nacey, Sarah Eggars, and Micah Towery, all of whom worked on the book. I am grateful to the many poets, near and far, who have talked over so many of the topics of poetry with me over the years. Their impress is everywhere apparent. My deep gratitude goes out to Lauren Watel, my love, who read this book through entry by entry, letter by letter, with her characteristically keen intelligence and scrupulous eye. I know I haven't always succeeded, but I've tried to meet her high standards.

Preface

This book — one person's work, a poet's glossary — has grown, as if naturally, out of my lifelong interest in poetry, my curiosity about its vocabulary, its forms and genres, its histories and traditions, its classical, romantic, and modern movements, its various outlying groups, its small devices and large mysteries — how it works. I hope it will be pleasurable to read and useful to study. It's intended for both initiated and uninitiated readers, something to keep at hand, a compendium of discoveries that has befriended me. It's a book of familiar and unfamiliar terms, some archaic, others modern, some with long and complicated histories, others newly minted. The alphabetical format may feel cool, but the hand that made the art was warm, and this book is animated by the practitioners who made poetry their own: the rational and the irrational, the lettered and the unschooled, those who would storm the barricades and tear down the castle, those who would rebuild it, the high priests of art, the irreverent tricksters, the believers and the skeptics, the long-lived purists and the doomed romantics, the holy eccentrics, the critics, the craftsmen, and the seers (singers, chanters, listeners, readers, writers); my quarrelsome friends, an extended family of makers. I've tried to figure out what they've been up to over the centuries.

This book is as definitive, inclusive, and international as I could make it — the reader will find terms from a wide variety of poetries, oral and written, lyric and epic. I've included examples whenever feasible. But it's also selective — I've inevitably followed my own interests and inclinations. This project has something of the madness of a Borgesian encyclopedia, since every culture has its own poetry, usually in its own language. It would be impossible to include all the terms in all the languages. I've explained what I can. I'm grounded in our moment, in the history of English and American literature, but I've also looked for guidance to Hebrew and Arabic poetry, to Greek and Latin poetry, to the European poetries, east and west, to Irish,

Welsh, and Scottish poetry, to Russian and Scandinavian poetry, to Chinese and Japanese poetry, to African, South Asian, and Latin American poetry. I've left things out, sometimes inadvertently, I'm sure. I've relied on many different sources — literary, historical, folkloric, anthropological, linguistic, and philosophical — and built on the work of others, but the mistakes are my own. I take responsibility for what's here and what's not. This is the result of years of engagement.

I've learned a tremendous amount in researching this book over the past fifteen years. As I've worked, I've often found myself transported to different time periods and countries, placing myself here and there, wondering what it would have been like to be a poet in the heady days of eighth-century China, or twelfth-century Provence, or thirteenth-century Florence, or fourteenth-century Andalusia, or fifteenth-century Wales, or seventeenth-century Japan, or early nineteenth-century England, or late nineteenth-century Ireland, or early twentieth-century Russia . . . I move freely among the bards, scops, and griots, the tribal singers, the poets of courtly love who sang for their mistresses, the court poets who wrote for their supper, the traveling minstrels, the revolutionaries, the flâneurs, the witnesses. I've encountered a series of recurring questions and debates about style and language, like the unresolved argument about the merits of the plain and the baroque style, or about the role of poetry in culture and society. There has been an ongoing quarrel, played out in many different countries, between tradition and innovation, the local and the international, the home-grown and the cosmopolitan. What language does one use, what forms does one employ? To whom is the poet responsible, and to what? Poetry, too, takes part in conversations about identity and nationalism. I've been surprised in my research by the sheer number of poetic contests throughout history. We may think of poetry as a noncompetitive activity, or as a competition with oneself, a struggle between the poet and the poem, but poetry competitions have kept cropping up over the years. The aesthetic debates, seldom good-natured, have also been fierce. I've tried to understand the intensities, to figure out what's at stake, and welcomed the contestants into the tent.

The devices work the magic in poetry, and a glossary gives names to those devices. It unpacks them. I believe its purpose is to deepen the reader's initiation into the mysteries. Here, then, is a repertoire of poetic secrets, a vocabulary, some of it ancient, which proposes a greater pleasure in the text, deeper levels of enchantment.

abecedarian An alphabetical acrostic in which each line or stanza begins with a successive letter of the alphabet. The word derives from the names of the first four letters of the alphabet plus the suffix "-arius" (*abecedarius*). The abecedarian, which generally starts with the first letter of the alphabet and runs to the final letter, is an ancient form often employed for sacred works. Most of the acrostics in the Hebrew Bible are alphabetical, such as Psalm 119, which consists of twenty-two eight-line stanzas, one for each letter of the Hebrew alphabet. The first eight lines all begin with the letter *aleph,* the next eight lines begin with the letter *beth,* and so on for 176 verses until the final *tav.* The completeness of the form, a tour de force, enacts the idea of total devotion to the law of God.

The abecedarian originally had powerful associations with prayer. In 393, Saint Augustine composed an alphabetical psalm against the Donatists, *"Psalmus contra partem Donati."* Geoffrey Chaucer was probably familiar with some vulgate translations of Psalm 119 into Medieval Latin, and he employed the abecedarian in his twenty-four-stanza poem entitled "An A.B.C." (ca. 1370), a translation of a French prayer ("The Prayer of Our Lady"). Each stanza begins with a letter of the Medieval Latin alphabet, progressing from A to Z. Ronald Knox adapts the biblical precedent in his re-creation from the Hebrew of the "Lamentations of the Prophet Jeremiah: An alphabet of Patience in Misery" (1950).

The Japanese *iroha mojigusari* (literally "character chain") is a specialized version of the abecedarian. The first letter of the alphabet kicks off the first line and the second letter of the alphabet concludes it. The third letter starts the second line and the fourth letter finishes it. This continues until all the letters of the alphabet have been used in order.

In 1940, Gertrude Stein set out to write a "book I would have liked as a child," an episodic A to Z poem, which eventually turned into a romp through the alphabet called *To Do: A Book of Alphabets and Birthdays* (1957). The abecedarian has been revived in contemporary poetry with experimental force. Paradoxically, the arbitrary structure triggers verbal extravagances. Thus Carolyn Forché follows a rigorous alphabetical order in her long poem "On Earth" (2003). The contents of Harryette Mullen's *Sleeping with the Dictionary* (2002) are arranged alphabetically, beginning with "All She Wrote" and ending with "Zombie's Hat." The title section of Barbara Hamby's *The Alphabet of Desire* (2006) contains twenty-six abecedarians. Karl Elder's *Gilgamesh at the Bellagio* (2007) contains two sequences of fifty-two ten-syllable lines: the first series, "Mead," consists of twenty-six abecedarians, the second series, "Z Ain't Just for Zabecedarium," runs backward through the alphabet twenty-six times.

SEE ALSO *acrostic.*

ab ovo Latin: "from the egg." The phrase *ab ovo* means "from the beginning," and refers to a poetic narrative that begins at the earliest possible chronological point. This is a logical way to commence, but it is not always the most dramatic way to tell a story. Horace uses the term in his *Ars Poetica* (ca. 19–18 B.C.E.) as a way of praising the skillfulness of Homer, the ideal epic poet, who does not begin his tale of the Trojan War with the twin egg from which Helen of Troy was born (*Nec gemino bellum Troianum orditur ab ouo*), but rather in the very middle of events (*in medias res*). The first book of the Hebrew Bible, Genesis (Greek: "birth," "origin"), or Bereshit (Hebrew: "In the beginning"), commences ab ovo or, perhaps, even before: "In the beginning God created the heaven and the earth."

SEE ALSO *in medias res.*

abstract, abstraction An abstract is a summary of any piece of written work. In poetry, abstraction refers to the use of concepts or ideas, things that come to us not through the senses but through the mind. Abstraction strips away the context and employs the immaterial properties of language. To employ abstraction is the opposite of embracing concrete particulars. Abstractions were a central feature of Victorian and symbolist poetry, one reason modern poets reacted against them. "Go in fear of abstractions," Ezra Pound declared in "A Retrospect" (1913): "Don't use such an expression as 'dim lands *of peace.*' It dulls the image. It mixes an abstraction with the concrete." But a postsymbolist modern poet such as Wallace Stevens, who claimed that "It Must Be Abstract" ("Notes Towards a Supreme Fiction," 1942), found ways to embrace abstraction by employing ideas and thinking in poetry. For Stevens, reality itself was an abstraction with multiple perspectives: "The major abstraction is the idea of man." There is also an abstract quality in the speculative language of T. S. Eliot's *Four Quartets* ("To be conscious is not to be in time," 1943) and the flowing consciousness of such book-length poems as John Ashbery's *Flow Chart* (1991) and A. R. Ammons's *Garbage* (1993).

Abstraction means the act of withdrawing. It is an active process, an act of moving away, a form of distancing and removal. This is how Frank O'Hara uses it in "Personism: A Manifesto" (1959), which takes off from an essay by Allen Ginsberg:

> Abstraction in poetry . . . appears mostly in the minute particulars where decision is necessary. Abstraction . . . involves personal removal by the poet. For instance, the decision involved in the choice between "the nostalgia *of* the infinite" and "the nostalgia *for* the infinite" defines an attitude towards degree of abstraction. The nostalgia *of* the infinite representing the greater degree of abstraction, removal, and negative capability (as in Keats and Mallarmé).

abstract poetry Dame Edith Sitwell coined this term to describe her own poems. Describing her 1922 book, she writes, "The poems in *Façade* are abstract poems, that is, patterns in sound." They try to use sound in much the same way that abstract painters use color, shape, and design. The aural parallels the visual. Abstract poetry never became a movement, though Lewis Carroll's nonsense poetry and Gertrude Stein's prose poems create some of the same effects. Sitwell praised Stein's "anarchic breaking up and rebuilding of sleepy families of words and phrases."

SEE ALSO *nonsense poetry, sound poetry.*

acatalectic, see *truncation.*

accent The vocal stress or emphasis placed on certain syllables in a line of verse. Stress varies from weak to strong. The word derives from the Latin *accentus,* meaning "song added to speech." Some poetries, such as Anglo-Saxon, count only accents, the number of stresses in a line. Other poetries, such as English, count both accents and syllables. Vocal stress is crucial to how we speak and hear the English language, how we say, scan, and sing poems in our language.

SEE ALSO *beat, meter, prosody, scansion.*

accentual verse, see *meter.*

accentual-syllabic verse, see *meter.*

acephalous Greek: "Headless." An acephalous line is a metrical line missing its first foot and thus "headless." In English poetry, this tends to be an iambic line that drops its first unstressed syllable, which is why it is sometimes called initial truncation. Take the foreshortened third line in the opening stanza of A. E. Housman's "To an Athlete Dying Young" (1896):

> Thĕ tíme yŏu wón yŏur tówn thĕ ráce
> Wĕ cháired yŏu thróugh thĕ márkĕt-pláce;
> Mán ănd bóy stŏod chéerĭng bý,
> Ănd hóme wĕ bróught yŏu shóuldĕr-hígh.

SEE ALSO *meter, truncation.*

Acmeism The word *acme* in Greek means "utmost," and this short-lived school of modern Russian poetry was one of the early twentieth-century pinnacles. In 1910, a group of young poets, which included Nikolay Gumilev (1886–1921), Anna Akhmatova (1889–1966), and Osip Mandelstam (1891–1938), set out to overturn the dominant mode of symbolism and reform Russian poetry. They sought Apollonian values, such as classical restraint, balance, and lucidity. The Acmeists focused on the texture of things, valued clarity of expression, and emphasized poetry as a craft. Their vision was neoclassical. The Acmeists believed that poetry was a kind of recognition and that poets of all ages echoed each other. Mandelstam characterized Acmeism as "nostalgia for world culture."

SEE ALSO *Apollonian/Dionysian, neoclassicism, symbolism.*

acrostic From the Greek: "at the tip of the verse." A poem in which the initial letters of each line have a meaning when read vertically. The acrostic reads down as well as across. The form may initially have been used as a mnemonic device in the transmission of sacred texts. The origin and history of the acrostic suggests that words have magical, incantatory, and religious power. In written poetry, the acrostic became a way both of hiding and revealing mysterious information, such as the names of lovers, authors, and titles. The writer engages the reader as the solver of a puzzle, inviting a more intimate bond. Thus Edgar Allan Poe spells out the name of his beloved in "Enigma" (1848), and Ben Jonson prefaces *The Alchemist* (1610) with an acrostic that spells out the name of his play:

The Argument

T he sickness hot, a master quit, for fear,
H is house in town, and left one servant there.
E ase him corrupted, and gave means to know
A Cheater and his punk, who now brought low,
L eaving their narrow practice, were become
C oz'ners at large; and, only wanting some
H ouse to set up, with him they here contract,
E ach for a share, and all begin to act.
M uch company they draw, and much abuse,
I n casting figures, telling fortunes, news,
S elling of flies, flat bawdry, with the Stone;
T ill it, and they, and all in fume are gone.

The abecedarian is possibly the oldest form of the acrostic. One type of acrostic uses the middle (*mesostich*) or final (*telestich*) letter of each line. A double acrostic employs both the first and last letters of the lines. A compound acrostic spells one word down the left-hand margin and another down the right-hand one.

A word square consists of a set of words, all of which have the same number of letters as the total number of words. Written out in a grid, the words can be read both horizontally and vertically. A famous example is this Roman palindrome, which was found as a graffito buried by ash at Herculaneum in 79 A.D.:

ROTAS
OPERA
TENET
AREPO
SATOR

One permutation of the word square:

SATOR
AREPO
TENET
OPERA
ROTAS

The meaning of this was obscure (one meaning may have been "the sower Arepo holds the wheels carefully"), but was interpreted as magical. One religious interpretation: the words were the "mystical names" of the five nails in Christ's cross.

The acrostic has frequently been employed as a clever device in light verse. John Dryden writes in *Mac Flecknoe* (1682):

Leave writing plays, and choose for thy command
Some peaceful province in acrostic land.
There thou may'st wings display and altars raise,
And torture one poor word ten thousand ways.

SEE ALSO *abecedarian, palindrome.*

adab The tradition of belles-lettres in Arabic poetry. The term suggests both the style of a cultured person and learning as a fulfilling way of life. The concept of adab dates to the sophisticated urban environment of eighth-century

Baghdad. Abu ʻUthman ʻAmr bin Bahr al-Jahiz (776–869) was one of its earliest significant proponents. S. A. Bonebakker points out that the term *adab* was widely used in the Middle Ages in the sense of "philology," "literary scholarship," and "literary culture," which may be the reason that translators in the nineteenth century adopted the plural ādāb to designate European works of literature. Adab anthologies, collections of poetry and anecdotes, promoted zarf, or refinement. Passages of poetry and prose were selected and arranged to serve as practical, moral, and rhetorical examples. The adab tradition developed both to edify and to entertain. It signals the crucial educational role that poetry played in medieval Arabic-Islamic culture.

SEE ALSO *didactic poetry, qasida.*

adonic In Greek and Latin poetry, an adonic verse is a five-unit metrical foot that consists of a dactyl and a spondee: / u u | / /. The last line of the Sapphic stanza is an adonic. Ezra Pound concludes his poem "The Return" (1912), which W. B. Yeats admired for "its real organic rhythm," with an accentual-syllabic adonic: "pállĭd thĕ léash mén."

SEE ALSO *meter, Sapphic stanza.*

adynaton Greek: "not possible." A figure of speech, a type of hyperbole in which something is magnified to such extreme lengths that it becomes impossible, which is why adynaton was known in Latin as impossibilia. The formal principle of adynata, "stringing together impossibilities," was a way of inverting the order of things, drawing attention to categories, turning the world upside down. The eclipse of the sun on April 6, 648 B.C.E., seems to have given Archilocus the idea that anything was possible now that Zeus had darkened the sun, and thus the beasts of the field could change their food for that of the dolphins (fragment 74). In Virgil's eighth Eclogue (37 B.C.E.), which was a great stimulus to later poetry, a shepherd forsaken by his beloved feels the world is out of joint: "Now may the wolf of his own free will flee the sheep, the oak bear golden apples, owls compete with swans, the shepherd Tityrus be Orpheus." Andrew Marvell begins "The Definition of Love" (1681):

> My love is of a birth as rare
> As 'tis for object strange and high:

It was begotten by Despair
Upon Impossibility.

SEE ALSO *hyperbole, rhetoric.*

Aeolic Two of the inventors of lyric poetry, Sappho and Alcaeus (late seventh to early sixth century B.C.E.), wrote in a Greek dialect known as Aeolic. The Greek colonies of Aeolis, a district of Mysia in Asia Minor, were one of the traditional birthplaces of lyric poetry. Aeolic subsequently became the name for a class of meters that brings dactyls and trochees close together to form a choriamb, a pattern of four syllables: long-short-short-long. In English prosody, this became two stressed syllables enclosing two unstressed ones. Horace both responded to the themes of Sappho and Alcaeus and used their meters, thus claiming: "I, passing from humble to mighty, / first found for Aeolic song a home / in Italian melodies" (*Odes,* book 3, 23–13 B.C.E.).

SEE ALSO *Alcaic, choriamb, dactyl, meter, Sapphic stanza, trochee.*

Aestheticism Aestheticism was a doctrine that art should be valued for itself alone. It should have no purpose or function beyond the cult of beauty. The aesthetic position provocatively opposed all instrumental or utilitarian views of art. It refused to let literature be subordinated to any other political or philosophical agenda or doctrine. The first self-conscious expression of the idea in modern literature was Théophile Gautier's preface to *Mademoiselle de Maupin* (1835) in which he denies that art can be useful in any way. In poetry, Charles Baudelaire (1821–1867) adopted the aesthetic view of experience and insisted on the sovereignty of the artist. In prose, J. K. Huysmans (1848–1907) and Gustave Flaubert (1821–1880) aligned themselves with the aesthetic position, which set itself against the chief value of the industrial era: productivity. Thomas Mann said of Aestheticism that it was "the first manifestation of the European mind's rebellion against the whole morality of the bourgeois age."

Gautier's notion of *l'art pour l'art* ("art for art's sake") became the rallying cry of the Aesthetic doctrine, which took hold in England in the second half of the nineteenth century under the influence first of John Ruskin, who taught a passionate commitment to beauty, and then of Walter Pater. At the end of *The Renaissance* (1873), Pater proposes the idea of life itself as a work of art whose goal is "To burn always with this hard, gemlike flame." He concludes that "to maintain this ecstasy, is success in life." The Aesthetic rejection of moralizing reached an apogee in Pater's extravagant disciple Oscar Wilde, who insisted that "all art is perfectly useless." Pater gave the name of the aesthetic poets to a group that included William Morris, Dante Gabriel Rossetti, and others associated with the Pre-Raphaelite brotherhood. The poets of the 1890s — Oscar Wilde, Ernest Dowson, Lionel Johnson, Arthur Symons, and the young W. B. Yeats — all wrote under the sign of what Pater called "poetic passion, the desire of beauty, the love of art for art's sake."

SEE ALSO *fin de siècle, Parnassians, Pre-Raphaelites, symbolism.*

affective fallacy When the meaning of a text is confused with how it makes the reader feel. W. K. Wimsatt and Monroe C. Beardsley defined the affective fallacy as the error of evaluating a poem by its effects. In *The Verbal Icon* (1954), they argued:

> The Affective Fallacy is a confusion between the poem and its *results*, (what it *is* and what it *does*) . . . It begins by trying to derive the standards of criticism from the psychological effects of the poem and ends in impressionism and relativism . . . The outcome . . . is that the poem itself, as an object of specifically critical judgment, tends to disappear.

Whereas the intentional fallacy confuses the meaning of a poem with its origin, the affective fallacy confuses the meaning with its results.

SEE ALSO *affective stylistics, intentional fallacy.*

affective stylistics The literary theorist Stanley Fish coined the phrase *affective stylistics* to describe the interpretation of reading as a process. His method focuses not on a text itself, but on how that text (*stylistics*) affects (*affective*) a reader in time. In "Literature in the Reader: Affective Stylistics" (1970), he intentionally committed the affective fallacy and advanced the argument "that all poems . . . were, in some sense, about their readers."

SEE ALSO *affective fallacy, reader-response criticism, stylistics.*

afflatus A Latin term for poetic inspiration. The noun *afflatus* derives from the Latin word meaning "to blow upon." Cicero wrote in *On Divination* (44 B.C.E.) that "no man was ever great without a touch of divine afflatus." The word presupposes a creative power — a divine breath — entering the writer. It names the nonrational aspect of poetic inspiration, which means "in-breathing," a mysterious force beyond the poet's conscious control.

SEE ALSO *inspiration, muse, spontaneity.*

age of reason, see *neoclassicism.*

age of sensibility, see *sensibility.*

agon Greek: "contest." In Greek drama, an agon is a verbal contest or dispute between two characters, each aided by one half of the Chorus, as in the debate between Aeschylus and Euripides in Aristophanes's comedy *The Frogs* (405 B.C.E.). Harold Bloom applies the term *agon* to the revisionary struggle of an author with his precursors. For example, John Keats displayed his agon toward the author of *Paradise Lost* when he declared in a letter, "Life to him would be death to me" (September 21, 1819).

SEE ALSO *anxiety of influence, poetic contest.*

air, ayre A song, a tune, or a melody. It can also suggest all three together. The English *ayre* derived from the French *air de cour* and generally referred to a solo song accompanied by a lute, which is why it is called the lute-song or lute-air. It was a subgenre of the lyric that flourished in the first two decades of the seventeenth century. The earliest publication of ayres was John Dowland's *The first Booke of Songs or Ayres* (1597). The lute-song hits its most beautiful notes in Thomas Campion's *Two Books of Ayres* (ca. 1613). "In these English Ayres," Campion wrote, "I have chiefly aymed to couple my Words and Notes lovingly together." He sets his program in "Now Winter Nights": "Let well-tun'd words amaze / With harmony divine."

SEE ALSO *lyric, song, songbook.*

aisling Irish for "dream." The *aisling* (pronounced "ashling") is a vision or dream poem, which developed in Gaelic poetry in Munster during the late seventeenth and eighteenth centuries. It has its origins in the Old French *reverdie,* which celebrates the arrival of spring, often in the form of a beautiful woman. The *aislingí* present and personify Ireland in the form of a woman, who can be young or old, haggard or beautiful, lamenting her woes. The woman is usually referred to as a *spéir-bhean* (sky-woman). Aodhagán Ó Raithille inaugurated the tradition of the political *aisling* with his eighteenth-century poem, "Mac an Cheannuidhe" ("The Merchant's Son"), which closes on a note of total despair. Throughout the eighteenth century, the form took on a strong political ethos, expressing a passion for Irish deliverance.

In *The Hidden Ireland* (1924), Daniel Corkery calls the *aisling* an "intimate expression of the hidden life of the people among whom it flourished." The *aisling* provides the legacy for such iconic female figures as Cathleen Ni Houlihan, the Shan Van Vocht, and Dark Rosaleen. The subgenre still reverberates, though reflexively. Seamus Heaney has several *aislings*, including "Aisling" (1974), "An Aisling in the Burren" (1984), and "The Disappearing Island" (1987), which he recognizes as "a form of *aisling,* a vision poem about Ireland, even though it is an *aisling* inflected with irony: 'All I believe that happened there was vision.' " In Paul Muldoon's mock-vision poem, "Aisling" (1983), written in light of the 1981 prison hunger strike in Northern Ireland, the maternal figure of Ireland is recast as Anorexia. In *A Kind of Scar* (1989), Eavan Boland calls the *aisling* tradition "that old potent blurring of feminine and national."

SEE ALSO *dream vision, Jacobite poetry, reverdie, vision.*

akam, puṟam Classical Tamil literature came to be known as *Cankam* ("an academy or fraternity"). A seventh-century commentator applied the term to poets and characterized three academies or *Cankams* of poets, which lasted for 4,440, 3,700, and 1,850 years, respectively. The fraternity of poets included kings, sages, and immortal gods. The 2,389 *Cankam* poems are collected in eight anthologies and classified as *akam* and *puṟam.* As A. K. Ramanujan explains in *The Interior Landscape* (1967): "*Akam* meant 'inner part,' *puṟam* meant 'outer part.' *Akam* poems were love poems; *puṟam* poems were 'public' poems." *Akam* was poetry of the "inner world," ideally expressed as the love between a man and woman, whereas *puṟam* was, in Ramanujan's words, "the 'public' poetry of the ancient Tamils, celebrating the ferocity and glory of kings, lamenting the deaths of heroes, the poverty of poets. Elegies, panegyrics, invectives, poems on wars and tragic events are *puṟam* poems." The Tamil poets created a spare and nuanced body of lyric poetry expressed through a common language of symbols, hence Ramanujan's observation: "The spurious name *Cankam* for this poetry is justified not by history but by the poetic practice."

akyn Before the twentieth century, Central Asian literature was circulated and popularized by itinerant minstrels who earned their living by traveling from town to town and giving traditional performances of poems, songs, and stories. These skilled improvisers who knew hundreds of poems were known as *akyn* or *yrchi* in Kazakh and Kyrgyz, and as *bakshi* or *dastanchi* in Turkmen and Uzbek, respectively. They came from all classes of nomad society and competed in festivals, called *toj,* which brought together thousands of pastoral nomads from the steppe. The *manaschi,* an elite category of *akyn,* specialized in reciting the national epic *Manas,* which could range up to half a million lines, nine times the length of the *Odyssey.* In his autobiography "Mein Leben" (1937), the Kazakhian *akyn* Dzhambul described the requirements for the traditional nomadic bard:

> He had to know all the tribes and families, all the tribal elders, all place-names and events. He had to be thoroughly familiar with all the questions of the time. Ready wit and resource, the ability to give quick answers — these were accomplishments without which the *akyn* found no popular esteem.
>
> Further, he must have sang-froid. Even when he was jeered at and when mockery was heaped upon him he must always remain calm. He might not, moreover, intoxicate himself with others' melodies, he must have a voice of his own, and must 'measure the earth with his own ell.' His every word must hit the mark like a dagger thrust. Nor might he feign emotion that he did not feel; he must take the words from his heart as water is taken from the source.

SEE ALSO *epic, minstrel, oral poetry, poetic contest.*

alba, see *aubade.*

Alcaic This classical Greek stanza was named for and possibly invented by Alcaeus, a poet of the late seventh and early sixth centuries B.C.E. It consists of four lines: the first two lines have eleven syllables each, the third, nine, and the fourth, ten. It has a complicated metrical scheme. Rosanna Warren points to "the principal beauty of the Alcaic, its shifts in rhythm in mid-course, its calculated imbalance as the iambic and choriambic first two lines yield to iambs in the third and resolve in racy dactyls in the fourth. An exemplum of poetry's task, it acts out the dynamic equilibrium between order and disorder."

Horace honored Alcaeus by adapting the Alcaic to Latin poetry; two-thirds of his *Odes* (23–13 B.C.E.) are written in it. The stanza was later adapted to Italian, French, German (Hölderlin's use of Alcaics is one of the high-water marks of the stanza's history), Hungarian, and English poetry. There are no true English equivalents of this quantitative meter, but there have been healthy imitations by the Countess of Pembroke (the sixteenth-century "Psalm 120"), Arthur Clough ("Alcaics," 1849), Robert Bridges ("Song: Chorus to Demeter," 1914), Thomas Hardy ("The Temporary the All," 1898), and Alfred, Lord Tennyson, who called it "the grandest of all measures" and used it to praise John Milton. Here is the first stanza of his "Experiment in Quantity" (1863), the Alcaics entitled "Milton":

O mighty-mouth'd inventor of harmonies,
O skill'd to sing of Time or Eternity,
  God-gift'd organ-voice of England,
    Milton, a name to resound for ages;

W. H. Auden took a Horatian stance and brilliantly employed the stanza in English in "In Memory of Sigmund Freud" (1939). In his book *Greek Lyrics* (1955), Richmond Lattimore fittingly used Alcaics to translate Alcaeus himself.

SEE ALSO *meter.*

Alcmanic verse This classical quantitative metrical form was used by and named after the Greek poet Alcman (seventh century B.C.E.). It refers to the dactylic tetrameter line. The Alcmanian strophe, also called the Alcmanian system, is a quatrain that combines the Alcmanic verse with a dactylic hexameter. It was employed in Greek drama and occasionally in Latin dramatic poetry. The closest approximation in English is Robert Southey's "Soldier's Wife" (1795), which begins

> Weary-way wanderer, languid and sick at heart,
>   Travelling painfully over the rugged road,
> Wild-visag'd Wanderer! ah for thy heavy chance!

SEE ALSO *dactyl, meter.*

aleatory From the Latin *alea,* a dice game. An aleatory work depends on randomness or chance — drawing lots, throwing dice — to generate fortuitous connections. Both the Dadaists and the Surrealists courted the mystique of accident, the liberation suggested by aleatory techniques. Tristan Tzara used random selections from newspapers to generate poems. His 1921 dada manifesto provided a recipe for creating a poem:

> Take a newspaper.
> Take some scissors.
> Choose from this paper an article of the length you want to make your
>   poem.
> Cut out the article.
> Next carefully cut out each of the words that makes up this article and
>   put them all in a bag.
> Shake gently.
> Next take out each cutting one after the other.
> Copy conscientiously in the order in which they left the bag.
> The poem will resemble you.
> And there you are — an infinitely original author of charming
>   sensibility, even though unappreciated by the vulgar herd.

André Breton pioneered the use of the *cadaver exquis* ("exquisite corpse") to explore the possibilities of chance. He described the game in *Dictionnaire abrége du surrealism* (1938): "A game with folded paper. Every participant makes a drawing without knowing what his predecessor has drawn, because the predecessor's contribution is concealed by the folded part of the paper." The Surrealists also played the game with words. The example, which has become a classic, and to which the game owes its name, was the first sentence produced by this method (in 1925): "Le cadavre exquis boira le vin nouveau" ("The exquisite corpse will drink the new wine").

In the early 1950s, John Cage famously used chance methods to create new music, as in his piece "Music of Changes" (1951), which he derived from using the ancient Chinese book of oracles, *I Ching* (third to second century B.C.E.). In the late 1960s he began using chance methods to create verbal works. He explored what he called *mesostics* as a means of "writing through" a source or precursor text according to chance operations. Between 1954 and 1960, Jackson Mac Low became a leading proponent of aleatory poetry by devising a series of chance operational methods, which he considered minimally egoic. Later, he relied instead on what he called "nonintentional" or "deterministic methods" because "what happens when they are utilized is not a matter of chance." So, too, the deterministic experiments of the Oulipo movement, a group of experimental French writers, are arbitrary but not accidental, and thus also anti-aleatory. There are seamless aleatory poems in Donald Justice's *Departures* (1973). The idea of the aleatory is to use accidental methods to liberate words from their usual meanings and habitual contexts, thus creating new meanings. An element of the accidental operates in all created work, thus the conflict between design and chance. Italo Calvino puts the matter forcefully in *Six Memos for the Next Millennium* (1988): "Poetry is the great enemy of chance, in spite of also being a daughter of chance and knowing that, in the last resort, chance will win the battle."

SEE ALSO *Dadaism, diastic, mesostic, Oulipo, Surrealism.*

alejandrino, see *cuaderna vía.*

aleluyas In Spain, *aleluyas* ("cries of hallelujah") were a form of a popular art, like strip cartoons. They consisted of rhymed octosyllabic couplets placed under wood-block prints and other religious pictures. The verses served as captions or moral lessons. Alleluias also served as illustrated pamphlets that were thrown out to crowds during Holy Week processions, like decorated valentines, to celebrate the Resurrection. This was the model for Federico García Lorca's play, *The Love of Don Perlimplín and Belinda in the Garden* (1925), which he called an "erotic *aleluya.*" Alleluias frequently became secular and political. With the rise of cheap printing, they were widely disseminated as broadside sheets in the nineteenth century.

SEE ALSO *octosyllabic verse.*

Alexandrian Hellenistic, or Alexandrian, literature was written in Greek from the fourth to the first centuries B.C.E. Literary activity was centered in the Egyptian city of Alexandria during the reign of the Ptolemies. Three of the major Alexandrian poets are Theocritus, who invented the pastoral and hailed from one of the Greek colonies in Sicily; Apollonius Rhodius, the author of the *Argonatica,* an epic on Jason's quest for the Golden Fleece; and Callimachus, who is known for his smoothly elegant short poems. In his prologue to the *Aetia,* Callimachus claimed that Apollo visited him and told him to "fatten your flocks, but keep your muse slender." Constantine Cavafy's modern poetry—refined, terse, historical—has clear affinities with the Greek poetry of the Alexandrian era.

SEE ALSO *pastoral.*

alexandrine A twelve-syllable poetic line used primarily in French poetry until the advent of *vers libre* (free verse) in the nineteenth century. It is the standard line of traditional French poetry since the sixteenth century and has an importance comparable to blank verse in English poetry. It was invented in the twelfth century—the name may have derived from a poem about Alexander the Great—and still circulates in the bloodstream of anyone classically educated in French poetry. The traditional alexandrine divided the line into two groups of six syllables with a fixed medial pause. There are strong stresses on the sixth and last syllables. The *Alexandrin classique* was perfected by the dramatists Pierre Corneille (1606–1684) and Jean Racine (1639–1699), its greatest exponent. The twelve-syllable *vers romantique,* or *Alexadrin trimètre,* divides the line into three parts. The twelve-syllable *tétramètre* divides the line into four parts with a caesura after the sixth syllable. Victor Hugo and other nineteenth-century poets challenged and reformed the alexandrine to give it greater rhythmic fluidity. Paul Verlaine expanded it so that it bordered on free verse.

The six strong accents of the English alexandrine give it a particularly sprawling, drawn-out feeling. In English poetry, Edmund Spenser employs an alexandrine as the last line of each stanza of his epic romance *The Faerie Queene* (1590–1596), and Milton cannily imitates him in his nativity ode (1629). Alexander Pope evokes what he criticizes in the second line of this couplet from "An Essay on Criticism" (1711):

> A needless Alexandrine ends the Song,
> That like a wounded Snake, drags its slow length along.

Robert Bridges employs what he calls "neo-Miltonics" or "loose alexandrines" for his long philosophical poem, *The Testament of Beauty* (1929):

> *What is beauty? saith my sufferings then.* — I answer
> the lover and poet in my loose alexandrines . . .

The Very Reverend William Ralph Inge (1860–1954), Dean of Saint Paul's, reputedly said that he hated "loose alexandrines" worse than loose living.

SEE ALSO *caesura, free verse, hexameter, meter, vers libre.*

allegory From the Greek *allēgoría* from *állos* ("other") and *-ēgorein* ("to speak"); that is, "speaking otherwise." Isidore of Seville (d. 636) wrote, "Allegory is other-speech. One thing is spoken, another is meant." An allegory is a story operating on two levels simultaneously. The narrative acts as an extended metaphor with a primary or surface meaning that continually discloses a secondary or representational meaning. The two levels provide a parallel experience: one entertains; the other instructs.

Allegory is a postclassical idea. Plutarch noted in *Moralia,* written around 100 C.E., that what was called *allēgoría* in his time had been previously called *huponoia,* or "under-meaning." It was a thought or meaning that existed underneath the surface of a text. The sense of underlying meaning or hidden thoughts expanded into a full-fledged method of speaking otherwise. The characters in an allegory are often personifications; that is, abstract ideas incarnated as persons. There is a one-to-one correspondence between what they are and what they mean. Think of the characters Death, Fellowship, Good-Deeds, and Beauty in the medieval morality play *Everyman,* or the characters Christian, Faithful, and Mr. Worldly Wiseman in Bunyan's

Pilgrim's Progress (1678). Consider the surrealist André Breton's characterization of reverie:

> Reverie . . . a magical young girl, unpredictable, tender, enigmatic, provocative, from whom I never seek an explanation of her escapades.

The characters of the great allegories go beyond merely representing their designated vices and virtues; they become them.

We are in the range of allegory whenever a writer explicitly indicates the relationship of the image to the precept. Northrop Frye writes: "A writer is being allegorical whenever it is clear that he is saying 'by this I *also* (*allos*) mean that.' " The hero of an allegory is also a cipher or a designated figure for the reader, since it's understood that the action takes place in the mental landscape of the audience. Allegory is a distinctive form. It treats the story as a means to an end and channels our affective responses. As William Empson explains in *The Structure of Complex Words* (1948),

> Part of the function of an allegory is to make you feel that two levels of being correspond to each other in detail and indeed that there is some underlying reality, something in the nature of things, which makes this happen. . . . But the effect of allegory is to keep the two levels of being very distinct in your mind though they interpenetrate each other in so many details.

Allegory is a method of critical analysis as well as a literary model. Critics interpret works allegorically when they perceive coherent analogies behind living characters and abstract ideas (hence psychoanalytic criticism). In *The Well Wrought Urn* (1947), Cleanth Brooks allegorizes the poems he explicates insofar as they become "parables about the nature of poetry." Frye suggests in *Anatomy of Criticism* (1957) that all criticism is covert allegorizing.

SEE ALSO *metaphor, personification.*

alliteration The audible repetition of consonant sounds at the beginning of words or within words. Listen to the letter *m* and the letter *d* in Gerard Manley Hopkins's striding, strutting, ecstatic evocation of a kestrel in "The Windhover" (1877):

> I caught this morning morning's minion, king-
> dom of daylight's dauphin, dapple-dawn-drawn Falcon . . .

Alliteration is part of the sound stratum of poetry. It predates rhyme and takes us back to the oldest English and Celtic poetries. It is known as *Stabreim* in the ancient Germanic languages. Alliterative meter was the principal organizing device in Anglo-Saxon poetry and continued to resound through the fourteenth century, as in the opening line of *Piers Plowman:*

> In a somer season, whan soft was the sonne . . .

The repetitive *s* here ties the four words together and urges their interaction upon us. Alliteration can reinforce preexisting meanings (*summer season*) and establish effective new ones (*soft sun*). A device of phonic echoes, of linked initial sounds, alliteration reverberates through most of the poetries of the world.

Robert Louis Stevenson argues for the purposefulness of alliteration and assonance in "On Some Technical Elements of Style in Literature" (1905):

> Each phrase in literature is built of sounds, as each phrase in music consists of notes. One sound suggests, echoes, demands, and harmonises with another; and the art of rightly using these concordances is the final art in literature. It used to be a piece of good advice to all young writers to avoid alliteration; and the advice was sound, in as much as it prevented daubing. None the less for that, was it abominable nonsense, and the mere raving of those blindest of the blind who will not see. The beauty of the contents of a phrase, or of a sentence, depends implicitly upon alliteration and upon assonance. The vowel demands to be repeated; the consonant demands to be repeated; and both cry aloud to be perpetually varied. You may follow the adventure of a letter through any passage that has particularly pleased you; find it, perhaps, denied a while to tantalise the ear; find it fired again at you in a whole broadside; or find it pass into congenerous sounds, one liquid or labial melting away into another. And you will find another, much stranger circumstance. Literature is written by and for two senses: a sort of internal ear, quick to perceive "unheard melodies"; and the eye, which directs the pen and deciphers the printed phrase.

Alliteration didn't predominate in later metrical verse, but it is a rough current in Sir Thomas Wyatt (1503–1542), if you listen, and thereafter becomes a subterranean stream in English-language poetry. It comes bubbling to the surface in such twentieth-century Welsh poets as David Jones and Dylan Thomas.

SEE ALSO *assonance, consonance.*

alliterative meter, see *meter.*

alliterative revival Alliteration was the organizing device of Anglo-Saxon poetry, but it was dying out by the fourteenth century until a group of poets established what has been called an "alliterative revival." Alliteration is the basic sound device of *Piers Plowman* (ca. 1360–1387) and *Sir Gawain and the Green Knight* (fourteenth century), and its heavy percussive use brings these poems close to oral poetry. Listen to the letter *v* in this line about the Green Knight, "And alle his <u>v</u>esture <u>v</u>erayly was clene <u>v</u>erdure," which Simon Armitage gleefully translates as "In all vestments he revealed himself veritably verdure."

SEE ALSO *alliteration.*

alloeostropha In the preface to *Samson Agonistes* (1671), John Milton uses this term to refer to poetry composed in irregular stanzas. "The measure of verse used in the chorus is of all sorts," he writes; "being divided into stanzas or pauses, they may be called Alloeostropha."

SEE ALSO *anisometric, counterpoint, verse paragraph.*

allusion A passing or indirect reference to something implied but not stated. The writer refers to something recognizable—a historical or fictional character, a specific place, a particular event or series of events, a religious or mythological story, a literary or artistic work. Allusion may serve as a compact between writer and reader, a means of summoning a shared world or tradition, a way of packing a work with meaning. Thus Dante alludes throughout the *Inferno* (1304–1309) to Virgil's *Aeneid* (29–19 B.C.E.), especially the sixth book that charts Aeneas's descent into the underworld, even as Virgil alludes to Homer's *Odyssey* (ca. eighth century B.C.E.), especially book 11 where Odysseus pours libations to the unnumbered dead and gathers the shades at the edges of the known world.

Throughout the history of poetry the song of Orpheus (according to Greek mythology, Orpheus's song was so enchanting that all the animals and even the rocks and trees gathered to listen) has been alluded to as the ideal of poetic creation. "When there is poetry, / it is Orpheus singing," Rainer Maria Rilke writes in his cycle *The Sonnets to Orpheus* (1922). Some contemporary readers are hostile to allusion as an elitist device, especially since there is now so little shared literary knowledge, and yet allusion is a crucial way that poems talk to each other and create meaning for us.

SEE ALSO *intertextuality, tradition.*

alternance des rimes, see *rhyme.*

alternate rhyme, see *rhyme scheme.*

ambiguity A word or sign is described as ambiguous when it is open to more than one explanation or interpretation. In rhetoric, ambiguity has been treated as both a stylistic fault (the Latin *ambiguitas*) and a potential literary virtue. William Empson introduced this term to modern critical discourse in *Seven Types of Ambiguity* (1930). Empson defines ambiguity as "any verbal nuance, however slight, which gives room for alternative reactions to the same piece of language." Empson's consideration of ambiguity, which moves from the least ambiguous (double meanings) to the most ambiguous (contradictory meanings), suggests the many linguistic plenitudes of verbal art. The division into exactly *seven* types of ambiguity now seems arbitrary, but Empson enlarged the reading of poetry by close verbal analysis and a careful textual consideration of the multiple meanings of words and passages. Following Empson, the formalist New Critics treated ambiguity as one of the crucial features of poetry.

SEE ALSO *New Criticism, plurisignation.*

American renaissance In the 1840s, '50s, and '60s, there was a remarkable flowering of American literature. Ralph Waldo Emerson, Henry David Thoreau, Herman Melville, Nathaniel Hawthorne, Walt Whitman, Emily Dickinson, Edgar Allan Poe, and others were all working during this time, which F. O. Matthiessen named the *American Renaissance* (1941). Matthiessen emphasized the devotion of these writers to the principles of democracy and traced their religious ideas to New England Puritanism. He established their near obsessive concern with the relationship between the individual and society. The idea of the American renaissance opened up American literature as a field of study, which was enlarged by such critics as R.W.B. Lewis (*The American Adam,* 1955), Charles Fiedelson (*Symbolism in American Literature,* 1956), Richard Chase (*The American Novel and Its Tradition,* 1957), Daniel Hoffman (*Form and Fable in American Fiction,* 1961), Quentin Anderson (*The Imperial Self,* 1971), and Ann Douglas (*The Feminization of American Literature,* 1977).

amhrán Irish: "song." The *amhrán*, or song poem, which had a long prehistory in Irish oral tradition, arose in the sixteenth century and predominated in Gaelic poetry for the next three centuries. The new stress meter of the amhrán — earlier Irish poetry was syllabic — had a regular rhythm based on the interplay of accented and unaccented syllables both within lines and between lines. The poem was divided into regular stanzas — the earliest examples are quatrains — and relied on ornamental assonance. Aodhgan Ó Raithille's eighteenth-century *aisling* or dream poem "Mac an Cheannuidhe" ("The Merchant's Son") is a good example of the amhrán or stress meter. It was common in the seventeenth century for Irish Gaelic poets to compose the body of a poem in syllabic verse and conclude with a stanza in the more modern accentual meter. For example, the Gaelic poet Dáibhí Ó Bruidair (1625–1698) is best known for his bitterly satirical poem "Is mairg nach bhfuil im dhubhthuata" ("O it's best to be a total bore," ca. 1674), which combines the strict *ae freislighe* form with a looser four-line amhrán at the end. He also sent up the tradition of amhrán poems, which may have become formulaic, with an amhrán in which the individual lines make sense but the whole poem is nonsensical.

SEE ALSO *aisling*.

amoebean verses Greek: "responsive verses." These verses in dialogue are found primarily in pastoral poetry, especially in the work of Theocritus and Virgil. Here two speakers chant alternate lines, couplets or stanzas. In Virgil's *Georgics,* book 3 (ca. 29 B.C.E.), the shepherd Menalcus asks the shepherd Dametas, "Do you want us to try alternately to see what each of us is capable of?" The speakers then try to match, debate, and outdo each other according to specified rules. Edmund Spenser imitated the form in *Shepheardes Calender* (1579). Responsive verses were rooted in the singing competitions of local peasant communities. As the pastoral genre developed, these responsive verses were modeled not on oral but on previous literary texts. The literary pastoral created fictions about rural life, which were eventually critiqued by poets writing counter-pastorals. Thus George Crabbe in *The Village* (1783):

> Fled are those times, when, in harmonious strains,
> The rustic poet praised his native plains:
> No shepherds now, in smooth alternate verse,
> The country's beauty or their nymphs' rehearse.

SEE ALSO *débat, georgic, pastoral, poetic contest.*

amour courtois, see *courtly love.*

amphibrach Greek: "short at both ends." A classical metrical foot consisting of one long syllable surrounded by two short ones. It would be approximated by a word like *remember.* The word remembers what it describes, since the foot is literally short at both ends. As Coleridge describes it in his poem "Metrical Feet" (ca. 1806):

> One syllable long, with one short at each side,
> Ămphībrăchy̆s hāstes with ă stātely̆ strīde;—

SEE ALSO *cretic, foot, meter.*

amphimacher, see *cretic.*

anacoluthon The transliteration of a Greek word meaning "without completion." It is primarily a grammatical term that designates a change of construction in a sentence that leaves its beginning uncompleted. It is a syntactical shift. The term is an academic one, but the experience is quite common in speech, where people often break off what they are saying and shift directions. In poetry, it can be used to focus on the syntax itself, on the way that something is being stated. It draws attention to the mechanics of meaning. By starting in one direction and then abruptly heading off in another, it can also suggest a state of mind, such as confusion, laziness, excitement. In his poem about Rimbaud and Verlaine ("Preludes for Memnon," 56, 1931), Conrad Aiken employs an anacoluthon even as he discusses it:

> Discussing, between moves, iamb and spondee
> Anacoluthon and the open vowel
> God the great peacock with his angel peacocks
> And his dependent peacocks the bright stars . . .

Anacreontic Anacreon (ca. 570–485 B.C.E.) was a Greek lyric poet who lived in Teos, in Asia Minor. Mere fragments survive of his graceful, lighthearted poems that deal with wine, women, and song. The *Carmina Anacreontea,* or anacreontic poems, consists of sixty texts in the manner of Anacreon on the simple pleasures of life. They survive from an appendix to the tenth-century codex of the *Palatine Anthology.* Abraham Cowley brought the word *Anacreontic* into English when he called a section of his poems "anacreontiques" because they were paraphrased out of the work of Anacreon, or his imitators (*Miscellanies,* 1656). They supposedly mimicked the Greek meter, which combined long (—) and short (u) syllables in the seven-syllable pattern u u — u — u —. Robert Herrick cultivated the Anacreontic and had his mistress promise him that in Elysium, "He bring thee Herrick to Anacreon / Quaffing his full-crown'd bowles of burning wine" ("The Apparition of His Mistresse Calling Him to Elizium. Dezunt Nonulla —," 1648). In 1800, Thomas Moore published a collection of erotic anacreontics (*Odes of Anacreon,* 1800) that try to catch "the careless facility with which Anacreon appears to have trifled." It begins:

> I saw the smiling bard of pleasure,
> The minstrel of the Teian measure;
> 'T was in a vision of the night,
> He beam'd upon my wondering sight.
> I heard his voice, and warmly prest
> The dear enthusiast to my breast.

The Anacreontic now tends to refer to any easy-going lyrical poem that mixes and serves wine with love.

anagogic An anagoge (from the Greek *anagoge,* "upward") is the mystical interpretation of a word, a passage, or a text, and especially refers to scriptural exegesis that detects allusions to the heavenly afterlife. An anagogic meaning refers to the ultimate underlying meaning. It is opposed to the literal, allegorical, and moral levels of biblical interpretation. Consider, for example, the anagogic perspective of the book of Revelation. Northrop Frye describes the anagogic in literature as "the imitation of infinite social action and infinite human thought, the mind of a man who is all men, the universal creative word which is all words."

anagram Greek: "transposition of letters." A word or phrase rearranged to form another word or phrase. Lying awake one November night in 1868, Lewis Carroll transposed "William Ewart Gladstone" into "Wilt tear down *all* images." He later came up with an even better one, "Wild agitator! Means well." The anagram is not a poetic form per se, but it can yield anagrammatic poems, such as David Shulman's rhyming sonnet, "Washington Crossing the Delaware" (1936), in which every line is an anagram of the title.

The Greek poet Lycophron (third century B.C.E.) was the first known practioner of onamastic anagrams, or anagrams relating to names. Anagrams were a common literary amusement in the Latin Middle Ages, when it was discovered that the letters comprising the words of the Annunciation, *"Ave Maria, gratia plena, Dominus tecum"* ("Hail Mary, full of grace, the Lord is with you") could be rearranged as *"Virgo serena, pia, munda et immaculata"* ("Virgin serene, holy, pure and immaculate"). George Puttenham tried to define the rules for the formation of anagrams in "Of the Anagram or Posy Transposed" (*The Art of English Poesie,* 1589) and so did the Scottish poet William Drummond of Hawthornden in his essay on the "Character of a Perfect Anagram" (written around 1615, collected in 1711). The historian William Camden gathered many anagrammatic samples in *Remains Concerning Britain* (1605). "Perhaps partly because of a continuing, post-Gutenberg fascination . . . with how words and letters looked in print, and how readily they could be rearranged into movable type," R. H. Winnick speculates, "English interest in onamastic anagrams, especially in court circles, reached a level of intensity by the late sixteenth century that would later surpass sonnet mania."

SEE ALSO *deconstruction, hypogram, intertextuality, metagram, palindrome, pun.*

analogy A resemblance between two different things, frequently expressed as an extended simile. William Blake talks back to ecclesiastical authority with this satirical analogy from "Proverbs of Hell" (1790–1793): "As the caterpillar chooses the fairest leaves to lay her eggs on, so the priest lays his curse on the fairest joys." The reader participates in the making of an analogy, especially an extended analogy, by testing the proposition against lived experience. It is the reader who decides to what extent Paul Valéry's analogy is true when he says that poetry is to prose as dancing is to walking.

Analogies and metaphors are both modes of relational thinking. An analogy works by suggesting similarity. A metaphor creates an identity between two different things. Some philosophers consider analogies and metaphors the same thing, a grammatical difference, while others think of them as two different forms of reasoning. Analogical thinking is nonlinear, nonconsecutive, indirect. It is an extended associative process. Thomas Aquinas believed that the fact that God created the world points to a fundamental "analogy of being" between God and the world. Henry David Thoreau concluded, "All perception of truth is the detection of an analogy."

SEE ALSO *conceit, metaphor, simile.*

anapest A metrical foot consisting of three syllables, two unaccented followed by one accented, as in the words "ĭn ă wár." The anapest was originally a Greek martial rhythm and often creates a galloping sense of action, a catchy, headlong momentum, as in these lines from the beginning of Lord Byron's "The Destruction of Sennacherib" (1815):

> Thĕ Ăssýr | iăn căme dówn | lĭke thĕ wólf | ŏn thĕ fóld,
> Ănd hĭs có | hŏrts wĕre gléam | ĭng ĭn púr | plĕ ănd góld;
> Ănd thĕ shéen | ŏf thĕir spéars | wăs lĭke stárs | ŏn thĕ séa,
> Whĕn thĕ blúe | wăve rŏlls níght | lў ŏn déep | Gălĭlée.

My own little antholology of eighteenth- and nineteenth-century anapestic poems in English would include Blake's "Ah! Sun-flower" (1794), Shelley's

"The Cloud" (1820), Poe's hypnotic "Annabel Lee" (1849), and Swinburne's "Before the Beginning of Years" (1865). The momentum of anapests has mostly been employed for comic or ironic effects in modern poetry, as in Thomas Hardy's "The Ruined Maid" (1901). David Rakoff used anapestic tetrameter, which trots along at four feet per line, for his posthumously published novel, *Love, Dishonor, Marry, Die, Cherish, Perish* (2013).

SEE ALSO *foot, meter.*

anaphora From the Greek, meaning "a carrying up or back." Anaphora is the repetition of the same word or words at the beginning of a series of phrases, lines, or sentences. The words accumulate mysterious power and resonance through repetition. In the first century, Longinus treated anaphora as an imitative action and a key feature of the sublime. Thomas Wilson dubbed anaphora "the marcher" (*The Arte of Rhetorique,* 1585), and George Puttenham deemed it the "figure of report" (*The Arte of English Poesie,* 1589). Anaphora serves as an organizing poetic strategy for long lists or catalogs, as in the Hebrew Bible. The piling up of particulars is itself a joyous poetic activity, a way of naming and claiming the world. Open almost any page of *Leaves of Grass* (1855) and you immediately encounter Walt Whitman's anaphoric method, his ecstatic iterations. Here is an excerpt from "A Broadway Pageant":

> For I too raising my voice join the ranks of this pageant,
> I am the chanter, I chant aloud over the pageant,
> I chant the world on my Western sea,
> I chant copious the islands beyond, thick as stars in the sky,
> I chant the new empire grander than any before, as in a vision it comes
>   to me,
> I chant America the mistress, I chant a greater supremacy,
> I chant projected a thousand blooming cities . . .

The key to anaphora is that each line is a repetition with a difference. Robert Alter calls it "a productive tension between sameness and difference, reiteration and development." Something is reiterated, something else added or subtracted. Our attention keeps shifting from the phrasing that is repeated to the phrasing that is freshly introduced. What recurs is also changed. Anaphora is a self-conscious and repeated turn back to beginnings, back to the origin of the line.

The counterpart of anaphora is *epiphora* or epistrophe: the repetition of a word or phrase at the end of successive clauses, sentences, or lines. Whitman uses the *epiphora* "it shall be you" fourteen times in seventeen lines in a passage from "Song of Myself" (1855), which begins "If I worship one thing more than another it shall be the spread of my own body, or any part of it," and concludes:

> Sun so generous it shall be you!
> Vapors lighting and shading my face it shall be you!
> You sweaty brooks and dews it shall be you!
> Winds whose soft-tickling genitals rub against me it shall be you!
> Broad muscular fields, branches of live oak, loving lounger in my
>   winding paths, it shall be you!
> Hands I have taken, face I have kiss'd, mortal I have ever touch'd, it
>   shall be you!

The repetition of the first words at the end of a sequence is called *epanalepsis.* Elizabeth Barrett Browning declares "Say over again, and yet once over again, / That thou dost love me"; Robert Frost writes in "The Gift Outright" (1941): "Possessing what we still were unpossessed by, / Possessed by what we now no more possessed."

SEE ALSO *catalog poem, parallelism, the sublime.*

anastrophe In Greek, *anastrophe* means literally "a turning back or about." It is an inversion of the normal syntactic order of words. Anastrophe is one of the ways that poetry wrenches language and thus departs from the expected. Edgar Allan Poe begins "The Raven" (1845), "Once upon a midnight dreary," rather than with the more predictable adjective-noun formation, "Once upon a dreary midnight." Gerard Manley Hopkins agonizingly writes in one of the so-called terrible sonnets, "Bitter would have me taste" (1885).

SEE ALSO *rhetoric.*

the Angry Penguins The Angry Penguins was a modernist movement that aimed to shake up the artistic establishment in Australia in the 1940s.

There were four poets in the movement, which also included the visual arts. Charles Rischbieth Jury is generally credited with naming the movement from Max Harris's line referring to "the angry penguins of the night." Harris was its primary spokesman and edited the magazine *Angry Penguins.* He recalled in a retrospective piece called "Angry Penguins and After" (1963) that the movement expressed "a noisy and aggressive revolutionary modernism." The two other young poets, D. B. Kerr and P. G. Pfeiffer, both died in the Second World War. The Angry Penguins were internationalists and thus aroused the furor of nativist Australian groups, such as the Jindyworobaks, who attacked their "pseudo-Europeanism."

The expressionist poetry of the Angry Penguins tended to be obscure and portentous, which left them open to what Harris called a "notable and complex jest," which became international news. James McAuley and Harold Stewart created a fictional poet named Ern Malley, who had just died, and his sister, Ethel Malley, who forwarded her brother's poems to the *Angry Penguins.* To test whether the Angry Penguins could distinguish between genuine poetry and poetry that was "a collection of garish images without coherent meaning and structure," McAuley and Stewart "concocted nonsense" and wrote haphazard poems. The poems were published and heralded under the cover title *The Darkening Ecliptic* in the 1944 edition of the *Angry Penguins.* The hoax was revealed in Sydney's tabloid paper, *FACT,* on June 5, 1944. The subsequent debate was then overshadowed when Harris was brought to trial and convicted for publishing Ern Malley's poems, which were labeled "indecent, immoral, or obscene." Modernism in Australia had suffered a comic blow and an ignoble setback.

SEE ALSO *Jindyworobak movement.*

anisometric Greek: "of unequal lengths." A stanza of unequal lines. Many free verse poets, from William Carlos Williams and e. e. cummings to Galway Kinnell and Louise Glück, have specialized in the off-balance rhythms of anisometric stanzas.

SEE ALSO *alloeostropha, free verse, verse paragraph.*

anthology Greek: "collection of flowers." A collection of poetry or prose. The earliest compilation of Greek poems dates to the fourth century B.C.E.

Around 90 B.C.E., Meleager of Gadara collected a "bouquet" of short epigrams, which represented some fifty poets, from Archilochus (seventh century B.C.E.) to himself. In the tenth century, Constantinus Cephalas, a Byzantine Greek, drew on previous anthologies and put together the *Palatine*, or *Greek Anthology*, the first major anthology of poems, and one of the great sourcebooks of lyric poetry.

antibacchius, see *foot.*

anticlimax Greek: "the opposite of a ladder." In the eighteenth century, Dr. Johnson defined an anticlimax as "a sentence in which the last part expresses something lower than the first." An anticlimax is literally an effect against the climax. It commonly refers to an endpoint (a sentence, a line, an act, a play) that is a disappointing contrast, or an ironic letdown. The result, frequently comic, is something lesser than one had expected.

SEE ALSO *bathos, climax, mock epic.*

anti-masque, see *masque.*

antimetabole, see *chiasmus.*

antiphon A song, hymn, or poem in which two voices or choruses respond to one another in alternate verses or stanzas, as is common in verses written for religious services. Antiphonal poetry has the quality of call and response, of liturgy. In George Herbert's "Antiphon (I)" (1633), for example, the chorus begins:

> Let all the world in ev'ry corner sing,
> *My God and King.*

The leader or minister calls back:

> The heav'ns are not too high,
> His praise may thither fly:
> The earth is not too low,
> His praises there may grow.

And the congregation responds again:

> Let all the world in ev'ry corner sing,
> *My God and King.*

antispast, see *foot.*

antipoems, antipoetry The Peruvian poet Enrique Bustamente Ballián published a book called *Antipoemas* in 1926. The Chilean poet Vicente Huidobro also used the term *antipoemas* in Canto IV of *Altazor* in 1931. But antipoetry became a full-fledged mode, a sacrilegious opponent to traditional poetry, in the 1950s when the Chilean poet Nicanor Parra used the term for some of the fierce, astringent, sardonic poems in his book *Poemas y Antipoemas* (*Poems and Antipoems,* 1954). Antipoetry vehemently opposes anything lyrical, rejecting traditional techniques and symbolic styles. It is mischievous, iconoclastic, antiheroic. It destroys literary norms. Parra has always used his flat colloquial voice and deadpan irony to take aim at poetry's high lyric pretentions. He offers a comic antidote to several generations of romantic Spanish and Latin American poets. He reminds us that modern poetry invariably needs gate crashers to keep it honest, to put it in touch with rude reality. Immersed in life and allergic to art for art's sake, to pretentiousness of any kind, to overblown rhetoric and imagery, Parra strips the lyric down to its solid core. He says that antipoetry "seeks to return poetry to its roots." "Viewed through the lens of antimatter," Liz Werner explains, "antipoetry mirrors poetry, not as its adversary but as its perfect complement . . . it is as opposite, complete, and interdependent as the shape left behind in the fabric where the garment has been cut out."

SEE ALSO *Aestheticism, naked poetry.*

antistrophe The middle section of a classical ode, following the strophe and preceding the epode. The structure of the classical ode is based on the odes of Pindar (early fifth century B.C.E.), who adapted this characteristic pattern from the songs chanted by the chorus in Greek drama. The chorus moved to the left during the strophe and to the right during the antistrophe.

SEE ALSO *epode, ode, strophe.*

antithesis, antithetical A rhetorical contrast or opposition between ideas, often enacted through a parallel structure. Antithesis is one of the favorite strategies of biblical poetry, as in the wisdom proverbs "When pride comes, then comes shame: but with the lowly is wisdom" (Prov. 11:2) and "The Lord is far from the wicked: but he hears the prayer of the righteous" (Prov. 15:29). Aristotle singled out antithesis as a pleasing device:

> When the style is . . . antithetical, in each of the two members . . . an opposite is balanced by an opposite, or two opposites are linked by the same word. For example . . . "By nature citizens, by law bereft of their city . . ." This kind of style is pleasing, because things are best known by opposition, and are all the better known when the opposites are put side by side; and is pleasing also because of its . . . logic — for the method of refutation is the juxtaposition of contrary conclusions. (*Rhetoric* III, 9, ca. 335–330 B.C.E.)

In *Paradise Lost* (1667), John Milton effectively contrasts Adam and Eve through the use of antithesis:

> For contemplation he and valour formed,
> For softness she and sweet attractive grace;
> He for God only, she for God in him.

In philosophy, antithesis is a second argument raised to oppose a first proposition, as in Hegel's dialectic of thesis, antithesis, and synthesis. Poetic contests are also founded on debate principles of argument and counterargument.

SEE ALSO *parallelism, poetic contest, rhetoric.*

antode Greek: "opposite song." During the intermission of a Greek Old Comedy, one half of the chorus sang a lyrical ode and the other half responded with an *antode,* an Answering Song in the same meter.

SEE ALSO *chorus, ode.*

antonomasia Greek: "naming instead." The substitution of an epithet or a phrase for a proper name, as when we refer to Shakespeare as "the Bard."

SEE ALSO *epithet.*

anxiety of influence Harold Bloom coined the phrase *anxiety of influence* to describe the crushing weight of poetic tradition. Bloom describes the agonizing struggle between the new poet, or ephebe, and the influential precursor, and theorizes that poetic history is indistinguishable from poetic influence. Bloom rebels against the New Critical idea that the meaning of a poem can be found in its internal structure, and he takes issue with genial and idealized ideas of poetic tradition. For him, a text is a psychic battlefield and a poem is inevitably a rewriting of an earlier poem, "for poetry lives always under the shadow of poetry." He finds that the poet must misread his precursors in order to survive: "the poet confronting his great original must find the fault that is not there." He defines his central principle, which he articulates and italicizes for emphasis, in *The Anxiety of Influence* (1973):

> *Poetic Influence — when it involves two strong, authentic poets — always proceeds by a misreading of the prior poet, an act of creative correction that is actually and necessarily a misinterpretation. The history of fruitful poetic influencing, which is to say the main tradition of Western poetry since the Renaissance, is a history of anxiety and self-saving caricature, of distortion, of perverse, willful revisionism without which modern poetry as such could not exist.*

For the Freudian-minded Bloom, the strong poet is locked in a deadly Oedipal struggle with the poets of the past, who make his work possible.

SEE ALSO *agon, belatedness, New Criticism.*

aoidos, aoidoi (pl) Greek: "singer." The Greek *aoidos* was a singing poet, a professional bard who performed at court or traveled from town to town. Homer gives us the name of Phemius ("man of fame"), the aoidos at Odysseus's palace in Ithaca, who sang the return of the Acheans: "And the famous bard (aoidos) sang to them, and they sat quietly listening." Homer also tells of Demodocus ("received by the people"), blind aoidos at the palace of Alcinous, king of the Phaeacians, who sang about the quarrel of Achilles and Odysseus. Homer says that they are "like gods in their *audê.*" He would most likely have considered himself an aoidos.

Aoidean poetry is sometimes used as a technical term for early Greek oral epic poetry. The Homeric corpus essentially refers to epic poems as *aoidê* or "singing," which is, as Andrew Ford points out, "an action noun, a word that names poetry not as text or aesthetic object but as activity and performance." Homer deemed poetry *thespis aoidê*, "divine song." It is a sublime voicing.

SEE ALSO *bard, epic, oral-formulaic method.*

Apollo Society In 1932, the poet Ahmad Zakī Abū Shādī (1892–1955) founded a society for poetry in Egypt, which was the center of the romantic movement in modern Arabic poetry. Abū Shādi hoped to introduce "a new sensibility" to Egyptian literature. Based on his reading of English and American free verse, he brought the use of mixed meters, or *shi'r hurr*, into Egyptian poetry with his collection of poems *al-Shafaq al-Bākī* (*The Weeping Twilight*, 1927). Many of the poets the Apollo Society brought together, such as Ibrāhīm Nājī (1893–1953) and 'Ali Mahmūd Tāhā (1902–1949), worked in a neo-romantic, modernist mode. The Apollonians were open-minded internationalists who yearned for liberation from the increasingly repressive politics of the 1930s. They opposed the conservative neoclassical trends, symbolized by the "school" of al-Bārūdī (*madrasat al-Bārūdī*), in Arabic poetry.

SEE ALSO *Apollonian/Dionysian, Dīwān school.*

Apollonian/Dionysian The twenty-seven-year-old Friedrich Nietzsche described *Apollonian* and *Dionysian* as two anthetical principles in his first book, *The Birth of Tragedy out of the Spirit of Music* (1872). Nietzsche derived the Apollonian from Apollo, the deity of light, and associated it with the genius of restraint, measure, and harmony, the superb clarity and refinement of ancient Greek sculptures and temples. He derived the Dionysian from Dionysus, the Thracian god of intoxication, and associated it with dark poetic ecstasy and the cult of the irrational, festive madness and the art of music.

Nietzsche's concept of these two polar forces of culture echoes Schopenhauer's *The World as Will and Idea* (1819). It resembles the distinction between romanticism and classicism. Nietzsche's emphasis on the Dionysian side of Greek culture opposed the prevailing nineteenth-century view, expressed by Winckelmann (1717–1768) and adapted by Goethe (1749–1832), that Greek culture expressed "noble simplicity, calm grandeur." Matthew Arnold would call this "sweetness and light." Greek culture was long identified with the triumph of rationalism. But Nietzsche recognized the darker, more barbaric side of Greek culture. He posited that tragedy developed out of the orgiastic festivals of Dionysius, where the participants felt possessed by the god.

Nietzsche suggested that the Apollonian and Dionysian reached a synthesis in tragedy. Aeschylus's tragedies embodied their greatest interaction. When Apollonian forces prevailed, when Socrates (470?–399 B.C.E.) taught the Greeks to separate appearance and reality, and Euripides (480?–406 B.C.E.) separated the "stage world" from the "real world," tragedy died. Nietzsche himself sought to be an "artistic Socrates." He argued that "the continuous development of art is bound up with the Apollonian and Dionysian duality." The Apollonian sets limits, the Dionysian dissolves them. Apollo is the god of form, clarity, contours, bright dreams, and individuality. Dionysius is the god of rapture, ectasy, orgiastic rites, and communal mergings. Nietzsche saw a dialectical struggle between Apollo and Dionysius, between classical reason and mantic power.

SEE ALSO *dithyramb, tragedy.*

aporia The term *aporia* derives from the ancient Greek *poros,* meaning way or road. The word *poria* suggests passage, and thus aporia literally means "impassable" or "without passage." In classical rhetoric, aporia suggests a situation of irresolvable difficulty, placing a claim in doubt by developing rival arguments. *Dubitatio* (from the Latin, "wavering in opinion"), a form of aporia, is the expression of feigned doubt about the capacity to speak well, as when Marc Antony says, "I come not friends, to steal away your hearts: / I am no orator . . ." (*Julius Caesar,* 1599). In philosophy, aporia denotes a philosophical puzzle, which often arises as a result of equally plausible but inconsistent premises. For Aristotle (384–322 B.C.E.), the aporia is created by the equal validity of contrary arguments.

Plato's early dialogues are called aporetic because they characteristically end with an irresolvable argument. Socrates (470?–399 B.C.E.) describes the purgative value of reducing someone to aporia in Plato's dialogue *Meno* (84 A.D.). Someone who knows something finds out that he merely thinks he knows something. Aporia instills in him the desire to investigate the truth. It becomes the deliberate act of talking about your inability to talk about something.

Jacques Derrida (1930–2004) makes aporia a central term in the philosophy of deconstruction. He locates an aporia as the site where the quest for meaning becomes blocked, and the text is charged with inconsistencies, discontinuities, fissures. The aporia is thus the place where the text undermines its own rhetorical structure. It deconstructs itself. The critic Paul de Man (1919–1983) treated the aporetic as a defining feature of the literary text, where we are inevitably faced with what we cannot know. De Man's readings demonstrate how texts do not practice what they preach, how they end in aporias.

SEE ALSO *deconstruction.*

apostrophe From the Greek, meaning "to turn away." Apostrophe is a poetic mode of direct address. Quintilian, speaking of oratory in the first century, defines apostrophe as "a diversion of our words to address some person other than the judge." Unlike the ideal orator, the poet turns away from the audience to address a God or gods, the muse, a dead or absent person, a natural object, a thing, an imaginary quality or concept. One of the distinctive marks of poetry is that anything can be addressed. Geoffrey Chaucer playfully addresses his purse, "The Complaint of Chaucer to His Purse" (ca. 1399); Anne Bradstreet addresses a book she has written, "The Author to Her Book" (1678); John Donne speaks to the sun, "The Sun Rising" (1633). Think of the fervor with which William Blake cries out, "O Rose thou art sick!" ("The Sick Rose," 1794) or the ritualistic formality with which Percy Shelley calls out, "O wild West Wind, thou breath of Autumn's being" ("Ode to the West Wind," 1819) or the unhinged grief with which Alfred, Lord Tennyson proclaims, "Ring out, wild bells" (*In Memoriam,* 1849). Apostrophe seems to take us back to the realm of magic ritual, to the archaic idea that the dead can be contacted and propitiated, the absent recalled, the inanimate and nonhuman formally humanized and invoked, and called upon for help.

SEE ALSO *invocation.*

Arcadia, Arcady Arcadia is an isolated mountainous region of Greece in central Peloponnese. In the ancient world, the sparsely populated region was known for its rustic simplicity, which became associated with the traditional singing and pipe playing of herdsmen, whose native god was Pan. It became famous throughout the ancient world as a Utopian ideal of pastoral harmony and simplicity. Theocritus set his idylls (third century B.C.E.)

in Arcadia. Virgil imagined Arcadia in his *Eclogues* (42–39 B.C.E.), where it bears a striking resemblance to northern Italy. Raymond Williams explains the transformation from the Arcadia of the Greek poet to the Arcadia of the Latin one in *The Country and the City* (1973):

> The pastoral landscape of Theocritus had been immediate and close at hand just outside the city . . . A transformation occurs, in some parts of Virgil, in which the landscape becomes in fact more distant, becomes in fact Arcadia, and the Golden Age is seen as present there, at once summoned and celebrated by the power of poetry . . . It is only a short step from a natural delight in the fertility of the earth to this magical invocation of a land which needs no farming.

Virgil's *Eclogues* were widely imitated in the pastoral poetry of the Italian, French, Spanish, and English Renaissance from the fourteenth to the seventeenth century. The landscape was the setting for Sir Philip Sidney's romance *Arcadia* (1580). The French painter Nicolas Poussin (1594–1665) employed the tradition in his painting of four shepherds, which is known as "The Arcadian Shepherds." The art historian Erwin Panofsky wrote an influential essay on the inscription in Poussin's painting, "ET IN ARCADIA EGO" ("I too am in Arcadia"), in which he showed that the statement was meant to be spoken by death itself, thus asserting the presence of mortality in the seemingly timeless pastoral world.

In 1690, an Italian poetic association named itself the Arcadian Academy. The members of the group wrote pastoral poetry and often dressed in shepherds' costumes for their meetings. The group sought "to exterminate bad taste and see to it that it shall not rise again," but bad taste survived and they produced little of lasting merit. Arcadia has retained its association as an ideal place of rustic simplicity and tranquility, which is perhaps no longer possible. The young W. B. Yeats entered poetry by declaring "The woods of Arcady are dead, / And over is their antique joy" ("The Song of the Happy Shepherd," 1885).

SEE ALSO *eclogue, idyll, nature poetry, pastoral.*

archaism A deliberately old or outdated use of language. To use an archaism in poetry is to resuscitate a word, an expression, or a form that has fallen out of use. Words are continually changing their meanings. Archaism is a way of holding on to or renewing something ancient, evoking an older style of speech and writing. In his book *Poetic Diction* (1928), Owen Barfield suggests that true archaism implies "not a standing still, but a *return* to something older."

In the history of poetry, one function of archaism was to maintain metrical regularity. The older form of a word sometimes has a different metrical weight. Thus poets continued to use the word *morn* for "morning" or treated the word *loved* as a two-syllable word. More deeply, older words have been used for the sake of their associations with the past. Thus Edmund Spenser uses archaic words to evoke the age of chivalry in *The Faerie Queene* (1590–1596), which relies on "strange inkhorn terms." In turn, Spenser and other Elizabethan poets became a source of archaisms for the romantic poets. In "The Rime of the Ancient Mariner" (1798), for example, Samuel Taylor Coleridge uses archaic words to give the feeling that his work belongs to the past of the ballad poets:

He holds him with his skinny hand,
"There was a ship," quoth he.
"Hold off! unhand me, grey-beard loon!"
Eftsoons his hand dropt he.

Sir Walter Raleigh said that the language of poetry always has "a certain archaic flavor." Poetry looks backward but it also looks forward and the archaizing impulse wars with the equally powerful impulse for poets to use a more common speech and to naturalize poetic diction. The use of archaism is at odds with the modern impulse to, in Pound's phrase, "make it new," though Pound's own work is filled with archaisms. Sometimes poets make poetry new by reviving something old. John Berryman, for example, often uses archaisms to render the feeling of a tormented postmodern spirit, a soul in stress.

archetype, archetypal criticism An original pattern or model, a prototype. Carl Jung pioneered the idea of the archetype as a "primordial image," a common psychic form that structures human experience. In Jungian theory, the archetype is a universal theme or idea, a "psychic residue" found in dreams and myths, in poems and other works of art, in different religions and philosophies. Archetypes belong to the "collective unconscious" of all peoples. The "outcast," who has been cast out of society, the "scapegoat," who gets blamed for everything, "the star-crossed lovers," who are destined for doom, are all common archtepypal figures. The idea of the archetype, especially as a fundamental quest, has been stimulating for many American poets — Theodore Roethke, Stanley Kunitz, Robert Bly, David Bottoms — who have tried to tap a primorodial imagery for their poems.

Literary critics adopted the Jungian notion of archetypes to consider permanently recurring symbols and patterns of action, images and character types, such as when youthful heroes battle dragons and journey to other worlds. In a major work of archetypal cultural criticism, Robert Graves describes the figure of the female divinity, a creator and destroyer, as "the cruel, capricious, incontinent White Goddess" (*The White Goddess,* 1948). Such critics as Richard Chase (*Quest for Myth,* 1949), Philip Wheelright (*The Burning Fountain,* 1954), and Joseph Campbell (*The Hero with a Thousand Faces,* 1949) study the recurrence of mythical patterns in literature. Northrop Frye authoritatively outlined the nature of archetypal criticism in *Anatomy of Criticism* (1957). Frye jettisoned Jung's notion of the collective unconscious as "an unnecessary hypothesis." He proposed that the totality of literary works constitute "a self-contained literary universe." Four *mythoi* or organizing plot forms, which correspond to the cycle of the four seasons, are incorporated into four major genres: comedy (spring), romance (summer), tragedy (fall), and satire (winter). For Frye, literature plays a key role in making humanly intelligible the external material universe. Archetypal criticism especially flourished in the 1950s and 1960s.

SEE ALSO *psychoanalytic criticism.*

Archilochian It is thought that Archilochus of Paros (eighth or seventh century B.C.E.), a Greek satirist, invented lines or couplets that combined different meters in complex patterns, including four different kinds of strophes. Horace used a series of Archilochian couplets in the *Odes* (23–13 B.C.E.) and *Epodes* (ca. 42–31 B.C.E.), thus immortalizing them.

arsis* and *thesis The terms *arsis* and *thesis* originally referred to the raising and lowering of the foot in ancient Greek dance. They were extended to Greek verse, which was quantitative. Arsis ("raising the foot in beating time") referred to the lighter or shorter part of the poetic foot and thesis to the heavier or longer part. The Latin poets, who associated poetry with the rising and falling of the human voice, reversed this. The Latin meaning has prevailed. In accentual poetry, arsis refers to the accented syllable and thesis to the unaccented one.

SEE ALSO *meter.*

ars poetica "Poetry is the subject of the poem," Wallace Stevens declares in "The Man with the Blue Guitar" (1937), and the *ars poetica* is a poem that takes the art of poetry — its own means of expression — as its explicit subject. It proposes an aesthetic. Self-referential, uniquely conscious of itself as both a performance and a treatise, the great ars poetica embodies what it is about. It enacts its subject.

Horace's *Ars Poetica* is our first known poem on poetics and the fountainhead of the tradition. Horace introduces himself as both poet and critic in what was probably his final work (ca. 19–18 B.C.E.), a combination of the formal epistle and the technical treatise. It is, among other things, an eloquent defense of freedom at a time when freedom was imperiled in Rome. Horace speaks of art and ingenuity, of the poet's need to fuse unity and variety, of the poet's dual function to delight and to be useful (*dulce* and *utile*). He wittily defends the usefulness of artistic constraints and the necessity for artistic freedom, and he writes on behalf of both the writer and the reader, the poet and the audience: "it is not enough for poems to be beautifully crafted, let them be attractive and drive as they wish the audience's emotion . . . if you want me to weep, you must first yourself feel grief: only then will I share the pain of your disasters." Horace also speaks of the sacred role of poets in earlier times.

An anthology of the *ars poetica* would include Alexander Pope's "An Essay on Criticism" (1711), the exemplary treatise of the Enlightenment; passages from William Wordsworth's *Prelude* (1805, 1850), which traces the growth of the poet's mind, and from Walt Whitman's "Song of Myself" ("I speak the password primeval . . . I give the sign of democracy," 1855); Emily Dickinson's poem number 1129, written around 1868 ("Tell all the Truth but tell it slant — "); Wallace Stevens's "Of Modern Poetry" (1940); and Hugh MacDiarmid's "The Kind of Poetry I Want" ("A poetry that takes its polish from a conflict / Between discipline at its most strenuous / And feeling at its highest," 1961). It would take into account Marianne Moore's adversarial *ars poetica* "Poetry," first published in 1921 ("I, too, dislike it") and Czeslaw Milosz's conditional "*Ars Poetica?*" ("The purpose of poetry is to remind us / how difficult it is to remain just one person," 1968). The *ars poetica,* like the defense of poetry, becomes a necessary form when poetry is called into question and freedom is endangered.

SEE ALSO *dulce et utile.*

arte mayor, arte menor, see *copla.*

ascending rhythm, see *rising rhythm.*

Asclepiad The Greek poet Asclepiades of Samos (ca. 290) gave his name to this meter, which is comprised of one spondee (two long syllables), two or three choriambs (two long syllables enclose two short ones), and one iamb (one short syllable and one long one). The Lesser Alcepiad has two choriambs, the Greater Asclepiad three. The Latin writers Horace (65–8 B.C.E.), Catullus (84–54 B.C.E.), and Seneca (ca. 4 B.C.E.–65 C.E.) all favored Asclepiads. In English, Sir Philip Sidney at times adapted this meter to accentual-syllabic verse in *Arcadia* (1590), as in this passage:

> O sweet woods, the delight of solitariness!
> O how much I do like your solitariness!
> Where man's mind hath a freed consideration,
> Of goodness to receive lovely direction.
> Where senses do behold th'order of heav'nly host,
> And wise thoughts do behold what the creator is;

W. H. Auden revived it for his poem "In Due Season" (1968). "I am . . . rather proud of *In Due Season,* an attempt to write accentual Asclepiadeans," Auden wrote to E. R. Dodds in September 1968. Auden refers to his attempt in stanza three: "Time for reading of thoughts, time for the trying-out / Of new metres and new recipes . . ."

SEE ALSO *choriamb, iamb, meter, spondee, trochee.*

ashough Armenian minstrel. *Ashoughs* traveled the Armenian countryside throughout the seventeenth and eighteenth centuries. The poet and folk singer Harutyun Sayatyan (1712–1795) was known as Sayat-Nova, or the "King of Songs" in Persian. *Ashoughs,* many of them blind singers, still perform on bridges and in town squares in Armenian cities. They are also honored guests at weddings and other festivities.

SEE ALSO *oral poetry.*

aşik The word for minstrel in Turkish, *aşik,* also means "lover." Turkish folk poets ("the ones who love") often sing poems of mystical quest, lyrics suggesting that God can be reached through love. Their songs are akin to mystical Sufi poetry. They traditionally sing with the three-stringed Turkish *saz,* an eight-stringed instrument similar to a mandolin.

SEE ALSO *ashough, the beloved, oral poetry.*

assonance The audible repetition of vowel sounds within words encountered near each other. Robert Latham defines assonance as the "resemblance of proximal vowel sounds." The word derives from the Latin *assonare,* meaning "to answer with the same sound." Listen to the interplay of vowels in these lines from Alfred, Lord Tennyson's "The Lotos-Eaters" (1833):

> And round about the keel with faces pale,
> Dark faces pale against that rosy flame,
> The mild-eyed melancholy Lotos-eaters came.

Notice the repetition of the letters *ou* in the words *round about;* the recurrence of the vowels *a* and *e* in "faces pale," which is repeated twice; how the soft *a* reverberates from the words *and* to *about* to *dark* to *against;* how the hard *a* is picked up again in the words *flame* and *came;* how the letter *o* moves as a hard sound from the word *rosy* to the first syllable of the word *Lotos* and as a soft sound from the word *melancholy* to the second syllable of the word *Lotos;* and how the letter *e* echoes from *mild-eyed* to *Lotos-eaters.* This is "vocalic rhyme."

John Keats was especially compelled by technical problems of assonance, of vowel music. "One of his favorite topics of discourse was the principle of melody in Verse," Benjamin Bailey remembered in 1849: "Keats's theory was, that the vowels should be so managed as not to clash one with another so as to mar the melody, — & yet that they should be interchanged, like differing notes of music." Keats's verbal tactics of repetition and variation, his subtle way of mixing long and short vowels, enabled him to fashion a sonorous music, and his vowels dilate the line into a numinous presence, creating a feeling both of intensity and spiritual easefulness. One notices, for example, how he grasps and modulates the pitch of a nightingale across several lines of "Ode to a Nightingale" (1819), how suggestively he invokes "a light-winged Dryad of the trees" who

In some melodious plot
Of beechen green, and shadows numberless,
Singest of summer in full-throated ease.

One hears the letter *i* in the words *In, singest,* and *in* again; the hard *e* repeating in *beechen green* and coming back in the word *ease;* the soft *e* echoing softly in the words *numberless* and *Singest;* the letter *o* vibrating from *melodious plot* to *shadows* and *full-throated;* and the letter *u* echoing from *numberless* to *summer* and then taking on a different valence in *full-throated.* All this imitates the effect of a nightingale singing melodiously in the trees.

Assonance preceded rhyme in the early verse of the Romance languages, Old French, Provençal, and Spanish, where it was a characteristic coordinating element. For example, each strophe or *laisse* closes with the same vowel sound in the epic *Chanson de Roland* (*The Song of Roland,* ca. 1090), the oldest surviving major work of French literature. As a binding element, assonance was later replaced by rhyme in European poetry. Nonetheless, poets have continued to experiment with assonance as an echo chamber within a poem. Assonance remains a key aural device, subtle and unsystematic, a form of internal vowel play that pleases the ear.

SEE ALSO *alliteration, bird song, consonance, rhyme.*

asyndeton The deliberate omission of conjunctions from a series of related phrases or clauses, as in Caesar's famous "Veni, vidi, vici" ("I came, I saw, I conquered"). It is the opposite of polysyndeton, the addition of conjunctions. Aristotle argues in his *Rhetoric* (ca. 335–330 B.C.E.) that it is more appropriate in spoken oratories than in written prose: "Thus strings of unconnected words, and constant repetitions of words and phrases, are very properly condemned in written speeches: but not in spoken speeches — speakers use them freely, for they have a dramatic effect." What works as an amplifying device for speeches also serves poetry, which thrives on being recited aloud. Petrarch highlights his mood when he writes, "vegghio, penso, ardo, piango" or "I lie awake, think, burn, weep" (Sonnet #164).

SEE ALSO *polysyndeton, rhetoric.*

astrophic, see *stichic.*

athletic poetry There's a long, jubilant tradition in poetry of celebrating athletic achievement. It begins with the Greek poet Pindar, who wrote a series of choral odes to commemorate athletic victories. Pindar's triumphal choral odes from the fifth century B.C.E. are the first truly written narrative texts of any length. Greek performers simultaneously sang the poems and danced to them at shrines or theaters, though now the words are all that remains of the complete Pindaric experience. The movement of the verse, which mirrors a musical dance pattern, tends to be emotionally intense and highly exalted.

Pindar's epinician odes (early fifth century B.C.E.) were commissioned victory poems (named for epi-Niké-an, the goddess of victory) about sports, and they had stories of gods and heroes woven into them. Each ode focuses on a triumphant athlete who has a symbolic connection to a god, and thus it incorporates a mythology. The poems have their roots in religious rites, and each one called for an ecstatic performance that communally reenacted the ritual of participating in the divine. Horace (65–8 B.C.E.) compared Pindar to a great swan conquering the air by long rapturous flights. He claimed that athletes were given more glory by Pindar's voice "than by a hundred statues standing mute / Around the applauding city" (*Odes,* 4.2). The poet Bacchylides (fifth century B.C.E.), who has often been considered a "lesser Pindar," also flew with appealing grace.

Since the mid-1970s, the Italian concrete and sound poet Arrigo Lora Totino has pioneered gymnastic poetry. It is a kind of mime poetry. In the catalog to the "International Week of performance" (1977), the critic Francesca Alinovi wrote that Lora Totino had offered "an excellent show of mimed and declaimed poetry, moving about with supremely graceful style and making all the strings of his body vibrate, which he transforms into a perfect musical instrument."

SEE ALSO *epinicia.*

aubade A dawn song expressing the regret of parting lovers at daybreak. The earliest European examples date from the end of the twelfth century. The Provençal, Spanish, and German equivalents are *alba, albada,* and *Tagelied.* Some scholars believe the aubade, which has no fixed metrical form, grew out of the cry of the medieval watchman, who announced from his tower the passing of night and return of day. Ezra Pound renders the Provençal "Alba Innominata" as "Ah God! Ah God! That dawn should come so soon!" In *The Spirit of Romance* (1910), he points out that romance literature dawned with a Provençal "Alba" from around the tenth century:

Dawn appeareth upon the sea,
  from behind the hill,
The watch passeth, it shineth
  clear amid the shadows.

However it began, the fact that the dawn song is found in nearly all early poetries suggests that its poignancy crosses cultures.

Chaucer gives a splendid example of an aubade in book 3 of *Troilus and Criseyde* (ca. 1380s). It begins when Criseyde hears the cock crow and then continues on for fourteen additional stanzas:

"Myn hertes lyf, my trist, and my plesaunce,
That I was born, allas! what me is wo,
That day of us mot make desseveraunce!
For tyme it is to ryse, and hennes go,
Or elles I am lost for evermo!
O night, allas! why niltow over us hove,
As longe as whanne Almena lay by Jove?"

The aubade recalls the joy of two lovers joined together in original darkness. It remembers the ecstasy of union. But it also describes a parting at dawn, and with that parting comes the dawning of individual consciousness; the separated, or day-lit, mind bears the grief or burden of longing for what has been lost. The characteristic or typal aubade flows from the darkness of the hour before dawn to the brightness of the hour afterward. It moves from silence to speech, from the rapture of communion to the burden of isolation, and the poem itself becomes a conscious recognition of our separateness. This is made evident in Shakespeare's *Romeo and Juliet* (act 3, scene 5, 1–36, 1597), which includes a debate about whether the two lovers are listening to the song of a nocturnal bird or a morning one:

Juliet: Will thou be gone? it is not yet near day:
It was the nightingale and not the lark,
That pierc'd the fearful hollow of thine ear;
Nightly she sings on yon pomegranate tree:
Believe me, love, it was the nightingale.

Romeo: It was the lark, the herald of the morn,
No nightingale: look, love, what envious streaks
Do lace the severing clouds in yonder east:
Night's candles are burnt out, and jocund day
Stands tiptoe on the misty mountain tops.

The aubade concludes with Romeo's heartfelt cry, "More light and light — more dark and dark our woes!" John Donne rebels against the convention of separation in his aubade "The Sun Rising" (1633), which begins by chiding the sun ("Busie old foole, unruly Sunne"). There is no beloved at all in Philip Larkin's last poem, "Aubade" (1977), a terrifying spiritual confrontation with oblivion. The direction of the aubade is irreversible. It moves from the song of the nightingale to the song of the lark and thus flows into time.

audition colorée, see *synaesthesia.*

Augustan Age One of the high moments in poetry: the period of Virgil (70–19 B.C.E.), Horace (65–8 B.C.E.), and Ovid (43 B.C.E.–18 C.E.), the three greatest poets, under the Roman emperor Augustus, "first among equals," who restored order and ruled alone from 27 B.C.E. to his death in 14 C.E. These poets of empire virtually reinvented pastoral poetry. Their work runs the gamut from the high themes of national glory sounded in Virgil's *Aeneid* (29–19 B.C.E.), whose subject is the greatness of Rome, to the keen clarity of Horace's *Satires* (35 B.C.E.), which describe the pleasures and irritations of daily life, to the mythological storehouse of Ovid's *Metamorphoses* (8 C.E.) and the urbane wit of his manual on seduction, *The Art of Love* (2 C.E.).

The Augustan Age also describes the literature of Britain during the first half of the eighteenth century, which is also called the Neoclassical Age or the age of reason. This is the era of John Dryden (1631–1700), Alexander Pope (1688–1744), and Jonathan Swift (1667–1745), all of whom self-consciously imitated the classical writers of the original Augustan period. They expressed themselves in tight heroic couplets and scathing satires. Thus, their writings reflect such neoclassical virtues as order, balance, and decorum, but also display a scathing wit and scapular wisdom, a rage against encroaching unreason.

SEE ALSO *aureate, couplet, eclogue, Enlightenment, georgic, the golden age, neoclassicism, pastoral, satire.*

aureate From the Middle English *aureat*, from Late Latin *aureātus*, from *aureus*, "golden," from *aurum*, "gold." The Augustan poets, especially Virgil (70–19 B.C.E.) and Horace (65–8 B.C.E.), were often described as "golden." Theirs was the golden age of Latin poetry, the Roman apex. The generation that followed, especially Lucan and Statius, were considered "silver poets." The term *aureate* was later marshaled and applied to the ornamental style, the eloquent poetic diction, of the fifteenth- and sixteenth-century English and Scottish poets. The Scottish Chaucerians, especially Robert Henryson (ca. 1460–1500) and William Dunbar (ca. 1460–1513), developed a virtuoso technique and an exotic, highly elaborated diction. In one of the recurring debates of literary history, their ornate "high style" was contrasted to the "low," "drab," or "plain" style.

SEE ALSO *Augustan Age, drab and golden poetry, the golden age, the plain style, Scottish Chaucerians.*

automatic writing, automatism The Surrealist poets advocated writing automatically without any conscious control. The method was a kind of Freudian free association, and the goal was to free the unconscious from the constraints of the ego or conscious mind. Poetry, the voice of desire, would be liberated by trancelike states, startling images. André Breton and Philippe Soupault created the first automatic book, the novel *Les Champs Magnétique* (*The Magnetic Fields*, 1919). Breton equated automatic writing with "pure psychic automatism" in his first *Manifeste de surréalisme* (1924) and dreamed of magical dictation. Maurice Blanchot summarizes the breakthrough of automatic writing:

> Automatic writing tended to suppress constraints, suspend intermediaries, reject all mediation. It put the hand that writes in contact with something original; it made of this active hand a sovereign passivitiy, no longer a means of livelihood, an instrument, a servile tool, but an independent power, over which no one had authority any more, which belonged to no one and which could not, which knew not how to do anything—but write . . .

William Butler Yeats conducted similar experiments in automatic writing with his bride Georgie Hyde-Lees, which eventuated in *A Vision* (1925). He described the experience: "On the afternoon of October 24th, 1917, four days after my marriage, my wife surprised me by attempting automatic writing. What came in disjointed sentences, in almost illegible writing, was so exciting, sometimes so profound, that I persuaded her to give an hour or two day after day to the unknown writer, and after some half-dozen such hours offered to spend what remained of life explaining and piecing together those scattered sentences. 'No,' was the answer, 'we have come to give you metaphors for poetry.' "

SEE ALSO *Surrealism.*

autotelic From the Greek *auto* and *telos,* meaning "self-directed" or "self-completing." This term suggests that a work of art has no other end or purpose but itself. The New Critics especially proposed and championed the idea of an autotelic text, the self-sufficient, autonomous individual poem.

SEE ALSO *New Criticism, objective correlative.*

avant-garde The term *avant-garde* literally meant the "advance-guard," the most forward-looking troops. It dates back to the Middle Ages as a term of warfare. In the nineteenth century, it was aggressively imported from the military into the realm of art and literature to blur the distinction between art and life, to challenge the social order and "shock" the bourgeoisie. It suggests something new and advanced, a revolutionary vanguard ahead of its time. In 1845, Gabriel-Désiré Laverant declared in *De la mission de l'art et du role des artiste:*

> Art, the expression of society, manifests, in its highest soaring, the most advanced social tendencies: it is the forerunner and the revealer.

> Therefore, to know whether art worthily fulfills its proper mission as initiator, whether the artist is truly of the avant-garde, one must know where Humanity is going, what the destiny of the human race is . . .

There is a paradox in the cultural idea of the avant-garde, which borrows a military notion to express its sense of noncomformism. Charles Baudelaire showed disdain in the 1860s for the "predilection of the French for military metaphors" (*My Heart Laid Bare,* 1887). A political vocabulary also infiltrated avant-garde notions of culture in the nineteenth century, as when Stéphane Mallarmé told an interviewer in 1891 that the modern poet is "on strike against society." The avant-garde set out with a dual purpose: to destroy and to invent. Matei Călenscu points out that Bakunin's anarchist maxim — "To destroy is to create" — applies to most of the activities of the twentieth-century avant-garde.

During the first decades of the twentieth century, the concept of the avant-garde widened to include all the new, antitraditional schools of art, music, and poetry (futurism, Cubism, etc.). Ever since, it has committed itself to rupture and change, to novelty, to aesthetic extremism. The avant-garde moved from modernism to postmodernism, and since the 1960s it has drawn its energy from a cross-polination of genres, playfulness in style, a commitment to experimentation. But ever since the late 1950s, critics such as Roland Barthes have also been declaring the death of the avant-garde. "It was dying," Călenscu summarizes, "because it was recognized as artistically significant by the same class whose values it so drastically negated." The novelist and semiotician Umberto Eco argues that the avant-garde hostility toward the past ultimately leads to silence. He explains in *Postscript to "The Name of the Rose"* (1984):

> The historic avant-garde . . . tries to settle scores with the past. "Down with the moonlight" — a futurist slogan — is a platform typical of every avant-garde; you have only to replace "moonlight" with whatever noun is suitable. The avant-garde destroys, defaces the past: *Les Demoiselles d'Avignon* is a typical avant-garde act. Then the avant-garde goes further, destroys the figure, cancels it, arrives at the abstract, the informal, the white canvas, the slashed canvas, the charred canvas. In architecture and the visual arts, it will be the curtain wall, the building

> as stele, pure parallelpiped, minimal art; in literature, the destruction of the flow of discourse, the Burroughs-like collage; silence, the white page in music, the passage from atonality to absolute silence (in this sense, the early Cage is modern). But the moment comes when the avant-garde (the modern) can go no further.

SEE ALSO *Cubist poetry, Dadaism, futurism, modernism, postmodernism, Surrealism.*

awdl, awdlau (pl) The *awdl,* the most highly considered form of Welsh bardic composition, has a complex history. The word *awdl* is a variant of *odl* ("rhyme"). It originally meant a metrical composition of any length with a single rhyme throughout. The *awdl* could stand alone as a discrete poem or else form part of a longer work, as in the medieval poem *The Gododdin.* Since the fourteenth century, the *awdl* has generally been established as a complete work with monorhymed sections, which are called *caniadau.* The separate sections are linked by repeating a word or sound between the end of one line and the start of another, or else by repeating the same word or phrase at the beginning of each section. The Poets of the Nobility, who flourished from the fourteenth to the seventeenth century, used a wide variety of meters, which were then codified into twenty-four strict meters. There are twelve *awdl* forms in the bardic tradition with complex harmonic rules, involving stress, alliteration, and rhyme. The rare "exemplary awdl" is a technical tour de force that employs all twenty-four of the meters. Since the nineteenth century, the form has been mostly confined to eisteddfod competitions, in which a "chair" is awarded to the greatest *awdl.*

SEE ALSO *cynghanedd, eisteddfod, englyn, strict-meter poetry.*

awen A Welsh word meaning poetic gift, or inspiration, the muse. The etymological sense of *awen* is "breathing-in," which makes it akin to the Latin *afflatus.* The very concept of *awen* embodies and recognizes the irrational power and magical potency of poetry. The Celtic bards inherited their authority from the Druids, and *awen* was the unconscious or supernatural energy that animated their words. It is what Dylan Thomas describes in his first book (1934) as "the force that through the green fuse drives the flower." In *The White Goddess* (1948), Robert Graves translates *awen* as "the divine spirit."

SEE ALSO *afflatus, bard, muse.*

bacchius, bacchiac The name of this Greek metrical foot, which consists of one short syllable followed by two long ones, may derive from ancient Greek drinking songs devoted to the god Bacchus. The bacchiac meter was common in Latin verse, especially in the plays of Plautus (ca. 254–184 B.C.E.). Such trisyllabic words and pairings, though aboveboard, are rare in English-language poetry.

SEE ALSO *wine poetry.*

badii'a This Arabic word refers to the poetry of the early Abbasid period (late eighth, early ninth century). The poets of this era developed a difficult new style, poetry of elaborate figuration, somewhat akin to English metaphysical poetry. Muslim Ibn al-Walid (d. 823) is said to be the first Arabic poet to employ this elaborated stylistic approach. Suzanne Stetkevych proposes that "*badii'a* poetry be defined not merely as the occurrence of this particular rhetorical device but rather that the *badii'a* style is first and foremost the intentional, conscious encoding of abstract meaning into metaphor. . . . The large number of . . . rhetorical devices in *badii'a* poetry is not a mere proliferation due to infatuation . . . but rather the product of a constant and ineluctable awareness of the logical and etymological relationship between words, and the intention to express this awareness." The Hebrew poets of Andalusia, especially Solomon Ibn Gabirol (ca. 1021–1058), frequently adopted the *badii'a* stylistic approach.

SEE ALSO *metaphysical poets.*

baile Spanish: "dance." The *baile* is a Spanish poetic form based on dance rhythms. It can also name a brief dramatic work that combines words, music, and pantomime. It is generally staged between the first two acts of a play.

bakshi, see *akyn.*

balada A Provençal dance song with no fixed form but an oft-repeated refrain, the *balada* is virtually indistinguishable from the *dansa,* which also marked the time for dancing.

balagtasan The *balagtasan,* a poetic contest, developed in Philippine poetry in the second quarter of the twentieth century. It is named after Francesco Balagtas (1788–1862), "the father of Tagalog poetry," and grew out of the popular folk form of the *duplo.* The *balagtasan* was primarily established by the poets Jose Corazon de Jesus and Florentino Collantes, who competed in a series of bouts in the 1920s, which drew enormous crowds. These highly publicized verse debates, which took place during the American colonial period in the Philippines, expressed a strongly nationalist and anti-colonial political consciousness. The most important ones centered on independence. The Tagalog *balagtasan* was so popular that it was taken up by other Filipino ethno-linguistic groups, such as the Kapampangans, who named their version *crissotan,* after Juan Crisostomo Soto (1867–1919), "the father of Pampango literature," and the Ilocanos, who named their version *bucanegan,* after the blind folk poet Pedro Bucaneg (1592–ca. 1630), "the father of Ilocano literature."

SEE ALSO *balak, bical, duplo, flyting, poetic contests.*

balak The seventeenth-century Spanish Jesuit Father Ignatio Francisco Alzina recognized the *balak* as one of the early forms of oral Waray literature in the Philippines. It has survived in the Cebuano-speaking region of Leyte, where some take it to be a generic term for poetry and others as a love joust, a poetic battle between the sexes. It thus overlaps with the *balitaw,* an extemporaneous debate simultaneously sung and danced. The Waray historian Charo N. Cabardo points out that the form has taken new names and adapted the language of the colonizers. It was labeled "amoral" during the

Spanish period and renamed *ismayling,* a term derived from the word "smile," during the American occupation.

SEE ALSO *poetic contests.*

ballad The traditional British ballad is a narrative song, a poem that tells a story, preserved and transmitted orally. It unfolds in four-line stanzas and customarily alternates four- and three-stress lines. The second and fourth lines rhyme. Here is the opening of "Earl Brand":

> Rise up, rise up, my seven brave sons,
> And dress in your armour so bright;
> Earl Douglas will hae Lady Margaret awa
> Before that it be light.

The word *ballad* derives from the Middle English *balade,* from Old French *ballade,* from Provençal *balada,* a dancing song. As the linguist Edward Sapir writes, "Poetry everywhere is inseparable in its origins from the singing voice and the measure of the dance." Over time, the ballad lost whatever connection it once may have had to dance, though Robert Graves believed, "When the word 'ballad' was adopted by English singers, though the association with dancing did not survive, there remained latent in it the sense of *rhythmic group action* whether in work or in play." Iceland is well known for its heroic ballads, the *sagas,* which were passed down orally for centuries. Once they were written down, their form was fixed and they were perceived as written poetry. The *rímur,* or sung ballads, were epic heroic songs. The English-language ballad originated in the fourteenth century—its most popular hero was Robin Hood. The most important collection is the Child ballads, which consists of 305 ballads from England and Scotland (and their American variants) collected by Francis James Child: *English and Scottish Popular Ballads* (1882–1898). The European ballad developed out of an earlier epic tradition. Medieval epic songs were transformed into shorter dramatic songs, such as the *romance* (a poem in octosyllabic meter) in France, Portugal, and Spain, which in turn crossed the ocean and became the Mexican *corrido.* Whereas epics were heroic songs sung by men, ballads were often sung by women, and told different kinds of stories.

As a form of great antiquity, the ballad has been built up and scoured down by oral transmission to a work of eloquent simplicity. It often opens abruptly, focuses on a single, crucial episode, and moves decisively toward a tragic conclusion. Dialogue carries the story and the narration is rapid, elliptical, and impersonal, though it retains vestiges of ritual participation. The individual singer stands in for the community, serving as the deputy of a public voice. The high degree of repetition is mnemonic, the refrain a way of creating and discharging intense emotion.

The broadside ballad was a poem printed on a broadside, a single sheet of paper, and sold in the streets. It was especially popular during the eighteenth century. "I love a ballad in print," Shakespeare writes in *The Winter's Tale* (act 4, scene 4, 1623). The written literary ballad, which emerged at the end of the eighteenth century as a viable and widely practiced subgenre, echoes the spirit, and often the language and form, of the traditional folk ballad. Thomas Percy's *Reliques of Ancient English Poetry* (1765) and Sir Walter Scott's collection *The Minstrelsy of the Scottish Border* (1802–1803) helped create the vogue. The ballad especially appealed to the romantic poets because it is an authentically popular form practiced by ordinary people, because of its "medieval" subject matter and "Gothic" taste, because it calls up deep feeling in the audience. Whitman loved Scott's offering of old ballads precisely because it seemed to take him back to the primitive origins of all poetry and thus offered a bardic model for his own "barbaric yawp." In England, think of Wordsworth and Coleridge (*Lyrical Ballads,* 1798) or John Keats ("La belle dame sans merci," 1884), in Germany of Wolfgang von Goethe ("Erlkönig," 1782) and Heinrich Heine ("Die Lorelei," 1822). The literary ballad resonates with nostalgia for a lost oral poetry. It has had powerful appeal for poets from the nineteenth century onward, and one could make a splendid anthology of twentieth-century literary ballads in English, including works by W. B. Yeats, Thomas Hardy, A. E. Housman, Robert Graves, Edwin Muir, and W. H. Auden. The writer of literary ballads seeks to transcend isolation and express a primordial collective will. The ballad writer also tends to be in quest of an archaic way of knowing, and thus the very form of the ballad becomes a way of attaining what Daniel Hoffman calls "barbarous knowledge."

SEE ALSO *broadside ballad, epic, folk song, incremental repetition, oral poetry, refrain, rima, romance, romanticism.*

ballade The most important of the fixed forms (*formes fixes*) of Old French poetry. The word *ballade* derives from an Old French word that means "dancing-song." It is a musical form that consists of three eight-line stanzas with a strict rhyme scheme (*ababbcbc*) and a four-line envoy (*bcbc*). The last line repeats in all three stanzas as well as the envoy. The entire poem turns on three rhymes, which build to the refrain. The lines are usually eight or ten syllables long. In English, the meter is customarily iambic tetrameter or pentameter. The envoy is a summary statement, traditionally an apostrophe to a head of state. Originally, this may have been the judge (the so-called prince) of a poetic competition. In these competitions, the host would often supply the first line and the poets would improvise from there. There are fifteen surviving poems, for example, that begin with the line that François Villon used so powerfully, "I die of thirst beside the fountain" ("*Je meurs de soif auprès de la fontaine*").

The ballade first rose to prominence in the fourteenth and fifteenth centuries when it was popularized by troubadour poets (Guillaume de Machaut, Eustace Deschamps, Christine de Pisan, Charles d'Orleans), but reached its greatest height in sixteenth-century France. Villon proved himself to be the undisputed master of the form in such works as "Ballade des pendus" ("Ballade of the Hanged," 1489) and "Ballade des dames du temps jadis" ("Ballade of Dead Ladies," 1450), with its famous refrain. Here is Dante Gabriel Rossetti's translation of the latter (1869):

Tell me now in what hidden way is
  Lady Flora the lovely Roman?
Where's Hipparchia, and where is Thais,
  Neither of them the fairer woman?
  Where is Echo, behold of no man,
Only heard on river and mere,—
  She whose beauty was more than human? . . .
But where are the snows of yester-year?

Where's Héloise, the learned nun,
  For whose sake Abeillard, I ween,
Lost manhood and put priesthood on?
  (From Love he won such dule and teen!)
  And where, I pray you, is the Queen

Who willed that Buridan should steer
    Sewed in a sack's mouth down the Seine? . . .
But where are the snows of yester-year?

White Queen Blanche, like a queen of lilies,
    With a voice like any mermaiden —
Bertha Broadfoot, Beatrice, Alice,
    And Ermengarde the lady of Maine, —
    And that good Joan whom Englishmen
At Rouen doomed and burned her there, —
    Mother of God, where are they then? . . .
But where are the snows of yester-year?

Nay, never ask this week, fair lord,
    Where they are gone, nor yet this year,
Except with this for an overword, —
    But where are the snows of yester-year?

In Germany, the ballade was a narrative poem or song, akin to the folk ballad, which flourished in the last quarter of the eighteenth and the first half of the nineteenth century. The French ballade was imported into English poetry by both Gower (1325?–1408), whose surviving ballades are written in French, and Chaucer — for example, "The Complaint of Chaucer to His Purse" (ca. 1399). The form had a vogue in late nineteenth-century England when it caught on with Austin Dobson, W. E. Henley, Alfred Noyes (who wrote a triple ballade of nine octaves and an envoy), and especially Algernon Charles Swinburne and Dante Gabriel Rossetti, both of whom translated Villon.

There are a number of variations on the original ballade formula. The ballade supreme consists of three ten-line stanzas that rhyme (*ababbccdcd*) with an envoy of five lines that rhyme (*ccdcd*). It turns on four rhymes. The refrain repeats as the last line of each stanza and of the envoy. The double ballade and the double ballade supreme have six stanzas of eight and ten lines, respectively, and follow the rhyme schemes of the ballade and the ballade supreme. The *hutain,* which is sometimes called the *Monk's Tale stanza,* is a complete poem composed of a single ballade stanza (*ababbcbc*). One form of the *dizain* is a complete poem composed of a single ballade supreme stanza (*ababbccdcd*). The ballade is now mostly a form of light verse, as in Dorothy Parker's "Ballade at Thirty-Five" (1924), "Ballade of a Great Weariness" (1937), and "Ballade of Unfortunate Mammals" (1931).

SEE ALSO *chant royal, dizain, formes fixes, Monk's Tale stanza, octave.*

barcarole The barcarole was originally a boating song sung by Venetian gondoliers. It has a rhythm suggestive of rowing. In the Middle Ages, the form expanded to include songs or pieces of music reminiscent of the Venetian *barcaroli* as they rowed their gondolas. It expanded further to include poems or songs whose subject is boats or water, or whose rhythms suggest the movement of water. Pablo Neruda's *La Barcarola* (1967) brought the barcarole into contemporary poetry. "I wrote a big book of poetry, I called it *La Barcarola,*" Neruda explained, "and it was a kind of ballad; I dabbled a little in all the materials I like to use, sometimes water or wheat, sometimes simple sand, an occasional hard and precise crag or quarry, and always the sea with its silence and its thunder, eternities at my disposal right outside my window and within reach of my paper." The Greek poet Pandelís Prevelákis's "Barcarole" (1941) begins with a lulling rhythm, "The waves rock me as in a cradle," but ends with a watchful cry, "Keep vigil! The land has let loose / her dogs upon me."

bard The word *bard* originally referred to the ancient Celtic order of minstrel-poets who composed verses celebrating the laws and heroic achievement of the people, of chiefs and warriors. The bards carried necessary cultural information and underwent rigorous technical training in order to tell the tale of the tribe. Ted Hughes noted that "tradition dwells on the paranormal, clairvoyant, somewhat magical powers of the Bards." The professional literary caste of the bardic order in Ireland lasted from the thirteenth to the seventeenth century. It was serious business to become a poet and serve the prince, and the training period could extend for as long as twelve years. In *The Book of Irish Verse* (1998), John Montague says that one way of describing the training is as "seven winters in a dark room," and quotes an early eighteenth-century memoir:

> Concerning the poetical Seminary or School . . . it was open only to such as were descended of Poets and reputed within their Tribes . . . The Structure was a snug, low Hut, and beds in it at convenient Dis-

> tances, each within a small Apartment . . . No windows to let in the Day, nor any Light at all us'd but that of Candles, and these brought in at a proper Season only . . . The reason of laying the Study aforesaid in the Dark was doubtless to avoid the Distraction which Light and the variety of Objects represented thereby commonly occasions.

The poets who came through this strict regimen created poems that sometimes let deep emotion break through their virtuoso technique. Some of their most poignant poems mourn the passing of their order. Some songs in the Irish language are a legacy of the bardic tradition, especially the repertoire of *sean nós* (old style). Emerson writes in his essay "The Poet" (1844): "The ancient British bards had for the title of their order, 'Those who are free throughout the world.' They are free, and they make free." In "Merlin I" (1846), he says: "Great is the art, / Great be the manners, of the bard."

The bardic poet in ancient Greece was called an *aoidos:* "And the famous bard (*aoidos*) sang to them, and they sat quietly listening," Homer states in the *Odyssey* (ca. eighth century B.C.E.). Medieval bards in Wales were frequently composers and not performers. They employed a harpist and a *datgeiniad,* who declaimed the bard's words. Since the eighteenth century, the term *bard* has often been used as a synonym for *poet.* One legacy of the Celtic bardic order is to preserve language, another to embody imaginative freedom. The creative use of technical poetic skill and wide literary and cultural knowledge makes for our greater freedom. Hence Emerson's dual claim that the poets are "liberating gods" and "America is a poem in our eyes." The poet offers us thought schooled by intuition, emotion deeper than thought, and soulfulness deeper than emotion. Such archaic ways of knowing go all the way down to the roots of being. "But trust my instinct," Robert Frost says jauntily in his poem "To a Thinker" (1936), arguing reasonably against excessive reason, "I'm a bard."

SEE ALSO *aoidos, fili.*

bardolatry The worship of William Shakespeare (1564–1616). George Bernard Shaw coined the term *bardolater* — one who idolized the Bard — in his preface to *Three Plays for Puritans* (1901). Shaw, who believed that the excessive adulation of Shakespeare stifled English drama, combined the term *bard* with the word *idolatry.* Shakespeare gradually became the national poet of England after 1660, and bardolatry began to set in. Ben Jonson had said, "I loved the man, and do honour his memory, on this side idolatry, as much as any." David Garrick, the supreme actor of his age, epitomized one form of bardolotry at the climax of his Jubilee in 1769 when he gesticulated toward a graven image of the Bard and called him "The god of our idolatry!" But it is not bardolatry to grapple with Shakespeare's universality, Harold Bloom contends: "Shakespeare has had the status of a secular Bible for the last two centuries."

baroque The word *baroque* probably derives from the Portuguese *barroco,* a jeweler's term for a rough and irregular pearl, which was imported from Goa to Portugal in the sixteenth century. In the eighteenth century, the French started using the word as an adjective meaning "bizarre" or "odd." The term was first used in the eighteenth century in a derogatory and pejorative sense to describe the bad taste, the noisy eccentricity, and overabundance of the art and architecture of the preceding era. The baroque was contrasted with the sober clarities and classicism of the Renaissance. In the nineteenth century, the term was rehabilitated by the art historian Heinrich Wölflin to describe any art that has become fully elaborated.

The term *baroque* refers both to an anti-naturalistic style and to a period in art, architecture, music, and literature. The baroque style is eccentric, excessive, and extravagant; it is lavish, ornamental, and ornate. The Baroque era in the visual arts refers to a European style of art and architecture that developed in the seventeenth century. In 1934, Erwin Panofsky argued that the Baroque was not the end of the Renaissance, but "the beginning of a fourth era, which may be called 'Modern' with a capital M." The Baroque era in music refers to the period roughly from 1600 to 1750. In poetry, the term is often used to refer to the elaborate poetic styles of the early seventeenth century, especially Gongorism, which derives from the work of the Spanish poet Luis de Góngora, and Marinism, which derives from the work of the Italian poet Giovanni Battista Marini. The mannerisms of the English Metaphysicals are often considered baroque. The baroque is colorful, decorative, and flamboyant. In *A Universal History of Infamy* (1935), Jorge Luis Borges defines baroque as "that style which deliberately exhausts (or tries to exhaust) all its possibilities and which borders on its own parody."

SEE ALSO *Gongorism, Marinism, metaphysical poets, Renaissance poetry.*

barzelletta Italian: "joke, funny story" or "carnival song." This Italian verse form, which is frequently written in octosyllabic couplets, began as a form of nonsense poetry, a series of disconnected subjects composed in haphazard meters. The fun was in the jumble. In the fourteenth century, it evolved into an epigrammatic vehicle for witty moral instruction. In the fifteenth and sixteenth centuries, it combined with the *frottola* (a joke with didactic content) and became the *frottola-barzalletta,* a type of whimsical love song for the courtly love poets.

SEE ALSO *epigram, nonsense poetry, octosyllabic verse.*

bathos *The American Heritage Dictionary* defines *bathos* as "An abrupt, unintended transition in style from the exalted to the commonplace, producing a ludicrous effect." It reaches for the sublime and tumbles into the absurd. In his second-century treatise *On the Sublime* (2.1), Longinus made *bathos* a synonym of *hypsos,* or the sublime, but Alexander Pope reversed the meaning and turned it into an antonym in his mock critical treatise, *Peri Bathous, or, Of the Art of Sinking in Poetry* (1728). Pope told his readers that he would "lead them as it were by the hand . . . the gentle downhill way to Bathos; the bottom, the end, the central point, the non plus ultra, of true Modern Poesy!" Pope's revisionary sense of bathos has held ever since. Pathos is an emotional height, but bathos (Greek, "depth") is a stylistic low. Pope illustrates bathos with lines he invented:

> Ye Gods! annihilate but Space and Time,
> And make two lovers happy.

There is overwriting in poetry, but it is also common for critics to insult extravagant writing by calling it bathetic. Whoever seeks a high style — Dylan Thomas (1914–1953), Hart Crane (1899–1932) — is vulnerable in an age of irony. As Willard Spiegelman puts it, "One reader's deftness is another's bathos." Wyndham Lewis and C. Lee's "anthology of bad verse," *The Stuffed Owl* (1930), presents bathos at its best — and worst.

SEE ALSO *the sublime.*

Battle of the Books, Battle of the Ancients and Moderns The argument between tradition and innovation, the old and the new — on the one hand, the authority of the classical; on the other, the originality of the modern — will never be resolved. It is a constant of literary history and tilts in different directions at different times. The dispute reached such a fever pitch in the seventeenth and eighteenth centuries in France and England that it took on comic proportions. It is now chiefly remembered under the satiric names, *La Querelle des Anciens et des Modernes* (The Quarrel of the Ancients and the Moderns) and The Battle of the Books.

The war, which was once well known but is now mostly forgotten, had many battles and a lot of side skirmishes, which involved intellectual luminaries and minor lights. The major question, as Gilbert Highet summarizes it, was this: "Ought modern writers to admire and imitate the great Greek and Latin writers of antiquity? or have the classical standards of taste now been excelled and superseded? Must we only follow along behind the ancients, trying to emulate them and hoping at most to equal them? or can we confidently expect to surpass them?"

In *Miscellaneous Thoughts* (1620), the Italian writer Alessandro Tassoni struck the first blow by attacking Homer and his admirers. He argued that the modern age of science and reason was superior to the superstitious worlds of the Greeks and Romans. In France, this position was taken up and vigorously extended by such writers as Bernard Le Bovier de Fontenelle in *Dialogues of the Dead* (1683) and Charles Perrault in a series of dialogues called *Parallel between the Ancients and the Moderns* (1688–1697). The neoclassicist Nicolas Boileau counterattacked and led the defense of antiquity. He satirized the modern age in his mock epic, *The Lectern* (1674–1683), which foreshadowed Alexander Pope's *The Dunciad* (1728). In England, Sir William Temple responded to Fontenelle by arguing that modern man was a dwarf standing upon the "shoulders of giants" and that the classics were an emanating source of clear light, which was reflected and refracted by the moderns (*An Essay upon the Ancient and Modern Learning,* 1690). The critic William Wotton responded with *Reflections upon Ancient and Modern Learning* (1694), and the classicist Richard Bentley produced his *Dissertation* (1697). Swift satirized the entire conflict in "The Battle of the Books," a short prolegomena to *A Tale of a Tub* (1704). Authors and ideas battle for supremacy in a literal contest between the books in the king's library, which was housed in Saint James's Palace.

SEE ALSO *Augustan Age, classic, mock epic, modernism, neoclassicism, satire, taste, tradition.*

Bāuls A small group of wandering folk poets and musicians from Bengal, male and female, Hindu and Muslim, who are known for describing their mystical experiences in song. They reject the caste system and sing of celestial love in earthly terms. Their name possibly derives from the ancient Sanskrit word for "wind" or "mad." They consider themselves mad about the soul of God that dwells within. They wear bright garments and typically sashay in tight, concentric circles as they sing. Rabindranath Tagore (1861–1941) identified strongly with the *Bāuls* ("I, a poet, am one of them") and collected the beautiful, enigmatic *Bāul* songs for most of his life. Gagan Harkara characterized the *Bāul* ethic when he sang

> Where shall I meet him, the Man of my Heart?
> He is lost to me and I seek him wandering from land to land.

This song inspired Tagore to write "Amar Shonar Bangla" ("My Golden Bengal," 1905), whose first ten lines later became the national anthem of Bangladesh.

SEE ALSO *bhakti poetry*.

beast epic, beast fable An animal story with a moral. These tales employ animals to tell human stories and dramatize human faults. The genre originated with the Greek writer Aesop, whose tales inspired countless fable collections throughout Western Europe. *Aesop's Fables* (*Aesopica,* sixth century B.C.E.) are still part of the moral education of children. Throughout the world, people know such tales as "The Tortoise and the Hare" and "The Boy Who Cried Wolf." Beast stories can be written in poetry or prose. The Aesopic fables conveyed moral and satirical lessons in brief, dry verses. Along with Buddhist Indic fable collections, such as the *Jatakas* (fourth century B.C.E.) and the *Panchatantra* (third century B.C.E.), they were widely circulated through medieval exemplum collections. Animal tales appeared in fable books throughout the Renaissance.

The term *beast epic* specifically applies to quasi-epic poems, like Pierre St. Cloud's twelfth-century *Roman de Renart.* There is a light mockery of epic themes in the story of the trickster Renart (Reynard the Fox), who first appeared in the Medieval Latin poem *Ysengrimus* (twelfth century). The Fox cycle of stories circulated in the Russian-Baltic area and in the southern

United States, where they, along with African traditions, fed into the Brer Rabbit tales.

Roman de Renart also tells the story of the Chanticleer, the anxious rooster at the center of Chaucer's "Nun's Priest's Tale" (ca. 1387–1400). The Scottish poet Robert Henryson composed *Morall Fabillis of Esope the Phrygian* in the 1480s. In his quasi-epic *Reineke Fuchs* (1793), Goethe refashioned the story of Reynard the Fox in classical hexameters, which he used to come to terms with the French Revolution. He called his poem "a profane secular Bible."

SEE ALSO *fable.*

beat The main rhythmic pulse in metrical verse. Sometimes called *ictus* (the Latin word for "beat"), sometimes *stress,* it is also referred to as *dynamic, intensive,* or *expiratory.* It is a way of keeping time. The oldest meaning of the word *beat* is "to strike repeatedly," and thus it carries the memory — the vestiges — of repeated physical action.

SEE ALSO *meter.*

Beats "Ah, this is nothing but a beat generation," Jack Kerouac told John Clellon Holmes, who then went on to write a *New York Times* article that carried the headline "This Is the Beat Generation" (1952). Kerouac also published a fragment of *On the Road* (1957) called "Jazz of the Beat Generation." Jazz musicians and hipsters used the word *beat* as slang for "down and out," flat broke. It also referred to those, in Allen Ginsberg's words, "who walked all night with their shoes full of blood on the snowbank docks waiting for a door in the East River to open to a room full of steam-heat and opium" (*Howl,* 1959). Kerouac and Ginsberg considered the Beats "beatific."

The Beat literary generation was a group of friends and writers who came together from the mid-forties on. It consisted of Kerouac and Neal Cassady (the prototype for the hero of *On the Road*), the fiction writers Holmes and William Burroughs, the hustler Herbert Huncke, and Ginsberg himself. The loosely affiliated group accumulated Carl Solomon and Philip Lamantia, next Gregory Corso, then Lawrence Ferlinghetti and Peter Orlovsky. It expanded to include Michael McClure, Gary Snyder, Philip Whalen, and the black poets Bob Kaufman and LeRoi Jones (later Amiri Baraka). All accepted the moniker "beat" at one time or another.

The Beat movement was launched when Allen Ginsberg read his apocalyptic poem "Howl" at a gallery in San Francisco in 1955. McClure later said that everyone immediately recognized that "a barrier had been broken, a human voice and body had been hurled against the harsh wall of America and its supporting armies and navies and academies and institutions and ownership systems and power-support bases." Ginsberg's blistering jeremiad is still the touchstone of Beat poetry, the poem heard round the world.

The Beat literary aesthetic has always been a boisterous one. It values a candid American speech and pursues, as Corso puts it, "the use of mixtures containing spontaneity, 'bop prosody,' surreal-real images, jumps, beats, cool measures, long rapid vowels, long long lines, and the main content, soul." Beat poetry rages against apathy and injustice, consumerism and war. It cherishes spontaneity, originality, and compassion. In the 1960s, the tenets of Beat literature melded with the counterculture, which championed free love, mystical self-awareness, drug experimentation, social protest, and the peace movement. The lifestyle has passed, but Beat poetry retains its brash spontaneity.

SEE ALSO *Black Mountain poets, New York school of poets, spontaneity.*

belatedness *Belatedness* is Harold Bloom's cunning critical term for the heavy burden of coming afterwards, for being a poetic latecomer. Bloom argues that all significant writers eventually become conscious of being overshadowed by "precursors," the great dead who influence and precede them. Himself influenced by W. Jackson Bate's *The Burden of the Past and the English Poet* (1970), Bloom developed the idea of belatedness into a full-scale theory of the poet's agonizing struggle with the precursors he chooses, who then threaten to overwhelm him. Thus the Hebrew Bible and the New Testament become "The Original and Belated Testaments." As Satan struggles with God in *Paradise Lost* (1667), so does John Milton struggle with the sixteenth-century titan Edmund Spenser, and the romantic poets subsequently struggle with Milton. A Freudian ambivalence toward one's precursors can itself become a kind of strength.

SEE ALSO *anxiety of influence.*

the beloved One who is dearly loved, a necessary object of desire, a sustained, often idealized, sometimes fictive source of inspiration. Dante immortalized Beatrice as his beloved in the *Vita Nuova* (*The New Life,* ca. 1292–1293) and the

Commedia (*The Divine Comedy,* ca. 1304–1321), and Petrarch built a shrine to Laura in the *Rime Sparse* (*Scattered Rhymes,* 1374). The poet traditionally promises to make the beloved immortal: "Your name from hence immortal life shall have," Shakespeare promises in sonnet 81 (1609). In Hebrew poetry, the beloved is often figured as a gazelle, a motif that originated in the Song of Songs (2:9): "Behold, my beloved is like a gazelle [*tzvi*] or a young hart [*'ofer ha'ayalim*]." In Arabic poetry, the beloved is also often compared to a gazelle (*ghazaal* or *zabi*). There seems to be a shadow of desire, a shadow of the beloved, looming over the love poem. Love crops up so often in lyric poetry because it is the soul's primary way of going out to another, of freeing itself through another from the pressures and distractions of ordinary existence. It is the soul's preferred mode of attainment. "In other words," Joseph Brodsky writes in "Alter Ego" (1997), an essay that makes a careful distinction between the beloved and the muse (the beloved dies, the muse finds another mouthpiece in the next generation), "love is a metaphysical affair whose goal is either accomplishing or liberating one's soul: winnowing it from the chaff of existence. That is and always has been the core of lyric poetry." Allen Grossman perceptively argues, "Poetry traditionally, and in my view fundamentally, deals in the continuity of the image *not* of the poet but of the poet's *beloved.*" Poetry therefore models the act of civilization, the act of presenting the image of a beloved Other. He says, "Poetry is a case of the magnanimity of the self toward the other — toward the beloved." There is a Sufi maxim, "The Beloved and I are one."

SEE ALSO *muse.*

bergerette, see *virelay.*

bertsolaritza The improvised oral poetry of the Basque-speaking people. The *bertsoak,* or Basque poems, are created in the Basque language (*Euskara*) and play an important role in the expression of Basque cultural identity. The *bartsolariak* (Basque poets) learn to improvise both on prompted and unprompted themes. Created in performance, the poems were at one time also circulated through broadsides called *bertso-paperak.* Today, they are generally performed in recitals and competitions, which culminate in the All Euskal Herria Championships, held every four years.

The contemporary champion *bertsolari* (singer of *bertso*) Andoni Egaña calls improvised *bertsoak* "one of the few cultural expressions wherein the moment of artistic creation and that of its exposition to the public are one and the same." He notes that the *bertso* "consists of a *sung, rhymed, and measured discourse,*" meaning that the air, the rhyme, and the meter are inseparable elements. For him, the "the soul of bertsolaritza" is the improvised oral confrontation, "in which one *bertsolari* faces another and they weave a performance of a greater or lesser number of *bertoak* between the two of them." He also refers to the principal strategy of first composing the end of the poem, which he calls "the sting of the tail."

SEE ALSO *broadside ballad, oral poetry, poetic contest.*

bestiary The bestiary is a collection of didactic pieces about the real or reputed characteristics of animals, many of them legendary, such as the unicorn. The genre seems to have originated in a lost Alexandrian work entitled *Physiologus* (*The Naturalist,* second century), a compendium of some fifty fabulous stories about animals, which was widely translated and imitated. Bestiaries can be written either in verse or in prose. In the fifth century, Herodotus collected oral accounts of animals, as did Aristotle a century later (*Historia animalium*). Plutarch noted the Egyptian belief that animals revealed mystical truths about the gods, and thus became the first philosopher to consider the theological symbolism of animal lore.

The bestiary flourished in Europe from the twelfth to the fourteenth century. The genre may have influenced the development of the exemplum and the fable. The French tradition was invoked and revived by Guillaume Apollinaire in his *Bestiare* (1919). Jorges Luis Borges reinvented the bestiary as a fabulist form in his whimsical *Book of Imaginary Beings* (1957), initially called *Manual de zoología fantástica* (*Handbook of Fantastic Zoology*), which contains 120 "of the strange creatures conceived through time and space by the human imagination."

SEE ALSO *allegory, beast epic, bird song, emblem, exemplum, fable.*

bhakti poetry In Hinduism, *bhakti* is a mystical devotion to God. The *Bhagavad Gita* ("Song of God," fifth to second century B.C.E.) was the first text to use the term *bhakti* to designate a religious path. Medieval bhakti poetry is the devotional genre of love poetry. The word *bhakti* derives from the Sanskrit root *bhaj,* meaning "to share, to possess," and bhakti poetry is an intense way of sharing in the divine. It is an ecstatic poetry. The Bhakti movement originated in the south of India in the sixth century and gradually spread to the rest of the subcontinent. From the seventh to the ninth century, the South-Indian poet-saints, the Vaisnava Alvars and Saiva Nayanars, traveled from temple to temple, singing of their gods and spreading bhakti energy throughout India. These itinerant poets drew upon Sanskrit models, but composed their hymns in their own local languages. They centered their work on the gods Visnu and Siva, and their poems establish direct, emotional bonds with these divines. Many of the bhakti poets came from the lower rungs of the Hindu caste ladder—among them, there is a cobbler, a tailor, a boatman, a weaver, a maidservent—and wrote in the vernaculars (Tamil, Telugu, Kannada, Marathi, Gujarati) rather than Sanskrit, the language of Brahmans. They reach from the lowest to the highest, the One Deity.

Scholars make a useful distinction between poet-saints who composed verses extolling God "with attributes" (*saguna bhaktas*) and those extolling God "without attributes" (*nirguna bhaktas*). One of the great *sagunas* was Mirabai (ca. 1498–ca. 1557), who sang passionately of her love for Krishna, her true husband, her *ishtadevata,* the god one makes through desire. One of the great *nirgunas* was Kabir (1440–1518), who questioned the hierarchies of the caste system and pondered God's greatness "without qualities." Both poets wrote out of personal experience. As Meena Alexander puts it in an essay on bhakti poetry: "There is a simplicity, a grace if you will, in the poetry of both. Mirabai and Kabir. A dwelling in the body that does not cut consciousness apart from the desiring, perishing body and sings, sings through sorrow into joy. A precarious joy that remains at the edge of the world."

SEE ALSO *the beloved.*

bical A poetic joust, which often pits men against women. The seventeenth-century Spanish Jesuit Father Ignatio Francisco Alzina documented a variety of poetic forms in the oral East Visayan Literature of the Philippines. One was the *bical,* a playful verbal war: "This one is used between two persons, either two men or two women. They answer one another in strict musical time and without any hesitation for one or two hours at a time, saying anything they wish even in satiric fashion and making public whatever faults the other may have. The shortcoming may be physical which is most common, or at times, moral, when these are not too offensive. All this is rendered with much jest, laughter and fun with the applause of those who are listening. Very often the listeners help one or the other, all of which add to the joy and amusement of all. When the *bical* and the party is over, everything remains forgotten without any resentment for the shortcomings or failure included in the rendition or contest" (*Historia de las Islas Bisayas,* 1668). The term *bical* is no longer in use, but the witty verbal sparring, often between the sexes, survives in Samar and Leyte, where it is sometimes called *baton-baton.*

SEE ALSO *oral poetry, poetic contest, siday.*

bird song The vocal music of birds has always had a great hold on poets. "Sir, we are a nest of singing birds," Samuel Johnson told James Boswell. The seventh century B.C.E. Greek poet Alcman of Sardis claimed to know the strains of all the birds. In *Bright Wings* (2012), Billy Collins points out that in early English poetry, "birds can be emblematic (the royal eagle), mythological (the reborn phoenix), or symbolic (the self-wounding pelican as Christ)." Over the centuries, poets have frequently identified with cuckoos ("Sumer is icumen in— / Lhude, sing cuccu!") and mockingbirds, seagulls, herons, and owls. They have also noted their difference from us. They have watched them in their backyards (John Keats, "Ode to a Nightingale," 1819; Anthony Hecht, "House Sparrows," 1979), followed them into the woods (Robert Burns, "Address to the Woodlark," 1795; Amy Clampitt, "A Whippoorwill in the Woods," 1990), and tracked them to the shore (May Swenson, "One of the Strangest," 1978; Galway Kinnell, "The Gray Heron," 1980). They have treated birds as messengers from the beyond, the embodiment of a transcendent vocation. One thinks of Edgar Allan Poe's raven, William Cullen Bryant's waterfowl, Gerard Manley Hopkins's windhover, W. B. Yeats's wild swans at Coole, Robinson Jeffers's hawks, Wallace Stevens's blackbird, Osip Mandelstam's goldfinch, Randall Jarrell's mockingbird . . . The tradition of imitating bird song is so strong that it sometimes begs for counterstatement, as in Michael Collier's poem "In Certain Situations I'm Very Much Against Birdsong" (2011).

The nightingale—a small, secretive, solitary songbird that goes on singing late into the night—has always had a special metaphorical and symbolic power. It fills an apparently irresistible need to attribute human feelings to the bird's pure and persistent song. Poets, who are often nocturnal creatures, have identified with "spring's messenger, the sweet-voiced nightingale," as Sappho (late seventh century B.C.E.) calls it. The romantic poets especially considered the bird a symbol of imaginative freedom. In "A Defence of Poetry" (1821), Shelley established the connection between the poet and the nightingale: "A poet is a nightingale, who sits in darkness and sings to cheer its own solitude with sweet sounds; his auditors are as men entranced by the melody of an unseen musician, who feel that they are moved and softened, yet know not whence or why." The singing of the nightingale becomes a metaphor for writing poetry, and listening to that bird, that natural music, becomes a metaphor for reading it. One of the romantic premises of Shelley's metaphor is that the poet "sings" in "solitude" without any consideration for an audience and that the audience, his "auditors," responds to the work of an "unseen musician."

The nightingale has had a rich history of representations in poetry, which begins with one of the oldest legends in the world, the poignant tale of Philomela, who had her tongue cut out and was changed into the nightingale, which laments in darkness, but nonetheless expresses its story in song. The tale reverberates through Greco-Roman literature. Ovid gave it a poignant rendering in *Metamorphoses* (8 C.E.), and it echoes down the centuries from Shakespeare (*Titus Andronicus,* 1589) and Sidney ("Philomela," 1595) to Matthew Arnold ("Philomela," 1853), T. S. Eliot ("The Waste Land," 1922), and John Crowe Ransom ("Philomela," 1923). Even without the mythological scrim, poets have often responded to the piercing woe-begotten quality of the nightingale's song, which Keats beautifully imitates in his nightingale ode. Samuel Taylor Coleridge was the first romantic poet to attack the idea that the nightingale's song was necessarily lonesome and sad ("The Nightingale," 1798). In the 1830s, the rural poet John Clare observed how nightingales actually look, sound, and behave. "I have watched them often at their song," he said. He objected to the old threadbare epithets such as "love lorn nightingale" and with a naturalist's eye remembered how assiduously he had observed one as a boy. Here is how he describes hearing a nightingale in his poem "The Progress of Rhyme" (1835):

> "Chew-chew chew-chew" and higher still,
> "Cheer-cheer cheer-cheer" more loud and shrill,
> "Cheer-up cheer-up cheer-up"—and dropped

Low — "Tweet tweet jug jug jug" — and stopped
One moment just to drink the sound
Her music made, and then a round
Of stranger witching notes was heard
As if it was a stranger bird:
"Wew-wew wew-wew chur-chur chur-chur
"Woo-it woo-it" — and could this be her?
"Tee-rew tee-rew tee-rew tee-rew
Chew-rit chew-rit" — and ever new —
"Will-will will-will grig-grig grig-grig."

SEE ALSO *bestiary, bird sound words, the language of the birds, shaman.*

bird sound words The Kaluli people of Papua New Guinea speak Bosavi. For them, "poetic language is bird language," Steven Feld points out in *Sound and Sentiment: Birds, Weeping, Poetics, and Song in Kaluli Expression* (1990). Whereas talk is pragmatic and serves utilitarian ends, song, Feld says, "is a communication from the point of view of a person in the form of a bird." The Kaluli use "bird sound words" (the systematic language of song poetics). Song is thus a special model of speech that goes beyond ordinary talk. Talk by the birds, talk for the birds, is the prototype for poetry and music. The Kaluli are avid ornithographers and categorize birds based on sound properties: there are birds that sing, weep, whistle, speak the Bosavi language, say their names, "only sound," and make a lot of noise. Bird songs are also heard as "talk" of the dead, communication from an invisible realm. "To you they are birds," one speaker told an anthropologist, "to me they are voices in the forest."

The Kaluli use the word *gisalo* both as a distinct song form and a generic term for "ceremony," "song," or "melody." *Sa-gisalo* refers to the "text," or the "words inside *gisalo*." "For ceremonies," Feld notes, "*gisalo* is composed with the deliberate intention of moving others to tears." The Kaluli have a host of terms for their poetics, such as *bali to* ("turned over words"), which includes euphemism and metaphor, and *hega* ("underneath"), which refers to the hidden or underlying meanings or motives in the text. Feld points out: "Kaluli assume that a song is constructed in the first person as a personal statement referring to the thoughts and feelings of the singer or of a spirit."

In the third volume of the *The Maximus Poems* (1974), Charles Olson, addressing poets, says that "the Airs which belong to birds have / led our lives to be these things instead of Kings." Nathaniel Mackey, who has three poems in *Splay Anthem* (2006) based on a Kaluli myth regarding the origin of poetry and music, writes: "To poeticize or sing is to talk like a bird, a way with words and sound given rise to by a break in social relations, a denial of kinship and social sustenance, as if the break were a whistling fissure, an opening blown on like a flute."

SEE ALSO *the language of the birds, oral poetry, sound poetry.*

birthday poems Statius closes the second book of his *Silvae* (ca. 89–96) with a poem on the birthday of the dead Lucan, which he names a *genethliacon* ("Genethliacon Lucani"), or birthday poem. It is a moving ode dedicated to Lucan's widow. There are many birthday poems in Latin literature, such as Propertius's celebration of Cynthia's birthday (3.10, ca. 23 B.C.E.) and Tibullus's birthday poems for his patron Messalla (1.7, ca. 27 B.C.E.) and for his friend Cornutus (2.2), which wasn't published until after his own death in 19 B.C.E. In his birthday poem for himself (*Elegies* 2.2, ca. 1490), the Italian poet and humanist Jacopo Sannazaro, who wrote fluently in Latin, repeated the structure of Propertius's poem and followed the events of the festive day, from dawn until midnight. Ovid wrote an anti-genethliacon from his exile in Tomis in *Tristia* (3.13, 9–12 C.E.): "For custom's sake and the day, I'll make one birthday wish — // that it not find me here a year from now."

Some Latin genethliaca are genuine birthday poems and take the day itself as their subject, some accompany or represent a birthday present, and some offer general good wishes. George Puttenham writes in *The Arte of English Poesie* (1589): "Reioysings . . . for magnificence at the natiuities of Princes children, or by custome vsed yearely vpon the same days, are called songs natall or *Genethliaca.*" The poem that apostrophizes the infant prince is necessarily political, as in the Scottish poet George Buchanan's "Genethliacon Jacobi Sexti Regis Scotorum," an ode on the birth of James in 1566. Hugh MacDiarmid uses the birthday poem to strike a note of hope in terrible times in "Genethliacon for the New World Order" (1934). The world seems to be coming to an end, MacDiarmid suggests, but as "A woman's labour, life's most terrible pain, / Suddenly into joy must pass . . ." Those especially interested in these celebratary lyrics should see Jason Shinder's anthology, *Birthday Poems: A Celebration* (2001).

Black Arts movement The separatist Black Arts movement, which thrived from 1965 to 1975, revolutionized black poetry. It had roots in the turmoil of the civil rights movement, in the culture of Malcolm X and the Nation of Islam, and in the Black Power movement. In a 1968 essay, "The Black Arts Movement," Larry Neal proclaimed Black Arts as "the aesthetic and spiritual sister of the Black Power concept." The Black Arts movement was overtly political and embraced social engagement as its primary aesthetic.

LeRoi Jones started out as a celebrated Beat poet (*Preface to a Twenty-Volume Suicide Note,* 1961, and *The Dead Lecturer,* 1964), playwright (*Dutchman,* 1964), small-press publisher (*Yugen* and *Floating Bear* magazines, Totem Press), and music critic (*Blues People,* 1963). Following the assassination of Malcolm X in 1965, he left Greenwich Village in Manhattan to establish the Black Arts Repertory Theater/School (BARTS) in Harlem. That exodus marked the symbolic beginning of the Black Arts movement. He changed his name to Amiri Baraka, repudiated white culture, and became the leader of a new movement. His 1965 manifesto poem "Black Art" declared "we want poems that kill." Baraka soon moved back to his hometown of Newark, but the Black Arts movement continued to burgeon, like Black Power. The poets of a surging new racial consciousness included Don L. Lee (later Haki Madhubuti), Sonia Sanchez, Mari Evans, Nikki Giovanni, Carolyn Rodgers, Audre Lorde, and Etheridge Knight. These poets, who distrusted and often despised white culture, embraced a black vernacular, revered black music, and raised their voices during the most volatile of times. A major poet such as Gwendolyn Brooks turned her work in a more populist direction. Concentrating on poetry, Dudley Randall's Broadside Press in Detroit was the most literary press of the movement, which also energized the development of African American theater groups.

The Black Arts movement was racially exclusive and dismissed all poets who did not embrace its ideological revolution, such as Robert Hayden. It has been criticized for being sexist, homophobic, and antisemetic. Yet it also motivated the radical consciousness of a new generation not just of black poets, but also of Native Americans, Latinos and Latinas, and gays and lesbians. It is a forerunner of multiculturism.

Black Mountain poets Charles Olson was the rector of Black Mountain College in western North Carolina from 1951 until 1956, when the school closed after twenty-three years. The innovative college, an educational experiment, became a center for a new poetics, an experimental approach to writing poetry. Olson's process-oriented anti-formalist manifesto, "Projective Verse" (1950), was an establishing document of the movement, which also included Robert Creeley and Robert Duncan, who were members of the staff. Ed Dorn, Joel Oppenheimer, Jonathan Williams, and John Wieners all studied at Black Mountain in the early fifties. In his influential anthology *The New American Poetry* (1960), Donald Allen also included Denise Levertov, Paul Blackburn, Larry Eigner, and Paul Carroll under "The Black Mountain School of Poetry," though they were never connected to the college. They published in the magazines *Origin* (First Series, 1951–1957), edited by Cid Corman, and *Black Mountain Review* (1954–1957), edited by Creeley, which provided two of the main outlets for the aggressively avant-garde "open-field" compositions opening up American poetry in the 1950s. Working in a line of descent from the modernists Pound and Williams, Olson proposed a kinetic poetry, "composition by field," as a radical alternative to "closed verse," traditional forms. Black Mountain poetry is "vehicular," to use Emerson's word, transitional, improvisatory, projective, on the move.

SEE ALSO *avant-garde, Beats, New York school of poets, organic form, postmodernism, projective verse.*

blank verse Unrhymed (hence "blank") iambic pentameter. The five-beat, ten-syllable line—a line of great flexibility and scope—was established in English between the fourteenth and sixteenth centuries, its emergence coterminous with the rise of Renaissance humanism. Blank verse was initially employed by Henry Howard, Earl of Surrey, in his translation of Virgil's *Aeneid* (ca. 1594). Christopher Marlowe (1564–1593) was the first English poet and playwright to explore the full potential of blank verse. The English dramatists used blank verse to move fluently between normal conversation and high rhetoric, and it became the standard form of drama in the era of Elizabeth I and James I. Many of the speeches in William Shakespeare's plays are written in blank verse, as in this famous soliloquy from *Macbeth* (1611):

> Tomorrow, and tomorrow, and tomorrow,
> Creeps in this petty pace from day to day,
> To the last syllable of recorded time;

And all our yesterdays have lighted fools
The way to dusty death. Out, out, brief candle!
Life's but a walking shadow, a poor player
That struts and frets his hour upon the stage
And then is heard no more: it is a tale
Told by an idiot, full of sound and fury,
Signifying nothing.

John Milton used blank verse in *Paradise Lost* (1667) to liberate poetry from the "troublesome and modern bondage of rhyming," thus establishing and confirming it as the pattern with the greatest equilibrium in English. Such eighteenth-century poets as James Thomson (*The Seasons,* 1730) and William Cowper (*The Task,* 1785) took up the mantle of Miltonic blank verse. Samuel Taylor Coleridge's "conversation poems" ("The Aeolian Harp," 1795; "Frost at Midnight," 1798), which were adapted from the classical ode, introduced the short blank verse poem into English. William Wordsworth, Percy Bysshe Shelley, and John Keats all wrote major poems in blank verse. Alfred, Lord Tennyson used blank verse to great effect, as in the final heroic lines of "Ulysses" (1842):

One equal temper of heroic hearts,
Made weak by time and fate, but strong in will
To strive, to seek, to find, and not to yield.

The American romantics Hart Crane and Wallace Stevens are also notable for their use of the noble blank verse line.

It has been estimated that three-fourths of all English poetry until the twentieth century is written in blank verse. This suggests that blank verse is the modal pattern in English, the pattern closest to natural speech, and therefore, as Allen Grossman puts it in "Summa Lyrica" (1992), "the form speech takes when it depicts the speech of persons in social situations." Blank verse has most often been used — from William Shakespeare's plays to Robert Frost's dramatic monologues — to evoke the spoken word, to create a speaker in a dramatic situation.

SEE ALSO *conversation poem, decasyllable, dramatic monologue, iambic pentameter, meter, rhyme, versi sciolti.*

blazon, blason A French heraldic term meaning "coat of arms." In literature, a *blazon* is a catalog of the beloved's physical features or attributes. The convention goes back to the thirteenth century. The blazon, a male form, relies on a series of comparisons, usually drawn from nature, that tend to come from a stock of images in the Song of Songs. Petrarch made the blazon a prominent part of his *Rime Sparse* (1374) and it thus became central to the Petrarchan tradition. Elizabethan lyricists are especially known for detailing the physical beauty of their mistresses. Spenser provides a well-known example in the tenth stanza of *Epithalamion* (1595):

Her goodly eyes like sapphires shining bright,
Her forehead ivory white,
Her cheeks like apples which the sun hath rudded,
Her lips like cherries charming men to bite,
Her breasts like to a bowl of cream uncrudded,
Her paps like lilies budded,
Her snowy neck like to a marble tower,
And all her body like a palace fair . . .

Ernst Robert Curtius uses the term *recipes* for medieval codes proscribing head-to-toe body descriptions. Mikhail Bakhtin speaks of the "dual fact, complete ambivalence, and contradictory fullness" of the blazon. Clément Marot launched a literary fashion with his erotic "Blazon du Beau Tétin" ("Blazon of the Beautiful Breast," 1536), which inaugurated the vogue for "anatomical blazons" (*blasons anatomiques*), descriptive poems in praise of the parts of the female body. John Davies of Hereford's poem "Some blaze the precious beauties of their loves" critiques those who write blazons for their hyperbolic comparisons ("Yet I by none of these will blazon mine"), and then proceeds to praise his beloved with a sense of wordless wonder (*Wit's Pilgrimage,* 1605). The convention inevitably became clichéd and thus led to parody, or the *contreblazon* (*anti-blazon*). Robert Greene mocks the traditional blazon in *Menaphon* (1589):

Thy teeth like to the tusks of fattest swine,
Thy speech is like the thunder in the air:
Would God thy toes, thy lips, and all were mine.

SEE ALSO *the beloved, catalog poem, conceit, Petrarchism.*

blues A secular form of African American folk song. Sung solo, the blues often express a deep stoic grief and despair, a dark mood of lamentation, but also a wry and ribald humor, a homemade political philosophy, a proverbial wisdom. Within the African American community, the blues have traditionally been contrasted to spirituals, a sacred form, and thus likened to devil's music. "You can bury my body down by the highway side / So my old evil spirit can catch a Greyhound bus, and ride," Robert Johnson sings in "Me and the Devil Blues." The *Oxford English Dictionary* states that the color blue was associated with the devil as early as the sixteenth century, hence the expression "blue devils."

The blues were first arranged, scored, and published early in the twentieth century, but have their roots in much earlier work songs, field hollers, group seculars, and sacred harmonies. The blues have retained a flexible style and structure, but classically tend toward a twelve-bar, three-line stanza with an *aab* rhyme pattern: a couplet stretched to three lines. The first line establishes the premise and scene; the second repeats (sometimes with slight variations) and hammers it in. This allows the singer to emphasize and modify the first line while improvising the next one. The third line punches, develops, or turns the premise. Each line is an intact entity, each stanza a complete unit.

I'm goin' to the river, take my rockin' chair,
Goin' to the river, take my rockin' chair,
If the blues overcome me, I'll rock on away from here.

The trick to singing the blues is to flatten the third, fifth, and seventh notes of the major scale, thus creating the "blue notes." Here is a durable vocal art, a living tradition, a foundational form, a shaping influence on American music, such as jazz and rock and roll. The blues have also been a major influence on African American written poetry from Langston Hughes and Sterling Brown to Michael S. Harper and Yusef Komunyakaa.

SEE ALSO *spirituals, work song.*

bob and wheel A metrical device of five short, rhyming, tightly metrical lines found mainly in Middle Scots and Middle English poetry, most notably in *Sir Gawain and the Green Knight* (fourteenth century). The bob is a short line, usually only two syllables long, and the wheel is a set of four slightly longer lines at the end of a stanza. Each one of the 101 stanzas of uneven length in *Sir Gawain and the Green Knight* ends with a bob and wheel. The bob serves as a bridge from the alliterated to the rhyming lines; the wheel concludes the stanza with four three-stress lines. The rhyme scheme is *ababa.* This is how the translator, Simon Armitage, renders it when Gawain turns up at an unknown court:

> This knight,
> whose country was unclear,
> now seemed to them by sight
> a prince without a peer
> in fields where fierce men fight.

bombast The term *bombast* (from the Latin *bombax,* cotton) originally referred to a cheap cotton wadding that was used as padding to exaggerate the size of clothing. In sixteenth-century drama, the term was extended from the realm of costume to the realm of speech. It came to mean an exaggerated speech or performance, as in Thomas Dekker's *Satiromastix* (1602): "You shall swear not to *bombast* out a new play with the old *linings* of jests." In Shakespeare's *Henry IV*, part 2 (1600), Prince Hal teases the verbose Falstaff, who is always overinflating his claims, as "my sweet creature of bombast." Shakespeare's mockery of bombast suggests that he preferred the more modest acting style favored by Hamlet (*Hamlet,* act 3, scene 2, line 1ff., 1603). In the *Biographia Literaria* (1817), Coleridge distinguished between what he called *verbal* bombast, "a disproportion of the expressions to the thoughts," and what he named *mental* bombast, "a disproportion of thought to the circumstance and occasion." He added, "This, by the bye, is a fault of which none but a man of genius is capable."

bouts-rimés French: "rhymed ends." In 1711, Joseph Addison defined *bouts-rimés* as "lists of words that rhyme to one another, drawn up by another hand, and given to a poet, who was to make a poem to the rhymes in the same order that they were placed upon the list." The game of rhyming terminations, which was supposedly invented around 1648 by a minor French poet named Dulot, had a great vogue in seventeenth- and eighteenth-century France. In 1654, Jean-François Sarasin skewered the fad in his extended satirical poem "Dulot vaincu" (Dulot Defeated, 1654). The *bouts-rimés* were popular with the nineteenth-century French Parnassians, who valued skillful rhymes almost above all else. The game had some life in nineteenth-century England, where it was prized, for example, by the three Rossetti's. William T. Dobson's chapter "Bouts Rimés," in *Literary Frivolities, Fancies, Follies and Frolics* (1880), is especially amusing.

SEE ALSO *Parnassians, rhyme.*

bowdlerize In 1815, Samuel Bowdler produced *The Family Shakespeare,* an edition of Shakespeare that expurgated any phrase or episode from Shakespeare's work that Bowdler considered indecent or offensive. "Those words and expressions are omitted," he said, "which cannot with propriety be read aloud in a family." The word *bowdlerize* subsequently became a notorious term for the way that literary texts are mutilated to conform to so-called family values.

brachycatalectic, see *truncation.*

bref double A minor French form, which originated in southern France, most likely in the tenth or eleventh century. Some think that it may simply have referred to a short irregular composition in troubadour poetry. Others believe that it was always considered a fourteen-line poem, or *quatorzain,* consisting of three four-line stanzas and a couplet at the end, which would make it an ancestor of the traditional Italian sonnet. The French fourteen-liner resembles the traditional sonnet, though the meter is open and the rhyme scheme is freer. The poem turns on three rhymes. Some critics think that every line must be rhymed, others suggest the form may contain some unrhymed lines. The first two rhymes, *a* and *b,* appear twice within each of the quatrains and once in the final couplet. The *c* rhyme concludes each quatrain.

SEE ALSO *quatorzain, rondelet, sonnet.*

British Poetry Revival The British Poetry Revival is a name given to a loose poetic movement, a sea change in British poetry in the 1960s and '70s. Reacting against the formal conservatism of the Movement, a number of poets throughout Britain turned to more innovative poetries. Whereas the

Movement poets took Thomas Hardy as their model, the poets of the British Poetry Revival looked to American modernists, such as Ezra Pound and William Carlos Williams, and to British modernists, such as David Jones, Basil Bunting, and Hugh MacDiarmid. Charles Tomlinson was a precursor to the innovative poets of the British Poetry Revival, who include Roy Fisher, Gael Turnbull, Bob Cobbing, Ian Hamilton Finlay, Edwin Morgan, Elaine Feinstein, Lee Harwood, and Christopher Logue. The innovative spirit of American modernism had come winging across the ocean.

SEE ALSO *modernism, the Movement, postmodernism.*

broadside ballad The eighteenth century popularized the broadside ballad, a ballad printed on a single sheet of paper (broadside) and sold in the streets. It may have developed as early as the fifteenth century. It thrived as a popular form of doggerel until the rise of the daily newspaper in the 1860s. Folk songs were sometimes written as broadsides, broadsides sometimes refashioned into folk songs. John Skelton's "A Ballade of the Scottysshe Kynge" (1513) may be the earliest printed broadside. Skelton mercilessly mocks the Scottish King, James IV, for his challenge to the English King, Henry VIII ("Kynge Jamy, Jomy your *Joye* is all go / Ye summnoed our kynge why dyde ye so / To you no thyng it dyde accorde / To sommon our kynge your souerayne lorde"). The broadside ballads, which carried news, have frequently been denigrated by purists who prefer ballads created anonymously and transmitted orally. Francis James Child expressed this point of view in an Appendix to the 1965 reprint of *The English and Scottish Popular Ballads:*

> The vulgar ballads of our day, the "broadsides" which were printed in such large numbers in England and elsewhere in the sixteenth century or later . . . are products of a low kind of *art,* and most of them are, from a literary point of view, thoroughly despicable and worthless.

Despite its negative connotations, the broadside ballad was an extremely popular and topical form of street poetry, a metrical form of journalism with an energetic vulgarity, a forerunner of the tabloid.

SEE ALSO *ballad, doggerel, folk song.*

broken rhyme, see *rhyme.*

bucolic, see *pastoral.*

bugarštica The term probably derives from the Serbo-Croatian word *bugariti,* meaning "to chant." It refers to the fifteen-syllable line, which has a strong break after the seventh syllable, found in certain Serbo-Croatian heroic songs. The Western Serbs of the Dalmatian coast called their long-line epic songs or ballads *bugarštica.* In the fifteenth century, Petar Hektorović first included these national songs, which he heard from local singers, in his poem *Ribańe,* or "Fishing."

SEE ALSO *ballad, epic, oral poetry.*

burden, burthen The common name for the refrain or chorus of a song until the seventeenth century, the burden carries a repetitive power, reinforcing a theme and feeling. Shakespeare plays on the meaning of *burden* in one of Ariel's songs in *The Tempest* (ca. 1611): "Foot it featly here and there, / And, sweet sprites, the burden bear." Songs and ballads with refrains were themselves sometimes called burdens. A burden can also be the leading idea or principal feeling of a poem or song.

SEE ALSO *refrain.*

burlesque From the Italian *burlesco,* from *burla,* "ridicule" or "joke." A burlesque is a satirical imitation, an exaggerated send-up of a literary work. The Greeks were addicted to it. "The rhapsodists who strolled from town to town to chant the poems of Homer," Isaac D'Israeli writes in *Curiosities of Literature* (1823), "were immediately followed by another set of strollers — buffoons who made the audiences merry by the burlesque turn which they gave to the solemn strains."

Samuel Johnson said, "Burlesque consists in a disproportion between the style and the sentiments, or, between the adventitious sentiments and the fundamental subject." Burlesque most commonly applies to drama and other stage entertainment, as in the play of Pyramus and Thisbe that Bottom and his friends perform in *Midsummer Night's Dream* (ca. 1595), which sends up earlier dramatic interludes, or *The Beggar's Opera* (1728), John Gay's satirical take on Italian opera. In 1648, the French dramatist Paul Scarron wrote a burlesque in verse entitled *Virgile travestie.* Nicolas Boileau-Despréaux burlesqued the classical epic in *Le Lutrin* (1674) — the mock epic is a burlesque form — and John Dryden made fun of the animal fable in *The Hind and the Panther* (1687). The burlesque sonnet was a rich comic take on the sonnet form. Miguel de Cervantes (1547–1616), the greatest Spanish novelist, prided himself on being a superior burlesque sonneteer.

SEE ALSO *Hudibrastic verse, mock epic, parody, satire.*

Burns stanza, Burns meter, see *sestet.*

Butzenscheibenpoesie, Butzenscheibenlyric The *Butschenscheib* is an old-fashioned target for archery. Technically, it is a round pane with a raised center ("bull's-eye glass"), which gives it a mock-medieval effect. In 1884, Paul Heyse coined the word *Butzenscheibenpoesie* as a derogatory term for a group of late nineteenth-century German poets with nationalistic values and a pseudo-medieval style. The three main practitioners were J. V. von Scheffel (1826–1886), Rudolph Baumbach (1840–1905), and Julius Wolff (1834–1910). "Archery target poetry" is a form of degenerate romanticism.

bylina, byliny (pl) From the Russian *byl,* which means "that which happened." The Russian peasants used the term *starina* ("what is old") for this form of epic folk song and poetry, which suggests "tales-of-things-that-have-been." Vladimir Nabokov described *byliny* as "anonymous medieval narrative poetry . . . botched by centuries of oral transmission," but if the *byliny* are "botched" by the process of oral transmission, then so are the Homeric epics. The poems were first collected in the late eighteenth century and the term *bylina* was then employed by collectors in the 1830s and 1840s. Byliny are oral heroic poems, epic entertainments performed by *skaziteli* ("narrators"), who chant or sing them, usually without musical accompaniment. The meter is a sort of accentual blank verse. The *byliny* mostly focus on legendary historical events that date from the eleventh to the sixteenth century. The heroes were *bogatyrs.* The *byliny* divide into two cycles: the Kievan cycle, which rotates around the eleventh-century court of Vladimir of Kiev ("the bright sun"), and the Novgordian cycle, which developed between the thirteenth and fifteenth centuries. Its main hero was the merchant-*bogatyr,* Sadko. The greatest literary work of Kievan Russia, *The Song of Igor's Campaign* (*Slovo o polku Igoreve*), which Nabokov subtitles "An Epic of the Twelfth Century," describes a failed raid in 1185 by Russian princes against the nomadic Turkic tribe of Kumans. Mikhail Lermontov captures the spirit of the anonymous *byliny* in his 1837 poem "A Song About Tsar Ivan Vasilevitch, the Young Bodyguard, and the Valorous Merchant Kalashnikov." Marc Slonim claims, "The musical rhythm of the *byliny*, the richness of their rhymes and alliterations, the freshness of their metaphors, the majestic pace of their descriptions, and the breadth of their style rank them with the world's greatest epic poetry."

SEE ALSO *ballad, epic, oral poetry.*

cabeza, see *zéjel.*

caccia Italian: "hunt" or "chase." The *caccia* is an Italian verse form with no fixed meter or structure. It is best known as a musical form popular in the thirteenth and fourteenth centuries. Musicologists have generally considered it synonymous with the "canon," a type of polyphonic "chase." Giosuè Carducci argued in 1896 that the *caccia* had a literary rather than a musical origin and pointed to the predominant subject of *cacce,* venery, or the hunting of wild animals, which becomes a metaphor for amorous pursuit, the sexual hunt. The fourteenth-century *caccia* does tend to depict a "hunt" or a bustling social scene, love or battle. Most scholars now consider the *caccia* a form of poetry for music. One of the most enchanting *cacce* is Franco Sacchetti's "Passando con pensier per un boschetto" ("As I walked pensively through a little wood," ca. 1362). Giovanni Boccaccio's *Caccia di Diana* (1334?) — the title can mean either "Diana's hunt" or "the chasing away of Diana" — describes a hunt for various beasts by fifty-nine beautiful women and their leader, Diana. The women change their allegiance to Venus, who then turns the beasts into men.

SEE ALSO *madrigal.*

cacoethes scribendi "Writer's itch," a mania for writing. The phrase derives from Juvenal, who writes in his *Satires* (late first to early second century) that *tenet insanabile multos / Scribendi cacoëthes,* "the incurable itch for scribbling (or writing) affects many." The *Oxford English Dictionary* quotes Joseph Addison (1713): "Juvenal terms [this distemper] a Cacoethes, which is a hard word for a disease called in plain English 'The itch of writing.' This Cacoethes is as epidemical as the small pox." Shelley wrote to his friend Thomas Peacock, "Your anathemas against poetry itself excited me to a sacred rage, or *cacoëthes scribendi* of vindicating the insulted Muses." Oliver Wendell Holmes's satirical poem "Cacoethes Scribendi" (1890) takes up the insatiable disease of writing:

> If all the trees in all the woods were men;
> And each and every blade of grass a pen;
> If every leaf on every shrub and tree
> Turned to a sheet of foolscap; every sea
> Were changed to ink, and all earth's living tribes
> Had nothing else to do but act as scribes,
> And for ten thousand ages, day and night,
> The human race should write, and write, and write,
> Till all the pens and paper were used up,
> And the huge inkstand was an empty cup,
> Still would the scribblers clustered round its brink
> Call for more pens, more paper, and more ink.

cacophony Jarring, discordant sound. Cacophony is generally associated with harsh consonants, rather than with vowels. It is the opposite of euphony. Sound is part of the context of a poem and should be judged in relationship to its other parts. The discordant sounds of poetry are often marshaled from Anglo-Saxon and other alliterative Germanic verses for special effect, as when Lord Byron writes of "Bombs, drums, guns, bastions, batteries, bayonets, bullets,— / Hard words, which stick in the soft Muses' gullets" (*Don Juan,* 1819–1824).

SEE ALSO *dissonance, euphony.*

cadence 1) Balanced, rhythmic flow. 2) The measure or beat of movement. 3) The general inflection or modulation of the voice, especially a falling inflection, as at the end of a sentence. The term *cadence* is used to describe the rhythmic movement of non-metrical poetry, of free verse, biblical poetry, highly charged prose. In "A Retrospect" (1918), Ezra Pound exhorted his contemporaries to write by the musical cadence and not by traditional meters: "As regarding rhythm: to compose in the sequence of the musical phrase, not in sequence of a metronome." F. S. Flint characterized free verse in 1920 as "unrimed cadence" and spoke of "the natural cadence of our emotion."

SEE ALSO *free verse, measure, rhymed prose, rhythm.*

caesura From the Latin *caedere,* meaning "to cut"; a pause in the poetic line. The caesura comes at the end of a unit of sense and is signaled either by a comma or a period. It is marked in scansion by a double vertical line (||). For example, there is a caesura after the semicolon in the first line and after the comma in the second line of this sonnet by William Wordsworth (ca. 1802):

> The world is too much with us; || late and soon,
> Getting and spending, || we lay waste our powers

SEE ALSO *meter.*

Cairo poets During World War II, the British military presence in Egypt had an unexpected side effect: a sudden influx of poets. There were two different types of British literary activity in Egypt. The journal *Personal Landscape,* which was run by Lawrence Durrell (1912–1990), Bernard Spencer (1909–1963), Robin Fedden (1908–1977), and Terence Tiller (1916–1987), sought an apolitical poetry that put a lyrical premium on personal experience during wartime. They kept alive the idea of the private individual. The "extrospective" Keith Douglas (1920–1944), killed in North Africa, was the most significant poet to emerge from this group. The Personal Landscape poets structured their lyrics around the bitter contrast between a prewar mobility of travel and the enforced stasis of wartime exile. Fedden's poem "Personal Landscape" (1966) is representative.

A rival group of soldier poets writing patriotic poems gathered around *Salamander,* run by Keith Bullen and John Cromer Braun, which also published a series of *Oasis* anthologies. The poems they published were old-fashioned and anti-modernist, Georgian and Kiplingesque. The group sought, in Roger Bowen's words, "to memorialize the soldier as amateur poet and oral historian." They ultimately collected an archive of seventeen thousand poems.

SEE ALSO *Georgian poets, martial verse.*

calligramme A form of modern visual poetry. Writing for the eye as well as the ear, Guillaume Apollinaire coined the term *calligrammes* (1918) for his attempts to create representational texts out of verbal compositions. He wanted to harness some of the visual power of painting for written compositions ("Moi aussi je suis peintre"). For example, the slanting lines in his poem "Il Pleut" ("It's Raining," 1918) create the sensation of rain running downward across a windowpane. The sound of the unpunctuated lines in French creates an incantatory murmuring that evokes the sadness and melancholy of a rainy day in Paris. They also create a sense of adventure. The *calligramme,* which pours a verbal text into a visual form, is a type of concrete, or pattern, poetry.

SEE ALSO *concrete poetry, pattern poetry.*

canciones Spanish: "songs." The word *cantar* means "to sing," and *canciones* are any compositions that are sung, especially in the lyric song tradition. Poets who write often use this term metaphorically to suggest the oral imperative of their work, poems that go beyond speech, as in St. John of the Cross's mystical sixteenth-century *Canciones.* Pablo Neruda entered poetry in 1924 with *Veinte poemas de amor y una canción desesperada* (*Twenty Love Poems and a Song of Despair*). The orality here is metaphorical; these songs are written poems. So, too, Neruda often uses the word *cantar* throughout his odes — he would "sing" them as poets did in ancient Greece — but in truth "singing" has become a metaphor, as in Catullus's *Carmina,* which date to the first century B.C.E. The *canción* also refers to Italianate verse forms that alternate seven- and eleven-syllable lines.

SEE ALSO *lira, song, songbook.*

Cankam, see *akam.*

cancrine, see *palindrome.*

canon A standard body of writings, a group of creative works that have been deemed authoritative. The word *canon* derives from a Greek word that meant either a measuring rod or a list. The first meaning was the basis for the idea of a model, a standard employed as a rule or principle. This was applied to the idea of "canon law" (ecclesiastical law). The second meaning forms the basis for the Roman Catholic concept of canonization, the practice of adding an individual to a "list" of saints.

The idea of a definitive canon was developed in the fourth century in relationship to the Hebrew Bible and the New Testament. It was a way of safeguarding a tradition. The biblical canon, which was formed over the centuries, comprised the books that the Christian church considered Holy Scripture. The apocrypha ("hidden books") became the books related to the Scriptural canon that were not officially recognized. Eleven books included in the Roman Catholic biblical canon are considered apocryphal by the Protestant church. A reading of the Bible that emphasizes the unity of the biblical texts tends to be called a canonical interpretation. This is in contrast to a historical interpretation, which suggests the different books of the Bible were authored by different writers working in different circumstances over time.

In late sixteenth-century England, the idea of canon was first applied to secular writings. In his poem "The Canonization" (1633), for example, John Donne expresses the hope of being canonized, which is to say, achieving a secular fame comparable to the Catholic saints. In his tract *Polimanteia* (1595), William Covell advocated canonizing literary works under the auspices of English universities. Critics later began to employ the idea of a canon to refer to the definitive works attributed to a given author, as in "the Chaucer canon" or "the Shakespeare canon." Works outside that established canon were considered apocryphal.

The word *canon* is now most frequently used as a collective term to refer to the totality of the most esteemed works in a culture. A church canon is determined by an institutional authority. A secular literary canon is more amorphous, more unofficial. Literary canons determine which writers are "major" and "minor," which works are "classics." They are often perceived as static, but canons are actually always in flux, under revision. New works force us to reconsider old ones. The metaphysical poets, for example, were largely ignored for centuries, but highly revalued in the period of early modernism. The romantic poets were undervalued by the modernists but came into greater prominence in the post–New Critical era.

Since the 1970s, literary critics and theorists have drawn attention to canon formation, the social processes that determine how certain authors and not others become recognized as standard. Pressure has been put on revising and opening up the canon. As John Ashbery recognizes, "The canons are falling / One by one."

SEE ALSO *metaphysical poets, poststructuralism, tradition.*

cantar de gesta *Cantar* means "to sing." The *cantar de gesta* is a "song of deeds," the Spanish equivalent of the French chanson de geste ("song of heroic deeds"). These folk epics, which narrated the legendary exploits of a heroic figure, were dramatically performed by roaming *juglares. Poema de mío Cid* (*Poem of the Cid,* literally *The Song of my Lord,* ca. 1142), the masterpiece of the genre, is Spain's oldest preserved complete literary work and stands at the top of what may have been a thriving epic tradition in medieval Spain.

SEE ALSO *chansons de geste, epic, jongleur, romances.*

cante fable The cante fable, a narrative form common in folk tales, tells a story partly in song. The term was coined in the only extant medieval (twelfth or thirteenth century) European cante fable, *Aucassin and Nicolette,* which contains the line, "*Non cantefable prent fin*" ("Our cante fable is coming to a close"). The distinguishing feature of the cante fable is the juxtaposition between the spoken sections, which set up the scene and explain the story, and the lyrical song sections, usually in dialogue, which are emotionally charged and often contain magical statements, animal calls, riddles, the sayings of poets. The cante fable is a hybrid form. Verse is embedded in *One Thousand and One Nights* and the *Panchatantra* (third century B.C.E.), in early Celtic literature and old Scandinavian sagas, in classic fairy tales. Listen to a traditional English ballad sung from African descendents in the West Indies, or, for that matter, in the southern United States, and you'll most likely hear a cante fable form. In the early 1960s, the folklorist Roger Abrahams found a profusion of the cante fable in an African American neighborhood in west Philadelphia (*Deep Down in the Jungle,* 1964).

SEE ALSO *folk song, narrative poetry.*

cante jondo *Cante jondo,* or "deep song," is an Andalusian term for a traditional type of Spanish folk song. It is intertwined with modern flamenco.

The poet Federico García Lorca and the composer Manuel de Falla organized the first *cante jondo* festival in Granada in 1922. Falla published an essay outlining what he believed to be the origin and values of deep song, and Lorca delivered a lecture in which he said that *cante jondo* "is truly deep, deeper than all the wells and seas that surround the world, much deeper than the present heart that creates it or the voice that sings it, because it is almost infinite . . . It comes from the first sob and the first kiss." The Sevillean poet Manuel Machado wrote a book of poems called *Cante Hondo* (1912), which was surpassed only by Lorca's 1921 series entitled *Poema del cante jondo* (*Poem of the Deep Song,* 1931). Lorca believed that deep song had two roots, love and death.

SEE ALSO *duende, folk song.*

cantica, canticum (pl) Part of the ancient Roman drama that was accompanied by music and either chanted or sung, the *cantica* was distinguished from the *diverbia,* or dialogue. There were two kinds: 1) those sung in lyric meters (i.e., anapests, cretics, bacchiacs); 2) those chanted melodramatically with music in the background. There is little certitude about the delivery of the *cantica.* For example, some scholars now contend that professional *cantores* came onstage to sing the *cantica,* leaving the actors free to pantomime or dance. Plautus (ca. 254–184 B.C.E.) employed *canticum* in his plays, which are among the earliest surviving works of Latin literature, to define characters and entertain the audience. Like operatic airs, favorite *canticum* were also sung at musical entertainments.

SEE ALSO *comedy.*

canticle, see *hymn.*

cantiga, cancioneiros The *cantiga* generally refers to some two thousand Galician-Portuguese lyrics written between the late twelfth and the early fourteenth centuries. The three great songbooks, or *cancioneiros,* of the fourteenth and fifteenth centuries refer to four main types: *cantigas de amigo,* which are sung by women about their lovers, *cantigas de amor,* which are addressed by men to their ladies, religious songs, and *cantigas d'escarnho e de mal dizer,* which are songs of mockery and insult. The *cantiga de escarnho* is comparable to the Provençal *sirventes,* a satirical poem.

SEE ALSO *sirventes, song, songbook, virelay.*

canto One of the major divisions of a long poem. The cantos of a narrative or epic poem are like the chapters of a novel, except more lyrical, since the word derives from the Latin word for "song." The division into separate cantos gave bards and minstrels the chance to structure a performance, to mark units within a longer work, and to rest between sections. Both oral and written poets use the canto to time a plot, to linger over individual sections, and to examine particular themes within an overarching structure. Dante's decision to divide his *Commedia* (ca. 1304–1321) into an even one hundred cantos, as opposed to breaking it into long books as Virgil does in the *Aeneid* (29–19 B.C.E.), suggests a commitment to new lyricism, a vernacular epic. Ariosto, Tasso, Pope, and Byron all divided their work into cantos. Ezra Pound spent much of his life working on his modernist epic, *The Cantos* (1915–1969).

canzone, canzoni (pl) The term *canzone,* which means "song" in Italian, suggests both art and popular music. A *canzoniere* is a maker of songs and/or a singer of songs. The canzone also refers to various kinds of medieval Provençal and Italian lyric poems, usually on the subject of love. Petrarch established the canzone as a form comprising five- or six-line stanzas and a concluding envoi (half-stanza). In *De Vulgari Eloquentia* (ca. 1302–1305), Dante called the canzone "the self-contained action of one who writes harmonious words to be set to music." He considered it the most perfect species of lyric. He composed a maddeningly difficult form of the canzone, which was modeled on the Provençal *chanso* — a poem that uses the same five end-words in each of the five twelve-line stanzas, intricately varying the pattern. There is also a five-line envoi (a *tornata*) that uses all five of the words. It operates with mathematical precision.

Stanza one:	1, 2, 1, 1, 3, 1, 1, 4, 4, 1, 5, 5
Two:	5, 1, 5, 5, 2, 5, 5, 3, 3, 5, 4, 4
Three:	4, 5, 4, 4, 1, 4, 4, 2, 2, 4, 3, 3
Four:	3, 4, 3, 3, 5, 3, 3, 1, 1, 3, 2, 2
Five:	2, 3, 2, 2, 4, 2, 2, 5, 5, 2, 1, 1
Envoi:	1, 2, 3, 4, 5

Dante knew that his rigorous philosophical poems could be challenging and relied on them to enchant with their beauty. Here he concludes the first canzone of the *Convivio* by radically addressing his own poem, which Shelley translates in *Epipsychidion* (1821):

My song, I fear that thou wilt find but few
    Who fitly shall conceive thy reasoning
        Of such hard matter does thou entertain,
    Whence, if my misadventure chance should bring
Thee to base company, as chance may do,
        Quite unaware of what thou dost contain,
        I prithee comfort thy sweet self again,
My last delight; tell them that they are dull,
And bid them own that thou art beautiful.

The Dantescan form of the canzone has been keenly employed in our time by W. H. Auden, L. E. Sissman, James Merrill, Anthony Hecht, and Marilyn Hacker. John Hollander explains two versions of the traditional canzone by enacting them in his handbook, *Rhyme's Reason* (1981). Ezra Pound entitled his fifth book of poems *Canzoni* (1911).

SEE ALSO *chanso, chanson, sestina, song, songbook.*

canzonet, canzonetta (Italian) A "little song." Thomas Morley adopted the name for "canzonets or little short songs" in the madrigal style (1593). The term was used in the Renaissance for short and light songlike poems, as in Michael Drayton's "To His Coy Love: A Canzonet" (1619), which concludes:

Clip me no more in those dear arms,
    Nor thy life's comfort call me;
O these are but too powerful charms,
    And do but more enthrall me.
But see how patient I am grown,
    In all this coil about thee;
Come, nice thing, let thy heart alone;
    I cannot live without thee.

Both Shakespeare and Ben Jonson employed the term as a ditty. Oscar Wilde penned a canzonet in 1888, and the American poet A. Bronson Alcott affected an Italian manner in *Sonnets and Canzonets* (1882). In the 1940s, Umberto Saba boasted about his twelve canzonettas: "Saba's *Canzonettas* are to common canzonettas what a Chopin waltz or a Bach gavotte was to the waltzes and gavottes that couples used to dance to."

SEE ALSO *ditty, madrigal.*

capitolo In Italian verse, the word for *chapter* refers to a form that either imitates or parodies Dante's terza rima. The name derives from Petrarch's term for the six parts or "chapters" of his *Trionfi* (*Triumphs*). It is, in effect, a satirical version of terza rima. It mimics and upends the effects of Dante's quintessential three-line stanza with interlocking rhymes (*aba, bcb, cdc*). Until the fifteenth century, the *capitolo* was used for didactic, allegorical, or political poems. Since the sixteenth century, it has been used for humorous and satirical subjects.

SEE ALSO *satire, terza rima.*

carmen The Latin word *carmen,* which means "song" or "lyric" (Catullus's *Carmina,* first century B.C.E.), has especially attracted English poets because of its closeness to the word *charm.* It is etymologically connected to *canere,* or "sing." In older Latin texts it also means a magic formula, an incantation to make things happen. Horace uses it in the *Odes* (23–13 B.C.E.) to suggest divine inspiration, the song of the poet as an instrument of the muse.

SEE ALSO *charm, incantation, muse.*

carmen figuratum, see *pattern poetry.*

carol A light-hearted religious song. The etymology of the word *carol* traces back to choric music, to a circle dance accompanied by singers. Originally a folk song, the carol seems to have traveled to England from France sometime in the Middle Ages. It was apparently an ancient church practice to sing carols, but medieval clerics sought to curtail the use of carols in religious celebrations, most likely because of their association with early pagan rites and their often erotic lyrics. The medieval carol had a more or less fixed form. The metrical style reflected its close connection with dance. But as that association faded so did the carol's formal strictures. Since the sixteenth century, the word *carol* has come to mean any festive, religious song. It follows secular rather than religious musical traditions. It is now mostly sung at Christmas in honor of the birth of Christ (in this sense it is akin to the French *Noël* and the German *Weihnachtslied*). Some examples: "Joy to the World" (1719), the seventeenth-century "I Saw Three Ships (Come Sailing In)," the Old English "Seven Joys of Mary," and "The Twelve Days of Christmas" (1780). John Milton, Henry Vaughan, George Herbert, Robert Southwell, and Ben Jonson all contributed to the carol genre. Romantic and modern poets have sometimes written poems that can't actually be sung, but which borrow motifs from the traditional carol. Some examples: Samuel Taylor Coleridge ("A Christmas Carol," 1799), C. Day Lewis ("A Carol," 1935), R. S. Thomas ("Carol," 1985), Donald Hall ("A Carol," 1987–1990), W. S. Merwin ("Carol of the Three Kings," 1952), and Joseph Brodsky ("A Martial Law Carol," 1983).

SEE ALSO *folk song, song.*

Caroline Age The name "Charles" is *Carolus* in Latin, and the Caroline Age is the literary era in England during the reign of King Charles I (1625–1649). The time was marked by civil war fought between supporters of the king, the "Cavaliers," and supporters of Parliament, the Puritan "Roundheads," led by Oliver Cromwell. The Cavalier poets — Robert Herrick (1591–1674), Edmund Waller (1606–1687), Richard Lovelace (1618–1657?), Abraham Cowley (1618–1667), and Sir John Suckling (1609–1642) — many of them courtiers, were royalists, classical, and conservative, who were influenced by Ben Jonson (1572–1637) and thus considered themselves "Sons of Ben." John Milton entered literature on the parliamentary side. This is the period of his masque *Comus* (1634), his pastoral elegy "Lycidas" (1638), and his political speeches and pamphlets, such as *The Doctrine and Discipline of Divorce* (1643), *Of Education* (1644), and *Areopatica* (1644), an impassioned tract against censorship: "For books are not absolutely dead things, but do contain a potency of life in them to be as active as that soul whose progeny they are; nay, they do preserve as in a vial the purest efficacy and extraction of that living intellect that bred them." John Donne (1572–1631), George

Herbert (1593–1633), and Richard Crashaw (1613?–1649) were religious "metaphysical poets," the Caroline Divines.

SEE ALSO *Cavalier poets, metaphysical poets, Renaissance poetry, Restoration poetry, Sons of Ben.*

carpe diem The notion of *carpe diem* — Latin for "seize the day" — is a recurring motif in poetry. Horace employs the motto in his *Odes* (23–13 B.C.E.), but the idea is present in poetry from its inception. It is found in ancient Egyptian poetry (in what are called "harper's songs" — mortuary poems inscribed on tombs) and Persian poetry (Omar Khayyám, 1048–1131). The idea that we are going to die is at the heart of lyric poetry, and carpe diem encapsulates an epicurean response to the ephemeral nature of life with an injunction: make the most of time, take seriously the pleasures of life. Religious poetry in general and Christian poetry in particular often appropriates the carpe diem theme to contrast the temporality of human life on earth with the eternal nature of the divine.

There is a long history of employing the rose as a symbol for life's brevity, which thus links it to the motif of carpe diem. The rose also came to symbolize the loss of virginity (*Roman de la rose*). Carpe diem has often been associated with sexuality, especially a fruitless chastity. One also detects an underlying cynicism toward the motif that runs from Catullus (84–54 B.C.E.) to the English Cavalier poets. Thus Andrew Marvell, "Had we but World enough, and Time, / This coyness, lady, were no crime" ("To His Coy Mistress," ca. 1650s), and Robert Herrick: "Gather ye Rosebuds while ye may, / Old time is still aflying: / And this same flower that smiles today / To morrow will be dying" ("To the Virgins, to Make Much of Time," 1648). Billy Collins playfully captures the spirit of the motif when he writes in his poem "Carpe Diem" (2008), "I knew this was one morning I was born to seize."

SEE ALSO *Cavalier poets.*

catachresis The misuse or misapplication of a word. Writing in the first century, the Roman rhetorician Quintillian defined catachresis (*abusio*, or abuse) as "the practice of adapting the nearest available term to describe something for which no actual [i.e., proper] term exists." In poetry, it is generally used to suggest a forced or mixed metaphor. George Puttenham described catachresis as a figure of "plain abuse, as he that bade his man go into his library and fetch him his bow and arrows." John Dryden characterized it as "wresting and torturing a word into another meaning." The catachresis need not always be a mistake. It can also be a deliberate way of wrenching a word from its usual context, as when Christopher Smart ironically compares his cat Jeoffry to a beast of burden, saying that "he camels his back to break the first notion of business." Or it can be a deliberately strained comparison, as when Hart Crane states, "Our tongues recant like beaten weathervanes." Northrop Frye speaks of "the violent or unexpected metaphor that is called catachresis." He says, "From Nashe's 'Brightness falls from the air' to Dylan Thomas's 'A grief ago,' the emotional crux of the lyric has over and over again tended to be this 'sudden glory' of fused metaphor."

Jacques Derrida has also made catachresis a key term in deconstruction, which locates those moments when texts expose their contradictions and dismantle themselves. Catachresis aggressively imposes a sign on a meaning. It has no original referent. Derrida explains that "philosophy is literary, not so much because it is *metaphor* but because it is *catachresis.* The term *metaphor* generally implies a relation to an original 'property' of meaning, a 'proper' sense to which it indirectly or equivocally refers, whereas catachresis is a violent production of meaning, an abuse which refers to no anterior or proper norm. The founding concepts of metaphysics — *logos, eidos, theoria,* etc. — are instances of *catachresis* rather than metaphors."

SEE ALSO *deconstruction, epic simile, metaphor, rhetoric.*

catalexsis, catalectic, see *truncation.*

catalog poem, catalog verse A list, or catalog poem, takes inventory of people, places, things, or ideas. Writing started with the making of practical lists around 3200 B.C.E. in ancient Mesopotamia. "The list is, perhaps, the most archaic and pervasive of genres," Jonathan Z. Smith explains. This ancient device, a structure of *parallelism,* is found in literatures around the world. One thinks of the genealogical lists in oral and written poetry, such as Genesis 10. "The Catalogue of Ships" in book 2 of the *Iliad* (ca. eighth century B.C.E.) served as a model for innumerable poetic catalogs to follow. Poets such as Christopher Smart and Walt Whitman give the catalog an incantatory quality and often use it to praise the diversity and unity of the universe. It thus becomes a form of praise poem. In his essay "Some Lines from Whitman" (1953), Randall Jarrell describes the pages of ecstatic listing in *Leaves of Grass* as "little systems as beautifully and astonishingly ordered as the rings and satellites of Saturn." The greatest catalogs in poetry instill a sense of wonder.

SEE ALSO *anaphora, blazon, incantation, litany, parallelism, praise poems.*

Catastrophism Czeslaw Milosz was one of the founders of *Zagary,* a Polish journal and movement of the 1930s. The name came from the Lithuanian word for "brushwood," or, more locally, dried twigs that were charred but still glowing in a fire. The two other original founders were Teodor Bujnicki and Jerzy Zagórski; the group also included Jerzy Putrament and Alexander Rymkiewicz. The *Zagary* poets supposedly prophesized the cataclysmic events of World War II and thus earned the label *Catastrophists.* Milosz's first two books, *A Poem on Frozen Time* (1933) and *Three Winters* (1936), are emblematic catastrophist works. Milosz later explained that catastrophism "was above all engaged with the great crisis of civilization. Only later was it acknowledged, somewhat superficially, as a Cassandra-like prophecy of the events of 1939–45, even though the Second World War was but a corollary of a far more protracted crisis." He added, "Leftist or not, 'catastrophism' was chary of the near future and foresaw decades, if not centuries, of tragedy."

SEE ALSO *Kraków avant-garde.*

catena rondo The Canadian poet Robin Skelton invented this form of rhyming quatrains (*abba*), which he describes in his guide to verse forms and meters, *The Shapes of Our Singing* (2002). The first line of each four-line stanza is also the last one, and the second line of each quatrain forms the first line of the next one. The final stanza repeats the first stanza. He took the name by combining the words *catena* (chain) and *rondo* (circle) "because the stanzas are linked together by repetition and the poem makes a circle by returning to its beginning."

catharsis Derives from *katharein* ("to cleanse"), which is the Greek word for purgation, cleansing, and purification. The word, which has both a religious and a medical history (it was employed early on in the writings of the Hippocratic School of Medicine), was first applied to Homeric poetry, to the poems of Hesiod, and to the mystery cults at Delphi and Eleusis, where cathartic actions were performed in rituals for spiritual and moral cleansing, which is the origin of tragedy. Aristotle famously states in the *Poetics* (350 B.C.E.) that tragedy "effects through pity and fear the proper catharsis of these emotions." Aristotle never defined or explained the term *catharsis,* and there has been an enormous ongoing (and still unresolved) debate about the term throughout the history of literary theory. He seems to suggest that tragedy has a therapeutic effect in arousing powerful feelings in the spectator. The storm of feelings leads to a release and resolution of tension. Adnan K. Abdulla argues that the meaning of catharsis mirrors the concerns of different historical periods. The term took on moral overtones during the Renaissance. The Augustan period focused on the purgative elements of tragedy. The focus moved from the spectator/reader to the poet during the romantic era, and the poem became a form of catharsis for its creator. In modern psychoanalytic terms, catharsis has also been linked to the need to release unconscious conflicts.

SEE ALSO *Augustan Age, confessional poetry, Renaissance poetry, romanticism, tragedy.*

Cavalier poets The Cavalier poets were a group of mid-seventeenth-century English lyric poets whose work has an unusual lightness, clarity, and grace. The group includes Robert Herrick (1591–1674), Thomas Carew (1595?–1640?), Edmund Waller (1606–1687), Richard Lovelace (1618–1657?), Abraham Cowley (1618–1667), and Sir John Suckling (1609–1642), who said, "For the People are naturally not valiant, and not much cavalier." These classically minded poets, influenced by Ben Jonson (1572–1637), worked during the reign of King Charles I. Most were courtiers. They were royalists during the civil war and supported the king against the Puritans, who supported Oliver Cromwell. The title *cavalier* began its political life in the early 1640s as an insult, an ironic term of abuse, which suggested a degenerate kind of person, a superficial fop, but it later became a sign of partisan pride, the mark of a royalist gentleman. The Cavalier poets were committed to the "good life." They were also "cavalier" in the sense that they distrusted the overearnest and the overly intense. Their poetry is witty, conservative, aristocratic, and devoted to an essentially English way of life. It has a nonchalant charm, a fastidious care for lucidity, and what Herrick calls "a wild civility."

The Cavaliers were especially good at tight, logical verse structures. They were compelled by friendship and haunted by erotic love.

SEE ALSO *Caroline Age, carpe diem, Sons of Ben.*

the Celtic Twilight, the Celtic Revival, see *Irish literary renaissance.*

cento From the Latin word for patchwork. A type of pastiche, the cento is a poetic composition that consists entirely of lines or passages from previous poems. Centos, or *Centones,* have been composed since at least the first century and may have begun as school exercises. Later, they became occasional pieces, sometimes humorous and off-color. They were also used to create Christian narratives out of pagan texts, as in the *Cento virgilianus* of Proba (fourth century). Homer (eighth century B.C.E.) was the most popular source of the Greek cento and Virgil of the Latin one. Two contemporary examples: John Ashbery's "The Dong with the Luminous Nose" (1998), which takes its title from an Edward Lear poem (ca. 1876), and Peter Gizzi's "Ode: Salute to the New York School" (2012), which works as both an homage and a bibliography. Maureen N. McLane includes two centos, an interlude and an envoi, in her prose book *My Poets* (2012).

SEE ALSO *collage.*

Centrifuge, see *futurism.*

chain rhyme, chain verse A type of verse that interlinks lines or stanzas through rhyme or repetition, as in Dante's terza rima (*aba bcb cdc*), or Robert Frost's interlocking rubaiyat, "Stopping by Woods on a Snowy Evening" (1923), which takes the unrhymed line in one stanza (*aaba*) and rhymes it with three lines in the next stanza (*bbcb*). These rhyme schemes and verse forms create a chain that connects the stanzas, like the rooms of a house.

SEE ALSO *rhyme, rhyme scheme, rubaiyat stanza, terza rima, villanelle.*

changga The Korean *changga*—a "long poem" or "long song"—consisted of ten or more lines or stanzas with a strong refrain, which combined verbal and musical rhythms with nonsense syllables and other onomatopoetic sounds. Peter H. Lee explains, "Consisting of pure onomatopoeia of drum sounds or nonsense jingles . . . the refrain sets up a mood or tone which carries the melody and spirit of the poem (as in 'Ode on the Seasons') or links a poem comprised of parts with differing contents (as in 'Song of Green Mountains'). The refrain attests, therefore, to the associations of verbal and musical rhythms in the *changga.*" These anonymous folk lyrics, which were sung in the eleventh to the fourteenth century, almost always expressed the joys and torments of love.

SEE ALSO *drum poetry, onomatopoeia, oral poetry, refrain.*

chanso, canso A love song. The *chanso* became the premiere genre of Provençal poetry (the other main branch was the *sirventes* or satire). It has been estimated that the *chanso* accounts for about one thousand poems, some 40 percent of the troubadour canon. The theme of the *chanso* was the troubadour ideal of courtly love. The typical structure consisted of four or five symmetrical stanzas and an envoy, or *tornado.* It was a measure of technical virtuosity, and each troubadour tried to mark the form with his own stanzaic structure and tune. The *chanso* was the model for the Italian *canzone. Vers* was the older term for *chanso,* though it was used more loosely and designated poems on almost any subject.

The *retroencha* essentially seems to have been a *chanso* or love song with a refrain at the end of each stanza, often with a satirical twist. There are only a few surviving examples of this form, which does not seem to have had a rigidly fixed structure. Jay Wright employs the *retroencha* in "The Hieroglyph of Irrational Space" (2000).

SEE ALSO *canzone, courtly love, sirventes, troubadour.*

chanson Ever since the Middle Ages, the French term for *song* has been used to refer to a wide variety of poetry and music, including the medieval epic songs (chansons de geste), the early story songs (*chansons d'histoire*), and the repertoires of the Provençal troubadours and the French trouvères. The troubadour Guillaume de Machaut (ca. 1300–1377), a great composer-poet, set the course for the French secular polyphonic songs of the fourteenth and fifteenth centuries.

SEE ALSO *chanso, chansons de geste, chansons de toile, song, troubadour, trouvère.*

chansonnier A manuscript or printed collection of French lyric poetry. It can also refer to a collection of musical settings of such lyric poetry.

chansons baladée, see *virelay.*

chansons de geste *Chansons de geste* is the term for the more than eighty Old French epic poems, "songs of heroic deeds," that date from the twelfth to the fifteenth century. The word *geste* carries an additional meaning of "history" or "historical document," and thus suggests that these poems were also songs of lineage. A large number of the chansons de geste, which were performed by jongleurs, revolve around the deeds of Charlemagne, who is accompanied by his Twelve Noble Peers and celebrated as the champion of Christendom. These legends are known as "the matter of France." The greatest chanson de geste is *La Chanson de Roland* (*The Song of Roland,* ca. 1090). A group of twenty-four poems center on Guillaume d'Orange. The tales about Roland and Oliver circulated widely and culminated in two Renaissance epics: Matteo Bolardo's *Orlando inamorato* (ca. 1478–1486) and Lucovico Ariosto's *Orlando Furioso* (1516).

SEE ALSO *epic, jongleur, laisse.*

chansons de toile "Weaving songs." These early French lyrics date to the beginning of the twelfth century. Sung by trouvères, the *chansons de toile* pretended to be songs that women sang at their looms while their husbands or lovers were away. Yet they are actually *chansons d'histoire,* or "story-songs," because they were sung by men about lovelorn women. They have a quality of feigned naiveté since they were poems that pretended to be folk songs, or songs sung by the people.

SEE ALSO *folk song, troubadour, trouvère.*

chant The term *chant* (from the Latin *cantare,* "to sing") has multiple meanings. It may refer to any song or melody; it may denote the particular melody to which a psalm or canticle is sung; it may refer to the actual psalm or canticle itself; it may suggest any religious recitative with a refrain. The Gregorian plainsong (*cantus firmus*) is the most influential form of religious chant. The chant may be part of special rites, as in the Navaho *yerbichai,* or "night chants," sung during "Night Way" rituals. Here is a strange chant, a pantheistic fragment, usually dated to the sixth century and attributed to Amergin, the chief bard of the Milesians and first poet of Ireland:

The Mystery

I am the breeze breathed at sea,
I am the wave woven of ocean,
I am the soft sound of spume,
I am the bull of the seven battles,
I am the cormorant upon the cliff,
I am the spear of the sun striking,
I am the rose of the fairest rose.
I am the wild bull of war,
I am the salmon stroking the flood,
I am the mere upon the moor,
I am the rune of rare lore,
I am the tooth of the long lance,
I am He who fired the head.

Who emblazons the mountain-meeting?
Who heralds the moon's marches?
Who leads the sun to its lair?
I am the Word, I am the Eye.

"The Mystery" is a rune, a Celtic incantation, with a deep archaic power.

Chanting also refers to a way of reciting a poem, giving it liturgical emphasis that is something between speaking and singing. William Hazlitt wrote, "There is a *chaunt* in the recitation both of Coleridge and Wordsworth, which acts as a spell upon the hearer and disarms the judgment." Chanting is a stylized mode of recitation that subordinates the musical element to the verbal one. It gives verse an oracular quality. One thinks of the many oral epic poets who composed and chanted their poems aloud: the Greek rhapsodists and Celtic bards, the Old English scops and Scandinavian skalds, the French trouvères and jongleurs. There are still *guslari* (minstrels) in Bosnia, Serbia, and Macedonia, who chant heroic poems aloud.

SEE ALSO *bard, guslar, jongleur, rhapsode, rune, scop, skald, troubadour, trouvère.*

chantey, see *sea shanties.*

chant royal A rich and difficult Old French verse form, the chant royal is a sixty-line poem. It is similar to, but even more demanding than, the ballade. The chant royal typically consists of five stanzas of eleven lines, each rhyming *ababcccddede,* and a five-line envoy rhyming *ddede.* The last line of the first stanza repeats as a refrain at the end of each succeeding stanza, including the envoy. Sixty lines rhyme on five sounds. The form has a regal element and was mostly used for elevated subjects, though it was probably considered "royal" because it was addressed to the "prince" who presided over a *puy,* a poetic contest.

The chant royal was first mentioned by Nicole de Margival around 1300. In his poem "Story of the Panther" he narrates a dream experienced by a lover who speaks in the first person. When the lover wakes up, he reports that he composed a series of poems in six types, including the chant royal. The form especially flourished in the fourteenth century. Some of those who excelled at it were Guillaume de Machaut (1300?–1377), Eustache Deschamps (1340–1406), Christine de Pizan (1364–ca. 1431), Charles d'Orléans (1394–1465), and Jean Marot (1457–1526). It was briefly revived in the nineteenth century by Théodore de Banville (1823–1891) and others. Paul Valéry claimed that "compared with the chant royal, the sonnet is child's play."

SEE ALSO *ballade, poetic contest.*

charm A spell or incantation (a word, a phrase, a verse, a song) spoken or sung to invoke and control supernatural powers. Charms, which are universally known, are among the earliest forms of recorded written literature. They carry the resonance of magic rites in archaic cultures. The Old English charms (against wens, against the theft of cattle, for taking a swarm of bees, for a land remedy) stand as some of the first written works in our language. A charm, such as *abracadabra,* which was used throughout the Middle Ages, gave the individual a feeling of protection through contact with higher powers. Charms can be used for positive or negative ends, to ward off the spirit of evil or invoke it, to destroy an enemy or attract a beloved, to enchant objects, to ensure good luck with supra-normal power. Here is the beginning of a charmed and charming poem by Thomas Campion:

> Thrice tosse these Oaken ashes in the ayre,
> Thrice sit thou mute in this inchanted chayre;

Then thrice three times tye up this true loves knot,
And murmur soft; shee will, or shee will not.

SEE ALSO *incantation, spell.*

chastushka A Russian folk poem that consists of one stanza of four lines, usually rhymed, sometimes unrhymed. There are variant two-line and six-line forms. Gleb Uspensky was the first collector to use the term *chastushka* in 1889, though the genre began to appear in Russian folklore collections in the 1860s and '70s. The word derives from the Russian *chastit,* meaning "to speak fast." Some *chastushkas* are known in villages all over Russia, others are improvised. All are performed at informal social gatherings, where they are either recited or sung, often accompanied by a balalaika or accordion. They cover a vast range of subjects from love to politics, and they are frequently biting, pithy, obscene. Here is one, recorded around 1920, about domestic life under Communism:

We Moscow folk, we live damn well,
Snug as corpses, don't you think?
Me and the wife sleep in a drawer,
Her's mother's tucked up in the sink.

Alexander Blok borrowed the folk form for the stanzaic structure of his revolutionary long poem "The Twelve" (1918), which Osip Mandelstam called "a monumental dramatic *chastushka.*"

SEE ALSO *quatrain.*

Chaucerian stanza, see *rhyme royal.*

cheikh, cheikha Wearing long white jellabas and turbans, the *cheikhs* of Western Algeria performed a popular form of poetry known as *melhûn,* which has its roots in the rural chants of Bedouin tribes. Their music is known as *bedoui.* They lived in cities and underwent a strict apprenticeship. The *cheikhs* flourished after World War I, especially in Oran, and performed wherever people gathered. One could stroll down to the local medina and listen to a *cheikh* praising Muslim saints and ancient freedom fighters. The venerable *cheikhs* chanted epic songs. As an alternative, a group of street poets confronted daily life by singing *zendanis* (from *zendan,* meaning "cellar"). These witty improvised cellar or bar songs combined bits of *melhûn* with bawdy rhymes to treat local subjects for the bottom part of society, the dispossessed. They interspersed their words and bought themselves time with cries such as "ya rai" ("it's my opinion"), and thus became the forerunners of *raï* music, a popular form of contemporary Algerian music. The word *raï* suggests an opinion, a view of the world. At the same time, *meddhahates* were itinerant female singers who toured in strictly supervised groups and sang the *medh* — lyrical songs in praise of the prophet. They performed exclusively for female audiences.

Cheikhas were women who moved beyond the pale of so-called decent society (they were known as "women of the cold shoulder") and performed in cafés and cantinas, hash dens and bordellos. They blended the Bedouin music of the *cheikhs,* the street style of the zendan poets, and the itinerant music of the *meddhahates,* and came up with a rough, slangy music — earthy, freewheeling. The *cheikhas* gave up their family names and surrounded themselves with mystery. Cheikha Remitta (1923–2006) exemplified the razor-sharp verbal wizardry of *cheikha* poetry, and has been called "the grandmother of Algerian *raï* music." The *cheikhas* see the source of their art in *mehna,* a form of dark inspiration. It is akin to the Andalusian notion of duende, so close to flamenco artists. Andy Morgan quotes the definition of *mehna* by Cheikha Djenia (the "she-devil"):

> Mehna is hard and terrible. Mehna is strong and dangerous. She who has never experienced it is lucky. It's better for her, for her peace of mind. Mehna is the love that hurts, the love that sickens. Mehna, God preserve us, is like a tumour, an evil that envelopes your being. That's mehna, that's suffering, that's life . . .

SEE ALSO *duende.*

Chhayavaad *Chhayavaad,* which in Hindi means "Shadowism," refers to the neo-romantic era (1917–1938) of Hindi literature, especially poetry. The four key figures are Jaishankar Prasad (1889–1937), Suryakant Tripathi 'Nirala' (1896–1961), Sumitranandan Pant (1900–1977), and Mahadevi Varma (1907–1987). The *Chhayavaad* poets reintroduced the individual, a sense of personal expression, a new subjectivity, into twentieth-century Hindi poetry.

chiasmus Greek: "a diagonal arrangement" or "placing cross-wise." The rhetorical device chiasmus is named after the Greek letter *X* and suggests a criss-crossing of sentence members, a grammatically balanced statement of contrasting or opposing ideas or sounds. Quintilian (first century C.E.) provided an example: "Write quickly and you will never write well; write well and you will soon write quickly." Samuel Johnson (1709–1784) said, "Those whose lot it is to ramble can seldom write, and those who know how to write very seldom ramble." Chiasmus was probably a Semitic inheritance in Greek culture, like the alphabet, and figures prominently in both the Hebrew Bible and the New Testament. It takes a specialized form in the figure known as *antimetabole* ("turn about"), which is used when identical words or phrases repeat in reversed order, as when Alexander Pope writes in *The Rape of the Lock* (1712–1714):

> Yet graceful ease, and sweetness void of pride,
> Might hide her faults, if belles had faults to hide.

SEE ALSO *hysteron proteron, rhetoric.*

Chicago literary renaissance Chicago was one of the hubs of a new American poetry in the first two decades of the twentieth century. Harriet Monroe founded *Poetry: A Magazine of Verse* there in 1912 to provide an exclusive forum for contemporary poetry in America's cultural life. The magazine took as its motto Walt Whitman's statement "To have great poets there must be great audiences too." Three of the poets it helped launch were Carl Sandburg (1878–1967), Vachel Lindsay (1879–1931), and Edgar Lee Masters (1869–1950), all of whom wrote a socially concerned, democratic poetry. These once popular, second-level modernists, who are now underappreciated, celebrate American life in the rough-hewn, free-verse vernacular of the Midwest.

SEE ALSO *modernism.*

Chicago school In the 1930s and 1940s, a group of critics and scholars at the University of Chicago defined themselves as neo-Aristotelians. The literary scholar and critic R. S. Crane and the poet and literary critic Elder Olson were the two primary apologists for the group, which also included

Richard McKeon, a philosopher, and the literary critics Bernard Weinberg, W. R. Keast, and Norman MacLean, later a novelist. The neo-Aristotelians turned to Aristotle's *Poetics* (350 B.C.E.) as a starting point for their study of poetry. They focused on the Aristotelian concepts of plot, character, and genre, and took their perspective from Aristotle's four causes of literary art: the efficient cause (the poet), the final cause (the effect on the reader), the material cause (the language), and the formal cause (the mimetic content). The group opposed New Criticism, and excoriated the New Critical fixation on analyzing language (ambiguity, irony, paradox) as the sole cause and distinguishing characteristic of poetry. The Chicago critics were intent on studying poems as concrete wholes of various kinds. They distinguished between imitative or mimetic poetry and nonimitative or didactic poetry, but essentially followed the Aristotelian idea that literary works are imitations of human actions, passions, thoughts, and characters. They aimed for objectivity and took a holistic approach to literary analysis. As Crane formulated it in his introduction to *Critics and Criticism* (1952), the main text or "manifesto" of the Chicago school, the job of the critic was to inquire into "the necessary constituent elements, of possible kinds of poetic wholes, leading to an appreciation, in individual works, of how well their writers have accomplished the particular sorts of poetic tasks which the nature of the wholes they have attempted to construct have imposed on them."

SEE ALSO *imitation, mimesis, New Criticism, rhetoric.*

chivalric romance A major type of medieval romance. From the twelfth century onwards, there were literary works, usually in verse, that described the adventures of legendary knights and celebrated an idealized code of behavior. As children, many of us read watered-down versions of the Arthurian romances that recount the adventures of Lancelot, Galahad, Gawain, and other Round Table knights. Thus did we enter the realm of magic and imbibe the codes of loyalty, honor, and courtly love. Chrétien de Troyes's *Lancelot* (late twelfth century), the anonymous *Sir Gawain and the Green Knight* (late fourteenth century), Sir Thomas Malory's prose romance *Le Morte d'Arthur* (1484), and Edmund Spenser's *Faerie Queene* (1590–1596) are all significant chivalric romances.

SEE ALSO *courtly love, quest-romance.*

chōka From the Japanese: "long poem." The *chōka,* the earliest genre of Japanese poetry, is written in alternating five- and seven-syllable lines and concludes on an extra seven-syllable line. It is unrhymed and often has one or more envoys at the end. The form, which can be any length, opened up the possibility for sustained narratives in Japanese poetry (the longest extant *chōka* is 149 lines) and flourished in the first half of the eighth century. But it did not survive. The impulse to a lyrical narrative was better expressed through *haibun,* which combines haiku and prose.

SEE ALSO *haibun, haiku, tanka.*

choliambus Greek: "lame iambic." Hipponax of Ephesus (ca. 540 B.C.E.) invented the *choliambus,* or *scazon* ("limping"), meter for his satires. He substituted a spondee or a trochee in the sixth foot of the normal iambic line, and thus created a "limping" feeling, a line that dragged its foot. "As a weapon this was rather a club or a cudgel than a rapier," William Ross Hardie notes. The sixth-century poet Ananius also substituted a spondee in the fifth foot, which was called *ischiorrhogic* ("with broken hips").

choree, see *trochee.*

choreus, see *foot.*

choriamb, choriambus A Greek metrical foot in which two long syllables enclose two short ones. This has been converted in qualitative verse into a foot in which two stressed syllables enclose two unstressed ones. A choriamb unites one trochee and one iamb into a single four-syllable metrical unit (/ u u /). "Few of us who burst out with 'Son of a bitch!' realize they have just given utterance to a classic choriamb," John Frederick Nims notes in a piece on what he calls "maverick meters." Sappho was fond of choriambic meters, as in her poem about a woman of little culture (#55), which Horace adapted to deride superstitions five hundred years later. The choriamb was frequently employed in Latin poetry. It is somewhat herky jerky in English and thus rarely used, though Swinburne experimented with it in his poem "Choriambics" (1878), which he modeled on Catullus. Each line consists of one trochee, three choriambs, and one iamb. Here is the first line:

> Lóve, whăt | aíled thĕe tŏ léave | lífe thăt wăs máde | lóvely, wĕ thóught, | wĭth lóve? —

SEE ALSO *Aeolic, foot, iamb, meter, trochee.*

chorography, see *topographical poetry.*

chorus 1) A body of singers. 2) A composition written for singers. The word *chorus* means "round dance." Among the ancient Greeks, the chorus was originally a group of masked singers who chanted or sang poetry while dancing at religious festivals. It consisted of fifty speaking dancers, all men, who performed poems devoted to the god Dionysius. The dithyramb was the music of the chorus. Pindar's choral odes, which derived from this genre, were simultaneously sung and danced at communal events honoring gods and Olympic victors. Choral poems were public poems, which had a civic function.

According to Aristotle (384–322 B.C.E.), Greek drama developed out of these choral rites. At some point, the leader of the chorus became semidetached, a kind of soloist. The origin of drama seems to be the question-and-answer, the give-and-take, between the soloist and the rest of the chorus. The chorus became an integral part of Greek tragedy, especially in the work of Aeschylus and Sophocles, where it provided a running commentary on the characters and events. The choral group represented the larger community. Aristotle claimed, "The chorus should be considered as one of the persons in the drama; should be part of the whole, and a sharer in the action: not as in Euripides, but as in Sophocles." In comedy as well as in tragedy, the chorus or communal element was originally prominent, but as the genres developed, as elements such as plot grew in importance, the chorus become increasingly out of place, eventually disappearing.

Roman playwrights, such as Seneca, borrowed the Greek chorus, but a full-scale chorus was not widely adopted by English dramatists. It was used by Milton in *Samson Agonistes* (1671) and notably revived by T. S. Eliot in *Murder in the Cathedral* (1935) and *The Family Reunion* (1939). The Elizabethans did adapt a "chorus" to apply to a single actor who presented the prologue and the epilogue, commented on the play and explained offstage events, as in Christopher Marlowe's *Dr. Faustus* (1592–1593).

In lyric poetry, a chorus is also a short stanza repeated as the refrain of a poem or song.

SEE ALSO *comedy, dithyramb, drama, ode, refrain, tragedy.*

Christabel meter The meter of Samuel Taylor Coleridge's unfinished but influential poem "Christabel" (1797–1800). The Gothic narrative is written in free couplets in *accentual verse* with four strong stresses per line. As Coleridge explained in the preface to "Christabel" (published as a pamphlet in 1816):

> I have only to add that the metre of Christabel is not, properly speaking, irregular, though it may seem so from its being founded on a new principle: namely, that of counting in each line the accents, not the syllables. Though the latter may vary from seven to twelve, yet in each line the accents will be found to be only four. Nevertheless, this occasional variation in number of syllables is not introduced wantonly, or for the mere ends of convenience, but in correspondence with some transition in the nature of the imagery or passion.

For Coleridge, the dramatic passion determines the varying line lengths. The gripping opening lines enact the rhythm:

> 'Tis the *mid*dle of *night* by the *cas*tle *clock,*
> And the *owls* have a*wak*ened the *crow*ing *cock;*
> *Tu-whit!* — *To whoo!*
> And *hark, again!* the *crow*ing *cock,*
> *How drow*sily it *crew.*

Coleridge's scandalous "new principle" was a form of accentual verse, the defining characteristic of Anglo-Saxon poetry.

SEE ALSO "accentual verse" in *meter, sprung rhythm.*

cielito, see *gaucho poetry.*

cinquain French: "a grouping of five." It is also called a quintet and refers to any five-line stanza or poem in five lines. Adelaide Crapsey developed a special form of five-line syllabic poem that was published in her posthumous book *Verse* (1915). It consists of twenty-two syllables: a two-syllable line followed by a four, six, eight, and ending with a two. It is akin to the five-line Japanese tanka. Here is "November Night":

> Listen . . .
> With faint dry sound,
> Like steps of passing ghosts,
> The leaves, frost-crisp'd, break from the trees
> And fall.

There is something asymmetrical in the five-line stanza, and the imbalance often enacts a feeling of something beyond reason, an out-of-kilter comedy, as in the limerick, or a deeper solemnity of feeling, as in Philip Larkin's despairing "Home Is So Sad" (1964).

SEE ALSO *limerick, quintet, tanka.*

circumlocution What the Greeks called periphrasis or "circling speech" is a roundabout way of naming or saying something. The Greeks also employed the rhetorical terms *ambages* (winding pathways; roundabout ways of talking) and *pleonasmus,* the use of more words than are necessary. The rhetorician Quintilian (first century C.E.) distinguishes between two uses of circumlocution: *circuitus eloquendi* or the euphemistic, which is employed for decoration, "a practice most frequent amongst the poets," and the descriptive, as in the phrase "the wandering stars" to signify the planets. The device probably has its roots in magical formulations, cult practices. Longinus (210?–273 C.E.) argues that circumlocution or pariphrasis "is a cause of Sublimity," exalting "the Sentiment." On the one hand, indirect statement, using a description instead of a name, is one of the heightened effects of poetry. Take the circumlocution for the beginning of spring, and thus love, in the Song of Songs: "The flowers appear on the earth, the time of singing has come, and the voice of the turtledove is heard in our land" (2:12). On the other hand, circumlocution is also open to abuse, slack thinking, avoiding the subject. The Tudor figure of rhetoric for circumlocution is *Selfe Saying,* as in this passage from *Antony and Cleopatra* (1623):

Lepidus: What manner o'thing is your crocodile?
Antony: It is shap'd, sir, like itself, and it as broad as it has breadth.
It is just so high as it is, and moves with its own organs. It lives
by that which nourisheth it, and the elements once out of it, it
transmigrates.
Lepidus: What colour is it of?
Antony: Of its own colour too.
Lepidus: 'Tis a strange serpent.
Antony: 'Tis so. And the tears of it are wet.

SEE ALSO *dróttkvætt, euphemism, kenning, praise poems, rhetoric.*

civic poetry, civic critics The Russian poet and revolutionary Kondrati Ryleyev (1795–1826) coined the term *civicism* to refer to a literature of political protest and social consciousness. For him, poetry and politics became virtually the same thing. His own poems were obsessed with the life of the Cossacks. The romantic poets and Decembrists Pavel Aleksandrovich Katenin (1792–1853), Pyotr Andreyevich Vyazemsky (1792–1878), and Wilhelm Küchelbecker (1797–1846) all shared the idea of creating a national poetry. The nineteenth-century Russian civic critics were known for their extreme socio-political and utilitarian approach to literature. They wanted art for society's sake.

More generally, we might use the term *civic poetry* to refer to a poetry concerned with *civitas,* the social engagement of citizenship, as in W. H. Auden's "The Unknown Citizen" (1940), William Meredith's "A Mild-Spoken Citizen Finally Writes to the White House" (1971), and Andrew Feld's socially minded first book, *Citizen* (2003). The critic Lowry Nelson uses the term *civic poetry* to refer to patriotic poetry. He writes: "Civic poetry is concerned with community, that is, with cohesion, duty, honor, honesty, belongingness, and communal survival." Popular poetry has had important civic and social functions in American culture.

classic, classical, classicism Matthew Arnold argues in *The Study of Poetry* (1888) that "the true and right meaning of the word *classic, classical*" is that the work of art "belongs to the class of the very best." It has the highest character. The classic work is the standard-bearer, worthy of imitation, fit to be studied by later generations. The word *classicus* originated as a Roman tax term for a member of the highest income bracket. It was distinguished from *proletarius,* a wage-earner below the taxable minimum. The scholars of Alexandria invented the classic status of early Greek literature, a system that was then inherited by the Romans. Thus in literary study, the term *classical,* which appeared in English criticism around the middle of the eighteenth century, came to refer to ancient Greek and Roman writing. The word *classicism* designated later writing influenced by the ancient models. T. S. Eliot notes in "What Is a Classic?" (1945) that a true classic can be determined "only by hindsight and in historical perspective." Frank Kermode adds that "the doctrine of classic as model or criterion entails, in some form, the assumption that the ancient can be more or less immediately relevant and available, in a sense contemporaneous with the modern."

Classicism in poetry represents a fundamental belief in order, in reason and rule. It emphasizes clarity, proportion, and restrained feeling. The classically minded poet has always looked forward by looking backward and building on the traditions of ancient Greece and Rome. Jacques Barzun characterizes classicism as "stability within known limits." In the eighteenth century, a new or revived classicism — a return to first principles — became a fundamental neoclassicism. Robert Herrick proposes a neoclassical attitude when he writes in "Rules for Our Reach" (1648):

Men must have Bounds how farre to walk; for we
Are made farre worse, by lawless liberty.

The classically minded artist is committed to objectivity and impersonality. "The word 'classic' has a somewhat chilly sound," Heinrich Wölfflin pointed out. Here is the poet Linda Gregg's personal three-line distillation "Classicism" (1979):

The nights are very clear in Greece.
When the moon is round we see it completely
and have no feeling.

SEE ALSO *neoclassicism, romanticism.*

clerihew The British detective writer Edmund Clerihew Bentley (1875–1976) invented this form of comic poetry. It consists of a skewed quatrain — two rhyming couplets (*aabb*) of unequal length that whimsically encapsulate a person's biography. The form spoofs metrical smoothness. There is usually something ludicrous in the deadpan send-up of a famous person, whose name appears as one of the rhymed words in the first couplet:

Geoffrey Chaucer
Could hardly have been coarser,
But this never harmed the sales
Of his *Canterbury Tales.*

Bentley prefaced his three volumes of capsule biographies, collected in *Clerihews Complete* (1951), with these "Introductory Remarks":

The Art of Biography
Is different from Geography.
Geography is about Maps,
But Biography is about Chaps.

G. K. Chesterton (1874–1936) and W. H. Auden (1907–1973) were both devotees of the clerihew.

SEE ALSO *light verse, limerick.*

cliché A trite, stereotyped expression or idea. In his *Dictionary of Clichés* (1940), Eric Partridge characterizes clichés as phrases that have become hackneyed, outworn, and tattered, though, as Christopher Ricks points out, "what, as a metaphor, could be more hackneyed than *hackneyed,* more outworn than *outworn,* more tattered than *tattered?*" Alexander Pope takes aim at the stereotypical phrases of eighteenth-century poets in "An Essay on Criticism" (1711):

Wher'er you find "the cooling western breeze,"
In the next line it "whispers through the trees";
If crystal streams "with pleasing murmurs creep,"
The reader's threatened (not in vain) with "sleep."

Clichés deaden and abuse language; they blunt ideas. Yet the cliché, so often banished by literary arbiters, also has its creative uses. Marshall McLuhan is one of the few critics to take the contrarian position that a cliché presents an opportunity, for a cliché is, as he puts it in *From Cliché to Archetype* (1970), "an active, probing, structuring feature of our awareness. It performs multiple functions from release of emotion to retrieval of other clichés from both the conscious and unconscious life." In *Structure & Surprise* (2007), Michael Theune identifies a "Cliché-and-Critique Structure" in poems that "strategically incorporate clichés to make their meanings." Such poems as Walt Whitman's "Death's Valley" (1892) and John Ashbery's "And *Ut Pictura Poesis* Is Her Name" (1987) begin with a cliché, which they then turn back to critique.

climax The apex, the moment when a crisis reaches its greatest peak of intensity, which is then resolved. A climax can refer to any form of narrative — a poem, a play, a story.

SEE ALSO *anticlimax.*

close reading, see *New Criticism.*

closet drama A dramatic work, usually written in verse, that is not intended for theatrical performance. It is meant to be read in one of two ways. It can be experienced by a solitary reader or else read aloud in a group. The tradition of closet dramas reaches its peak in Milton's *Samson Agonistes* (1671) and Goethe's *Faust* (1808–1832), in Byron's *Manfred* (1817), Shelley's *The Cenci* (1819) and *Prometheus Unbound* (1820), Browning's *Pippa Passes* (1841), and Hardy's *The Dynasts* (1904–1908). James Merrill resurrected and reinvented the genre in his trilogy, *The Changing Light at Sandover* (1976–1982). Richard Howard's *Two-Part Inventions* (1974) takes the dramatic monologue in the direction of the closet drama, though these five highly performative pieces for reading, especially "Wildflowers," a dialogue between Oscar Wilde and Walt Whitman, are a long way out of the closet.

SEE ALSO *drama.*

cobla The word for *stanza* in Old Provençal or Old Occitan, the language of the troubadours. An isolated or standalone stanza in troubadour poetry was called a *cobla esparsa.* It was called *coblas unissonans,* stanzas in unison, when the rhyme scheme and the rhyme sounds were consistent from stanza to stanza. It was named *coblas singulars* when the rhyme scheme remained the same but each stanza had its own rhyme sounds, *coblas doblas* when the sounds changed every two stanzas, and *coblas ternas* when the sounds changed every three stanzas. It was called *coblas capcaudadas* ("head-tailed") when the last rhyme of one *cobla* became the first rhyme sound of the next and *coblas capfinidas* ("head-finished") when the last rhyme word of one stanza appeared in the first line of the next. It was called *coblas alternadas* ("alternated stanzas") when the patterns stayed the same but the actual rhyme sounds differed. It was common for one troubadour to write a *cobla* that inspired an answering *cobla* in the same form.

SEE ALSO *stanza, tenson, troubadour.*

the Cockney school of poetry In October 1817, *Blackwood's Edinburgh Magazine* launched a notorious series of articles "On the Cockney School of Poetry," a derisive term for the Londoners Leigh Hunt, John Keats, Percy Bysshe Shelley, and William Hazlitt, who constituted a coterie group. The venomous Tory attacks used the low birth of the Cockneys, especially Hunt and Keats, to dismiss their colloquial verse and radical social and political views. Keats came from a lower-middle-class milieu in an extremely class-bound society and thereby entered poetry without the advantages of birth, wealth, or university education. An aura of class still sometimes hovers around his achievement and reputation. From the first, there seem always to have been readers who could not abide his liberal sympathies and "Cockney" roots, his radical sensuality and democratic feeling for literary culture, his mask of—to use W. B. Yeats's phrase—"deliberate happiness."

collage The word *collage* derives from the French *coller,* meaning "to glue," and the first meaning of collage is as an artistic composition made of various materials glued on a surface. As an assembly of different forms, the collage made a dramatic entry into modern art early in the twentieth century. In 1912, Georges Braque and Pablo Picasso started making paper collages according to the principles of Cubism. The subversive and creative strategy spread to other modernist movements—the Futurists used collage to create works of dynamic speed, the Surrealists for unconscious connections—and to the other arts as well. Hans Arp, Marcel Duchamp, Kurt Schwitters, and

Max Ernst were all collage artists who worked by the principle that you don't just make art, you find it. A literary collage is a creative work that incorporates various materials or elements, a work that puts together disparate scenes in rapid succession without transitions.

Collage has been crucial to modern poetry. Ezra Pound's *Cantos* (1915–1969) and T. S. Eliot's "The Waste Land" (1922) are based on principles of collage, which David Antin defines as "the dramatic juxtaposition of disparate materials without commitment to explicit syntactical relations between elements." For example, think of "The Waste Land" as an open structure of fragments, a poem without a fixed center. It has no single interpretation or truth, no one narrator or narrative thread to hold it together. It disseminates the self. It contains scenes and vignettes from a wide variety of times and places: agitated scraps of conversations, parodies, intertextual allusions, unattributed and often broken quotations, a medley of radically shifting languages, a disturbing cacophony of voices. It is rhetorically discontinuous.

In his book on Joseph Cornell, *Dime-Store Alchemy* (1992), Charles Simic argues, "The collage technique, the art of assembling fragments of preexisting images in such a way as to form a new image, is the most important innovation in the art of this century. Found objects, ready-mades (mass-produced items promoted into art objects), abolish the separation between art and life." So, too, Tony Hoagland explains the practice of collage in contemporary poetry:

> Collage is really the practice of a theory of knowledge: antirational and semi-intentional, it takes coincidence and chance materials as part of its method and inspiration. By eliminating transition, it embraces ambiguity, improvisation, speed, and multiplicity of meaning. It is expressive, but not primarily self-expressive. It does not place priority on closure, nor on conventional notions of completeness. In the constant conversation between unity and disunity, juxtaposition plays with omission and collision. It loves the energy of disruption and dislocation.

SEE ALSO *cento, Cubist poetry, found poem, fragment, futurism, Surrealism.*

comedy "Comedy has been particularly unpropitious to definers," Samuel Johnson cautioned in 1755 and there is no single definition that can encompass the wide scope of what is considered comic. Comedy and tragedy are the two most common and familiar kinds of drama. The term *comedy* derives from the Greek *komos,* "a processional celebration," which suggests that comedies date back to festivals of revelry. The primal archaic drive of comedy is the power of renewal, of rebirth. The first recorded performance of a comedy took place in March 486 B.C.E. in the Theater of Dionysius, an open-air structure located on the southern slope of the Acropolis in Athens. Five comic poets, each with a single play, competed in the five-day festival City Dionysia. Thus, as George Meredith puts it, "comedy rolled in shouting under the divine protection of the Son of the Wine-jar, as Dionysius is made to proclaim himself by Aristophanes" (*An Essay on Comedy,* 1877).

Historically, in Greek drama, comedies were stage plays with happy endings. Comedies end well, whereas tragedies end badly. Aristotle argues in the *Poetics* (350 B.C.E.) that, whereas tragedy presents "noble actions" of "noble personages," comedy presents "actions of the ignoble." Comedy was initially devoted to "invective" or to "the ridiculous," which Aristotle calls "a species of the ugly," that is "a mistake or deformity not productive of pain or harm to others." Both tragedy and comedy originated in "improvisations," he says, but tragedy derives from "dithyrambs" and comedy from "phallic songs." There was always an element of the low mimetic in comedy.

Old Comedy was essentially topical satire directed against individuals. Aristophanes (ca. 450–ca. 388 B.C.E.) embodies the spirit of Old Comedy when he skewers Socrates (470?–399 B.C.E.) as the worst kind of sophist in *The Clouds* (423 B.C.E.) and makes fun of his rival tragic playwrights, Sophocles (496?–406 B.C.E.), Aeschylus (525–456 B.C.E.), and Euripides (480?–406 B.C.E.) in *The Frogs* (405 B.C.E.). The New Comedy of Menander (342–291 B.C.E.) ridiculed types of characters rather than well-known figures. It treated human foibles by mocking ordinary people. This comedy of manners became the model for Roman playwrights, such as Terence and Plautus (both second century B.C.E.), who in turn transmitted a typical structure to Renaissance playwrights, including Shakespeare (1564–1616). As Northrop Frye explains it in *A Natural Perspective* (1965): "The normal action is the effort of a young man to get possession of a young woman who is kept from him by various social barriers: her low birth, his minority or shortage of funds, parental opposition, the prior claims of a rival. These are eventually circumvented, and the comedy ends at a point when a new society is crystallized, usually by the marriage or betrothal of hero and heroine.

The birth of a new society is symbolized by a closing festive scene featuring a wedding, a banquet, or a dance. This conclusion is normally accompanied by some change of heart on the part of those who have been obstructing the comic resolution. Tragedy ends in a 'catastrophe,' and Ben Jonson uses this term for the end of a comedy also, but in a comedy the end might better be called an anastrophe, a turning up rather than turning down."

In the medieval era, comedy expanded beyond the drama to include any narrative that ends positively, as in Dante's *Commedia* (*The Divine Comedy,* ca. 1304–1321). In Christian literature, comedy is enacted as the theme of salvation. The Renaissance brought the term *comedy* back to the theater, but without the connotation of satire.

The Italian *Commedia dell'arte* ("Comedy of Art" or "Comedy of the profession") was a type of unwritten drama, a form of improvised "sketches," that especially flourished in the sixteenth and seventeenth centuries. It was performed by traveling players, the first truly professional actors in Europe. It gave us stock characters that have had a strong afterlife in poetry and other genres, such as Pierrot the sad clown and Harlequin the sly servant.

The *commedia erudita* was the written comic drama of the Italian Renaissance.

The comedy of manners was the dominant form of Restoration comedy (1660–1700). It depicted the manners, customs, and outlook of a particular society. It was often satirical and sent up the fashionable members of a social set, as in William Congreve's *Way of the World* (1700).

The comedy of humours was a form of drama inspired by the theory of "humours." The humours were believed to be the fluids that regulated the body and thus the human temperament. There were four main ones: blood, phlegm, black bile, and yellow bile. In the comedy of humours, each character embodied a particular "humour" and what it represented, as in Ben Jonson's *Every Man in His Humour* (1598). It was a satirical mode. Moliére, the leading comic dramatist of seventeenth-century France, writes: "I am telling you that I now abandon you to your poor constitution, to the intemperance of your bowels, to the corruption of your blood, to the bitterness of your bile and to the starchiness of your humours" (*La malaide imaginaire,* act 3, scene 5, 1673).

Comedy, especially satirical comedy, is generally more topical than tragedy. It tends to exploit a local situation. William Hazlitt suggested that the satirical impulse in comedy inevitably dissipated itself: "Comedy naturally wears itself out — destroys the very food on which it lives; and by constantly and successfully exposing the follies and weaknesses of mankind to ridicule, in the end leaves itself nothing worth laughing at" ("On Modern Comedy," 1817). Yet comedies, too, can reach beyond the local moment, as in Samuel Beckett's *Waiting for Godot* (1952). Over the centuries, comic absurdity has increasingly taken over some of the subject matter of tragedy.

Comedy is a form of playfulness. The comedy of errors was a type of play heavily dependent on coincidences, on serendipity, as in Shakespeare's early comedies, such as *The Comedy of Errors* (1592–1594), which drew on two Latin farces by Plautus (ca. 254–184 B.C.E.). Kenneth Burke follows Nietzsche and argues that comedy takes a humane attitude toward existence. In *Attitudes Toward History* (1937), Burke defends comedy by saying that "the progress of humane enlightenment can go no further than in picturing people not as vicious, but as mistaken. When you add that people are necessarily mistaken, that *all* people are exposed to situations in which they must act as fools, that *every* insight contains its own special kind of blindness, you complete the comic circle." Comedy becomes a mode of enlightened thinking that concentrates on human folly.

SEE ALSO *satire, tragedy, tragicomedy.*

common measure, common meter, see *hymn* and *ballad.*

compensation In verse, compensation refers to the adjustment for an omitted or additional syllable or foot in a metrical line. The space is sometimes filled by a pause or rest. Compensation fulfills a law of completion.

SEE ALSO *inversion, meter, prosody, verse.*

complaint The complaint goes against Robert Frost's dictum of "grief without grievance." It is a plaintive poem, which defines itself by its grievance, often wistful, sorrowful, or sad. In the history of poetry, the complaint has frequently operated as a poem to an inconstant or unresponsive mistress, as in the Earl of Surrey's "A Complaint by Night of the Lover Not Beloved" (1557). The medieval love-complaint turned into a Petrarchan convention, one of the staples of Renaissance love poetry. The pastoral complaint, a popular Elizabethan genre, stressed the dangers of ambition and the virtues of simple life. The Elizabethans often called epistolary poems of love or complaint elegies, as in Christopher Marlowe's innovative translation of Ovid's *Amores* (16 B.C.E.), which he called *Ovid's Elegies* (1594–1595). There is a telling moment when the poet asks his lover to love him so that she can become the subject of his books: "Be thou the happy subject of my books, / That I may write things worthy thy fair looks."

There are poetic complaints that mourn the general state of the world. So, too, there are pointed political complaints, such as the Scottish poet David Lyndsay's "The Dreme" (1528), an allegorical lament on the misgovernment of Scotland, which includes an espistle to the king, "Complaynt to the King" (1529), and "Complaynt of Our Soverane Lordis Papyngo" (1530), a bird poem that is by turns mournful, exhortatory, satirical. Thomas Sackville's "Complaint of Henry, Duke of Buckingham" (1563) attributes the duke's misery to his ruthless ambition. There are occasionally light-hearted complaints, as in Chaucer's "The Complaint of Chaucer to His Purse" (ca. 1399). At times the complaint is indistinguishable from the lament, as in "Deor's Lament" (ninth or tenth century), the complaint of a scop fallen from favor. Thomas Percy included a song entitled "The Complaint of Conscience" in *Reliques of Ancient English Poetry* (1765). There will always be complaints as long as the poet has a conscience and the world is flawed.

SEE ALSO *pastoral, Petrarchism, scop.*

computer poetry Poets started experimenting with computers in the 1950s, a decade that set in motion the beginning of the computer revolution. Poets first used computer programs to synthesize databases. They fed the computer a series of instructions, which established a work's shape and content. "Labeled by its authors as 'Computer Poetry' and 'computer-poems' (among other terms)," C. T. Funkhouser explains, "these works are generated by computer algorithm, arranged as a sequence of words, or signs and symbols according to a programming code":

> All works of text generation, or archetypal computer poetry, can be seen as performing some type of permutation in that they transform or reorder one set of base texts or language (word lists, syllables, or pre-existing texts) into another form . . . I measure the permutation procedures of algorithmically generated poems into three classifications. Works are either permutational (recombining elements into

> new words or variations), combinatoric (using limited, pre-set word lists in controlled or random combinations), or slotted into syntactic templates (also combinatoric but within grammatical frames to create an image of "sense").

Charles O. Hartman lays out the basics of programming and poetry in *Virtual Muse: Experiments in Computer Poetry* (1996).

SEE ALSO *digital poetry, hypertext poetry.*

conceit From Italian: *concetto,* "conception." An elaborate figure of speech comparing two extremely dissimilar things. A good conceit discovers or creates a surprisingly apt parallel between two otherwise unlikely things or feelings. It is an arresting mental action that draws attention to the artificial process of figuration. "Shall I compare thee to a summer's day?" Shakespeare famously asks in a sonnet that goes on to develop and extend the analogy. The process invites the reader to participate in the making of the analogy, in playfully developing and extending it.

The Petrarchan conceit, borrowed from Italian poetry, compares the beloved to a rose, the sun, a statue, a summer day. Shakespeare employs these conceits even as he satirizes them in the first eight lines of "Sonnet 130" (1609):

> My mistress' eyes are nothing like the sun;
> Coral is far more red than her lips' red;
> If snow be white, why then her breasts are dun;
> If hairs be wires, black wires grow on her head.
> I have seen roses damasked, red and white,
> But no such roses see I in her cheeks,
> And in some perfumes is there more delight
> Than in the breath that from my mistress reeks.

T. S. Eliot defined the metaphysical conceit as the elaboration "of a figure of speech to the furthest stage to which ingenuity can carry it." Since its ingenious employment by the metaphysical poets in the seventeenth century, the conceit has often been associated with poems about erotic love or the most intense spiritual or sensual experiences. In this famous example from John Donne's "A Valediction: Forbidding Mourning" (1669), he compares two lovers to the two complementary legs of a compass:

If they be two, they are two so
  As stiffe twin compasses are two,
Thy soule the fixt foot, makes no show
  To move, but doth, if the'other doe.

And though it in the center sit,
  Yet when the other far doth rom,
It leanes and hearkens after it,
  And growes erect, as that comes home.

Such wilt thou be to mee, who must
  Like th'other foot, obliquely runne;
Thy firmness draws my circle just,
  And makes me end, where I begunne.

SEE ALSO *analogy, metaphor, metaphysical poets, simile.*

Conceptism, Conceptismo, see *Gongorism.*

concordia discors, discordia concors Horace employed the Latin term *concordia discors* ("harmony in discord") in his *Epistles* (20–14 B.C.E.) to summarize the ancient Greek doctrine that the perpetual strife between the four elements (earth, air, fire, and water) paradoxically creates harmony in the world. He directly referred to Empedocles's philosophy that Love ordered the four elements into a jarring unity or, in musical terms, "a dissonant harmony." Ovid also dramatized *discors concordia* — each warring element a harmonic of the other — in *The Metamorphoses* (8 C.E.).

The idea of a discordant harmony was central to the Renaissance humanism of the seventeenth and eighteenth centuries. John Denham summarized the English royalist version of the doctrine in his 1642 poem "Cooper's Hill":

Wisely she [Nature] knew, the harmony of things,
As well as that of sounds, from discord springs.
Such was the discord that did first disperse

> Form, order, beauty through the Universe;
> While dryness moisture, coldness heat resists,
> All that we have, and that we are, subsists.

Alexander Pope also spoke of a world harmoniously confused: "Where order in variety we see, / And where, though all things differ, all agree" ("Windsor-Forest," 1736). Referring to metaphysical poetry, Samuel Johnson inverted the term to *discordia concors* in his *Life of Cowley* (1779):

> Wit, abstracted from its effects upon the hearer, may be more rigorous and philosophically considered as a kind of discordia concors, a combination of dissimilar images or discovery of occult resemblances in things apparently unlike. Of wit defined they [Donne and his followers] have more than enough.

SEE ALSO *metaphysical poets, wit.*

concrete poetry A poem of visual display, a form of spatial prosody. Each concrete poem presents itself in a different physical shape—a lyric typed out to look like a typewriter, the word *SHRINK* printed in gradually smaller letters, and so forth. All written poems have spatial dimension, but the concrete poem foregrounds the visual configuration (how a poem looks) and pushes the pictorial boundaries of poetry.

The term *concrete poetry* was coined in the 1950s, but the desire to bring together literary and visual impulses into a shaped poem is ancient. There are poems in the shape of objects, such as a shepherd's pipe or a pair of wings, that date to the Hellenistic era (third to second century B.C.E.) in Greece. Guillaume Apollinaire's *calligrammes* are a lively avant-garde manifestation of what was once known as *technopaignia* or pattern poetry, verses arranged in distinctive shapes on the page. The pioneers of the 1950s international movement were the Bolivian-born Eugen Gomringer, who was working in Switzerland and initially called his poems "constellations" (the visual poem is a "constellation" in space), and three Brazilian poets, Haroldo de Campos, Augusto de Campos, and Décio Pignatari, who formed the avant-garde group Noigrandes, which adopted its name from a puzzling Provençal word in Ezra Pound's "Canto XX" ("Noigrandes, eh, noigrandes / now what the DEFIL can that mean!"). The concrete poetry movement was launched at the National Exhibition of Concrete Art in São Paulo in 1956. The movement was influenced by the symbolist writings of Stéphane Mallarmé and the modernist concretizations of Ezra Pound, James Joyce, and e. e. cummings, by Alexander Calder's mobiles and Piet Mondrian's space-structures, especially his Boogie-woogie series, and by Anton Webern's "Klangfarbenmelodie." Augusto de Campos defines concrete poetry as "tension of things-words in space-time."

The German concrete poet Max Bense said in 1965: "Concrete poetry does not separate languages; it unites them, it combines them." Some international examples: the Vienna Group; the German "Darmstadt Circle"; the Icelander Dieter Roth; the Czech Ladislav Novak; the Swede Öyvind Fahlström, whose "Manifesto for Concrete Poetry" (1954) prefigured the visual poetry movement; the Japanese Katasono Katué, who embraced the idea that poetry that "started with a quill" should "come to an end with a ballpoint pen"; the French poet Henri Chopin, who was also a pioneer of sound poetry; the English experimentalist Bob Cobbing; the American concretists Emmet Williams and Dick Higgins, both of whom were involved with the international intermedia movement called Fluxus; and the "Scots Makar" Edwin Morgan. Anyone interested in environmental poetry should wander through Little Sparta, Ian Hamilton Finlay's five-acre garden near Edinburgh, where his poems are inscribed on stones. Mary Ellen Scott suggests that "the pure concrete poem extracts from language an essential meaning structure and arranges it in space as an ideogram or a constellation — as a structural word design — within which there are reticulations or play-activity." The most powerful concrete poems still follow the example of Renaissance figure poems where the words are arranged to form a perceivable design on the page that mimics or enacts the subject.

SEE ALSO *calligramme, pattern poetry.*

concrete universal Hegel introduced this term into metaphysics by arguing that a universal is concrete rather than abstract. Hegel argued that ideas or concepts operate as historical forces, which have actual effects in the real world. The notion that a true universal is self-specifying, that it, as Hegel contends in *The Science of Logic* (1812–1816), "possesses in its own self the moment of particularity and externality," was adapted from idealist philosophy to literary criticism. The idea of the concrete universal engages and tries to reconcile the long critical opposition between what is often called "general," "abstract," or "universal" and what is frequently called "individual," "particular," or "concrete." The Hegelian idea was especially debated in modern criticism by W. K. Wimsatt Jr., who proposed *concrete universal* as a key term for a holistic poetics, and John Crowe Ransom, who opposed holistic theories of literature. The question revolves around how specific or general, concrete or universal, a verbal representation needs to be in order to achieve its effects.

SEE ALSO *New Criticism, universality.*

confessional poetry Reviewing Robert Lowell's book *Life Studies* in 1959, the critic M. L. Rosenthal claimed that the poems invoked "the most naked kind of confession." Rosenthal considered the word *confessional* appropriate, and later said, "because of the way Lowell brought his private humiliations, sufferings, and psychological problems" into his poems, which were thus "one culmination of the Romantic and modern tendency to place the literal Self more and more at the center."

The controversial term *confessional poetry* applies most appropriately to Lowell and a group of three younger poets associated with him: W. D. Snodgrass (*Heart's Needle,* 1959), Anne Sexton (*To Bedlam and Part Way Back,* 1960, and *All My Pretty Ones,* 1962), and Sylvia Plath (*Ariel,* 1965). These poets reacted against the New Critical focus on impersonality, which fetishized technique, as well as the modernist separation between, as T. S. Eliot put it, "the man who suffers and the mind which creates." They collapsed the distinction between the persona and the writer so that readers felt they were getting "the real Robert Lowell" or "the real Sylvia Plath." The idea that the reader was being presented with an actual person was an enabling fiction.

In her essay "What Was Confessional Poetry?" (1993), Diane Middlebrook identifies the chief characteristics of the group: "Their confessional poetry investigates the pressures on the family as an institution regulating middle-class private life, primarily through the agency of the mother. Its principal themes are divorce, sexual infidelity, childhood neglect, and the mental disorders that follow from deep emotional wounds received in early life. A confessional poem contains a first-person speaker, 'I,' and always seems to refer to a real person in whose actual life real episodes have occurred that cause actual pain in the poem."

These poets, along with Theodore Roethke (1908–1963), John Berryman (1914–1972), and Randall Jarrell (1914–1965), introduced a raw sensibility and a broken subjectivity into their poems. They confronted experience head-on. As Lowell put it near the end of his life, "why not say what happened?" But the narrow definition of "confessional poetry" equates poetry too closely with psychological trauma and defines it too restrictively as a way of writing about such illicit subjects as sexual guilt, alcoholism, and mental illness. There is a more honorific sense of confession, which after all goes back as far as the *Book of the Dead* and other ancient Egyptian literary texts. It can be traced to autobiographical writing from Saint Augustine (354–430) to Jean Jacques Rousseau (1712–1778). Confessional writers in the autobiographical vein declare, disclose, and defend the individual self as a representative figure, who writes not just about the inner self but also about the outer world. Thus in the 1860s Charles Baudelaire exposes "Mon Coeur mis à nu," or "My heart laid bare," in a book that was meant to gather all his rage, but which he never completed.

SEE ALSO *impersonality, the Middle Generation, New Criticism.*

congé A farewell poem. There are two distinct types of French medieval goodbye poems. One type, the *congé d'amour* (the troubadour *conjat*), was a consolation poem about the separation of lovers. The poet takes reluctant leave of his lady, a cruel or withholding mistress. The military *congé d'amour* was written on the occasion of a departure for military service, usually for the Crusades. There was a practice in such poems of giving a miniature of oneself as a pledge of love. Arthur Marotti locates John Donne's poem "A Valediction: Forbidding Mourning" (1669) within the tradition of the military *congé d'amour,* "which moralizes the gift-giving act in the ceremony as a sign of constancy and mutual fidelity," and notes that "conventionally this pledge and the promise of safe return are the two assurances the lover tries to give his beloved on such an occasion."

The second type of farewell poem, the *congés d'Arras,* consists of three poems by trouvères in the city of Arras in the thirteenth century. Jean Bodel (d. 1210) and Baude Fastoul (d. 1272), both forced into exile because of leprosy, wrote their fellow citizens a poem "to ask for permission to leave." Bodel's congé said goodbye to forty-two friends in forty-two stanzas. Ironically, one of the friends was Fastoul, who would later write his own leave-taking poem from the same hospice. Adam de la Halle (1237?–1288), who left Arras by choice in 1276 or 1277, turned the lyric congé into a satirical genre. He railed against the injustices and scandal-mongering rampant in the city.

connotation, see *denotation.*

consolations The Latin *consolatio* (pl. *consolationes*) was a work of consolation spoken or written to expound religious or philosophical themes as comfort and aid for the misfortunes of life. The consolatio literary tradition broadly encompasses poems, speeches, personal letters, and essays. Crantor of Soli (ca. 325–ca. 375 B.C.E.), a member of Plato's academy, inaugurated the genre, which in turn became famous in Latin through Cicero's now lost treatise consoling himself on the death of his daughter Tullia in 45 B.C.E. Seneca (ca. 4 B.C.E.–65 C.E.) wrote three consolatory works, which characterize his Stoic teachings. Plutarch's *Consolatio ad Uxorem* (early 90s) is the letter that Plutarch wrote to his wife when he received news of the death of their two-year-old daughter Timoxena. Boethius's treatise *The Consolation of Philosophy* (ca. 524), in which philosophy consoles the author for his misfortunes, claims a strong connection with the *consolatio.* The *Oxford Classical Dictionary* summarizes some of the typically recurring arguments or topoi that characterize the consolation genre: "All are born mortal; death brings release from the miseries of life; time heals all griefs; future ills should be prepared for; the deceased was only 'lent' — be grateful for having possessed him. Normally grief is regarded as natural and legitimate, though not to be indulged in." One consolatio in verse form that has come down to us is the *Consolatio ad Liviam* (ca. 9 B.C.E.), a lament on the death of Drusus, which was once attributed to Ovid, but now is generally considered the work of an anonymous poet working in the Ovidian vein.

consonance The audible repetition of consonant sounds in words encountered near each other whose vowel sounds are different. Thus W. H. Auden presses the consonants from "rider to reader" and from "farer to fearer" and from "hearer to horror" in the last stanza of his poem from the 1930s, " 'O where are you going?' " Consonance is seldom a structuring device in poetry. Rather, it is a strategic way of enforcing relation. It has an echoic effect. Consonance overlaps with alliteration. Whereas alliteration repeats the first letter of a word, consonance repeats sounds within a word. Listen to the letters *f* and *l* woven through these lines from Wilfred Owen's World War I poem "Insensibility" (posthumously published in 1920):

> The front line withers,
> But they are troops who fade, not flowers
> For poets' tearful fooling:
> Men, gaps for filling:
> Losses, who might have fought
> Longer; but no one bothers.

SEE ALSO *alliteration, assonance.*

conte, see *lai.*

conte dévot The *conte dévot,* or "pious tale," was a thirteenth- and fourteenth-century French genre, a tale in verse or prose designed to instruct. It was a "good story." Many of these medieval short stories were inspired by the *Vitae Patrum* (Lives of the Desert Fathers, 1628) and the *Miracles de Nostre-Dame* (The Miracles of Our Lady, early thirteenth century).

SEE ALSO *didactic poetry.*

Los Contemporáneos The Mexican vanguard group Los Contemporáneos ("The Contemporaries") was active in the late 1920s and early 1930s. The founding members of the group were José Gorostiza (1901–1973), Carlos Pellicer (1897–1977), Bernardo Ortiz de Montellano (1899–1949), Enrique González Rojo (1899–1939), and Jaime Torres Bodet (1902–1974), who started the magazine *Contemporáneos* (1928–1939). They were committed to "contemporary cultural universalism" and succeeded in expanding the horizons of Mexican poetry. They were devoted internationalists. Octavio Paz (1914–1998) praised Los Contemporáenos for opening Mexican literature to outside influences, but criticized them for ignoring Mexican realities. He would himself try to navigate the space between the national and the cosmopolitan, the local and the international.

Contrasto, Contrasti (pl) A type of improvised poetry in the Tuscan dialect, the *Contrasto* ("contrast") is a poetic contest that dates back to the

Middle Ages, a heated debate that is still recited during public events and festivals throughout the Italian regions of Tuscany, Lazio, and Abruzzo. It is performed by adversarial pairs of poets called *Poetí Bernescanti* (literally, poets in Berni's style, a name taken from the sixteenth-century Tuscan poet Francesco Berni), *Poetí a Braccio,* or *poetí.* The audience chooses themes and the poets respond in alternating eight-line stanzas. Each stanza is composed of eleven syllables and rhymes *abababcc.* The rhyming couplet, which concludes the stanza, signals the other poet to respond. It is linguistically creative, mixing codes and registers, bending syntactical rules, and frequently political. "In the Contrasto," Valentina Pagliai writes, "each poet proposes a different view of causality, or what motivates people, or the facts of human relationships, including what is the meaning of relations of exploitation and how they come to be created, and especially how they can be changed. The poets in the Contrasto do not just present different views of reality, they discuss how those realities could be modified. In this sense, the Contrasto is also a metapragmatic genre. The poets do not merely assume a political reality, but modify the political realities that they enact."

SEE ALSO *octave, ottava rima, poetic contest.*

convention An implicit agreement between a writer and a reader, or a speaker and an audience, an accepted device, procedure, principle, or form. "What we mean by a 'convention' in art ranges from an accepted distortion of reality, as when a character speaks in meter, to an expected system of feeling," David Perkins writes in *A History of Modern Poetry* (1987). Art is a form of play, and to accept a convention is to accept the rules of a game. It is a convention of the apostrophe, for example, that the poet turns aside from the audience to address someone or something else. What would be madness in life can be both playfully serious and seriously comic in poetry. Conventions enable us to make meaning in poetry. Samuel Johnson famously explains the convention of dramatic illusion in his *Preface to Shakespeare* (1765):

> Delusion, if delusion can be admitted, has no certain limitation; if the spectator can be once persuaded, that his old acquaintance are Alexander and Caesar, that a room illuminated with candles is the plain of Pharsalia, or the bank of Granicus, he is in a state of elevation above the reach of reason, or of truth, and from the heights of empyrean

> poetry, may despise the circumscriptions of terrestrial nature. There is no reason why a mind thus wandering in ecstasy should count the clock, or why an hour should not be a century in that calenture of the brains that can make the stage a field. The truth is, that the spectators are always in their senses, and know, from the first act to the last, that the stage is only a stage, and that the players are only players.

Conventions are both liberating and restrictive. They also change over time to accommodate innovations and challenges, new types of work, new eras. Some conventions continue more or less unchanged, others become outmoded, but there is no ongoing poetry without them. As Paul Fussell puts it, "The notion that convention shows a lack of feeling, and that a poet attains 'sincerity' . . . by disregarding [convention], is opposed to all the facts of literary experience and history."

SEE ALSO *decorum, sonnet.*

conversation poem A type of poem that is intimate, informal, and serious. It has an element of address, like the verse epistle, and most likely has its origins in Horace's epistles and satires. Coleridge entitled his poem "The Nightingale. A Conversation Poem" (1798). George Harper coined the term *Conversation Poems* in 1928. He was following up on Coleridge's subtitle, and taking a lead from the Horatian motto: *Sermoni propriora* (*Satires,* 1.4, ca. 36 B.C.E.), "more fitted to conversation or prose." Harper thus gave a name to this kind of poem, which Coleridge developed and mastered in such lyrics as "The Aeolian Harp" (1795), "Reflections on Having Left a Place of Retirement" (1796), "This Lime-tree Bower My Prison" (1797), "Frost at Midnight" (1798), "The Nightingale" (1798), "Fears in Solitude" (1789), "Dejection: An Ode" (1802), and "To William Wordsworth" (1807). Coleridge's conversation poems introduced the short blank verse poem into English.

The conversation poem simulates a speaking voice, usually in blank verse, but it does not record a conversation per se because it is really only animated by one solitary speaker. It tends to be a poem of friendship specifically addressed to a living person, who is not a lover. This type of poem puts the reader in the position of feeling that he or she is overhearing one side of a conversation. But this intimate address is not a secret; it is meant to be overheard.

SEE ALSO *blank verse, letter poem.*

copla The Spanish term *copla* can simply mean stanza. It can also refer specifically to two rhyming lines (a couplet) in a ballad. And it is used generally to refer to a popular song or ballad. There are many different kinds of *coplas* in Spanish-language poetry. For instance, the *copla real* is a ten-line octosyllabic strophe widely used in fifteenth- and sixteenth-century Spanish poetry. The *copla de arte mayor* ("the stanza of the major art") is a Spanish metric term for any line of nine or more syllables. It usually refers to a stanza of eight alexandrines, when it is also called the *octava de arte mayor* or the *copla de Juan de Mena*. The *colpa de arte menor* ("the stanza of the minor art") refers to a stanza of eight syllables (octosyllabic) or less. The *copla de pie quebrado* ("the stanza of the broken foot") or *manriquen sextain* is a six-line stanza of alternating eight- and four-syllable lines. It was created by Gómez Manrique (ca. 1412–ca. 1490) and reached its zenith in the fifteenth century.

The most common form of *copla* is the rhyming eight-syllable quatrain. For example, this is one of the staples of vernacular Puerto Rican poetry. In one type of *copla* between two dueling poets, the last line of the first *copla* becomes the initiating line of a second one. The last line of the second *copla* becomes the first line of the third one, and so forth until the competition ends. The *copla* has an artful simplicity and lends itself to terse and impromptu comments. Robert Márquez explains in his anthology, *Puerto Rican Poetry* (2007), "By turns pithily incisive, witty, and grave; humorous, festive, and flippant; didactic and unapologetically romantic and sentimental; and frankly insolent, serenely philosophical, or subversively revealing, the *copla* is the most concise, democratically accessible, and agilely adaptable of the popular verse forms of Puerto Rico."

SEE ALSO *alexandrine, octosyllabic verse.*

corona, see *sonnet.*

coronach From the Gaelic: "wailing together." A *coronach* (coranich, corrinoch, coranach, cronach, etc.) is a dirge or lament for the dead chanted or sung at funeral ceremonies of clan heads or other important people. It was practiced in Ireland and the Highlands of Scotland. In his presentation of the ballad "Glenfinlas, or Lord Ronald's Coronach," Sir Walter Scott characterized the *coronach* as "a lamentation for a deceased warrior, sung by the aged of the clan" (*The Minstrelsy of the Scottish Border,* 1802–1803). The words led to women clapping their hands in grief, shrieking, wailing. Scott characterizes it in his "Coronach" in *Lady of the Lake* (1811):

> The hand of the reaper
>   Takes the ears that are hoary,
> But the voice of the weeper
>   Wails manhood in glory.

SEE ALSO *keening*.

correlative verse When relationships among the words in one group balance and parallel the relationships among the words in a second group. This kind of symmetry dates to some of the epigrams in the *Greek Anthology*, which date to the tenth century. Listen to the opening stanza of George Herbert's "The Call" (1633):

> Come, my Way, my Truth, my Life:
> Such a Way, as gives us breath:
> Such a Truth, as ends all strife:
> And such a Life, as killeth death.

Each of the three presiding nouns that describe Christ in the first line (Way, Truth, Life) becomes the subject of the three following lines (Such a Way, Such a Truth, And such a Life). The poem is enriched by the way that the Christian speaker adopts Christ's own words to make Christ his listener.

counted verse This type of poem simply counts the number of words per line, as in May Swenson's self-explanatory "Four-Word Lines" (1967). William Carlos Williams's "The Red Wheelbarrow" (1923) consists of eight lines broken into four stanzas. The first line of each stanza contains three words and the second line has one word. Counted verse purposefully does not count accents or syllables, as in metrical poetry. It has a willful, arbitrary, and mathematical orderliness.

counterpoint, counterpoint rhythm In the second half of the nineteenth century, Gerard Manley Hopkins coined the term *counterpoint rhythm* to describe two simultaneous rhythms in a poetic line: ". . . two rhythms are in some manner running at once and we have something answerable to counterpoint in music, which is two or more strains of tune going on together." Hopkins considered Milton the great master of counterpoint, especially in the choruses of *Samson Agonistes* (1671). For example:

> Or do my eyes misrepresent? Can this be he,
> That heroic, that renowned,
> Irresistible Samson? whom, unarmed,
> No strength of man, or fiercest wild beast, could withstand; . . .

Hopkins was trying to account for changes of rhythm, multiplicities and cross-rhythms, formal substitutions and irregularities, "which all natural growth and motion shews."

SEE ALSO *organic form, running rhythm, sprung rhythm.*

counting-out rhymes Some bits of poetry are hiding in childhood memories. Remember playing the game of It? Someone stands in the middle and starts counting: Eeny, meeny, miny, mo . . . The self-appointed leader points to each player in turn, one child per word, until the end, the last syllable. Someone is It. You may have balked, but you accepted your fate.

The rhyme starts the game and marks it as a type of play, which is why it is removed from ordinary speech. It is a form of gibberish or near-gibberish that signals the roles in the coming game. In England and America, this children's game is called counting-out or telling out. It was once called rimbles. In Scotland it is called chapping-out or titting-out. Some British children call it dips or grace. The one who is It is called the Wolf in Germany; the *Loup* in France; the *Pupule,* or crazy one, in Hawaii; the *Boka,* or leper, in the Malagasy tribe of Madagascar; the *Oni,* the devil or evil spirit, in Japan. There is an ancient terror lurking in these childhood rhymes. For example, the scholars G. W. Boswell and J. R. Reaver argue, "Eeny, meeny, miny, mo" derives "from Druid days when victims were taken across the Menai Strait to the island of Mona for sacrifice."

Counting-out rhymes are one of many types of traditional rhymes passed on by children to each other in games, such as ball-bouncing rhymes and jump rope rhymes, which subdivide into different rhymes for different jumps (the plain jump, call in/call out, speed jumps, and so forth). These ancient rhymes come down to us through the schoolyard bearing relics of the past, some of them religious. Children love nonsense and preserve charms and chants, sometimes holy phrases, which have been smoothed down by quick, frequent repetition.

SEE ALSO *nonsense poetry, tongue twister.*

country-house poem The country-house poem, which was especially popular during the seventeenth century, typically praises the virtues of a powerful patron's country estate. It also praises the virtues of retirement, of life far from the city. It is a subgenre of Renaissance poetry. Ben Jonson provided the model for country-house poems in "To Penshurst" (1616), which compliments Robert Sidney, the younger brother of Sir Philip Sidney, on his Penshurst Place. It opens by alluding to Horace's *Odes* (2.18, 23–13 B.C.E.):

> Thou art not, Penshurst, built to envious show,
> Of touch or marble, nor canst boast a row
> Of polished pillars, or a roof of gold;
> Thou hast no lantern, whereof tales are told,
> Or stair, or courts; but stand'st an ancient pile,
> And, these grudged at, art reverenced the while.

Two other key examples: Thomas Carew's "To Saxham" (1640) and Andrew Marvell's "Upon Appleton House" (ca. 1650). Alastair Fowler suggests the term *estate poems* to account for those poems that do not deal with the architecture of a country house, but promote the values of a country house ethos. The country-house poem typically contrasts the "natural" world of the country, the uncorrupted natural realm, to the worldliness of the city, the corrupted urban realm. It also carries a set of social values and morals related to aristocracy. Raymond Williams argues that there is a mystification of actual social relations, especially in regard to rural laborers, in the country-house poem.

SEE ALSO *topographical poetry.*

couplet The couplet, two successive lines of poetry, usually rhymed (*aa*), has been an elemental stanzaic unit—a couple, a pairing—as long as there has been written rhyming poetry in English. It can stand as an epigrammatic poem on its own, a weapon for aphoristic wit, as in Pope's "Epigram Engraved on the Collar of a Dog which I gave to his Royal Highness" (1734):

I am his Highness' Dog at Kew;
Pray tell me Sir, whose Dog are you?

The couplet also serves as an organizing pattern in long poems (Shakespeare's "Venus and Adonis," 1592–1593; Marlowe's "Hero and Leander," 1593) or part of a larger stanzaic unit. It stands as the pithy conclusion to the ottava rima stanza (*abababcc*), the rhyme royal stanza (*ababbcc*), and the Shakespearean sonnet (*ababcdcdefefgg*).

The rhyming iambic pentameter or five-stress couplet—later known as the heroic couplet—was introduced into English by Chaucer in "The Prologue to the Legend of Good Women" (1386), in imitation of French meter, and employed for most of *The Canterbury Tales* (ca. 1387–1400). It has sometimes been nicknamed riding rhyme, probably because the pilgrims reeled them off while they were riding to Canturbury. It was taken up and used with great flexibility by the Tudor and Jacobean poets and dramatists. Nicholas Grimald's pioneering experiments with the heroic couplet should be better known (*Tottel's Miscellany,* 1557). Christopher Marlowe employed the heroic couplet for his daring translation of Ovid's *Amores* (16 B.C.E.), which he called *Ovid's Elegies* (1594–1595). The mighty two-liner was also used by William Shakespeare, George Chapman, and John Donne, and then stamped as a neoclassical form by John Dryden, Alexander Pope, and Samuel Johnson, who wrote:

Let Observation with extensive View
Survey Mankind, from China to Peru . . .

This closed form of the couplet is well suited to express aphoristic wit.

The octosyllabic or four-stress couplet, probably based on a common Latin meter, became a staple of English medieval verse (such as *The Lay of Havelok the Dane,* ca. 1280–1290), then was virtually reinvented by Samuel Butler in his mock-heroic satire *Hudibras* (1663–1680), whose couplets became known as *Hudibrastics,* and raised to a higher power by Milton ("L'Allegro" and "Il Penseroso," both 1645), Marvell ("To His Coy Mistress," ca. 1650s), and Coleridge ("Christabel," 1797–1800).

We call a couplet closed when the sense and syntax come to a conclusion or strong pause at the end of the second line, thus giving a feeling of self-containment and enclosure, as in the first lines of "To His Coy Mistress":

> Had we but world enough, and time,
> This coyness, Lady, were no crime.

We call a couplet open when the sense carries forward past the second line into the next line or lines, as in the beginning of Keats's *Endymion* (1818):

> A thing of beauty is a joy for ever:
> Its loveliness increases; it will never
> Pass into nothingness, but still will keep
> A bower quiet for us, and a sleep
> Full of sweet dreams . . .

Ben Jonson told William Drummond that he deemed couplets "the bravest Sort of Verses, especially when they are broken." All two-line stanzas in English carry the vestigial memory of closed or open couplets.

SEE ALSO *end-stopped line, enjambment, meter, octosyllabic verse, stanza.*

courtly love "The history of love is the history of a passion but also of a literary genre," Octavio Paz writes in *The Double Flame* (1996). In the Middle Ages, the troubadour poets invented the idea of courtly love — a fantasy love, a noble passion in which the courtly lover idolizes a sovereign lady, his true beloved. He longs for union with her. The poet or knight is enobled by his passion for an ideal beauty, a paragon of virtue who is married to another. Thus his ideal love is also extramarital and so inevitably thwarted, illicit, adulterous. The historian Barbara Tuchman describes the stages of courtly love:

> The chivalric love affair moved from worship through declaration of passionate devotion, virtuous rejection by the lady, renewed wooing with oaths of eternal fealty, moans of approaching death from unsatisfied desire, heroic deeds of valor which won the lady's heart by prowess, [very rarely] consummation of the secret love, followed by endless adventures and subterfuges to a tragic denouement.

The troubadour concept of courtly love, the exaltation of an untouchable beloved, owes something both to the feudal courts and to medieval Christianity, especially the cult of the Virgin. The troubadours were almost certainly influenced by Ovid (43 B.C.E.–18 C.E.) as well as by the Arabic poets of Andalusia and elsewhere in the Islamic world. The passionate ideal — masochistic, spiritual — traveled like wildfire to Europe. In Italy, one thinks of Cavalcanti (ca. 1250–1300), Guinicelli (ca. 1230–1276?), and especially Dante (1265–1321). In northern France, courtly love became central to the trouvères and to the romances, such as Chrétien de Troyes's *Le Chevalier de la Charrette* (ca. 1170s). In Germany, it was a staple of the minnesingers. In England, Chaucer transformed it into *Troilus and Criseyde* (ca. 1380s). Courtly love had a tremendous influence on Petrarch, and thus on subsequent love poetry influenced by him. It became one of the formative influences on sixteenth-century English poetry.

Courtly love was a prevailing literary ideal, but there is scant evidence that it was actually ever practiced. As a term, *courtly love* is a relatively late invention. It derives from the phrase *amour courtois,* which was coined by Gaston Paris in 1883 to describe the medieval experience. The medieval terms were *amor honestus* (honest love) and *fin'amor* (refined love). A. J. Denomy writes in *The Heresy of Courtly Love* (1947): "The novelty of Courtly Love lies in three basic elements: first, in the ennobling force of human love; second, in the elevation of the beloved to a place of superiority above the lover; third, in the conception of love as ever unsatisfied, ever increasing desire." He calls these three things the "skeleton framework" of courtly love because they distinguish it from all other kinds of love.

SEE ALSO *allegory, dolce stil novo, minnesinger, Petrarchism, romances, troubadour, trouvère.*

cowboy poetry Cowboys have been composing verse, some of it recited around campfires and in bunkhouses, some of it sung as lyrics, ever since the cattle drives of the 1860s. The folk poems were firmly rooted in the oral traditions of working cowboys and rodeo men. Traditionally, cowboy poets made no particular distinction between song and verse. The "singing cowboy" is a recognizable figure in popular culture, but the poems themselves were mostly unknown outside range country until 1985 when the Western Folklife Center started sponsoring the annual National Cowboy Poetry Gathering, held in Elko, Nevada. It defines cowboy poetry this way:

> Cowboy poetry is rhymed, metered verse written by someone who has lived a significant portion of his or her life in the Western North American cattle culture. The verse reflects an intimate knowledge of that way of life, and the community from which it maintains itself in tradition.

There is a strong oral and storytelling component to cowboy poetry, a decided emphasis on performance, and cowboy poets have tended to favor the traditional four-line ballad stanza, sometimes in rhyming couplets, though there are also cowboy poems in free verse. The poems are rooted in the rural past of the West. They often focus on horses and cattle, the loneliness of life on the trail, the strong codes of behavior, the daunting challenges and sublimity of the natural world. Since the nineteenth century, cowboy poetry has brooded about its vanishing subject, a dangerous and endangered way of life.

SEE ALSO *gaucho poetry*.

Crambo Robert Burns (1759–1796) liked to play the game of Crambo, also known as Capping the Rhyme, a form of doggerel poem that tries to exhaust all the possible rhymes on a word. He confessed, "Amaist as soon as I could spell, / I to the crambo-jingle fell" ("Epistle to J-L-k"). In Lowland Scots, *crambo-clink* or *crambo-jingle* refers to rhyming doggerel and other types of bad verse, which Douglas Jerrold calls "verse and worse." As Burns declares in "On a Scotch Bard, Gone to the West Indies" (1786):

> A' ye wha live by crambo-clink,
> A' ye wha live an' never think,
> Come mourn wi' me!

SEE ALSO *doggerel*.

Creationism, Creaciónismo (Spanish) The Chilean poet Vicente Huidobro (1893–1948) initiated Creationism, which was not so much a school of art as "a general aesthetic theory." Huidobro declared the three duties of the poet: "to create, to create, and to create." From 1917 through the 1920s, he trumpeted the idea of pure creation and traveled between the European and Latin American vanguards. He sought a poetry that magically obliterates the empirical external world and replaces it with a new creation. One of his mottos was "Non serviam": "I shall not be your slave, Mother Nature." Another was: "The poet is a little God" ("Ars Poetica," 1916). He wrote:

> A [created poem] is a poem in which every constituent part, and the whole, show a new fact, independent of the external world, not bound to any reality save its own, since it takes a place in the world as a singular phenomenon, separate and distinct from other phenomena.

crepuscolarismo Italian: "twilight school." The *crepuscolari* were a group of early twentieth-century Italian poets. These world-weary and disillusioned poets — the Italian equivalent of the Irish Celtic Twilight — embodied a poetics of aftermath or belatedness. They wrote in a direct, unadorned way that rejected the ornamental rhetoric and grandiosity of Giosue Carducci (1835–1907), Gabriele D'Annunzio (1863–1938), and others. The critic Giuseppe Borgese named the group in a 1910 article, "Poesie crepuscolare," which characterized their poetry as the sunset of a more glorious time. The term later came to characterize the gently nostalgic and rustic poetry of this group, which included Guido Gozzano (1883–1916), who was its most significant poet, Fausto Maria Martini (1886–1931), Sergio Corazzini (1886–1907), Marino Moretti (1885–1979), and Aldo Palazzeschi (1885–1974). Dino Campana (1885–1932) and Eugenio Montale (1896–1981) both grew out of *crepuscolarismo.* The movement was overshadowed by futurism, which burst out in 1909 and made a more strident break with the past. It darkened for good in the 1920s.

SEE ALSO *decadence, futurism, Hermeticism, Irish literary renaissance.*

cretic Greek: "long at both ends." A Greek quantitative foot, which consists of one short syllable between two long ones. It is the opposite of the amphibrach. William Blake's poem "Spring" (1789) imitates the meter by substituting two stressed syllables for long syllables and an unstressed syllable for the short one.

> Sóund thĕ Flúte!
> Nów ĭt's múte.

> Bírd's dĕlíght
> Dáy ănd Níght.

Coleridge imitated the meter in describing it: "First and last being long, middle short, Amphimacer / Strikes his thundering hoofs like a proud high-bred Racer" ("Metrical Feet," ca. 1806).

SEE ALSO *amphibrach, foot, meter.*

cross rhyme, see *rhyme.*

crown of sonnets, see *sonnet.*

cuaderna vía The *cuaderna vía* is a Spanish verse form of fourteen-syllable lines especially popular in the Middle Ages. Each line breaks down into two seven-syllable hemistiches or half-lines separated by a caesura or strong break in the middle. It is monorhymed (*aaaa, bbbb,* etc.), a form for purists. It is also called the *verso alejandrino* (fourteen). Both the name and the form derive from the *Libro de Alejandro* (ca. 1240), a poem celebrating the legendary exploits of Alexander the Great. The Spanish clergy seem to have introduced syllabic poetry to Spain under the influence of French poetry, especially the French alexandrine, which is why the *cuaderna vía* is also called the *mester de clerecía* or art of the clerics (in contrast to the *mester de juglaría* or minstrel's art) and the *nueva maestría.* The poet-deacon and priest Gonzalo de Berceo (ca. 1190–1264) was the first known writer consistently to use the *cuaderna vía.* John Keller explains Berceo's medium: "The full rhyme of *cuaderna vía*'s quatrains has power. It catches the reader in its net and carries him along with force and sometimes with violence. Once entrapped, once caught up in the metrics and trained to march to the regular and unchanging cadence, once taught to expect each line in each quatrain to rhyme completely with each of the other lines, the reader surrenders to *cuaderna vía*'s spell and reads on tirelessly." The alejandrino was replaced in the fifteenth century by the *arte major.* Rubén Dario (1867–1916) restored it to use in Spanish, and it was then taken up by such twentieth-century Spanish-language poets as Jorge Luis Borges (1899–1986), Pablo Neruda (1904–1973), and Blas de Otero (1916–1979).

SEE ALSO *alexandrine, copla.*

Cubist poetry Guillaume Apollinaire defined Cubism in 1913 as "the art of painting new structures out of elements borrowed not from the reality of sight, but from the reality of insight." Cubist poetry was an experimental attempt to create in language something roughly equivalent to the work of the Cubist painters, especially Pablo Picasso (1881–1973), who called a painting "a sum of destructions," Georges Braque (1882–1963), and Juan Gris (1887–1927). The Cubist painters were dissatisfied with conventional ways of representing objects as the eye sees them. They shattered surfaces, analyzed broken objects, and reassembled the fragments in a nonobjective or abstracted form. Every subject was depicted from a multitude of perspectives. The planes interpenetrated. So, too, Cubism in poetry was, as Kenneth Rexroth characterized it, "the conscious, deliberate dissociation and recombination of elements into a new artistic entity made self-sufficient by its rigorous architecture." The goal was to restructure experience.

The French poets associated with Analytical and Synthetic Cubism are Apollinaire (1880–1918) and Reverdy (1889–1960), Blaise Cendrars (1887–1961), Jean Cocteau (1889–1963), André Salmon (1881–1969), and Max Jacob (1876–1944), who states in his poem "The Cock and the Pearl," the longest piece in *The Dice Cup* (1917):

> When one paints a picture, it changes completely with each touch, it turns like a cylinder and is almost endless. When it stops turning, that's because it's finished. My last one showed a tower of Babel in lighted candles.

In the United States, one thinks of Parker Tyler (1904–1974); Charles Henri Ford (1913–2002); Walter Conrad Arensberg's last works, especially "For Shady Hill" (1917); and the early poems of Rexroth, collected in *The Art of Worldly Wisdom* (1949). William Carlos Williams (1883–1963) moved beyond the pictorialism of imagism and experimented with Cubist techniques, especially in *Al Que Quiere* (1917), which Conrad Aiken commented upon: "We get the impression from these poems that [Williams's] world is a world of plane surfaces, bizarrely coloured, and cunningly arranged so as to give an effect of depth and solidity." Consider, too, the different perspectives in some of Wallace Stevens's early poems, such as "Thirteen Ways of Looking at a Blackbird" (1917) and "The Man with the Blue Guitar" (1937). Gertrude Stein's *Tender Buttons* (1914) is perhaps the most sustained literary work of Analytical Cubism. Stein describes objects without ever naming them, and approaches each subject from a multiplicity of perspectives, like a Cubist painter.

SEE ALSO *ekphrasis.*

Cubo-futurism, see *futurism.*

cultism, cultismo, culteranismo, see *Gongorism.*

cyberpoetry Cyborgian poetry is work that is cocreated by human beings and digital machinery. It combines randomness with order. Catherine Daly explains that cyberpoetry is "concerned with the machine control of the writing process, delivery of poetry in more than one medium, and machine-mediated interactivity, between audience and reader or writer and text."

SEE ALSO *digital poetry.*

Cyclic poets The early oral epic poets who worked approximately at the same time as Homer (eighth century B.C.E.) are sometimes called the Cyclic poets because they covered the entire cycle of the Trojan War. Only small fragments of their work survive.

SEE ALSO *epic.*

cynghanedd In Welsh poetry, *cynghanedd* (or "harmony") is a highly elaborated system of sound arrangements and correspondences, involving stress, alliteration, and rhyme. *Cynghanedd* as a poetic art was well developed by the fourteenth century, but was not codified until the *Caerwys Eisteddfod,* or Bardic Assembly, of 1524. These consonant chimes show up in the definitions of all traditional Welsh forms. The sound patterns, which are some of the most sophisticated in the world, are impossible to reproduce accurately in English. In *The White Goddess* (1948), Robert Graves defines *cynghanedd* as "the repetitive use of consonantal sequences with variations of vowels," and invents this example:

Billet spied,
Bolt sped.

Across field
Crows fled,
Aloft, wounded,
Left one dead.

There are three types of *cynghanedd*: 1) consonantal; 2) *sain,* which involves both rhyme and alliteration; and 3) *lusg* (dragging), which involves internal rhyme. The consonantal type divides into three prevalent kinds: "crossing" (*groes*), "leaping" (*draws*), and "interlinked" crossing. In crossing or cross-harmony, the alliteration connects two stressed vowels: the last before the medial caesura and the last in the line.

In *groes,* the consonants in the first half of the line are repeated in the second part in the same order. In *draws,* the middle consonants are ignored, and there are consonants in the second half of the line that are not part of the echoed consonants. In *sain,* the line divides into three parts, each with a primary stress. The first two parts rhyme, and the second part is linked to the third by consonance or alliteration. In *lusg,* the last unaccented syllable in the first half of the line rhymes with the stressed penultimate syllable of the line.

These complicated meters took years for poets to master in the bardic orders. In "The Wreck of the Deutschland" (1875–1876), Gerard Manley Hopkins employed, as he said, "certain chimes suggested by the Welsh poetry I had been reading (what they call *cynghanedd*)." Dylan Thomas (1914–1953) followed Hopkins's example and experimented with using cynghanedd in modern English-language poetry. Alan Llywd writes that "Rhydwen Williams, a Welsh poet, discussed *cynghanedd* . . . with Thomas, and Dylan is reported as saying, 'If I was writing in Welsh, I would write *cynghanedd.*' " The Scottish poet Hugh MacDiarmid (1892–1978) desired a "poetry full of *cynghanedd,* and hair-trigger relationships, / With something about it that is plasmic" ("The Kind of Poetry I Want," 1961). In the 1970s, Llwyd and other Welsh poets formed a society called *Barddas* (Poetic Art), which brought a new energy to the study of *cynghanedd.*

SEE ALSO *alliteration, bard, cywydd, eisteddfod, rhyme.*

cywydd A traditional Welsh metrical form that has been employed from the fourteenth century to the present day. It was developed by the medieval poet Dafydd ap Gwilym, who assimilated Welsh verse into European poetry, and became the favorite meter of the Poets of the Nobility (ca. 1350–ca. 1600), who were also called the *Cywyddry,* the masters of the *cywydd* meter. The term *cywydd* originally meant "harmony" or "song." It is a flexible form with four variations. The type most commonly practiced by the Celtic bards was the *cywydd deuair hirion.* It consists of a series of seven-syllable lines in rhyming couplets. In each couplet, one of the end rhymes is stressed and one unstressed. Each line employs the devices of *cynghanedd.* It is this meter that is usually meant when one refers to the *cwydd.* The other three meters are *awdl-gywydd, cywydd deair fyrion,* and *cywydd llosgyrnog.* The *cwydd* has no set length, but generally runs to sixty or seventy lines.

The *cywydd* has proved wily, flexible, and all-purposeful. It has been employed for love poetry, whether joyous or despairing. It has served for prayers to the Virgin and appeals to patrons. As Gwen Jones puts it in *The Oxford Book of Welsh Verse in English* (1977):

> It was a jousting spear or switch of nettles for poetic rivals; *conte,* homily, beast-fable, social comment, friendly invitation, autobiography, tribute, elegy—whatever the need the *cywydd* supplied it. Stylistically it lent itself perfectly to such poetic devices as description by comparison (*dyfalu*), allegory, the break in syntactic flow (*sangiad*), or between what in English are words so closely related as to be inseperable (*trychiad*).

SEE ALSO *awdl, cynghanedd, dyfalu, strict-meter poetry.*

dactyl A metrical foot consisting of three syllables, one accented syllable followed by two unaccented ones, as in the word *póĕtrÿ*. The word *dactyl* means "finger" in Greek. Tennyson's "The Charge of the Light Brigade" (1854) deploys dactyls, as do many nursery rhymes, the earliest poems we learn by heart. Here is the haunting opening of Thomas Hardy's dactylic poem "The Voice" (1912): "Wómăn mŭch / míssed, hŏw yŏu / cáll tŏ mĕ, / cáll tŏ mĕ."

SEE ALSO *double dactyl, foot, meter.*

Dadaism, Dada Surrealism grew directly out of the flamboyantly self-conscious and joyously nihilistic movement known as *Dada,* which began in the Café Voltaire in Zurich in 1916 when a group of young writers and artists, including Tristan Tzara (1896–1963), Hans Arp (1886–1966), Richard Huelsenbeck (1892–1974), Hugo Ball (1886–1927), Emmy Hennings (1885–1948), and Sophie Taeuber (1889–1943), decided to shower their contempt on the decadent values of bourgeois society and the moral insanity of World War I. The word *dada,* chosen at random from a dictionary, is baby talk for "hobbyhorse" in French. "This is the song of a dadaist / who had dada in his heart," Tzara chants in "Chanson Dada": "he tore his motor apart / he had dada in his heart." In his "Dada Manifesto on Feeble and Bitter Love" (1920), he asserts:

> DADA is a virgin microbe
> DADA is against the high cost of living

> DADA
> limited company for the exploitation of ideas
> DADA has 391 different attitudes and colours according to the sex of the president
> It changes — affirms — says the opposite at the same time — no importance — shouts — goes
> fishing.
> Dada is the chameleon of rapid and self interested change.
> Dada is against the future. Dada is dead. Dada is absurd. Long live Dada.
> Dada is not a literary school, howl

The Dadaists' favorite word was *nothing,* and there is a wildly subversive, childlike energy in their manifestos, sound poems, simultaneous lyrics, noise music, and provocative public spectacles aimed at destroying rational logic, social restraints and conventions, traditional art and literature. Dada was subsumed by Surrealism and formally laid to rest in a mock funeral service in Paris in 1923, though there have been reported sightings wherever nonsense thrives and the spirit of anarchy reigns. In *The Posthuman Dada Guide* (2009), Andrei Codrescu interprets all of twentieth-century history as a chess game between the libertine Tristan Tzara and the control freak Vladimir Lenin. He maintains Dada's contemporary relevance as a model for wildness, action, and inclusive participation, an antidote to consumerism.

SEE ALSO *sound poetry, Surrealism.*

daimon, daemon The intermediary. There is no precise equivalent in English for this word that suggests divine power, fate, god. Empedocles believed that the daimon persisted through successive incarnations. Whereas the psyche was at home within the body, the daimon was seeking a dwelling place beyond its mortal limits. It stands as a source of our possible divinity. In the *Symposium* (ca. 385–370 B.C.E.), Plato defined the daimon as "a very powerful spirit . . . halfway between god and man." He has Diotima explain to Socrates the mediating role and function of the daimons:

> They are the envoys and interpreters that ply between heaven and earth, flying upward with our worship and our prayers, and descending with the heavenly answers and commandments.

The gods don't communicate to mortals directly, Plato suggests, but rely on intermediate spirits. So, too, mortals need figures to communicate with the gods, and thus the daimon becomes the figure of the petition, a source evolving into sacrifices and initiations, incantations and prophecies, divinations and magic spells, sacred poems. Plato further suggests in the *Republic* (ca. 380 B.C.E.) that it is possible for the soul to choose its own daimon, its own potential source of immortality.

Harold Bloom proposes that the ancient idea of the daimon, of a divine or magical inner self, an occult self that is even older than the body, is the origin of all Gnosticisms — Jewish, Christian, and Islamic — and the crucial source for the Hermetic Corpus, which was foundational for the Italian Renaissance. It is at the core of all heretical mysticism. The daimon evolved over time into the figure of the demon, a word which, taken in its root sense, means an attendant, ministering, or indwelling spirit. In ancient Greek mythology, the daimon referred to a class of supernatural beings less individualized than the gods. The daimones were spirits associated with particular places, such as nymphs, who dwelled in trees, springs, and mountains; satyrs, who moved through wooded areas; and Nereids, who were confined to the waves of the sea.

The idea of the daimon has had strong appeal to poets. To cite but two examples: Ralph Waldo Emerson referred often to an inner or alternative secret self, "a sort of alter ego or Socratic daemon," as his biographer Robert Richardson explains, "a free prophetic voice or persona who was, of course, himself and yet not his daylight self"; W. B. Yeats was powerfully attracted to the notion that, as he expressed it when writing about Shakespeare, the Greeks "considered that myths are the activities of the Daimons, and that the Daimons shape our characters and our lives." He fancied the idea that for each of us there existed one archetypal story, a single explanatory myth, which, if we but only understood it, would clarify all that we said and did and thought. That is why he was so drawn to the Greek notion that "the Daimon is our destiny," which he expanded into a summary doctrine in "Anima Hominis" (1917):

> When I think of life as a struggle with the Daimon who would ever set us to the hardest work among those not impossible, I understand why there is a deep enmity between a man and his destiny, and why a man loves nothing but his destiny.

daina A traditional form of Latvian folk song. Latvian song-poetry is closely akin to Lithuanian traditional songs called *dainos.* The *daina,* which dates to well before the twelfth century, retains vestiges of a preliterate, agricultural culture. The form is compact and typically consists of four unrhymed lines. The meter is normally trochaic, as in Finnish runo-songs. Between 1904 and 1915, Krišjánis Barons put together six volumes of *Latvju Dainas,* still the most well-known and popular collection of Latvian song texts. More than two hundred thousand *dainas* have now been recorded and collected. The daina is the mother lode of Latvian culture. It has been estimated that nearly 70 percent of Latvian *dainas,* anonymous folk songs, have been composed by women. There are men's songs, but the *daina* frequently expresses the emotional life of women, especially in villages. Modern Latvian poetry in particular and written Latvian literature in general are deeply affected by the *daina.* The twentieth-century poet Zinaīda Lazda (1902–1957) especially captures the spirit of *daina.*

SEE ALSO *folk song.*

dastanchi, see *akyn.*

dead metaphor A metaphor that has supposedly been used so often that it has lost its capacity to describe one thing in terms of another, and no longer operates as a metaphor. Do we think of the heart when we say that this definition strikes *the heart of the matter?* The question of whether or not a dead metaphor is still a metaphor has been debated in recent years. Metaphors may not be surprising — I'm *skating on thin ice* here — but they can still work as metaphors. Zoltán Kövecses explains: "The 'dead metaphor' account misses an important point. . . . The metaphors . . . may be highly conventional and effortlessly used, but this does not mean that they have lost their vigor in thought and that they are dead. On the contrary, they are 'alive' in the most important sense — they govern our thought — they are 'metaphors we live by.' " Some poets, such as Samuel Johnson in "The Vanity of Human Wishes" (1749), make a point of invigorating dead metaphors. Giambattista Vico contended in *The New Science* (1725) that all language begins with metaphor and that the first metaphors were drawn from the human body. A great deal of what we think of as literal speech consists of dead metaphors, as when we say "the mouth of a river," "veins of minerals," "murmuring waves," "weeping willows," "the bowels of the earth," and "smiling skies." We speak the vestiges of ancient metaphorical language.

SEE ALSO *cliché, convention, metaphor, personification.*

deaf poetry Deaf poets have demonstrated that there is a poetry independent of sound. John Keats's declaration that "Heard melodies are sweet, but those unheard / Are sweeter" ("Ode on a Grecian Urn," 1819) has been marshaled as a defense of deaf poetry. One type of written deaf poetry focuses on the "inner music" of poems as an alternative to the "outer music," another intensifies the other senses, like sight. Deaf poets create poems that reverberate in silence, or partial silence. "Such is the story made of stubbornness and a little air," Ilya Kaminsky writes in "Deaf Republic" (2009), "a story sung by those who danced before the Lord in quiet."

There is also a form of deaf poetry that does not depend on writing. Signing, which is native to deaf culture, has given rise to a poetry that subverts the paradigm of hearing. Whereas hearing poets may make poems out of "a mouthful of air" (W. B. Yeats), hearing-impaired poets may make it out of "a handful of air." The body is the text in American Sign Language (ASL) poetry, which is expressed through the hands, the stance, the movements, and the facial expressions of the signer. There is a strong distinction between everyday signing and poetic signing. There are also pidgin poems that combine signing with words. Dorothy Miles explains in *Gestures: Poetry in American Sign Language* (1976) that in certain poems she had "tried to blend words with sign-language as closely as lyrics and tunes are blended in song." Her poems "should be seen as well as read."

débat A popular literary genre of the twelfth and thirteen centuries, the *débat* dramatizes a quarrel or debate between two opposing perspectives. For example, the twelfth-century Middle English poem *The Owl and the Nightingale* sets up a debate between a sober owl, who represents the didactic or religious poet, and a merry nightingale, who represents the love poet. The owl sings in the somber mood of winter, the nightingale in the joyous mood of summer. The allegorical *débat* poem sets up a dramatic model for a verbal contest of wits, which in the end is referred to a judge.

There are pastoral contests of wit in the eclogues of Theocritus and Virgil, and many examples in Old French and Provençal literature, such as the fifteenth-century "Débat du cors et du l'âme." Later, François Villon wrote a great *"Débat du coeur et du corps"* (1461). The theme of the soul versus the body has a pedigree that dates to Old English literature. Andrew Marvell presents two examples in his metaphysical poems "A Dialogue, between the Resolved Soul and Created Pleasure" (1681) and "A Dialogue between the Soul and Body" (1681). Here the soul inquires:

> What magic could me thus confine
> Within another's grief to pine,
> Where, whatsoever it complain,
> I feel, that cannot feel, the pain,
> And all my care itself employs,
> That to preserve, which me destroys:
> Constrained not only to endure
> Diseases, but, what's worse, the cure:
> And read oft the port to gain,
> Am shipwrecked into health again?

And the body responds:

> But physic yet could never reach
> The maladies thou me dost teach:
> Whom first the cramp of hope does tear,
> And then the palsy shakes of fear;
> The pestilence of love does heat,
> Or hatred's hidden ulcer eat;
> Joy's cheerful madness does perplex,
> Or sorrow's other madness vex;
> Which knowledge forces me to know,
> And memory will not forgo.
> What but a soul could have the wit
> To build me up for sin so fit?
> So architects do square and hew,
> Green trees that in the forest grew.

SEE ALSO *dialogue, dit, poetic contest.*

decadence "I like the word *decadent,*" the French poet Paul Verlaine said in the 1880s: "All shimmering with purple and gold . . . it throws out the brilliance of flames and the gleam of precious stones. It is made up of carnal spirit and unhappy flesh and of all the violent splendors." The word *decadent* comes from the Latin *decadere,* which means "to fall down or away." It was used for centuries to characterize conditions of decline, as in the corruption that led to the fall of the Roman Empire. For example, in 1770 Voltaire counseled his friend LaHarpe: "Don't hope to re-establish good taste; we are in a time of the most horrible decadence." It wasn't until the mid-nineteenth century in France that a pejorative turned into an honorific and decadence was put forward as a full-fledged aesthetic stance and posture. It proudly opposed any notion of "normalcy," the triumphant idea of progress and its associated bourgeois optimism. Charles Baudelaire (1821–1867), whom George Poulet called "the poet of the irretrievable," was the first poet of decadence, and his masterpiece *Les Fleurs du Mal* (*The Flowers of Evil,* 1857) represented its moral and spiritual side. Decadence is both a style and an attitude.

The 1880s and '90s was the first period when *decadence* and *decadents* were used as proper nouns. In England, the poet Algernon Charles Swinburne (1837–1909), the artist Aubrey Beardsley (1872–1898), and the supreme aesthete Walter Pater (1839–1894) were all affiliated with the decadent stance. Oscar Wilde (1854–1900) became the "High Priest of the Decadents." The fatalistic mood, languorous glamor, and overaffected thinking of decadence were taken up by the poets Lionel Johnson (1867–1902), who said that decadence occurs "when thought thinks upon itself, and when emotions become entangled with the consciousness of them," and Arthur Symons (1865–1945), who said that "what decadence in literature really means is that learned corruption of language by which styles ceases to be organic and becomes, in the pursuit of some new expressiveness or beauty, deliberatedly abnormal." In 1898, William Butler Yeats lyrically described the Decadent movement as a reflection of "the autumn of the body."

SEE ALSO *Aestheticism, fin de siècle, Pre-Raphaelites, symbolism.*

de casibus A poem or prose work on the seemingly inevitable fall of great men. Boccaccio's *De casibus virorum illustrium* (*Concerning the Falls of Great Men,* 1360–1373), which consists of fifty-six moral biographies about the misfortunes and calamities of famous people, set the tradition of *de casibus tragedies.* The *de casibus* tradition directly influenced Geoffrey Chaucer's "The Monk's Tale," probably the earliest of *The Canterbury Tales* (ca. 1387–1400), which is subtitled "*De Casibus Virorum Illustrium,*" and states its theme at the outset:

> I will lament what we see in tragedies,
> The sorrows of those who stood in high degree
> And fell so far there was no remedy
> To bring them back from their adversity.
> For surely, once wild Fortune turns and flees
> No living man can hope to block her road.
> Let no one trust in blind prosperity:
> Be warned by these examples, true and old.
> *(tr. Burton Raffel)*

John Lydgate's encyclopedic *Fall of Princes* (1431–1438) recounts the sad stories of famous men and women in nine books consisting of more than thirty-six thousand lines of verse. It is an English rendering of Laurent de Premierfait's *Des Cas de nobles hommes et femmes* (1409), a prose redaction of Boccaccio's work. The popular English book *Mirror for Magistrates* (1559) consisted of nineteen tragic stories written in verse by a variety of authors. Both Shakespeare (1564–1616) and Marlowe (1564–1593) created characters in the *de casibus* tradition.

SEE ALSO *Monk's Tale stanza, tragedy.*

decastich Any whole poem of ten lines. The *decastich* is equivalent to the French *dizain* and the Spanish *décima.* Some of Ben Jonson's *Epigrammes* (1616) are well-balanced *decastichs,* such as his ingratiating dedicatory poem "To King James":

> How, best of Kings, do'st thou a scepter beare!
> How, best of *Poets,* do'st thou laurel weare!
> But two things, rare, the *Fates* had in their store,
> And gave thee both, to shew they could no more.
> For such a *Poet,* while thy days were greene,

Thou wert, as chiefe of them are said t'have beene.
And such a Prince thou art, wee daily see,
As chiefe of those still promise they will bee.
Whom should my *Muse* then flie to, but the best
Of Kings for grace; of *Poets* for my test?

SEE ALSO *décima, dizain.*

decasyllable A ten-syllable line, as in "Where are the songs of Spring? Ay, where are they?" (John Keats, "To Autumn," 1820). The decasyllable line appeared in French poetry in the eleventh century (*décasyllabe*) and in Italian poetry in the twelfth century (*decasillabo*). It was often called "heroic verse" because it was used for the medieval French heroic epics, the *chansons de geste,* such as *La Chanson de Roland* (*The Song of Roland,* ca. 1090). An oddity: because French and Italian lines often have multisyllabic or feminine endings, the decasyllable itself often has eleven or twelve syllables. One classic formulation divides the line into two parts of four and six syllables, with a strong caesura after the fourth syllable. In French poetry, the decasyllable was essentially replaced by the twelve-syllable alexandrine, in Italian by the eleven-syllable hendecasyllable.

The decasyllable is the basic unit of the rhythmical epic poetry of South Slavic epic poetry. The linguist Roman Jakobson points out that the basic type of the decasyllable not only exercises "a complete hegemony over contemporary Serbocroatian epic lore, but it survives to this day in the oral tradition of other Slavic areas, while remaining alien in a non-Slavic environment." He finds it a living element in the Slovenian, Macedonian, and West Bulgarian epic traditions.

The decasyllable has usually been treated in English as a five-stess iambic pentameter line, the standard-bearer for English poetry until the twentieth century.

SEE ALSO *alexandrine, blank verse, chansons de geste, epic, hendecasyllabics, iambic pentameter.*

décima Spanish: "tenth." The *décima* is a ten-line poem, or a work that consists of ten-line stanzas, composed in eight-syllable lines that commonly rhyme *abbaaccddc.* One popular type opens with a four-line stanza (called a *redondilla* or *planta*) or five-line *quintilla,* which establishes the theme of the poem. The *décima* is also known as the *espinela* in honor of Vicente Martínez Espinel (1550–1624), a Spanish writer who standardized the form in his *Rimas* (*Rhymes*, 1591). The form was brought to Latin America by Spanish sailors and conquistadors. The Mexican poet Sor Juana Inés de la Cruz (1651–1695), who is known, like Sappho (late seventh century B.C.E.), as *la décima musa*, the Tenth Muse, famously composed *décimas*.

The *décima* has flourished as a form of oral poetry that has been practiced throughout Latin America since the early sixteenth century. Traditionally accompanied by guitar music (*socabón*), it is, as Richard Bauman states, "perhaps the most widely distributed form of folk poetry in the Western Hemisphere." It flourished in Mexico in the nineteenth century. It is still the favored genre of Cuban and Puerto Rican popular poets. *Décimas* are often improvised by poet-singers (*trovadors*). Those who specifically practice them are called *decimistas* or *decimeros*. The *decimistas* from the Province of Esmeraldas in Ecuador distinguish between two categories: the *décima a lo humano* (about human matters) and the *décima a lo divino* (about divine matters).

Ten-verse *décimas* were competitively improvised along the Texas-Mexican border in the late nineteenth century. According to Américo Paredes:

> The satirical décima was not so much a jibe as a song-making challenge. The victim was supposed to answer and he would acquit himself very well indeed if he was able to reply in a gloss of four *décimas* based on the same *planta* (initial quatrain) used by his challenger.

When a writer such as the Cuban poet Eugenio Florit composed *décimas* (*Trópico*, 1930), he was in part associating himself with the oral folk tradition. The same could be said for the Spanish poets of the Generation of 1927, such as Jorge Guillén and Luis Cernuda, who cultivated the *décima*.

The *decima Italiana* consists of ten eight-syllable lines that rhyme *ababcdedec*. Traditionally, the last words of the fifth and tenth lines are stressed, and the sixth line begins a new sentence.

SEE ALSO *glose, oral poetry, quintilla.*

decir, dezir A medieval poem, the *decir* was intended to be read or recited, not sung. It was often a long narrative or didactic poem. It was one of the two major forms of Castilian court poetry from the late fourteenth through the early sixteenth century. The other was the *cantiga,* which was sung, and dealt mainly with the subject of love. The two forms were not always distinguishable in their early uses. For example, the first twenty poems of Alvarez de Villasandino (fl. 1370?–1425?) were in the form of *decirs* but called *cantigas* and dealt with love. They were mostly likely also sung.

The typical form of the *decir* was a sequence of octosyllabic stanzas *de arte menor* ("the stanza of the minor art"), a metric term for a stanza with lines of eight syllables or less, *reales, castellanas o mixtas.* They were also composed, however, in *coplas de pie quebrado* ("the stanza of the broken foot"), a sextilla with the third and sixth lines foreshortened, in hexasyllables and in the *copla de arte mayor* ("the stanza of the major art"), which is a metric term for a line of nine or more syllables. Many *decirs* are written in eight-line stanzas of octosyllables, rhyming *abbaacca,* with the rhyme carrying through the first four-line half stanzas to the second. The rhyme is assonantal. The rhymes are interlinked by repeating the rhymes of the first stanza in subsequent stanzas (*unisonancia plena*), by repeating the rhymes of the first and last lines of the half stanzas (*unisonancia media*), by beginning all the stanzas with the same line, and so forth. As the form developed, it became customary to conclude it with a brief stanza, which was linked to the rhyme of the main stanza. This final stanza was usually half the length of the other stanzas. It was a conclusion known at first by the Gallego Portuguese name *finida* and later as *fin* or *cabo.* One of the main sourcebooks for the *decir* is the *Cancionero de Baena* ("Songbook of Baena"), which was compiled toward the mid-fifteenth century.

SEE ALSO *cantiga, copla, didactic poetry, narrative poetry, octosyllabic verse.*

deconstruction The French philosopher Jacques Derrida gave the name *deconstruction* to an approach or endeavor that rigorously pursues the meaning of a text until it unravels, showing its contradictions, its unstable or impossible foundations. It is a notoriously difficult and sometimes maddeningly elusive project of critical thought that takes apart and exposes the problems in a given text. Meaning, which can be accessed only through language, is always indeterminate because language itself is indeterminate. Derrida calls the moment that a work shows its incompatibility with itself the "aporia" in a text. The philosopher Richard Rorty notes that "the term 'deconstruction' refers in the first instance to the way in which the 'accidental' features of a text can be seen as betraying, subverting, its purportedly 'essential' message." J. Hillis Miller argues that "Deconstruction is not a dismantling of the structure of a text, but a demonstration that it has already dismantled itself. Its apparently-solid ground is no rock, but thin air."

Derrida adapted the term *deconstruction* from Martin Heidegger's word *Destruktion,* or *Abbau.* He recalls that deconstruction began with a particular attention to structures, but was necessarily an "antistructuralist gesture" because "Structures were to be undone, decomposed, desedimented." Derrida borrowed from the linguist Ferdinand de Saussure the notion that "in language there are only differences" and coined the term *différance,* which derives from both "to defer" (to put off or delay) and "to differ" (to be unlike, not identical) to refer to "the 'active,' moving discord of different forces, and of differences of forces." He conjoins the temporal sense of defer and the spatial sense of unlikeness to undermine the "metaphysics of presence," the idea of origins, which has been so central to Western culture. "What defers presence . . . is the very basis on which presence is announced or desired in what represents it, its sign, its trace." Deconstruction understands language not as speech but as writing. Meaning does not originate from an original logos or word. It is forever deferred. Derrida writes: "Writing thus enlarged and radicalized no longer issues from a logos. Further, it inaugurates the destruction, not the demolition, but the de-sedimentation, the de-construction, of all the significations that have their source in that of the logos."

Deconstruction became a self-reflexive mode of analysis for a group of American literary theorists, including the Yale critics Geoffrey Hartman and Paul de Man. Deconstructive readings tend to emphasize the endlessly deferred meaning in texts and the open-ended nature of interpretation. They indicate how poems say one thing and perform another, how they simultaneously assert and deny their own rhetorical modes, how they take themselves apart. Or as De Man puts it in *Allegories of Reading* (1979): "Poetic writing is the most advanced and refined mode of deconstruction; it may differ from critical or discursive writing in the economy of its articulation, but not in kind."

SEE ALSO *aporia, catachresis, intertextuality, poststructuralism, structuralism.*

decorum Propriety, an appropriate sense of form, subject matter, language. Aristotle used the word *propon* to describe propriety of style (*Rhetoric,* ca.

335–330 B.C.E.), and Cicero claimed that *decorum* was the Latin equivalent of *propon* (*Orator,* 46 B.C.E.). Horace illustrated the purposefulness of decorum as a concept in poetry in his *Ars Poetica* (ca. 19–18 B.C.E.), where he argues that each style should find and keep its proper place. It matters who speaks — a slave, a hero, or a god — and comic and tragic themes are distinct and should be kept separate. The doctrine of decorum was aesthetically influential throughout the Renaissance and beyond. Hence John Milton's recognition of poetry in his *Tractate on Education* (1644) as "that sublime art which in Aristotle's *Poetics,* in Horace, and the Italian commentaries of Castelvetro, Tasso, Mazzoni, and others, teaches what the laws are of a true epic poem, what of a dramatic, what of a lyric, what decorum is, which is the grand masterpiece to observe." The neoclassical theory of decorum emphasized a hierarchy of styles (plain, moderate, grand) and a distinct division of poetic genres. One of the primary impulses of romanticism was the breaking of these rules, especially in relationship to language. In the preface to *Lyrical Ballads* (1798), William Wordsworth explained how he changed decorum by using situations from "humble and rustic life" in a "selection of language really used by men."

Decorum has sometimes proved useful as an established concept of propriety. Hence Wilfred Owen's ironic use of Horace's phrase "Dulce et Decorum Est" ("It is sweet and right") for the title of one of his greatest war poems. Horace's full phrase becomes the bitter last lines of Owen's lyric: "Dulce et Decorum Est / Pro patria mori" ("It is sweet and right / to die for your country"). Owen calls this patriotic saying "the old Lie."

Decorum is now mostly outdated as a concept, though it still functions in the social constraints and usages of poetry, often unconsciously. Occasional poems, for example, are deemed appropriate (or not) and fitted to their occasions. Some genres — the epithalamium, the elegy — work within social norms and decorums. It is unlikely that one would read a wedding poem at a funeral, or a dirge at a wedding, even if called for. A fastidious and skillful contemporary formal poet such as Richard Wilbur is both praised and criticized for his cultivated sense of artistic decorum. In *Dark Harbor* (1993), Mark Strand writes of admiring "the pursuit of rightness" in a poet: "Balance, some ineffable decorum, the measured, circuitous / Stalking of the subject, turning surprise to revelation."

SEE ALSO *elegy, epithalamium, neoclassicism, occasional poem.*

deep image Robert Kelly coined this term in an essay, "Notes on the Poetry of Deep Image" (1961), to identify a new energy entering American poetry. Deep imagism was never a movement, but the term is mostly associated with the poetry of Robert Bly, James Wright, Louis Simpson, William Stafford, Donald Hall, W. S. Merwin, Galway Kinnell, David Ignatow, and other poets of "the emotive imagination" working in the 1960s and '70s. These poets deployed the image to concentrate inner and outer energies, to unite the psyche and the cosmos.

In his magazine *The Fifties,* which subsequently turned into *The Sixties* and then *The Seventies,* Robert Bly argued that American poetry after Pound and Eliot had exalted the conscious mind at the expense of the unconscious mind. He sought a more passionate, irrational kind of poetry modeled after such earlier twentieth-century Spanish-language poets as Pablo Neruda (1904–1973), César Vallejo (1892–1938), Antonio Machado (1875–1939), and Federico García Lorca (1898–1936). In his essay "A Wrong Turning in American Poetry" (1963), Bly differentiated the Spanish poets from the American modernists ("the phrase 'objective correlative' is astoundingly passionless") and distinguished the kind of image he was seeking from the Imagist movement per se:

> The only movement in American poetry which concentrated on the image was Imagism, in 1911–13. But "Imagism" was largely "Picturism." An image and a picture differ in that the image, being the natural speech of the imagination, cannot be drawn from or inserted back into the real world. It is an animal native to the imagination.

The deep imagist poets navigated a space between the automatism of the French Surrealists and the hyperrationality of the New Critics. They used rational means to summon the irrational and retrieve forgotten relationships. Influenced by both Jungian psychology and Zen Buddhism, the deep imagists sought to unite both the conscious and unconscious mind through "psychic leaps," thus filling their poems with spiritual energy. The large word *imagination,* Bly reminds us, "has the smaller word 'image' in it."

SEE ALSO *image, imagism, leaping poetry, New Criticism, objective correlative, Surrealism.*

defective foot An incomplete foot, a foot lacking one or more unstressed syllables, in a line of metrical verse. The term itself, which was once common in traditional metrical analysis, is somewhat defective because it suggests that anything short of absolute metrical regularity is defective or faulty. In his essay "The Rationale of Verse" (1843), Edgar Allan Poe quotes Byron in order to show "how absurd it often is to cite a single line from amid the body of a poem, for the purpose of instancing the perfection or imperfection of the line's rhythm."

Della Cruscans Robert Merry (1755–1798) founded this circle of late eighteenth-century sentimental English poets. Taking a name from the Accademia della Crusca in Florence, which was founded for linguistic purity, he began writing as "Della Crusca," and thus initiated the romantic mannerisms of the group, some of whom lived in Italy, some in England. William Gifford savaged the group in *The Baviad* (1791) and *The Maeviad* (1795), and the term *Della-cruscan* thereafter came to refer to a pedantic, affected literary style.

SEE ALSO *romanticism.*

denotation, connotation Denotation (from the Latin "to mark out") is the exact or dictionary meaning of a word. The denotative qualities of a word are stated, explicit, and definable. Connotation (from the Latin "to mark [a thing] with or in addition [to another]") is the force of a word's associations. It is suggestive and reflects the emotional and/or cultural meanings radiating from a word beyond its lexical meaning.

Take the rose, for example, which has a long history as a symbol in poetry. It denotes a particular kind of flower, but it is often used to connote life's brevity, passion, beauty. In some medieval poems, it symbolized the loss of virginity. One thinks of the many ways that W. B. Yeats employed it in his book *The Rose* (1893). He explained: "The Rose is a favourite symbol with the Irish poets. It has given a name to more than one poem, both Gaelic and English, and is used, not merely in love poems, but in addresses to Ireland, as in De Vere's line, 'The little black rose shall be red at last,' and in Mangan's 'Dark Rosaleen.' " The rose suggests earthly love in Yeats's poem "The Rose of Peace" (1892), but it becomes a refuge from earthly love in his poem "The Rose of Battle" (1892). It connotes the power of creative imagination and occult philosophy in "To the Rose upon the Rood of Time" ("Red Rose, proud Rose, sad Rose of all my days!"). Yet it always continues to denote a flower.

Dertigers The Dertigers ("writers of the thirties") were a group of South African poets crucial to the formation of an independent literature in Afrikaans. The key figures were N. P. Van Wyck Louw (1906–1970) and his younger brother, W.E.G. Louw (1913–1980), whose book *Die ryke dwaas* (*The Rich Fools,* 1934) kicked off the movement; Uys Krige (1910–1987); and Elisabeth Eybers (1915–2002). Modern Afrikaans poetry begins with the Dertigers, who wanted to break through the gentilities to create something more emotionally honest and intense than the work of their predecessors, the *Tweede Asem* ("Second Breath"), who wrote in the first decades of the twentieth century. They were well aware of national politics, but treated poetry as a universal impulse, a sublime activity. Van Wyck Louw encapsulated the Dertiger ideal, the goal of poetry, in *Field Reports* (1939): "The themes of all great poetry . . . are also the content of this Afrikaans poetry," he wrote: "Poetry is to us a high and compelling task . . . not pleasurable play or pastime . . . or decoration of life, but a form of life itself without which we as humans and we as Afrikaans people could not as a people have a full human and national existence."

descending rhythm, see *falling rhythm.*

descort A type of discordant Provençal song in which each stanza takes a different shape. In many Old Occitan forms, such as the *sestina,* everything is formally prescribed, but here irregularity is the rule and liberty prevails. The troubadour Raimbaut de Vaqueyras (ca. 1180–1207) created a special kind of *descort* that used a different language in every stanza (one stanza is in Occitan, a second in Italian, a third in Northern French, a fourth in Gascon, a fifth in Gallician-Portuguese, and a sixth in a medley of the five languages). He thus enacted a linquistic discord that matched his subject, a lover's complaint over being deserted by his mistress. "Her heart is changed," he sings, "and therefore in these discordant measures do my words, and my music, and my language flow." Yet the fact that he could alternate between these five languages also suggests a poetry culture that extends beyond national borders.

SEE ALSO *lai, nonce forms, sestina, troubadour.*

descriptive poetry Poetry that describes something, that pictures and represents it in words. *Wasf,* or descriptive verse, was one of the four main categories of medieval Arabic poetry. (The other three were the *fakhr,* or "boast"; the *hija,* or "invective"; and the *marthiya,* or "elegy"). The *wasf* tradition was highly developed, and poets elaborately described single subjects, such as hunting animals or seeing different kinds of flowers. They described natural scenes and memorable occasions. The medieval Hebrew poets adapted this tradition and used poetry to describe gardens and palaces, the pleasures of wine, the beauties of young men and women.

Descriptive verse also flourished in Europe in the sixteenth, seventeenth, and eighteenth centuries, especially in landscape and topographical poetry. James Thomson's nature poem *The Seasons* (1730) is one of the defining classics of descriptive poetry. Description can seldom be sustained as an end in itself in poetry—Thomson's many imitators seemed to prove this—and thus descriptive poetry gave way in the nineteenth century to description *in* poetry. The descriptive impulse has often been derided by critics. Thus John Keats's ode "To Autumn" (1820), one of the most beautiful poems in the language, was once condescended to as "mere description." Everything starts with description, the pictorial impulse, the visual representation of the world, in a range of poets extending from William Wordsworth to Elizabeth Bishop.

SEE ALSO *fakhr, hija, nature poetry, topographical poetry, wine poetry.*

deus ex machina Latin: "god from the machine." A plot device in which something unexpectedly appears—a person, a group, an object—to help a character overcome a seemingly insolvable difficulty. In ancient Greek theater, a crane (*mekhane*) was frequently used to transport gods onto the stage, where they intervened in the action. More than half of Euripides's extant tragedies, for example, employ a *deus ex machina.* The Latin phrase comes into English through Horace's *Ars Poetica* (ca. 19–18 B.C.E.), where he instructs poets that they should never resort to a god from the machine in order to solve their plots. Friedrich Nietzsche argues in *The Birth of Tragedy* (1872), "The *deus ex machina* has taken the place of metaphysical solace."

SEE ALSO *tragedy.*

dialogue In a general sense, we think of dialogue as a verbal exchange between two or more imaginary speakers in fiction, drama, or poetry. This kind of exchange is obviously at the heart of drama. A literary dialogue is also a genre, either in prose or in poetry, in which a subject is discussed at length, as in Plato's celebrated *Dialogues,* which may have their origins in the mimes of the Sicilian poets Sophron and Epicharmus (fifth century B.C.E.). This sort of dialogue is not intended for the stage. Poetic contests, which have a long history, from the pastoral singing match to the Scottish flyting to the urban game of the dozens, are essentially dialogues. Two speakers go back and forth and, in many traditions, respond to each other by matching poetic forms. The dialogue poem written by a single poet tends to stand between the conversation poem, which has one speaker, and the play, which has any number of speakers. Narrative poems, such as ballads and epics, often employ dialogue. The *débat* poem, which was especially popular in England and France in the medieval era, depicts a dialogue between two opposing forces, such as the sun and moon, winter against summer, and, especially, the body and soul. Andrew Marvell's "A Dialogue Between the Soul and Body" (1681) stands behind such modern poems as T. S. Eliot's "First Debate Between the Body and Soul" (1910) and W. B. Yeats's "A Dialogue of Self and Soul" (1928). The dialogue poem can also simulate speech, two people talking to each other in time, which is how it is effectively used in William Barnes's nineteenth-century dialect poems and the verse dialogues in Robert Frost's *North of Boston* (1914).

SEE ALSO *conversation poem, débat, drama, dramatic monologue, flyting, pastoral, poetic contest.*

diastic An arbitrary method of selecting words from one text to create a new text. It is akin to *acrostic.* In *The Virginia Woolf Poems* (1986), Jackson Mac Low explained the "diastic" or "spelling-thru" method that he developed in a series of eleven poems. He began with a striking phrase from Virginia Woolf's *The Waves* (1931): "ridiculous in Picadilly." He reread the novel, looking for the first word that began with an *r,* then the next word that had an *i* as its second letter, then the next word that had a *d* as its third letter, and so forth until he had "spelled through" the whole phrase. He also had other rules for such things as line breaks and punctuation. Charles O. Hartman later embodied these rules in a computer program called *Diastext* (1996).

SEE ALSO *acrostic, aleatory, mesostic.*

dibrach, see *foot.*

didactic poetry From the Greek *dĭdak,* "apt at teaching." Didactic poetry is a type of literature that seeks to instruct, poetry with direct intention. Didactic poetry originated in the proverb, a miniature form. The Book of Proverbs in the Hebrew Bible is an anthology of didactic poetry whose goal is to teach wisdom. The ancient Greeks established a traditional model for didactic poetry, verse with a purpose, which operated in one of two ways. It taught *how* to do something, like keep bees or handle a plough, or it taught *what* to know about something, such as mathematics or philosophy. Thus Hesiod, the father of didactic poetry, signals his pedagogical vocation in two ways. He conveys practical information and teaches about farming in *Works and Days* (ca. 700 B.C.E.), whereas he explains the geneaology and myths of the gods, the origins of the cosmos, in *Theogony* (ca. 700 B.C.E.). Virgil's *Georgics* (29 B.C.E.) teaches "how to farm" and thus follows the practical model; Lucretius's *De Rerum Natura* (*On the Nature of Things,* 50 B.C.E.) is an exposition of science, ethics, and the nature of materialism, and thus follows the philosophical model.

Is poetry an art that entertains or instructs? The geographer/philosopher Strabo explained the Stoic position about the didactic value of poetry in his *Geography* (ca. 17 C.E.), where he argues against the Alexandrian scholar Eratosthenes's (ca. 275–194 B.C.E.) view that poetry is entertainment:

> Every poet, according to Eratosthenes, aims at entertainment (psuchagögia), not instruction. The ancients held a different view. They regarded poetry as a sort of primary philosophy, which was supposed to introduce us to life from our childhood, and teach us about character, emotion, and action in a pleasurable way. My own school, the Stoics, actually said that only the wise man could be a poet. This is why Greek communities give children their first education through poetry, not for simple "entertainment" of course, but for moral improvement. Even the musicians lay claim to this, when they teach plucking the strings with the fingers, or playing the lyre, or *aulos* [oboe or clarinet]; they are, as they say, educators and correctors of character.

He contended that, like Aristoxenus and the Pythagoreans, "Homer himself regards bards as moral guides." Horace (65–8 B.C.E.) tried to solve the divide by arguing that poetry should be both *dulce et utile,* "sweet and useful," enjoyable and instructive. Robert Frost picked up the Horatian idea when he said that a poem "begins in delight and ends in wisdom" ("The Figure a Poem Makes," 1939).

From the second millennium B.C.E., Sumerian poetry had a central role in the educational system, and thus was didactic. The Christian poetry of the Middle Ages is almost entirely didactic. The fable, which often employs speaking animals, is a didactic genre and so is the *conte dévot* ("pious tale"). The eighteenth century turned one type of didactic poetry, which teaches a moral, into a predominant mode. Alexander Pope's "Essays" ("An Essay on Criticism," 1711; *Moral Essays,* 1731–1735; "An Essay on Man," 1733–1734) epitomize the best argumentative moral verse. Much political poetry has a didactic intention. John Keats rebelled against didactic poetry when he declared in a letter (1818), "We hate poetry that has a palpable design upon us — and if we do not agree, seems to put its hand in its breeches pocket. Poetry should be great and unobtrusive." Yet Keats also spoke of "doing the world some good" through poetry. "Every great Poet is a Teacher," William Wordsworth told a friend in 1808, "I wish to be considered as a teacher or as nothing." In *The Didactic Muse* (1989), Willard Spiegelman observes that "even those who try to evade the didactic impulse embrace it." To examine the didactic impulse in poetry is to study strategies of instruction.

SEE ALSO *conte dévot, dulce et utile, fable, proverb, rhetoric, verse essay, wisdom literature.*

di-iamb, see *iamb.*

différance, see *deconstruction.*

digital poetry Digital poetry or e-poetry is a genre of electronic literature created, preserved, and displayed by computer codes. It is born digital. It does things instead of saying them and covers a spectrum of computerized literary art. The genre grew out of experiments that poets did with computers in the late 1950s. In their introduction to *P0es1s: Aesthetics and Digital Poetry* (2004), Frederick Brock, Christiane Heibach, and Karen Wenz suggest that digital poetry "applies to artistic projects that deal with the medeal changes in language and language-based communication in computers and digital networks. Digital poetry thus refers to creative, experimental, playful and also critical language art involving programming, multi-media, animation, interactivity, and net communication." They argue that the forms derive from "installations of interactive media art," "computer- and net-based art," and "explicitly from literary traditions." Janez Strehovec claims that digital poetry is "a new genre all of its own," which incorporates "kinetic/animated poetry, code poetry, interactive poetry, digital sound poetry, digital 'textscapes' with poetry features, and poetry generators." Digital poetry is depersonalized. It relies on mechanistic chance methods to compose poetry.

SEE ALSO *computer poetry*.

dimeter, see "accentual syllabic meter" in *meter*.

Dinggedicht German: "poems of things." Rainer Maria Rilke's early work is intensely subjective, but beginning in 1902, when he first came to Paris and put himself under the wing of the sculptor Rodin, he started to conceive a poetry that belonged more to the world of things than to the realm of feelings. The twenty-seven-year-old focused on the artist's labor, the actual process of making something material, and objectified his practice to match something of what he referred to as Rodin's "art of living surfaces." He called his new work *Dinggedichte,* or "thing-poems," and wrote two books of *Neue Gedichte* (*New Poems,* 1907, 1908).

In 1926, Kurt Oppert gave the name *Das Dinggedicht* to a genre of German poetry ranging from the nineteenth to the early twentieth century that stressed the self-sufficiency of objects. The idea was to describe objects, as if from within them. He found examples in the poetry of Edvard Mörike ("To a Lamp," 1846) and C. F. Meyer ("The Roman Fountain," 1882). These poems break with the German tradition, predominant since the 1770s, of *Erlebnisdichtung,* or the poetry of personal experience. Rilke's sculptural treatment of subjects, which are "separated from chance and time," culminate the genre. Strictly speaking, *dinggedicht* refers to German poetry, but there are strong analogies to other "thing poems," such as the French poet Francis Ponge's phenomenological prose poems, *The Voice of Things* (1942), and the Polish poet Zbigniew Herbert's object poems, *Study of the Object* (1961).

Dionysian, see *Apollonian/Dionysian*.

dipody, dipodic verse Greek: "two footed." Two metrical feet considered as a single unit or measure. In classical prosody, dipodic verse is rhythmically constructed so pairs of feet are taken together. In English poetry, it refers to a meter that can be scanned according to two different feet, heard in two ways. This especially happens in nursery rhymes, children's songs, and ballads. It tends to happen in long-lined poems when strong beats get emphasized and weaker ones get subsumed. Here is A. E. Stallings's couplet, "Dipodic Verse" (2007):

> What is it? Is it catching, is it common, is it rare?
> Is it something you have heard, and maybe uttered, unaware?

Stallings gives an example of a line from Gilbert and Sullivan's "Modern Major General" (1879) that can be scanned in two different ways. The first way has seven iambs:

> I *am* the *ve*ry *mo*del *of* a *mod*ern *ma*jor *gen*eral

In performance, it might sound like this:

> I *am* the very *mod*el of a *mod*ern major *gen*eral

Whole words — "of," "very," and "major" — are unstressed or "demoted." It might be more accurate to say that this is how we hear it:

> I AM the *ve*ry Model of a MOdern *ma*jor GENer*al*

dirge A song of grief, a lament that commemorates the dead. The dirge is close to the elegy, but less consoling, less meditative. The genre comes from the Greek *epicedium,* a song sung over the dead, and the Greek *threnody,* a song sung in memory of the dead. In fifth-century Greece, lyric dirges were sung, not just at funerals and other ceremonies commemorating the dead, but also at festivals. Catullus (84–54 B.C.E.) commemorates Simonides's Greek dirges with the phrase "Sadder than the tears of Simonides."

The dirge was also an ancient Near Eastern literary form that was used to memorialize disasters. The term *dirge* derives from the first words of the Latin antiphon in the Office of the Dead, which is adapted from the Psalms (5.9): *Dirige, Domine, Deus meus, in conspectus tuo via meam* ("Direct my way in your sight, O Lord my God"). The Latin meter was the hexameter (elegiac distich). In English, one hears the mournful tones of the dirge in Henry King's *Exequy* (1624) on his young wife, in Percy Shelley's "Autumn: A Dirge" (posthumously published in 1824), in Thomas Lovell Beddoes's "Dirge" (1825–1844), and in George Meredith's "Dirge in Woods" (1870), which reads

A wind sways the pines,
    And below
Not a breath of wild air;
Still as the mosses that glow
On the flooring and over the lines
Of the roots here and there.
The pine-tree drops its dead;
They are quiet, as under the sea.
Overhead, overhead
Rushes life in a race,
As the clouds the clouds chase;
    And we go,
And we drop like the fruits of the tree,
    Even we,
    Even so.

In American poetry, there is a leitmotif of ritual grief that runs from Ralph Waldo Emerson's "Dirge" (1838), Herman Melville's "A Dirge for McPherson" (1864), and Walt Whitman's "Dirge for Two Veterans" (1867) to Kenneth Fearing's "Dirge" (1935), Edna St. Vincent Millay's "Dirge without Music" (1928), and Thomas Merton's "Dirge for the World Joyce Died In" (1940–1942), to Heather McHugh's "Etymological Dirge" (1999) and David Wojahn's "Dirge and Descent" (1995). The African dirge is also what G. M. T. Emezue calls "one of the elevated forms of poetry."

SEE ALSO *elegy, epicedium, keening, lament.*

discordia concors, see *concordia discors.*

dispondee, see *spondee.*

discursive Discursive poetry moves from topic to topic, digressing, relying on argumentation. It is the essayistic movement of a text, which crosses wide swatches of terrain. It tends to put things in rather than take them out.

Often it is a reaction against a radically stripped-down poetry, such as imagism. In "The Discursive Mode" (1965), the Australian poet A. D. Hope characterized the discursive as "that form in which the uses of poetry approach closest to the uses of prose, and yet remain essentially poetry." Robert Pinsky champions discursive poetry in *The Situation of Poetry* (1978), where he argues for poetry as speech, "organized by its meaning, avoiding the distances and complications of irony on one side and the ecstatic fusion of speaker, meaning, and subject on the other. The idea is to have all of the virtues of prose, in addition to those qualities and degrees of precision which can be called poetic." Pinsky practices what he preaches as a mode of inclusion in his discursive book-length poem *An Explanation of America* (1979).

SEE ALSO *imagism, verse essay.*

disinterestedness Impartiality, free of bias. Matthew Arnold championed disinterestedness as a critical ideal. In "The Function of Criticism at the Present Time" (1864), Arnold writes: "And how is criticism to show disinterestedness? By keeping aloof from what is called 'the practical view of things'; by resolutely following the law of its own nature, which is to be a free play of the mind on all subjects which it touches. By steadily refusing to lend itself to any of those ulterior, political, practical considerations about ideas, which plenty of people will be sure to attach to them." One critique of the idea of critical disinterestedness is that it disguises its own subjectivity. Marianne Moore made the case for "disinterestedness" not as a critical ideal but a formalist criterion for her scientifically oriented verse: "Precision, economy of statement, logic employed to ends that are disinterested, drawing and identifying, liberate — at least have some bearing on — the imagination."

dissociation of sensibility T. S. Eliot coined this phrase, a historical idea, in his essay "The Metaphysical Poets" (1921) to describe a shift of sensibility between the Jacobean dramatists and metaphysical poets, such as Donne (1572–1631) and Marvell (1621–1678), and later writers, such as Milton (1608–1674) and Dryden (1631–1700). The phrase suggests a divorce between thinking and feeling. Eliot used the idea of dissociation of sensibility to privilege the Metaphysicals and disparage the romantics and Victorians. For a time, his somewhat questionable idea that thinking was severed from experience during the seventeenth century had a remarkable influence on literary criticism, especially the New Criticism. Frank Kermode argues in *Romantic Image* (1957) that the idea of dissociation of sensibility was misleading because it shored up the idea that the image was the central element in poetry. He suggests that discourse, too, has an important part to play.

SEE ALSO *discursive, New Criticism, sensibility.*

dissonance A harsh sound or rhythm. It is nearly equivalent to cacophony. If there is any difference between them, it is that cacophony tends to refer to conflicting sounds, whereas dissonance refers to the deliberate lack of harmony of the things around it. "The Waste Land" (1922), for example, is a dissonant text, which works by disjunction. In *Paradise Lost* (1667), Milton writes of "the barbarous dissonance / Of Bacchus and his revellers, the race / Of that wild rout that tore the Thracian bard / In Rhapsode."

SEE ALSO *cacophony.*

distich A stanzaic unit of two metrical lines, which usually rhyme and express a complete thought. It was commonly used in Greek and Latin elegiac poetry. The two-line epigram, for example, is a distich. At Pembroke, a student named Penlycross included this Latin motto with an essay he thought would be rejected for a contest:

> Distichon ut poscas nolente, volente, Minerva,
> Mos sacer? Unde mihi distichon? En perago.
>
> Without a distich, vain the oration is;
> Oh! for a distich! Doctor, e'en take this.

SEE ALSO *couplet, epigram.*

dit French: "something said." In medieval French poetry, the *dit* was literally a poem meant to be spoken, not sung. The term applied to a wide variety of poetic forms, and seems closely related to other forms, such as the fabliau, the *débat,* and the *lai.* It was most commonly written in octosyllabic couplets. It could be either narrative or expository, and ranged in length from one hundred to several thousand lines. It could be a love poem or a eulogy, a political satire, a spiritual testament. According to *The New Oxford Companion to Literature in French* (1995), certain traits can nonetheless be associated with the *dit:* "It is always constructed on first-person discourse. Thus the narrative *dits,* in which a narrator identified with the author recounts events that he or she experienced or observed, can be distinguished from the *lai,* narrated in the third person and often set in the distant past." Some medieval examples: Rutebeuf's "Le dit de l'herberie" ("The Tale of the Herb Market"), a comic monologue from the point of view of a seller of quack medicines; Guillaume de Mauchat's "Le livre dou voir dit" ("The Book of the True Poem"), which tells the "true story" of the aged poet's romance with a young admirer; and Christine de Pizan's "Ditié de Jehanne d'Arc," which was inspired by Joan of Arc's early victories.

SEE ALSO *débat, fabliau, lai.*

dithyramb The dithyramb began as a frenzied choral song and dance in honor of Dionysius, the god of wine, fertility, and procreation. It was a performed hymn, a processional danced song. What we now think of as three distinct genres — poetry, music, and dance — were completely intertwined. Archilochus (seventh century B.C.E.) first used the term *dithyramb* to describe the "beautiful song of Dionysius"; Plato (427?–347? B.C.E.) mentions "the birth of Dionysus called, I think, the dithyramb"; and Aristotle (384–322 B.C.E.), who claimed that the Dionysiac Arion was the first to lead a circular chorus, argued that the dithyramb evolved into Greek tragedy. C. M. Bowra suggests that Arion "seems to have found in existence an improvised, ecstatic song to Dionysius and to have transformed it into a formal, choral hymn attached to definite festivals and accompanied by regular dancing." He argues that the dithyramb was thought of as a narrative in lyric form.

The first dithyrambs were probably composed in Athens around the seventh century B.C.E. Lasus of Hermione, presumably Pindar's teacher, is said to have introduced dithyrambic competitions into Athens. Aristophanes reports in *The Wasps* (422 B.C.E.): "A contest rose 'twixt Lasus and Simonides / (The day has long gone by) who show'd most mastery / In music." These large-scale compositions were performed at festivals in Athens, Delphi, and Delos. The dithyramb reached its peak in the work of Simonides (ca. 556–468 B.C.E.), Bacchylides (fifth century B.C.E.), and Pindar (ca.

522–443 B.C.E.). A. W. Pickard-Cambridge describes the Pindaric dithyramb as "an anti-strophic composition dealing with special themes taken from divine and heroic legend, but still maintaining its particular connection with Dionysus, who is celebrated, apparently at or near the opening of the song, whatever its subject." Pindar says in one dithyrambic fragment, "The Muse set me up as the chosen herald of skillful verses for Greece with its beautiful choruses as I was praying in might-charioted Thebes."

Dithyrambs are now considered any wild, vehement, and enthusiastic piece of writing. Dithyrambs are relatively rare in English, though John Dryden composed one called "Alexander's Feast" (1697), which contains this praise:

The praise of Bacchus then the sweet musician sung,
    Of Bacchus ever fair, and ever young:
        "The jolly god in triumph comes;
        Sound the trumpets; beat the drums;
            Flush'd with a purple grace
            He shews his honest face:
Now give the hautboys breath; he comes, he comes.
        Bacchus, ever fair and young,
            Drinking joys did first ordain;
        Bacchus' blessings are a treasure,
        Drinking is the soldier's pleasure:
            Rich the treasure,
            Sweet the pleasure,
        Sweet is pleasure after pain."

Two examples in contemporary poetry: Richard Katrovas, "Three Dithyrambs" (1993), and David Wojahn, "Dithyramb and Lamentation" (2006).

SEE ALSO *Apollonian/Dionysian, chorus, paean, poetic contest, tragedy.*

ditrochee, see *trochee.*

ditty A short simple song. The ditty can refer to a composition to be sung, sometimes a *lai,* occasionally even a ballad, as in Rudyard Kipling's *Departmental Ditties & Barrack-Room Ballads* (1899):

I have eaten your bread and salt,
  I have drunk your water and wine,
The deaths ye died I have watched beside,
  And the lives that ye led were mine.

Was there aught that I did not share
  In vigil or toil or ease, —
One joy or woe that I did not know,
  Dear hearts across the seas?

I have written the tale of our life
  For a sheltered people's mirth,
In jesting guise — but ye are wise,
  And ye know what the jest is worth.

The ditty can also suggest the words of a song, its burden or theme. The term *ditty* now has a disparaging tone, but that was not always so. Thomas Campion's chapter "Of Ditties and Odes" in *Observations in the Art of English Poesy* (1602) suggests that for him the ditty and the ode were essentially the same thing.

SEE ALSO *ballad, burden, lai, ode, roundelay.*

divan, diwan A gathering of one poet's poems, usually a "selected" or "collected poems." *Divan* is a Persian word, which derives from the Persian *dibir* ("writer, scribe"), and suggests, among other things, a historical record. Thus Ibn Khaldun's declaration in the fourteenth century, "Poetry is the divan of the Arabs." The term was also used in Urdu, Arabic, Armenian, Turkish, Hebrew, and other poetries. Attributed to Radaki (d. 940), the first poet of modern classical Persian, it has been widely employed to name a collection of poems, as in Hafiz's fourteenth-century *Divan* or Rumi's thirteenth-century work of about forty thousand lines, *Divan-e Shams-e Tabrizi.*

In the West, Goethe reacted to the first German translation of Persian poetry with his book of poems, *West-East Divan* (1819). In 1923, Muhammad Iqbal responded with a book of Persian poems, *The Message of the East.* The Arabic-German dialogue has continued in the magazine *Divan* (2000), which takes as its motto: "The Occident cannot exist without the Orient, and the Orient cannot exist without the Occident. They differ from one another and are similar to one another."

The term has been periodically used in Western poetry to connect poets to the East, as when the Spanish poet Federico García Lorca signaled his abiding love for Arabic poetry with *The Divan at Tamarit* (1931–1934).

Dīwān school The Dīwān school of poets flourished in Egypt for nearly a decade between 1913 and 1921. 'Abbās Mahmūd al-'Aggād (1889–1964), Ibrāhim 'abd al-Qadir al-Māzinī (1889–1964), and 'Abd al-Rahmān Shukrī (1886–1958) formed the Dīwān school in Cairo. Shukrī's collection of poems, *The Light of Dawn* (1909), and al-'Aggād's critical essays launched the movement. These three writers were so deeply influenced by English romantic poetry that they were dubbed "the English school" by contemporaries. They reacted against traditionalism in Arabic poetry, the way that contemporary neoclassical poets imitated the ancient Arabic poets. Rather, they stood, as A.M.K. Zubaidi suggests, "for humanism and individuality, faithfulness to nature, truth and simplicity against national fanaticism, artificiality, rhetoric and imitativeness." The poet Khalīl Matrān (1872–1949), who believed in the poet's faithfulness both to himself and to his own era, was a key transitional figure between Arabic neoclassicism and modern romanticism. The writers of the Dīwān school called themselves *madras at al-tajdid* (The School of Innovation), but are generally recognized by the name of their collective critical writings, *Al-Diwan.* They believed that the voice of the individual was more important than the voice of the tribe and anticipated the modernist revolution in Arabic poetry.

SEE ALSO *Apollo Society.*

dizain From the French: a stanza or poem of ten lines. The *dizain* with ten syllables per line (or more rarely eight) was especially favored by French poets of the fifteenth and sixteenth centuries, either as an independent poem or as a stanza within a longer structure, as in the *ballade* and the chant royal. Philip Sidney wrote the first crown or corona in English verse as a song of ten linked *dizains* (*Old Arcadia,* #72, 1590). The stately ten-line stanzas of John Keats's great odes are technically *dizains.* Keats grafted a Shakespearean quatrain (*abab*) onto a Petrarchan sestet (*cdecde*) and thus established the central pattern of "Ode to a Nightingale" (1819), "Ode on a Grecian Urn" (1819), "Ode on Melancholy" (1819), and "Ode on Indolence" (1819).

SEE ALSO *ballade, chant royal, decastich, décima.*

dochmiac, see *foot.*

dodecasyllable In Spanish verse, the dodecasyllable, or twelve-syllable verse, is divided into two equal half lines or hemistiches. It can also divide into five- and seven-syllable units, the rhythm of several traditional poetic forms. Rubén Dario (1867–1916) brought it back into modern Spanish-language poetry.

dodoitsu A Japanese form that consists of twenty-six syllables in four lines. Lengthwise, it operates between the haiku and the tanka. It is unrhymed and nonmetrical. The first three lines have seven syllables and the last line has five syllables. This creates a kind of foreshortening effect at the end. In Japanese, the word *dodoitsu* suggests a folk song of love or work.

SEE ALSO *folk song, haiku, tanka.*

doggerel *Doggerel* has been used as a derogatory term for bad poetry since the thirteenth century. It is a trivial form of verse, loosely constructed and rhythmically irregular. It often has forced rhymes, faulty meters, and trite sentiments. It has also been purposefully employed as a source of comedy and a type of satire. In German, doggerel is known as *Knittelvers* ("cudgel verse"). Doggerel is verse that is too willful. Northrop Frye points out, "Doggerel is not necessarily stupid poetry; it is poetry that begins in the conscious mind and has never gone through the associative process. It has a prose initiative, but tries to make itself associate by an act of will, and it reveals the same difficulties that great poetry has overcome at a subconscious level."

In "The Nature and Phenomena of Doggerel" (1906), George Saintsbury usefully distinguishes between two different kinds of doggerel: "there is doggerel which is doggerel, and doggerel which is not." The doggerel "which is doggerel" is merely bad verse, a lyric that aspires to a certain standard and fails. The doggerel "which is not," on the other hand, consists in "the using of recognized forms of verse, and of diction recognized and unrecognized, with a willful licentiousness which is excused by the felicitous result. The poet is not trying to do what he cannot do; he is trying to do something exceptional, outrageous, shocking."

Chaucer uses the term *rhyme doggerel* in the mock-courteous "Tale of Sir Thopas" (ca. 1387–1400), and Shakespeare puts doggerel into the mouths of his comic characters (think of Bottom and his companions in *Midsummer Night's Dream*, ca. 1595). Jonathan Swift (1667–1745), who rhymes "Profane is" and "Aristophanes," is one of its satirical masters. And so is John Skelton (1460–1529), who writes:

> For though my rhyme be ragged,
> Tattered and jagged,
> Rudely rain-beaten,
> Rusty and moth-eaten,
> If ye take well therewith,
> It hath in it some pith.

Doggerel is one of the staples of comic verse, from Samuel Butler (1612–1680) to Ogden Nash (1902–1971). It is easily memorized and still very much present in limericks and nonsense poetry, in children's games, popular songs, and advertising jingles.

SEE ALSO *Crambo, jingle, Knittelvers, light verse, limericks, nonsense poetry, Skeltonics.*

dohā This common Hindi form is a self-contained rhyming couplet. Each twenty-four-syllable line divides into unequal parts of thirteen (6, 4, 3) and eleven syllables (6, 4, 1). A *sorthā,* an inverted *dohā,* transposes the two parts of the line. The simple form of the *dohā,* which conveys an image or idea in two verses, has made it especially useful to describe devotional, sensual, and spiritual states, as in the mystical poetry of Kabir (1440–1518) and Nanak (1469–1539). It often has a proverbial feeling. Goswami Tulsidas employed *dohās* to adapt the Sanskrit epic *Ramayana* (fifth to fourth century B.C.E.). His *Ramcharitmanas* (sixteenth century) are as well known among Hindus in northern India as the Bible is in rural America.

dolce stil novo Italian: "sweet new style." Dante Alighieri invented this term, which he used in the *Purgatorio* (ca. 1308–1312) to describe the new poetic, the mellifluous lyricism, of a group of late thirteenth-century love poets. The three words suggest the originality of their manner (*"novo"*), the new themes and content of their style (*"stil"*), and the audibly as well as intellectually pleasing quality of their poetry (*"dolce"*). Dante hailed the Bolognese poet Guido Guinizzelli (1230–1276) as the "Father" of a fresh poetry that harmonized form and content in a clear style. "Love always has its home in the noble heart," Guinizzelli writes. Dante did not designate precisely who belonged to the *stilnovsti,* but the Florentines Guido Cavalcanti (ca. 1250–1300), whom he calls his "first friend" in the *Vita Nuova* (1295), and Cino da Pistoia (1270–1336/7) are usually included under this rubric because of the strong musicality and shared subject matter of their work. These poets reworked the themes of courtly love invented by the troubadours and theologized romantic love; they played a fundamental role in the development of the Italian sonnet, providing a bridge to Petrarch; and they established the Italian vernacular as the language of poetry. Dante himself was the consummate poet of the *dolce stil novo,* and his own early work embodies the muscular eloquence of the vernacular, a sweet new style.

SEE ALSO *courtly love, sonnet, troubadour.*

double dactyl Two dactyls in a row (/ / u / / u), as in the word *mónŏmănĭácăl.* The double dactyl is also a comic verse form, an offshoot of the clerihew invented by Anthony Hecht and Paul Pascal (1961). It is an elaborate form of doggerel, also known as *Higgledy Piggledy.* The double dactyl consists of two four-line stanzas. Most of the lines are double dactyls. The first line is usually a jingle or nonsense phrase, often "Higgledy Piggledy" or "Jiggery-pokery." The second line is the name of a person, who is the subject of the poem. The truncated fourth and eight lines rhyme. One line in the second stanza should consist of a single word. As John Hollander describes it in *Rhyme's Reason* (1989):

> Higgledy-piggledy
> Schoolteacher Hollanders
> Mutter and grumble and
> Cavil and curse,
>
> Hunting long words for the
> Antepenultimate
> Line of this light-weight but
> Intricate verse.

SEE ALSO *clerihew, dactyl, doggerel, light verse.*

the dozens Playing the dozens is an African American verbal street game of escalating insults. In different communities, it is also called woofing, sounding, joning, screaming, cutting, capping, and chopping, among other things. There is a slight shift in the rules from place to place. Played by both males and females, it is sometimes "clean," more often "dirty." In the *Dictionary of Afro-American Slang* (1970), Clarence Major defines the Dirty Dozens as "a very elaborate game traditionally played by black boys, in which the participants insult each other's relatives, especially their mothers. The object of the game is to test emotional strength. The first person to give in to anger is the loser."

No one knows the origins of the dozens, which probably derives its name from an eighteenth-century meaning of the verb *dozen,* "to stun, stupefy, daze." Lawrence Levine points out that all the ingredients of the dozens were present in the slaves' environment. He quotes the earliest documentation of the dozens in a Texas song collected in 1891:

Talk about one thing, talk about another;
But if you talk about me, I'm gwain to talk about your mother.

The dozens is a way of using language to stun someone in front of an audience, as in this opening rhymed couplet:

I don't play the dozens, the dozens ain't my game
But the way I fucked your mama is a god damn shame.

There is a structural turn in the couplet: the first line disclaims the game, which the second line then contradicts.

The sociolinguist William Labov codifies the "Rules for Ritual Insults" in *Language in the Inner City* (1972):

1. A sound opens a *field,* which is meant to be sustained. A sound is presented with the expectation that another sound will be offered in response, and that this second sound may be built formally upon it. The player who presents an initial sound is thus offering others the opportunity to display their ingenuity at his expense.
2. Besides the initial two players, a third-person role is necessary.
3. Any third person can become a player, especially if there is a failure by one of the two players then engaged.

4. Considerable symbolic distance is maintained and serves to insulate the event from other kinds of verbal interaction.

In his autobiography, *Die Nigger Die!* (1969), H. Rap Brown remembers that in school his teachers tried to teach him "poetry" in the classroom when he was actually talking poetry in the streets. "If anybody needed to study poetry," Brown says, "[my teacher] needed to study mine. We played the Dozens for recreation, like white folks play Scrabble." He grew up in Baton Rouge and distinguishes between the dozens, which are a "mean game because what you try to do is totally destroy somebody else with words," and "Signifying," which was "more humane." He says, "Signifying allowed you a choice — you could either make a cat feel good or bad. If you had just destroyed someone (verbally) or if they were just put down already, signifying could help them over." Claudia Mitchell-Kernan recalls that in Chicago, games of verbal insult were called sounding in general. The dozens was a specific type of game that broadened the target from an individual adversary to his relatives and ancestors, especially his mother. There were direct insults, called sounds, and indirect insults, called signifying.

Langston Hughes imitates the dozens, and uses it to structure his wittiest and most ambitious work, the twelve-part sequence *Ask Your Mama: 12 Moods for Jazz* (1961).

SEE ALSO *signifying*.

drab and golden poetry In his book *English Literature in the Sixteenth Century: Excluding Drama* (1954), the novelist and critic C. S. Lewis distinguished between the "Drab" poets of the mid-sixteenth century (George Gascoigne, Barnabe Googe, George Turberville) and the "Golden" poets of the late Elizabethan era (Sidney, Surrey, Shakespeare). Lewis claimed that these were descriptive terms, not value judgments, and that he was merely describing a shift from simple, plain writing to colorful, gorgeous writing, but his characterization helped to establish one set of writers at the cost of the other. "Drab" was a somewhat misleading term and is now commonly known as "the plain style." In *Forms of Discovery* (1967) and other books, Yvor Winters argued for the fundamental centrality of the plain style. What Lewis called the drab style, J. V. Cunningham called "the moral style." It is the iambic style of Sir Walter Raleigh's "The Nymph's Reply to the Shepherd" (1600):

Time drives the flocks from field to fold
When rivers rage and rocks grow cold,
And Philomel becometh dumb;
The rest complains of cares to come.

SEE ALSO *aureate, the plain style.*

drama, dramatic poetry Drama applies to the entire corpus of work written for the theater. We speak of English Drama and Russian Drama. We also classify plays by their content or style, as in Restoration Drama and the Drama of the Absurd. In general, a drama is a work performed by actors on a stage or in front of an audience. The fundamental situation of a drama or play, then, is when actors take on the role of characters, uttering dialogue, performing actions. The audience participates with the actors in the realm of make believe. The pact between them relies on dramatic convention, the way that literary practice simulates reality—that time is compressed, that masks or personae represent real people, and so forth. All this helps to simulate a play world. There is a perceptible or psychic distance between the performers and the audience. A play is different from a game because the outcome is predetermined, the resolution foreknown. The *dramatis personae* (Latin for "persons," literally masks) are the characters in a play. The dramatic structure is the plan that creates and resolves conflict in a literary piece. For example, the Elizabethan dramatists borrowed from the Roman playwrights the idea of dividing their plays into five acts, beginning with an introduction, proceding through a rising action, climaxing, moving through a falling action, and then concluding with a final resolution, a denouement. Lyric poetry borrows from dramatic poetry the idea of a dramatic situation—that is, a situation that brings into contention different conflicting forces. At the core, drama represents conflict.

The drama, which dates to the fifth century B.C.E. in Greece (the word derives from the Greek word for "doing"), has its roots in religious practice and ritual. Comedy developed from festivals of revelry, tragedy out of ritual hymns sung during an animal sacrifice at Dionysian festivals. Drama, which retains a ritual element, initially served as a way of honoring the divine. A verse drama, sometimes called a poetic drama, is a play in which the dialogue is written in verse. It incorporates poetry.

Literary works have conventionally been divided into three generic types or classes, dependent upon who is supposedly speaking:

> *epic* or *narrative:* in which the narrator speaks in the first person, then lets the characters speak for themselves.
> *drama:* in which the characters do all the talking.
> *lyric:* uttered through the first person.

This useful but flawed textbook division evolved from Aristotle's fundamental distinction between the three genres of poetic literature: epic, drama, and lyric. All were radically presentational: recited, spoken, chanted, sung. "Like all well-conceived classifications," the Portuguese poet Fernando Pessoa writes in "Toward Explaining Heteronymy" (ca. 1915),

> this one is useful and clear; like all classifications, it is false. The genres do not separate out with such essential facility, and, if we closely analyze what they are made of, we shall find that from lyric poetry to dramatic there is one continuous gradation. In effect, and going right to the origins of dramatic poetry — Aeschylus, for instance — it will be nearer the truth to say that what we encounter is lyric poetry put into the mouths of different characters.

Pessoa conceived different "heteronyms" or fictive poets for himself, each with his own style and sentiments, and thus considered himself "a dramatic poet writing in lyric poetry." In *A Common Stage* (2007), her study of theatrical documents in thirteenth-century Arras, Carol Symes demonstrates that "the generic definition of a play as such was in flux for most of the Middle Ages." The distinction between lyrics, dialogues, and plays has been more permeable than is generally recognized.

Jonas Barish points out in *The Anti-Theatrical Prejudice* (1985) that the theater has aroused ferocious antagonisms over the centuries. He traces the history of philosophical repudiations from Plato (427?–347? B.C.E.) onward. These repudiations carry the haunting acknowledgment of the genuine fictive potency of drama. A dramatic or theatrical element spills over into everyday life. The term *drama* applies to any situation in which there is conflict. We keep playing roles and acting out, putting or finding ourselves in situations that are framed with a beginning, middle, and end. In his book

Frame Analysis (1976), the sociologist Erving Goffman convincingly demonstrates some of the ways we frame experience, how drama operates and acts in ordinary life.

SEE ALSO *closet drama, comedy, dialogue, dramatic monologue, monologue, tragedy.*

dramatic monologue "Everything written is as good as it is dramatic," Robert Frost declared in the preface to his play, *A Way Out* (1929). Poems become dramatic when we get the sensation of someone speaking, when we hear a poem, in Frost's words, "as sung or spoken by a person in a scene — in character, in a setting." A monologue presents a single person speaking alone, but a dramatic monologue presents an imaginary or historical character speaking to an imaginary listener or audience, as in Robert Browning's "Andrea del Sarto" (1853), "My Last Duchess" (1842), and "The Bishop Orders His Tomb at St. Praxed's Church" (1844). Browning termed such poems "dramatic lyrics." Browning and Tennyson are the Victorian inaugurators of this type of poem.

The speaker of the dramatic monologue is decidedly *not* the author, and thus the poem requires a high degree of impersonation. It enacts the displacement of the poetic self into another being. The utterance tends to take place in a specific situation at a critical moment, the speaker addresses and sometimes interacts with one or more auditors (this is revealed by what the speaker *says*), and the speaker reveals his or her character to the reader. The dramatic monologue imagines a speaker into being over the course of a poem, and we collaborate in the construction of that self. It engages us in the very act of poetic making and reminds us that the poem is always an artificial utterance.

Many poets have explored and exploited the possibilities of the dramatic monologue over the past 150 years — from Tennyson ("Ulysses," 1833) and Browning ("Fra Lippo Lippi," 1855) to Yeats (Crazy Jane poems, 1933), Eliot ("The Love Song of J. Alfred Prufrock," 1920, which gives us what Hugh Kenner calls "a name plus a voice"), and Frost (*North of Boston,* 1914). In Edwin Arlington Robinson's favorite poem of his own, "Rembrandt to Rembrandt" (1927), one phase of the painter's soul converses with another through the surface of his mirror. One could make a wonderful anthology of American dramatic monologues from midcentury onward, beginning with the Middle Generation, Robert Lowell, John Berryman, Elizabeth Bishop, and Randall Jarrell, highlighting the work of Richard Howard, the Robert Browning of our time, and marching forward to include recent pieces by Frank Bidart, Louise Glück, Norman Dubie, and Garrett Hongo.

SEE ALSO *monologue.*

drápa The *drápa* is an encomium, an Old Norse poetic form used for hymns of praise. It is an elaborate skaldic poem that consists of a number of stanzas with the same metrical pattern, often the *dróttkvætt.* It has a refrain (*stef*) of two or more half-lines. The *drápa* is well-suited to highly formal occasions, such as recitations at court, and has always been considered more prestigious than the *flokkr,* which is a shorter series of these stanzas without a refrain. The *drápa* became the only form used for praise of kings. *Geisli,* an encomium on Saint Óláfr (twelfth century), is the earliest *drápa* that has been preserved intact. It is also the earliest skaldic poem to which a definite date can be attached. It was composed by Einarr Skúlason, the most prolific skald and prominent Norse poet of the twelfth century, who recited it to a gathering of dignitaries in the Trondheim Cathedral in 1153. Longfellow loosely adapted the *drápa* to free verse in his poem "Tegner's Drapa," first entitled "Tegner's Death," a memorial for the Swedish poet Esias Tegner (1782–1846). On October 14, 1847, Longfellow noted: "Went to town, after finishing a poem on Tegner's death, in the spirit of the Old Norse poetry."

SEE ALSO *encomium, praise poems, skald.*

dream vision, dream allegory A narrative poem that tells the story of a dream. The dream vision — a narrator falls asleep and dreams a tale, which has moral or allegorical significance — was a favored medieval genre. It offered a type of vision literature, a tour of the marvelous, and a didactic conclusion. The conventions are strong. It is spring and a protagonist starts out walking through a natural landscape, a garden or wood, before falling into a visionary slumber. He then beholds a spectacle — characters acting symbolically or abstractions personified. It is as if the medieval convention embodied and enacted the way that walking can cross the threshold into visionary dreaming. Guillaume de Lorris and Jean de Meung's thirteenth-century *The Romance of the Rose* influenced the visionary dreams to come, such as Chaucer's "Parlement of Foules" (ca. 1381–1382), William Langland's apocalyptic *Piers Plowman* (ca. 1360–1387), and the fourteenth-century anonymous masterpiece *Pearl.* Shelley took the dream vision into the romantic era with "The Triumph of Life" (1824).

dróttkvætt "Lordly meter." This alliterative royal meter was the most stylized, prestigious, and common measure in skaldic poetry. It is still practiced in Icelandic poetry. Its name comes from combining the words *drótt* (the king's retainers) and *kveoa* (to recite), thus suggesting a poem recited before the king's retainers. Bragi Boddason is generally revered as the first skald, and his ninth-century poem "Ragnarrsdrápa" is the earliest extant poem in the *dróttkvætt* meter.

In this elaborate form, each stanza consists of eight lines, which are divided into two half-stanzas of four lines each. There is a syntactic break between the half-stanzas. The meter is syllabic: each line consists of six syllables, three stressed and three unstressed. The last two syllables are always a trochee (one long, stressed syllable followed a short, unstressed one). Every two lines are held together by alliteration, which binds them into parts. The alliterative sounds fall on the first stressed syllable of the second line. There are two alliterations in the first line as well. There is also internal rhyming. The even-numbered lines have full rhymes and the odd-numbered lines have half or assonant rhymes. The sentence structure is intricate — the *dróttkvætt* is notorious for its use of convoluted word order — and so is the system of kennings, metaphoric circumlocutions.

SEE ALSO *alliteration, circumlocution, kenning, skald.*

drum poetry Drum poetry — literally, poetry delivered through the drums — is an instrumental form of oral poetry. The instruments do not accompany a verbal text or communicate through a prearranged code. The drum actually transmits the words themselves. The talking drums imitate the precise sounds of the human voice. Drum poetry exists in tonal languages, and it is widespread in the tropical forests of Africa, where the sounds can carry telegraphically across long distances. It has been found in parts of the Far East and Oceania, in New Guinea and Indonesia. It has also been employed in Native American poetries.

Drum poetry is especially strong in Yoruba, a tonal language that has seven vowels. The syllables tend to consist of one consonant followed by a vowel or by a vowel itself. As Ulli Beier explains in the introduction to *Yoruba Poetry* (2002):

> It is this tonal quality of Yoruba and its vowel structure that enables the drummer to recite poetry. The Yoruba *dundun* drum is probably the most complex drum in the world. It cannot only reproduce all speech tones, but also the glides. Its wooden body is shaped like an hourglass and the two membranes at each end are connected with leather thongs. The drummer presses these to heighten the pitch of the drum, and the average musician can produce a range of an octave. Thus, the famous Yoruba talking drum does not operate on a code system, but is simply an accurate imitation of speech melody and rhythm.

Drum poetry includes panegyric poems, historical poems, hunters' songs, and dirges. The drummers also accompany chanted or sung poetry, and the talking drum often syncopates poetry across a dance rhythm.

SEE ALSO *hunting chants, oral poetry, oríkì, panegyric.*

dub poetry Dub poetry, which refers to adding or "dubbing" words over an instrumental rendering of a popular song, developed in the West Indies in the 1970s and spread to West Indian communities abroad, especially London, Toronto, and New York. It began with Jamaican disc jockeys who recited and sang their own words over the dub versions of reggae records. DJs like U-Roy borrowed something from scat, the vocal improvisations of jazz. Dee Jaying, also known as Toasting, is an improvised form of chat, but dub poetry developed into a type of performance poetry. The poems are prepared in advance and recited in public, often to the accompaniment of music. Dub poetry, the origin of rap, now refers to any poetry that incorporates reggae musical rhythms.

There is a precedent for dub poetry in the work of Kamau Brathwaite, who brought the indigenous rhythms of African and West Indian drumming as well as jazz into his poetry in the 1960s, when he often read in a Jamaican theater accompanied by Count Ossie on drums. The term was popularized by Oku Onuora for his own work as well as for the work of other Jamaican poets, such as Michael Smith ("Me a one writer first, me a one actor second, and me a one director third"), Noel Walcott, and Jean Breeze. Ras Michael Jueune picked up dub poetry in Guyana. In Trinidad, the performer Brother Resistance combined dub with rap and calypso to produce a new form he dubbed *rapso.* Some key performances: Linton Kwesi Johnson's *Dread Beat an' Blood* (1978), Oku Onuoro's *Reflection in Red* (1979), and Benjamin Zephaniah's *Rasta* (1983). There is a powerful stream of social activism in dub poetry.

SEE ALSO *hip hop poetry, jazz poetry, performance poetry, spoken word poetry.*

duende From the Spanish, *duen de casa,* "lord of the house." The *duende* has generally been considered in Spanish folklore an imp, a hobgoblin, a sly poltergeist-like trickster who meddles and stirs up trouble. The duende connects to Gypsy culture, since the Spanish Romany word *duquende* has virtually the same meaning. The spirit may have ridden the rails of Gypsies moving east. It may also have crossed the ocean with the Spaniards, because the duende haunts the rural households of many Latin American countries as a malign, unruly, and anarchic spirit.

In Andalusia, as Christopher Maurer points out, "the word duende is also applied to the ineffable, mysterious charm of certain gifted people, especially flamenco singers. The Andalusian says that a cantaor *has* duende." The singer who has duende is driven and possessed. Thus, while one flamenco glossary defines *duende* as "ghost, demon or spirit in folk music and dancing," another characterizes it as "deep, trance-like emotion," and a third calls it "the indefinable life force that illuminates flamenco performers and listeners." It is both a troublesome spirit and a passionate visitation. It seems to suggest both contact with the depths and access to our higher selves.

Federico García Lorca (1898–1936) uses the word *duende* in a special Andalusian sense as a term for the obscure power and penetrating inspiration of art. He describes it, quoting Goethe on Paganini, as "a mysterious power which everyone senses and no philosopher explains." For him, the concept of duende, which could never be entirely pinned down or rationalized, was associated with the spirit of earth, with visible anguish, irrational desire, demonic enthusiasm, and a fascination with death. It is an erotic form of dark inspiration. Lorca liked to repeat the legendary Gypsy singer Manuel Torre's statement, "All that has black sounds has duende." Duende becomes a metaphor for the demonic inspiration of art. "The duende does not come at all unless he sees that death is possible," Lorca says. Duende, then, means something like artistic inspiration in the presence of death. It has an element of mortal panic and fear, the power of wild abandonment. It speaks to an art that touches and transfigures death, both wooing and evading it. Every art, every country, is capable of duende. It is a power (not a work), a struggle (not a thought). It seems to come up from the earth, it suggests a radical change in forms, and it signals closeness to death.

Duende exists for readers and audiences as well as for writers and performers. Lorca states: "The magical property of a poem is to remain possessed by duende that can baptize in dark water all who look at it, for with duende it is easier to love and understand, and one can be sure of being loved and understood."

dulce et utile Latin: "sweet and useful." In his *Ars Poetica* (ca. 19–18 B.C.E.), the Roman poet Horace recommends that poetry should be sweet, which is to say that it should give enjoyment, and also useful, which is to say that it should provide instruction. Horace's idea of providing sweetness and light had a long critical life, and especially influenced Renaissance thinkers. In his *Apology for Poetry* (1583), Sir Philip Sidney suggests that poets "imitate both to delight and teach, and delight to move men to take that goodness in hand, which without delight they would fly as from a stranger."

SEE ALSO *ars poetica, didactic poetry, rhetoric.*

duma, dumy (pl) The *dumy,* Ukrainian epic songs, deal with the struggles of the Ukrainians against the Poles and Tartars in the late Middle Ages. They were first collected and written down in the nineteenth century. These epic songs, which reached their zenith between 1850 and 1930, have tremendous national power because they are seen as legitimizing the Ukraine both as a separate culture and as a seprate independent state. They were traditionally performed by itinerant Cossack bards called *kobzari.*

SEE ALSO *epic, kobzari.*

duplo The *duplo,* a poetic debate, a proto-drama in verse, was a popular folk form in the rural Philippines. This traditional Filipino matching of wits by *Makatas* (folk poets) was frequently played as a game at wakes, usually on the ninth night of a funeral vigil, to entertain the family of the dead and other mourners. The participants in the game role-played a court procedure investigating the loss of the king's ring or the king's favorite bird. The most advanced or master poet usually played the role of a *fiscal,* a kind of prosecutor. The other poets acted as the accused or as the lawyer for the accused. "In the *duplo,* the collective virtually acts as the chief protagonist," E. San Juan Jr. explains. "With the rite itself — for it was functionally a rite — the opponents, the *belyako* (male) and *belyaka* (female) performed, with the dead in the background, man's affirmation of life and the ceaseless pursuit of justice and truth."

SEE ALSO *balagtasan, poetic contest.*

dūta kāvya The Sanskrit *dūta kāvya* was a message poem with a lyrical feeling and a two-part narrative structure. The first part describes the journey of the messenger. The second part describes the delivery of the message. Kālidāsa's fifth-century masterpiece "The Cloud-Messenger," which is written in the magisterial meter of *mandakranta* (the "slow stepper"), tells the story of a *yaksha* ("divine attendant on Kubera, god of wealth") who is forcibly exiled for a year from his young bride. After months away from home, he asks a passing cloud to convey a message to his distant lover ("Cloud, you who are the refuge of the tormented, please take a message from me to my beloved"). The first section of the poem then vividly describes the route the cloud would take during the rainy season, what it might see and encounter from the Vindhyas to the Himalaya Mountains. The second section concentrates on the message and the reception of the beloved.

"The Cloud Messenger" gained popularity in Southern India around the fourteenth century and developed its own offshoot genre, the *sandesa kāvya,* which was generally a message in verse carried by a bird and addressed to a deity. It was typically a petition asking for a benediction on a king or some other important personage. The *sandesa* genre also became important to the poets of Sri Lanka in the fourteenth and fifteenth centuries. As H.B.M. Ilangasinha explains:

> The secular outlook of the *sandesas,* in contrast with the exclusively religious character of the earlier literary works, allowed more freedom of expression for the Sinhalese poets. Thus the poets began to describe contemporary life and what they saw around them, the

beauties of nature, the forms of worship, seats of learning, men of eminence, etc., to an extent never done before. These *sandesas* were intended as messages to various gods and distinguished personalities in the country and they differ in their subjects. They have considerable historical value, for their authors seem to have taken great pains to depict a faithful picture of the society of their time.

dyadic line A line of Hebrew verse that contains two parallel units or half-lines, which are called *versets,* as in 2 Samuel (22:29): "For you are my lamp, O Lord, / the LORD lights up my darkness." The dyadic line is the prevailing pattern in biblical poetry.

SEE ALSO *verset.*

dyfalu In Welsh poetry, *dyfalu* is the piling on of comparisons, definition through conceit. The word also means "to guess" in Welsh, and many poems of *dyfalu* have an element of guesswork, a fanciful and riddling dimension. "The art of *dyfalu,* meaning 'to describe' or 'to deride,' rests in the intricate development of a series of images and extended metaphors which either celebrate or castigate a person, animal, or object," the encyclopedia of *Celtic Culture* explains. Dafydd ap Gwilym's poems to the mist and the wind are classic fourteenth-century examples. *Dyfalu,* or something akin to it, has also influenced English-language poets steeped in Welsh poetry. For example, the sixth stanza of Henry Vaughan's poem "The Night" (1655) has been called "a perfect example of *dyfalu.*"

God's silent, searching flight;
When my Lord's head is filled with dew, and all
His locks are wet with the clear drops of night;
His still, soft call;
His knocking time; the soul's dumb watch,
When spirits their fair kindred catch.

SEE ALSO *cywydd.*

Dymock poets Between 1911 and 1914, a group of poets lived near the Gloucestershire village of Dymock in England. The poets included Robert

Frost (1874–1963), Edward Thomas (1878–1917), Lascelles Abercrombie (1881–1938), Rupert Brooke (1887–1915), Wilfrid Wilson Gibson (1878–1962), and John Drinkwater (1882–1937). The group—the only one to which Robert Frost ever willingly belonged—broke up because of World War I. Wilfrid Gibson captures a sense of what the gatherings were like in his nostalgic poem "The Golden Room" (1926). Much of the poetry of the Dymock poets was triggered by a genuine love of the English countryside, a feeling for the mysteries of nature. Frost and Thomas especially made a lasting bond there. Frost recognized the lyric element in Thomas's prose writings about nature and persuaded him to start writing poetry. Thomas, who also began writing under the stimulus of World War I, always delighted in what he called "this England." His friend Walter de la Mare remembered that "England's roads and heaths and woods, its secret haunts and solitudes, its houses, its people—themselves resembling its thorns and juniper—its very flints and dust, were his freedom and his peace." Like Thomas Hardy, Thomas loved the oldest English poetry, traditional ballads and folk songs, which come down to us, he said, "imploring a new lease of life on the sweet earth."

SEE ALSO *Georgian poets.*

dysphemism, see *euphemism.*

early modern period, see *Renaissance poetry.*

echo A recurrence of the same sound or combination of sounds. The repetitions of rhymes and near rhymes, the patterns of alliteration, of assonance and consonance, of refrains, are all varieties of echo, part of the sound chamber of lyric poetry. An echo can also be a means of allusion, a way of evoking an earlier text. Thus John Milton echoes the Hebrew Bible at the beginning of *Paradise Lost* (1667): "In the beginning how the heav'ns and earth / Rose out of chaos . . ." In *The Figure of Echo* (1984), John Hollander points out that the sonic origin of the term creates an association between a written echo and "a lurking and invisible vocal presence."

SEE ALSO *alliteration, assonance, consonance, echo verse, refrain, rhyme.*

echo verse An echo verse is a lyric in which lines conclude with (or are followed by) a word or phrase that echoes the preceding syllable, word, or phrase. The echo verse dates to the *Greek Anthology,* which spans the classical and Byzantine periods of Greek literature. Ovid tells the story in *Metamorphoses* (8 C.E.) of how the Nymph Echo, who keeps vainly repeating the words of Narcissus, dwindles down to a mere voice. This bodiless sense of missed connection also haunts the tradition of echo poems, which flourished in sixteenth- and seventeeth-century Italian, French, and English verse. Pastoral poetry especially employed the figure of echo when the shepherds, who serve as their own audience, delight in hearing their voices resounding through the natural world.

The echo can be used for light effects, as in Barnabe Barnes's "Sestine 4" from *Parthenophil and Parthenophe* (1593), which begins:

Eccho, what shall I do to my Nymphe, when I goe to behold her?
Eccho, hold her.

And it can create a sense of crossed dialogue, as in George Herbert's "Heaven," which commences:

O who will show me those delights on high?
Echo. I.
Thou Echo, thou art mortal, all men know.
Echo. No.

SEE ALSO *ovillejo, pastoral.*

eclogue The word *eclogue,* which derives from the Greek word *eklegein,* "to choose," originally suggested "a choice poem," the title given to choice collections of extracts from longer works. An eclogue is a short dialogue or soliloquy. The term defines the structure and not the content of this type of poem, though almost all eclogues turn out to be pastorals. The name was first applied to Virgil's *Bucolica,* which date from the mid-30s B.C.E., and later became known as the *Eclogues.* These formal pastoral poems extend a pattern, first established by Theocritus in his idylls (third century B.C.E.), in which urban poets turn to the rural countryside for sustenance.

In the Middle Ages and Renaissance, the term *eclogue* was often misconstrued as "goat song," falsely derived from *aix,* "goat," and *logos,* "speech." As a genre, the eclogue was revived by Dante (1265–1321), Petrarch (1304–1377), and Boccaccio (1313–1375), and flourished throughout the early modern era. One aspect of the eclogue is an often coded or allegorical dimension. In *The Art of English Poesie* (1589), George Puttenham recognized that the eclogue was devised

> not of purpose to counterfeit or represent the rustical manner of loves or communications, but under the veil of homely persons and

> in rude speeches, to insinuate and glance at great matters, and such as perchance had not been safe to have been disclosed of any other sort.

He thus contended that the eclogue makes it possible for writers to consider "great matters" that would otherwise be unacceptable for them to take on more directly. For example, in the course of his pastoral dialogues Virgil could also address political subjects, attitudes toward power, specifically toward the house of Julius Caesar and Octavian (Augustus).

Some of the English poems that explicitly descend from Virgil's *Eclogues:* Edmund Spenser's *The Shepheardes Calender* (1579), Philip Sidney's double sestina "Ye Goatherd Gods" (1593), Christopher Marlowe's "The Passionate Shepherd to His Love" (1599, 1600), Andrew Marvell's "Mower" poems (1681), John Milton's "Lycidas" (1638), Alexander Pope's "Pastorals" (1709), book 8 of William Wordsworth's *The Prelude* (1805, 1850), Percy Shelley's "Adonais" (1821), and Matthew Arnold's "Thyrsis" (1866). Robert Frost's "Build Soil—A Political Pastoral" (1936) illustrates the artistic difficulty of reviving the eclogue in modern poetry. Jonathan Swift probably wrote the greatest nonpastoral eclogue in *A Town Eclogue. 1710. Scene, The Royal Exchange* (1710).

SEE ALSO *georgic, nature poetry, pastoral.*

edda The *edda* encompasses two collections of Old Norse literature and stands as the fountainhead of Germanic mythology. The Icelandic poet and historian Snorri Sturluson (1179–1241) put together a mythographic treatise, largely a handbook of poetics or book of instruction for skalds, which he termed an *edda,* a word that in fourteenth-century Icelandic came to mean "poetics," seemingly derived from the word for poetry, *odr.* The nineteenth-century philologist Jacob Grimm later defined the word *edda* somewhat nostalgically as "great-grandmother" based on its usage in one poem, the *Rígsthula* (*The Song of Ríg,* fourteenth century). He skewed the edda into the folkloristic "Tales of a Grandmother." The Icelandic scholar Eirikr Magnusson came up with the now widely accepted determination that *edda* derives from the proper name "Oddi," a settlement in southwest Iceland, the home of Snorri Sturluson and Saemund the Wise (1056–1133). Snorri's treatise was thus conventionally named *The Book of Oddi.*

Snorri's *Edda,* written in the thirteenth century, is now generally referred to as the *Younger Edda* or the *Prose Edda.* It consists of a prologue and three distinct books. The *Gylfaginning* ("the tricking of Guilfi") tells the story of how Guilfi, the king "of the land men now call Sweden," travels to find out about the origin and destruction of the world of the Nordic gods. This survey of Old Norse mythology is written in prose, but contains lines and stanzas from skaldic poetry. The next section *Skáldskaparmál* ("poetic diction" or "the language of poetry") presents a systematic list of specifically poetic words, kennings for various people, places, and things, and explains them by retelling many of the old mythological stories. The last section *Háttatal* ("list of verse-forms") is Snorri's *ars poetica,* a poem consisting of 102 stanzas in 100 different meters. It systematizes the material with a practical commentary in prose.

In 1643, Brynjolfur Sveinsson discovered a manuscript of twenty-nine poems (ca. 1270), both partial and complete, which contained lines and stanzas referenced in Snorri's *Edda.* The collection, now referred to as the *Codex Regius,* was attributed to Saemund the Wise, Snorri's predecessor and compatriot, and thus was referred to as *Saemund's Edda.* It is now generally called the *Elder Edda,* or the *Poetic Edda.* The linguistic and literary evidence shows that these poems were orally transmitted sometime between 900 and 1100 and were written down only in the thirteenth century. They were circulated in many different regions (Denmark, Germany, Iceland, Norway) and composed by many different hands.

The *Poetic Edda* and a similar group of poetry fragments from other manuscripts, the *Eddica minora,* suggest that the language of Eddaic poetry is simpler, more direct, and less adorned than the later Old Icelandic poetry and prose of the skalds. The *Poetic Edda* work has fevered the imagination of such English-language poets as Thomas Gray (1716–1771), William Morris (1834–1896), and W. H. Auden (1907–1973).

SEE ALSO *alliteration, ars poetica, kenning, lai, saga, skald.*

Edwardian Age The Edwardian Age covers the reign of King Edward VII (1901–1910). This brief epoch is usually extended to the beginning of World War I. It marks a pre-war transition from the Victorian era to the modern world. W. B. Yeats (1865–1939) and Thomas Hardy (1840–1928) are the major poets of an era that can also be represented, perhaps more characteristically, by A. E. Housman (1859–1936) and Rudyard Kipling (1865–1936),

John Masefield (1878–1967), G. K. Chesterton (1874–1936), Alfred Noyes (1880–1958), Robert Bridges (1844–1930), Laurence Binyon (1869–1943), and Walter de la Mare (1873–1956). These popular poets tended to be learned traditionalists, mildly conscious of the modern spirit, but primarily dedicated to the ideal of Beauty. Kenneth Millard argues that they were preoccupied with the changing and perhaps fading value of the idea of England. Their conservative formalist bent, their distrust of the overreaching creative imagination, makes them forerunners to the Movement poets, such as Philip Larkin and Kingsley Amis, who were also obsessed with England's declining place in the world.

SEE ALSO *fin de siècle, Georgian poets, modernism, the Movement, Victorian period.*

ego-futurism, see *futurism.*

egotistical sublime John Keats (1795–1821) coined this somewhat derogatory term in reference to William Wordsworth (1771–1850). It refers to the way the poet projects his inner self onto the outer world. Keats believed in the egoless or "self-annuling character" of the poet and defined his notion of negative capability ("A Poet is the most unpoetical of any thing in existence; because he has no identity") as an alternative to the poetic imagination that retains its identity and projects itself onto everything, including the landscape. One kind of genius has no self; another is always itself. Thus, he wrote to Richard Woodhouse: "As to the poetical Character itself, (I mean that sort of which, if I am any thing, I am a Member; that sort distinguished from the wordsworthian or egotistical sublime; which is a thing per se and stands alone) it is not itself—it has no self—it is everything and nothing—It has no character . . ."

SEE ALSO *negative capability, the sublime.*

eisteddfod Welsh: "session." The first recorded *eisteddfod,* a Welsh festival of poetry and music, was held under the auspices of the Lord Rhys at his castle in Cardigan in 1176. He invited poets and musicians from all over the country to gather for a set of competitions. In the Middle Ages, the bardic order or guild used the *eisteddfod* to examine and license performers. At the Carmathen Eisteddfod of 1450, for example, the bards were required to show their skill in a combination of twenty-four elaborate metrical forms. The professional bardic order had died out by the 1690s. The *eisteddfod* was subsequently revived in the eighteenth century using amateur competitors. In 1858, the *eisteddfod* of Llangolden turned the gathering into a national festival. Today, the annual National Eisteddfod of Wales is the largest festival of competitive poetry and music in Europe.

SEE ALSO *bard, cynghanedd, poetic contest, strict-meter poetry.*

eisthesis A rarely used word for the indentation of a line or lines by one or more spaces from the left margin. The indentation is a way of setting off a line, or creating partner lines, thus establishing linkages and connections.

SEE ALSO *ekthesis, line.*

ekphrasis, ekphrastic (also ecphrasis, ecphrastic) *The Oxford Classical Dictionary* defines *ekphrasis* as "the rhetorical description of a work of art." The prototype of all ekphrastic poetry is Homer's description of the shield that Hephaestus is making for Achilles in the *Iliad* (ca. eighth century B.C.E.). This description, which takes up 130 lines of Greek verse, is a "notional ekphrasis," the representation of an imaginary work of art.

There is something transgressive in writing about the visual arts, in approaching the painter, the sculptor, or the photographer's work in words. A border is crossed, a boundary breached, as the writer enters into the spatial realm, traducing an abyss, violating the silent integrity of the pictorial. Writing about Camille Corot, Paul Valéry warned: "We should apologize that we dare to speak about painting." Yet Valéry also acknowledged, "There are important reasons for not keeping silent [since] all the arts live by words. Each work of art demands its response." Works of art imitate and provoke other works of art; the process is a source of art itself. There is an intricate history of reciprocity and sibling rivalry between "the sister arts," poetry and painting. John Hollander describes ekphrastic poetry as "poems addressed to silent works of art, questioning them, describing them as they could never describe—but merely present—themselves; speaking for them; making them speak out or speak up."

The long occidental tradition of ekphrasis includes the Greek, Latin, and Byzantine anthologists. Homer's description of the shield of Achilles leads directly to Virgil's account of Aeneas's shield in the *Aeneid* (29–19 B.C.E.) and Dante's description of the sculptures on the terrace of the proud in the

Purgatorio (1308–1312). The tradition extends in a more or less unbroken line from the rhapsodists of late antiquity to Keats and Shelley, Baudelaire and Gautier, Rilke and Yeats; it extends from Horace (whose famous phrase *ut picture poesis* — "as in painting, so in poetry" — has had a controversial history of its own) to W. H. Auden and John Ashbery, Marianne Moore, William Carlos Williams and e. e. cummings, Randall Jarrell and Elizabeth Bishop, Joseph Brodsky, Anthony Hecht, and Howard Nemerov. Ekphrastic modes inevitably address — and sometimes challenge — the great divide between spatial and temporal experience, eye and ear, visual and verbal mediums. They teach us to look and look again more closely. They dramatize with great intensity the actual experience of encounter.

SEE ALSO *ut pictura poesis.*

ekthesis A rarely used word for the setting of line or lines at the left margin. The use of the justified left margin emphasizes the poem as a continuous sequence of lines and distinguishes it from prose.

SEE ALSO *eisthesis, line.*

elegiac distich, see *elegy.*

elegiac stanza, see *heroic quatrain.*

elegy A poem of mortal loss and consolation. The word *elegy* derives from the Greek *élegos,* "funeral lament." It was among the first forms of the ancients, though in Greek literature it refers to a specific verse form as well as the emotions conveyed by it. Any poem using the particular meter of the elegiac couplet or elegiac distich was termed an elegy. It was composed of a heroic or dactylic hexameter followed by a pentameter. Here are two lines from Longfellow's "Elegiac Verse" (1882):

> So the Hexameter, rising and singing, with cadence sonorous,
> Falls; and in refluent rhythms back the Pentameter flows.

There were elegies, chanted aloud and traditionally accompanied by the flute, on love (amatory complaints) and war (exhortatory martial epigrams) as well as death. But, as Peter Sacks puts it, "behind this array of topics there may have lain an earlier, more exclusive association of the flute song's elegiacs with the expression of grief."

Since the sixteenth century, the elegy has designated a poem mourning the death of an individual (as in W. B. Yeats's "In Memory of Major Robert Gregory," 1918) or a solemn meditation on the passing of human life (as in Thomas Gray's "Elegy Written in a Country Churchyard," 1751). The elegy does what Freud calls "the work of mourning." It ritualizes grief into language and thereby makes it more bearable. The great elegy touches the unfathomable and originates in the unspeakable, in unacceptable loss. It allows us to experience mortality. It turns loss into remembrance and delivers an inheritance. It opens a space for retrospection and drives a wordless anguish toward the consolations of verbal articulation and ceremony.

The sense of overwhelming loss that powers the poetry of lamentation exists in all languages and poetries. It has roots in religious feeling and ritual. The process, the action of mourning, of doing something to pass on the dead, thus clearing a space between the dead and the living, has residual force in the ceremonial structure of the elegy. Classical antiquity had several literary vehicles for the formal expression of deep sorrow. The dirge was a song of lament deriving from the Greek *epicedium,* a mourning song sung over the body of the dead. The threnody was a Greek "wailing song" sung in memory of the dead. Originally a choral ode, it evolved into the monody (Greek: "alone song"), an ode sung by a single actor in a Greek tragedy or a poem mourning someone's death. Milton described "Lycidas" (1638), a poem inspired by the death of Edward King, as a monody; Matthew Arnold also termed "Thyrsis" (1866), a lament for Arthur Clough, a monody.

These two poems, along with Spenser's "Astrophel" (1586), a lament for Sidney, and Shelley's "Adonais" (1821), a lament for Keats, belong to a subspecies of the tradition called the pastoral elegy. The laments of three Sicilian poets writing in Greek—Theocritus (third century B.C.E.), Moschus (second century B.C.E.), and Bion (second century B.C.E.)—inspired the pastoral conventions of the later English elegy. These highly elaborated conventions (the invocation to the muse, the representation of nature in the lament, the procession of mourners, and so forth) become the formal channel of mourning. "The elegy follows the ancient rites in the basic passage from grief or darkness to consolation and renewal," Sacks writes. The pastoral conventions are dropped in a poem such as Tennyson's *In Memoriam* (1849), his heartbroken book on the death of Arthur Hallam, but the ritualistic feeling remains. There is a sense of lineage and inheritance in Swinburne's hieratic Baudelairean elegy for Baudelaire, "Ave atque Vale" ("a mourning musical of many mourners," 1868), and Hardy's Swinburnean elegy for Swinburne, "A Singer Asleep" (1910). The dignified formality opens out into elegies commemorating a public figure, such as Whitman's poem for Abraham Lincoln, "When Lilacs Last in the Dooryard Bloom'd" (1865) and W. H. Auden's "In Memory of Sigmund Freud" (1939). It empowers the elegy for a friend who is also a public figure, such as García Lorca's "Lament for Ignacio Sánchez Mejías" (1935).

Coleridge was thinking of the elegy as a de-particularized form, a poem with a certain meditative mood or style, when he described it as "the form of poetry natural to the reflective mind." The definition of the elegy as a serious reflection on a serious subject applies to the so-called Anglo-Saxon elegies, some of the earliest poems in the English tradition, such as "The Wanderer" (tenth century) and "The Seafarer" (tenth century), which are poems of great personal deprivation shading off into meditations on mutability and petitions for divine guidance and consolation. This sense of the elegy carries forward through Thomas Nashe's "A Litany in Time of Plague" (1600), Samuel Johnson's "The Vanity of Human Wishes" (1749), Gray's "Elegy Written in a Country Churchyard" (1751), Edward Young's *Night Thoughts* (1742–1746), and Rilke's *Duino Elegies* (1923).

The sense of a highly self-conscious dramatic performance, of a necessary and sometimes reluctant reentry into language, continues to power the elegy in our century, but the traditional consolations and comforts of the elegy have often been called into question. For example, Thomas Hardy radicalizes the genre by speaking from a position of uncompromising isolation in emotionally unsheltered elegies for his dead wife, *Poems of 1912–13*. Think, too, of Wilfred Owen's ironically titled "Dulce et Decorum Est" (1917) and his poems "Greater Love" (1917) and "Anthem for Doomed Youth" ("What passing-bells for those who die as cattle?," 1917), of Isaac Rosenberg's "Dead Man's Dump" (1917) and Edward Thomas's "Tears" ("It seems I have no tears left," 1915), of Edith Sitwell's "Dirge for the New Sunrise" (1945) and Dylan Thomas's "A Refusal to Mourn the Death, by Fire, of a Child in London" (1945).

The American elegist in particular seems to suffer from what Emily Dickinson calls a "polar privacy," a dark sense of isolation, of displacement from the traditional settings of grief and the consolations of community. This is accompanied by a more naked experience of grief. A saving and even ceremonial formality still comes to the aid of Allen Tate's "Ode to the Confederate Dead" (1928), James Merrill's *The Changing Light at Sandover* (1976–1982), Amy Clampitt's "A Procession at Candlemas" (1981), Charles Wright's *The Southern Cross* (1981), Richard Howard's deeply aggrieved elegies for dead friends. How many dead paternities stalk like ghosts through the precincts of American poetry! One thinks of Dickinson ("Burgler! Banker — Father!") and Plath ("Daddy, daddy, you bastard, I'm through"), of Robert Lowell (*Life Studies*, 1959), Philip Levine (*1933*, 1974), and Sharon Olds (*The Father*, 1992), of mournful poems to the father by James Agee, John Berryman, Stanley Kunitz, Stanley Plumly, William Matthews, Garrett Hongo, Li-Young Lee, Alberto Rios. I have been moved over the years by William Meredith's memorial poems to his beloved friends in poetry, by Robert Hayden's "Elegies for Paradise Valley" (1978), by L. E. Sissman's self-elegies (*Hello, Darkness*, 1978), by Mark Doty's elegies for a lover dying of AIDS (*My Alexandria*, 1993), by Larry Levis's posthumous collection, *Elegy* (1977). These poems continue to ask, as W. H. Auden writes in his elegy "At the Grave of Henry James" (1941), "What living occasion can / Be just to the absent?"

SEE ALSO *dirge, keening, lament, marsiya.*

elision From the Latin, "striking out." *Elision* is a metrical term for the blurring or omission of an unstressed vowel or syllable to preserve the regular meter of a line of verse. This line from Shakespeare's Sonnet 129 provides an example: "Th' expense of spirit in a waste of shame." So, too, Robert Burns deliberately substitutes "o'er" for "over" in "Tam O'Shanter" (1791): "Whiles holding fast his guid blue bonnet, / Whiles crooning o'er an auld Scots sonnet . . ."

Elizabethan Age Queen Elizabeth's reign (1558–1603) was the high-water mark of the English Renaissance, the age of the great dramatists Christopher Marlowe (1564–1593), Ben Jonson (1572–1637), and William Shakespeare (1564–1616). The first public theater was established in London in 1576 and the Globe was built in 1599. Marlowe also gave a daring new erotic voice to the English lyric, Jonson defined and mastered the plain style, and Shakespeare famously developed the English sonnet, whose enduring subjects are love and time. It was an era of romantic exuberance and distinguished courtly poetry, such as Edmund Spenser's *Shepheardes Calender* (1579) and *The Faerie Queene* (1590–1596) as well as Philip Sidney's sonnet sequence *Astrophel and Stella* (1591), which brings the weight of the Petrarchan tradition into English. The poets were influenced by Italian forms and genres and created a vogue for the sonnet, the classical pastoral, the allegorical epic. Elizabethan poets, many anonymous, notably wrote songs — Thomas Campion (1567–1620), Thomas Nashe (1567–1601) — which were collected in miscellanies and songbooks, such as Richard Tottel's *Songes and Sonettess* (1557), generally called *Tottel's Miscellany*, the first printed anthology of English poetry.

SEE ALSO *allegory, epic, pastoral, Petrarchism, the plain style, Renaissance poetry, sonnet.*

ellipsis From the Greek: "leaving out." An ellipsis is a form of compression, the intentional omission or non-expression of something understood, an expected word or phrase in a sentence. It is secondly a sudden leap from one topic to another. Ellipsis goes back as far as the ancient Greek and Hebrew poets (there are ellipses in Homer, in the Hebrew Bible), but it was an especially favored device of the modernists, such as T. S. Eliot, who made it one of the disjunctive strategies of "The Waste Land" (1922).

The ellipsis is also a three-point punctuation mark (. . . or * * *) used in writing and printing to indicate an intentional omission or pause.

SEE ALSO *collage, elliptical poetry, modernism.*

elliptical poetry In *The Idiom of Poetry* (1946), Frederick Pottle used the term *elliptical* for a kind of pure poetry that omits prosaic information. He recognized ellipticism in various historical works, but contended that "the modern poet goes much farther in employing private experiences or ideas than would formerly have been thought legitimate." To the common reader, he says, "the prime characteristic of this kind of poetry is not the nature of its imagery but its obscurity, its urgent suggestion that you add something to the poem without telling what that something is." He names that something "the prose frame." Robert Penn Warren used the term "elliptical" in his essay "Pure and Impure Poetry" (1943) to summarize T. S. Eliot's notion that some poets "become impatient of this meaning [explicit statement of ideas in logical order] which seems superfluous, and perceive possibilities of intensity through its elimination."

Stephen Burt redeployed the term *elliptical poetry* to characterize a kind of oblique, gnomic poetry. He calls elliptical poets "post-avant-gardist, or post-'postmodern.' " Emily Dickinson and Marina Tsvetaeva could be considered two great precursors to the elliptical mode, since they charged their sometimes secretive and oblique poems with maximum intensity and meaning.

SEE ALSO *ellipsis, pure poetry.*

emblem An image accompanied by a motto and a brief verse. The emblem, which was intended as a moral lesson, was a pictorial representation of an idea. The *Oxford English Dictionary* defines it as a verbal form, a "fable or allegory that might be constructed pictorially," or an image, "a drawing or picture expressing a moral fable or allegory." It is both an image and a text. There is a riddling or hieroglyphic element to the emblem, which is also related to the epigram. The dialogue or tension between the picture and the words creates a space for the audience to interpret the meaning.

The emblem emerged as a distinct literary form in the sixteenth century. It was a major Renaissance type. It is also known in vernacular as *device,* or *impresa* in Italian, *empresa* in Spanish. The first European emblem book was Andrea Alciati's *Emblematum liber* (1531), which inspired several episodes in Spenser's *The Faerie Queene* (1590–1596); the first English emblem book was George Whitney's *A Choice of Emblemes* (1586); the most well-known Protestant emblem book was Francis Quarles's *Emblemes* (1635). Quarles called the emblem a "silent parable." Henri Esteinne described it as "A sweet and morall Symbole, which consists of pictures and words" (1646). Both as a form in and of itself and as a fund of imagery, the emblem influenced not only Spenser and Shakespeare, but also Ben Jonson, Richard Crashaw, John Donne, and George Herbert, whose pattern poems, such as "The Altar" (1633), have a strong emblematic quality. William Blake's illuminated books evoke the tradition of emblem books. Robert Louis Stevenson playfully revived the form in *Moral Lessons* (1881). The emblem book slows down the pace of reading and invites associations between the image and the word.

SEE ALSO *epigram, pattern poetry.*

empathy and ***sympathy*** Empathy is the projection of ourselves into the lives of others, the identification of the self with animate or inanimate objects. Sympathy is a feeling for the thoughts and feelings of others, which may also involve fellow feeling with animals. The *International Encyclopedia of the Social Sciences,* 2nd ed. (2008) suggests that empathy involves imagining the thoughts and feelings of other people from their own perspectives; sympathy involves imagining them as if those thoughts and feelings were our own.

The word *empathy* derives from the Greek *empatheia,* meaning "physical affection, partiality." It comes into English from the German *Einfühlung.* The word *sympathy* derives from the Latin *sympatha,* meaning "feeling with." Empathy unites us with other beings, sympathy connects us to them. Walt Whitman enacts a feeling of empathy when he writes in "Song of Myself" (1855):

> I do not ask the wounded person how he feels, I myself become the
> wounded person,
> My hurt turns livid upon me as I lean on a cane and observe.

Whitman also put sympathy at the center of his national aesthetic, arguing that Americans were distinguished from other nationalities by "their self-esteem and wonderful sympathy." He recognizes the necessity of sympathy when he writes in "Song of Myself":

> I am he attesting sympathy,
> (Shall I make my list of things in the house and skip the house that
> supports them?)

He also declares: "And whoever walks a furlong without sympathy walks to his own funeral drest in his shroud."

encomium, encomia (pl) Originally "revel songs," then "songs of praise." A formal expression of praise, the *encomium* was a Greek choral song in celebration of a hero. It was sung at a joyous procession, the *komos* — the Latin word *encomium* derives from a Greek word meaning "in revel" — that praised the victor of athletic matches. Pindar (ca. 522–443 B.C.E.) and Simonides (ca. 556–468 B.C.E.) wrote the great early encomia. Aristotle (384–322 B.C.E.) remembered the encomium as part of all early poetry, but considered it a subdivision of declamatory oratory. He also argued that praise is one of the two essential forms of poetry (the other is blame). Later, the term *encomium* came to suggest any laudatory composition in poetry or prose.

SEE ALSO *epideictic poetry, praise poems.*

endecha The Spanish *endecha* is a dirge or lament. It uses quatrains of six- or seven-syllable lines with assonant rhyme (*asonancia:* the vowels following the vowel that carries the accent rhyme) in the even-numbered lines. Francisco Salinias describes in *De musica libri septem* (1577) how the *endecha* was used throughout the Iberian Peninsula as a song or poem of lamentation for the dead. Sor Juana Inés de la Cruz (1651–1695) made it a particular specialty and introduced a range of metrical variations. The *endecha real* or "royal lament" employs a series of quatrains (three seven-syllable lines with one eleven-syllable line), which utilize assonant rhyme in the second and fourth lines. It is sometimes called a *romancillo,* as in Lope de Vega's "Pobre barquilla mia" ("Poor little boat of mine").

SEE ALSO *dirge, elegy, lament.*

end rhyme, see *rhyme.*

end-stopped line A poetic line in which a natural grammatical pause, such as the end of a phrase, clause, or sentence, coincides with the end of a line. An end-stopped line, the alternative to an enjambed or run-on line, halts the movement of the verse and creates the sensation of a whole syntactical unit, which gives the line an additional rhetorical weight and authority, a meaning unto itself. It imparts a feeling of completeness, though that feeling is temporary, since the poem then proceeds on until its end. It gains additional force by its relationship to the whole. The halting effect is increased when each end-stopped line concludes with an emphatic punctuation mark, as in the first eight lines of Gerard Manley Hopkins's ecstatic sonnet, "The Starlit Night" (1877):

> Look at the stars! look, look up at the skies!
>   O look at all the fire-folk sitting in the air!
>   The bright boroughs, the circle-citadels there!
> Down in dim woods the diamond delves! the elves'-eyes!
> The grey lawns cold where gold, where quickgold lies!
>   Wind-beat whitebeam! airey abeles set on a flare!
>   Flake-doves sent floating forth at a farmyard scare!
> Ah well! it is all a purchase, all is a prize.

SEE ALSO *enjambment, line.*

englyn In Welsh poetry, the *englyn* is a strictly regulated rhyming verse form with four lines and thirty syllables. It employs the patterns of stress, alliteration, and rhyme that are called *cynghanedd.* There are eight different measures or kinds of *englynion* among the twenty-four traditional Welsh strict-meters. Two of the early meters, used for gnomic, saga, and nature poetry, have only three lines. Gwen Jones explains: "The *englyn* can be used magnificently for every poetic purpose comprised within a loose definition of epigram: amatory, satiric, elegiac, exhoratory, descriptive, reflective, religious, cautionary, and comic." The four-line *englyn* has remained popular with folk poets from the eighteenth century to the present day. D. R. Johnson explains that there is a strong nationalistic dimension to the modern usage of *englyn,* "since the composition of an englyn . . . can be seen as an act of defiance against the dominant Anglo-American culture which threatens to smother the Welsh language."

SEE ALSO *awdl, cynghanedd, epigram, strict-meter poetry.*

enjambment Enjambment (or what the French call *emjambement*) is the carryover of one line of poetry to the next without a grammatical break. A runover or enjambed line is the alternative to an end-stopped line. Enjambment creates a dialectical motion of hesitation and flow. The lineation bids the reader to pause at the end of each line even as the syntax pulls the reader forward. This creates a sensation of hovering expectation. In 1668, John Milton called enjambment "the sense variously drawn out from one verse into another." Enjambment breaks the sense of the line as a final terminus.

Here is a stanza from William Carlos Williams's "To a Poor Old Woman" (1935) in which he breaks down a sentence three times in order to present an old woman sensuously eating plums. The first and fourth lines are end-stopped, the middle lines enjambed:

> They taste good to her.
> They taste good
> to her. They taste
> good to her

Each line break emphasizes something different (that the plums taste good to *her;* that they taste *good;* that they *taste*) and the lineation is a signpost to the meaning.

Nicholson Baker describes enjambment in his novel *The Anthologist* (2009):

> [E]njambment is a word that means that you're wending your way along a line of poetry, and you're walking right out to the very end of the line, way out, and it's all going fine, and you're expecting the syntax to give you a polite tap on the shoulder to wait for a moment. Just a second, sir, or madam, while we rhyme, or come to the end of our phrasal unit, or whatever. While we rest. But instead the syntax pokes at you and says hustle it, pumpkin, keep walking, don't rest. So naturally, because you're stepping out onto nothingness, you fall. You tumble forward, gaaaah, and you end up all discombobulated at the beginning of the next line, with a banana peel on your head and some coffee grounds in your shirt pocket. In other words, you're "jammed" into the next line — that's what enjambment is.

SEE ALSO *end-stopped line, line.*

Enlightenment A European literary and philosophical movement that lasted from around 1660 to 1770. It is generally called the age of reason in England and the *Zeitalter der Aufklärung* in Germany. The French called the men of the Enlightenment *philosophes.* Some of the key eighteenth-century philosophes or philosophers per se are Voltaire (1694–1778), Denis Diderot (1713–1784), Gotthold Ephraim Lessing (1729–1781), Moses Mendelssohn (1729–1786), Jean-Jacques Rousseau (1712–1778), David Hume (1711–1776), and Immanuel Kant (1724–1804), who defined the Enlightenment as "man's emergence from his self-imposed tutelage" and suggested its motto, "*Sapere aude!* — Dare to know!" ("What Is Enlightenment?," 1784). These writers had a firm faith in the power of reason and a strong devotion to clear thought. In *A History of English Literature* (1987), Alastair Fowler states categorically that what characterizes the Enlightenment "everywhere was a commitment to clarity." The Enlightenment thinkers were aggressively secular and assailed Christianity for its hostility to reason, which meant for them reasonableness, a commitment to scientific method, a trust in facts

(Voltaire's motto was "Droit au fait — Let facts prevail"). They believed in progress. Two monumental and universalizing intellectual feats of the era are Diderot's *Encyclopédie* (1751–1772) and Samuel Johnson's *Dictionary of the English Language* (1755).

The poetry of the Enlightenment also extols rational reflection, thus the predilection for didactic poetry, moral verse, teaching through satire. Alexander Pope invented the "verse essay" for his long poems that proceed through well-balanced heroic couplets, "An Essay on Criticism" (1711) and "An Essay on Man" (1733–1734). His utterances have a feeling of epigrammatic clarity, polished finality, such as

> True ease in writing comes from art, not chance,
> As those move easiest who have learned to dance.

Pope's work promotes propriety and order, the virtues of learning and reason. Jonathan Swift used his savage wit as a weapon against the mean-spirited and arrogant modern world, which he believed had fallen far from ancient ideals. As he put it in "To Mr. Congreve" (1693), he placed his faith in

> My hate, whose lash just Heaven has long decreed
> Shall on a day make sin and folly bleed.

Swift was a representative Enlightenment figure — a misanthrope who used his furious indignation to serve human liberty.

SEE ALSO *didactic poetry, satire, Sturm und Drang, universality, verse essay.*

ennui A feeling of extreme tedium, utter weariness, reflective boredom. The term seems to stem from the Latin *odium* or *odio,* probably from the expression "esse in odio" (to be an object of hate). The notion of ennui originated in the ancient Greek concept of *acedia,* a kind of spiritual listlessness or torpor, which was stigmatized by the monks in the Middle Ages as "a state of restlessness and inability either to work or to pray" (*The Concise Oxford Dictionary of the Christian Church,* revised ed., 2006). Reinhard Kuhn points out that ever since the Middle Ages the word has had two very different meanings:

> On the one hand, it designated something, often of a petty nature, that proved vexatious and irritating. It is in this sense that the Provençal troubadours of the twelfth and thirteenth centuries used it for their "enuegs," poems that complain of the annoyances of life. . . . On the other hand, in the twelfth-century *Eneas* the word "ennui" is used to designate a profound sorrow; in this stronger sense it recurs throughout French medieval epics and romances.

Ennui is connected to melancholia, which became a fashionable disease of inwardness during the Renaissance. Charles Baudelaire (1821–1867) famously suffered from ennui or spleen, which he considered "a delicate monster" that would someday swallow the world in a yawn. Ennui was for him a true form of acedia, the struggle toward spiritual life, a sense of implacable mental torpor. It is woe without a particular source, which can make it seem nameless. Sylvia Plath characterized it as "doom's blank door" ("Ennui," 1948), Conrad Aiken as "a blest misery" ("Psychomachia," 1924). The pride of ennui comes in its determined isolation, its refusal to connect to others. It can also serve as a spur, an inspiration, to poetry. Paul Valéry writes in his poem "Chanson à part" (1938):

> What do you know? Ennui.
>
> What do you know? Dreams
> To transform ennui.

ensalada Spanish: "salad." *Ensaladas* are poems that combine lines from different poems, or intermingle diverse meters, often in different languages, usually for comic effect. These saladlike lyrics were commonly sung in sixteenth-century Spain.

envelope A pattern of repetition, the envelope is a line or stanza that encloses the rest of the poem. It recurs in the same form or with a slight variation. The structural pattern of recurrence gives the line or stanza deeper resonance, additional power, by being brought back propitiously at the end of the poem. This strategy was one of the favorites of the Biblical poets. For example, Psalm 8 begins and ends with the same line, "O Lord our Lord, how excellent is thy name in all the earth!" Robert Alter explains that "the repetition of this vertically ordered poetic review of cosmic hierarchy is felt as a climactic completion, a symmetric framing-in by praise of the panorama of creation."

It is called an envelope rhyme when a pair of outer rhymes encloses a pair of inner ones, as in Tennyson's *In Memoriam* (1849) stanza (*abba*).

SEE ALSO *In Memoriam stanza, refrain, repetition, rhyme.*

environmental poetry, see *nature poetry.*

envoi, envoy A "send-off." The half-stanza that concludes certain French forms, such as the *ballade* and the *sestina.* The troubadours called their envoys *tornados* (returns). The envoy is a final return to the subject, a valedictory summing up, and a clever send-off.

SEE ALSO *sestina, troubadour.*

epanalepsis, see *anaphora.*

ephymnion, see *proode.*

epic A long narrative poem, exalted in style, heroic in theme. The earliest epics all focus on the legendary adventures of a hero against the backdrop of a historical event: think of the Trojan War and Odysseus's action-packed journey home in the eighth century B.C.E.; Homeric epics the *Iliad* and the *Odyssey,* the models for epic poetry ever since; or the territorial battles of a warrior culture in the Anglo-Saxon epic *Beowulf,* dated between the eighth and eleventh centuries; or the preservation of a city and a civilization in the Babylonian *Gilgamesh* (ca. 1600–1000 B.C.E.). These epics seem to be the written versions of texts long sung and retold, composed and recomposed by many epic singers over time, all telling the tale of a tribe. The first audiences for the epics were listeners, the later ones readers. Aristotle (384–322 B.C.E.) considered the Homeric epic the prototype of tragedy. The epic carried important cultural truths but, as M. I. Finley puts it, "Whatever else the epic may have been, it was *not history.* It was narrative, detailed and precise, with minute description of fighting and sailing, and feasting and burials and sacrifices, all very real and vivid; it may even contain, buried away, some kernels of historical fact — but it was not history." The epic is inherently nostalgic. It looks back to greater and more heroic times — the emergence of tribes, the founding of countries, the deeds of legendary figures. It is removed from the contemporary world of the audience and looks back to what Goethe and Schiller called the *vollkommen vergangen* or "perfect past." It moves beyond individual experience. It binds people to their own outsize communal past and instills a sense of grandeur.

The epic singer of tales brings together a powerful memory and strong improvisatory technique, using formulaic phrases, lines, and half-lines; propulsive rhythms; stock descriptions; recurrent scenes and incidents, to build a tale with encyclopedic range and cyclical action. The epic is purposefully recited in segments. In the epic, Bakhtin writes, "It is, therefore, possible to take any part and offer it as the whole . . . the structure of the whole is repeated in each part, and each part is complete and circular like the whole." The epic poets who worked at the same time as Homer are sometimes called the Cyclic poets because they covered the entire war cycle. "The cyclical form of the classical epic is based on the natural cycle," Northrop Frye explains. "The cycle has two main rhythms: the life and death of the individual, and the slower social rhythm which, in the course of years . . . brings cities and empires to their rise and fall."

Some examples: the great Sanskrit epics of ancient India are the *Mahābhārata* (ninth to eighth century B.C.E.) and the *Rāmāyana* (fifth to fourth century B.C.E.); the major epic poem in Persian is the Iranian epic *Shāhnāma* (ca. 977–1010). The epics of Mesopotamia survived in tales written in Sumerian and Akkadian. The *Nibelungenlied* (ca. 1180–1210) is the great epic of Middle High German. *La Chanson de Roland* (*The Song of Roland,* ca. 1090) is the pinnacle of the French epic tradition of chansons de geste ("songs of heroic deeds [lineage]"), which influenced the most complete example in the thriving Spanish epic tradition, the *Poema de mío Cid* (*Poem of the Cid,* twelfth century). The Irish epic *Táin Bó Cuailnge* (*Cattle Raid of Cooley*) was first written down by monks in the ninth century, but the story dates to the La Tène period of civilization, possibly about 100 B.C.E. It intersperses lyrics and verse duologues with the main tale told in prose. The story, which narrates the great deeds of the warrior Cuchulainn, has attracted a large number of subsidiary tales called *remscéla,* or introductory tales, and *iarscéla,* or after-tales. In his translation from Old Russian, Vladimir Nabokov calls *The Song of Igor's Campaign: An Epic of the Twelfth Century* (1960) "a harmonious, many leveled, many hued, uniquely poetical structure created in a sustained and controlled surge of inspiration by an artist with a fondness for pagan gods and a percipience of sensuous things." In the early nineteenth century, a group of medieval German texts were grouped together as *Spielmannsepen,* or "minstrel epics." These historic legends included *König Rothar* (ca. 1160), *Herzog Ernst* (ca. 1180), *Der Münchener Oswald* (fifteenth century), *Orendel* (late twelfth century), and *Salman und Moralf* (late twelfth century). In the 1830s, the folklorist Elias Lönnrot linked and organized Finnish runo-songs (*runolaulu*) to create the *Kalevala,* a magisterial Balto-Finnish epic ("It is my desire, it is my wish, / my desire to recite, / to get ready to sing"). In the 1860s, the folklorist F. Reinhold Kreutzwald followed suit and used Estonian runo-songs to compose Estonia's national epic, *Kalevipoeg.*

There are two main types of European songs that tell stories: epics and ballads. Whereas the ballad is a short strophic form that focuses on a primary event, the epic song is a long non-strophic form that focuses on a variety of events. But the genres sometimes blur and there is considerable thematic overlap between the longer ballads and the shorter epic songs, often dramatic, that have been collected in a wide range of cultures.

The Serbs, Croatians, Montenegrins, Bulgarians, and Albanians all have epic songs, which are performed by *guslars* (the *gusle* or *gusla* is a single-stringed instrument). The *guslars* specialized in *junačke pesme* ("men's songs"), heroic narratives chanted or sung on aggressively masculine themes, like war. They also performed *narodne pesme* ("people's songs") — the word *pesma* also means "poem." There are nine epic cycles of these popular narrative poems based on historical events, which were collected in the nineteenth century by the Serbian scholar Vuk Karadžić. The *guslari* provided the models for Milman Parry and Albert Lord's theories of an oral-formulaic method that stretches back to the Homeric bards. The slow-moving, unrhymed, and typically unaccompanied Russian epic songs are called *byliny.* The Ukrainian version of the epic is a body of songs called *dumy,* which were traditionally performed by itinerant Cossack bards called *kobzani.* The Tibetan *Epic of King Gesar* (ca. twelfth century), one of the major epic cycles of Central and East Asia, is performed both by amateurs and professional epic bards. A typical episode of the story contains five to ten thousand lines of verse (fifty to one hundred songs) linked by a spoken narration. The Mande epic of Son-Jara is recited by professional *finah* (poet-historians) and runs to more than three thousand lines. The Kyrgy national epic, *Manas* (ca. eighteenth century), can range close to half a million lines and take up to three weeks to recite.

Sïrat Banï Hilāl (ca. eleventh century) is the epic history of the Banï Hilāl

Bedouin tribe. It has been told and retold throughout the Arab world from the Indian Ocean to the Atlantic Coast for almost a thousand years. Dwight Fletcher Reynolds points out that "in different regions and over different historical periods the epic has been performed as a complex tale cycle narrated entirely in prose, as a prose narrative embellished with lengthy poems, as a narrative recited in rhymed verse, and as a narrative sung to the accompaniment of various musical instruments." It is both a textual and a performance tradition. Al-Bakātūsh, a village in northern Egypt, is known throughout the Nile Delta as the "village of the poets" because of its large community of hereditary epic singers who recite and perform the poem.

Ezra Pound called the epic "a poem including history." Literary or secondary epics — one thinks not just of Virgil's *Aeneid* (29–19 B.C.E.), but also of Dante's *Divine Comedy* (ca. 1308–1321), Ariosto's *Orlando furioso* (1516), Camões's *The Lusiads* (1572), Spenser's *Faerie Queene* (1590–1596), Tasso's *Jerusalem Delivered* (1581), Milton's *Paradise Lost* (1667) — adopted many of the conventions and strategies of the traditional epic, even though they are written poems meant to be read (and reread) rather than oral ones intended to be told and sung. "Homer makes us hearers," Alexander Pope said, "and Virgil leaves us readers." The editors of *Epic Traditions in the Contemporary World* argue, "Epic conceived as a poetic narrative of length and complexity that centers around deeds of significance to the community transcends the oral and literary divide that has long marked the approach to the genre." Byron playfully satirizes the epic apparatus he employs in this stanza from *Don Juan* (1819–1824):

> My poem's epic, and is meant to be
>   Divided in twelve books; each book containing,
> With Love, and War, a heavy gale at sea,
>   A list of ships, and captains, and kings reigning,
> New characters; the episodes are three:
>   A panoramic view of Hell's in training,
> After the style of Virgil and of Homer,
>   So that my name of Epic's no misnomer.

The epic also generated several types of revisionary and even anti-epics, such as the epic with a recent action (Lucan's *Pharsalia,* ca. 61–65 C.E.) or Christian "brief epics" (Abraham Cowley's *Davideis: A Sacred Poem of the Troubles of David,* 1656, or John Milton's *Paradise Regained,* 1671), which were supposedly modeled on the book of Job but more closely followed the classical epic. "All the types of Biblical epic developed during the Divine Poetry movement [in sixteenth-century England] answered the pagan epic repertoire feature by feature," Alastair Fowler explains. The pagan muse was replaced by the Holy Spirit, or a prayer to God, and the national or legendary action became the redemptive history of Scripture.

Pound's *Cantos* (1915–1969) were a bid to revive the epic as a modernist form. Nikos Kazantzakis's Greek poem *The Odyssey: A Modern Sequel* (1924–1938), David Jones's Welsh poem *Anathemata* (1952), and Derek Walcott's West Indian *Omeros* (1990) all make epic bids. From a Turkish prison cell, Nazim Hikmet wrote a five-volume epic novel in verse, *Human Landscapes from My Country* (1963), which he regarded as a historical synthesis of oral poetry, designed to be sung, and the printed novel, designed to be read silently in private. An epic apparatus has been employed by American poets from Anne Bradstreet's *Exact Epitome of the Four Monarchies* (1650), which could be called the first North American epic, to William Carlos Williams's *Paterson* (1940–1961), H. D.'s *Helen in Egypt* (1974), Louis Zukofsky's *"A"* (1928–1968), Charles Olson's *The Maximus Poems* (1950–1970), and James Merrill's *The Changing Light at Sandover* (1976–1982).

All in all, as Jorge Luis Borges wrote, "the epic is one of the necessities of the human mind."

SEE ALSO *aoidos, ballad, bard, bylina, Cyclic poets, duma, epic question, epic simile, epithet, guslar, in medias res, invocation, kobzari, mock epic, oral-formulaic method, oral poetry.*

epicedium, epicedia A funeral ode or hymn, a mourning song in praise of the dead. The word itself is the Latin spelling of the Greek "funeral song." The *epicedium* was sung in the presence of the dead, which gave it a raw, ritualistic feeling and made it a functional form, like the wedding song. This differentiates it from the dirge, which isn't limited to time or place. The elegiac statements over the bodies of Hector and Achilles are *epicedia.*

My anthology of the Latin *epicedia* would include "Catullus 101" (57 B.C.E.), Catullus's grief-stricken elegy for his brother ("A journey across many seas and through many nations / has brought me here, brother"); Virgil's *Eclogues* 5.20–44 (42–39 B.C.E.) and *Aeneid* 6.860–86 (29–19 B.C.E.); Horace's *Odes* 1.24 (23–13 B.C.E.), Propertius's 3.7.18 (18–23 B.C.E.); Ovid's

Amores 3.9 (16 B.C.E.) and *Expistulae ex ponto* 1.9 (9–12 C.E.); Martial's *Epigrams* 5.37 (89 C.E.), 6.28, 29, and 85 (90 C.E.); and Statius's *Silvae* 2.1.6 (90 C.E.), 3.3 (93 C.E.), 5.1, 3, and 5 (in or after 96 C.E.).

SEE ALSO *dirge, elegy.*

epic question The traditional epic often begins *in media res.* The singer of tales invokes the muse, states his theme, and raises a large question about the nature and cause of the conflict. The answer initiates the narrative. "What god drove them to fight with such a fury?" the Homeric singer asks at the beginning of the *Iliad* (ca. eighth century B.C.E.). Milton raises an epic question at the beginning of *Paradise Lost* (1667) when he asks, "What cause / Mov'd our Grand Parents, in that happy state / Favour'd of Heaven so highly to fall off / From their Creator?"

SEE ALSO *epic, in medias res.*

epic simile An extended comparison. An epic simile is a verbal comparison (usually using *like* or *as*) that is literally epic in scale. This fully developed analogy is sometimes called a Homeric simile, since it is a minor convention of the epic and plays a prominent role in Homer's poems. The epic simile is lingering and digressive — it can extend for twenty or more lines — and tends to suspend the action. It often shifts perspective. Thus Homer compares a battle to a snowstorm and Virgil compares the ghosts of the dead on the shores of Lethe to a swarm of bees.

SEE ALSO *epic, simile.*

epideictic poetry Poetry of display. One of the three branches of classical rhetoric, epideictic oratory was used to praise or blame someone or something in public. Epideictic poetry is poetry for special occasions, which utilizes the rhetoric of praise or blame in public, as in wedding odes and funeral orations. Epideictic oratory, which was categorized by Menander in *On Epideictic Oratory* (third century), continued as a strong influence throughout the Renaissance. O. B. Hardison asserts, "Renaissance lyric is more obviously influenced by epideictic rhetoric than by any other."

SEE ALSO *encomium, epithalamium, occasional poem, oríkì, panegyric, political poetry, praise poems, rhetoric.*

epigram From the Greek *epigramma,* "to write upon." An epigram is a short, witty poem or pointed saying. Ambrose Bierce defined it in *The Devil's Dictionary* (1881–1911) as "a short, sharp saying in prose and verse." In Hellenistic Greece (third century B.C.E.), the epigram developed from an inscription carved in a stone monument or onto an object, such as a vase, into a literary genre in its own right. It may have developed out of the proverb. *The Greek Anthology* (tenth century, fourteenth century) is filled with more than fifteen hundred epigrams of all sorts, including pungent lyrics on the pleasures of wine, women, boys, and song.

Ernst Robert Curtius writes in *European Literature and the Latin Middle Ages* (1953): "No poetic form is so favorable to playing with pointed and surprising ideas as epigram — for which reason seventeenth- and eighteenth-century Germany called it 'Sinngedicht.' This development of the epigram necessarily resulted after the genre ceased to be bound by its original definition (an inscription for the dead, for sacrificial offerings, etc.)." Curtius relates the interest in epigrams to the development of the "conceit" as an aesthetic concept.

Samuel Taylor Coleridge defined the epigram in epigrammatic form (1802):

> What is an epigram? A dwarfish whole;
> Its body brevity and wit its soul.

The pithiness, wit, irony, and sometimes harsh tone of the English epigram derive from the Roman poets, especially Martial, known for his caustic short poems, as in 1.32 (85–86 B.C.E.): "Sabinus, I don't like you. You know why? / Sabinus, I don't like you. That is why."

The epigram is brief and pointed. It has no particular form, though it often employs a rhymed couplet or quatrain, which can stand alone or serve as part of a longer work. Here is Alexander Pope's "Epigram from the French" (1732):

> Sir, I admit your general rule,
> That every poet is a fool:
> But you yourself may serve to show it,
> That every fool is not a poet.

Geoffrey Hartman points out that there are two diverging traditions of the epigram. These were classified by J. C. Scaliger as *mel* and *fel* (*Poetics Libri Septem,* 1561), which have been interpreted as *sweet* and *sour, sugar* and *salt, naïve* and *pointed.* Thus Robert Hayman, echoing Horace's idea that poetry should be both "dulce et utile," sweet and useful, writes in *Quodlibets* (1628):

Short epigrams relish both sweet and sour,
Like fritters of sour apples and sweet flour.

The "vinegar" of the epigram was often contrasted with the "honey" of the sonnet, especially the Petrarchan sonnet, though the Shakespearean sonnet, with its pointed final couplet, also combined the sweet with the sour. "By a natural development," Hartman writes, "since epigram and sonnet were not all that distinct, the pointed style often became the honeyed style raised to a higher power, to preciousness. A new opposition is frequently found, not between sugared and salty, but between pointed (precious, over-written) and plain."

The sometimes sweet, sometimes sour, and sometimes sweet-and-sour epigram has been employed by contemporary American formalists, such as Howard Nemerov, X. J. Kennedy, and especially J. V. Cunningham. Here is a two-line poem that Cunningham translated in 1950 from the Welsh epigrammatist John Owen (1.32, 1606):

Life flows to death as rivers to the sea,
And life is fresh and death is salt to me.

SEE ALSO *aureate, conceit, dulce et utile, epitaph, proverb, sonnet, wit.*

epinicia, epinicean (epinician or epinicion) Victory songs. The Greek *epinician* odes were commissioned victory poems (named for *epi-Níké-an,* the goddess of victory) about sports. They had stories of gods and heroes woven into them. Each ode focused on a triumphant athlete who had a symbolic connection to a god, and thus it incorporates a mythology. The poems have their roots in religious rites, and each one called for an ecstatic performance that communally reenacted the ritual of participation in the divine. Albin Lesky explains: "The epinicean elevates the significant event of victory into the realm of values, the world from which the poet's creation flows. This world of values is displayed and exemplified in its various spheres: in the divine itself, in the tales of the heroes, in the rules of conduct and not least in the poet's own creative activity as an artistic realm in its own right."

The tradition of celebrating athletic achievement begins with Pindar, whose choral odes to commemorate athletic victories from the fifth century B.C.E. are the first truly written narrative texts of any length. Greeks simultaneously sang the poems and danced to them at shrines or theaters, though now the words are all that remains of the complete Pindaric experience. The movement of the verse, which mirrors a musical dance pattern, tends to be emotionally intense and highly exalted. Horace (65–8 B.C.E.) compared Pindar (ca. 522–443 B.C.E.) to a great swan conquering the air by long rapturous flights. He claimed that the athletes were given more glory by Pindar's voice "than by a hundred statues standing mute / Around the applauding city."

Simonides also wrote *epinician* odes. C. M. Bowra explains that the *epinicean* ode became something "serious and stately; it assumed characteristics which had hiterhto belonged to the hymn; it told instructive and illuminating stories; it contained aphorisms on man's relations with the gods. All these can be found in Pindar's *Odes*, and we cannot doubt that Simonides did something to prepare the way for them." A special place should also be reserved for the *epinicean* odes of Bacchylides, who has often been considered a "lesser Pindar." Bacchylides was known after antiquity by a mere 107 nonsequential lines (in 69 fragments) until 1896, when a papyrus in Egypt was discovered containing his work. The papyrus was cut up into sections, smuggled from Egypt, and delivered to the British Museum. There a papyrologist reassembled 1,382 lines, including fifteen *epinician* odes and five dithyrambs.

SEE ALSO *ode.*

epiphany From a Greek word meaning "to appear." An epiphany is a sudden spiritual manifestation, a luminous or visionary moment. Epiphany means the manifestation of a god or spirit in the body, and thus the Christian epiphany is literally the manifestation of Christ to the Magi. James Joyce (1882–1941) secularized the term so that it came to mean a sudden manifestation of spiritual meaning, an unexpected revelation of truth in the commonplace, a psychological and literary mode of perception. It disrupts the ordinary, a moment out of time. The epiphany is akin to what Virginia Woolf termed "Moments of Being" and Wordsworth called "spots of time." In book 8 of *The Prelude* (1805, 1850) he recalls the "instant," for example, when he first crossed in a stagecoach the "threshold" of London and the "trivial forms / Of houses, pavements, streets, of men and things" suddenly radiated with significance:

'twas a moment's pause,—
All that took place within me came and went
As in a moment; yet with Time it dwells,
And grateful memory, as a thing divine.

The spiritual insight or luminous moment has frequently been considered the motivating pulse of lyric writing itself. It is "Within a Moment: a Pulsation of the Artery," Blake writes, when "the Poets Work is Done."

epiphora, epistrophe, see *anaphora, lyric, vision.*

epistle, see *letter poem.*

epitaph Greek: "on a tomb." An epitaph can be either a commemorative short poem inscribed on a gravestone or a poem that imitates one. The imitative type creates the fiction of a memorial site. The epitaph generally refers to the dead in the third person ("Here lies one whose name was writ in water") and serves as an abbreviated elegy. The inscribed poem addresses itself to the stranger passing by. Roman tombs were placed along the highways near Rome and thus a typical Roman epigraph began, "Read, passing friend . . ." The earliest epitaphs are Egyptian pieces carved on sarcophagi and coffins. The classical epitaphs found in book 4 of the *Greek Anthology* (tenth century) have influenced writers of epitaphs ever since—from the Latin poets to the English and American ones—from Ben Jonson to William Wordsworth to Edgar Lee Masters, who employed the fictive epitaph to create the voices of an entire village in *Spoon River Anthology* (1916). The most famous Greek epitaph memorializes the dead at Thermopylae:

Go, tell the Lacedaimonians, passer-by,
That here obedient to their laws we lie.

Jonathan Swift imitated the Roman tradition of addressing passing strangers in his epitaph in Latin, which appears above his tomb in Saint Patrick's Cathedral, Dublin. W. B. Yeats called it "the greatest epitaph in history":

> Hic depositum est corpus
> Jonathan Swift, S. T. P.
> Hujus ecclesiae cathedralis Decani
> Ubi saeva indignatio
> Ulterius cor lacerare nequit
> Abi, viator,
> Et imitare, si poteris,
> Strenum pro virili liberatatis vindicem

Jonathan Middleton Murry renders this: "The body of Jonathan Swift, Dean of this Cathedral Church, is buried here, where fierce indignation can lacerate his heart no more. Go, traveler, and imitate if you can one who strove his utmost to champion liberty."

SEE ALSO *elegy*.

epithalamium (Latin), ***epithalamion*** (Greek) From the Greek, "at the bridal chamber." An epithalamium is a poem or song celebrating a marriage. It was intended to be recited or sung outside the bridal chamber on the wedding night. Traditional marriage songs exist in most cultures (the Song of Solomon is a notable example), though Sappho (late seventh century B.C.E.) is credited with first using it as a distinct literary form ("Raise high the roofbeams, carpenters!"). Most of her epithalamia are lost. In the *Iliad* (ca. eighth century B.C.E.), Homer describes wedding processions accompanied by torches, music, dancing, and song. The epithalamium reached classical peaks with Theocritus in Greek (*Eclogue* 18 on the marriage of Helen and Menelaus) and Catullus in Latin (*Carmina* 61, 62). Philip Sidney first imported the wedding song into English in the 1580s ("A Ditty"); Edmund Spenser influentially marked the form with his *Epithalmion* (1595), which was written for his own wedding and consists of twenty-four stanzas that progress from first awakening until late at night. In 1595, he invented a new title, "Prothalamion" (i.e., before [in time or place] the bridal chamber), for his poem commemorating a betrothal ceremony, thus perhaps suggesting a separate genre ("Sweete *Themmes* runne softly, till I end my Song").

The epithalamium is a ceremonial poem with no specific formal requirements. It marks an occasion. Some notable examples: John Donne's "Epithalamium Made at Lincoln's Inn" (1633), Robert Herrick's "An Epithalamie to Sir Thomas Southwell and His Ladie" (1648), Andrew Marvell's "Two Songs at the Marriage of the Lord Fauconberg and the Lady Mary Cromwell" (1657), and Percy Shelley's "Fragment. Supposed to Be an Epithalamium of Francis Ravaillac and Charlotte Cordé" (1810). Alfred, Lord Tennyson's *In Memoriam* (1849) opens with a funeral for a friend and concludes with an epithalamium for his sister. A. E. Housman imitated an antique idiom in "He Is Here, Urania's Son" (1922) and so did e. e. cummings in "Epithalamion" ("Thou aged unreluctant earth . . . ," 1923). Guillaume Apollinaire helped to inaugurate the modern epithalamium with his 1909 "Poem Read at André Salmon's Wedding" ("I know that only those will remake the world who are rooted in poetry").

epithet A fixed formula, usually an adjective or adjectival phrase, used to characterize a person or thing. The Homeric epithet refers to Homer's repeated way of conjoining adjectives and nouns to make stock phrases, as in "wine-dark sea" and "rosy-fingered dawn" or "divine Odysseus" and "swift-footed Achilles." In the 1930s, the scholar Milman Parry analyzed these Homeric epithets and demonstrated that Homer's language was a structure built up from fixed formulas. He considered the formula "a group of words regularly employed under the same metrical conditions to express a given essential idea." These prefabricated phrases and repeated repetitions were part of the formulaic method, particularly important because they satisfied the needs of the Homeric meter, which was dactylic hexameter. They were a crucial rhythmic device for oral poets, who were sewing things together from memory (*rhapsode* means "sewer of songs"). The Homeric epithet was thus essential to the oral-formulaic compositional method. It was also a way of capturing something essential about a person or thing.

The spelling out of a hero's special praise name is not exclusively an epic device. There are many places in Africa and elsewhere where the use of someone's praise name is at the heart of public life. These names, which live in everyday public life, are elaborated upon by praise singers at times of heightened public display events. One's praise name often includes references not only to past deeds but also to one's ancestors. These epithets thus live in rituals and public ceremonies.

SEE ALSO *antonomasia, epic, oral-formulaic method, oral poetry, oríkì, panegyric, praise poems, rhapsode.*

epitrite, see *foot.*

epode From the Greek, meaning "after-song," and referring to the third section of a classical ode, which differs in meter from the first two sections, the strophe and the antistrophe. It suggests a coming together, a unified and completed movement. Horace entitled his fifth book of odes *Epodon libor,* or *The Book of Epodes* (ca. 29 B.C.E.).

SEE ALSO *antistrophe, ode, strophe.*

epopee The word *epopee,* which means "epic poem" or "epic poetry," came into English in the late seventeenth century and derives from the French *épopée,* which in turn comes from the Greek word for "poem making." This indicates the status of the epic in ancient Greece.

SEE ALSO *epic.*

epyllion The *epyllion* or "little epic" is a brief narrative poem with a romantic and mythological theme. The term came into vogue in the nineteenth century to describe classical poems that told a love story in mythological terms. The tradition dates from Theocritus and was defined by Ovid, whose *Metamorphoses* (8 C.E.) set the terms for erotic treatment of mythological narratives in the Renaissance, such as Shakespeare's "Venus and Adonis" (1592–1593) and Marlowe's "Hero and Leander" (1593).

SEE ALSO *epic.*

esemplastic "To shape into one." Samuel Taylor Coleridge coined this outlandish word "because, having to convey a new sense, I thought that a new term would both aid the recollection of my meaning and prevent its being confounded with the usual import of the word, imagination" (chapter 10 of *Biographia Literraria,* 1817). Coleridge was trying to convey the active rather than passive quality of the imagination, which he believed had a tremendous capacity — an *esemplastic* power — to shape disparate and discordant things into a unified whole. He also gave the word the form *esenoplastic,* which he apparently thought of as a translation of the German *Einbildungskraft,* Kant and Schelling's word for imagination. He wrote, "How excellently the German word 'Einbildungskraft' expresses the prime and loftiest faculty, the power of coadunation, the faculty that forms the many into one, In-Eins-bildung. Esenoplasy or Esenoplastic power is contradistinguished from fantasy or mirrorment, repeating simply or by transposition." Coleridge's imagined etymology shows him treating the imagination as a force that brings together and reconciles opposites.

SEE ALSO *imagination.*

espinela, see *décima.*

estrambote A Spanish term for extra lines or verses irregularly added to a fixed form. The *soneto con estrambote* is a tailed sonnet, or sonnet with additional lines. Miguel de Cervantes often uses the *estrambote* for comic effect, adding three additional lines to the traditional fourteen-line sonnet, as in his burlesque poem "To the Tomb of Phillip II in Seville" (1598). The novelist María de Zayas has one poem in which the *estrambote* is four times longer than the sonnet itself. It is sung by the character Carlos in the "Second Tale of Disillusion" (1647).

SEE ALSO *sonnet.*

estribillo A refrain in Spanish lyrics and ballads, the *estribillo* originated in the Arabic *zéjel.* It first operated as the introductory stanza of a poem (the *cabeza* or *texto*), which repeated at the end of each stanza. Later, it was dropped as an initiating burden and became a refrain that recurred at the end of each stanza of a poem.

SEE ALSO *refrain, zéjel.*

Estridentismo Mexico's first self-conscious avant-garde movement, *Estridentismo* ("Stridentism") spanned all the arts and flourished between 1921 and 1927. In the aftermath of the Mexican revolution, the cosmopolitan *estridentistas,* who were akin to the Italian futurists and the Spanish ultraists, rebelliously provoked and attacked the bourgeois establishment. The poetry of Manuel Maples Arce (1898–1981), who started the movement, José Juan Tablada (1871–1945), and Luis Quintanilla (1893–1978), who liked to sign his last name Kin-Taniya, illustrated how the *Estridentistas* tried, in Arce's words, "to relate or merge disparate terms so that they produced surprise or expectation." Germán List Arzubide's 1927 book *El movimiento entridentista* ironically marked the end of the movement it sought to promote.

SEE ALSO *futurism, Ultraism.*

ethnopoetics In the late 1960s, George Quasha asked Jerome Rothenberg to create a term using the words *ethnos* and *poetics* on the model of *ethnomusicology,* and thus was born *ethnopoetics.* Rothenberg's anthology *Technicians of the Sacred* (1964) was a foundational text. The anthropologist Dennis Tedlock also shaped the interest in what he calls "a decentered poetics, an attempt to hear and read the poetries of distant others, outside the Western tradition as we know it now." The Dada and surrealist poets Tristan Tzara, Benjamin Peret, and Antonin Artaud were all interested in exploring the oral poetics of Africa, the Pacific, and the Americas. Ethnopoetics expanded the modernist interest in archaic art forms and focused on the oral poetries of different cultures, cross-fertilizing the work of poets, folklorists, linguists, and anthropologists. Tedlock summarizes, "Ethnopoetics originated among poets with an interest in anthropology and linguistics and among anthropologists and linquists with an interest in poetry, such as David Antin, Stanley Diamond, Dell Hymes, Jerome Rothenberg, Gary Snyder, Nathaniel Tarn (E. Michael Mendelson), and myself. The emphasis has been on performances in which the speaking, chanting, or singing voice gives shape to proverbs, riddles, curses, laments, praises, prayers, prophecies, public announcements, and narratives." The magazine *Alcheringa* (1970–1980) established itself as "the first magazine of the world's tribal poetries."

SEE ALSO *Dadaism, oral poetry, primitivism, Surrealism.*

euphemism, dysphemism *The American Heritage Dictionary* defines *euphemism* as "The act or an example of substituting a mild, indirect, or vague term for one considered harsh, blunt, or offensive." Euphemism has its root in a Greek word meaning the "use of auspicious words." The poetic use of euphemism, substituting one word for another, using words of good omen, probably has its origins in magical practice. In "Politics and the English Language" (1946), George Orwell alerted us to the ways that language corrupts thought and "the inflated style is itself a kind of euphemism." Concentration camps become "pacification centers" and bombing one's own troups becomes "friendly fire." Yet saying one thing and meaning something else is a necessary strategy in poetry. Euphemisms sometimes provide a way of voicing something — erotic, religious, political — that cannot be said or written directly. Euphemism gets around the censors, which can be personal, social, or political, sometimes internal, sometimes external.

The opposite of a euphemism is a dysphemism (Greek: "not fair speech"), which exaggerates the negative. There is a moment in *Romeo and Juliet* (1595), for example, where Mercutio mocks and derides with low derogatories the great romantic lovers of history: "Laura was but a kitchen maid; Dido a dowdy; Cleopatra a gipsy, Helen and Hero hildings and harlots." In 1927, the French psychologist Albert J. Carnoy characterized dysphemism as "unpitying, brutal, mocking." He said: "It is also a reaction against pedantry, rigidity, and pretentiousness, but also against nobility and dignity in the language."

SEE ALSO *circumlocution, metaphor, rhetoric.*

euphony A pleasing or sweet sound. The word *euphony* derives from a Greek word meaning "good sound." It is the opposite of cacophony. Vowel sounds are usually considered more euphonious than consonants. The liquids and semi-vowels (*l, m, n, r, y, w*) are generally deemed the most euphonic of the consonants. This is a matter of taste. Since the ancients, the emphasis on beautiful sounds has been an essential part of poetry, but harmonic sounds are a means to an end, not an end in and of themselves. Some poets have always preferred a more dissonant music. Poetry in English is a river fed by two streams: the more euphonic Latinate words and the more cacophonous Anglo-Saxon ones.

Listen for how John Keats grasps and modulates the pitch of a nightingale across several lines in "Ode to a Nightingale" (1819), how suggestively he invokes "a light-winged Dryad of the trees" who

> In some melodious plot
> Of beechen green, and shadows numberless,
> Singest of summer in full-throated ease.

Or of how he captures the sound of the wind (listen for the light *i* sounds as well as the *f* and *w* consonants in a famous line from "To Autumn," one of the most euphonic poems in the English language: "Thy hair soft-lifted by the winnowing wind."

SEE ALSO *assonance, cacophony.*

euphuism An affected, highly elaborated and ornate style. John Lyly popularized the name and the artificial style in his prose works *Euphues: The Anatomy of Wyt* (1578) and *Euphues and his England* (1580). Lyly's high-flown style, which provided a model for many of the courtiers and wits at the court of Queen Elizabeth, depended on balanced phrasing, excessive alliteration, far-fetched figures of speech. Here is a brief sample:

> Though the chamomile the more it is trodden and pressed down, the more it spreadeth, yet the violet the oftener it is handled and touched, the sooner it withereth and decayeth.

"[T]hough we cannot say that euphuism is verse," John Dover Wilson writes in his 1905 book on Lyly, "we can say that it partakes of the nature of verse."

Lyly's influential style dated rapidly. Shakespeare notably parodies Lyly's euphuistic manner in *Henry IV* (1598). Falstaff sounds comically bombastic in lecturing Prince Harry in the person of the king:

> For though the chamomile, the more it is trodden on, the faster it grows, yet youth, the more it is wasted, the sooner it wears. That thou art my son I have partly thy mother's word, partly my own opinion, but chiefly a villainous trick of thine eye, and a foolish hanging of thy nether lip, that doth warrant me. If then thou be son to me, here lies the point. Why, being son to me, art thou so pointed at? Shall the blessed son of heaven prove a micher, and eat blackberries? — A question not to be asked. Shall the son of England prove a thief, and take purses? — A question to be asked.

SEE ALSO *bombast, Gongorism.*

eye rhyme, see *rhyme.*

exemplum, exempla (pl) A short narrative that makes a moral point. The term is primarily applied to illustrative stories within longer prose works, such as medieval sermons, though there are examples in poetry, such as John Gower's thirty-thousand-line poem, *Confessio Amantis* (ca. 1385), which employs the exempla to illustrate sins against Love.

explication de texte, explication A pedagogical tool of the French school system, *explication de texte* suggests a method of reading, a basic, detailed, step-by-step explanation of a literary work. The educational use is close to paraphrase and generally refrains from interpretation. In English, *explication* suggests a detailed formal or textual analysis of a work, considering such elements as structure, style, and imagery. It examines each part and considers how it relates to the whole. Some of the key twentieth-century critical texts in the development of this kind of analytic reading: Laura Riding and Robert Graves, *A Survey of Modernist Poetry* (1928), I. A. Richards, *Practical Criticism* (1929), and William Empson, *Seven Types of Ambiguity* (1930).

SEE ALSO *New Criticism, paraphrase.*

expressionism The words *expressionism* and *expressionist* started cropping up around 1911 to describe various types of European avant-garde art. More specifically, expressionism was employed to designate a group of German artists and writers who flourished from around 1912 through the early 1920s. Expressionism was powerfully expressed through the paintings of *Die Brücke* (The Bridge), founded in Dresden in 1905, and *Der Blaue Reiter* (The Blue Horseman), founded in Munich in 1912. These artists championed a feverish, anti-mimetic form of art that moved between abstraction and visionary distortion. Between 1910 and 1920, the "Expressionist decade," a group of German expressionist poets emerged, which includes Elsa Lasker-Shüler (1869–1945), Ernst Stadler (1883–1914), Georg Heym (1887–1912), and Georg Trakl (1887–1914). Their work is extremely diverse, but they all focused on the visual element of the imagination and wrote a poetry of crisis — terrifying, visionary, spiritual. The 1920 expressionist anthology *Dawn of Humanity* marked the end of the movement, but also launched its reputation.

fable A fable is a short allegorical narrative, in verse or prose, that makes a moral point. The fable is a didactic genre and the fabulist, whether an oral storyteller or a writer, traditionally anthropomorphizes animals, plants, and inanimate objects to dramatize human weakness. Many of the great fables employ speaking animals. The first collection of fables is attributed to Aesop in the sixth century B.C.E., and *Aesop's Fables* (*Aesopica*) are known throughout the world. The Roman Phaedus employed iambic trimeters to imitate Aesop and expand his tales in the first century; Babrius wrote a series of Aesop-like fables in choliambic verse in the second century. Jean de la Fontaine's *Fables,* which began to appear in the 1660s, raised the fable to a new level of artistry. La Fontaine combined the openness of a child with a sophisticated literary taste, a quality captured in nineteenth-century Russian by Ivan Andreyevich Krylov and in twentieth-century American English by Marianne Moore (*The Fables of La Fontaine,* 1965). The term *fable* has sometimes widened to suggest a kind of pointed narrative, as in John Dryden's *Fables, Ancient and Modern* (1700), which included original poems as well as adaptations of Homer, Ovid, and others. John Crowe Ransom suggested that Thomas Hardy's poems were best described as fables: "They offer natural images of the gods in action or, sometimes unfortunately, in inaction." Most people in the West now think of fables as animal stories to educate children.

SEE ALSO *beast epic.*

fabliau A short, comic, often bawdy tale in verse. This literary genre — part farce, part dirty story — was especially popular in France during the Middle

Ages. It was performed by jongleurs. The vogue spread to Italy and England, where Chaucer re-created the genre in "The Miller's Tale" and "The Reeve's Tale" in *The Canterbury Tales* (ca. 1387–1400). The French *fabliau* was gradually replaced by the short story, but its influence lived on in the works of such writers as Boccaccio and Molière.

SEE ALSO *dit, jongleur.*

fakhr An Arabic term meaning "pride," the *fakhr* is a form of poetic boasting. This type of self-vaunting or self-advertising often came at the end of the *qasida,* or ode. In pre-Islamic Arabic poetry, the poet was a spokesman not just for himself but also for his tribe, and the *fakhr* was a way of instilling strength in people through poetry. The poetic boast was subsequently taken up as a motif in Arabic and Andalusian medieval poetry as a way of staking one's claim in the competitive arena of poetry. The boast is the flip side of the taunt. If there were an equivalent term in American poetry, it would apply to Walt Whitman's "Song of Myself" ("I celebrate myself, and sing myself / And what I assume you shall assume / For every atom belonging to me as good belongs to you").

SEE ALSO *poetic contest, qasida.*

falling rhythm, descending rhythm Rhythm in which the stress comes first. Trochaic (/ u) and dactylic (/ u u) meters are falling rhythms and thus give a sense of "falling" or "descending" from a stressed syllable to an unstressed one. Here is a trochaic line and thus a falling rhythm from Henry Wadsworth Longfellow's "The Song of Hiawatha" (1855):

> Shóuld yŏu | ásk mĕ, | whénce thĕse | stóriĕs?

The first three feet are dactylic, and thus a descending rhythm, in Robert Browning's "The Lost Leader":

> Júst fŏr ă | hándfŭl ŏf | sílvĕr hĕ | léft ŭs

The term *falling rhythm* can be misleading because it seems to suggest something about the emotional movement or impact of the verse, though it is merely a technical term.

SEE ALSO *dactyl, rocking feet and rhythms, rising rhythm, trochee.*

fame The traditional dream of eternal fame was a longstanding literary ideal that goes back to Homer and such ancient Greeks as Theognis (sixth century B.C.E.), who promised his beloved she would be "known / To people of all time, your name imperishable." Horace (65–8 B.C.E.) famously boasted: "I have built a monument more lasting than bronze" (3.30), thus suggesting that his words were more solid than the architecture of the Roman Empire. Jacob Burckhardt pointed out that Dante had "the fullest consciousness that he was the giver of fame and immortality." He could also consign people to oblivion. Shakespeare followed the Horatian example when he declared, "Not marble, nor the gilded monuments / Of princes, shall outlive this powerful rhyme." John Keats prophesied, "I think I shall be among the English poets after my death."

SEE ALSO *the beloved, topos.*

familiar verse, see *vers de société.*

fancy Samuel Taylor Coleridge distinguished fancy, an abbreviation of fantasy, from imagination. Fancy is like "ordinary memory," he wrote in *Biographia Literaria* (1817), because it "must receive all its materials ready made from the law of association." Imagination is a higher power: "It dissolves, diffuses, dissipates, in order to recreate . . . it struggles to idealize and to unify." Fancy, then, is mechanical and passive, whereas imagination is organic and active.

SEE ALSO *imagination.*

les fantaisistes A group of French poets who came together in Paris in 1911. Francis Carco and Tristan Derème were the principle spokesmen for this Montmartre-based group, which included Blaise Cendrars, Jean-Marc Bernard, Tristan Klingsor, Valery Larboud, and Paul Jean Toulet. Max Jacob was a *fantaisiste* with a heartbreaking wit and eccentric verbal ingenuity. The ironist Jules Laforgue, an inventor of *vers libre,* was one of the primary models. Guillaume Apollinaire, perhaps the unofficial leader, was another inspiration for this loosely affiliated group of poets who reacted against the lofty obscurities of symbolist poetry. They also rebelled against the social and humanitarian concerns of French poetry at the time. Instead, they embraced a modern poetry of blithe ironies and whimsical grotesqueries.

SEE ALSO *Cubist poetry, Dadaism, modernism, symbolism, vers libre.*

fatras, fatrasie, fratrasie, resverie *Fatras* is a type of sophisticated nonsense poetry that flourished in medieval France. It is written in a kind of invented dialect. One scholar distinguished the *fatras possible,* which seems to offer a coherent text, from the *fatras impossible,* which makes no coherent sense at all. But both types have the irrational logic of nonsense poetry. Jacques Prévert (1900–1977) gave the name *Fatras,* which is translated as *Hodgepodge* or *Rubbish* (1966), to his incongruous mix of surrealist poems and collages.

SEE ALSO *nonsense poetry.*

feigning There is a long philosophical debate around the idea that poetry pretends or creates fictions. In the *Republic,* Plato condemned the "lies" of poets such as Homer and Hesiod, who are "only imitators, who do but imitate the appearance of things." He banished poets from the ideal commonwealth because imitative poetry, which is "devoid of knowledge," undermines the understanding of truth. Aristotle responded in the *Poetics* by arguing that imitative poetry is a higher undertaking than historical fact. The poet imitates the ideal. The idea of poetry as feigning, as "a fervid and exquisite invention" (Boccaccio, *Geneology of the Gods,* ca. 1360), has been part of its long conversation and quarrel with philosophy. Thus Philip Sidney argues in his "Defence of Poesie," "Now for the poet he nothing affirmeth, and therefore never lieth."

This whole debate stands behind the moment in *As You Like It* when the court clown Touchstone tries to woo the country girl Audrey:

> Touchstone. Truly, I would the gods had made thee poetical.
> Audrey. I do not know what "poetical" is. Is it honest in deed and in
> word? Is it a true thing?
> Touchstone. No, truly; for the truest poetry is the most feigning.

Touchstone betrays his doubtful motives by his punning of the word *faining* (desiring) with *feigning* (to pretend). W. H. Auden plays with Touchstone's "ingenious fibs" in his poem "The Truest Poetry Is the Most Feigning" (1955). Man is "the only creature ever made who fakes," Auden suggests, and poetry is "truest" that acknowledges its own artificial nature.

SEE ALSO *imitation, mimesis, verisimilitude.*

Félibrige, Felibritge (Occitan) The word *Félibrige* derives from a Provençal word meaning "pupil" or "follower." This noble French association was founded in the mid-nineteenth century by the fiction writer Joseph Roumanille, who is called "le pere de Félibrige" and founded the group's official journal, *Armana provençau*; the poet Fredéric Mistral, who received the Nobel Prize in literature in 1909; and others to revive the Provençal language, poetry, and culture. The troubadour poets used the Romance language *langue d'oc* in Provence in the Middle Ages, but it had been banned by Francis I when he made French the official language in 1591. Mistral spoke of the language as a whole, with all its local variations, as *Occitan,* now the preferred term. The language of the troubadours is *Old Occitan.* Mistral's first book, *Mireio* (1859), was one of the decisive books of the movement. Zbigniew Herbert wrote that Mistral's entry into literature was unusual. "In an age of declining romanticism, there emerges a poet that is the embodiment of romantic ideals: a spontaneous folk singer writing in the tongue of the most perfect medieval lyrics. If he had not existed, he would have been invented, like Ossian." The Félibrige movement lasted from 1854 through the 1920s.

SEE ALSO *troubadour.*

feminine rhyme A rhyme of two syllables, the first stressed and the second unstressed (*trances/glances*). It is also called double rhyme and has often been employed for light verse, as when Lewis Carroll playfully riffs through the opening stanza of "Rules and Regulations":

> A short direction
> To avoid dejection,
> By variations
> In occupations,
> And prolongation

Of relaxation,
And combinations
Of recreations,
And disputation
On the state of the nation
In adaptation
To your station,
By invitations
To friends and relations,
By evitation
Of amputation,
By permutation
In conversation,
And deep reflection
You'll avoid dejection.

SEE ALSO *masculine rhyme, rhyme.*

feminist poetry, feminist criticism The premise of feminist poetry and feminist criticism is that writing is a gendered practice. The personal is political. From the 1960s to the 1980s, self-consciously feminist poetry articulated the motives and commitments of women writing and reading *as women.* "What would happen if one woman told the truth about her life?" Muriel Rukeyser asked in her poem "Käthe Kollwitz." "The world would split open." Such poets as Sylvia Plath, Adrienne Rich, Audre Lorde, and June Jordan told the truth about their lives and thus split open the literary world.

Feminist approaches to literature became an important influence on literary study during the 1970s. One crucial aspect of feminist criticism has been to recover neglected and lost literary works by women. Another has been to study the image of women in literature and culture. Feminist critics have attempted to recover how women have written and read over the centuries. In doing so, they stand against the patriarchal erasure of women's experiences. In *Stealing the Language,* Alicia Ostriker argues that women poets "steal" patriarchal language, preserving its denotative meanings, while at the same time radically revising its connotations, in order to create a distinctive "women's poetry." Mary Wollfstenecraft

(1759–1797) was the first English woman to systematically investigate the causes of women's oppression. In *A Room of One's Own* (1929), Virginia Woolf insisted that women must have independence, both financial and intellectual, to create a vital literature. Simone de Beauvoir argued in *The Second Sex* (1949) that patriarchal society fostered mythologies about women — ideas of femininity, the equation of women with biology — in order to sustain masculine privilege and power. In *The Madwoman in the Attic* (1979), Sandra Gilbert and Susan Gubar concentrated on the destructive power of Victorian stereotypes on women. Despite a withering critique of Freud, feminist theorists have powerfully linked feminism to psychoanalysis, to deconstruction and other modes of poststructuralism. Such French thinkers as Luce Irigaray, Hélène Cixous, and Julia Kristeva developed the idea of *écriture feminine,* which in turn inspired the American feminist critic Elaine Showalter to come up with the idea of gynocriticism, which she defines as "the study of women *as writers,* and its subjects are the history, styles, themes, genres, and structures of writing by women; the psychodynamics of female creativity; the trajectory of the individual or collective female career; and the evolution and laws of a female literary tradition." Gertrude Stein writes in her 1927 prose poem "Patriarchal Poetry": "Let her be let her be let her be let her be to be to be let her be let her try."

fescennine verse A form of early Latin poetry, fescennine verses were coarse and caustic songs — ribald, crude, sometimes abusive — sung at festivals celebrating the gathering of the harvest and the grape crops. They were also performed at weddings. The format was a dialogue between peasants. The name probably derives from Fescennium, the Etruscan town of its origin. In the *Epistles* (21, 20 B.C.E.), Horace refers to the *Fescennina licentia* or "the license of the Fescennine verses" and suggests a formulaic structure of reciprocal insults (*versibus alternas*) among the country people. The invective in these songs reached such a pitch that a law was eventually passed against their circulation. They were a precursor to Roman comedy and satire.

SEE ALSO *drama, poetic contest, satire.*

figures of speech The various rhetorical uses of language are considered figures of speech. These nonliteral expressions employ words in imaginative or "figurative" ways. Think of how John Donne addresses the sun as a "busy old fool" ("The Sun Rising," 1633) or Christopher Smart treats his cat's daily activitities as a form of devotion to God in "Jubilate Agno" (1759–1763):

> For I will consider my cat Jeoffry.
> For he is the servant of the Living God duly and daily serving him.
> For at the first glance of the glory of God in the East he worships in his way.
> For is this done by wreathing his body seven times round with elegant quickness.
> For then he leaps up to catch the musk, which is the blessing of God upon his prayer.
> For he rolls upon prank to work it in.
> For having done duty and received blessing he begins to consider himself.

The study of figurative speech and thought was originally a branch of rhetoric, but gradually became part of poetics. Henry Peacham delights in them in *The Garden of Eloquence* (1593):

> The most excellent Ornaments, Exornations, Lightes, Flowers, and Formes of Speech, commonly called the Figures of Rhetorike. By which the singular Partes of Man's Mind, are most aptly expressed, and the sundrie Affections of his Heart most effectualie uttered.

George Puttenham defines and illustrates 121 figures of speech in "Of Ornament," the third section of *The Arte of English Poesie* (1589). Figures of speech were once considered "ornaments" of poetry, something added on, but they are actually at its core, the quintessence of poetic thinking, a way of knowing through language.

SEE ALSO *metaphor, metonymy, poetics, rhetoric, trope.*

fili, filídh (pl) The *filídh* were a professional caste of poets in early Ireland who were often credited with the supernatural power of prophecy. The words *fili* and *filídh* are etymologically connected to "seer." These poets, who were the successors of the druids and could practice divination, were magicians and lawgivers. They were the highest-ranking members of a group called the *áes dána* (literally, "the people of skill, craft"). In English, the word *bard* usually denotes a Celtic poet, but the *filídh* were in fact more aristocratic and enjoyed greater privileges than the bards. Their poetry is nonetheless called bardic, since they were entrusted with an oral tradition, the full knowledge of the tribe, which predated Christianity. Their education was daunting and they spent years at a dedicated school where poetry was studied as a craft. There were seven orders of *filídh;* the highest grade, the *ollamh,* studied for twelve years. The *filídh* practiced an elaborate form of syllabic poetry and mastered complex metrical forms, which employed both internal and end-rhymes, consonance, alliteration, and other devices of sound. They learned by heart at least 300 poetic meters, 250 primary stories, and 100 secondary stories. They recited traditional tales and topographical lore. They also served as crucial advisors and historical chroniclers, who remembered the genealogies of their patrons. They were so bound by tradition that there is little change in their work for the four centuries from 1250 to 1650. The poet Giolla Bríghde Mac Con Midhe explained in the thirteenth century:

> If poetry were to be suppressed, my people,
> if we were without history, without ancient lays,
> forever, but the father of each man,
> everyone will pass unheralded.

Ted Hughes said that the *fili* "was the curator and re-animator of the inner life which held the people together and made them what they were."

SEE ALSO *bard, oral poetry.*

fin de siècle This French term, which means "end of the century," was almost immediately applied to the final years of the nineteenth century in Europe and associated with effete sophistication, moody decadence. In England, it had an especially foreign, exotic ring. Holbrook Jackson observed in 1913, "Anything strange or uncanny, anything which savored of freak or perversity was swiftly labeled *fin de siècle.*" Much of the poetry of the 1890s (sometimes called *The Mauve Decade* or *The Yellow Decade*) has a world-weary self-consciousness that suggests the end of civilization, but also seems underscored by a lively cultural scene, especially in London. The decade begins with the narrative gusto of Robert Louis Stevenson's *Ballads* (1890) and Rudyard Kipling's *Departmental Ditties, Barrack-Room Ballads, and Other Verses* (1891); it reaches one of its peaks in the elegiac nostalgia of A. E. Housman's *A Shropshire Lad* (1896); and it concludes with Oscar Wilde's *The Ballad of Reading Gaol* (1899) and W. B. Yeats's *The Wind Among the Reeds* (1899). A group of women poets consolidated their reputations during the 1890s: Mary Coleridge, Michael Field (Katherine Bradley and Edith Cooper), E. Nesbit, Dollie Radford, and Alice Meynell. The era has been largely characterized by the bohemian London circle of Arthur Symons, Ernest Dowson, John Davidson, and Lionel Johnson, amongst others, which Yeats identified as "The Tragic Generation."

SEE ALSO *decadence, symbolism, Young Vienna.*

the fireside poets The fireside poets, also known as the "Schoolroom" or "Household" poets, refers to a group of highly popular nineteenth-century New England poets, which includes Henry Wadsworth Longfellow, John Greenleaf Whittier, James Russell Lowell, William Cullen Bryant, and Oliver Wendell Holmes. These poets wrote in traditional forms ("I love the old melodious lays," Whittier declared) and their rhyming, metrical poems made them suitable for memorizing in the schoolroom as well as at home. The light of the fireside was one of their cherished images; their poems seem to create a space where the writer and reader meet in its soft glow. This light brings together Longfellow's travelers: "Around the fireside at their ease / There sat a group of friends, entranced / With the delicious melodies" (*Tales of a Wayside Inn,* 1863) and radiates through the conclusion of Whittier's "Snow-Bound" (1866):

> Sit with me by the homestead hearth,
> And stretch the hands of memory forth
> To warm them at the wood-fire's blaze!
> And thanks untraced to lips unknown
> Shall greet me like the odors blown
> From unseen meadows newly mown,
> Or lilies floating in some pond,
> Wood-fringed, the wayside gaze beyond;
> The traveller owns the grateful sense

> Of sweetness near, he knows not whence,
> And, pausing, takes with forehead bare
> The benediction of the air.

Time seems to have passed by these bearded poets, who were deeply learned, socially engaged, and politically astute. Their sometime radical views were couched in soft tones. Their work was reassuring precisely because it stood up for eternal truths at the very moment America was undergoing such vast urban and industrial changes.

flarf Garry Sullivan coined the term *flarf* in 2000 for intentionally bad poems, such as "Flarf Balonacy Swingle." The term became a catch-all for poems that use Internet search engines to collage search results, randomly substitute words, and use other electronic cut-up procedures. Hence Morton Hanley's *Anthology of Spam Poetry* (2007), a form of found poetry, which consists of spam and other junk mail found in e-mail in boxes. Spoetry or spoems are poems that are made up from the subject lines of spam e-mails. The detritus of electronic culture gets recycled as purposefully bad poetry.

SEE ALSO *found poem.*

flokkr, see *drápa.*

fleshly school of poetry, see *Pre-Raphaelites.*

flyting A contest of insults, cursing matches in verse. The *flyting,* which derives from a Scots word meaning "scolding," is a formal exchange of taunts, a form of rhetorical one-upmanship in which poets alternately blast and assail each other. In early heroic narratives, there is often an exchange of boasts and insults between two warrior-heroes in a public setting (the mead hall, the battlefield), which often ends in a trial of arms, as in the quarrel between Beowulf and Unferth in *Beowulf.* These heroic *flytings* became the model for "*ludic flytings.*" The finest example of the *ludic flyting* in Scottish literature is the early sixteenth-century poem "The Flyting of Dunbar and Kennedy," which pitted William Dunbar against his rival Walter Kennedy. Here is a translated sample of Dunbar's invective:

Gaelic robber poet, vile beggar with your brats,
    Cunt-bitten coward Kennedy, natural coward,
Ill-fared and excreted, like a Dane on the wheels,
    It's as if the hawks had dined on your yellow snout;
Poorly-made monster, out of your mind on each full moon,
    Renounce, rogue, your rhyming, you only rave,
Your traitorous tongue has taken a highland strain;
    A lowland arse (=Erse/Gaelic) would make a better noise.

The *flyting* is crucial to Scottish poetry, but cursing matches in verse have also been found in a startlingly wide range of poetries.

SEE ALSO *poetic contest.*

folía Portuguese, Italian: "insanity." The *folía* is a Spanish stanzaic form of quatrains in which the lines may be octosyllabic or shorter. It was first mentioned in late fifteenth-century Portuguese documents and probably originated in a Portuguese fertility dance-song, whose original name comes from the furious tempo and lunatic action of the dancers. It was associated with wild singing and dance in Spain in the early seventeenth century. A variation of the four-line *seguidilla,* it is now commonly used for nonsense and other types of light verse. The term is wide-ranging and refers to light and popular music in local fiestas and other celebrations. It has the sound and movement of a Spanish dance.

SEE ALSO *octosyllabic verse, quatrain, seguidilla.*

folio The word *folio* derives from the Latin *folium,* "leaf." A folio is a large book that consists of sheets folded once only, into halves. The folio format was especially prestigious and primarily used for the work of leading theologians, historians, and philosophers during the early modern era. A quarto is much smaller and consists of sheets folded twice, into quarters. An octavo is folded three times and even smaller. During his lifetime, many of Shakespeare's plays were issued as quartos, which were less prized than the more expensive folios. The First Folio appeared in 1623, seven years after his death. This was the first time that a folio was devoted entirely to plays. There were three other subsequent Folios, in 1632, 1663, and 1685.

folk song A traditional song. The essential trait of folk song, a large part of the repertoire of folk verse, is that it is sung aloud. Folk songs are composed by individuals, usually untrained, nonprofessional musicians, and passed on by word of mouth, which is why there are so many variants of a given song. There are also many types of folk song, such as children's songs and lullabies, ballads and carols, spirituals and work songs. The folk song is composed by an individual and perpetuated by oral tradition, honed and changed by usage, which is how it becomes the expression of a group of people. There is often a strong connection between written songs and oral ones, as in the interchange between ballads and broadside ballads. Some nineteenth-century scholars naively believed that folk songs were created by people improvising in groups, which is untrue, though many people make changes to these songs over time in a process known as "communal re-creation." Folk songs were traditionally considered rural, but they can thrive both in the country, as in the rural blues, and in the city, as in the urban blues. They are both preindustrial and postindustrial. Individual singers continually modify the songs, which tend to be in a relatively simple style. The lyrics are memorized and carried along by the music. Folk songs often have highly formalized structures. The meters are frequently short, the verses fluent and melodic, the stanzas regular, reinforced by refrains. There is a specialized form, the cumulative song, or *randonnée,* in which the content as well as the length of each stanza expands by the introduction of new elements, which are then repeated. Many songs revolve around rites of passage, such as births, weddings, and deaths, which give them a functional dimension, recognized and understood by a wide swatch of a community. The cultural idea of folk song significantly changed in the mid-twentieth century because of the widespread folk song movement. The rubric of "folk song" widened to include new compositions and performances, some recorded, some adapted orally, by artists working in the mode of traditional folk songs. Here the line blurs between folk songs and popular songs.

SEE ALSO *ballad, blues, carol, copla, lullaby, oral poetry, pastourelle, refrain, romances, sea shanties, song, spirituals, work song.*

foot A group of syllables forming a metrical unit. The poetic foot is a measurable, conventional unit of rhythm. The term derives from Greek meter, which is quantitative. Rhythm in Greek poetry is based on units in which the balance of syllables is based not on loudness or stress, but on quantity, the time taken to speak it. The word *foot* relates to dance, and it seems likely that individual "feet" were based on dancing steps, on the balance and difference between short and long movements. The steps were matched by music. Later, written poetry was severed from dance (and music), but the notion of the foot was retained as a conventional unit of measurement. Quantitative meter depends on the relation of long (—) and short (u) syllables in each line. Every two- or three-syllable unit constituted the equivalent of a foot, which was called a *metron*. The main feet or *metra* were: the iamb (u —), the trochee or choree (— u), the anapest (u u —), the dactyl (— u u), the pyrrhic (u u), the spondee (— —), and the tribach (u u u).

The concept of the foot may be a useful abstraction since there are no poetic feet in nature, few pure examples of any of the standard feet in English verse. "For that matter," as Hugh Kenner puts it, "you will never encounter a round face, though the term is helpful . . . The term 'iambic foot' has the same sort of status as the term 'round face.' " Yet there is also some controversy over the adaptation of Greek meter to English meter and the usefulness of classical scansion in English.

The most common feet in English versification are:

iamb: a pair of syllables with the stress on the second one, as in the word *ădóre.*

trochee: a pair of syllables with the stress on the first one, as in the word *árdŏr.*

dactyl: a triad consisting of one stressed syllable followed by two unstressed ones, as in the word *rádĭănt.*

anapest: a triad consisting of two unstressed syllables followed by one stressed one, as in the words *ĭn ă bláze.*

spondee: two equally stressed syllables, as in the word *ámén.* It is the most common syllabic variation or substitution.

Here is Coleridge's witty illustrative poem "Metrical Feet" (ca. 1806):

Trochee trips from long to short;
From long to long in solemn sort
Slow Spondee stalks; strong foot! yet ill able
Ever to come up with Dactyl trisyllable.

Iambics march from short to long;—
With a leap and a bound the swift Anapests throng.

Here are some classical feet. The three-syllable feet are:

amphimacher, cretic — u —
amphibrach u — u
antibacchius, palimbacchius — — u
bacchius, bacchiac — — u
molossus — — —

The four-syllable feet are:

antispast u — — u
choreus (by resolution) u u u u
choriamb — u u —
di-iamb u — u —
dispondee — — — —
ditrochee — u — u
epitrite u — — — (known as the first, second, third, or fourth, according to the position of the first syllable)
ionic majore — — u u
ionic minore u u — —
paeon (known as first, second, third, or fourth according to the position of the stressed syllable) — u u u
proceleusmatic u u u u

The dochmiac is a five-syllable foot: u — — u — .

I have not included separate entries for feet that generally can't be applied to English-language poetry, such as the *antispast* ("pulling against"), a four-syllable foot (u — — u), which in English resolves into an iamb (u /) and a trochee (/ u), or the *molossus,* a unit of three long syllables (— — —), which, as George Saintsbury points out, is "practically impossible in English verse."

SEE ALSO *amphibrach, anapest, bacchius, choriamb, cretic, dactyl, iamb, ionic, meter, paeon, pyrrhic, spondee, trochee.* SEE ALSO the discussion of "accentual-syllabic meter" under the entry for *meter.*

form Latin: "shape." Form is the shape and structure of an object, which can be distinguished from its material and determined by the sum of its parts. A poetic form refers to the shape and structure of a literary work, the manner in which it is made, which is different than its subject matter, what it is about. The formal shape and underlying structure of a poem are the way it unfolds, its mode of being and method of understanding. Written poetic forms have their origins in oral musical forms. John Hollander explains, "Poetic form, as we know it, is an abstraction from, or residue of, musical form, from which it came to be divorced when writing replaced memory as a way of preserving poetic utterance in narrative, prayer, spell, and the like."

Critics often use the word *form* to designate the genre or type of a work (lyric form, epic form) or the pattern of metrical lines and rhymes. A prescribed or fixed form is thus a poetic form with a set of rules, such as the sonnet or villanelle, but it is not simply a container. The poet plays with the traditional structure, which creates a series of expectations that are fulfilled or defied in various ways. An organic form is an individual form that grows from within, taking shape as it develops, like a plant. Each of Walt Whitman's free verse poems, for example, has its own organic form. A larger critical sense of form treats it as the underlying principle of a work, the concept or idea that determines its organization.

SEE ALSO *genre, organic form.*

formes fixes "Fixed forms." Three structurally *formes fixes* — the ballade, the rondeau, and the virelay — characterized secular French poetry in the fourteenth and fifteenth centuries. The *bergerette,* a related form, was popular in the late fifteenth century. Each of the traditional *formes fixes* is characterized by a complex pattern of repetitions and a refrain. The lyrics were translated into musical forms until the end of the fifteenth century. After that, they were written but no longer sung. The medieval poet and composer Guillaume de Machaut compiled the first comprehensive repertory of these forms.

SEE ALSO *ballade, rondeau, virelay.*

fornyrðislag, see *edda.*

found poem A borrowed text, a piece of writing that takes an existing text and presents it as a poem. Something that was never intended to be a poem—a newspaper article, a street sign, a letter, a scrap of conversation—is refashioned as a poem, often through lineation. The found poem works by changing the concept in a piece of writing, by distorting its original intent. Something mundane takes on a new layer of meaning. "Art must not look like art," Marcel Duchamp said, and the found poem is similar to his ready-mades and other found objects that appear in Pop Art, such as Andy Warhol's soup cans. "The original meaning remains intact, but now it swings between two poles," as Annie Dillard puts it in her book of found poems, *Mornings Like This* (1995). In essence, W. B. Yeats created a found poem when he turned Walter Pater's prose description of the Mona Lisa from *The Renaissance* (1873) into free verse and published it as the first poem in *The Oxford Book of Modern Verse* (1938). Without calling what they are doing found poetry, many modern poets have taken portions of previous texts and incorporated them into longer poems. One thinks, for example, of the way that Ezra Pound includes an array of official and unofficial historical documents into *The Cantos* (1915–1969). The found poem suggests that something was hidden or lost that has now been discovered or "found." In French, found poetry is called *Poésie d'emprunt,* which translates as "borrowed poetry" or "expropriated poetry." George Hitchcock put together the first anthology of found poetry in *Losers Weepers: Poems Found Practically Everywhere* (1969).

SEE ALSO *collage.*

Four Ages of Poetry Thomas Love Peacock's treatise "The Four Ages of Poetry" (1820) divided poetry into four periods: iron, gold, silver, and brass. It also criticized contemporary poetry, making the case that poetry is useless in an advanced industrial society. This argument excited his friend Percy Bysshe Shelley into "a sacred rage." Shelley's "A Defence of Poetry" (1821) argues that all literature radiates from the same deep wellspring and creative source.

SEE ALSO *ars poetica, romanticism.*

fragment A part broken off, something cut or detached from the whole, something imperfect. Much of the work of the ancients comes down to us in fragments and tatters, cut pieces. As W. R. Johnson puts it in *The Idea of Lyric* (1982):

> No experience in reading, perhaps, is more depressing and more frustrating than to open a volume of Sappho's fragments and to recognize, yet again — one always hopes that somehow this time it will be different — that this poetry is all but lost to us. . . . Even though we know that Greek lyric is mere fragments, indeed, *because* we know that Greek lyric is mere fragments, we act, speak, and write as if the unthinkable had not happened, as if pious bishops, careless monks, and hungry mice had not consigned Sappho and her lyrical colleagues to irremediable oblivion.

In the medieval and Renaissance eras, fragments were often allegorical, suggesting something broken off from a divine whole. They were survivals from an earlier era. Readers had become so accustomed to reading unfinished texts by the early nineteenth century that it became acceptable and even fashionable to publish poems that were intentionally fragmentary. The passion for ruins as well as the taste for poetic relics and antiquities contributed to the acceptance of the romantic fragment, which we now recognize as a genre in its own right and a prototype of romantic poetry in general. One of Friedrich Schlegel's fragments defines the genre: "A Fragment must as a miniature work of art be entirely isolated from the surrounding world and perfect in itself, like a hedgehog." Coleridge's "Kubla Khan: or a Vision in a Dream. A Fragment" (1816), Keats's "Hyperion. A Fragment" (1818–1819), and Byron's "The Giaour. A Fragment of a Turkish Tale" (1813) all were presented as lyrics with a purposeful partiality. Anne Janowitz characterizes the romantic fragment as "a *partial whole* — either a remnant of something once complete and now broken or decayed, or the beginning of something that remains unaccomplished." It becomes a radiant moment out of time, which can never be completed because it aspires to the infinite.

The modernist poets reinvented the fragment as an acutely self-conscious mode of writing that breaks the flow of time, leaving gaps and tears, lacunae. They created discontinuous texts, collages and mosaics, fragmentary epics such as Ezra Pound's *The Cantos* (1915–1969), Louis Zukofsky's *"A"* (1927–1978), and T. S. Eliot's "The Waste Land" (1922), which he summarizes as "These fragments I have shored against my ruins." There is even greater vertigo in the destabilizing fragments of contemporary poetry, sometimes cooly giddy, as in John Ashbery, sometimes desperate for insight, as in Jorie Graham. In general, postmodernism is less regretful and nostalgic than modernism — it no longer yearns for wholeness — and postmodern poets typically view the fragment as a kind of emancipation that breaks the omnipotence of totalizing systems. As a genre of disruption, the postmodern aesthetic of the fragment revels in its own incompleteness, its partiality, since all texts are incomplete and all poetic language insufficient. "The interruption of the incessant," Maurice Blanchot writes, "that is the distinguishing characteristic of fragmentary writing."

SEE ALSO *allegory, collage, epiphany, modernism, postmodernism, romanticism.*

frasca The Italian word *frasca* means "a little twig" or "a trifle" and also suggests a "light, frivolous person." In the Renaissance, it referred to a short occasional poem, a concise epigram, sometimes frivolous, sometimes more serious and philosophical. The Polish poet Jan Kochanowski's collection of court poems in this form was called *Fraszki* (1584), which he uses to meditate on poetry, "To the Muses" ("Maidens . . . I do not ever want to separate from you"), as well as "On Human Life" ("Everything that we think is trifles, / Everything that we do is trifles").

SEE ALSO *occasional poem.*

free-meter poetry, see *strict-meter poetry.*

free verse A poetry of organic rhythms, of deliberate irregularity, improvisatory delight. Free verse is a form of nonmetrical writing that takes pleasure in a various and emergent verbal music. "As regarding rhythm," Ezra Pound writes in "A Retrospect" (1918): "to compose in the sequence of the musical phrase, not in sequence of a metronome." Free verse is often inspired by the cadence — the natural rhythm, the inner tune — of spoken language. It possesses visual form and uses the graphic line to differentiate itself from prose. "The words are more *poised* than in prose," Louis MacNeice states in *Modern Poetry* (1938); "they are not only, like the words in typical prose, contributory to the total effect, but are to be attended to, in passing, for their own sake." The dream of free verse: an originary verbal music for every poem. Jorge Luis Borges explains: "Beyond its rhythm, the typographical appearance of free verse informs the reader that what lies in store for him is not information or reasoning but emotion."

The term *free verse* is a literal translation of *vers libre,* which was employed by French symbolist poets seeking freedom from the strictures of the alexandrine. It has antecedents in medieval alliterative verse, in highly rhythmic and rhymed prose, in Milton's liberated blank-verse lines and verse paragraphs. But the greatest antecedent is the King James version of the Psalms and the Song of Songs, based in part on the original Hebrew cadences. The rhetorical parallelism and expansive repetitions of the Hebrew Bible inspired Christopher Smart, who created his own canticles of praise in *Jubilate Agno* (1759–1763); William Blake, whose long-lined visionary poems have the power of prophetic utterance; and Walt Whitman, the progenitor of American free verse, who hungered for a line large enough to express the totality of life:

> My voice goes after what my eyes cannot reach,
> With the twirl of my tongue I encompass worlds and volumes of
>   worlds.
> Speech is the twin of my vision, it is unequal to measure itself . . .

Whitman's rhythms directly influenced Gerard Manley Hopkins's long-lined metrical experiments and William Carlos Williams's exercises in a new measure, the three-ply line and the variable foot. They are an influence, mostly repressed, on T. S. Eliot, who initiated modern poetry with the iambic-based free-verse rhythms of "The Love Song of J. Alfred Prufrock" (1920), and Ezra Pound, whose poem "The Return" (1912) W. B. Yeats praised as the "most beautiful poem that has been written in the free form, one of the few in which I find real organic rhythms." Some of Whitman's international progeny: Apollinaire (France), Pessoa (Portugal), Lorca (Spain), Vallejo (Peru), Neruda (Chile), Paz (Mexico), Borges (Argentina), Martí (Cuba), Darío (Nicaragua). Whitman leads a long line of visionary poets, such as Hart Crane and D. H. Lawrence, Galway Kinnell, Gerald Stern, and Muriel Rukeyser. Formally, Whitman is the progenitor of C. K. Williams's rangy inclusive cadences and Charles Wright's use of a two-part dropped line, a long line with an additional rhythmic (and spatial) thrust. So, too, Whitman stands behind the improvisatory free-verse rhythms of such poets as Langston Hughes, Philip Levine, and Michael Harper, all influenced by jazz, and such New York poets as Frank O'Hara, John Ashbery, and James Schuyler, all influenced by abstract expressionism. Jazz and action painting are two good American analogues for modern free verse.

"If one thinks of the literal root of the word verse, 'a line, furrow, turning — *vertere,* to turn . . . ,' he will come to a sense of 'free verse' as that instance of writing in poetry which 'turns' upon an occasion intimate with, in fact, the issue of its own nature," Robert Creeley explains in "Notes Apropos 'Free Verse' " (1966). Free verse also turns in the space of short-lined poems. The short line often gives a feeling that something has been taken away, which has proved especially suitable for poems of loss. It can also give the feeling of clearing away the clutter and has thus proved useful for the imagist poems of T. E. Hulme, F. S. Flint, and H. D., and the objectivist works of George Oppen, Charles Reznikoff, and Louis Zukofsky. As the length of the lines varies in free-verse poems, so the reader participates in the making of poetic thought. The free-verse poem fits no mold; it has no preexistent pattern. The reader supplies the verbal speeds, intonations, emphasis. Or as Frank O'Hara says: "You just go on your nerve."

SEE ALSO *Beats, blank verse, cadence, jazz poetry, line, prose poem, variable foot, vers libre.*

fu The word *fu* means "rhyme-prose" in Chinese. This narrative form — a mixed genre of prose and verse — often started with a narrative or expository passage, and then shifted into long descriptions in verse. It sometimes concluded with a short poem called a *tz'u* or *fan tz'u.* Some early examples, such as the "Rhapsody on Mount Kao-t'ang," which is attributed to Sung Yü (290?–222 B.C.E.), suggest that the form may have originated in the magical incantations of shamanism. Over time, the *fu* became regularized into a style of parallelism, which created balanced units, as in Yü Hsin's sixth-century "Lament for the South" on the fall of the Liang Dynasty. The master work of the poet and critic Lu Chi (261–303) is his "Wen-fu" or "The Art of Writing," a poetic treatise on the nature of the creative process, which begins: "The poet stands at the center of the universe."

SEE ALSO *parallelism, rhymed prose, shaman, tz'u.*

the Fugitives The Fugitives were a group of sixteen Southern poets and critics who met at Vanderbilt University and gathered often in Nashville, Tennessee. John Crowe Ransom, Allen Tate, Donald Davidson, and the young Robert Penn Warren were all closely associated with the group and helped to publish the magazine *The Fugitive* from 1922 to 1925. The Fugitives conducted a furious war on behalf of concrete particularity against scientific abstractionism. In their commitment to the historical past, their anti-industrialism, their hatred of abstraction, their diagnosis of what Tate called the "deep illness of the mind," dissociation of sensibility, their belief in what Ransom defined as the "antipathy between art and science," and their prevailing sense of the tragedy of modern man, the Fugitives developed a brand of what might be called Traditionalist Modernism. They believed that the free-verse revolution needed a countercurrent and worked within traditional forms. Ransom, Tate, and Warren all became leading New Critics, which redefined the way that American poetry was read in the classroom.

The Fugitives were classicists in literature and traditionalists in religion: they also became regionalists. By the end of the 1920s, they had regrouped as Agrarians, a movement that culminated in the manifesto *I'll Take My Stand* (1930). This rear-guard group, which was not purely literary in focus, defended an agrarian economy and looked back nostalgically to a preindustrial Christian south.

SEE ALSO *dissociation of sensibility, modernism, New Criticism.*

fustian The word for thick cotton cloth came to mean, in literary terms, inflated, bombastic language. Hence these lines from Alexander Pope's "Epistle to Dr. Arbuthnot" (1735) about a writer "whose fustian's so sublimely bad / It is not poetry, but prose run mad."

SEE ALSO *bombast.*

futurism Filippo Tommaso Marinetti (1876–1944) dramatically launched the futurist movement on February 20, 1909, with his "violently upsetting, incendiary manifesto" called "The Founding and Manifesto of Futurism" ("We had stayed up all night, my friends and I") and then bombarded Europe with his proclamations about the future. The word *futurism* had a startling success, and the new movement spread rapidly through Italy, France, Spain, England, and Russia. The hyperkinetic Marinetti, who christened himself "the caffeine of Europe," the self-proclaimed "primitive of a new sensibility," was the driving force of futurism. "I felt, all of a sudden, that articles, poetries, and polemics no longer sufficed," he said. "You had to change methods, go down in the street, seize power in all the theatres, and introduce the fisticuff into the war of art." The manifesto was his weapon, and he used it to praise danger and revolt, aggressive action, "the beauty of speed" (he famously proclaimed that "A racing car . . . is more beautiful than the *Victory of Samothrace*"), "the metallization of man," the violent joys of crowds and cities. He also showed appalling innocence about war, which he glorified as "the world's only hygiene."

The Italian futurists include the poets Paolo Buzzi and Corrado Govani; the painters Umberto Boccioni, Gino Severini, Carlo Carra, and Giacomo Balla; the composers Luigi Russolo and Francesco Balilla Pratella; and Il Duce himself, Benito Mussolini. Even in Italy, there were a variety of futurisms, including *Noisism* or *Bruitism,* which wanted to join experiences and senses to each other (Carlo Carra called it "The Painting of Sounds, Noises, and Smells," 1913), and *Tactilism* (the futurism of touch) and a *Futurism of Woman* (Valentine de Saint-Point, "Manifesto of Futurist Woman," 1912). As Apollinaire noted in his parody manifesto "L'Antitradition futuriste" (1913), futurism was the first collective effort to suppress history in the name of art. There is no greater critique than Walter Benjamin's summary judgment at the end of "The Work of Art in the Age of Mechanical Reproduction" (1936):

> Fascism attempts to organize the newly created proletarian masses without affecting the property structure which the masses strive to eliminate. Fascism sees its salvation in giving these masses not their right, but instead a chance to express themselves. The masses have a right to change property relations; Fascism seeks to give them an expression while reserving property. The logical result of Fascism is the introduction of aesthetics into public life.
>
> All efforts to make politics aesthetic culminate in one thing: war. War and only war can set a goal for mass movements on the largest scale while respecting the traditional property systems.
>
> *Fiat ars—pereat mundus,* says Fascism, and, as Marinetti admits, expects war to supply the artistic gratification of a sense of perception that has been changed by technology. This is evidently the consummation of *l'art pour l'art.* Mankind, which in Homer's time was an object of contemplation for the Olympian gods, now is one for itself. Its self-alienation has reached such a point that it can experience its own destruction as an aesthetic pleasure of the first order. This is the situation of politics which Fascism is rendering aesthetic. Communism responds by politicizing art.

Russian futurism was an offshoot of futurism that was so rich, various, and contradictory that it became its own complex movement. The Russian avant-garde poets and artists did not think of themselves as futurists per se (the name was pinned on them by newspapers). The poet, painter, and publisher David Burliuk (1882–1967) organized the Hylean poets, as they first called themselves, and convinced them to issue the joint manifesto "A Slap in the Face of Public Taste" (1912), which he signed along with Alexei Kruchenykh (1886–1968), Vladimir Mayakovsky (1893–1930), and Velimir Khlebnikov (1885–1922). It announced that "*We* alone are the *face* of our *Time*"; it pledged "to stand on the rock of the word 'we' amidst the sea of boos and outrage"; and it predicted "the New Coming Beauty of the Self-sufficient (self-centered) Word." Mayakovsky's poetry faces the future and his defiant, revolutionary early work testifies to futurist energies. Khlebnikov was possibly the most radical experimenter in futurism. He cofounded with Kruchenykh the wildly imaginative, disruptive sound poetry called *zaum.*

There were four distinct Russian futurist groups: Cubo-futurism, ego-futurism, the Mezzanine of Poetry, and Centrifuge. What these groups shared was a dedication to modernism and a determination to denounce each other.

The Hylean Group developed into the Cubo-futurists, a group of painters who combined the Cubist techniques of Pablo Picasso, Georges Braques, and Juan Gris with the dynamism of the Italian futurists. Painters such as Mikhail Larionov, Natalia Goncharova, and Kazimir Malevich were inspired by futurist poems, and they included various letters, at times even whole words, in their compositions. They treated words as material things.

The ego-futurist collective paid direct homage to Marinetti and introduced the word *futurism* to the Russian literary scene. The aristocratic poet Igor Severyanin tried to create a new trend within futurism in 1911 with his small brochure *Prolog (Ego-Futurism)* that attacked the extreme objectivity of the Cubo-futurists and proposed an alternative subjectivity, which included a more ostentatious egoism and sensuality. "All of history lies before us," Graal-Arelsky (the pseudonym of Stepan Stepanovich Petrov) argued in "Egopoetry in Poetry" (1912): "Nature created us. Only She should rule us in our actions and efforts. She placed egoism inside of us; we should develop it. Egoism unites us all, because we are all egoists."

Lev Zak introduced the short-lived movement the Mezzanine of Poetry, which consisted of Konstantin Bolshakov, Riuruk Ivnev, Vadim Shershenevich, Marinetti's eager translator, and Zak himself. "Darling! Please come to the opening of our Mezzanine!" Zak wrote in his invitation to the movement: "The image of the Most Charming One, which each of us has locked in his soul, makes all things, all thoughts, and all passions equally poetic."

Centrifuge was the last offshoot of futurism before the Russian Revolution. It was launched in 1914 by Sergei Bobrov, Nikolay Aseyev, and Boris Pasternak with the almanac *Rukonog* (a trans-rational coinage that meant *Handfoot*). Pasternak cosigned a scurrilous charter denouncing rival futurists. This led to a settling of accounts between the anti-Centrifuge futurists and the Centrifuge futurists at a Moscow café on a hot day in May 1914. But at the meeting, Pasternak was infatuated with Mayakovsky, his supposed enemy, and immediately opted out of the proposed feud. "I carried the whole of him with me that day from the boulevard into my life," he said later. "But he was enormous; there was no holding on to him when apart from him. And I kept losing him."

SEE ALSO *avant-garde, collage, Cubist poetry, Dadaism, modernism, Oberiu, parole in libertà, Russian formalism, Silver Age, sound poetry, spontaneity, verbless poetry, zaum.*

gai saber (*gaia sciensa*) A Provençal term for the "poetic skill" of the troubadours. It especially suggests the troubadour art of composing love poems, as set forth in the fourteenth-century work *Leys d'amors.* The Old Provençal phrase *gai saber,* which means "gay knowledge" or "gay science," refers to the art of poetry. *Gai Saber* became the name of a group of seven troubadours who gathered in Toulouse in 1324 to restore the lost glory of the Provençal language. In 1872, Ralph Waldo Emerson said, "Poetry is the gai science." Ten years later, Friedrich Nietzsche borrowed the expression for *The Gay Science.*

SEE ALSO *troubadour.*

galliambic This Greek meter took its name from the priests, the Galli, who worshiped in the cult of Cybele, the great mother-goddess. The technical name of the *galliambic* is *ionic tetrameter catalectic,* which has four ionic feet per line (*ionic majore* — — u u or *ionic minore* u u — —) with a final syllable suppressed. Walter Savage Landor said that "the Galliambic has a grave and severe majesty about it, such as haunted the forests of Ida and befitted the sanctuary of the great goddess. It is grand and awful, and approaches nearer to the pure ideal of poetry than perhaps any other in any language." It was adopted in the Alexandrine era by Callimachus and his contemporaries, used in Latin by Catullus in the *Attis* poem (*Carmen 63*), and adapted into English by George Meredith in *Phaéthôn,* subtitled *Atempted in the Galliambic Measure* (1887), and Lord Tennyson in *Boädicea* (1864). Tennyson gives a sense of the stately measure in the opening lines, each of which breaks in the middle and speeds up at the end:

> While about the shore of Mona those Neronian legionaries
> Burnt and broke the grove and altar of the Druid and Druidess,
> Far in the East Boädicéa, standing loftily charioted,
> Mad and maddening all that heard her in her fierce volubility,
> Girt by half the tribes of Britain, near the colony Cámulodúne,
> Yelled and shrieked between her daughters o'er a wild confederacy.

SEE ALSO *foot, ionic, meter.*

the Gang (Di Khalyastre) The Warsaw poets Peretz Markish (1895–1952), Uri Zvi Greenberg (1896–1981), and Melech Ravitch (1893–1976) expressed the impudent rebelliousness of youth in their futurist Yiddish poems. The nightmare of World War I stands behind the explosive work of the "poetic triumvirate," who treated the cosmos, rather than the shtetl, as their true home. Markish proclaimed, "Our standard *is not the beautiful,* but the horrible." Hillel Zeitlin gave these poets the derogatory nickname *Di Kkalyastre,* the Gang, because of their outrageous behavior, such as holding readings on Saturday mornings, the Jewish Sabbath. The group took Zeitlin's insulting name as a badge of honor and called their short-lived literary magazine *Di Khalyastre,* which was followed by *Albatros,* a journal that exalted an extreme individualism and revolutionary spirit, a renewed Yiddish and secular Jewish national culture. The group dispersed when Markish left for Soviet Russia, Ravitch moved to Australia, and Greenberg immigrated to Palestine in 1925.

SEE ALSO *futurism.*

garcilasistas The poets who began writing in the years before the Spanish Civil War modeled their work on the sixteenth-century golden age poet Garcilaso de la Vega (ca. 1501–1536). The most astonishing *garcilasista* was Miguel Hernández (1910–1942), a shepherd boy from the village of Orihuela in eastern Spain who, under the guidance of a local priest, educated himself in the Spanish golden age. His early manner culminated in the sonnets of his second book, *The Unending Lightning* (1936), where the poet's volcanic feelings collide with the classical restraints of the traditional form.

Luis Rosales (1910–1992) was the first *garcilasista* to ease into a more flexible poetry, and Hernández followed suit in his embrace of larger free-verse rhythms and more surrealistic imagery, which coincided with his growing commitment to the anti-Fascist cause.

SEE ALSO *the golden age, pure poetry, Surrealism.*

gaucho poetry Gaucho poetry refers to the poetry *by* as well as *about* the gauchos, those cowboy figures who are a deep part of Argentina's national consciousness. The gaucho is also celebrated as a trailblazer in southern Brazil and Uruguay. The gauchos were generally nomads who lived on the pampas, and the gaucho genre originated in the Río de la Plata region early in the nineteenth century. It includes the poetry of the *payadores,* illiterate peasants who roamed the vast, open land singing ballads and strumming guitars, often competing in improvised musical face-offs called *payadas,* or *contrapuntos.* It also includes the traditional Spanish ballads brought to South America by Spanish explorers and conquerors as early as the sixteenth century, as well as the rustic dialogues of colonial country people, a form of folk drama. Finally, it includes the so-called cultivated and contemporary poetry written about the romantic life of the gauchos.

Most gaucho poetry consists of literary imitations of the folk style of the early *payadores.* The first of these poets was the Uruguyan Bartolomé Hidalgo (1788–1822), who specialized in *cielito* ("little heaven"), an octosyllabic quatrain rhyming in the second and fourth lines. Hidalgo was followed by the Argentines Hilario Ascasubi (1807–1877), whose poetry Jorge Luis Borges calls "happy and valiant"; Estanislao del Campo (1834–1880); and José Hernández (1834–1886), whose masterpiece *Martín Fierro* (1872, 1879) has generally been considered the fountainhead of Argentine literature. Martin Fierro is a gaucho, a free, poor, pampas dweller, who is illegally drafted into the Argentine military for a border war, eventually deserts, and becomes a *gaucho matrero,* an outlaw, an emblematic figure who stands against corruption. Leopoldo Lugones first made the claim for the poem as a national epic in *El Payador* (1916). With Margarita Guerrero, Borges wrote a book of essays about the poem and its reception, *El "Martín Fierro"* (1953), and emphasized that "gauchesque" poetry was not written by gauchos, but by educated literary writers who adopted the eight-syllable line of the folk ballad and successfully impersonated the *payadores.* Borges noticed that *Martín*

Fierro was written in "a gauchesco-accented Spanish," but that the actual *payadores,* whom he heard in the surroundings of Buenos Aires, reject the idea of versifying in street slang and seek a higher-sounding language. Borges greatly admired the artistry of the poem, which he viewed less as an epic and more as a verse novel that brought together two Argentine literary traditions, rural and urban, oral and written.

SEE ALSO *cowboy poetry, octosyllabic verse, payada, verse novel.*

Generation of '98 Miguel de Unamuno (1864–1936), Antonio Machado (1875–1939), and Juan Ramón Jimenez (1881–1958) created a road into the twentieth century for Spanish poetry. Azorín (the pseudonym of José Martinez Ruiz) called them the Generation of '98 and thus labeled a group of writers and intellectuals linked by a rebellious spirit and a determination to help Spain escape from its dispiriting loss to the United States in the Spanish American War in 1898. As Hardie St. Martin puts it, "Unamuno, Machado, and Jiménez especially hated literary realism, positivism, middle-class morality, and the muddled politics of nineteenth-century Spain." The Nicaraguan poet Rubén Dario arrived in Spain and helped propel Spanish poetry out of its provincialism.

Each poet in the Generation of '98 was influenced by Dario's *modernismo* and rebelled against it. Unamuno believed that a poet should express himself as naturally and plainly as possible, like a man. His poetry expressed his philosophy that reason offers no consolation for the tragedy of death in human life. Machado's poetry takes a deeply inward path ("I thought that the substance of poetry does not lie in the sound-value of the word, nor in its color, nor in a complex of sensations but in the deep pulse of the spirit; and this deep pulse is what the soul contributes, if it contributes anything, or what it says, if it says anything, with its own voice"). Jiménez cut through the bramble of *modernismo* in his search for a new *poesía desnuda,* or naked poetry. He concentrated on the interior of the poem and created a poetic ethic for the poets to come, the Generation of '27.

SEE ALSO *Generation of '27, modernismo, naked poetry.*

Generation of '27 Nineteen twenty-seven was the tercentenary anniversary of the death of the Spanish poet Luis de Góngora (1561–1627), and a group of young poets gathered to celebrate the baroque master. That was the official starting point — a turn to Gongorism — for a generation of Spanish poets, who created a new Spanish golden age after the *Síglo de Oro* of the sixteenth and seventeenth centuries. The talented group included Federico García Lorca (1898–1936), Jorge Guillén (1893–1984), Vicente Aleixandre (1898–1984), Dámaso Alonso (1898–1990), Luis Cernuda (1902–1963), Rafael Alberti (1902–1999), Geraldo Diego (1896–1987), Emilo Prados (1899–1987), and Manuel Altolaguirre (1905–1959). Cernuda preferred the term "the generation of 1925," but 1927 stuck as the initiating point, which was marked by Lorca's essay "The Poetic Image in Don Luis de Góngora"; Alonso's prose edition of Góngora's *Soledades* (*Solitudes*); an anthology of neogóngorist efforts, *Antología poética en honor de Góngora;* and what Diego called "all sorts of serious and frivolous youthful manifestations," including, the legend goes, a mock ceremony in which Alonso and Alberti burned effigies of Góngora's enemies, which was followed the next day by a "solemn requiem mass" for Góngora himself. Guillén remembered in *Language and Poetry* (1936): "There was no program, there was no manifesto attacking or defending fixed positions. There were dialogues, letters, dinners, walks, and friendship under the bright light of Madrid." The heady atmosphere of the Second Republic contributed to the freedom of these internationally minded young poets, who were all lacerated by the Spanish Civil War: murdered like Lorca, forced into exile like Alberti, or silenced at home like Aleixandre, who explained in 1953: "They all left, all together at one moment, on very different paths." Spanish Fascism crushed modern Spanish poetry.

SEE ALSO *Generation of '98, the golden age, Gongorism, modernism, Surrealism.*

Generation of 1930 George Seféris (1900–1971), Odysseus Elytis (1911–1996), and Yannis Ritsos (1909–1990) reinvigorated Greek poetry after the Asia Minor disaster and cultural defeatism of 1922. They discarded old verse forms, wedded ancient mythology to the situation of modern man (Seferis), celebrated the Aegean as an ideal sensuous world (Elytis), and married a startling simplicity, a wild creativity, and a furious social vision (Ritsos). Seféris published *The Turning Point* in 1931, but the real turning point may have been 1934 and 1935 when the liberating winds of modernism, of Surrealism and free verse, spread through Greek poetry.

SEE ALSO *free verse, modernism, Surrealism.*

Generation of 1930 (Generación del Treinta) In Puerto Rico, the Generation of 1930, also known as the "generation in crisis," sought to investigate and define Puerto Rican culture. Two of the founding members, Samuel R. Quiñones and Vicente Géigel Polanco, had belonged to the avant-garde poetry group of the twenties, *noísmo* or "Grupo No," whose philosophy was based on cultural skepticism and denial. Now they sought something more educationally useful. The generation included the essayist Antonio S. Pedreira, whose *Insularismo* (1934) was the first in-depth study of what it means to be Puerto Rican; the playwright Manuel Méndez Bellester; the novelist Enrique A Laguerre; the poet and educator Cesário Rosa-Nieves; and the poet Julia de Burgos, the bedrock of Puerto Rican poetry, who was a Puerto Rican *independista.* Their work is a quest for Puerto Rican identity. They were forerunners to the *Generación del 1940,* who sought cultural and political independence from both Spain and the United States.

genethliacon, see *birthday poems.*

genre The word *genre* derives from the Latin *genus,* meaning "kind" or "sort." A genre is a class or species of texts. It is a subgroup of literature. We move from the particular work (*King Lear,* 1608) to the general literary category or genre (*tragedy*). The works within a genre — "Every work of literature belongs to at least one genre" (Alistair Fowler) — are marked by conventions and norms, resemblances and differences, which suggest possibilities of meaning. A genre provides a mode of discourse, a horizon. It exists in relationship to other genres. Genres are interdependent. Each genre creates a set of expectations, an implicit agreement between an oral performer and an audience, or else a writer and a reader. Genres are time-bound and continually change. Modulation is the norm. The conventions that determine a genre are often fulfilled and expanded, sometimes thwarted, frequently violated.

Genre criticism has traditionally been concerned with both the development of literary forms and the classification and description of literary texts. Literary theory brought the account of genres to the forefront of literary studies. "An account of genres should be an attempt to define the classes which have been functional in the processes of reading and writing, the sets of expectations which have enabled readers to naturalize texts and give them a relation to the world," Jonathan Culler prescribes in *Structuralist*

Poetics (1976), "or, if one prefer to look at it in another way, the possible functions of language which are available to writers at any given period."

SEE ALSO *kind.*

Georgekreis Stefan George (1868–1933) was surrounded by a group of disciples who shared his views and supported his efforts to renew German civilization. This fluid inner circle, this "secret Germany," comprised a kind of cultural elite. George and his group believed in the spiritual renewal of German culture through the development of a pure poetic language that celebrated pagan ideals and recognized the power of myth. They opposed what they viewed as an anemic modern civilization. The group included Ernst Bertram (1884–1957), Max Dauthendey (1867–1918), Friedrich Gundolf (1880–1931), the Jewish poet Karl Wolfskehl (1869–1948, whose gravestone is chiseled with the words *Exul Poeta* (a poet in exile), and, for a little while, the Austrian modernist Hugo von Hofmannsthal (1874–1929), who ultimately refused membership in the circle. Some of George's disciples were anti-Semetic, others were Jewish. Some critics considered his work proto-fascist, but George himself rejected any attempts to appropriate his work for political ends.

Georgian poets Between 1912 and 1922, Edward Marsh edited five anthologies of English poetry entitled *Georgian Poets.* Strictly speaking, the Georgian poets are the lyric poets who worked in this ten-year period during the reign of King George V. Loosely speaking, the term can refer to poets writing with a conservative bent in traditional fixed forms between 1912 and 1940. Georgian poetry is a countercurrent to modernism. The Georgians thought of themselves as modern — they lowered the diction of Victorian poetry — but turned away from the cataclysms of the twentieth century. They looked nostalgically toward romantic poetry and favored bucolic subjects. Their poetry is genteel, but also keenly alert to the character of the English countryside. In contrast to the modernists, they turned toward and not away from middle-class readers. The first anthology included Rupert Brooke (1887–1915), Walter de la Mare (1873–1956), and G. K. Chesterton (1874–1936). The major war poets all developed out of the Georgian movement, such as Wilfred Owen (1893–1918), Isaac Rosenberg (1890–1918), and Edward Thomas (1878–1917). The Georgian poets stand as an important link in the chain that runs between Thomas Hardy (1840–1928) and Philip Larkin (1922–1985).

SEE ALSO *Dymock poets, Edwardian Age, modernism.*

georgic From Latin, *georgicus,* "agricultural," which derives from the Greek word for earth, *gê.* The georgic is a how-to or didactic poem that gives instructions about some skill, art, or science. In "Essay on the Georgics" (1697), Joseph Addison points out that this "class of Poetry . . . consists in giving plain and direct instructions," which is what distinguishes it from other types of the pastoral poem. Its subject is nature. Its practical strategy is to instruct readers on rural occupations, such as farming, shearing, etc. It puts physical labor into poetry and regards nature in terms of necessary work. It is written in the past or present tense, but directed toward the future.

The archaic poet Hesiod inaugurated the tradition in his *Works and Days* (eighth century B.C.E.), which consists of agricultural advice, with frequent digressions for mythological lore and philosophical considerations. Formulaic elements in the poem suggest that Hesiod was an oral poet or, possibly, inherited an oral tradition. The poem is directed toward a second person and broods on the inevitability of work: *labor omnia vincit.* Virgil's *Georgics* (37–30 B.C.E.), which John Dryden called "the best poem of the best poet," is the centerpiece of the genre. Virgil's four long poems take up plowing and the weather, the cultivation of trees and vines, the rearing of cattle, and the care of bees. Virgil makes the farmer's hard work a basis for living.

Virgil's influence was far-reaching, especially in eighteenth-century Britain, where the country tradition was developed by James Thomson ("the English Vergil") in *The Seasons* (1730), which vividly treats the seasons in succession, and William Cowper in *The Task* (1785), his spiritual autobiography: "God made the country, and man made the town." Andrés Bello, who was born in Venezuela and later became a Chilean citizen, inaugurated a tradition of American Georgics in his two-volume epic poem *América* (1823, 1826). The tradition includes Gregorio Gutiérrez González's *Memoir on the Cultivation of Maize in Antioquia* (1881) and Leopoldo Lugones's *Secular Odes* (1910). Robert Frost, like Henry David Thoreau, had georgic tendencies. Both writers emphasize rural labor and hard knowledge, the knowledge born of labor. The Kentucky poet and farmer Wendell Berry forcefully brings the georgic into contemporary poetry.

SEE ALSO *didactic poetry, eclogue, pastoral.*

gest, geste, see *chansons de geste.*

gestalt *Gestalt* is a psychological term that means "unified whole." It has been adapted to describe the holistic effect of a piece of literature. A poem is more than the sum of its parts, and the gestalt of a poem characterizes the overall effect or experience of wholeness. Poetry has also had a place in gestalt therapy. For example, in *Creative Process in Gestalt Therapy* (1977), Joseph Zinker compares poetry writing to psychotherapy and argues that both are involved with change and transformation. He refers to the process of writing as dynamic: "A poem can be rewritten a thousand times, each attempt a new way of experiencing the process of one's thoughts. The new words themselves modify one's experience, one's ideas, words, and images. Analogies and metaphors move fluidly into one another like the conversation of good friends. Each rewritten poem, like each unit of an ongoing relationship, has its own internal validity."

ghazal A lyric form of Eastern poetry, which dates to seventh-century Arabia and has flourished in Arabic, Persian, Turkish, Urdu, and Pashto. It developed as an offshoot of the praise poem. One meaning of the word *ghazal* is "the talk of boys and girls"; in other words, sweet talk or verbal lovemaking. Another meaning of *ghazal* is the cry of the gazelle when it is cornered in a hunt and knows it must die. This explains, as Ahmed Ali puts it, "the atmosphere of sadness and grief that pervades the ghazal" as well as its "dedication to love and the beloved." The *ghazal* tends to blur the distinction between erotic and divine love. So, too, wine-drinking is one of the most common metaphors for spiritual intoxication.

The form consists of five named parts:

1. *Sher:* Five or more autonomous couplets. Each two-line unit is independent, disjunctive. This is the most consistent — and sometimes the only — rule followed by English-language *ghazals.*
2. *Beher:* Metric consistency, counted syllables. There are nineteen *beher*

in Urdu, which can be classified as short, medium, and long. The key formality is that the lines of each couplet should be of equal *beher,* or length.

3. *Radif:* The second end word of each couplet should repeat: *aa, ba, ca, da,* etc. The two-line stanzas thus set up a kind of echo chamber.
4. *Qafia:* The poem contains internal rhyme in each line of the first couplet and in the last line of each couplet.
5. *Mahkta:* The poet often signs his name in the final couplet.

Each couplet in a *ghazal* is a separate entity, and yet, as Agha Shahid Ali states, "There is, underlying the ghazal, a profound and complex cultural association and memory and expectation, as well as an implicit recognition of the human personality and its infinite variety."

The early *ghazals* were short and easy to sing. Later, the form began to take on mystical and philosophical themes. The Persian or Farsi master is Hafez (1325–1389), the Urdu master Ghalib (1797–1869). The Pakistani poet Faiz Ahmad Faiz (1911–1984), who wrote in both Urdu and Panjabi, used the *ghazal* to address secular and political themes, as in this "Ghazal," translated by Shahid Ali:

In the sun's last embers, the evening star burns to ash.
Night draws its curtains, separating lovers.

Won't someone cry out, protest Heaven's tyranny? An era has passed,
and Time is still stranded, its caravan of day and night lost.

Nostalgia for friends and wine: to crush that sorrow,
we'll allow memory nothing, neither the moon nor the rain.

Once again the breeze knocks on the prison door.
It whispers, Don't give up, wait a little, Dawn is near.

Since the eighteenth century, the *ghazal* has played a central role in many literary and musical cultures from the Middle East to Malaysia. In Afghanistan, for example, the *ghazal* form is a key feature of intimate musical gatherings. The *ghazal* came to India via Persian Muslims, and the Indian *ghazal* tends to be more songlike than its Urdu counterpart, which is often performed at *mushairas,* or poetry gatherings. It is especially popular among

Northern Hindus. The Indian film industry even co-opted the *ghazal* into *filmi-ghazali,* which used Western harmonies and lush orchestral interludes.

The *ghazal* was introduced into Western poetry by the German romanticists: Schlegel, Rückert, and von Platten. It became widely known through Goethe's faithful imitations of the Persian in his *West-East Divan* (1819). Federico García Lorca wrote *gacelas,* which evoked the tradition of Arabic and Hebrew *ghazals* in medieval Andalusia. In the past decades, the form, loosely constructed, has had a particular vogue amongst some American poets, such as Robert Bly and Adrienne Rich. Shahid Ali called *ghazals* ravishing disunities. "There is a wilderness within a wilderness," Ghalib wrote, "I saw the desert and remembered home."

SEE ALSO *the beloved, mushaira, praise poems, wine poetry.*

ghinnawa This "little song" is a highly stylized form of folk poetry practiced in Bedouin cultures. The Bedouins have always cherished love poetry and most *ghinnawas* are love poems, usually dark and plaintive, like the blues. They are mostly sung by women, sometimes by boys, only occasionally by men, and convey hidden feelings that are otherwise unexpressed in daily life. In her study of Bedouin women's poetry, *Veiled Sentiments* (1986), Lila Abu-Lughod notes, "Poetry cloaks statements in veils of formula, convention, and tradition, thus suiting it to the task of carrying messages about the self that contravene the official cultural ideals." She also recognizes that the use of a stylized formula "renders content impersonal or non-individual, allowing people to dissociate themselves from the sentiments they express, if revealed to the wrong audience, by claiming that 'it was just a song.' " *Ghinnawas* are now written and recited as well as sung.

gisalo, see *bird sound words.*

gleeman In Anglo-Saxon England, the gleeman was a singer of songs and a teller of tales. He had something of the status of the Teutonic scop. The gleeman reemerged as a figure in the fourteenth century a bit lower on the social scale, as an itinerant minstrel, a juggler and performer. John Davidson romanticized the figure in his poem "The Gleeman" (1891), which begins, "The gleeman sang in the market town; / The market folk went up and down." In *The Celtic Twilight* (1893), W. B. Yeats called the blind Irish minstrel, Michael Moran (ca. 1794–1846), "the last gleeman": "He was a true gleeman, being alike poet, jester, and newsman of the people."

SEE ALSO *minstrel, scop.*

glose, glosa (Spanish) A Spanish form, the *glose* opens with a quotation from another author, which is subsequently repeated as a refrain in succeeding verses. Some scholars argue that the opening text (in Spanish *texto, cabeza,* or *retuécano*) must be a quatrain and the rest of the poem follows a special pattern, such as four ten-line stanzas. Others insist the only restriction is that the quotation must be repeated line by line as a refrain. The key to the form is that it incorporates the words of another. The *glosser,* or *glosador,* advertises a connection to a prior text. The Spanish *glosa,* which was frequently used in poetic contests, was especially popular among European writers from the fifteenth to the eighteenth century. Marilyn Hacker develops four quoted lines into four rhyming four-line stanzas in a series of poems she calls "Glose" (2006).

SEE ALSO *décima, poetic contest.*

gnome, gnomai (pl), ***gnomic*** A proverbial expression, a brief reflection or maxim that expresses a general truth or fundamental principle. The gnome is a form of wisdom literature.

Aristotle defines it as "a statement not relating to particulars . . . but to universals; yet not to all universals indiscriminately as, e.g., that straight is the opposite of crooked, but to all such things as are the objects of (human) action and are to be chosen or avoided in our doings." He then gives examples from Homer and other Greek poets. More than twelve hundred gnomai, which were originally part of a living oral tradition, have been identified in the works of the archaic Greek poets.

Gnomai are among the oldest literary expressions in the world and can be found in ancient Sumerian and Egyptian literature. In *The Growth of Literature* (1932), H. Munro Chadwick and Nora Chadwick divide gnomai from around the world into three categories: 1) those which exhort moral behavior by listing human virtues; 2) those which observe human activities or the workings of destiny or fate, but which do not pass judgment; 3) all other gnomai, which observe natural processes. Gnomai have a proverbial quality, but some scholars distinguish them from proverbs. Kenneth Jackson writes:

"A gnome need not be, and usually is not, a current popular saying with an implied moral, as the proverb is . . . and it need contain no advice or exhortation like the precept."

The primary Old English gnomai, *Maxims 1* and *II,* are found in *The Exeter Book* (ca. 960–990) and the eleventh-century *Cotton Psalter.* They tend to be generalizations about the natural or human world, as in "Frost shall freeze, fire eat wood" or "A king shall win a queen with goods." A gnomic strain runs through all of Old English poetry as well as through early Icelandic, Irish, and Welsh poetry.

SEE ALSO *proverb, wisdom literature.*

the golden age A *golden age* refers to a cultural high point, the apex of a civilization. *The golden age* is inevitably a retrospective or nostalgic term, which is symbolically linked to metals, since gold sets the standard. Golden ages are always past, always "lost." In *Works and Days* (eighth century B.C.E.), the Greek poet Hesiod first divided time into five mythological ages — the Golden Age, the Silver Age, the Bronze Age, the Heroic Age, and the Iron Age. The Golden Age was a period of serenity, spring, and eternal peace ("It is said that *men lived among the gods, and freely mingled with them*"). Ovid takes up the subject in *Metamorphoses* (8 C.E.) when he writes, "The golden age was first, when man, yet knew, / No rule but uncorrupted reason rule, / And with a native bent did good pursue."

Over the centuries, the notion of a golden age came to refer to the high-water cultural moments of a society. For example, many people refer to the fifth century B.C.E. in classical Greece — the time of the great dramatists Aeschylus, Euripides, and Sophocles — as a golden age. So, too, it is possible to speak about the golden age of Elizabethan theater, the era of William Shakespeare, Ben Jonson, and Christopher Marlowe, or the medieval golden age of Jewish Culture in Spain (from 900 to 1100), or the Dutch golden age (seventeenth century), or the golden age of Russian poetry, the nineteenth-century period that revolved around the sun of Alexander Pushkin. In his 1923 poem "Vek," or "The Age," the Russian poet Osip Mandelstam combined two uses of the Latin *aureus* "golden" (golden measure, golden age) in his line "Meroi veka zolotoi" ("With the *golden* measure of the *age*").

The sixteenth and seventeenth centuries were an unprecedented *Síglo de Oro,* or golden age, in Spanish poetry. The Spanish Empire reached both its greatest height and its lowest depth, since the creative flowering of the Spanish Renaissance was shadowed by the despotism of the Inquisition. The poets turned away from the institutionalized religious and political persecution, which they were forbidden to write about, toward an idealized golden age of the past. They mastered traditional forms, such as the Latin eclogue and the Italian sonnet. The central poets were Garcilaso de la Vega (ca. 1501–1536), who "nationalized the Petrarchan esthetic so successfully that, during the Renaissance, Italianate meters and attitudes came to seem native to Spain" (Edith Grossman); Fray Luis de León (1527–1591), a *converso* Jew who "Christianized" Spanish poetry; the sublime mystic San Juan de la Cruz (1542–1591), known in English as Saint John of the Cross; Luis de Góngora (1561–1627), the master of the *culteranista* or euphuistic style; Lope de Vega (1562–1635), whom Miguel Cervantes supposedly called "a monster of nature" because of his prodigious creativity, which included some three thousand sonnets; and Francisco de Quevedo (1580–1645), who was associated with *conceptismo,* a poetry of ingenious puns, conceits, and concepts.

SEE ALSO *Arcadia, eclogue, Four Ages of Poetry, Generation of '27, Gongorism, Silver Age, sonnet.*

goliardic verse A type of medieval lyric poetry. Goliardic verse probably derives its name from the tribe of "Golias" or the philistine giant "Goliath," who was slain by David. One standard anthology on Medieval Latin points out: "It was common by the ninth century to associate Goliath with Satan and to describe particularly evil clerics as belonging to the family of Golias. Bernard of Clairvaux, in condemning Peter Abelard, called him a new Goliath, perhaps setting off the new lease on life that Golias achieved in the twelfth century. By the middle of the century, indeed, Golias had become a more affable figure, a poet-beggar who served as a patron saint to poetic practitioners of the genre named after him."

The goliardic poets were the wandering scholars or *vagantes* of the twelfth and thirteenth centuries, academic drifters who composed secular songs in rhymed and accented Latin verse. Their boisterous youthful poems strike a pose, parodying religious hymns, mocking institutions, reveling in gambling, and celebrating physical love and excessive drinking ("Let's away with study

/ Folly's sweet"). The foundational examples of goliardic verse (*Vagantenlider*) are found in the *Carmina Burana,* a thirteenth-century compendium of Latin and German poems, which was discovered in Munich in the nineteenth century. The greatest poet of the tradition is the shadowy figure known as the Archpoet. Ten of his poems have survived, including a scathing mock confession, *Estuans intrinsecus / ira vehemnti* ("Burning inside / with violent rage"), the most famous poem of the Middle Ages. Here is a sample of his blasphemous wit, which puns *potatori* and *peccatori.* He takes a line from the Apostle's prayer: *Deus propitius esto mihi peccatori* ("God have mercy on this sinner") and turns it into *Deus sit propitius huic potatori* ("God have mercy on this drunk").

Meum est propositum in taberna mori,
Ut sint vina proxima morientis ori.
Tunc cantabunt lætius angelorum chori:
"Sit Deus propitius huic potatori!"

For I propose to die in a tavern
so that wine will be close to my dying mouth.
Then the angelic choirs will jubilantly cry:
"God have mercy on this drunk!"

Gongorism, Gongorismo Gongorism, or *cultismo* ("cultism"), suggests a studied obscurity, a florid ornate style, the elaborate use of learned words, Hispanized from Greek and Latin, as well as puns and conceits. Gongorism takes its name from the flamboyant baroque master Luis de Góngora (1561–1627), "a book-nosed and dangerous beast from Córdoba" (Rafael Alberti), who had a gift for extravagant comparisons and metaphorical thinking. At the end of "The First Solitude" (*Soledades,* 1613–1618), for example, he refers to the marriage bed as *"a batallas de amor, campo de pluma,"* or "a field of feathers for the strife of love."

Cultismo can be surprisingly close to its supposed rival in Spanish literary history, *Conceptismo* (Conceptism), exemplified by Francisco de Quevedo y Villegas (1580–1645). In theory, the style of conceptism is characterized by the ingenious use of concepts and conceits, whereas cultism is characterized by the ingenious use of a new poetic vocabulary. In essence, Quevedo virulently disapproved of Góngora's vocabulary. But in practice, both Góngora and Quevedo are Baroque poets. Góngora's opponents labeled his movement *culteranismo,* which blends *culto* ("cultivated") and *luteranismo* ("Lutheranism"), to suggest the heresy committed against true poetry. The backlash against Gongorism subsequently became so strong that his poetry virtually disappeared for three centuries. Góngora's method of rapid associations looked forward to the Surrealists, who adopted him as one of their patron saints. He was taken up by a new generation of twentieth-century Spanish poets (Federico García Lorca, Rafael Alberti, Luis Cernuda, Geraldo Diego, Jorge Guillen) who first met in Seville in 1927 to mark the three-hundreth anniversary of his death.

SEE ALSO *baroque, conceit, Generation of '27, the golden age, pun, Surrealism, wit.*

grand style Matthew Arnold characterized the grand style in his lectures *On Translating Homer* (1861–1862). It is exemplified, he said, "when a noble nature, poetically gifted, treats with simplicity and severity a serious subject." Arnold believed that the grand style enlarges and enriches us. "For Homer is not only rapid in movement, simple in style, plain in language, natural in thought; he is also, and above all *noble.*" Arnold considered Homer the finest model of the simple grand style and Milton the best model of the severe grand style. Dante exemplified both. Arnold's understanding of the grand style, which he never exactly defined, is close to Longinus's concept of the sublime.

SEE ALSO *the sublime.*

Graveyard poets, also ***Churchyard poets*** In the second half of the eighteenth century, a group of melancholy, pre-romantic English poets wrote in the shadow of the graveyard. They were night poets who rejected the decorum of the Augustans and foreshadowed gothic literature. They were sometimes derided as the school of the drowned-in-tears. Much of it is "skulls and coffins," but the mode reached a sublime height in James Thomson's *The Seasons* (1730), Edward Young's *Night Thoughts* (1742), and Thomas Gray's "Elegy Written in a Country Churchyard" (1751). The graveyard poets were never a formal school, but their dark sensibilities, their feeling for the uncanny, and their spooky supernaturalism helped to create the climate for romantic poetry.

SEE ALSO *Augustan Age, keening, romanticism, sensibility, the uncanny.*

greater romantic lyric In his essay "Structure and Style in the Greater Romantic Lyric" (1965), M. H. Abrams gave the name "the greater Romantic lyric" to one of the most distinctive kinds of English romantic poem. He includes under the rubric of descriptive-meditative poems Coleridge's "Aeolian Harp" (1796), "Frost at Midnight" (1798), "Fears in Solitude" (1789), and "Dejection: An Ode" (1802); Wordsworth's "Tintern Abbey" (1798) and "Ode: Intimations of Immortality" (1807); Shelley's "Stanzas Written in Dejection" (1818) and "Ode to the West Wind" (1819); and Keats's "Ode to a Nightingale" (1819). He characterized the greater romantic lyric as spoken by a poet in a particular, identifiable locale, usually outdoors, conversing with a silent human auditor:

> The speaker begins with a description of the landscape; an aspect or change of aspect in the landscape evokes a varied but integral process of memory, thought, anticipation, and feeling which remains closely interinvolved with the outer scene. In the course of this meditation the lyric speaker achieves an insight, faces up to a tragic loss, comes to a moral decision, or resolves an emotional problem. Often the poem rounds upon itself to end where it began, at the outer scene, but with an altered mood and deepened understanding which is the result of the intervening meditation.

SEE ALSO *conversation poem, ode, romanticism.*

green poetry, see *nature poetry.*

griot, griotte (feminine) The West African griot or *jeli* is a praise-singer, a poet-historian who preserves the genealogies, historical narratives, and oral traditions of a people. The griots are members of a hereditary caste who hold the memory of West Africa by maintaining an oral tradition that is more than six centuries old (the first portrait of a griot dates to the fourteenth century). Until the late nineteenth century, griots were attached to the courts of local kings. We have no equivalent for the complex social role of these oral storytellers and official chroniclers — "the people of the spoken word" — who also serve as trusted advisors, messengers, mediators, teachers, and ambassadors. The griots are skilled musicians who often play a wooden xylophone called a *balafon,* a plucked lute called a *koni,* or *ngoni,* and a twenty-one-stringed instrument called a *kora,* a cross between a lute and a harp. They specialize in reciting the epic of Son-Jara (also known as "Sunjata" or "Sundiata"), which celebrates the exploits of the warrior-prince and legendary founder of the "Empire of Old Mali" some 750 years ago. The griots have a formidable knowledge of local history, a gift for extemporizing on current events, and the capacity to cut their enemies with devastating wit. Licensed to sing and dance alone, to behave outlandishly, these singers of praise and scandal at the center of the artistic universe of most sub-Saharan African societies are commonly considered outcasts, both scorned and feared, called on at times of ritual elevation to represent power. They are allied by caste with other craftsmen who work with sacred, dangerous, and unclean materials: leather, wood, iron, gold. They are frequently considered to carry contagion with them wherever they live and work. All the dimensions of deep stereotype are attributed to them: they are diabolical, insane, creatures of the brush, devils. Yet they also bring playfulness and ecstasy with them.

The term *griot* is itself controversial. The most common view is that the word derives from the French *guiriot* and thus smacks of colonialism. Others maintain that it has a Portuguese, Spanish, Catalan, or Arabic origin. Yet others suggest that it has an African origin. In *Griots and Griottes,* Thomas Hale posits that the term goes as far back as the Ghana Empire and moved by way of the slave trade through Berber to Spanish and then French: *Ghana-agenaou-guineo-guiriot-griot.* He calls the griot a time-binder, "a person who links past to present and serves as a witness to events in the present, which he or she may convey to persons living in the future."

Amiri Baraka assumes the role of a griot in *Wise Why's Y's* (1995). He includes variant spellings in the subtitle (*The Griot's Song: Djeli Ya*), lists his name as Amiri Baraka, *Djali,* and states: "*Why's/Wise* is a long poem in the tradition of Djali (Griots) but this is about African American (American) History."

SEE ALSO *oral poetry, praise poems, song.*

Group 42 *Skupina* 42, or Group 42, formed during World War II in Czechoslovakia. The poets included Jiří Kolář (1914–2002), Josef Kainar (1917–1972), Jan Hanc (1916–1963), and Ivan Blatny (1919–1990). Their wartime aesthetic was rough, even deliberately crude, fragmented, prosaic. They were influenced by František Halas (1901–1949) and inspired by Jiří

Orten (1919–1941), who loved poetic spontancity, clung to personal truths, and helped take Czech poetry in a more inward direction. They wanted to capture the dissonance of contemporary urban life and turned for models to Walt Whitman and T. S. Eliot, Carl Sandburg and Edgar Lee Masters. The organizer of the group, Jindřich Chalupecký, outlined the basic premise in his 1942 article "Generation": "the progress of the arts at the present day does not depend on the — much-vaunted! — practice of attributing personal significance to hundreds of subtleties of meaning. . . . On the contrary, it can reach fulfillment only through increasing intensity, vehemence and harshness — by which we mean absolutely strict *accuracy*." The government dissolved the group in 1948, but the radical juxtapositions in their work continued to resonate in Czech literature.

Group 47 (Gruppe 47) Founded in 1947, hence its name, *Gruppe 47* was a postwar literary association in Germany. It was the idea of Hans Werner Richter as a follow-up to the magazine *Der Ruf*, or *The Call*, which was published in Munich from August 1946 to August 1947. Group 47 sought to be a forum for "authors from all zones, all classes, all trends." It included most, if not all, major German writers until 1968. Its goal was to create a new *Nachkriegsliteratur*, or "post-war literature." Prose writers such as Gunter Grass and Heinrich Böll initially rejected lofty generalizations in favor of a deliberately bare unsentimental style, which became known as *Kahlschalg* ("root and branches"). Gunter Eich's stripped-down poetry was one response to postwar conditions; the epic theater of Bertolt Brecht's *Berliner Ensemble* was another. Paul Celan and Ingeborg Bachman were both members of Group 47.

guslar, guslari (pl) These oral poets, who specialize in southern Slavic epic songs, play the *gusle* (or *gusla*), a single-stringed lute-shaped instrument common to all Slavic people. The Serbs, Croatians, Bosnians, Bulgarians, and Albanians all have *guslari*, male singers who perform heroic narratives.

SEE ALSO *epic, oral-formulaic method.*

haibun *Haibun* is a work that combines haiku and prose. Matsuo Bashō's book *The Hut of the Phantom Dwelling* (1690) is generally considered the first outstanding example of *haibun* literature. It was closely modeled on Kamo no Chōmei's extended prose essay, *Ten-Foot Square Hut* (1212), which is, as Haruo Shirane puts it, "an extended prose poem in a highly elliptical, hybrid style of vernacular, classical Japanese and classical Chinese, with Chinese-style parallel words and parallel phrases." Bashō's subsequent travel journal, or *nikki, The Narrow Road to the Deep North* (1694), established the *haibun* as a major form that connects individual haiku with a surrounding prose narrative. The prose of the travel diaries — precise, elliptical — is written in the same spirit as the poems, which emerge from the prose. The prose has the aesthetic of *haikai.* The link between each prose passage and each subsequent poem is implicit, a leap made by the reader. Bashō's disciple Morikawa Kyoriku, who edited the first important anthology of *haibun, Prose Collection of Japan* (1706), noted:

> Works such as *The Tale of Genji* and *The Tale of Sagoromo* . . . should be called handbooks for composing classical poetry. Both these texts follow the principles of classical poetry and classical linked verse. There is not a single word that offers a model for haikai prose. Bashō, my late teacher, was the first to create such a model and breathe elegance and life into it.

Some of the Japanese poets best known for *haibun* are Yosa Buson (1716–1783), the samurai Yokoi Yayū (1702–1783), and Kobayashi Issa (1763–

1827), whose autobiographical book, *The Year of My Life* (1819), was his culminating work. The climax responds to the death of his daughter:

This world of dew
is a world of dew,
and yet, and yet . . .

The *haibun* has sometimes provided a model for the crossing of genres in contemporary poetry, from poetic diaries by Gary Snyder and lyrical prose works by Jack Kerouac, who saw much of his work as prose written by a haiku poet, to the six *haibun* in John Ashbery's *A Wave* (1984), the *haibun* sensibility in the Canadian poet Fred Wah's 1985 book *Waiting for Saskatchewan* (he characterizes the *haibun* as "short prose written from a haiku sensibility and, in this case, concluded by an informal haiku line"), and the mixture of poetic plays and photo-documentary poems in Mark Nowak's *Shut Up Shut Down* (2004). Sam Hamill's *Bashō's Ghost* (1989) is structured as a series of *haibun* around his visit to Japan.

SEE ALSO *haikai, haiku.*

haikai A Japanese term, the *haikai no renga,* abbreviated to *haikai,* is an inclusive type of *renga,* a major form of Japanese poetry that especially flourished in the fourteenth and fifteenth centuries. *Renga* literally means "linked poetry." The *renga* began as a courtly form written by a team of poets with a circumscribed subject matter and a strict set of rules. The *haikai* (the word means "playful style") was a light-hearted type of linked poetry. It was more aesthetically relaxed and employed a more colloquial style. It democratized poetry by embracing the language and the emotions of common people.

Matsuo Bashō (1644–1694) was the first major poet of *haikai,* combining spiritual depth with comic playfulness. *Haikai* more generally refers to all types of literature derived from *haikai no renga,* such as *hokku* (the opening verse of a *renga* sequence), haiku (an independent verse form that follows a 5–7–5 pattern), *haiga* (a form of painting that combines a *hokku* and a visual image), and *haibun* (a genre that links haiku and narrative prose). Bashō believed that all these genres embodied the "haikai spirit" (*haii*). Bashō'school especially cherished *sabi,* or lonely beauty, a kind of impersonal sadness or melancholy latent in nature, a recognition in humble scenes, such as the light of dusk in autumn or the solitary voice of a cuckoo in the trees.

SEE ALSO *haibun, haiku, renga, yūgen.*

haiku A Japanese poetic form usually consisting, in English versions, of three unrhymed lines of 5, 7, and 5 syllables. The Japanese haiku is divided into seventeen phonic units, which are the equivalent of syllables. It is written as a single vertical line that is broken into three metrical units or phrases. The English spacing tries to replicate the aural effects of the Japanese. The haiku has its roots in the Middle Ages, or earlier, in the classic poetic form of the *tanka* and the *renga.* The *hokku,* or opening verse of the *renga* sequence, consists of seventeen syllables, which include a season word. At some point during the late Edo period (1600–1868), the *hokku* began to be appreciated in its own right, eventually achieving its own status. Matsuo Bashō was the first poet to elevate the *hokku* to a major form. Here is his well-known *hokku* on a cicada:

> The cry of the cicada
> Gives no sign
> That presently it will die.
> *(tr. W. G. Aston, 1899)*

Bashō was followed by Yosa Buson and Kobayashi Issa. In the late nineteenth century, the poet Masaoka Shiki decided to distinguish more clearly between the *hokku* as the initial verse of a larger sequence and the *hokku* as a self-contained poem. He named the autonomous seventeen-syllable poem a haiku. The 5–7–5 format may be ancient, but the word *haiku* is a modern invention. *Haijin* is an honorific name for a person who writes *haikai* or haiku.

The haiku, invariably written in the present tense, almost always refers to a time of day or season (the *kigo* is a season word), focuses on a natural image, and captures the essence of a moment. Its goal: a sudden insight or spiritual illumination. R. H. Blythe states, "A haiku is an open door that looks shut." His monumental four-volume *Haiku* (1949–1952), the first work in English based on the *saijiki,* is a dictionary of haiku in which the poems are arranged by seasons. He states in volume 4:

> It is not merely the brevity by which the haiku isolates a particular group of phenomena from all the rest; nor is it suggestiveness, through which it reveals a whole world of experience. It is not only in its remarkable use of the season word, by which it gives us a feelng of a quarter of the year; not its faint all-pervading humor. Its peculiar quality is its self-effacing, self-annihilative nature, by which it enables us, more than any other form of literature, to grasp the thing-in-itself.

Haiga is a style of Japanese painting that combines a haiku and a visual image, as in Buson's poetry-paintings.

The *senryū* (the word means "river willow" in Japanese) has the same structure as the haiku. But whereas the haiku deals with nature, the *senryū* deals with human nature. It is often satiric and treats human foibles. The haiku, on the other hand, seeks the momentary and the eternal.

SEE ALSO *renga, tanka.*

hain-teny In Madagascar, *hain-teny* ("the knowledge of words") is a form of oral poetry structured as a poetic duel, a competitive exchange between two "opponents" on the subject of love. It is a playful, proverbial, and highly metaphorical form of dispute and debate. Here is a scene that Jean Paulhan, who collected eight hundred examples of *hain-teny,* observed in a Madagascar village and described in 1913:

> After the evening meal, the children spread a clean mat over the floor, and a group of village men . . . are admitted. They sit down on the mat next to the householders. One of them opens the session by reciting a few verses. He pronounces them with a forceful rhythm and with such energy that he seems to be voicing a complaint or in some way demanding his due. And then one of the inhabitants of the house . . . will answer him in the same tones — sometimes brusquely, sometimes ironically. The discussion continues. The audience now and again takes part, interjecting a few rhythmic words that seem meant to redirect the discussion toward its real object. Bit by bit the speeches of the two opponents become longer, more forcefully accentuated; by now each speaker has acquired a cheering section to encourage him with their bravos and their laughter. At the end the opponents are

> shouting, until suddenly one of them finds the decisive words—or so one discovers when the other hesitates and finds no answer; that speaker then acknowledges defeat and the crowd rushes to congratulate the winner.

SEE ALSO *oral poetry, poetic contest.*

hājis "Poetic genius." The Khawlānis of North Yemen (the Yemen Arab Republic) have two general terms for poet. One is the general Arabic word for poet, *shā*^{c}*ir,* which applies to any poet, and the other is *hājis,* which is used especially for the poet with an inexhaustible talent, who can create poetry *min rās-ah* (off the top of his head). Steven C. Caton writes: "Tribal poetry is thought to be as ancient as the spoken language. I heard the opinion expressed more than once that Adam spoke in verse all the time and that the ancestors, the kings of Saba' and Himyār, did likewise, for the gift of *hājis* (poetic genius) was as much part of their constitution as walking or breathing." The term *hājis* also refers to the muse, to poetic talent or inspiration.

Poets and critics of written dialect poetry, which is known as *humēnī,* categorize poetry on the basis of subject matter: love poetry, nature poetry, social verse, and political poetry. Verse is also considered religious or historical. Caton points out that "a poem is only composed in response to an *actual* situation, a momentous occasion (*munāsibah*) or a sociohistorical issue (*gadīyah*)." For the Khawlānis, poetry is fundamentally purposeful, efficacious, and has always been so. In *Travels through Arabia and other countries in the East* (1792), the Danish explorer Carsten Niebuhr tells the story of the Yemeni fascination with the poetic word:

> The best poets are among the Bedouins of Dsjof. The Schiech of that country was, a few years since, imprisoned in Sana'a. The Schiech, observing a bird upon the roof of a house, recollected the opinion of those pious Musulmans, who think it a meritorious action to deliver a bird from a cage. He thought that he himself had as good a right to liberty as any bird, and expressed this idea in a poem; which his guards got by heart, at length reached the Monarch's ears, who was so pleased with it, that he set the Schiech at liberty, although he had been guilty of various acts of robbery.

Khawlānis tribesmen connect poetry and vocal music. They distinguish between two kinds of vocalizing in the performance of poetry: *ghinā* (singing) and *sayhah* (chanting, literally "yelling," "shouting"). The two main performative genres are *bālah* and *zāmil.* Both are composed in performance, spontaneously, before an audience. The *bālah* is a poetic competition between a group of poets, which is performed indoors at night, whereas the *zāmil* is a two-line poem composed by a single poet, performed outdoors, day or night. The poets in the *bālah* genre take turns performing in a circle of six to ten men facing inward with their arms clasped around each other and moving in a simple side step. Caton describes it: "One rank or *saff* chants a refrain, and the other chants a certain part of the verse, the two groups thus alternating their chanting throughout the performance of a single poem." Thus the poets compete within a dancing circle before an audience.

SEE ALSO *ghazal, oral poetry, poetic contest, qasida, shiʿr.*

Hallucinism The Brazilian poet Mário de Andrade (1893–1945) began his modernist book of poems *Hallucinated City* (1922) with a parody of his own avant-garde project. He founded the school of Hallucinism at the beginning of his preface ("Hallucinism has been launched") and disbanded it at the end ("So the poetic school of 'Hallucinism' is finished"). "I sing in my own way," Andrade claims, which is the true meaning of this most short-lived of movements. But what persists is Arthur Rimbaud's rhythmic quest for a mystical "hallucination of the word."

SEE ALSO *avant-garde, modernism.*

Hammond's meter, see *heroic quatrain.*

Harlem renaissance The Harlem renaissance included all the arts and roughly spanned the years from the end of World War I to the start of the Depression. Centered in the cultural hub of Harlem, it was first named after Alain Locke's anthology, *The New Negro* (1925), and known as the "New Negro Movement." It marked a vital stage in black consciousness. It was also a coming of age for a new black American poetry. James Weldon Johnson (1871–1938) became the first true anthologist of black poetry with his two editions of *The Book of American Negro Poetry* (1922, 1931). Langston Hughes (1902–1967) summed up the renaissance spirit when he declared that younger black writers "now intend to express our individual dark-skinned selves without fear or shame."

Hughes would go on from his first book, *The Weary Blues* (1926), to become known as the "poet laureate" of black America. His poetry expressed his feeling for ordinary black people, his hatred of social injustice, and his reverence for black musical arts, like jazz and blues. Some of the other key poets of the Harlem renaissance were the Jamaican-born Claude McKay (1890–1948), who started out writing dialect verse and used his lyrical art to protest vehemently against racial injustice (*Harlem Shadows,* 1922); Jean Toomer (1894–1967), whose greatest poetry survives in his prose book *Cane* (1923); James Weldon Johnson, who turned the folk art of the black sermon into poetry in *God's Trombones* (1927); and Countee Cullen (1903–1946), who embraced traditional forms, wrote movingly about racism, and explored the paradox of being a black poet. In the sonnet "Yet Do I Marvel" (1925), he marveled that God could do "this curious thing: / To make a poet black and bid him sing!" Additionally, Georgia Douglas Johnson (1880–1966) wrote genteel love poems, Arna Bontemps (1902–1973) wrote meditative verse, Helene Johnson (1906–1995) wrote poems of black pride, and Anne Spencer dedicated herself to modernism. Sterling Brown (1901–1989) engaged in a different but parallel poetic revolution. He explored the social nature of the southern black experience in a sensitive folk idiom. As Hughes experimented with jazz rhythms to render Harlem nightlife (at first in *Fine Clothes to the Jew,* 1927, and later in *Montage of a Dream Deferred,* 1951), so Brown turned to rural folk forms like the blues, spirituals, and work songs to create an accurate, unsentimentalized, and dignified portrait of southern black life (*Southern Road,* 1931).

hecho poético "Poetic fact" or "poetic event." Federico García Lorca coined this term for the free-standing image, an illogical phenomenon, like "rain from the stars." In the late 1920s he suggested that *hechos poéticos* were images that followed a strange inner logic "of emotion and poetic architecture," metaphors that arose so quickly that in order to be understood they demanded a sympathetic attentiveness, a capacity for rapid association and for structured reverie, and a willing suspension of disbelief. As an example of a *hecho poético,* he cited his love poem "Sleepwalking Ballad," with its radiant refrain: *Verde que te quiero verde* ("Green, how much I want you green").

He said: "If you ask me why I wrote 'a thousand glass tambourines / were wounding the dawn,' I will tell you that I saw them, in the hands of angels and trees, but I will not be able to say more." Lorca's myriad crystal tambourines wounding the new day are an extrasensory event that strikes the reader or the listener as something that has been creatively added to nature, something beyond natural description, something visionary.

SEE ALSO *willing suspension of disbelief.*

heelloy A form of modern Somali sung poetry that developed in the turbulent period after the Second World War. The *heelloy* emerged out of a shorter form known as *balwo,* which developed in the early 1940s. There are four genres — the *wiglo,* the *dhaanto,* the *hirwo,* and the *balwo* — that comprise what John Johnson terms *The Family of Miniature Genres.* The *balwo* was about four lines, the *heelloy* much longer. Both unfold in couplets. One of the first innovators of the form, Abdilahi Qarshi, explains the renaming from *balwo* (a loan-word meaning "misfortune") to *heelloy:*

> But in Somali usage, the word had acquired the implication of profligacy in matters of sex, womanizing, drinking, and so on. Thus we see that the name *balwo,* which had negative connotations in Somali, was adding to the unacceptability of the "*balwo* movement" in respectable society. It provided the religious leaders with ammunition to have it suppressed and outlawed. So we changed the name to *heello* and began the first few bars of the song not with "*balwo*" but with the acceptable, traditional invitation to dance "*heelloy heellelloy* . . ."

This dynamic form became a crucial vehicle for freedom songs in the 1950s.

hemistich A half-line of verse. A hemistich can stand as an unfinished line, usually for emphasis, or form half of a complete line, which is divided by a caesura. Virgil isolated half-lines in the *Aeneid* (29–19 B.C.E.) to great effect, but the strategy troubled his neoclassical translator John Dryden, who called his hemistiches "the imperfect products of a hasty Muse." The principal line of medieval Arabic and Hebrew poetry was divided into two symmetrical hemistiches. In Hebrew, this was known as the *delet* (door) and the *sogair* (latch or lock). In Arabic, it was known as the *sadr* (chest, front) and the *'ajouz* (backside or rump). So, too, the hemistich was used as the fundamental metrical structural unit in Old English, Old High German, Old Saxon, and Old Norse. Think of the two halves of the Old English four-beat line, which divides near the middle. It has two metrical stresses on either side of the divide (caesura). "Caedmon's Hymn," probably the earliest extant Old English poem, begins:

> Nu we sculan herian   heofonrices Weard,
> Metodes mihte   and his modgeþonc,
> weorc Wuldorfæder;   swa he wundra gehwæs,
> ece Dryhten,   ord onstealde.

SEE ALSO *caesura, stichomythia, verset.*

hendecasyllabics Lines of eleven syllables. The term *hendecasyllable* usually refers to the precise metrical line used by the ancient Greek poets, which consists of an opening pair of syllables (u u, u —, — u, or — —) followed by a dactyl (— u u) and three trochees (— u). It was perfected by the Roman poet Catullus (84–54 B.C.E.), who created a Latin verse that is rapid, light, and emphatic. He used it for 40 of his extant 113 poems. It later became the standard verse line of Italian poetry, exploited by Dante in *The Divine Comedy* (ca. 1304–1321) and Petrarch in his sonnets. Popularized by Garcilaso de la Vega (ca. 1501–1536), it is also one of the primary verse forms in Spanish poetry since the Renaissance, where it is customarily accentuated on the sixth and tenth syllables, or else on the fourth, eighth, and tenth syllables. Hendecalsyllabics are relatively rare in English, though Tennyson experimented with them in his poem "Hendecasyllabics" (1863), which he calls "a tiny poem / All composed in a metre of Catullus." Swinburne followed with his own "Hendecasyllabics" (1866), and Robert Frost employs them in his poem "For Once, Then, Something" (1920). James Wright referred to it as "the difficult, the dazzling / Hendecasyllabic" ("The Offense," 1972).

SEE ALSO *meter, silva, versi sciolti.*

hendiadys Hendiadys is a rhetorical figure of speech that comes from the Greek and literally means "one through two." Two words are connected by a conjunction to express a single complex idea. Rather than one word subordinating the other, the two words are united in duplication, as when Macbeth famously declares that life "is a tale / Told by an idiot, full of *sound and fury,* / Signifying nothing." He doesn't say that life is full of "furious sound." The hendiadys was strategically employed in Latin poetry, especially in Virgil's *Aeneid* (29–19 B.C.E.). In *The Art of English Poesie* (1589), George Puttenham refers to hendiadys as "the figure of Twynnes." He considered it of "little or no use" in English, though four hundred uses of hendiadys have now been counted in Shakespeare.

A *hendiatris* ("one through three") is a figure of speech in which three words are employed to express an idea, as in Thomas Jefferson's tripartite motto for the Declaration of Independence: "Life, liberty, and the pursuit of happiness."

heptameter, see "accentual syllabic meter" in *meter, rhetoric.*

heptastich, see *septet.*

heresy of paraphrase Cleanth Brooks introduced this phrase in his essay "The Heresy of Paraphrase" in *The Well Wrought Urn* (1947). Brooks argues that if paraphrase means "to say the same thing in other words," then it is impossible to summarize or paraphrase a poem. He suggests that "paraphrase is not the real core of meaning which constitutes the essence of the poem." Brooks's phrase has religious overtones, perhaps unconscious, as if to suggest that the poem is a sacred text and the critic is its priest, distinguishing true from heretical readings. Yet Brooks's recognition is a crucial one. A poem is not a statement made by the poet, but an experience. The poem is an act beyond paraphrase because what is being said cannot be separated from how it is said. Samuel Taylor Coleridge posited the untranslatableness of poetry. Osip Mandelstam suggested that if a poem can be paraphrased, then the sheets haven't been rumpled, poetry hasn't spent the night.

SEE ALSO *New Criticism, translation, untranslatableness.*

Hermeticism The term *Hermeticism* derives from the work of the ancient mystical author Hermes Trismegistos, "thrice-great Hermes." In general, it applies to mystical nineteenth- and early twentieth-century poetry that employs occult symbolism. It has its roots in the work of Novalis and Poe. It is associated with the French symbolist poets (Baudelaire, Mallarmé, Rimbaud, and Valéry) and their international heirs, such as Maeterlinck, Claudel, Hauptman, Strindberg, and the early Yeats.

In particular, Hermeticism refers to a movement in modern Italian poetry. In his book *La poesía ermetica* (1936), the Italian critic Francesco Flora borrowed *Ermetismo,* or "Hermeticism," to describe a new kind of Italian poetry with its roots in French symbolist poetry. He found it exemplified by the cryptically inward and allusive work of Guiseppe Ungaretti. The Italian pioneer of Hermeticism was Arturo Onofri, who created a kind of aesthetic mysticism or "pure poetry" that emphasized the suggestiveness of language. Reacting to the disillusionment of World War I and the bombastic propaganda of Fascism, the hermetic poets, especially Salvatore Quasimodo, sought to pare down language to its essential elements. Eugenio Montale refused to claim membership in any movement, but the secretive, astringent, and highly personal music of first book *Cuttlefish Bones* (1925) has a decidedly hermetic quality.

SEE ALSO *pure poetry, symbolism.*

heroic couplet, see *couplet.*

heroic quatrain Four iambic pentameter lines rhyming alternately (*abab*). The heroic quatrain, also known as the elegiac stanza and Hammond's meter, is used in Thomas Gray's "Elegy Written in a Country Churchyard" (1751) and James Hammond's *Love Elegies* (1732), which contains the exemplary stanza:

> Beauty and worth in her alike contend
> To charm the fancy and to fix the mind:
> In her, my wife, my mistress, and my friend,
> I taste the joys of sense and reason join'd.

SEE ALSO *quatrain.*

heterometric stanza A stanza that consists of lines of varying length. The Pindaric ode, the Sapphic stanza, and the medieval bob and wheel are all heterometric. John Donne's early poem "Song" (1635), for example, pushed the limits of heterometric verse in English. The first stanza establishes the pattern. Notice especially the short seventh and eighth lines.

> Go and catch a falling star,
>   Get with child a mandrake root,
> Tell me where all past years are,
>   Or who cleft the Devil's foot,
> Teach me to hear mermaids singing,
>   Or to keep off envy's stinging,
>   And find
>   What wind
> Serves to advance an honest mind.

SEE ALSO *bob and wheel, isometric stanza, ode, Sapphic stanza, stanza.*

hexameter The hexameter is a six-foot metrical line, as when Shelley writes "In profuse strains of unpremeditated art" ("To a Skylark," 1820), which scans as an iambic hexameter:

> Ĭn pró | fŭse stráins | ŏf ún- | prĕméd- | ĭtát- | ĕd árt

The Homeric hexameter is the oldest type of Greek verse. The classical dactylic hexameter also reached its pinnacle in Greek and Latin epic poetry (the *Iliad* and the *Odyssey*, ca. eighth century B.C.E.; the *Aeneid*, 29–19 B.C.E.). It was successfully adapted to German and Russian poetry by Goethe and Pushkin, among others. Despite many experiments, such as Longfellow's epic poem *Evangeline* (1847), it has never found a natural place in French, English, or American poetry. In his essay "Notes Upon English Verse" (1842), Edgar Allan Poe prints a line that he describes as "an unintentional instance of a perfect English hexameter upon the model of the Greek." He seems to have made it up himself:

> Man is a | complex, | compound, | compost, | yet is he | God-born.

The dactylic hexameter is to classical verse what iambic pentameter is to English-language poetry. Coleridge wittily discriminates between them in "The Ovidian Elegiac Metre" (1799):

> In the hexameter rises the fountain's silvery column;
> In the pentameter aye falling in melody back.

SEE ALSO *alexandrine, dactyl, foot, iambic pentameter, meter.*

hexastich, see *sestet.*

hiatus In classical prosody, a hiatus refers to the gap between one word ending in a vowel (or diphthong) and another word beginning with a vowel (or diphthong). It was frequently avoided through elision.

SEE ALSO *elision.*

hija, hijaa', hajw *Hija* (invective, satire) was one of the main modes of classical Arabic poetry. The Arabic word may originally have meant "murmuring, casting a spell." This type of poetry possibly originated in magic, where a well-aimed curse can destroy the honor of a person by naming his shameful characteristics. The invective can also be directed against an entire tribe. It was often brutally insulting. Everyone recognized the destructive power of *hija,* which is the polar opposite of the praise poem. The epigram was one of the most packed and lethal forms of *hija* in both medieval Arabic and Hebrew poetry. The tradition of *hija* has carried into the present. During the Gulf War in 1991, for example, Iraqis and Saudis traded poetic insults on a daily basis in rival radio and television broadcasts.

SEE ALSO *epigram, flyting, lampoon, panegyric, poetic contest, praise poems, satire.*

hip hop poetry, rap poetry Rap is the rhythmic vocal style of rap or hip hop music. Rapping (emceeing) is the style in which a performer speaks rhythmically, and in rhyme, generally to a strong beat. The lyrics fit a metrical pattern. As Jerry Quickley puts it in "Hip Hop Poetry" (2003):

> Hip hop incorporates many of the technical devices of other forms, including slant rhymes, enjambment, A-B rhyme schemes, and other techniques, usually parsed in sixteen-bar stanzas, and generally followed by four-to-eight-bar hooks.

Rap is poetry, Adam Bradley notes, "but its popularity relies in part on people not recognizing it as such." He points out that rappers prefer similes to metaphors because similes "shine the spotlight on their subject more directly than do metaphors." Sometimes rappers perform pieces they have already written, other times they improvise and freestyle new poems in front of an audience. Their poetry, a form of public art, is always pitched to their listeners. Rappers call it flow when rhythm sparks and overtakes. Kanye West is boasting about his flow when he raps on "Get Em High" (2004): "my rhyme's in the pocket like wallets / I got the bounce like hydraulics." The synergy of beats and rhyme is what Bradley calls "rap's greatest contribution to the rhythm of poetry: the *dual rhythmic relationship.*"

Hip hop, which arose in the 1970s, has its roots in African American and West African music. It started with Jamaican DJ music, where DJs spin dub versions of rhythm tracks with MCs, who are part singers, part rappers, "chatting" over them. Hip hop strongly connects to other types of contemporary oral poetry, such as slam and performance poetry, which also provide voices for the disenfranchised.

SEE ALSO *dub poetry, oral poetry, performance poetry, rhythm, slam poetry.*

hobo poetry People have been hopping rides as long as there have been freight trains. The life of homeless migrants and itinerant travelers developed its own distinctive vocabulary and culture in the second half of nineteenth- and first half of twentieth-century America. Hoboes camped and congregated in trackside "jungles." Older "jockers" lured younger "preshuns" (road kids) into hobo life. You didn't want to Grease the Track (get run over by a train) or Catch the Westbound (die). You could use a moniker (nickname). During the Depression, the number of hoboes radically increased. Many were radicalized and became "Wobblies" or members of the I.W.W. (Industrial Workers of the World). Such legendary figures as Joe Hill and T. Bone Slim spread the word through wobbly songs and ballads. In 1923, the sociologist Nels Anderson contended, "Much so-called hobo verse which has found its way into print was not written by tramps, but by men who knew enough of the life of the road to enable them to interpret its spirit. The best hobo poems have been written behind prison bars. Many of the songs of the I.W.W. have been written in jail" (*The Hobo: The Sociology of the Homeless Man,* 1923). The finest hobo poems capture a life that was hard, lonely, moving, and adventurous.

holopoetry A holopoem is quasi-dimensional, a poem experienced in space. The artist Eduardo Kac defines a holographic poem or holopoem as "a poem conceived, made and displayed holographically. This means, first of all, that such a poem is organized non-linearly in an immaterial three dimensional space and that even as the reader or viewer observes it, it changes and gives rise to new meanings."

Homeric epithet, see *epithet.*

Homeric simile, see *epic simile.*

homoeomeral Greek: "having like parts." *Homoeomeral* is a prosodic term for two parts or sections of a poem that are metrically identical, as in a strophe and antistrophe.

SEE ALSO *antistrophe, strophe.*

Horatian ode, see *ode.*

Horatian satire, see *satire.*

hortus conclusus Latin: "sealed garden." A key image in the Song of Songs (4:12): "A garden inclosed is my sister, my spouse; a spring shut up, a fountain sealed." It is an image of a sealed Arcadia, the earthly Paradise. Medieval theologians often interpreted it as a symbol of Mary's fruitfulness but perpetual virginity, hence the common iconography of the Madonna and Child seated in an abundant fenced-in garden cut off from the world. The bower, the space of the sealed secret garden, appears often in romantic poetry, and sometimes beyond. "Language is intent on entering / its hidden garden," Miranda Fields writes in her poem "Hortus Conclusus" (2002).

hovering accent In *Understanding Poetry* (1938), Cleanth Brooks and Robert Penn Warren coined this term to refer to two consecutive syllables of indeterminate but approximately equal stress. They were seeking a term for syllables that approximate the rhetorical weight of a quasi-spondaic foot. It is also referred to as hovering stress and distributed stress.

Thinking about two lines from John Donne's "Holy Sonnet IX" (1631):

If lecherous goats, if serpents envious
Cannot be damned, alas, why should I be?

Warren said: " 'Why should I be?' — you can't tell how to accent it even: it's spondaic but not *spondees;* it's hovering."

SEE ALSO *New Criticism, spondee.*

Hudibrastic verse A type of comic narrative poetry, Hudibrastic verse (Hudibrastics) consists of jangling eight-syllable rhyming couplets. It is named after Samuel Butler's satirical long poem *Hudibras* (1663–1680), which uses deliberately absurd, iambic tetratmeter couplets to ridicule and attack the Puritans. Here is an example from Canto III:

He would an elegy compose
On maggots squeez'd out of his nose;
In lyric numbers write an ode on
His mistress, eating a black-pudden;
And, when imprison'd air escap'd her,
It puft him with poetic rapture.

Jonathan Swift used the octosyllabic rhyming couplet with greater variety, as in these lines from "Vanbrugh's House" (1703):

So, Modern Rhymers strive to blast
The Poetry of Ages past,
Which having wisely overthrown,
They from it's Ruins build their own.

Swift's use of Hudibrastics provided a model for contemporaries, such as Oliver Goldsmith ("New Simile, in the Manner of Swift," 1765) and Alexander Pope ("The Seventh Epistle of the First Book of Horace, Imitated in the Manner of Dr. Swift," 1739), and pointed the way to the use of modern Hudibrastics, such as W. H. Auden's 1940 "New Year Letter." John Barth, who based his novel *The Sot-Weed Factor* (1960) on a poem in Hudibrastics by Ebenezer Cook (ca. 1672–1732), declared: "The Hudibrastic couplet, like Herpes simplex, is a contagion more easily caught than cured."

SEE ALSO *burlesque, couplet, doggerel, mock epic, octosyllabic verse.*

huitain A French stanzaic form, the *huitain* consists of eight lines (an octave) of either eight or ten syllables each, which usually rhyme *ababbcbc* or *abbaacac.* It may stand as a poem in its own right or form part of a longer work, as in the ballade. Chaucer used the stanza in "The Monk's Tale" (1387–1400) and François Villon employed it in his "Testament" (1461).

SEE ALSO *ballade, Monk's Tale stanza, octave.*

hunting chants, hunting songs Wherever there are hunters in traditional societies, there is also a tradition of hunting chants or songs. From the Ammassalik Eskimo to the Navajo and the Zuni, Native American tribes had a powerful tradition of offerings to deceased hunters, of words to summon game and prayers before killing animals ("Prayer Before Killing an Eagle," "Before Butchering the Deer"). These poems incarnate a belief that everything is holy and words have the power to make things happen.

Hunting chants are found throughout Africa. "Like a poet," Judith Gleason writes in *Leaf and Bone: African Praise-Poems* (1994), "the African hunter is a mediator between the unknown and the familiar." The hunter moves away from the cultivated world of the village, which is filled with the talk of other people, into the uncultivated, spirit-saturated, natural world of the forest, which is a place for listening. The forest is a dangerous setting that opens up the imagination.

The Yoruba have an especially powerful tradition of hunting chants, which are called *ijala.* The poetry of hunters is customarily recited during festivals of Ogun, the god of iron. The chanter typically recites the *oríkì* or praise names of important hunters as well as of Ogun, who is worshiped by all those who use iron. Inspiration comes from a divine source and the poet taps Ogun's power to create and transmit his poem. S. A. Babalola quotes some illuminating comments by members of the Yoruba hunting societies in *The Content and Form of Yoruba Ijala* (1966):

> No hunter can validly claim the authorship of an ijala piece which he is the first to chant. The god Ogun is the source and author all ijala chants; every ijala is merely Ogun's mouthpiece.
>
> It is often through inspiration that ijala artists compose new ijala chants. They receive tuition from the god Ogun in dreams or trances.

SEE ALSO *oríkì.*

hymn From the Greek *hymnos:* "song in praise of a god or hero." In the classical world, odes were composed in honor of gods and heroes and chanted or sung at religious festivals and other ceremonial occasions. One thinks of the ringing hexameters of the so-called Homeric hymns, which provided models for the hymns of Callimachus (ca. 305–ca. 240 B.C.E.), and the Orphic hymns chanted by initiates in the Orphic mysteries. Hymns were also a major genre in ancient Egyptian literature, where they served as poems worshiping a deity or a divine king, or, more occasionally, praising a city, such as Thebes, or an object, such as the Red Crowns of Egypt. Charles Boer explains that the word *hymn* derives from the East. The Greek *hymnos* is connected to the word *woven* or *spun:* "in its primal sense, a hymn was thought of as what results when you intertwine speech with rhythm and song." Bacchylides refers to "weaving a hymn."

Songs in praise of gods and heroes became in Christianity "Praise of God in song." Hymns as scriptural texts, shared songs, came into the church in the fourth century (early examples include the nativity song "*Gloria in excelsis*" and the three Gospel canticles) and have been part of devotional services ever since. Latin hymns were written throughout the Middle Ages. Isaac Watts (1674–1748) wrote modern hymns that have a radiant clarity and take great joy in God's created world. He envisioned the Promised Land, as on a clear day, and dramatically adapted the Psalms to his own purposes, as when he "translated the scene of this psalm — 67 — to Great Britain":

Sing to the Lord, ye distant lands,
  Sing loud with solemn voice;
While British tongues exalt his praise,
  And British hearts rejoice.

Charles Wesley (1707–1788) had a gift for transposing and adapting Holy Scriptures into memorable metrical verses, and his hymns have a powerful devotional urgency. He brought a stately grace to the hymnal stanza, as in this passage from Psalm 17:

Hear him, ye deaf; his praise, ye dumb,
  Your loosened tongues employ;
Ye blind, behold your Saviour come.
  And leap, ye lame, for joy!

The hymnal stanza, also known as common measure, is traditionally the same as the ballad stanza, but has the stricter rhythms and rhymes found in the hymnal. Susan Stewart explains, "The phrase *common meter* joins with the terms from music, *common measure* and *common time,* to signify the two pulses to a measure, 4/4 rhythm, under which the entire musical system is coordinated and out of which variations proceed. Common meter presents itself as the most suitable for group singing — the coordination of song and the coordination of social life under a common temporal framework emphasize integration and solidarity." The hymn has accrued terrific liturgical importance as a source of communal devotion. Think, then, of what it meant for Emily Dickinson to fracture the common measure, thus invoking the hymn tradition and responding to its communal nature with a radical individuality of her own. We hear the distinctiveness of her voice against a traditional nineteenth-century social and religious backdrop.

SEE ALSO *ballad, ode, psalm, short meter.*

hypallage Greek: "exchange." A common device in which words are interchanged. The use of hypallage shifts the application of words, reversing their syntactic relation. It transfers and perturbs one's understanding. Thomas Gray declares, "The plowman homeward plods his weary way, / And leaves the world to darkness and to me." Technically, it is the plowman and not the way that is weary, but Gray gains some additional intensity, some greater heaviness, by projecting the weariness onto the path. The surrealist Jean Arp creates a discordant effect when he declares, "The bed was sleeping soundly."

SEE ALSO *metonymy, rhetoric.*

hyperbaton, see *anastrophe.*

hyperbole Hyperbole is a rhetorical figure for "overshooting" or "excess" (Greek), for bold exaggeration. It is a deliberate extravagant statement not intended to be taken literally. George Puttenham called it a "loud liar" and claimed it is used "to advance or . . . abase the reputation of any thing or person" (1589). Hyperbole can be rhetorically marshaled to great effect, for as Oliver Goldsmith put it in 1837, "Poetry is animated by the passions; and all the passions exaggerate. Passion itself is a magnifying medium" ("On the Use of Hyperbole"). Hyperbole is crucial for panegryrics and other forms of praise poetry. The poetry of the Hebrew Bible is filled with prophetic hyperboles. So, too, Jesus was fond of hyperbole as a strategy: "it is easier for a camel to go through the eye of a needle than for a rich man to enter the kingdom of God" (Mark 10:25, Luke 18:25).

Hyperbole is a central device of love poetry from the Song of Songs onwards. Think of John Donne's poem "The Flea" (1633), a witty attempt to seduce a lady by comparing various aspects of their relationship to a flea he has found on her body ("This flea is you and I") or Andrew Marvell's exaggerations in trying to overcome his lady's "coyness" in "To His Coy Mistress" (ca. 1650s):

My vegetable love should grow
Vaster than empires, and more slow.
An hundred years should go to praise
Thine eyes, and on thy forehead gaze.
Two hundred to adore each breast:
But thirty-thousand to the rest.

SEE ALSO *panegyric, praise poems, rhetoric.*

hypercatalectic, see *truncation.*

hypermetric, see *truncation.*

hypertext poetry An electronic text, poetry composed of blocks of words linked electronically. Hypertext poetry, which is created using computer software tools, has its roots in modernism, a poetry of juxtapositions, and challenges the strict linearity of poetic texts. Theodor H. Nelson, who coined the term *hypertext* in the 1960s, explains that by hypertext he means "non-sequential writing—text that branches and allows choices to the reader, best read at an interactive screen. As popularly conceived, this is a series of text chunks connected by links which offers readers different pathways." Hypertext poetry allows the reader to traverse or interact with it in different ways. Lawrence Rainey points out that it "can take two forms, a read-only hypertext, where readers could discover paths already embedded by the creator of the hypertext, and a read/write hypertext, where readers could add their own links and screens."

SEE ALSO *computer poetry, digital poetry, modernism.*

hyphaeresis Taking away a letter from the body of a word. Thus Thomas Moore drops the letter *v* from the word *over* in his poem "Come O'er the Sea" (1823). We employ a *hyphaeresis* every time we sing "The Star-Spangled Banner" (1814):

> O, say, does that star-spangled banner yet wave
> O'er the land of the free, and the home of the brave?

SEE ALSO *elision.*

hypogram The linguist Ferdinand de Saussure filled a series of nearly one hundred notebooks with diagrams of "polyphonic hypograms" from the *Rig-Veda* (1700–1100 B.C.E.), Homer, and the Latin Saturnians. Saussure tried to demonstrate that the sounds in a series of Latin poems showed the same principles as anagrams or *hypograms,* as he sometimes called them: "a hypogram highlights a name or word by artfully repeating its syllables, thus giving it a second, artificial mode of existence, added, as it were, to the word's original form." Saussure thus redefined the anagram around a theme-word, which he related to the addressee of a literary text or else to its subject matter. It was not the transposition of letters, but the repetition of the phonemes in this theme-word that defined the anagram, which disseminated sounds throughout a text "outside of the temporal order of its elements." The *hypogram,* often the name of a hero or deity, is encrypted in the verse line, lying under it, as Jean Starobinski says, or mounted upon it, as Oliva Emmet puts it. "Saussure's specialized notion of the 'hypogram,' " Garrrett Stewart writes, is "an absent 'theme-word' that deliberately organizes the line *from without,* like an absconded prime mover." Starobinski explains:

> The hypogram is for Saussure nothing more than a piece of material data, whose function, which was perhaps initially sacred, was limited very early on to that of a mnemonic aid for the improvising poet and then a regulating process that is intrinsic to the *écriture* itself—at least in Latin. Saussure never stated that the final text preexists in the theme-word; the text builds itself *around* the theme word, and this is quite different.

Saussure's revised idea of the anagram, however flawed, has had a great influence on subsequent literary theorists, who define literature by the materiality of language. In *Semiotics of Poetry* (1978), for example, Michael Riffaterre redefines the *hypogram* as a structural pre-text, a poetic generator. He argues that a poetic text revolves around a semantic nucleus and repeats many different variants of the same invariant. Julia Kristeva prefers the term *paragram* to *anagram* to point to the phonic patterns of a literary text. A *paragram,* Walter Redfern explains, is "a play on words involving the alteration of one or more letters — one of the commonest forms of punning." For the psychoanalytically minded semiotician, these sounds function dynamically to make meaning rather than to express it. A tabular rather than a linear network of sounds presumably uncovers the unconscious principles operating in a literary text, which can sustain a plurality of readings.

SEE ALSO *anagram, metagram.*

hysteron proteron From the Greek: "latter before" or "the latter (in place of) the former." This dignified-sounding term is a figure of speech in which the logical order of ideas is reversed, as when Virgil writes, "Let us die, and rush into the midst of the fray" (*Aeneid,* 29–19 B.C.E.), or Shelley claims, "I die, I faint, I fail" ("The Indian Serenade," 1822). George Puttenham characterized it in *The Art of English Poesy* (1589):

> Ye have another manner of disordered speech, when ye misplace your words or clauses and set that before which should be behind *et è converse,* we call it in English proverb, the cart before the horse, the Greeks call it *hysteron proteron,* we name it *Preposterous,* and if it be not too much used is tolerable enough.

Noting the reversal of "far and wide" to "wide and far" in a translation of the *Aeneid,* Samuel Taylor Coleridge said, "I fear a something ludicrous in this hysteron-proterizing of a familiar idiom, so bare-facedly for rhyme's sake."

iamb A two-syllable metrical foot, the first unstressed, the second stressed, as in the word *ŭnknówn.* It is an upbeat followed by a downbeat. In classical poetry, the iamb or iambus consisted of a short and a long syllable. Two iambs in a row constituted a di-iamb. Iambic rhythm was considered close to ordinary speech in ancient Greek and Latin verse. Aristotle argues that "the iambic is, of all measures, the most colloquial: we see it in the fact that conversational speech runs into iambic lines more frequently than any other kind of verse." Michael Schmidt points out that iambic poetry "described at first a genre as much as a metre. The genre presumed that humour would be an ingredient, but humour of a specific kind, humour at someone's expense . . . The term 'iambic' may derive from the name of the maidservant Iambe, whose tart wit, expressed perhaps in metrical form, brought laughter back to the heart of bereaved and grieving Demeter." Archilochus, Semonides, and Hipponax are the three classical writers of iambics (*iambopoioi*).

Despite similarities, the English iamb is not precisely equivalent to the Greek one. The iamb is by far the most typical foot in English because it fits the natural stress pattern of English words and phrases. Shakespeare understood this and thus employed it in many of his greatest dramatic speeches. The iamb functions, as Alexander Pope puts it, "Tŏ wáke | thĕ sóul | bÿ tén- | dĕr strókes | ŏf árt" ("Prologue to Mr. Addison's 'Cato,' " 1713).

SEE ALSO *foot, iambic pentameter, meter.*

iambe In French poetry, the *iambe* is a satirical poem of variable length composed of verses of twelve and eight syllables, which alternate on cross rhymes or *rimes croisés* (*abab, cdcd,* etc.).

This form of invective, which is rooted in the deadly satirical iambics of the Greek poet Archilochus, came into French poetry with the posthumous *Iambes* of André Chénier (1762–1794), who was executed during the French Revolution, and *Les iambes* (1830–31) of August Barbier, which George Saintsbury called "a series of extraordinarily brilliant and vigorous satires, both political and social." In *Iambe IX,* Chénier uses the alternating syllabics to mimic the rise and fall of the guillotine blade in Saint Lazare prison:

> Le messager de mort, noir recruteur des ombres,
>   Escorté d'infâmes soldats,
> Ebranlant de mon nom ces longs corridors sombres,
>   Où seul dans la foule à grands pas
> J'erre, aiguisant ces dards persécuteurs du crime,
>   Du juste trops faibles soutiens,
> Sur mes lèvres soudain va susprendre la rime.

iambic pentameter A five-stress, roughly decasyllabic line. This fundamental line, established by Chaucer (1340?–1400) for English poetry, was energized when English attained a condition of relative stability in the late fifteenth and early sixteenth centuries. It might be the traditional formal line closest to the form of our speech and thus has been especially favored by dramatists ever since Christopher Marlowe, whose play *Tamburlaine* (1587) inaugurated the greatest Elizabethan drama, and William Shakespeare, who used it with astonishing virtuosity and freedom. John Milton showed just how supple and dignified the pentameter line could be in *Paradise Lost* (1667):

> Of man's first disobedience, and the fruit
> Of that forbidden tree, whose mortal taste
> Brought death into the world, and all our woe,
> With loss of Eden, till one greater Man
> Restore us, and regain the blissful seat,
> Sing, Heav'nly Muse . . .

The iambic pentameter line was strategically employed by most of the great nineteenth-century English poets, from William Wordsworth and

Samuel Taylor Coleridge to Robert Browning and Alfred, Lord Tennyson. It was given a distinctly American stamp in the cadences of Robert Frost, Wallace Stevens, and Hart Crane.

SEE ALSO *blank verse, decasyllable, meter.*

ictus, see *beat.*

identifical rhyme, see *rhyme.*

idyll A short poem (or prose piece) that deals with rustic life. There are no formal requirements for this poem of innocent tranquility, but the description of a picturesque rural scene is a quintessential element. The term derives from *eidyllion,* meaning "little picture," and the idyll is indeed a framed picture, a portrait fantasy of rural life. The ten pastoral poems of the Greek poet Theocritus (third century B.C.E.) defined the genre. Theocritus assembled shepherds and goatherds who are either musicians playing on the syrinx (the reed pipe of Pan) or poets singing of their feelings in pastureland beyond cultivated fields, in hills where there are flowering trees and flowing streams. His idylls ("Begin the pastoral song, dear Muses, begin the song") established the conventions that would be imitated in Virgil's *Eclogues* (42–39 B.C.E.), Dante's Latin idylls, Spenser's *Shepheardes Calender* (1579), Milton's "Lycidas" (1638), and other poems of the Italian, French, and English Renaissance.

In the seventeenth century, there was a critical attempt to apply the term *eclogue* to pastoral poems in dialogue, and reserve the term *idyll* for pastoral poems in narrative, though the words are now mostly interchangeable. Since the Renaissance, there have been many idyllic moments in poetry, but very few major poems that are idylls per se. In the nineteenth century, Robert Browning widened the term for his poems of psychological crisis, *Dramatic Idylls* (1879–1880), and Alfred, Lord Tennyson applied the word to his Arthurian verse romance, *Idylls of the King* (1856–1885).

SEE ALSO *eclogue, nature poetry, pastoral.*

Ifa divination verses *Odu Ifa* (Ifa divination verses) are the sacred texts of the Yoruba people of Nigeria. These verses, which revolve around the Yoruba god of divination, Ifa, are recited and interpreted by the *babalawo,* or priest. The Yoruba have developed a poetics of chance, a complex system of divination and interpretation. The priest dials or rotates sixteen sacred palm nuts sixteen different times, and then translates the configuration into fixed verse texts and interpretations. The visual signs are termed "signatures of an Odu," and the method of oral interpretation is called *Dídafa,* or "reading the signs." Thousands of poems comprise the canonical 256 *Odu,* which regulate terrestrial and cosmic forces. It is through the coded form of Ifa that one's destiny is disclosed.

Henry Louis Gates points out that Ifa's process of oral narration is often compared to writing: "Ifa is frequently called 'scribe' or 'clerk,' or 'one who writes books' (*akowe, a-ko-iwe*). He wrote for his fellow gods, and taught each *babalawo* to write the figures of Ifa on his tray of divination. Ifa speaks or interprets on behalf of all the gods through the act of divination. Ifa, however, can speak to human beings only by inscribing the language of the gods onto the divining tray in visual signs that the *babalawo* reads aloud in the language of the lyrical poetry called *ese.*"

SEE ALSO *oríkì.*

ijala, see *hunting chants.*

image, imagery (collective noun) The image, which Wyndham Lewis calls the "primary pigment" of poetry, relates to the visual content of language. It speaks to our capacity to embody meaning through words. The *Princeton Encyclopedia of Poetry and Poetics* (1993) defines the image as "the reproduction in the mind of a sensation produced by a physical perception." Cleanth Brooks and Robert Penn Warren define it in *Understanding Poetry* (1938) as "the representation in poetry of any sense experience," whereas another handbook characterizes it as "a mental picture evoked by the use of metaphors, similes, and other figures of speech." These are, then, the two bases for its definition: the image is sensuous ("I give you my sprig of lilac"); the image is figurative ("The star my departing comrade holds and detains me"). The literal literally bubbles over into the symbolic in Walt Whitman's "When Lilacs Last in the Dooryard Bloom'd" (1865): "All over bouquets of roses, / O death, I cover you over with roses and early lilies."

The poetic image is always delivered to us through words. Poetry engages our capacity to make mental pictures, but it also taps a place in our minds that has little to do with direct physical perceptions ("Heard melodies are sweet," Keats writes, "but those unheard / Are sweeter"). There are poetic images that give us the remembrance of things past ("When to the sessions of sweet silent thought / I summon up remembrance of things past") or that summon up the memory of the dead, as in the opening of W. B. Yeats's "In Memory of Major Robert Gregory" (1918), where he broods about his lost friends ("All, all are in my thoughts to-night being dead"). There are images that have the character of daydreams, and images that have the hallucinatory power of fevers and dreams. The term *imagination* originally meant the image-making faculty of the mind, and the sense of an image is thus buried in the very concept of imagination. "We cannot speak of imagining without speaking of images," as Mary Warnock puts it.

The imagist movement (1912–1917) placed the image at the center of modern poetry. Ezra Pound, F. S. Flint, and other imagists treated the image as something directly apprehended in a flash of perception. In the 1960s, Robert Bly, James Wright, and others rejected the pictorial image and replaced it with the deep image, that is, an image saturated with psyche, welling up out of the unconscious and thus uniting the inner and outer worlds. In *The Poetics of Space* (1958), the French phenomenological critic Gaston Bachelard recognizes the poetic image as "a sudden salience on the surface of the psyche," something free of causality and thus escaped from time, something with its own ontology, which places us "at the origin of the speaking being." The reader enters into the "dreaming consciousness" and functions in a state of receptivity to language "in a state of emergence." In *Reading the Written Image* (1991), the literary theorist Christopher Collins contends that since every literary image is also a mental image and since every mental image is a representation of an absent entity, then the imagination itself is a poiesis, a making-up, an act of free play for both the writer and the reader.

SEE ALSO *archetype, deep image, imagination, Imaginism, imagism, metaphor, simile, symbol, trope.*

imagination The term *imagination* originally meant the faculty that forms mental images. For Aristotle, the word translated as imagination meant "how the object appears." It referred both to objects present and sensed as well as to those absent and merely thought about. Imagination was thus a practical term for picturing things, a mode of visualization, though the term evolved during the Renaissance to suggest a greater creative faculty, a deeper power of mind. Shakespeare brings together these two senses of imagination in a passage in *A Midsummer Night's Dream* (1590–1596):

> The poet's eye, in a fine frenzy rolling,
> Doth glance from heaven to earth, from earth to heaven,
> And as imagination bodies forth
> The forms of things unknown, the poet's pen
> Turns them to shapes, and gives to airy nothing
> A local habitation and a name.

The poet pictures unknown things and magically transforms them into poetry.

The imagination looks beyond the immediate and enables us to make fictions. David Hume treated ideas as images and recognized the crucial place the imagination plays in thinking. Immanuel Kant's word for the imagination, *Einbildungskraft,* suggested forming a picture in the mind, the power of making images, representing things. Taken together, Hume and Kant developed an account of the imagination, as Mary Warnock explains, "as that which functions both in the presence of an object of perception in the world, and in its absence, when we turn to it in our thoughts. Imagination both presents and re-presents things to us." How we account for the world is dependent upon this faculty, which is also engaged, provoked, and accompanied by the emotions. The romantic poets especially made the imagination the hallmark of their poetics, something almost godlike in its power. For Byron, the imagination was a psychological release: "Poetry is the lava of the imagination, whose eruption prevents an earthquake." For Keats, "The Imagination may be compared to Adam's dream—he awoke and found it truth." For Wordsworth, it was "but another name for absolute strength / And clearest insight, amplitude of mind / And reason in her most exalted mood" (*The Prelude,* 1805, 1850). For Blake, however, imagination's greatest apostle, it was the absolute enemy of reason, a sign of inspiration, and an entrance into the larger world of truth, a vision of the infinite. In *Biographia Literaria* (1817), Coleridge distinguished between two kinds of imagining, which he deemed fancy and imagination. He describes the imagination as a power that "dissolves, diffuses, dissipates, in order to recreate or where the process is rendered impossible, yet still at all events it struggles to idealize and to unify." The fancy, however, merely "receive[s] all its materials ready made from the law of association." Coleridge also distinguishes between primary imagination ("the living power and prime agent of all human perception") and secondary imagination ("an echo of the former, co-existing with the conscious will").

For many poets, the imagination takes something from life — a remote scene, a distant detail — and creates a full-blown vision out of it. Memory is the spark; imagination the process of enlargement. This is the process of poetry. It is also a gift. "But when we refuse what has been offered to the empty heart, when possible futures are given and not acted upon, then the imagination recedes," Lewis Hyde writes in *The Gift* (1983). "And without the imagination we can do no more than spin the future out of the logic of the present; we will never be led into new life because we can work only from the known. . . . The artist completes the act of imagination by accepting the gift and laboring to give it to the real." The power of the imagination is to work from the known to the unknown, and then from the unknown back to the known, to incorporate the world. Emily Dickinson radically declared in poem #632 (ca. 1862):

> The Brain — is wider than the Sky —
> For — put them side by side —
> The one the other will contain
> With ease — and You — beside —

SEE ALSO *esemplastic, fancy, image, invention, leaping poetry, negative capability, organic form, romanticism.*

Imaginism Vadim Shershenevich was the leader of this Russian poetic movement, which was founded in Moscow after the Russian Revolution and flourished between 1919 and 1922. Sergei Yesenin, Rurik Ivnev (the pseudonym of Mikhail Aleksandrovich Kovalyov), and Anatoly Marienhof were the main poets. The Imaginists distanced themselves from futurism, but seem to have taken their name from the futurist Fillipo Marinetti's claim that "a poem is an uninterrupted series of images [*immagini*]." They often wrote verbless poems and created an alternative poetry based on startling images and long chains of metaphors.

SEE ALSO *futurism, verbless poetry.*

imagism Imagism was the movement (and doctrine) of a small group of British and American poets who called themselves imagists or *Imagistes* between 1912 and 1917. T. S. Eliot said: "The point de repère usually and conveniently taken as the starting-point of modern poetry is the group denominated 'imagists' in London about 1910." The group included Ezra Pound, who edited the first anthology, *Des Imagistes: An Anthology* (1914), Richard Aldington, H. D. (Hilda Doolittle), F. S. Flint, and others. Amy Lowell became a strong advocate for the movement and edited three anthologies, all of which were called *Some Imagist Poets* (1915–1917). Pound, who had defected to a new movement called vorticism, sneeringly called it Amygism.

The image was the prevailing aesthetic device of the movement. Pound offered a one-sentence definition of an image as "that which presents an intellectual and emotional complex in an instant of time." He added: "It is the presentation of such a 'complex' instantaneously which gives the sense of sudden liberation; that sense of freedom from time limits and space limits; that sense of sudden growth, which we experience in the presence of the greatest works of art." The image here becomes a moment of revelation.

The Imagists practiced directness and concision. They focused on concrete language and avoided abstractions. Their short poems have no extra verbiage and seek "direct treatment of the thing." The one-image poem of the Imagists owes a strong debt to the Greek lyricists and to the Japanese haiku poets. They were against fixed meters, vague language, and moral reflections. Their precise, free-verse poems were meant to extricate poetry from the nineteenth century. Imagism died as a movement, but its values influenced the poetry not only of Pound and H. D., but also of such poets as Wallace Stevens and William Carlos Williams. The question for poets after imagism was how to maintain imagist precision while introducing larger poetic structures. It purged the lyric of discourse, which then had to be reintroduced into modern poetry.

SEE ALSO *discursive, objectivism, vorticism.*

imayō Japanese: "modern." The *imayō* was originally a Japanese folk song form that became especially popular during the Heian period (794–1185). It was favored by courtesans and Shirabyoshi dancers and then taken up by imperial court poets. The form contains four lines, each with units of seven and five syllables, like all traditional Japanese poetry. The Emperor Go-Shirakawa (1127–1192) took great pains to train himself in the art of *imayō.* He brought to court an elderly woman named Otomae, the undisputed authority on *imayō,* who taught him her singing style and repertoire of songs over nearly a decade. "As a practitioner of imayō," Yung Hee-Kim writes, "Go-Shirakawa helped to create a new culture milieu in which commoners and aristocrats could enjoy and learn from each other's artistry." Go-Shirakawa had an esoteric belief in the mystical power of song. He described his complete absorption in *imayō:*

> Ignoring both summer's heat and winter's cold, and favoring no one season over another, I spent my waking hours in singing; no day dawned without my having spent the whole night singing. Even at dawn, with the shutters still unopened, I kept on singing, oblivious of both sunrise and noon. Hardly distinguishing day from night, I spend my days and months in this manner.

SEE ALSO *waka.*

imitation The Latin word *imitatio* is a translation of the Greek *mimesis.* The concept of imitation began its long history in aesthetics with Plato's critique of poetry and other "mimetic arts," which he considered dangerous and inferior to philosophy. In Book X of *The Republic* (ca. 380 B.C.E.), Plato characterizes mimesis—counterfeit "creations"—as the method of all poetry. He condemns the poet as a "creator of phantoms" who knows "only how to imitate." For him, the world of appearances imitates the real world of ideal forms, and since poetry imitates the appearance of the world of objects, it is the imitation of an imitation and thus "three removes from reality" or "at the third remove from truth." Plato never revised or withdrew his attack on poetry, though the later Neo-Platonists affirmed the value of poetry as imitation by arguing that it is a sensuous embodiment of the ideal realm. Plotinus argues in *The Enneads* (ca. 270) that poetry imitates "the Ideas from which Nature itself derives." This notion would become important to

German romanticists, such as F.W.J. Schelling, who considered poetry a representation of the Absolute.

Aristotle accepted the assumption that art is representational and defined poetry as imitation, but he rejected Plato's transcendental world of ideas and widened the scope of the notion of mimesis beyond mere "copying." In the *Poetics* (350 B.C.E.), he calls imitation "one instinct of our nature" and considered human beings "the most imitative of living creatures," who relish the pleasures of imitation or representation. He redefined mimesis to mean not merely a counterfeiting of the sensible world, but a representation of "universals." Aristotle characterized all poetry as imitating general truths, an idea revived in the eighteenth century by Samuel Johnson, who famously argued, "The business of a poet is to examine, not the individual, but the species; to remark general properties and large appearances: he does not number the streaks of the tulip." For Aristotle, poetry essentially imitated human beings in action. Thus, tragedy and epic represented the "noble actions of noble heroes," whereas "Comedy is an imitation of baser men." The literary work itself represents a preexistent reality, though it is not a mere copy or reflecting surface but an object in its own right.

This Aristotelian stress on formal harmony links to a second idea of imitation: the classical and neoclassical notion of formal models, the imitation of the classics, the following of one writer by another. Alexander Pope believed that nothing recommended itself to modern production so much as the imitation of the ancients. John Dryden developed the idea of imitation as a mode of translation, and here imitation comes to mean adaptation or re-creation. The romantic poets replaced the idea of poetry as imitation with a notion of poetry as spontaneous creation, and imitation fell into disrepute as a critical term. Edward Young sneered at "that meddling ape imitation," and declared: "We read imitation with somewhat of his languor who listens to twice-told tales: our spirits rouse at an original." Modern and contemporary poets have almost exclusively used the word *imitation* to refer to a freer mode of translation, the adaptation of a previous poem. In modern criticism, especially post-Aristotelian criticism, *imitation* has been used as synonymous with *mimesis* and roughly means "representation."

SEE ALSO *Chicago school, comedy, epic, feigning, mimesis, originality, romanticism, tragedy, translation, verisimilitude.*

immram, immrama (pl) Irish: voyage tale. The *immram* (the noun derives from an Old Irish compound verb meaning "rows around") is a medieval Irish narrative that relates a sea journey, often to the Otherworld. The *immram* narrates a perilous ocean voyage and overlaps with the genre of *echtrai,* or "otherworldly adventures." The earliest extant Celtic voyage poem is the *Immram Brain mac Febail* (The voyage of Bran son of Febal), which possibly dates to the seventh or eighth century. It consists of two poems of twenty-eight stanzas each, which are connected by introductory, linking, and final prose passages. The prose-tale *The Voyage of St. Brendan* (ca. 900), which narrates the seven-year journey of Saint Brendan to the Promised Land of the Saints, is a Latin counterpart to the Celtic *immram.* It inspired many European imitations. W. B. Yeats was enamored with the medieval *immrama* and drew on P. W. Joyce's version of *The Voyage of Maildun* (1894) in writing *The Wanderings of Oisin* (1889). Louis MacNeice gives readers a modernist *immram,* the myth of the voyager, in his radio parable play "The Mad Islands" (1962), and Paul Muldoon parodies the Irish voyage tale in his picaresque long "Immram" (1981), which is based on the Gaelic poem *The Voyage of Maél Dúin* (eleventh century). In her fourteen-poem sequence "Immram" (1992), Nuala Ní Dhomhnaill dramatizes the journey to a holy city, the mysterious island of Irish folklore, as a psychic adventure connected to writing poetry.

impersonality T. S. Eliot brought this term into modern poetry criticism in his influential essay "Tradition and the Individual Talent" (1919). Eliot argued for "an impersonal theory of poetry." He suggested that the poet must develop and procure a full consciousness of the past: "What happens is a continual surrender of himself as he is at the moment to something which is more valuable. The progress of an artist is a continual self-sacrifice, a continual extinction of personality." The artist surrenders his own personality to the tradition. Eliot's classical position sought to sever poetry from the personality and subjectivity of the poet. He devalued the emotionalism of romantic poetry. "Poetry is not a turning loose of emotion, but an escape from emotion; it is not the expression of personality, but an escape from personality." This formulation was so powerful for New Critics and others, who valued objectivity and scientific method, that it was forty years before anyone really noticed the next sentence: "But, of course, only those who have personality and emotions know what it means to want to escape from these things." Impersonality is an ideal, which never can be entirely realized.

SEE ALSO *confessional poetry, dissociation of sensibility, New Criticism, objective correlative, tradition.*

impure poetry, see *pure poetry.*

incantation A formulaic use of words to create magical effects. *Incantation* derives from a Latin word meaning "to consecrate with charms or spells," and, indeed, charms, spells, chants, and conjurations all employ the apparatus of sympathetic magic. Incantations, whether spoken or chanted, are characteristic of archaic poetries everywhere, which have always employed the rudimentary power of repetition to create enchantment. Oracular and prophetic poets rely on what Roman Jakobson calls "the magic, incantatory function" of language to raise words beyond speech, to create dream states and invoke apocalyptic forces, dangerous transcendent powers. The Orphic poets and Hebrew prophets, as well as those outsize vatic figures who identify with them (Christopher Smart, William Blake, Walt Whitman, Robert Desnos), deliver incantations formally, not haphazardly, and harness the rhythmic power of repetition through parallel structures and catalogs. Here is a statement from "The Song of Amergin," which was said, as Robert Graves has pointed out, to have been chanted by the chief bard of the Milesian invaders as he set his foot on the soil of Ireland, in the year of the world 2736 (1268 B.C.E.).

> Invoke, People of the Sea, invoke the poet, that he may compose
>   a spell for you.
> For I, the Druid, who set out letters in Ogham,
> I, who part combatants,
> I will approach the rath of the Sidhe to seek a cunning poet
>   that together we may concoct incantations.
> I am a wind of the sea.

SEE ALSO *anaphora, catalog poem, charm, parallelism, repetition, rune, spell, vatic.*

incremental repetition This term, coined by Francis Gummere in *The Popular Ballad* (1907), describes one of the key rhetorical devices of the ballad form. It refers to the repetition of succeeding stanzas with small substitutions or changes. The refrain, modified each time it is repeated, takes on additive power even as the changes in crucial words build, develop, and heighten the suspenseful dramatic situation, as in the traditional Scottish ballad "Lord Randal":

> "What d'ye leave to your mother, Lord Randal, my son?
> What d'ye leave to your mother, my handsome young man?"
> "Four and twenty milk kye: mother, mak my bed soon,
> For I'm sick at the heart, and I fain wad lie down."
>
> "What d'ye leave to your sister, Lord Randal, my son?
> What d'ye leave to your sister, my handsome young man?"
> "My gold and my silver; mother, mak my bed soon,
> For I'm sick at the heart, and I fain wad lie down."

The poetry of the Hebrew Bible commonly relies on a type of incremental repetition. As Robert Alter puts it in *The Art of Biblical Poetry* (1985), "Something is stated; then it is restated verbatim with an added element." Here is an example from The Song of Deborah (Judges 5:23):

> Curse Meroz, says the Lord's angel.
> Curse, O curse *its inhabitants.*
>
> For they came not to the aid of the Lord,
> to the aid of the Lord *among the warriors.*

SEE ALSO *ballad, refrain.*

in medias res Latin: "into the middle of things." Horace coined this phrase in his *Ars Poetica* (ca. 18–19 B.C.E.) to describe a way of commencing a story at a crucial point in the action. It is opposed to *ab ovo,* or starting a story at the beginning. Homer provides the model for leaping into the midst of things. *In medias res* is a formulaic prescription for the epic poem, a license to enter a tale at a peak moment. It is as if the story is already familiar to the audience—"the epic is indifferent to formal beginnings," as Bakhtin puts it in "Epic and Novel" (1941) — and thus the poet has greater narrative freedom to tell it out of chronological order, a license for contingency, shuttling back and forth in time, linking events. The epic poet can also end at any time. He does have a dramatic mandate, however, to engage and move the listener.

SEE ALSO *ab ovo, epic.*

In Memoriam stanza This stanza — a quatrain in iambic tetrameter (ta TUM | ta TUM | ta TUM | ta TUM) with an envelope rhyme scheme of *abba* — is named for the pattern Alfred, Lord Tennyson used in his poem *In Memoriam* (1849). Tennyson did not invent the stanza, as he had thought — Ben Jonson uses it in his 1640 "An Elegy" ("Though beauty be the mark of praise"), as does Lord Herbert of Cherbury in "Ode upon a Question Moved, whether Love Should Continue for ever" (1665) — but he did reserve it for all his poems dealing with the death of his friend, Arthur Hallum, and turned it into one of the most striking and ingenious elegiac devices of nineteenth-century poetry. Notice how the rhyme scheme, which begins with an expectation and concludes by looking back, is self-enfolding.

VII

Dark house, by which once more I stand,
    Here in the long unlovely street,
    Doors, where my heart was used to beat
So quickly, waiting for a hand,

A hand that can be clasped no more —
    Behold me, for I cannot sleep,
    And like a guilty thing I creep
At earliest morning to the door.

He is not here; but far away
    The noise of life begins again,
    And ghastly through the drizzling rain
On the bald street breaks the blank day.

SEE ALSO *envelope, octosyllabic verse, quatrain, stanza.*

inscape and ***instress*** Gerard Manley Hopkins invented these terms in the 1860s. By inscape he means the "individually-distinctive" form, the complex of characteristics that give each thing its uniqueness, its "oneness." By instress he means the natural force, the energy of being, ultimately divine, that holds all things together. This relates to what Shelley called "the One Spirit's plastic stress," which sweeps through "the dull dense world." "There lives the dearest freshness deep down things," Hopkins writes, and the sudden perception of that freshness, the sensation of a deeper pattern of order and unity, is provided by instress. He believed that his poetic style was influenced and shaped by the inscape of organic natural forms. As he wrote to Robert Bridges:

> No doubt my poetry errs on the side of oddness . . . But as air, melody, is what strikes me most of all in music and design in painting, so design, pattern, or what I am in the habit of calling *inscape* is what I above all aim at in poetry. Now it is the virtue of design, pattern, or inscape to be distinctive and it is the vice of distinctiveness to become queer. This vice I cannot have escaped.

SEE ALSO *epiphany, organic form.*

inspiration Inspiration means in-breathing, indwelling. It may be a form of spiritual alertness. It is connected to "enthusiasm," which derives from the Greek word *enthousiasmos,* or "inspiration," which in turn derives from *enthousiazein,* which means "to be inspired by a god." Such passion is ardent, consuming, fanatic. Shelley's "A Defence of Poetry" (1819) makes clear that he considered poetic composition both an uncontrollable force beyond the dispensation of the poet's conscious intellect ("Poetry is not like reasoning, a power to be exerted according to the determination of the will. A man cannot say, 'I will compose poetry' ") and an internal phenomenon of the deeper mind:

> for the mind in creation is as a fading coal which some invisible influence, like an inconstant wind, awakens to transitory brightness; this power arises from within, like the color of a flower which fades and changes as it is developed, and the conscious portions of our natures are unprophetic either of its approach or its departure.

There is a long lineage for the idea that, as Cicero put it, "I have heard that—as they say Democritus and Plato have left on record—no man can be a good poet who is not on fire with passion and inspired by something like frenzy" (*On the Orator,* 55 B.C.E.). There is always a point in creation where voluntary effort merges with something else, something involuntary, and some unknown force takes over. "Henceforward, in using the word *Poetry,*" Robert Graves writes in *On English Poetry* (1922), "I mean both the controlled and the uncontrollable parts of the art taken together, because each is helpless without the other."

There are two views of inspiration—that it comes as a force from beyond the poet; that it comes as a power from within the poet—but these views keep intertwining. In *The Greeks and the Irrational* (1951), E. R. Dodds suggests that Democritus was the first writer—at least the first we know about from ancient Greece—who held that the finest poems were composed "with inspiration and a holy breath." Dodds points to the ancient Greek belief that minstrels derive their creative power from a supreme source: "I am self-taught," says the bard Phemius. "It was a god who implanted all sorts of lays in my mind" (the *Odyssey,* ca. eighth century B.C.E.). So, too, Pindar begged the Muse to grant him "an abundant flow of song welling from my own thought" ("Nemean III," 475 B.C.E.). These poets characterize inspiration as a power from without that is also a deep source within.

Poets have always known they are trying to invoke something that can't be entirely controlled. This is the necessary touch of madness that Plato made so much of, the freedom that terrified him. Here is Socrates (470?–399 B.C.E.) in the dialogue *Phaedrus* (ca. 370 B.C.E.):

> There is a third form of possession or madness, of which the Muses are the source. This seizes a tender, virgin soul and stimulates it to rapt passionate expression, especially in lyric poetry, glorifying the countless mighty deeds of ancient times for the instruction of posterity. But if any man comes to the gates of poetry without the madness of the Muses, persuaded that skill alone will make him a good poet, then shall he and his works of sanity with him be brought to nought by the poetry of madness, and behold, their place is nowhere to be found.

Dodds notes that for Plato, "the Muse is actually *inside* the poet." The Neo-Platonic Shelley spoke of "the visitations of the divinity in man." The philosopher Benedetto Croce echoes Shelley when he states, "The person of the poet is an Aeolian harp which the wind of the universe causes to vibrate."

Creativity is the celebration of the unexpected, and no one entirely understands the relationship between trance and craft, between conscious and unconscious elements, in the making of poetry. On one side, we have the idea of poetry as something entirely inspired by an outside force. Hesiod claimed that he heard the Muses singing on Mount Helicon, and they gave him a poet's staff and told him what to sing. English poetry begins with just such a vision, since it commences with the holy trance of a seventh-century figure called Caedmon, an illiterate herdsman, who now stands at the top of the English literary tradition as the initial Anglo-Saxon or Old English poet of record, the first to compose Christian poetry in his own language. The story goes that when it was his turn to sing during a merry social feast, Caedmon invariably fled, ashamed he never had any songs to contribute. But one night a voice came to Caedmon in a dream and commanded him to sing about the beginning of created things. "Thereupon," as Bede tells it in his *Ecclesiastical History of the English People* (731), "Caedmon began to sing verses which he had never heard before in praise of God the Creator." That is the legendary origin of the inspired poem known as "Caedmon's Hymn." So, too, in tribal societies, the poet is considered the instrument of a power, an external source, which speaks through him.

Edgar Allan Poe took a contrary view by arguing that poetry is created not by inspiration, but out of a conscious method of trial and error. He makes his point in "The Philosophy of Composition" (1846):

> Most writers—poets in especial—prefer having it understood that they compose by a species of fine frenzy—an ecstatic intuition—and would positively shuder at letting the public take a peep behind the scenes, at the elaborate and vacillating crudities of thought—at the true purposes seized only at the last moment—at the innumerable glimpses of an idea that arrived not at the maturity of full view—at the fully matured fancies discarded in despair as unmanageable—at the cautious selections and rejections—at the painful erasures and interpolations—in a word, at the wheels and pinions—the tackle for scene-shifting—the step-ladders and demon-traps—the cock's leathers, the red paint and the black

> patches, which, in ninety-nine cases out of the hundred, constitute the properties of the literary histrio.

Here Poe privileges the nature of calculated reason in the creative process. He provides a counterargument for the work of deliberation. Paul Valéry spoke of "une ligne donné" — the given line — and suggested that everything else was labor, a matter of making. Yet he also declared: "the fact is that every act of the mind itself is always somehow accompanied by a certain more or less perceptible atmosphere of indetermination." As the Polish poet Wislawa Szymborska declares in "The Poet and the World" (1996), "Whatever inspiration is, it is born from a continuous 'I don't know.' "

Longinus added a crucial dimension to the idea of inspiration by considering the way the sublime affects not the speaker but the listener. Poetry also instills a sense of inspiration in the listener or reader. Valéry goes so far as to claim that this is the function or purpose of a poet's work. Thus he writes in "Poetry and Abstract Thought" (1954):

> A poet's function — do not be startled by this remark — is not to experience the poetic state: that is a private affair. His function is to create it in others. The poet is recognized — or at least everyone recognizes his own poet — by the simple fact that he causes his reader to become "inspired."

SEE ALSO *afflatus, the sublime.*

intensity John Keats said, "The excellence of every Art is its intensity, capable of making all disagreeables evaporate, from their being in close relationship with Beauty & Truth." Keats's evocation of intensity — exceptionally great concentration, power, or force — is a crucial feature of romantic poetry. It dates back to Longinus's use of ecstasy as a value and criterion in his early treatise *On the Sublime* (100 C.E.). As M. H. Abrams explains in *The Mirror and the Lamp* (1953), "the opinion of some nineteenth-century critics that only the intense and necessarily brief fragment is quintessential poetry had its origin in Longinus's emphasis on the transport that results from the lightning revelation, the shattering image, or the stunning burst of passion."

SEE ALSO *fragment, romanticism, the sublime.*

intentional fallacy When the meaning of a poem is equated with the author's intention. W. K. Wimsatt and Monroe Beardsley used this phrase to describe what they considered a common critical mistake: "The Intentional Fallacy is a confusion between the poem and its origins, a special case of what is known to philosophers as the Genetic Fallacy. It begins by trying to derive the standard of criticism from the psychological *causes* of the poem and ends in biography and relativism" (*The Verbal Icon,* 1954). The Wimsatt-Beardsley hypothesis was a corrective to reductive criticism, usefully focusing on the poem itself as a work of art, but it ignores the reality that a whole range of contextual formation, including an author's so-called intentions, can help us better understand a literary work. Intentions are complicated and can refer to something more than what is locked up in the private mind of a writer.

SEE ALSO *affective fallacy.*

interlaced rhyme An interlaced rhyme is a medial rhyme that occurs in long rhyming couplets, especially the hexameter. Words in the middle of each line rhyme at the caesura. Swinburne employs the device in "Hymn to Proserpine" (1866):

> Thou art more than the day or the *morrow,* the seasons that laugh or that
>   weep;
> For these give joy and *sorrow;* but thou, Proserpina, sleep.

SEE ALSO *hexameter, rhyme.*

intermedia The Fluxus artist Dick Higgins (1938–1998) came up with the term *intermedia* to describe the fusion of different art forms, a crossing of genres, as in visual poetry or sound poetry. He championed art "between media." Higgins often pointed out that Coleridge had used the word "intermedium" in a lecture on Spenser (1818). Intermedia is an avant-garde art that crosses boundaries and combines forms.

SEE ALSO *avant-garde, concrete poetry, postmodernism, sound poetry.*

internal rhyme, see *leonine rhyme, rhyme.*

intertextuality In the late sixties, the French semiotician Julia Kristeva created the word *intertexualité* (*intertextuality*). She derived it from the Latin *intertexto,* meaning "to intermingle by weaving," to suggest the interdependency of texts, the way that texts necessarily derive from other texts. "Every text takes shape as a mosaic of citations," Kristeva writes in *Semiotikè* (1969), "every text is the absorption and transformation of other texts." A work, then, can be read only relative to other works, which precede it and make its meanings possible. As Roland Barthes writes in "Theory of the Text" (1973):

> Any text is a new tissue of past citations. Bits of code, formulae, rhythmic models, fragments of social languages, etc., pass into the text and are redistributed within it, for there is always language before and around the text. Intertextuality, the condition of any text whatsoever, cannot, of course, be reduced to a problem of sources or influences; the intertext is a general field of anonymous formulae whose origin can scarcely ever be located; of conscious or automatic quotations, given without quotation marks.

Every writing is thus always a rewriting, an open-ended reiteration, and every text is an intermingled weaving, an unfolding tapestry.

SEE ALSO *aporia, deconstruction, iqtibas, shibbus, structuralism.*

the Introspectivists (Di Inzikhistn) Jacob Glatstein (Yankev Glatshteyn, 1896–1971), Aron Glantz-Leyles (1889–1966), and N. B. Minkov (1893–1958) were the first full-fledged modernist Yiddish poets. After World War I, in the late teens in New York, they formed the group *Di Inzikhistn,* which called for Yiddish writers to express their own individual voices. The Introspectivists turned Yiddish poetry away from collectivist concerns and toward an expression of individual life. The group declared their principles in the introduction, which became known as the "Introspectivist Manifesto," to their first anthology, *In zikh* (In Oneself, 1919):

> The world exists and we are part of it. But for us, the world exists only as it is mirrored in us, as it touches *us.* The world is a non-existent category, a lie, if it is not related to us. It becomes an actuality only *in* and

> through *us.* This general philosophical principle is the foundation of our trend. We will try to develop it in the language of poetry.

The title of their journal was contracted into one word, *Inzikh,* which became the name of their trend, *Inzikhism* (Introspectivism). The poets were *Inzikh-ists,* or Introspectivists.

The idea that poetry should explore the inner self was anticipated by the Yiddish poets of *Di Yunge,* but the Introspectivists rejected the traditional high romanticism of the Young Ones and created more vibrant linguistic structures. They employed a taut free verse, rebelled against symbolic formalisms, and stylistically took Yiddish poetry into the twentieth century.

SEE ALSO *the sweatshop poets, the Young Ones.*

invention The word *invention* began its long critical life in classical rhetoric, where *inventio* was listed as the first of five parts of oratory, concerned with the discovery and deployment of arguments. The noun *inventio* corresponds to the verb *invenire,* meaning "to find, to discover, to come upon." One of the ancient criticisms of rhetoric is that it is an art without a proper subject matter and can be manipulated at will. This charge, which Plato launches against the sophist philosophers, such as Gorgias, whom he accuses of empty words, is the source of *inventio* as an old term of abuse. Aristotle countered that *inventio* is a term for how rhetoric discovers truth. In *De invention* (ca. 87 B.C.E.), Cicero, who views rhetoric as the source of civilization, hedges the argument when he defines *inventio* as "the discovery of valid or seemingly valid arguments that render one's thoughts plausible." The idea of finding valid or true arguments was always dogged in classical rhetoric by its evil twin, arguments that only seem valid, which suggests duplicity, lying. This was also a charge of philosophy against poetry.

Invention migrated from rhetoric to poetics and at first referred to the discovery of subjects for poems. Leonardo de Vinci stated: "The poet says that his science consists of invention and measure, and this is the main substance of poetry—invention of the subject-matter and measurement in metre." Invention was sometimes contrasted with the "imitation" of prior literary models, and thus came to signal new and original discoveries. It has had a bewildering variety of uses. It was equated with wit and applied to the fanciful and the incredible. It was associated with the imagination and thus came to refer to "creating" rather than "finding" new truths. It was used to describe fictional, i.e., "invented," rather than historical truths — or the combination of them. It was characterized as an originating power and thus contrasted with judgment. It was used in opposition to convention. In his *Life of Pope* (1781), Samuel Johnson defined invention as the faculty "by which new trains of events are formed and new scenes of imagery displayed . . . and by which extrinsic and adventitious embellishments and illustrations are connected with a known subject." In modern times, invention tends to suggest innovation in either content or form — or both. There remains a sliding ambiguity in the concept that dates back to its origins in rhetoric. The invention that poetry undertakes suggests either the discovery of something previously overlooked or unknown, or else the creation of something utterly new, fresh, and original.

SEE ALSO *convention, fancy, imagination, imitation, inspiration, originality.*

inversion In rhetoric, inversion is the turning of an opponent's argument against him. In poetry, it refers to a grammatical reversal of normal word order, sometimes for the sake of rhyme or meter. It is a notorious device in bad poetry, where words are often wrenched to fit a rhyme scheme, but it can also be used for rhetorical and metrical effect. In her poem beginning "There's a certain Slant of light / Winter Afternoons" (1861), Emily Dickinson places a direct object before a subject and verb and thus writes, "Heavenly Hurt, it gives us." In Book III of *Paradise Lost* (1667), John Milton purposefully inverts the word order in identifying with prophetic poets of the past, "Blind Thamyris and blind Maeonides, / And Tiresias and Phineus prophets old."

SEE ALSO *compensation, rhetoric.*

invocation An apostrophe asking a god or goddess, asking the muse, for inspiration, especially at the beginning of an epic, as when John Milton calls out at the beginning of *Paradise Lost* (1667), "Sing, Heavenly Muse." The invocation — a prayer to initiate a story — recognizes that a poet has a complex indebtedness to tradition. The invocation also acknowledges the uncontrollable aspect of art. Poetry is helpless without an element of mania, an element of the demonic or the irrational or the unconscious. Thus the invocation becomes a plea for an uncontrollable power, a prayer for creativity.

SEE ALSO *apostrophe, epic, inspiration, muse, tradition.*

ionic The Ionians of Asia Minor seem to have used ionic verses for the orgiastic worship of Dionysius and Cybele. The greater ionic foot (*Ionicus a maiore*) was composed of two long syllables followed by two short ones. The lesser ionic foot (*Ionicus a minore*) reversed the order; two short syllables preceded two long ones. Anacreon employed ionics in lyric poetry, Euripides (480?–406 B.C.E.) in tragedy.

SEE ALSO *Anacreontic, foot,* "quantitative meters" in *meter, tragedy.*

iqtibas Arabic: "the lighting of one flame from another." In poetry, it suggests acquisition or adoption. The medieval Arabic poets were adept at *iqtibas,* the process of "borrowing" and weaving scriptural fragments of the Koran into poems. It is a special case of *tadmīn* or "quotation" because it is an unacknowledged borrowing, a mode of intertextuality.

SEE ALSO *allusion, intertextuality, shibbus.*

Irish literary renaissance, the Celtic Twilight, the Celtic Revival The title of W. B. Yeats's book *The Celtic Twilight* (1893, 1902) became a tag for the Irish literary revival. The term *the Celtic Twilight* evoked the moody, mournful, mystical years of the 1890s — after the Celtic Twilight, as Austin Clarke puts it, "All that is vague, wistful, and dreamful was assumed to be characteristic of the Celtic race, here and elsewhere" — but the Irish ferment was much deeper and the mist began to burn off in the early years of the twentieth century.

Yeats liked to quote the Fenian leader John O'Leary's maxim, "There is no great literature without nationality, no great nationality without literature." The revival was an attempt to emancipate Irish literature from English literature, creating a national literature by turning to Irish Celtic culture. The contemporary folklore of the Irish countryside, the tales and beliefs of Irish peasants, and the ancient Gaelic culture served as sources for a new Irish literature. For the writer George Russell (AE), the Celtic Twilight was about reviving contact with the supernatural. For the folklorist Douglas Hyde, it was about revitalizing the Gaelic language. For Yeats, it was about creating a new Irish literature based on ancient sources. The sense of a renaissance in Irish literature was reflected in the Irish Literary Theatre (1898), which developed into the Abbey Theatre (1902) and became the home for Anglo-Irish drama. As John Synge wrote in the Preface to *The Playboy of the Western World* (1907):

> In Ireland, for a few years more, we have a popular imagination that is fiery, and magnificent, and tender; so that those of who wish to write start with a chance that is not given to writers in places where the springtime of local life has been forgotten, and the harvest is a memory only, and the straw has been turned into bricks.

W. B. Yeats mourned the death of one kind of Irish culture with the lines "Romantic Ireland's dead and gone, / It's with O'Leary in the grave" ("September 1913," 1916). James Joyce praised "the delicate skepticism" in Yeats's "happiest book, *The Celtic Twilight,*" but he scorned the romantic sentimentalities of the late nineteenth-century movement, which he mocked in *Finnegans Wake* (1939) as the "cultic twalette."

iroha mojigusari, see *abecedarian.*

irony Greek: "dissimulation." *Irony* is a notoriously slippery term. Eric Heller noted in 1958: "Every attempt to define irony unambiguously is in itself ironical. It is wiser to speak about it ironically." Nonetheless, there are some traditional ways of looking at this shifty concept. Until the eighteenth century, irony referred to the rhetorical mode of dissembling ignorance, saying something less or different than one means. In Greek comedy, the *eirön* was the underdog, a weak but clever dissembler, who pretended to be less intelligent than he was and ultimately triumphed over his adversary, the *alazon,* a dumb braggart. In Plato's dialogues (fourth century B.C.E.), the philosopher Socrates (470?–399 B.C.E.) takes up the role of the *eirön,* or "dissembler." He asks seemingly innocuous questions that gradually undermine the arguments of his interlocutor, thus trapping him into discovering the truth. This became known as Socratic irony. John Thirwall named this dialogue form "Dialectical Irony" (*On the Irony of Sophocles,* 1833). The sense of dissembling still clings to the word *irony.*

Verbal irony. A speaker states one thing, but means something else, often the opposite of what one thinks. Samuel Johnson defined irony in verbal terms as "a mode of speech in which the meaning is contrary to the words: as, *Bolinbroke was a pious man.*" The *Princeton Encyclopedia of Poetry and Poetics* (1993) includes various rhetorical terms under the rubric of irony, such as *hyperbole* (overstatement), *litotes* (understatement), *antiphrasis* (contrast), *chleuasm* (mockery), *mycterism* (the sneer), and *mimesis* (imitation). We can add to this *pastiche, puns, parody,* and *conscious naïveté.*

Dramatic irony. A situation turns out to be different than it seems. As a plot device, dramatic irony operates in a number of established ways: 1) the spectators know more than the protagonist; 2) the character acts in an unwise or inappropriate way; 3) characters or situations are compared; 4) there is a marked difference between what the character recognizes and understands and what the play suggests. Think of Sophocles's *Oedipus* (ca. 429 B.C.E.) in which the king hunts for the incestuous father-murderer who has brought a plague to Thebes. The protagonist gradually discovers what the audience knew all along: that the hunter is the hunted, that Oedipus has been looking for himself all along and blinds himself. This is an instance of tragic irony.

Cosmic irony is the irony of fate. A deity, a destiny, the universe itself, leads a character to a sense of false hope, which is duly frustrated and mocked. This characteristic plot device works so well for Thomas Hardy because it reflects his world view.

Friedrich Schlegel and late eighteenth- and early nineteenth-century German writers introduced the notion of romantic irony. The author builds the illusion of representing external reality, but shatters it by revealing that the author himself, an artist, is self-consciously manipulating the scene. Lord Byron's narrative poem *Don Juan* (1819–1824) repeatedly draws attention to itself in this way.

The New Critics enlarged and generalized irony into a criterion of value. Thus I. A. Richards defined irony in poetry as the equilibrium of opposed attitudes and evaluations. As he writes in *Principles of Literary Criticism* (1924):

> Irony in this sense consists in the bringing in of the opposite, the complementary impulses; that is why poetry which is exposed to it is not of the highest order, and why irony itself is so constantly a characteristic of poetry which is.

Robert Penn Warren ("Pure and Impure Poetry," 1942), Cleanth Brooks ("Irony as a Principle of Structure," 1949), and other New Critics developed the idea that weaker poems are vulnerable to a reader's skepticism, but that greater poems are invulnerable because they incorporate into their very being the poet's ironic awareness of opposite or complementary attitudes.

In *On the Concept of Irony with Constant Reference to Socrates* (1841), the philosopher Soren Kierkegaard considers irony, especially Socratic irony, a mode of seeing things, a way of viewing life. To be ironic is to be double-minded.

SEE ALSO *ambiguity, hyperbole, imitation, litotes, New Criticism, parody, pun, rhetoric, satire.*

isochronism, isochrony In mechanics, isochronism is "the propery of having a uniform rate of operation or periodicity," as in a pendulum or a watch balance. In prosody, the term applies to the metrical organization of a poem into equal time units, such as feet, lines, and stanzas. The term is usually employed to describe quantitative verse. Some theorists have nonetheless maintained that it is a natural feature of the English language.

SEE ALSO *meter, prosody.*

isocolon Greek: "of equal members or clauses." The repetition of phrases of equal length and, usually, corresponding structure. *Isocolon* is a rhetorical term that includes what the Latin rhetoricians called *compar,* the balancing of two clauses of the same length, and *parison,* the corresponding structure in a series of phrases or clauses, as in these three lines from John Donne's "Love's Alchemy" (1635):

> I have lov'd, and got, and told,
> But should I love, get, tell, till I were old,
> I should not find that hidden mystery.

SEE ALSO *rhetoric.*

isometric stanza A stanza using lines of the same length. Verse forms and stanzas that employ a single kind of metrical line—all the traditional fixed forms, for example, or poems in blank verse, heroic couplets, or terza rima—are isometric. "It is a simple fact," T.V.F. Brogan states, "that most of the poems written in English from Chaucer to Tennsyon and Browning are isometric."

SEE ALSO *blank verse, couplet, formes fixes, heterometric stanza, stanza, terza rima.*

ivory tower The phrase *ivory tower* comes from the *Song of Songs* (7:4): "Thy neck is a tower of ivory." In 1837, the French critic Sainte-Beuve applied the phrase *tour d'ivoire* to the poet Alfred de Vigny (1797–1863). The term was intended as an insult signaling his isolation from daily life, his blinkered elevation of art above everything else. "Ivory tower" has been used ever since as a derogatory for an artistic or intellectual unworldliness, an indifference to practical life, an art insulated from social concerns. Perhaps the term should be rehabilitated as a descriptive metaphor for the beloved.

Jacobean Age The reign of King James I, which lasted from 1603 to 1625, was the era of courtly masques and violent dramas obsessed with bloody death and sexual passion. It is the most prolific era of English drama. One thinks of the plays of Cyril Tourneur (*The Revenger's Tragedy*, 1606), John Webster (*The Duchess of Malfi*, 1623), Thomas Middleton (*The Changeling*, 1622, with Thomas Rowley), and John Ford (*'Tis Pity She's a Whore*, 1629). This was the period of William Shakespeare's *Macbeth* (1611) and *King Lear* (1608). And it was also the era of Ben Jonson's sophisticated collaborations with Inigo Jones. In poetry, Jonson and the "sons of Ben" flourished during these two decades, and so did the metaphysical poets. Poetry, too, was by turns sophisticated and savage, courtly and violent. The King James Bible (1611), the cornerstone of English prose and the prototype for free verse, was also produced during this era.

SEE ALSO *masque, metaphysical poets, Sons of Ben.*

Jacobite poetry For a period of the eighteenth century (1705–1775), many of the leading Gaelic poets (Eoghan Ruadh Ó Súilleabháin, who was called Eoghan an Bhéil Bhinn or Owen of the Sweet Mouth; Seaghan Clàrach Mac Domhnaill; Piaras Mac Gearailt; and Aodhagán Ó Rathaille) expressed a strong desire for a Jacobite restoration. They championed the cause of James II (whose name in Latin is *Jacobus*, hence Jacobite) and his descendents. Their poems frequently foretell the restoration of the rightful king by an Irish prophet. Munster was a great center of literary activity in the eighteenth century, and most of the Munster poets were Jacobites. One of the main forms of Jacobite poetry was the political *aisling,* or dream poem. Here in James Clarence Mangan's somewhat flowery but telling nineteenth-century version is Ó Rathaille's "Gile na Gile" or "Brightness Most Bright," which expresses his feeling about the state of Ireland at the time:

The Brightest of the Bright

The Brightness of the Bright met me on my path so lonely;
    The Crystal of all Crystals was her flashing dark-blue eye;
Melodious more than music was her spoken language only;
    And glorious were her cheeks, of a brilliant crimson dye.

With ringlets above ringlets her hair in many a cluster
    Descended to the earth, and swept the dewy flowers;
Her bosom shone as bright as a mirror in its luster;
    She seemed like some fair daughter of the Celestial Powers.

She chanted me a chant, a beautiful and grand hymn,
    Of him who should be shortly Éire's reigning King—
She prophesied the fall of the wretches who had banned him;
    And something else she told which I dare not sing.

Trembling with many fears I called on Holy Mary,
    As I drew nigh this Fair, to shield me from all harm,
When, wonderful to tell! she fled far to the Fairy
    Green mansions of Sliabh Luachra in terror and alarm.

O'er mountain, moor and marsh, by greenwood, lough and hollow,
    I tracked her distant footsteps with a throbbing heart;
Through many an hour and day did I follow on and follow,
    Till I reached the magic palace reared of old by Druid art.

There a wild and wizard band with mocking fiendish laughter
    Pointed out me her I sought, who sat low beside a clown;
And I felt as though I could never dream of Pleasure after
    When I saw the maid so fallen whose charms deserved a crown.

Then with burning speech and soul, I looked at her and told her
    That to wed a churl like that was for her the shame of shames

When a bridegroom such as I was longing to enfold her
    To a bosom that her beauty had enkindled into flames.

But answer made she none; she wept with a bitter weeping,
    Her tears ran down in rivers, but nothing could she say;
She gave them a guide for my safe and better keeping,—
    The Brightest of the Bright, whom I met upon my way.

SEE ALSO *aisling*.

jazz poetry Poetry informed by jazz. Jazz is an art of improvisation (the performance of music without following a prearranged score), which is also the core value in jazz poetry, a kind of verbal music that seeks to bring the lyric "into the moment," whether it is composed spontaneously with music in the background, or deliberately by the poet in solitude. Jazz has provided a particular beat for American poetry from the 1920s to the present. Hart Crane declared: "Let us invent an idiom for the proper transposition of jazz into words! Something clean, sparkling, elusive!" The transposition of jazz into words takes place in the work of the poets of the Harlem renaissance, the Beat movement, and the Black Arts movement. The music of jazz and blues has been central to the emerging aesthetics of African American poetry, but it has also had a reach throughout modern and contemporary poetry, whether black or white. Langston Hughes was the first poet devoted to jazz. He used its syncopated rhythms and repetitive phrases as a way to address the struggles of African American life, especially in Harlem, in such early short poems as "Jazzonia" and "The Weary Blues" (1923). Jazz was a joyous antidote to suffering. His later jazz poems relate to jazz more directly, especially *Ask Your Mama: Twelve Moods for Jazz* (1961) and *Montage of a Dream Deferred* (1951), which he said was "like be-bop, marked by conflicting changes, sudden nuances, sharp and impudent interjections, broken rhythms, and passages sometimes in the manner of the jam session, sometimes the popular song, punctuated by the riffs, runs, breaks, and distortions of the music of a community in transition."

Jazz entered American poetry in the 1920s. T. S. Eliot sounded some jazz notes in "The Waste Land" (1922), which made it especially appropriate for Crane to marshal the affirmations of jazz against the poetry of negation and despair. Vachel Lindsay and Carl Sandburg both summoned the rhythmic drive of jazz. Hughes, Kenneth Rexroth, and Maxwell Bodenheim all started reciting poetry with jazz bands. Rexroth defined jazz poetry in 1958 as

> The reciting of suitable poetry with the music of a jazz band, usually small and comparatively quiet. Most emphatically, it is not recitation with "background" music. The voice is integrally wedded to the music and, although it does not sing notes, is treated as another instrument, with its own solos and ensemble passages . . .

Kenneth Patchen, a Beat precursor, read his poetry with Charles Mingus's jazz combo in the 1950s and later with the musician Allyn Ferguson, who composed and arranged jazz accompaniments for each individual poem, including "I Went to the City" and "The Murder of Two Men by a Young Kid Wearing Lemon-colored Gloves" (1957). He was one of the first to record his poetry with a jazz group. Jack Spicer also read poems with jazz accompaniments. During the Beat era, reading poetry to jazz became part of the San Francisco club scene. Lawrence Ferlinghetti introduced *A Coney Island of the Mind* (1958) with the statement that the poems were written not for the page but for oral presentation with jazz accompaniment. Jack Kerouac called his work "spontaneous bop poetry" and collaborated with David Amram, who would scat as Kerouac read. Kerouac was a jazz aficionado, like Ted Joans, who was also a musician, and LeRoi Jones, later Amiri Baraka, who collaborated with musicians such as Max Roach and helped to pioneer jazz studies with his book *Blues People* (1963). Black jazz musicians were symbolically important to the Beats, who were white hipsters, as artistic outcasts, symbols of outlaw spirituality. The spirit of jazz also crossed the ocean, and in the 1950s a group of young British writers were deemed the Jazz Poets for reading their work to jazz accompaniment. The group included Christopher Logue, Pete Brown, and Roy Fisher.

Jazz also operates as a metaphor and subject matter, a rhythmic base, in poems such as Frank O'Hara's "The Day Lady Died" (1964), Paul Blackburn's "Listening to Sonny Rollins at the Five-Spot" (1967), and Michael Harper's "Dear John, Dear Coltrane" (1970). My short list of other poets in the jazz tradition includes Sterling Brown, Hayden Carruth, Joy Harjo, Garrett Hongo, T. R. Hummer, Yusef Komunyakaa, Philip Levine, Mina Loy,

William Matthews, Robert Pinsky, Sonia Sanchez, Charles Simic, Lorenzo Thomas, and Al Young.

SEE ALSO *Beats, Black Arts movement, blues, Harlem renaissance, sound poetry.*

jeli, see *griot.*

je ne sçai quoi, je ne sais quoi "I don't know what." This phrase entered French criticism in the seventeenth century to suggest the indescribable or inexpressible qualities of a work of art or literature, including poetry. It was first used in England in the mid-seventeenth century to characterize a sudden illness, a strange malady, that had no apparent cause, but it migrated to critical discourse in the eighteenth century, where it once more referred to an indefinable quality, an intangible element, in a poem. The English poet William Whitehead, who became poet laureate in 1757, entitled a playful love poem "The Je Ne Sçai Quoi. A Song" (1772):

> Yes, I'm in love, I feel it now,
>   And Cælia has undone me;
> And yet I'll swear I can't tell how
>   The pleasing plague stole on me.
>
> 'Tis not her face which love creates,
>   For there no graces revel;
> 'Tis not her shape, for there the Fates
>   Have been rather uncivil.
>
> 'Tis not her air, for sure in that
>   There's nothing more than common;
> And all her sense is only chat,
>   Like any other woman.
>
> Her voice, her touch, might give th' alarm—
>   'Twas both perhaps, or neither;
> In short, 'twas that provoking charm
>   Of Cælia altogether.

jeremiad A lamentation, a doleful complaint, a sustained invective. The jeremiad, named after the prophet Jeremiah, is a long literary work, usually in prose, sometimes in poetry. The Lamentations of Jeremiah is a series of poems mourning the desolation of Jerusalem and the sufferings of her people after the siege and destruction of the city and the burning of the temple by the Babylonians. The poet is Jeremiah crying out to the assembly to witness the folly unprecedented in both West (Cyrus) and East (Kedar) of a people who forsake the fountain of living waters for the stagnant water at the bottom of a leaky cistern. The prophet is wild, unsparing, oracular, and ruthless.

In *The New England Mind: From Colony to Province* (1953), Perry Miller first identified the jeremiad as a New England specialty, which was formalized in Puritan sermons as a response to a tragedy and a warning of greater tribulations to come. It also holds out hope for a brighter future. The sermon comes as a verse jeremiad in Michael Wigglesworth's "God's Controversy with New England," which he composed during the drought of 1662. It begins:

Good Christian Reader, judge me not
  As too censorious,
For pointing at those faults of thine
  Which are notorious.
For if those thoughts be none of thine
  I do not thee accuse:
But if they be, to hear thy faults
  Why shouldest thou refuse?

In a piece on the Puritan jeremiad, Emory Elliot explains: "Taking their texts from Jeremiah and Isaiah, these orations followed—and re-inscribed—a rhetorical formula that included recalling the courage and piety of the founders, lamenting recent and present ills, and crying out to return to the original conduct and zeal." In current scholarship, the term *jeremiad* has expanded to include not only sermons but also other like-minded texts, such as captivity narratives, letters, and covenant renewals, as well as some histories and biographies. The Puritan poet Edward Taylor took Samuel Hooker's death as an occasion to preach a verse jeremiad in "An Elegy upon the Death of that Holy and Reverend Man of God, Mr. Samuel Hooker" (1697).

jikaawase, see *utaawase.*

Jindyworobak movement In 1937, Rex Ingamells took a Woiwurrung word meaning "to join" or "to annex" and founded the Australian Jindyworobak Movement. He outlined its values in "On Environmental Values" (1937), later expanded to "Conditional Culture" (1938), which set out a nativist Australian agenda. The group, which consisted of white writers, believed that Australian literature should attend to the land, history, and values of Australia, especially its indigenous culture. Some of the most interesting Jindyworobak poems appropriate the Aboriginal concept of "altijira," or "dream time." In 1941, A. D. Hope ridiculed the Jindyworobaks as "the Boy Scout school of poetry," though he later apologized in *Native Companions* (1975). The movement was over by the 1950s, but continued to influence such poets as Peter Porter and Les Murray.

SEE ALSO *the Angry Penguins.*

jingle Any catchy little verse. The jingle, which is marked by repetitive rhythms and emphatic rhymes, strikes a light chord and sticks in the mind, a memorable piece of nonsense. In "A Literary Nightmare" (1876), later re-titled "Punch, Brothers, Punch!," Mark Twain tells the story of catching a viruslike jingle in the morning paper, which he can't dislodge from his mind until he "infects" someone else ("Punch brothers! Punch with care! / Punch in the presence of the passenjare!"), who continues the cycle. The term is sometimes used to deprecate poetry that is too tinkling. William Dean Howells reported that Ralph Waldo Emerson contemptuously dismissed Edgar Allan Poe as "*the jingle man.*"

SEE ALSO *doggerel, light verse, nonsense poetry, nursery rhymes.*

joc partit (Provençal), ***jeu parti*** (French), see *tenson.*

jongleur A wandering minstrel and entertainer of the Middle Ages. Jongleurs existed in France from the fifth to the fifteenth century. The name first applied to all entertainers, including actors and acrobats — they considered themselves to be "jugglers" — but from the tenth century on it referred exclusively to musicians and performers of verse. "A jongleur is a being of multiple personalities," Edmond Faral declared. The names *jongleur* and *trou-*

badour were also at one time used interchangeably, but later the term for jongleur came to refer to entertainers who presented the material of others, such as the chansons de geste. The gulf had widened between creative and performing artists. Troubadours composed but did not perform their own work. Yet some troubadours fell on hard times and became jongleurs, some inventive jongleurs became troubadours. The two were equally received at court. The jongleurs were outsiders, frequently treated as madcaps and fools, but there was a lordship of jongleurs in Arras. In 1221, a member of the *carite de nostre dame des ardents,* which was known in the later Middle Ages as the "confraternity of the jongleurs and the townspeople of Arras," declared:

> This Carité was founded by jongleurs, and the jongleurs are the lords of it (*li iogleor en sont signor*). And those whom they put in, are in. And whoever they keep outside cannot be in, unless they say so. Because there is no lordship with us, save that of jongleurs (*Car sor iogleors ni a nus signorie*).

Carol Symes writes that "the Carité de Nostre Dame des Ardents was not only the first lay confraternity in Europe to produce its own documents, it was one of the first entities to develop a vocabulary of power based on — and in — texts." The lively jongleurs played a crucial role in transmitting poetry from one country to another. Marius Barbeau points out in *Jongleur Songs of Old Quebec* (1962) that "the New-World settlers brought the songs to North America as part of their French heritage two or three hundred years ago."

SEE ALSO *chansons de geste, juglar, troubadour.*

Jugendstil The term *Jugendstil* ("Youth Style") took its name from the Munich journal *Die Jugend* ("Youth"), founded in 1896, which featured Art Nouveau designs. It was primarily used in Germany and Austria to describe a style of decorative art and architecture (ca. 1895–1905) and then spread northward into Scandinavian countries. Jugendstil extended to poetry to include the symbolist work of Stefan George (1868–1933) and the neo-romanticism of Richard Beer-Hofmann (1866–1945) and Hugo von Hofmannsthal (1874–1929). The early work of Rainer Maria Rilke (1875–1926), especially *The Book of Hours* (1903), has affinities with the youthful exultation and rapt intensities of the Jugendstil movement. The Judgenstil writers reacted against naturalism and yearned for an escape from modern industrialism. They sought cosmic wholeness. Walter Benjamin said that Judgendstil "represents the last attempted sortie of an art besieged in its ivory tower by technology. This attempt mobilizes all the reserves of inwardness."

SEE ALSO *symbolism, Young Vienna.*

juglar, juglares The Spanish name for wandering minstrels and entertainers. The name of the French *jongleur* and the Spanish *juglar* — they are equivalent — derives from the Latin word *ioculari,* jokes, or *ioculator,* a clown or joker, someone who entertains. One theory is that they derive from the wandering street entertainers of Rome. They are known to have existed by the seventh century in Spain, but emerged only in the twelfth century as creators and performers of epic *cantares,* sung poems. The *mester de juglaria* (art of the minstrel) refers to the oral and epic narrative poetry of the twelfth, thirteenth, and fourteenth centuries.

SEE ALSO *jongleur, romances.*

junačke pesme, see *epic* and *ženske pesme.*

Juvenalian satire, see *satire.*

Kantan Chamorrita The Chamorros, the indigenous people of Guam, have an ancient style of improvised rhyming debate known as *Kantan Chamorrita.* It was first documented in 1602—it is obviously much older—and remains a vital part of Chamorro culture. The word *chamorritta* originally referred to a love song, and *Kantan Chamorrita* (Chamoritta Singing) is an improvised folk song with a call-and-response pattern in rhyming couplets. Verses are chanted and sung back and forth between individuals and groups, who spontaneously trade witty comments and jibes as a kind of dialogue and debate. During World War II, the Chamorros used this form of double talk to communicate with each other and mock the occupying forces.

SEE ALSO *poetic contest.*

kasa Korean: "song words." The *kasa* is an extended narrative verse form (some run for several thousand lines) that consists of eight-syllable lines arranged in balanced couplets. Each line is broken into two equal four-syllable units. The *kasa* emerged in Korean poetry around the mid-fifteenth century. The traditional *naebang kasa* ("inner room" kasa), which deals with women's lives, is still composed today.

SEE ALSO *sijo.*

katabasis From an ancient Greek word meaning "a going down." In epic poetry, a *katabasis* is a descent into the underworld, as when Odysseus goes down into Hades in book 11 of the *Odyssey* (ca. eighth century B.C.E.) and

Aeneas journeys into the underworld in Book VI of the *Aeneid* (29–19 B.C.E.). Both of these archetypal journeys echo through Dante's *Inferno* (1304–1309), which is an extended *katabasis.* Alexander Pope uses the Cave of Spleen to parody *katabasis* in *The Rape of the Lock* (1712–1714).

SEE ALSO *epic.*

katharsis, see *catharsis.*

kávya A word from Sanskrit, an ancient language of India. In classical Sanskrit literature, which roughly dates from the fourth century B.C.E. to the eighth century C.E., *kávya* was the term for elegant or ornate poetry characterized by its artistry. The Kavi were court poets who created and circulated a body of literary texts with highly developed aesthetic ideas, such as *rasa* (poetic emotion), *dhvani* (poetic sound), and *vakrokti* (poetic obliqueness). *Kávya,* which was distinguished from the rougher epic called *Alkyana,* or tale, reached a high peak in three poems by Kālidāsa created in the fifth century: the lyric monologue of nature, *Maghadūta* (The Cloud Messenger), and two long lyric narratives, *Raghuvamsa* (The Lineage of Ramsu) and *Kumārasambhava* (The Birth of Siva's Son).

SEE ALSO *dūta kāvya, rasa, shloka.*

keening The Irish form of lamenting over the dead, "Raising the Keen," was primarily a form of women's oral poetry, a public display of grieving, sometimes sung by relatives and neighbors of the deceased, sometimes by professional mourners. It was once common, both in Europe and in Africa, to hire professional mourners to keen one's relatives. In the *Aeneid* (29–19 B.C.E.), Virgil notes the ancient practice among the Phoenicians: "*Lamentis gemituque et femineo ululatu / tecta fremunt*"; "Lamentations, keening, and shrieks of women / sound through the houses." The Ossian corpus may be made up of keenings for the dead warrior king.

Keening, which derives from the Irish word *caoineadh,* is a more verbally articulated expression of grief than the high-pitched moaning of the death wail, the *ullagone.* Seán Ó Súilleabháin explains that "many of the lamentations about the corpse at wakes and funerals were in the form of extempore poetry in Irish." It was common for a relative of the dead to recite some mournful poetry in praise of the deceased, lamenting his death. Eugene

O'Curry described a nineteenth-century scene in his introduction to *On the Manners and Customs of the Ancient Irish* (1873):

> I once heard in West Muskerry, in the county of Cork, a dirge of this kind . . . improvised over the body of a man who had been killed by a fall from a horse, by a young man, the brother of the deceased. He first recounted his genealogy, eulogized the spotless honor of his family, described in the tones of a sweet lullaby his childhood and boyhood, then changing the air suddenly, he spoke of his wrestling and hurling, his skill at ploughing, his horsemanship, his prowess at a fight in a fair, his wooing and marriage, and ended by suddenly bursting into a loud, piercing, but exquisitely beautiful wail, which was again and again taken up by the bystanders. Sometimes the panegyric on the deceased was begun by one and continued by another, and so on, as many as three or four taking part in the improvisation.

Gaelic keening—atonal, primitive—has informed the elegies and dirges that form an essential part of Irish poetry and drama. Keening is expressed in traditional folk ballads, such as "The Keening of the Three Marys," which Douglas Hyde collected and translated in *The Religious Songs of Connacht* (1906). John Synge describes the rhythmic power of keening among a group of neighbors in *The Aran Islands* (1907): "While the grave was being opened the women sat down among the flat tombstones, bordered with a pale fringe of early bracken, and began the wild keen, or crying for the dead. Each old woman, as she took her turn in the leading recitative, seemed possessed for the moment with a profound ecstasy of grief, swaying to and fro, and bending her forehead to the stone before her, while she called out to the dead with a perpetually recurring chant of sobs."

W. B. Yeats evokes the keening tradition in the song "Do Not Make a Great Keening" in his play *Cathleen ni Houlihan* (1902), and so does Pádraic Pearse in his lyric "A Woman of the Mountain Keens Her Son" (*Songs of Sleep and Sorrow,* 1914). Traditional keening has now mostly died out in Ireland, and contemporary Irish poets continue to lament its loss, which is associated with ritual grief. As Seamus Heaney notes, "we pine for ceremony, / customary rhythms" ("Funeral Rites," 1993). In Scots Gaelic the term of *coronach,* and the practices of lament, have not been completely lost.

SEE ALSO *coronach, dirge, elegy, oral poetry.*

kenning A standard phrase or metaphoric compound used in Old Norse and Old English poetry as a poetic circumlocution for a more familiar noun. In *Beowulf* (ca. eighth to eleventh century), for example, the human body is called *banhus* ("bone house"), a ship is termed *saewudu* ("sea wood"), and the sea is named *swanrud* ("swan road"). Darkness is "the helmet of night." There is a riddling element to the kenning, which is a way of renaming and thus re-envisioning an object. Andrew Walsh calls it "a riddle in miniature." This idea can be illustrated by turning the declaration into a question. "What is the sky's candle (*rodores candel*)"? *The sun.* "What is the home of the winds (*windgeard*)?" *The sea.*

The word *kenning* derives from the Old Norse phrase *kenna eitt vio,* meaning "to express or describe one thing in terms of another." The term came into English in the nineteenth century through the medieval Iceland treatises on poetics. The word *ken,* meaning "to know," is still used in Scottish dialects. The kenning, a metaphoric transfer, is a way of knowing.

SEE ALSO *circumlocution, metaphor, riddle.*

khamriyyat, see *wine poetry.*

kharja, see *muwashshah, zéjel.*

Kiev Group A cadre of Yiddish poets, playwrights, and novelists who made the case for Soviet Yiddish literature in the Ukraine in the 1920s. David Bergelson (1884–1952) and Der Nister (the pen name of Pinchus Kahanovich, 1884–1950) were the leaders of the movement, which also included the poets David Hofstein (1889–1952), Leib Kvitko (1890–1952), and Peretz Markish (1895–1952). The Kiev Group was socialist and non-Zionist. The writers agreed that Yiddish, "the people's tongue," was the appropriate language for modern Jewish national literature. Under Stalinism, all but Nister, who died earlier, were executed for alleged crimes against the state.

kind In the seventeenth and eighteenth centuries, the term *kind* was used to suggest a literary genre, such as the epic. The very notion of kind implies that formal genres are characterized both by their intrinsic values and their particular social usefulness. Susan Stewart explains: "The notion of poetic *kinds* is tied to the specificity of their use and occasion: the epithalamion, the elegy, the audade are at once works of art independent of their particular contexts of production and use and social acts tied to specific rules of decorum. Poems are in this sense acts of social intent and consequence and not things in a world of things." Literary kinds also have histories, and new kinds are continually made out of old ones. The concept of genre is often broadened by foreign models.

SEE ALSO *decorum, genre.*

kitsch The term *kitsch* originally applied to cheap, trashy, ephemeral works of art: sentimental illustrations and paintings, sentimental poems and novels. Kitsch is pseudoart, art in bad taste, what in Yiddish goes by the terms *schlock* (stuff of low quality) and *schmaltz* (sentimental exaggerations). The art critic Clement Greenberg explained in "Avant-Garde and Kitsch" (1939):

> Where there is an avant-garde, generally we also find a rear-guard. True enough — simultaneously with the entrance of the avant-garde, a second new cultural phenomenon appeared in the industrial West: the thing to which the Germans gave the wonderful name of *Kitsch* . . . Kitsch is vicarious experience and faked sensations. Kitsch changes according to style, but remains always the same. Kitsch pretends to demand nothing of its customers except the money — not even their time.

Kitsch was first used in Munich in the 1860s and '70s among painters and art dealers to characterize cheap artistic stuff. It became an international term in the first decades of the twentieth century. *Kitsch* is such a derogatory word that, perhaps inevitably, it began to reappear in the modern domain of high art. Matei Calinescu notes: "From Rimbaud's praise of 'poetic crap' and 'stupid paintings' through Dada and Surrealism, the rebellious avant-garde has made use of a variety of techniques and elements directly borrowed from kitsch for their ironically disruptive purposes."

SEE ALSO *avant-garde, modernism.*

Knittelvers, Knütttelvers, Knüppelvers, Klippelvers A German form of rhyming couplets, using four stressed syllables. In its earliest incarnation, the line contained any number of unstressed syllables. It was later regularized by Hans Sachs (1494–1576) and others to eight or nine syllables. *Knittelvers* was the most popular meter in German poetry in the fifteenth and sixteeth centuries. It was given its derogatory name (the word means "badly knit verse" or "cudgel-verse") and considered doggerel by the German classical poets of the seventeenth century. It was revived by Gottsched in the eighteenth century, who used it for comedy, and then by Schiller (*Wallensteins Lager,* 1798), and especially Goethe ("The Poetical Mission of Hans Sachs," 1776, and the older parts of *Faust,* 1808–1832), who discovered the literary potential of doggerel and other forms of popular entertainment. On a bumpy local train in June 1774, Goethe declaimed to a drowsy friend the *Knittelvers* from his epic fragment *The Wandering Jew.*

SEE ALSO *doggerel, meistersinger, octosyllabic verse, Silesian school.*

kobzari Ukrainian minstrels. These singers were blind mendicants who wandered from village to village. They are mostly known for their performance of *dumy,* or epic songs built around historial events, but they also had an extensive repertoire of religious (*psalmy*) and historical (*istorchni pisni*) songs. They knew lyrical and satirical songs as well as dance melodies both with and without words. They traditionally accompanied themselves on a twenty-stringed lute, the *kobza.* There are many individual blind singers in different traditions, and blindness is often legendary in different oral traditions (think of the blind *aoidos* in Homer's *Odyssey,* ca. eighth century B.C.E.), though most epic singers are actually sighted. But blindness has been obligatory for Ukrainian minstrels since the early 1800s. The Ukrainian minstrels, who are members of an elaborate system of professional guilds, probably reached their greatest heights between 1850 and 1930.

SEE ALSO *aoidos, duma.*

Kraków avant-garde A Polish poetry movement of the 1920s and '30s. The group is usually divided into *The First Vanguard* (1920s) — Julian Przybós (1901–1970) and Tadeusz Peiper (1891–1969) were the theoreticians of the movement — and *The Second Vanguard* (1930s), "whose claim to solidarity," Czeslaw Milosz declares, "was based on a certain intellectual climate rather than on any common programs." The Kraków avant-garde, which grouped around the magazine *Zwrotnica* (*The Switch*), rejected the traditional formalism of the rival *Skamander* poets, whom they called "organ-grinders," and cultivated a more dynamic free-verse idiom. They treated poets as engineers of words who conveyed emotion by finding equivalent images. They were socialists who believed in the relevance of art to modern cities and showed a touching, misplaced faith in the future of technological civilization.

In the early 1960s, a group of Polish émigrés in London, the *Kontynenty*, or Continents Group, set out to continue the program of the Kraków avant-garde and other related interwar groups. One fruition of their work was the 1965 anthology *Ryby na piasku* (*Fish on the Sand*). Julian Przybós's preface testified to the continuity of interests between the poets of the twenties and the exiled poets in the sixties.

SEE ALSO *Skamander*.

kyrielle This French form is composed of any number of four-line stanzas, usually rhymed. The last line of the first stanza repeats, sometimes with meaningful variations, as the final line of each quatrain. Repeated lines in any style of poetry are sometimes called *rime en kyrielle*. The name of the *kyrielle* is a foreshortened form of the response "Kyrie eleison!" ("Lord, have mercy upon us") from the Roman liturgy. A number of Anglican hymns preserve the form. Thomas Campion's "With broken heart and contrite sigh" (1613) fits the letter and law of *kyrielle*. It repeats the plea "God, be merciful to me" for four stanzas and concludes with the recognition, "God has been merciful to me." William Dunbar's "Lament for the Makers" (ca. 1508), a dirge for the makers, or poets, is a secular *kyrielle* that concludes with the Latin phrase, "*Timor Mortis conturbat me*" ("The fear of death disturbs me"). It poignantly begins:

> I that in heill [health] wes and gladnes,
> Am trublit now with gret seikness [sickness],
> And feblit with infermité:
> *Timor Mortis conturbat me.*

Theodore Roethke takes a different tact with the *kyrielle* in his comic poem "Dinky" (1973), which concludes with the memorable assertion, "*You* may be dirty dinky."

SEE ALSO *quatrain*.

lai (French), ***lay*** (English) The term *lay* is now virtually synonymous with *song*. In Old French poetry, a *lai* was originally a short lyrical or narrative poem. Gautier de Dargies wrote the earliest lyrical *lais* in the thirteenth century. Marie de France's short romantic tales (contes), usually written in octosyllabic verse, are the oldest narrative *lais* and date to the twelfth century. Later, the term became synonymous with *contes*. In Provençal poetry, the *lai* was a love song set to a popular tune. In fourteenth-century Britain, the term *Breton lay* applied to poems set in Brittany, which echoed the spirit and theme of Marie de France's poems. Two examples: the anonymous Middle English poem *Sir Orfeo* (late thirteenth or early fourteenth century) and Chaucer's "Franklin's Tale" in *The Canterbury Tales* (written between 1387 and 1400 but not published until the 1470s).

In the nineteenth century, the term *lay* was often used for a short historical ballad, as in Sir Walter Scott's *The Lay of the Last Minstrel* (1805). The term seemed to invoke antiquity, and Scott associated the minstrel with the French trouvère.

The way was long, the wind was cold,
The Minstrel was infirm and old;
His withered cheek, and tresses gray,
Seemed to have known a better day;
The harp, his sole remaining joy,
Was carried by an orphan boy.

> The last of all the Bards was he,
> Who sung of Border chivalry . . .

SEE ALSO *dit, octosyllabic verse, trouvère.*

laisse The *laisse* is the basic lyric, dramatic, and narrative unit of Old French poetry. The medieval French epics (chansons de geste), such as *La Chanson de Roland* (*Song of Roland,* ca. 1090), are written in *laisses* or *tirades,* which are stanzas of varying length. The early works were assonanced and thus used the same vowel sound in the last accented syllable of each line. The later ones were monorhymed. Old French poetry was highly formulaic, and there were many strong repetitions that carried material from one *laisse* to the next. The scholar Jean Rychner first named the use of block repetitions — stanzaic correspondences — *laisses similaires.*

SEE ALSO *chansons de geste, oral-formulaic method.*

Lake poets This name applies to the nineteenth-century romantic poets William Wordsworth, Samuel Taylor Coleridge, and Robert Southey, who lived in the Lake District of Cumberland and Westmorland (now Cumbria) in northwest England. Wordsworth spent most of his life in what he called his "dear native regions." He was followed there for a time by Coleridge and later by Southey. Francis Jeffrey derided these poets for twenty years in the *Edinburgh Review.* In 1807, reviewing Wordsworth's *Poems, in Two Volumes,* he associated the "new school" with the Lake District: "[The] author is known to belong to a certain brotherhood of poets, who have haunted for some years about the Lakes of Cumberland." The phrase *Lake poets* itself seems first to have been used in 1812. Lord Byron later mocked Wordsworth and Southey in a similar way in *Don Juan* (1819–1824), where he wonders if Southey is "With all the Lakers, in and out of place?," and declares:

> You — Gentlemen! by dint of long seclusion
> From better company, have kept your own
> At Keswick, and, through still continu'd fusion
> Of one another's minds, at last have grown
> To deem as a most logical conclusion,
> That Poesy has wreaths for you alone:

> There is a narrowness in such a notion,
> Which makes me wish you'd change your lakes for Ocean.

A *laker* was also an old cant term for an actor. The local name Lake poets stuck and eventually turned into an honorific for a few romantic poets. The idea of a "school" of Lakers was a fiction, though the Lake District mattered especially to Wordsworth, whose work directly describes and celebrates the region with a quasi-religious feeling. Yet his work ultimately goes beyond its apparent place of origin.

SEE ALSO *romanticism*.

Lallans, see *Scottish renaissance*.

lament A poem or song expressing grief. The lament is powered by a personal sense of loss. The poetry of lamentation, which arose in oral literature alongside heroic poetry, seems to exist in all languages and poetries. One finds it, for example, in ancient Egyptian, in Hebrew, in Chinese, in Sanskrit, in Zulu. A profound grief is formalized as mourning, as in Lamentations 2:10:

> The elders of the daughter of Zion sit upon the ground, *and* keep silence: they have cast up dust upon their heads; they have girded themselves with sackcloth: the virgins of Jerusalem hang down their heads to the ground.

The poetry of intense grief and mourning, such as the Lamentations of Jeremiah or David's lament for Saul and Jonathan, has its roots in religious feeling and ritual. The Hebrew Bible is filled with both individual laments (a worshiper cries out to Yahweh in times of need) and communal laments, which mourn a larger national calamity.

Laments may have developed from magic spells to call back what was lost—a destroyed temple, a dead god. The "Lament for the Destruction of Ur" (early second millennium B.C.E.) memorialized the catastrophic destruction of the Third Dynasty of Ur (2112–2004 B.C.E.) and turned out to be the last great masterwork of Sumerian civilization. It is one of five known Mesopotamian "city laments," which were the province of elegists called *gala* ("The Lament for Sumer and Ur," "The Lament for Nippur,"

"The Lament for Eridu," and "The Lament for Uruk"). Thorkild Jacobsen points out that "the great laments for destroyed temples and cities usually divide into a part called *balaĝ* 'harp,' which was to be sung to the strains of the harp, and a following *ershemma,* a lament to be accompanied by a tambourine-like drum called *shem.*" He suggests that the laments served ritual purposes. The ones for dead gods were performed during annual mourning processions of weeping; the ones for destroyed temples were "originally performed in the ruins to induce the gods to rebuild the destroyed structure."

A few other haunting early examples of laments: the scop, or minstrel, in the Anglo-Saxon poem "Deor's Lament" (ninth or tenth century) is a poet who is no longer favored and consoles himself by reciting the misfortunes of others ("That trouble passed. So can this"). The medieval poet Yosef Ibn Avitor's "Lament for the Jews of Zion" (eleventh century) is a mournful Spanish-Hebrew poem written after Jews were attacked by Bedouins from the tribe of Bnei Jaraakh in Palestine in 1024 ("Weep, my brothers, and mourn"); Avraham Ibn Ezra's "Lament for Andalusian Jewry" (mid-twelfth century) is an elegy for the Jewish communities of Spain and North Africa destroyed in 1146 by the invading Almohads ("Calamity came upon Spain from the skies, / and my eyes pour forth their streams of tears").

The late eighteenth-century poet Eibhlín Dubh Ní Chonaill, or Dark Eileen, majestically mourns the death of her husband in "Lament for Art O'Leary" (1773). "The Hag of Beare" (ninth century), the greatest of all early Irish poems written by a woman, is a piercing lament not just for one but for many loves, an outcry against aging. The Polish poet Jan Kochanowski's *Laments* (1580) consists of nineteen poems that wrestle with his grief over the death of his two-and-a-half-year-old daughter ("Wisdom for me was castles in the air; / I'm hurled, like all the rest, from the topmost stair"). They desperately try to "Bear humanly the human lot." Here is Shelley's ten-line "A Lament" (*Posthumous Poems,* 1824):

I

O World! O life! O time!
On whose last steps I climb,
    Trembling at that where I had stood before;
When will return the glory of your prime?
    No more — Oh, never more!

II

Out of the day and night
A joy has taken flight;
    Fresh spring, and summer, and winter hoar,
Move my faint heart with grief, but with delight,
    No more — Oh, never more!

SEE ALSO *dirge, elegy, keening.*

lampoon A harsh, personal, and often scurrilous type of satire. The term came into use in the mid-seventeenth century as a cross between the French *lampons* ("let us drink") and the slang *lamper* ("to guzzle"). But the satiric attack on an individual goes back at least as far as ancient Greek drama, when Aristophanes lampooned Euripides in *The Frogs* (405 B.C.E.) and Socrates in *The Clouds* (423 B.C.E.). The lampoon was also one of the modes of classical Arabic poetry known as *hija* (invective, satire). It is the opposite of the panegyric, or praise poem. The Scottish *flyting* was a contest of insults, a formal exchange of taunts, and similar cursing matches have been found in a wide variety of other poetries.

In English poetry, the lampoon took on particular life in Restoration and eighteenth-century England. Samuel Johnson defined lampoon as "a personal satire; ridicule; abuse." Johnson considered the lampoon a lesser form of satire because of the particularity of its reflections. John Dryden declared that the type of satire "which is known in *England* by the name of lampoon, is a dangerous sort of weapon and for the most part unlawful. We have no moral right on the reputation of other men" (*Discourse Concerning the Origin and Progress of Satire,* 1693). He was nonetheless a terrific lampooner, which he demonstrates in his lampoon of Thomas Shadwell, whom he names Og in *Absalom and Achitophel* (1681–1682):

Now stop your noses, Readers, all and some,
For here's a tun of Midnight work to come,
Og from a Treason Tavern rowling home.
Round as a Globe and Liquored ev'ry chink,
Goodly and Great he Sayls behind his Link,
With all this Bulk there's nothing lost in Og,

For ev'ry inch that is not Fool is Rogue:
A Monstrous mass of foul corrupted matter,
As all the Deveils had spew'd to make the batter,
When wine has given him courage to Blaspheme,
He curses God, but God before curst him;
And if man cou'd have reason, none has more,
That made his Paunch so rich and him so poor.

SEE ALSO *flyting, hija, panegyric, poetic contest, satire.*

landay Often considered the quintessential Pashto verse form, the *landay* (or *ṭappā*) is a folk couplet with nine syllables in the first line and thirteen syllables in the second. The poem is traditionally sung aloud, often to a drumbeat, and ends on the sound *na* (*-īna, -ūna, -āna*) or *ma* (*-āma*). It is sometimes rhymed, mostly not. The *landays,* which probably began with nomads, may date as far back as the Indo-Aryan caravans to Afghanistan, Pakistan, and India around 1700 B.C.E. One thinks of the call-and-response pattern, the movement back and forth, the challenge and retort, of verses along a long caravan train.

Landays are considered a form of women's poetry. For centuries they circulated in oral tradition, and thus they belong historically to women who were, and still are, largely illiterate. Some are fueled by sexual passion; others aggressively challenge masculine codes of chivalry or ideals of honor. Even when they are composed by men, they are almost all sung in the voices of women. In *I Am the Beggar of the World: Landays from Contemporary Afghanistan* (2014), Eliza Griswold points out that the internal lilt of these short poems, which often sound like lullabies, "belies the sharpness of their content, which is distinctive not only for its beauty, bawdiness, and wit, but also for the piercing ability to articulate a common truth about war, separation, homeland, grief, or love." These poems often articulate dangerous truths, transgressive ideas. Here is Griswold's rendition of one biting *landay:*

When sisters sit together, they always praise their brothers.
When brothers sit together, they sell their sisters to others.

the language of the birds In many traditional and archaic cultures, the shaman is a mediator between the human and animal worlds. As Mircea Eliade points out in *Shamanism* (1951): "All over the world learning the language of animals, especially of birds, is equivalent to knowing the secrets of nature and hence to being able to prophesy. Bird language is usually learned by eating snake or some other reputedly magical animal. These animals can reveal the secrets of the future because they are thought to be receptacles for the souls of the dead or epiphanies of the gods. Learning their language, imitating their voice, is equivalent to ability to communicate with the beyond and the heavens . . . Birds are psychopomps. Becoming a bird oneself or being accompanied by a bird indicates the capacity, while still alive, to undertake the ecstatic journey to the sky and the beyond." The shaman is a "technician of the sacred." Jerome Rothenberg refers to the shaman as a "proto-poet, for almost always his technique hinges on the creation of special linguistic circumstances, i.e., of song & invocation." The shamans become masters of magic words, which they refer to as the "Language of the Birds." Eliade points out that the secret language of shamans is actually "the 'animal language' or originates in animal cries."

Elif Batuman points out that in various esoteric traditions "the language of birds" is a code phrase for total knowledge. The Kabbalists and alchemists referred to the perfect language that would unlock ultimate knowledge as "the language of birds" or "the green language." Given the gift of prophecy by Athena, Tiresias could suddenly understand the language of the birds. Solomon exclaims in the Koran (27:16), "O mankind! Lo! We have been taught the language of the birds and have been given abundance of all things."

SEE ALSO *bird sound words, ethnopoetics, shaman, sound poetry, wordless poetry.*

L=A=N=G=U=A=G=E poetry The L=A=N=G=U=A=G=E school of poets is a self-conscious American avant-garde group that developed in the 1970s. It was first associated with the small literary magazines *This* and *L=A=N=G=U=A=G=E*. The visual strangeness of the term itself emphasizes the nonrepresentational nature of language itself. Such poets as Charles Bernstein, Bob Perelman, Bruce Andrews, Ron Silliman, and Susan Howe have all concentrated on how language determines and dictates meaning rather than the other way around. "Language is nothing but meanings, and meanings are nothing but a flow of contexts," Lyn Hejinian writes in *The Language of Inquiry* (2000). The L=A=N=G=U=A=G=E poets view poetry as a cultural production opposed to official power structures. They depersonalize poetry. L=A=N=G=U=A=G=E poetry marshals a central modernist recognition: all poetry, even the most subjective, is language centered.

SEE ALSO *avant-garde, modernism.*

lauda, laude (pl) The *lauda,* or "canticle of praise," is an Italian verse form with religious content. It flourished from about the thirteenth to the sixteenth century. The first Italian *lauda* was Saint Francis's moving "Laudes creaturarum" ("Praise of the Creatures") or the "Cantico del Sole" ("Canticle of the Sun") from 1224. The thirteenth-century Franciscan poet Jacopone da Todi, who wrote many vernacular *laudi spirituali* ("spiritual canticles"), reputedly wrote the Latin *lauda* or hymn, "Stabat mater dolorosa."

SEE ALSO *muwashshah, zéjel.*

leaping poetry Robert Bly coined this term for poems that enact "a long floating leap from the conscious to the unconscious and back again, a leap from the known part of the mind to the unknown part and back to the known" (*Leaping Poetry,* 1975). *Leaping poetry* is Bly's term for the rapid associative imagination that moves through different levels of consciousness. Bly adapted the ancient Chinese phrase "riding on dragons" to describe the "time of inspiration," the movement between worlds, between planes of thought. He found this ecstatic mode of exploration in nineteenth-century French poets, such as Gérard de Nerval and Charles Baudelaire, and in twentieth-century Spanish ones, such as Juan Ramón Jiménez, Rafael Alberti, and Antonio Machado. Machado says, "Everyone who moves on / walks like Jesus, on the sea" ("Moral Proverbs and Folk Songs," in *Campos de Castilla,* or *The Countryside of Castille,* 1907–1917). Bly's method courted the irrational and denigrated the poetics of rationality, i.e., "dull poets who give off a *steady light.*" He distinguished hopping, which entails a short jump in consciousness, from leaping, and maintained that we notice far leaps of association in many ancient works of art.

SEE ALSO *deep image.*

Leich (German), see *lai.*

leonine rhyme In English poetry, a leonine rhyme occurs when a word near the middle of the line rhymes with a word at the end. Thus Alfred, Lord Tennyson writes in *The Princess* (1847):

> The splendor *falls* on castle *walls*
>   And snowy summits old in story:
> The long light *shakes* across the *lakes,*
>   And the wild cataract leaps in glory.

Leonine rhyme dates to the classical age (Ovid uses it in *The Art of Love,* 2 C.E.), but was especially favored in the Latin poetry of the European Middle Ages. It was referred to as *rime leonine* in the anonymous twelfth-century romance *Guillaume d'Angleterre.* The name has been fancifully attributed both to Pope Leo I (ca. 400–461) and to Leonius, a twelfth-century Parisian canon and Latin poet who was fond of the device. In Latin and French poetry, it is called a leonine rhyme when the last word in the line rhymes with the word before the caesura, as in the ecclesiastical "Stabet mater."

SEE ALSO *rhyme.*

letrilla Spanish diminutive of *letra,* "a short gloss." The *letrilla*—a brief poem, usually light and satirical, with short lines and a refrain—was a favored form of the golden age poets of the seventeenth century. Two of the most lasting examples: Góngora's "Letrilla" (1581), which begins "Ándeme yo caliente, / y ríase la gente" ("Just let me be warm and easy / and let them laugh, if they will") and Quevedo's "Letrilla satírica" (1670), which commences "Poderoso caballero / es don Dinero" ("Sir Money / is a Powerful Gentleman").

SEE ALSO *estribillo, the golden age, light verse.*

letter poem, epistle A kind of letter in poetry. The verse epistle, as it was once called, is a poem specifically addressed to a friend, a lover, or a patron. In his *Epistles* (20–14 B.C.E.), Horace established the type of epistle poem that reflects on moral and philosophical subjects. In his *Heroides* (ca. 25–16 B.C.E.), Ovid established the type of epistle poem that reflects on romantic subjects. They are fictional letters from the legendary women of antiquity (Helen, Medea, Dido) to their lovers. Horace's letters on the art of poetry, known since Quintilian as the *Ars Poetica* (ca. 18–19 B.C.E.), are also verse epistles, and so are Ovid's poignant poems of exile, *Tristia* (9–12 C.E.).

Ovid's *Heroides* particularly influenced the troubadours and their poems of courtly love, which are shaped as love songs from a distance. The Horatian epistle had a lasting influence throughout the Renaissance and the eighteenth century. There are Petrarch's *Epistulae metricae* (1331–1361) in Latin, Ariosto's *Satires* (1517–1525) in vernacular Italian, Garcilaso's *Epístola a Boscán* (1543) in Spanish, and Boileau's *À mes vers* (1695) and *Sur l'amour de Dieu* (1698) in French. Ivan Funikov's ironic verse epistle, "Message of a Nobleman to a Nobleman" (1608), is the oldest dated Russian work in verse. It jokes about his misfortunes in riotously funny rhymed couplets. Epistolary poetry was also the most popular literary genre in fourteenth-century Uzbekistan. Elif Batuman explains, "Poems during this period took the form of love letters between nightingales and sheep, between opium and wine, between red and green. One poet wrote to a girl that he had tried to drink a lake so he could swallow her reflection: this girl was cleaner than water."

Samuel Daniel introduced the epistle into English in his *Letter from Octavia to Marcus Antonius* (1599) and in *Certain Epistles* (1601–1603). Ben Jonson employed the Horatian mode in *The Forest* (1616), which was also taken up by John Dryden in his epistles to Congreve (1694) and to the duchess of Ormond (1700). Alexander Pope modeled "Eloisa to Abelard" (1717) on Ovid's *Heroides,* and adapted the Horatian epistle in his *Moral Essays* (1731–1735) and *An Epistle to Dr. Arbuhnot* (1735). The epistle fell into disuse in the romantic era. Since then, it is occasionally revived and renamed as a letter, as in W. H. Auden and Louis MacNeice's *Letters from Iceland* (1937). Richard Hugo brings the form closer to a real letter in *31 Letters and 13 Dreams* (1977). Robert Lowell created a controversy in the 1970s by taking actual letters from Elizabeth Hardwick and reshaping them as unrhymed sonnets.

The letter poem is addressed to a specific person and written from a specific place, which locates it in time and space. It imitates the colloquial familiarity of a letter, though sometimes in elaborate forms. Some create fictive speakers, as in Ezra Pound's adaptation of Li Po, "The River-Merchant's Wife: A Letter" (1915). Some are addressed to those long dead, as in W. H. Auden's "Letter to Lord Byron" (1937), others to contemporaries. But unlike an actual letter, the letter poem is never addressed to just its recipient; it is always meant to be overheard by a third person, a future reader.

Lettrisme A Paris-based avant-garde movement of the 1940s that gained recognition in the 1960s and '70s. With messianic zeal, the Lettristes insisted on the primacy of the letter over the word. They created a radical lexicon for deconstructing words into their constituent parts and synthesizing poetry and music. Isidore Isou (1925–2007), who founded the movement with Gabriel Pomerand in 1946, made up a fresh alphabet of sounds in vocal performance, which he first presented in *Introducion à une nouvelle poésie et à une nouvelle musique* (1947). "Le Nouvel Alphabet Lettrique," based on letters and on body noises, was later expanded by the other Lettristes.

The early Lettristes included François Dufrêne, who joined the group at the age of sixteen; Maurice Lemaître; Jean-Louis Brau; and Gil J. Wolman, who broke loose with his first *mégapneumie,* or mega-breath, a form of physical poetry. "This was not the breath of the lyrical poet," Frédéric Acquaviva explains, "but a brutal and quintessential reduction, like Antonin Artaud crossed with Isou." The anarchic spirit of youth was very much present in the group of more than two dozen Lettristes, cultural provocateurs, theoreticians on the edge of violence, noisy sound poets who set out to outdo the Dadaists and surpass the Surrealists.

Here is Isou's Lettriste diagram of the step-by-step development of French experimentation. He uses the word *anecdote* to mean content and suggests that he is the end of a lineage.

Ch. Baudelaire (destruction of the anecdote for the form of the POEM)
P. Verlaine (annihilation of the poem for the form of the line of poetry)
A. Rimbaud (destruction of the line for the WORD)
St. Mallarmé (arrangement of the WORD perfected)
T. Tzara (destruction of the word for NOTHING)
I. Isou (arrangement of a NOTHING—THE LETTER—for the creation of the anecdote)

SEE ALSO *Dadaism, L=A=N=G=U=A=G=E poetry, sound poetry, Surrealism.*

light verse Light verse, which is both lightfooted and lighthearted, sets out to amuse and entertain. It seems to imply an opposite, "heavy verse," and thus is sometimes taken less seriously than "serious poetry," which it makes light of and often takes to account. It measures itself against the high pretensions of its own era. Its power lies in its irreverent spirit and technical skill, its witty daring-do, its punch and accuracy, the way it turns things upside down. Its strategy is to laugh rather than to cry.

Light verse is a broad category that includes a wide variety of poetic types, from the clerihew, the double dactyl, the limerick, and *vers de societé* to burlesques and mock heroics, nonsense poetry and occasional verse, pointed epigrams, ironic epitaphs, parodies. Its subject can be trivial or carry deep poetic significance, as in, say, Petrarchan love poems and Cavalier lyrics. A. E. Milne accounts for light verse in *Year In, Year Out* (1952):

> Light Verse obeys Coleridge's definition of poetry, the best words in the best order; it demands Carlyle's definition of genius, transcendent capacity for taking pains; and it is the supreme exhibition of somebody's definition of art, the concealment of art. In the result it observes the most exact laws of rhythm and metre as if by a happy accident, and in a sort of nonchalant spirit of mockery at the real poets who do it on purpose . . .

One characterization of light verse is "poets at play." In "To Minerva" (posthumously published in 1862), Thomas Hood desperately, comically, needs a break from the high poetry of Wisdom:

My temples throb, my pulses boil,
    I'm sick of Song, and Ode, and Ballad—
So, Thyrsis, take the Midnight Oil,
    And pour it on a lobster salad.

My brain is dull, my sight is foul,
    I cannot write a verse, or read,—
Then, Pallas, take away thine Owl,
    And let us have a lark instead.

SEE ALSO *clerihew, comedy, doggerel, double dactyl, epigram, limerick, nonsense poetry, parody.*

limerick The only English stanzaic form used exclusively for light verse, the limerick is a five-line verse that rhymes *aabba.* The first, second, and fifth lines have three beats, the third and fourth lines two beats. The dominant rhythm is anapestic. It is sometimes written in four lines. The origin of the limerick is lost in oral tradition. One theory is that it was brought to the Irish town of Limerick in 1700 by veterans returning from the French War; another is that it originated in the nursery rhymes published in *Mother Goose's Melody* (ca. 1765); a third is that it stems from a refrain in a nonsense verse, "Will you come up to Limerick?" (One version goes: "Oh will you come up, come up, / Oh will you come up, I say, / Oh, will you come up, all the way up / All the way up to Limerick?") The most convincing theory is that it was used by the poetic school Fili na Maighe in County Limerick in the mid-eighteenth century. The form is undoubtedly much older, but there are limericks collected in the *History of Sixteen Wonderful Old Women* (1820), such as

> There was an old woman of Lynn,
> Whose nose very near reach'd her chin;
>   You may easy suppose
>   She had plenty of beaux,
> This charming old woman of Lynn.

There are also limericks in *Anecdotes and Adventures of Fifteen Gentlemen* (1822). Edward Lear mastered and popularized the form in his *Book of Nonsense* (1846), though he never used the word *limerick* himself. A friend introduced him to the limerick "as a form of verse lending itself to limitless variety for Rhymes and Pictures," and he started composing verses and drawings for children, who responded with "uproarious delight and welcome at the appearance of every new absurdity." M. Russel, SJ, coined the term *learic* for this type of nonsense:

> There was an old Person of Sparta,
> Who had twenty-five sons and one "darta;"
> He fed them on Snails, and weighed them in scales,
> That wonderful Person of Sparta.

One of the charms of the limerick is that it taps the odd magic of place. Eudora Welty points out, "There's something unutterably convincing about that Old Person of Sparta who had twenty-five sons and one darta, and it is surely beyond question that he fed them on snails and weighed them in scales, because we know where that Old Person is *from* — Sparta!"

Alfred, Lord Tennyson (1850–1892), Algernon Charles Swinburne (1837–1909), Rudyard Kipling (1865–1936), Robert Louis Stevenson (1850–1894), Dante Gabriel Rossetti (1828–1882), Mark Twain (1835–1910), W. S. Gilbert (1836–1911), Morris Bishop (1893–1973), and Edward Gorey (1925–2000) are just some of the poets who have continued to experiment with the limerick form for the past two centuries, adding additional twists and surprises. The limerick is a popular oral form, invariably bawdy and off-color. The scholar Gershon Legman maintained that the folk limerick is always obscene. An anonymous lyric that makes his point:

A limerick packs laughs anatomical
Into space that is quite economical.
    But the good ones I've seen
    So seldom are clean,
And the clean ones so seldom are comical.

SEE ALSO *double dactyl, light verse, nonsense verse, quintet.*

line A unit of meaning, a measure of attention. The line is a way of framing poetry. All verse is measured by lines. On its own, the poetic line immediately announces its difference from everyday speech and prose. It creates its own visual and verbal impact; it declares its self-sufficiency. Paul Claudel called the fundamental line "an idea isolated by blank space." I would call it "words isolated by blank space," because the words can go beyond the idea, they can plunge deeper than thought. Adam Zagajewski says, "Tragedy and joy collide in every line."

"Poetry is the sound of language organized in lines," James Longenbach asserts in *The Art of the Poetic Line* (2008). "More than meter, more than rhyme, more than images or alliteration or figurative language, line is what distinguishes our experience of poetry as poetry, rather than some other kind of writing." There are one-line poems called monostiches, which are timed to deliver a single poignancy. An autonomous line in a poem makes sense on its own, even if it is a fragment or an incomplete sentence. It is end-stopped and completes a thought. An enjambed line carries the meaning over from one line to the next. Whether end-stopped or enjambed, however, the line in a poem moves horizontally, but the rhythm and sense also drive it vertically, and the meaning continues to accrue as the poem develops and unfolds.

In "Summa Lyrica" (1992), Allen Grossman proposes a theory of the three modular versions of the line in English:

1. Less than ten syllables more or less.
2. Ten syllables more or less.
3. More than ten syllables more or less.

The ten-syllable or blank verse line provides a kind of norm in English poetry. Wordsworth (1771–1850) and Frost (1874–1963) both perceived that the blank verse line could be used to give the sensation of actual speech, a person engaging others. "The topic of the line of ten is conflict," Grossman says, which is why it has been so useful in drama, where other speakers are always nearby. It has a feeling of mutuality. In the line of less than ten syllables, then, there is a sense that something has been taken away or subtracted, attenuated or missing. There is a greater silence that surrounds it, a feeling of going under speech, which is why it has worked well for poems of loss. It has also proved useful for the stripped-down presentation of objects, what the Imagists called "direct treatment of the thing." We feel the clutter has been cleared away to create a clean space. Poems with drastically reduced lines aspire to be lyrics of absolute concentration, rhythmic economy. The line of more than ten syllables consequently gives a feeling of going above or beyond the parameters of oral utterance, or over them, beyond speech itself. The long lines widen the space for reverie. "The speaker in the poem bleeds outward as in trance or sleep toward other states of himself," Grossman says. This line, which has a dreamlike associativeness, also radiates an oracular feeling, which is why it has so often been the line of prophetic texts, visionary poetry.

SEE ALSO *blank verse, end-stopped line, enjambment, free verse, imagism, monostich, objectivism, verse.*

lineation The organization of a poem into lines. Lineation specifies that we are in the presence of a poem, which requires a special act of attention.

lin-ga In Burma, *lin-ga* (transliterated *lankā,* from the Sanskrit *alamkāra,* and used in Burmese to suggest "ornamentation" or "embellishment") is a generic term for poetry of all kinds. It especially refers to verse that is not in one of the recognized forms, such as *e-gyin* (historical ballads) or *maw-gun* (panegyric odes).

SEE ALSO *than-bauk, ya-du.*

lipogram A lipogram (from the Greek *lipagrammatos,* "missing letter") is a text that purposefully excludes a letter of the alphabet. It can be written in either verse or prose. It is reported, for example, that the Egyptian Tryphiodorus's lost *Odyssey* (fifth century) had no *A* (alpha) in the first book, no *B* (or beta) in the second, and so on for twenty-four books. The Oulipian writer Georges Perec, who dispensed with the letter *e* in his novel *La Disparition* (*The Disappearance,* 1969), wrote a "Histoire du lipogramme" that traces the genre back to such figures in the sixth century B.C.E. as Lasus of Hermione, who wrote the asigmatic poems *Centaurs* and *Hymn to Demeter* (the sigma or sibilant *s* is one of the most frequent and least esteemed consonants in ancient Greek), and Nestor of Laranda, who composed a lipogrammatic version of the *Iliad.* "A lipogrammatist is a letter-dropper," Isaac Disraeli noted in *Curiosities of Literature* (1824), adding

> The Orientalists are not without this literary folly. A Persian poet read to the celebrated Jami a gazel of his own composition, which Jami did not like: but the writer replied, it was notwithstanding a very curious sonnet, for the *letter Aliff* was not to be found in any one of the words! Jami sarcastically replied, "You can do a better thing yet; take away *all the letters* from every word you have written."

SEE ALSO *Oulipo, pangram.*

lira A Spanish stanzaic form. Garcilaso de la Vega (1501–1536) invented a new five-line stanza that consisted of three eleven-syllable and two seven-syllable lines that rhyme *ababb.* The rhyming second and fifth lines are the ones stretched to eleven syllables. Garcilaso was imitating the Italian poet and courtier Bernardo Tasso (1493–1569), who was in turn reaching back to antiquity and imitating Horace (65–8 B.C.E.). The name *lira* derives from the last word in the first line of Garcilaso's poem "Ode ad florem Gnidi" (1543), which he titled in Latin. The form, which he created for the occasion and never employed again, is sometimes known as *lira garcilasiana.* The stanza is the basis for the great poetry of San Juan de la Cruz (1542–1591) and Fray Luis de León (1527–1591), which is why it later came to be known as *estrofa de Fray Luis de León, lira de Fray Luis de León,* and *quintilla de Luis de León.*

The *lira* now refers to any Spanish stanzaic form of four, five, or six (occasionally more) lines that employ eleven-syllable and seven-syllable lines. It is also loosely used as a term for any Spanish poem with short stanzas in Italianate verse. It thus recalls the indebtedness of Spanish to classical Italian poetry.

SEE ALSO *canciones, the golden age.*

list poem, see *catalog poem.*

litany Greek: "prayer" or "supplication." In Christian worship, the litany is a type of liturgical prayer used in services and processions. It is chanted between the clergy and the congregation and consists of a series of supplications and fixed responses. The frequent repetition of the "Kyrie" was probably the original form of the litany in the early church. The Litany of the Saints continues to be a sacred prayer. Seventeenth-century religious poets, especially those with a taste for complicated forms, mined the formal possibilities of the litany, hence John Donne's "A Litany" (1608–1609) and Robert Herrick's "His Litany, to the Holy Spirit," (1647), which mimics a sense of call and response:

> In the hour of my distress,
> When temptations me oppress,
> And when I my sins confess,
>   Sweet Spirit, comfort me!

In contemporary usage, the litany now suggests any long, syntactically repetitive work, such as the Book of Psalms, Walt Whitman's "Song of Myself" (1855), or Allen Ginsberg's "Kaddish" (1961). The litany has in essence become a catalog poem, a witness of marvels. John Ashbery takes the original idea of the litany—a sacred community ritual meant to be repeated—and turns it into an experimental form in his sixty-eight-page

"Litany" (1978), a poem in two columns "meant to be read as simultaneous but independent monologues."

SEE ALSO *anaphora, catalog poem, parallelism, praise poems.*

Literatura de Cordel "Stories on a String." Folk poets throughout northeast Brazil publish their poems in pamphlets that they hang on clotheslines strung across stalls in marketplaces. The pamphlets (*folhetos*) are printed on newsprint with hand-drawn illustrations and sold with uncut pages. The poets often sing or perform their work to try to peddle it to passing shoppers. Some tell of local events, some narrate stories about the famous bandit Lampião, or Padre Cícero, who performed miracles. The anthropologist Candace Slater calls these narrative poems "the world's richest and most varied heirs to a centuries-old ballad and chapbook tradition once embracing most of Europe."

litotes Greek: "plainness," "simplicity." Litotes is no ordinary rhetorical device. It is a figure of deliberate understatement. It can also be used to affirm something in the form of a negative contrary, as when we say that an accomplishment is *no mean feat.* It would be an example of litotes to say that litotes itself is not bad as a form of irony. The device was widely utilized in Old English poetry and the Icelandic sagas. The *Beowulf* poet (ca. eighth to eleventh century) lets his audience know that a sword was useful by announcing "The edge was not useless / to the warrior now." Speaking of the reaction of the Danes to the death of Grendel, the poet says, "his fatal departure / did not seem painful to any warrior." At times the deepest feeling shows itself in restraint.

SEE ALSO *hyperbole, meiosis, rhetoric.*

locus amoenus Latin: "pleasant place." Homer's description of the garden of Alcinous in book 8 of the *Odyssey* (ca. eighth century B.C.E.) helped to establish the literary topos of *locus amoenus,* the representation of an idyllic natural scene, often with singing birds and a rustling stream, a fresh breeze in a flowering meadow. The *locus amoenus,* which is a backdrop for the pastoral poetry of Theocritus (third century B.C.E.) and Virgil (70–19 B.C.E.), became a bravura descriptive performance in its own right in later poetry. It forms, as Ernst Robert Curtius puts it, "the principal motif of all nature description" from the Roman Empire to the sixteenth century. The description of an ideal landscape evolves into various characterizations of the earthly paradise.

SEE ALSO *nature poetry, pastoral.*

logaoedic Greek: "prose-poetic." Roman metricians, such as Hephaestion (ca. 356–324 B.C.E.) and Aristides Quintilianus (ca. third century), coined the word *logaoedic* to describe a rhythm that mixes several meters, most specifically, dactyls and trochees, or anapests and iambs. It thus created a rhythm that seemed more suggestive of prose.

SEE ALSO *anapest, dactyl, iamb, trochee.*

logic of metaphor In 1926, Hart Crane wrote that "the entire construction of the poem is raised on the organic principle of a 'logic of metaphor,' which antedates our so-called pure logic." Crane believed that poetry preceded other types of logical or philosophical thinking. It consists of a series of "metaphorical inter-relationships." He organized poems through the "implicit emotional dynamics" of sudden conjunctions. He was arguing for an associative mode of poetic thinking, what Rimbaud called a systematic "disordering of the senses." His idea of the logic of metaphor harkens back to the way that Keats exalted poetic thinking freed from habitual trains of thought, from analytic logical procedures. "I am the more zealous in this affair," Keats wrote in 1817, "because I have never yet been able to perceive how any thing can be known for truth by consequitive reasoning."

SEE ALSO *hecho poético.*

logopoeia The linguistic qualities of a poem, particularly as they pertain to intelligence. In *How to Read* (1929), Ezra Pound uses this term for one of three "kinds of poetry":

> LOGOPOEIA, "the dance of intellect among words," that is to say, it employs words not for their direct meaning, but it takes count in a special way of habits of usage, of the context we *expect* to find with the word, its usual concomitants, of its known acceptances, and of ironical play.

Pound is pointing to the rhythmical progression of ideas, the capacity of poetry to estrange language, to charge words and phrases with new meanings. Pound found an elegant use of *logopoeia* in the Latin of Propertius (50?–15? B.C.E.) and the French of Jules Laforgue (1860–1887). Richard Sieburth characterizes *logopoeia* as "language commenting upon its own possibilities and limitations as language." K. K. Ruthven calls it "a proto-deconstructive term."

SEE ALSO *deconstruction, melopoeia, phanopoeia.*

long meter The long meter of the hymn books is a variant of the ballad stanza. The ballad meter follows a pattern of alternating stresses: 4, 3, 4, 3. The long meter lengthens the trimeters and equalizes the stresses: 4, 4, 4, 4. The meter is usually iambic. Instead of the *abcb* rhyme scheme, long meter usually rhymes *abab* or *aabb.* Isaac Watts employed long meter in a hymn he wrote for a 1707 Communion service, which begins:

> When I survey the wondrous cross
> On which the Prince of Glory died,
> My richest gain I count but loss,
> And pour contempt on all my pride.

SEE ALSO *ballad, hymn, short meter.*

luc-bat Vietnamese: "six eight." A Vietnamese form that alternates lines of six and eight words in tightly rhymed couplets. Vietnamese is a tonal language and its six tones are divided into two types, sharp and level, for the purposes of rhyming. Each rhyme of the *luc-bat* recurs three times: at the end of the first eight-syllable line, at the end of the next six-syllable line, and as the sixth syllable of the next eight-syllable line. The final line rhymes back to the opening couplet and thus creates a circle. Another form — seven/seven, six/eight — is called *song that de luc bat.* The *luc-bat* was popular both in folk poetry, such as the songs of peasants working in the rice paddies, and in long narrative works, such as Nguyen Du's *The Tale of Kieu* (1813), a *luc-bat* vernacular poem (*nom*) of more than three thousand lines, the masterpiece of nineteenth-century Vietnamese poetry.

Lucilian satire, see *satire.*

lullaby A bedtime song or chant to put a child to sleep. Lullabies typically begin "Hush-a-bye baby, on the tree top," or "Rock-a-bye, baby," or "Sleep, my child," or "Hush, little baby, don't say a word." The English term *lullaby* may derive from the sounds *lu lu* or *la la,* a sound that mothers and nurses make to calm babies, and *by by* or *bye bye,* another lulling sound or else a good-night term. The oldest lullaby to survive may be the lullaby of Roman nurses recorded in a scholium on Persius: "Lalla, Lalla, Lalla, / aut dormi, aut lacte" (Lullaby, Lullaby, Lullaby, / either go to sleep or suckle). As ancient folk poems, lullabies range from meaningless jingles to semi-ballads. They are closely related to nursery rhymes. Rodrigo Caro called these soothing melodies, which are found all over the world, the "reverend mothers of all songs."

Federico García Lorca noted that "Spain uses its very saddest melodies and most melancholy texts to darken the first sleep of her children" and concluded: "The European cradle song tries only to put the child to sleep, not, as the Spanish one, to wound his sensibility at the same time" ("On Lullabies," 1928). Lorca reminds us that cradle songs were invented by women desperate to put their children to sleep. The women soothe their children by expressing their own weariness. The poems thus have a double purpose. He found the most ardent lullaby sung in Béjar and said, "This one would ring like a gold coin if we dropped it on the rocky earth." It begins:

> Sleep, little boy,
> sleep, for I am watching you.
> God, give you much luck
> in this lying world.

Joseph Brodsky's poignant late poem to his infant daughter, "Lullaby" ("Birth I gave you in a desert") echoes one of W. H. Auden's most beautiful early lyrics, "Lullaby" ("Lay your sleeping head, my love"). Reetika Vazirani (1962–2003) wrote a startling and inconsolable three-line poem called "Lullaby" (2002), which wounds:

> I would not sing you to sleep.
> I would press my lips to your ear
> and hope the terror in my heart stirs you.

SEE ALSO *carol, nursery rhyme.*

lyric The short poem has been practiced for at least forty-five hundred years. It is one of the necessary forms of human representation, human speech, one of the ways we invent and know ourselves. It is as ancient as recorded literature. It precedes prose in all languages, all civilizations, and it will last as long as human beings take pleasure in playing with words, in combining the sounds of words in unexpected and illuminating ways, in using words to convey deep feeling and perhaps something even deeper than feeling. The lyric poem immerses us in the original waters of consciousness, in the awareness, the aboriginal nature, of being itself.

The Greeks defined the lyric as a poem to be chanted or sung to the accompaniment of a lyre (*lyra*), the instrument of Apollo and Orpheus, and thus a symbol of poetic and musical inspiration. The Greek lyric has its origins, like Egyptian and Hebrew poetry, in religious feeling and practice. The first songs were most likely written to accompany occasions of celebration and mourning. Prayer, praise, and lamentation are three of the oldest impulses in poetry. Aristotle (384–322 B.C.E.) distinguished three generic categories of poetry: epic, drama, and lyric. This categorization evolved into the traditional division of literature into three generic types or classes, dependent upon who is supposedly speaking in a literary work:

epic or *narrative:* in which the narrator speaks in the first person, then lets the characters speak for themselves;
drama: in which the characters do all the talking;
lyric: uttered through the first person.

The lyric, which offers us a supposed speaker, a person to whom we often assign the name of the author, shades off into the dramatic utterance ("All poetry is of the nature of soliloquy," John Stuart Mill writes), but has always been counterposed to the epic. Whereas the speaker of the epic stands in as the deputy of a public voice, a singer of tales narrating the larger tale of the tribe, the lyric offers us a solitary singer or speaker singing or speaking on his or her own behalf. Ever since Sappho (late seventh century B.C.E.), the lyric poem has created a space for personal feeling. It has introduced a subjectivity and explored our capacity for human inwardness. The intimacy of lyric — and the lyric poem is the most intimate and personally volatile form of literary discourse — stands against the grandeur of epic. It asserts the value and primacy of the solitary voice, the individual feeling.

The definition of the lyric as a poem to be sung held until the Renaissance, when poets routinely began to write their poems for readers rather than composing them for musical presentation. The words and the music separated. Thereafter, lyric poetry retained an associational relationship to music. Its cadences and sound patterns, its tonal variations and rhythms, all show its melodic origins (hence Yeats's title *Words for Music Perhaps*). But writing offers a different space for poetry. It inscribes it in print and thus allows it to be read, lingered over, reread. Writing fixes the evanescence of sound and holds it against death. It also gives the poem a fixed visual as well as an auditory life. With the advent of a text, the performer and the audience are physically separated from each other. Hence John Stuart Mill's idea that "eloquence is *heard;* poetry is *overheard,*" and Northrop Frye's notion that the lyric is "a literary genre characterized by the assumed concealment of the audience from the poet." Thereafter, the lyric becomes a different kind of intimate communiqué, a highly concentrated and passionate form of communication between strangers. It delivers on our spiritual lives precisely because it gives us the gift of intimacy and interiority, of privacy and participation. Perhaps the asocial nature of the deepest feeling, the "too muchness" of human emotion, is what creates the space for the lyric, which is a way of beating time, of experiencing duration, of verging on infinity.

SEE ALSO *dramatic monologue, epic, poetry.*

lyrisme romantique The notion of romantic lyricism is used to describe a deep subjectivity in nineteenth-century French romantic poetry. Such major poets as Victor Hugo (1802–1885), Alphonse de Lamartine (1790–1869), Alfred de Musset (1810–1857), and Alfred Victor de Vigny (1797–1863) introduced a new musicality into their poems driven by personal feelings and experiences.

SEE ALSO *romanticism.*

macaronic verse Poetry in which two or more languages are mixed together. Strictly speaking, macaronic verse incorporates words from the poet's native language into another language and subjects them to its rules, thus creating a comic effect. It was first used in the late fifteenth century by interspersing vernacular Italian with Latin. Teofilo Folengo made the form famous in his mock epic *Macaroneae* (1517–1521). The humor came in bending the vernacular to a high literary language, as in doggerel. Later, the term came to be applied to any poem, humorous or serious, in which languages are intermingled. By this criterion, modernists such as T. S. Eliot and Ezra Pound often wrote macaronic verse. Alexander Pushkin, for example, liked to rhyme Russian words with foreign ones. We could extend the term to include the work of Chicano and other English-language poets who incorporate vernacular Spanish into their poems and thus create a new idiomatic American poetry. The fusion of languages speaks to complex modern identities.

SEE ALSO *doggerel, mock epic.*

madrigal A verse to be sung to music; a secular vocal composition for two or more voices. The madrigal originated as a pastoral song (*matricale* was the Medieval Latin name for a country song) in northern Italy in the fourteenth century. The simple rustic song consisted of two or three three-line tercets followed by one or two rhyming couplets. The lines were either seven or eleven syllables long.

The madrigal was revived by composers throughout Europe in the sixteenth century. It was freed of its traditional formal strictures; all that remained of the original form was the final rhyming couplet, which has also been abandoned in most modern madrigals. The English madrigal especially flourished from the 1580s to the 1620s. Thomas Morley (1557–1602), Thomas Weelkes (1576–1623), and John Wilbye (1574–1638) were all great English madrigal composers. Here is one of my favorite anonymous Elizabethan madrigals:

> My Love in her attire doth show her wit,
> It doth so well become her;
> For every season she hath dressings fit,
> For Winter, Spring, and Summer.
> No beauty she doth miss
> When all her robes are on:
> But Beauty's self she is
> When all her robes are gone.

SEE ALSO *lyric, pastoral.*

mal-mariée A type of Old French song or poem about an unhappily married woman mistreated by her husband. There are many variations that center on the female protagonist. In one type, a coquettish young wife complains about her cruel and jealous older husband and fantasizes about a young lover, real or imaginary, who sometimes comes to rescue her. In another, a nun laments her marriage to the church and longs for a lover to take her away from the convent. The poems were often written (and sung) in ballade meter.

SEE ALSO *ballade.*

mannerism When capitalized, the term *Mannerism* specifically refers to the artistic period of the "Late" Renaissance, basically the years between Michelangelo (1475–1564) and Rubens (1577–1640). Vasari (1511–1574) used the word *maniera* to refer to the impressive or distinctive quality in a work of art, the way it fuses particular characteristics into a beautiful whole. In the seventeenth century, the term *mannerism* came to suggest a highly affected or exaggerated literary style. Ernst Robert Curtius broadens the concept of mannerism to represent "the common denominator for all literary tendencies which are opposed to Classicism, whether they be pre-classical, post-classical, or contemporary with any Classicism," and thus mannerism becomes a complementary phenomenon to classicism in all periods, "a constant in European literature." Whereas classicism values clarity and restraint, mannerism looks for ingeniousness and ornamentation. Its aim is to dazzle and astonish. It embraces complex forms and moves on the wings of a high rhetoric, piling up words, preferring circumlocution to straightforwardness, elaboration to plainness. One thinks of the virtuosity of the poet Giambattista Marino (1569–1625) or the highly artificial style of Gabriele D'Annunzio (1863–1938).

SEE ALSO *baroque, circumlocution, classic, Gongorism, Marinism, metaphysical poets.*

maqāma An Arabic term for picaresque stories in rhymed prose. The word *maqāma* means "assemblies" or "sessions," and the tales were recited in social gathering places. The two greatest masters of this prolific genre were Ahmed ibn al-Husain al-Hamadhanī (968–1008), known as Badī' al-Zamān (the Marvel of the Age), who most likely invented it, and his emulator, Abū Muhammad al-Qasim ibn 'Alī al-Harīrī (1054–1122).

The *maqāma* is comprised of a single continuous narrative or a series of independent stories. It is created in rhythmical rhyming prose and often interspersed with metrical poems, which are comparable to arias in an opera. The story classically included two characters: a wandering narrator of solid social standing, and a mischievious, itinerant protagonist, who has fallen from grace and will do anything for personal gain. He is conventionally an eloquent poet. The genre was adapted into Persian, Syriac, and Hebrew, where it flourished for centuries. It is a forerunner of the picaresque novel.

SEE ALSO *rhymed prose.*

Marinism *Marinism* takes its name from the extravagant Italian poet Giambattista Marino (1569–1625). His sonnets, madrigals, and narrative poems are marked by a startling wordplay, a taste for elaborate conceits, and a sonorous music. His ornate style was the primary influence on seventeenth-century Italian poetry. *Marinismo* is a nineteenth-century term for the themes and techniques of Marino and his followers. "It continues to be used synonymously with *secentismo* and *concettismo,*" James Mirollo explains, "although the former has more pejorative connotations as well as wider cultural implications, while the latter embraces the European practice of the witty style." The work of Marino and his followers was part of the extreme baroque reaction against classicism, and it is thus kin to other European movements of the same period, such as Gongorism in Spain and metaphysical poetry in England. The Italian literary academy was founded in Rome to combat Marinism. The movement died out with the baroque period. It stands as a highly decorated, much maligned monument to the ornamental style of poetry.

SEE ALSO *aureate, baroque, Gongorism, mannerism, metaphysical poets.*

marsiya An elegy, often on the death of a family member or close friend. In Urdu, the *marsiya* is a specialized lamentation that commemorates the martyrdom of Imām Husayn, the grandson of the Prophet Muhammad, and his clan who were killed by their Ummayad enemies at Karbalā, in Iraq, in 680. The first Urdu *marsiyas* were written in the sixteenth century in South India and had no fixed structure. They were chanted or sung, either singly or in a chorus. The genre migrated to North India in the nineteenth century. The poets at Lucknow and Faizabad standardized the form, which now typically consists of a six-line stanza called a *masaddas* that brings together a rhyming quatrain and a rhyming couplet (*aaaa, bb*). The *marsiya* has discernible sections: *cihra* (prologue), *sārapā* (physical and spiritual qualities of the hero), *rukhsat* (departure for battle), *jang* (battle), *shahādat* (martyrdom), and *bain* (lament).

SEE ALSO *elegy, lament.*

martial verse War verses, battle poems, marching songs. There has sometimes been poetic accompaniment to military campaigning. At such times, poetry sounds a drumbeat of fury. According to Plutarch, the Athenian statesman and elegiac poet Solon (ca. 638–558 B.C.E.) was given leadership for the Athenian war against Megara on the basis of a poem he wrote about Salamis Island. He used his martial verse ("Let us march to Salamis") to inspire his men to take Salamis from the Megerians. So, too, the Spartan poet and general Tyrtaeus (seventh century B.C.E.) used his poems to rally his men to quell the Messenian revolt. According to the Athenian orator Lycurgus, Tyrtaeus's exhortations were recited to men in front of the king's tent. There are also less martial settings for military exhortations to fight bravely.

Martial verse is prevalent in pre-Islamic poetry, as in the eighth-century *Romance of Antar.* Indeed, there is a category of martial verse in most tribal poetries. All wars inspire patriotic poems. Two poems of martial verse that survived the American Civil War are James Ryder Randall's fervent "Maryland, My Maryland" (1861) and Julia Ward Howe's "Battle Hymn of the Republic" (1862). One conventional kind of martial verse is the military elegy, a type of public poetry that extols the heroic valor of the fallen warrior. Martial verse, which generally shows a patriotic and even warmongering spirit, should be distinguished from the poetry of war, which frequently dramatizes the horrors encountered there. "Despite these ancient connections, war and poetry are fundamentally different activities," James Anderson Winn writes in *The Poetry of War* (2008). "War dismembers bodies, scattering limb from limb. Poetry re-members those bodies and the people who lived in them, making whole in verse what was destroyed on the battlefield."

SEE ALSO *epic.*

Martian poets British poets in the late 1970s and early 1980s tried to break the grip of convention by de-familiarizing ordinary things and writing about them as though through a Martian's eyes. James Fenton's article "Of the Martian School" (1979) named the movement based on Craig Raine's book *A Martian Sends a Postcard Home* (1979) and Christopher Reid's collection *Arcadia* (1979). Martin Amis promoted the movement and carried the strategy into his 1981 novel, *Other People: A Mystery Story.* The word *martianism,* which is generally applied both to fiction and poetry, is an anagram of his name.

In a different context, the American poet Jack Spicer (1925–1965) claimed that he was a radio transmitting poetic messages that were dictated to him by a mysterious unknown source he sometimes called Martians, who contacted him from the Outside, the spirit world.

SEE ALSO *Surrealism.*

Marxist criticism, Marxist poetry Marxist criticism is a type of literary criticism grounded in the economic and cultural theory of Karl Marx (1818–1883) and Friedrich Engels (1820–1895). Marxist poetry is a social poetry driven by Marxist ideology, especially the commitment to proletarian class struggle. To give a rough summary of Marxism: according to Marx and Engels, the modes of "material production" essentially determine the history of humanity, its social structures and cultural institutions. Historical changes in the modes of production lead to changes in class structure, establishing dominant and subordinate classes. Human consciousness is created by ideology, the complex way that human beings view reality through the lens of social class. Ideology is the product of economic structure, which determines class relations and class interests. The "scientific" or Marxist view of history recognizes that it unfolds according to economic determinants. Whoever controls the means of production basically controls the way that reality is viewed in any given era. What seems natural and inevitable is actually historically determined. The present era of capitalism emerged in the eighteenth century, and the subsequent ideology incorporates the interests of the dominant or "bourgeois" class over the "proletariat" or working class. Bourgeois culture, its various social and cultural institutions, operates to legitimize and maintain the interests of the ruling class.

Marxist criticism tends to explain the literature of any given era as the product of economic factors. Early Marxist critics concentrated on the literary representation of the working class. One of the vulgar consequences of Marxist ideology was the notion of "social realism," the idea that works of art should represent the current stage of the class struggle. This was a way of forcing literature to conform to party politics, stripping it of its autonomy, a policy that had disastrous consequences in the Soviet era. More significantly, Marxist criticism taught writers and critics to view literature not as a timeless art but as a historically determined one, subject to external material conditions. It focused on the way that culture intersects with power. Some of the key twentieth-century Marxist literary critics are Georg Lukács, Antonio Gramsci, Louis Althusser, and Raymond Williams.

Marx and Engels themselves ignored poetry. Marxist criticism primarily focused on "realistic" social fiction, but at times forayed into poetry and theater. Official Marxist poetry and criticism are hard to stomach, especially from the Soviet Bloc, but, as an alternative, one thinks of the way that the German Marxists, the poet and playwright Bertolt Brecht and the critic Walter Benjamin, used historical ideas gleaned from Marxist writings to explain and support modernist art. Brecht's epic theater is a case in point. Historically, Marxism was a global phenomenon, and it influenced poetry around the world. One thinks, for example, of the class-conscious, socially engaged, human-centered poetry of the modernist poets Nazim Hikmet (Turkey) and César Vallejo (Peru), or the large polemical embrace of the Scottish modernist Hugh MacDiarmid. Twentieth-century Latin American poets, such as the Nicaraguan priest Ernesto Cardenal, the Cuban poet Nicholás Guillén, and the Chilean poet Pablo Neruda, frequently committed to a vanguard revolutionary poetry. In Africa, the anti-colonial revolutionary affirmations of Négritude had Marxist affinities.

American Marxist poetry had a brief doctrinaire moment of engagement in the 1930s, and a wide range of English-language poets, from W. H. Auden to Muriel Rukeyser, underwent a Marxist phase. The poet Kenneth Fearing sustained his commitment and created a coherent body of Marxist poetry. At the height of his Black Nationalist phase, Amiri Baraka employed an aggressive Marxist rhetoric to argue that the "central task" of poetry was to build a Marxist/Leninist Communist party in the United States. The San Francisco poet Jack Hirschman writes a Marxist poetry of class struggle.

SEE ALSO *Négritude.*

masculine rhyme A rhyme on a terminal syllable (*Pan/man*). The commonest kind of rhyme, masculine, or single-syllable rhyme, is contrasted to feminine or multisyllabic rhyme. The engendering of the terms is arbitrary. The one-syllable rhyme makes emphatic connections; it creates a force field of relation — as when this anonymous sixteenth-century poet declares in "To Her Sea-Faring Lover":

> Alas! say nay! say nay! and be no more so dumb,
> But open thou thy manly mouth and say that thou wilt come.

SEE ALSO *feminine rhyme, rhyme.*

masnavi, also ***masnawi, mathnavi*** A characteristic type of Persian verse, the *masnavi* consists of a series of rhyming couplets (*aa, bb, cc,* etc.). The lines are hemistiches or half-lines and thus the poet rhymes the first and second half of each line. The couplets are horizontal. It is a narrative form that originated in the Middle Persian period, which extended from the third century B.C.E. to the ninth century. The *masnavi* enabled the poet to thread a story through thousands of verses. Each type of *masnavi* — the didactic, the heroic, the romantic — had its own prescribed meter and diction. No line was more than eleven syllables long. In Arabic literature the form is known as *muzdawij.* Jalâl al-Din Rumi's twelfth-century Sufi travelogue, *Masnavi-ye ma*ʿ*navi* (Spiritual Couplets), is the single greatest *masnavi* work. Rumi's magnum opus consists of some twenty-six thousand verses divided into six books. "This is the book of the Masnavi," Rumi said. "It contains the roots of the roots of the roots of the Faith, and treats of the mysteries of 'Union' and 'Certitude.' "

SEE ALSO *hemistich.*

masque A Renaissance form, the masque was a brief and festive poetic entertainment usually performed at court, a lavish spectacle that incorporated poetic drama with singing and dancing to ornate music. The masked performers wore sumptuous costumes and extravagant jewelry. Professional actors and musicians performed the speaking and singing parts, while masked courtiers assumed the other roles. The stage designs were elaborate.

The masque may derive from a folk tradition when masked players would unexpectedly call on a nobleman, dancing and bringing gifts to commemorate a special occasion, as in the rustic presentation of "Pyramus and Thisbe" as a wedding entertaining in *A Midsummer Night's Dream* (1590–1596). Many traditions contributed to its development, such as morris dancing, "disguisings," also called "a mumming" (the disguised performers say nothing that betrays their identity), and mummers' plays, when English ritual maskers performed an age-old drama on Christmas day. From these folk forms with their roots in archaic religious rites, the masque evolved into an elaborate court spectacle, a form that reached its zenith in the first half of the seventeenth century in the courts of the English monarchs James I, who ruled from 1603 to 1625, and Charles I, who ruled from 1625 to 1649. The masque was characteristically a complimentary offering to a patron, and the image of an idealized feudal court was at the heart of the entertainment. The masque celebrates the audience, and the figure of the monarch is the center of the universe.

The structure of the masque was simple, the action highly ritualized. A prologue introduced a group of actors to a social gathering. The masked revelers then entered. The procession introduced a sequence of vices or figures of topical interest. The more elaborate masques presented a short drama with a theme that was frequently mythological, allegorical, or symbolic. The moralizing was evident: good defeats evil, light triumphs over darkness. In the concluding dance, the masquers took off their masks and danced with partners from the audience. One kind of royal entertainment turned into another.

Ben Jonson transformed the masque into a significant poetic form. From 1605 to 1631, he collaborated with the set designer Inigo Jones, who brought a new architectural style to English theater. Jonson considered the words the key feature of the masque and quarreled with his collaborator, who considered the spectacle of primary importance. As he put it "An Expostulation with Inigo Jones" (1631):

> Oh, to make boards to speak! There is a task!
> Painting and carpentry are the soul of masque!
> Pack with you peddling poetry to the stage!
> This is the money-get, mechanic age.

Jonson also invented the anti-masque—an antic and unruly revelry, which presented grotesque or comic figures to contrast with the main mythological figures of the masque itself. Robert Adams points out that the opposition between the masque's goodly forces and the anti-masque's negative ones is "heraldic, not dramatic; good appears, declaring itself, and the figures of evil withdraw like the shades of night when the sun rises."

Jonson's major masques are *Hymenaei* (1606), *The Masque of Beauty* (1608), *The Masque of Queens* (1609), *The Masque of Augurs* (1621), *Neptune's Triumph for the Return of Albion* (1624?), and *The Fortunate Isles and Their Union* (1624). Shakespeare contributed the masque of Juno and Ceres within the fourth act of *The Tempest* (ca. 1611), and the form reached one of its peaks in Milton's *Comus,* performed at Ludlow Castle in 1634. The masque died as a primary form with the outbreak of the English Civil War and the closing of the theaters by the Puritans. What was learned from masques was essentially turned into the production of plays. Over the centuries, the form has occasionally been adapted into a different kind of entertainment, as in Robert Frost's *A Masque of Reason* (1945) and *A Masque of Mercy* (1947).

SEE ALSO *allegory, drama.*

Matinée Poétique The Matinée Poétique, or "First Postwar Wave," was a small, cosmopolitan, left-wing Japanese group formed in 1942. The group was founded, amongst others, by Fukinaga Takehiko, Nakamura Shin'ichirō, and Katō Shūichi, who recalls how the Matinée Poétique took their flamboyant name from the morning poetry readings of Jacque Copeau's troupe in Paris. "Nakamura came up with the idea of having private recitals amongst ourselves," Katō remembers. "In a playful mood, we called the first of our poetry recitals a *matinée poétique.* The same name served for the title of a poetry collection we published after the war, and that was how it came to be known to the general public." The First Postwar Wave writers repudiated nationalistic and patriotic poetry — their name stylishly signals their internationalism — and embraced a wide range of world literature, especially French poetry.

mawwāl, mawāwīl (pl) The Egyptian *mawwāl* is a poly-rhymed form of vernacular poetry, usually in five, seven, or nine lines, which is sung in colloquial rather than classical Arabic. The form, which was first mentioned in a thirteenth-century manuscript, has been popular in Arab countries from Iraq to North Africa. Somewhat confusingly, the term, which means "affiliated with" or "connected to," can be used to refer to the poetic form, to the musical style used to perform it, or to its characteristically sad, aphoristic content. Dwight Fletcher Reynolds points out: "The most common theme of the folk mawwāl, and perhaps the most ubiquitous and enduring theme in all of Egyptian folk poetry, is that of *s̲hakwà,* literally 'complaint.' S̲hakwa, however, is specifically a complaint that addresses the forces of the world: Time (*al-zaman*), the Days (*al-ayyām*), the Nights (*al-layālī*), the Era (*al-awān*), Fate (*al-dahr*), Destiny (*qadar*), the World (*al-dunyā*), and Separation (*al-bēn;* SA *al-bayn*)." He paraphrases one of the songs:

1. As a strong man, when the time comes, I should shoulder life's burdens,
2. Yet Fate seized me, despite my intentions, and bore me away from what I had hoped my life would be.
3. O my heart, strengthen yourself against the difficulties of life [or: against your enemies],

4. I ask you, O Lord, I ask you, O Lord, You who cause milk to flow in the breast,
5. You who give the young hope despite their troubles,
6. You who have the power to grant me prosperity,
7. Let me continue to prosper. Yet all the forces of the world are trying to overcome me!

measure "Verse has always been associated in men's minds with 'measure,' i. e., with mathematics," William Carlos Williams said in "On Measure—Statement for Cid Corman" (1954). The word *measure,* which is linked to counting, is often used interchangeably with *meter,* which derives from *métron,* meaning "measure." It was once, as George Santayana notes, "a condition of perfection, for perfection requires that order should be pervasive, that not only the whole before us should have a form, but that every part in turn should have a form of its own, and that those parts should be coördinated among themselves as the whole is coördinated with the other parts of some greater cosmos."

A single measure is a rhythmic unit that refers to a foot in English-language prosody, or to two feet, dipody, in classical Greek prosody. In contemporary poetry, it tends to refer to the rhythmic cadence of a line or a group of lines. Williams categorically states in a letter: "Poetry began with measure, it began with the dance, whose divisions we have all but forgotten but are still known as measures. Measures they were and we still speak of their minuter elements as feet." Williams imagines the origins of poetry in the ritual divisions of dance. *Measure* is an ancient word in poetry and Williams sought "a new measure by which may be ordered our poems as well as our lives." Or as Robert Kelly puts it in his poem, "Prefix: Finding the measure" (1968): "Finding the measure is finding the / specific music of the hour."

SEE ALSO *cadence, meter, rhythm.*

Mehian Group The word *Mehian* means "temple" in Armenian, and the Mehian Group, formed in Constantinople in 1914, sought to connect Armenian culture to its pagan, pre-Christian past and free it from tyranny in the future. Daniel Varoujan led this modernist movement for an Armenian renaissance. He was butchered at the age of thirty-one by the "Young Turks" as part of the Armenian genocide. Adom Yarjanian, who used the pen name Siamanto, was also murdered in the execution of 250 Armenian intellectuals and leaders in 1915. The movement was carried on by Vahan Tekeyan, Aharon Dadourian, Hagop Oshagan, and Kostan Zaryan, among others. Here is part of the Mehian Group's declaration of principles:

> We announce the worship and the expression of the Armenian spirit, because the Armenian spirit is alive, but appears occasionally. We say: Without the Armenian spirit there is no Armenian literature and Armenian artist. Every true artist expresses only his own race's spirit . . . We say: External factors, acquired customs, foreign influences, diverted and deformed emotions have dominated the Armenian spirit, but were unable to assimilate it.

meiosis Meiosis is a "lessening," a rhetorical figure of speech that contains an ironic understatement, as when Monty Python calls an amputated leg "just a flesh wound." It is generally synonymous with *litotes,* but sometimes considered more general. George Puttenham labeled it "the disabler or figure of extenuation." It is often used by a clever speaker to gain credibility by deprecating himself.

Shakespeare is the master of ironic understatement. Trevor McNeeeley argues, "*Meiosis* may well be the most devious of all rhetorical tricks, having the effect simultaneously of disarming the hearer and of subtly flattering the speaker; and as Shakespeare uses it particularly it has an effect of special challenge, for his favorite ploy is to have the character affect modesty in *verbal skill* itself—an affectation which is blatantly contradicted by the skills the speaker displays in its very utterance." He points to Richard of Gloucester ("Cannot a plain man live and think no harm"), to Prince Hal and Hotspur, and especially to the end of the funeral oration of Marc Antony in act 3 of *Julius Caesar* (1599), which he calls "the *meisosis* to end *meiosis.*"

> I come not, friends, to steal away your hearts.
> I am no orator, as Brutus is,
> But, as you know me all, a plain blunt man,
> That love my friend; and that they know full well
> That gave me public leave to speak of him.
>
> For I have neither wit, nor words, nor worth,
> Action, nor utterance, nor the power of speech
> To stir men's blood. I only speak right on . . .

Meiosis may also suggest a moment of striking understated simplicity. In the *Inferno* (1304–1309), Dante breaks off the Paolo and Francesca episode with the statement, "We read no more that day." And in *King Lear* (1608), just a moment before he dies, the old king says, "Pray you, undo this button."

SEE ALSO *litotes, rhetoric.*

meistersinger The German burgher poets of the fourteenth to sixteenth centuries formed guilds, which were governed by town councils, to perpetuate and emulate the art of the minnesingers, the lyric poets of the twelfth and thirteenth centuries. They established hierarchical categories for the study and performance of *Meistergesang,* poetry for singing to melodies. One began as an apprentice (*Schüler*), next became a journeyman or school friend (*Schulfreund*), progressed through the positions of singer and poet (*Dichter*), and, hopefully, reached the summit as a master (*Meister*). These middle-class artists worked with regularized *Töne,* certain set metrical patterns and tunes, and held singing contests (*Singschulen*) during religious festivals at Easter, Whitsuntide, and Christmas. Three of the most well-known *meistersingers* are the Swabian weaver Michel Beheim (1416–ca. 1472); the master barber-poet Hans Folz (ca. 1437–1513), who expanded the repertoire by adding twenty-seven new tones to the original twelve allowed by the old masters (*Alten Meister*); and the Nuremberg shoemaker-poet Hans Sachs (1494–1576), who became the hero of Wagner's sunniest opera *Die Meistersinger von Nürnberg.* Adam Puschman's song book (1571) is the richest collection of *meistersinger* tunes.

SEE ALSO *Knittelvers, minnesinger, poetic contest, Silesian school.*

melic poetry The Greeks spoke of melic poetry, which derives from the word *melos* or song. It is the root of melody and means "connected with music." They applied the name to all forms of lyric poetry. Melic poetry especially flourished in the hands of the Aeolians and the Dorians between the seventh and the fifth centuries B.C.E. It was divided into two classes: the solo or monodic lyric, which was sung by a single voice and expressed the emotions of an individual (Sappho, Alcaeus, and Anacreon), and the choral lyric, which was sung by a chorus and expressed the emotions of the group

(Alcman, Stesichorus, Simonides, Pindar, and Bacchylides). In essence, melic poetry became the lyric.

SEE ALSO *lyric, melopoeia, ode.*

melopoeia Greek: "song making." *Melopoeia* refers to the aural qualities of a poem, the making of music. In *How to Read* (1929), Ezra Pound employed this term for one of three "kinds of poetry":

> MELOPOEIA, wherein the words are charged, over and above their plain meaning, with some musical property, which directs the bearing or trend of that meaning.

In Greek, the infinitive form of *melopoeia* is the verb for composing lyric poems, or composing music, or composing lyric poems set to music. Pound, who may have discovered the term in Aristotle's 350 B.C.E. *Poetics* (*melopoiia*) or Longinus's treatise on the sublime, argued that there are three kinds of *melopoeia,* or poetry on the borders of music: "(1) that made to be sung to a tune; (2) that made to be intoned or sung to a sort of chant; and (3) that made to be spoken." Pound might also have picked up the Irish poet Thomas MacDonagh's distinction between song-verse, chant-verse, and speech-verse (*Thomas Campion and the Art of English Poetry,* 1913). The notion of *melopoeia* is what Samuel Taylor Coleridge called "poetry of the ear" ("On the Principles of Genial Criticism," 1814).

SEE ALSO *logopoeia, melic poetry, phanopoeia.*

Menippean satire, see *satire.*

Merz In Hanover, Germany, in 1919, the avant-garde artist Kurt Schwitters extracted the word *Merz* (as in *Kommerz,* which means "commerce") from one of his collages, and used it to explain his totalizing concept of art, which erased the boundaries between genres:

> My aim is the total Merz art work, which combines all genres into an artistic unity. First I married off single genres. I pasted words and sentences together into poems in such a way that their rhythmic com-

> position created a kind of drawing. The other way around, I pasted together pictures and drawings containing sentences that demand to be read.

Schwitters also composed and regularly performed an early groundbreaking example of sound poetry, the thirty-five-minute *Ursonate* or "Primal Sonata" (1924). He published his score in the final issue of his magazine, *Merz* (1932).

SEE ALSO *Optophonetics, sound poetry.*

mesode, see *proode.*

mesostic A poem, or other typographical arrangement, in which a vertical word or phrase intersects lines of horizontal texts. In the 1970s, John Cage wrote a series of *mesostic* poems with a key word in capital letters running through the middle of a typescript. This word or phrase, which can be a name or a quotation, determines the words that will be chosen from various source texts. As Cage explained: "Like acrostics, mesostics are written in the conventional way horizontally, but at the same time they follow a vertical rule, down the middle not down the edge as in an acrostic, a string which spells a word or name, not necessarily connected with what is being written, though it may be. This vertical rule is lettristic and in my practice the letters are capitalized. Between two capitals in a perfect or 100% mesostic neither letter may appear in lower case. . . . In the writing of the wing words, the horizontal text, the letters of the vertical string help me out of sentimentality. I have something to do, a puzzle to solve." One result was his *mesostic* text "Writing Through Finnegans Wake" (1977), which used the string JAMES JOYCE. He "wrote through" the entire novel from front to back. All in all, Cage wrote four *mesostics* using *Finnegans Wake* as a source text. He also applied the procedure to Ezra Pound's *Cantos* (1982), Franz Kafka's *Die Verwandlung* (1983), Marcel Duchamp's *Notes* (1984), and Henry David Thoreau's "On the Duty of Civil Disobedience" (1985). Jim Rosenberg developed *Mesolist* as a computer program that re-creates the *mesostic* procedure.

SEE ALSO *acrostic, aleatory, diastic.*

mester de juglaria, see *juglar.*

metagram The *Oxford English Dictionary* defines a metagram as "a kind of puzzle turning on the alteration of a word by removing some of its letters and substituting others." The surrealist poet and novelist Raymond Roussel (1877–1933) especially played with the metagram, which had for him the elements of a chess problem — overdetermined, arbitrary — though one that estranged language. In "How I Wrote Certain of My Books" (1935), Roussel explained his use of what he called "the device" (*le procédé*): "I would choose two different words (suggesting the metagram). For example, *billard* and *pillard.* Then I would add similar words selected for two different meanings, and I would obtain identical sentences."

SEE ALSO *anagram, hypogram, Surrealism.*

metaphor A figure of speech in which one thing is described in terms of another — as when Whitman characterizes the grass as "the beautiful uncut hair of graves." The term *metaphor* derives from the Greek *metaphora,* which means "carrying from one place to another," and a metaphor transfers the connotations of one thing (or idea) to another. It says *A* equals *B* ("Life is a dream"). It is a transfer of energies, a mode of energetic relation, of interpenetration, a matter of identity and difference, a collision, or collusion, in the identification of unlike things. There is something dreamlike in its associative way of thinking. Kenneth Burke calls this "perspective by incongruity." In "The Constant Symbol" (1946), Robert Frost says, "There are many other things I have found myself saying about poetry, but the chiefest of these is that it is metaphor, saying one thing and meaning another, saying one thing in terms of another, the pleasure of ulteriority."

In *The Philosophy of Rhetoric* (1936), I. A. Richards distinguished the two parts of a metaphor by the terms *tenor* and *vehicle.* The tenor stands for what is being talked about. It is the subject. The vehicle stands for the way it is being talked about and carries the weight of the comparison. When Macbeth says that "life is but a walking shadow," "life" is the tenor and "walking shadow" is the vehicle.

One philosophical tradition maintains that there is no logical difference between metaphors and similes. Metaphors are considered literal comparisons with the explicit "like" or "as" suppressed. Another tradition, the one to which I belong, holds that there is a radical difference (or should be) between saying that A is *the same as* B and saying that A is *like* B. ("I am crossing the word *like* out of the dictionary," Mallarmé declared.) Metaphor operates by condensation and compression, simile by discursiveness and digression.

Metaphor works by a process of interaction. It draws attention to the categories of language by crossing them. The language of poetry, Shelley writes in "A Defence of Poetry" (1821), is "vitally metaphorical; that is, it marks the before unapprehended relations of things and perpetuates their apprehension." Shelley suggests that the poet creates relations between things unrecognized before, and that new relations create new thoughts and thus revitalize language.

Readers actively participate in making meaning through metaphor, in thinking through the conjoining — the relation — of unlike things. The philosopher Ted Cohen suggests that one of the main points of metaphor is "the achievement of intimacy." He argues that the maker and the appreciator of a metaphor are brought into deeper relationship with each other. That's because the speaker issues a concealed invitation through metaphor that the listener makes a special effort to accept and interpret. Such "a transaction constitutes the acknowledgement of a community." So, too, in poetry meaning emerges as an intimate collaborative process.

SEE ALSO *figures of speech, metonymy, rhetoric, simile, trope.*

metaphysical poets The metaphysical poets were a group of early seventeenth-century poets, including John Donne, George Herbert, Abraham Cowley, Henry Vaughan, Andrew Marvell, Thomas Carew, and Richard Crashaw. They were not a school or a movement — most of them didn't know each other — but their work shares some common characteristics: a bold wit, a clever sense of inventiveness, a love of intellectual elaboration. They have a special gift for constructing arguments and finding analogies, for discovering likeness in unlike things. They explore metaphysical concerns.

The Scottish writer William Drummond seems to have been first to apply the term *metaphysical poets* to particular poets. Around 1630, he objected to his contemporaries who attempted to "abstract poetry to metaphysical Ideas and Scholastic Quiddities." In 1693, John Dryden remarked that Donne "affects the Metaphysics . . . not only in his satires, but in his amorous verses, where only nature should reign." He criticized his "nice speculations of philosophy." In his *Life of Cowley* (1779), Samuel Johnson subsequently expanded the term to name a "school" of poets: "about the beginning of the seventeenth century appeared a race of writers that may be termed the metaphysical poets." He added that "the metaphysical poets were men of learning, and to show their learning was their whole endeavor." Johnson characterized their work by "a kind of *discordia concors;* a combination of dissimilar images, or discovery of occult resemblances in things apparently unlike," and described their method of wit as "the most heterogeneous ideas . . . yoked by violence together." Johnson thus put intellectual ingenuity and the use of conceits, or wit, at the heart of the metaphysical endeavor.

Johnson's largely negative evaluation of the metaphysical poets held sway until the 1890s and the early part of the twentieth century. T. S. Eliot helped elevate John Donne and bring the metphysical poets back into favor. In his essay "The Metaphysical Poets" (1921), a review of Herbert J. C. Grierson's anthology *Metaphysical Lyrics and Poems of the Seventeenth Century,* Eliot argued that the metaphysical poets embodied a fusion of thought and feeling that was unavailable to later generations because of a "dissociation of sensibility." Eliot argued that Donne could "feel [his] thought as immediately as the odour of a rose. A thought to Donne was an experience; it modified his sensibility." He found in the metaphysical "a direct sensuous apprehension of thought, or a recreation of thought in feeling." Donne and the other metaphysical poets became the central objects of study for the New Critics of the 1940s and 1950s. I have always loved their work for its passionate argumentation and its furious wit.

SEE ALSO *concordia discors, dissociation of sensibility, wit.*

meter The word *meter* derives from the Greek term *metron,* meaning "measure." Meter is a way of describing rhythmic patterning in poetry, of keeping time, of measuring poetic language. Meter is one quality that marks a poem as verse, as a made thing, a work of art. Barbara Herrnstein Smith writes in *Poetic Closure* (1968): "Meter serves . . . as a frame for the poem, separating it from a 'ground' of less highly structured speech and sound. . . . Meter is the stage of the theater in which the poem, the representation of an act of speech, is performed. It is the arena of art, the curtain that rises and falls as well as the music that accompanies the entire performance."

The first pleasures of meter are physical and intimately connected to bodily experience — to the heartbeat and the pulse, to breathing, walking, running, dancing, working, lovemaking. The meter of a poem can slow us down or speed us up; it can focus our attention; it can hypnotize us. Imagine you have gone down to the ocean in the early morning. You stand in the water and feel the waves breaking against the shore. You watch them coming in and going out. You feel the push and pull, the ebb and flow, of the tide. The waves repeat each other, but no two waves are exactly the same. Think of those waves as the flow of words washing across the lines and sentences of a poem. To measure the rhythmic pattern of those waves is to establish its meter. It is something you are observing, but also something you are experiencing. As I. A. Richards puts it in *Principles of Literary Criticism* (1952):

> Its effect is not due to our perceiving a pattern in something outside us, but to our becoming patterned ourselves. With every beat of the metre a tide of anticipation in us turns and swings, setting up as it does extraordinarily extensive reverberations. We shall never understand metre so long as we ask, "Why does temporal pattern so excite us?" and fail to realize that the pattern itself is a vast cyclic agitation spreading all over the body, a tide of excitement pouring through the channels of the mind.

Meter has to do with beating out time, with counting and naming. Syllables are temporal and meters restructure time.

The terminology of metrics is problematic because it is borrowed from classical languages and applies only imperfectly to English. Still, there are readers who find metrical analysis an important constitutive feature of poetic meaning, and it is useful for all readers of poetry to know the four generally distinguishable metrical systems.

- **pure accentual meter:** This system, which we all recognize from nursery rhymes, measures only the number of stressed or accented syllables in each line. Accentual meter — the four-stress line with a caesura after the second stress — is common to all Germanic poetries. English poetry began in a pure accentual meter (*Piers Plowman, Beowulf*). The standard line throughout the Old and Middle English periods consists of four accents with a strong medial pause (*caesura*) and a pattern of repetitive consonants (*alliteration, consonance*), as in this line from Ezra Pound's version of the tenth-century poem "The Seafarer":

Wáneth the wátch, | but the wórld hóldeth.

Robert Graves speculated that the rhythm of accentual meter was based on the steady, synchronized rowing of oars across rough northern seas. The fifteenth-century poet John Skelton came up with a version of accentual meter called Skeltonics, Coleridge experimented with pure accentual verse in "Christabel" (1797–1800), and Gerard Manley Hopkins developed a creative form of it he called "sprung rhythm," his most important metrical discovery.

- **pure syllabic meter:** This system measures only the number of syllables in each line. It pays no attention to accentuation. Some languages are accent-timed, such as German and English, whereas other languages are syllable-timed, such as Japanese. Thus Japanese court poetry, Toda songs, Balinese poetry, Malay verse, and a good deal of Chinese, Korean, and Mongolian poetry are all syllabic. In Arabic poetry, the meter (*wazn*) is based on the length of syllables (a short syllable is a consonant followed by a short vowel; a long syllable is a vowelled letter followed by an unvowelled consonant or a long vowel). Pure syllabic verse frustrates and works against what Paul Fussell calls "our own Anglo-Saxon lust for stress."

  Both Robert Bridges (1844–1930) and his daughter Elizabeth Daryush (1887–1977) experimented with syllabics. Marianne Moore (1887–1972) is the great practitioner of syllabics in the twentieth century. Her compositions in verse—she was reluctant to call them "poems"—make the syllable a visible particle of language. This gives a scrupulously observed, slightly clinical feeling to her measures. Moore intermingles her line lengths, and each stanza repeats the syllabic pattern exactly. The syllabics are used contrapuntally to the rhythm of the phrase.
- **quantitative meter:** This system measures duration—the time it takes to pronounce a syllable—rather than contrasting stresses or accents. Sanskrit, Greek, and Latin meters were all quantitative. Greek verse was connected to the ecstatic beat of dancers moving around a sacred altar. It has its origins in ritual or play. The foot in classical prosody was something like a musical measure. Syllables were long or short, and one long syllable took the same length of time it took to utter two short ones. Every unit of two or three syllables

constituted a foot. A verse was two to six feet. Thus, the Homeric hexameter is a meter based on quantity. "Scarcely any facet of the culture of the ancient world is so alien to us as its quantitative metric," Paul Maas writes in *Greek Metre* (1923). Latin forms provide the model for almost all modern imitations of quantitative verse. Robert Bridges experimented interestingly with quantitative meters, though we don't know how Greek poetry actually sounded: applying durational values to English verse has generally failed because English is such a heavily accented language. It was only when classical feet were replaced with pairs or triads of stressed and unstressed syllables that meter began to have any applicability to the evolution of English poetry.

- **accentual-syllabic meter:** This system counts both the number of accents and the number of syllables in each line. Rhythm results from the interplay between them. Accentual-syllabic meter, which is sometimes called syllable-stress meter or foot verse, comprises the main tradition of English poetry from the late sixteenth century to the early twentieth century. It is traditionally discussed as a sequence of feet. Each foot usually consists of a nucleus of one stressed syllable and one or two unstressed syllables. The main feet in English versification are the iamb (a pair of syllables with the stress on the second one), trochee (a pair of syllables with the stress on the first one), dactyl (a triad of one stressed syllable followed by two unstressed ones), and anapest (a triad of two unstressed syllables followed by a single stressed one).

A meter is determined by the prevailing accentual pattern (iambic, trochaic, dactylic, anapestic) plus the number of feet per line. The monometer is one foot, as in Robert Herrick's "Upon His Departure Hence" (1648). The dimeter is two feet, as in Tennyson's "The Charge of the Light Brigade" (1854). The trimeter is three feet, as in Theodore Roethke's "My Papa's Waltz" (1942). The tetrameter is four feet, as in Andrew Marvell's "To His Coy Mistress" (ca. 1650s). The pentameter is five feet, as in William Shakespeare's sonnets. The hexameter is six feet, as in the first sonnet of Sir Philip Sidney's "Astrophil and Stella" (1591). The heptameter or septenary is seven feet, as in Rudyard Kipling's "Tommy" (1890). The octometer is eight feet, as in Robert Browning's "A Toccata of Galuppi's" (1855). The most common meters in English verse are: iambic u /; trochaic / u; anapestic u u /; dactylic

/ u u; spondaic / /; paeonic / u u u (first paeon). A line of verse in which one or more extra syllables are added to the first and/or last lines is called hypermetric.

The native four-beat rhythm, which is rooted in the Old English line, has an inescapable feeling of symmetry. It establishes the rhythm of ballads and hymns, of most folk, rock and roll, and rap songs. The very reason that iambic pentameter (five beats) became the preferred meter in our language is that, as Derek Attridge observes in *The Rhythms of English Poetry* (1982), "it is the only simple metrical form of manageable length which escapes the elementary four-beat rhythm, with its insistence, its hierarchical structures, and its close relationship with the world of ballad and song."

It has been estimated that three-fourths of all English poetry from Chaucer (1340?–1400) to Frost (1874–1963) has been written in rhymed or unrhymed iambic pentameter. The Irish tradition developed a technique of craftsmanship based on the hammer and anvil. "When two hammers answer each other five times on the anvil — *ti-tum, ti-tum, ti-tum, ti-tum, ti-tum* — five in honour of the five stations of the Celtic year," Graves suggests, "there you have Chaucer's familiar hendecasyllabic line."

> A knight there was, and that a worthy man
> That fro the time that he first began
> To ryden out, he loved chivalrye . . .

Iambic pentameter was the modal line in English for over three hundred years — the meter that Chaucer used for most of *The Canterbury Tales* (ca. 1387–1400), Spenser employed for *The Faerie Queene* (1590–1596), Shakespeare used with great versatility through most of his plays, Milton employed for his epics, Pope used judiciously for nearly all his verse, Wordsworth used with great flexibility in *The Prelude* (1805, 1850), Robert Browning carried through *The Ring and the Book* (1868–1869), and Yeats, Frost, Stevens, and Crane re-created for many of their greatest poems.

Every meter has accrued a history, and that history haunts later usages. It becomes part of its conscious and unconscious associations, its meanings and memories.

SEE ALSO *alliteration, ballad, blank verse, caesura, consonance, foot, hymn, iambic pentameter, measure, rhythm, Skeltonics, sprung rhythm,* and the entries for individual feet: *anapest, dactyl, iamb, spondee,* and *trochee.*

metonymy From the Greek, meaning "change of name." A figure of speech that replaces or substitutes the name of one thing with something else closely associated with it. We say, "The pen is mightier than the sword" (and mean that writing is more powerful than warfare). We say "Homer says" rather than "In the *Iliad* it is written" (and thus substitute the name of an author for his work). Metonymy strategically employs concrete, tangible, or corporeal terms to convey abstract, intangible, or incorporeal states, as when we speak of "the heart" and mean "the emotions." It's a way of embodying emotive and spiritual experiences. "If you trail language back far enough," Kenneth Burke explains, "you'll find all our terms for 'spiritual' states were metonymic in origin."

Synecdoche, the most crucial kind of metonymy, substitutes the name of a part for that of a whole (e.g., "hired hand" for "worker"). Burke argues that "all such conversions imply an integral relationship, a relationship of convertibility between the two terms." In "The Four Master Tropes" (1941), Burke goes on to argue for the synecdochic nature of ancient metaphysical doctrines:

> The "noblest synecdoche," the perfect paradigm or prototype for all lesser usages, is found in metaphysical doctrines proclaiming the identity of "microcosm" and "macrocosm." In such doctrines, where the individual is treated as a replica of the universe, and vice versa, we have the ideal synecdoche, since microcosm is related to macrocosm as part to whole, and either the whole can represent the part or the part can represent the whole.

The metonym and the metaphor are complementary figures. Whereas a metaphor establishes a radical likeness between two different things, a metonym establishes a contiguous or associative relationship between them. It is a form of associative or representational thinking. The linguist Roman Jakobson (1896–1982) famously extended the field of complementary figures, metaphor and metonym, to encompass dreams, myths, psychoanalysis, types of aphasia, and other things. Metonymy and metaphor offer the creative reader two different ways of organizing experience and making meaning.

SEE ALSO *figures of speech, metaphor, rhetoric, trope.*

metrical variation Any number of techniques, such as swapping one foot for another ("substitution") to vary a basic metrical pattern. For example, John Milton substitutes a trochee (/ u) for an iamb (u /) in the second foot of this iambic pentameter line in *Paradise Lost* (1667):

> Ă mínd | nót tŏ | bĕ chánged | bў pláce | ŏr tíme

SEE ALSO *counterpoint, foot, meter.*

metrics Metrics is the study of meter. It implies measurement. A metrist is a practitioner or student of meter. Paul Maas explains in *Greek Metre* (1923): "The art of metric is the means by which a regular rhythm is imposed upon the natural rhythm of language in a work of literature."

SEE ALSO *measure, meter, prosody, rhythm.*

metron, metra (pl) The unit of measurement in classical prosody. A *metron* is composed of long (—) and short (u) syllables, which roughly corresponds to a foot in English poetry.

SEE ALSO *foot, measure,* "quantitative meter" in *meter.*

the Mezzanine of Poetry, see *futurism.*

mGur Tibetean *mGur* ("poetical songs") are religious songs based in experience. They are songs of "positive personal experience," which probably originated in Tibetan literature as a subgenre of *glu,* the oldest type of songs. The greatest Tibetan poet, Mi la ras pa (1040–1123), composed songs "that combined the imagery, structural parallelism and expressive directness of ancient *glu* with distinctively Buddhist themes and Indian-inspired metrical schemes" (Roger Jackson). "Myriad things, whatever appears to the mind," he writes: "Ah, cyclic events of the triple world, / Nonexistent, yet appearing — how wondrous!"

There are seven major types of *mGur:* those that 1) remember the guru's kindness; 2) indicate the source of one's accomplishments; 3) inspire the practice of Dharma; 4) give instructions on how to practice; 5) answer disciples' questions; 6) admonish the uprooting of evil; 7) serve as missives to gurus or disciples.

Nyams mGur are "songs of experience," if we think of experience as an inner spiritual awareness or realization. These songs, which are a form of religious poetry, may be the most popular of Tibetan literary genres. Allen Ginsberg believed that the Buddhist poetic tradition is a repository "of millennial practical information on the attitudes and practices of mind speech & body that Western poets over the same millennia have explored individually, fitfully, as far as they were able — searching thru cities, scenes, seasons, manuscripts, libraries, backalleys, whorehouses, churches, drawing rooms, revolutionary cells, opium dens, merchants' rooms in Harrar, saloons in Lissadell."

SEE ALSO *sNyan ngag.*

the Middle Generation The Middle Generation of American poets flourished in the decades of the 1940s through the 1970s. Robert Lowell, Elizabeth Bishop, John Berryman, Randall Jarrell, Delmore Schwartz, Theodore Roethke, Robert Hayden, and Lorine Niedecker are just some of the poets who worked past midcentury. As Eric Harelson puts it, "Both formally and politically, their poetry constitutes *the* center of twentieth-century American poetry: the bull's eye, pulsating heart, eye of the storm." These poets came after the great moderns, and thus struggled with feelings of belatedness. After the heroic impersonality of modernism itself, their work seems quickened by losses, freshened by warmth, scaled down to human size. They were highly personal writers who began under the austere sign of New Criticism, but, ironically, ended up using their ironic sensibilities to bring a messy humanity, a harsh luminosity, a well of tenderness, back into poetry.

SEE ALSO *confessional poetry, irony, modernism, New Criticism, postmodernism.*

middle rhyme, see *rhyme.*

mimesis A transliteration of the Greek word for "imitation" and a key term in aesthetics since Aristotle asserted in the *Poetics* (350 B.C.E.) that tragedy is the imitation of an action. *Mimesis* has come to mean "representation," especially in terms of verisimilitude. We call a work "mimetic" or "realistic" when it gives the semblance of truth, the illusion of transparency, the sense of fidelity to an external reality. Philip Sidney argues in his *Apology for Poetry* (1583) that "Poesy . . . is an art of imitation, for so Aristotle termeth it in the word mimesis—that is to say, a representing, counterfeiting, or figuring forth—to speak metaphorically, a speaking picture." Poetry is not reality itself, Sidney suggests, but a representation modeled closely on reality.

We tend to think of imitation as something static, a frozen copy, but George Whalley usefully defines *mimesis* as "the continuous dynamic relation between a work of art and whatever stands over against it in the actual moral universe, or could conceivably stand over against it." Mimesis—the act of responding to the outside world—is actually a dynamic process, a convention with its own evolving aesthetic properties. It responds to reality by redefining it and challenges received notions of what is real.

SEE ALSO *Chicago school, imitation, verisimilitude.*

minnesinger The minnesingers (*minnesänger*) were German lyric poets and singers of the twelfth and thirteenth centuries. They were mostly knights of the lower nobility who carried on the tradition of the Provençal troubadours and sang of courtly love, hence the German name *minneseinger,* which derives from the word *Minne,* or love. The term *Minnesang* first referred to courtly love poems, which were indeed sung in open court, but later expanded to include the entire corpus of *Sprüche* (political, social, and religious songs).

The oldest songs consisted of a strophe with three movements. The tripartite structure developed naturally into a poem with three stanzas. The first two formally identical sections or "doorposts," which were called *Stollen* individually and *Aufgesang* collectively, stated and developed the argument. The third section, called *Abgesang,* concluded it. The terms derive from the later *meistersingers* (mastersingers), the musical guilds that carried on the minnesinger tradition from the fourteenth to the seventeenth century.

Some of the well-known minnesingers: Dietmar von Aist, Friedrich von Hausen, Heinrich von Morungen (the subject of the fifteenth-century ballad "The Noble Moringer"), Reinmar (the "scholastic philosopher of unhappy love"), Walther von der Vogelweide (the greatest German lyric poet of the Middle Ages), and Tannhaüser, the legendary figure at the center of Wagner's opera *Tannhaüser and the Singers' Contest at Wartburg* (1845).

SEE ALSO *meistersinger, troubadour.*

minstrel A musician or poet. The professional entertainers of the Middle Ages were generically termed *minstrels.* The Middle English *minestral* ultimately derived from the Latin *minister* ("servant") and especially referred to a singer of verses accompanied on the harp. The minstrel was a man who lived by song. The troubadours were the poet-musicians of Provence or the South of France, the trouvères were the poet-musicians of Northern France, and the minnesingers were the poet-musicians of Germany. Minstrels also were a class of acrobat-musicians who were called jongleurs in France, *Gauklers* in Germany, and gleemen in Britain.

From the eleventh to the fourteenth century, minstrels tramped across Europe, alone or in company, carrying musical instruments on their backs and providing entertainment to welcoming local audiences. There were different grades of minstrels. At the top of the profession and the hierarchy, there were accomplished poet/musicians permanently attached to royal or noble households. Next on the rung were itinerant bands of players who had a repertory of short dramas, songs, and debates, such as the *dit* and *fabliaux* of France. On the lowest rung, there were the anonymous jugglers, rope-walkers, acrobats, conjurors, animal trainers, and others. These performers were the forerunners of the circus and the music hall.

The minstrel became a romantic emblem and symbolic term for the itinerant poet endangered by changing times, as in Sir Walter Scott's *The Lay of the Last Minstrel* (1805), which he wrote after reading the metrical romances of the Middle Ages, and John Clare's *The Village Minstrel, and Other Poems* (1821). Today the word *minstrel* is a generic term for all types of popular entertainers.

SEE ALSO *dit, fabliau, gleeman, jongleur, minnesinger, troubadour, trouvère.*

mise-en-page A French term meaning "put-on-the-page." There is always a visual dimension to written poetry, to the design of a manuscript or printed page, and the actual layout of a poem is an integral part of our experience of it. It is something we see as well as read. The use of lowercase and capital letters, of bold type or italics, makes a difference, and so does the utilization or absence of punctuation, the spacing and length of lines, the use of an epigraph, and other visual devices. The spatial dimension is most aggressively employed and foregrounded in the concrete or patterned poem.

SEE ALSO *concrete poetry, emblem, pattern poetry.*

the Misty poets, also known as ***the Obscures*** For ten years, from the Beijing Spring in 1979 to the student protests in 1989, a new generation of Chinese poets challenged the strictures of social realism and rebelled against the ideology of the Cultural Revolution. They were subjective poets with a gift for deep, hermetic images and metaphors. The new poets were denounced by an older generation for the "gloomy obscurity" of their work, and thus a name was born, though later, as with the metaphysical poets, the insult turned into an honorific. Four of the main poets — Bei Dao, Gu Cheng, Duo Duo, and Yang Lian — were exiled after the Tiananmen Square massacre. This two-line poem by Gu Cheng is summary:

A Generation

a black night gave me black eyes
still I use them to see the light
(tr., Aaron Crippen)

SEE ALSO *deep image, obscurity.*

mock epic, mock heroic A fake epic, a satiric poem that takes the low and trivial and elevates it to absurd heights. The mock epic ludicrously imitates the tone, content, and/or formal requirements of heroic narratives. The anonymous burlesque of Homer, the *Batrachomyomachia* (*War between the Mice and the Frogs,* first century B.C.E.), is possibly the earliest manifestation of a parody epic. "This is an *image of the Homeric style,*" M. M. Bakhtin writes. "It is precisely style that is the true hero of the work." This is also true of the seven books of Paul Scarron's *Virgil travesti* (1638–1653). The mock epic especially flourished in the late seventeenth and early eighteenth centuries when it was often used to observe how far the contemporary world had fallen from the classical age. For example, Alexander Pope's *Rape of the Lock* (1712–1714) treats the theft of a lock of hair as if it were comparable to the events that sparked the Trojan War.

The term *mock epic* is sometimes used in a modern context to suggest a long poem that is not a full-fledged or classical epic, such as Ezra Pound's *Cantos* (1915–1969) or Ted Hughes's *Crow* (1970). These serious and self-conscious poems imply that a fragmented or parody epic is more suitable for the modern age.

SEE ALSO *burlesque, epic, parody, satire.*

modernism The modernism that we still recognize, the modernism that is ours, originated in the middle of the nineteenth century as a movement against conventional taste. It was fresh, convulsive, and transgressive. But the idea of the modern as a break with the past, as something forward-looking, has a much longer history and goes back to medieval times. Christianity's eschatological understanding of history raises the inevitable question of linear progress, of changing times, the either-or of *modernus* versus *antiquus.* For much of the last millennium, the idea of the modern was an entirely negative one. It was associated with the degradation of past achievements. In Shakespeare (1564–1616), for example, the modern is used to connote what is common. During the Enlightenment, however, modernism began to take on more positive connotations. The emphasis on the capacity of human reason as well as the renewed belief in the possibility of human progress made the future seem like a promising alternative to antiquity.

Charles Baudelaire (1821–1867) is the first hero of modernism and a key figure in the transformation of modernity as a concept, which he vaunted as "the ephemeral, the fugitive, the contingent, the half of art whose other half is the eternal and the immutable." Baudelaire inaugurated our modernity by emphasizing what is current ("Every old master has had his own modernity"), what is immediate and fresh, unadorned and uninhibited by the shackles of the past. Arthur Rimbaud turned the Baudelairean premise into an injunction in *A Season in Hell* (1873) with his anarchic motto: "One must be absolutely modern."

Matei Calinescu identifies a radical division that takes place within modernity. At some point in the first half of the nineteenth century, he argues, a split occurred between "modernity as a stage in the history of Western civilization — a product of scientific and technological progress, of the industrial revolution . . . and modernity as an aesthetic concept." On the one side, you have the "bourgeois idea of modernity . . . the doctrine of progress, the confidence in the beneficial possibilities of science and technology." On the other side, you have an alternative anti-bourgeois modernity, "the one that was to bring into being the avant-gardes." Since then the relations between the two modernities have been irreducibly hostile.

Some of the major cultural precursors to modernism as a literature of crisis: Friedrich Nietzsche (1844–1900), Karl Marx (1818–1883), Sigmund Freud (1856–1939), and James Frazer (1854–1941), who linked Christian tenets to pagan myths and rituals in the *Golden Bough* (1890–1915). Albert Einstein (1879–1955) transformed our perception of the universe. Some date modernism to 1890, some to the pivotal years around the turn of the century, some to 1910. The period of high modernism is generally thought of as 1910–1930. The fifty-two slaughterous months of World War I called all values and certainties into question. "All my beautiful safe world blew up," F. Scott Fitzgerald said. In the 1920s, the term *modernism* underwent a sea change — it moved from a general sense of sympathy with modern things to a more particular association with experimentation in the arts. The rallying cry was Ezra Pound's jaunty slogan, "Make it New!"

Modernism in poetry is a laceration within language. One of the recurring strategies of modern poetry (from Arthur Rimbaud to Dino Campana) is to break up traditional ways of making meaning, to use asyntactical, nonlinear language to create new semantic relationships. The American modernist poets also begin with a sense of what Pound called "a botched civilization" ("Hugh Selwyn Mauberley," 1920). T. S. Eliot's "The Waste Land" (1922) — with its sense of the unreal city and the walking dead, hysterical voices and fragmented experiences — was unquestionably the central summary text of generational despair over the decline of the West. The technique was collagist.

I detect at least three evolving traditions within American modernism. Eliot and Pound created an American version of continental modernism. They treated American poetry as an offshoot of European literature. William Carlos Williams (1883–1963), e. e. cummings (1894–1962), and Marianne Moore (1887–1972) wrote in what Moore called "plain American which cats and dogs can read." They created and defined a modernist poetry of the New World, a local, homemade American poetic. Robert Frost (1874–1963) shared with them a taste for the vernacular but favored blank verse, like Wallace Stevens (1879–1955) and Hart Crane (1899–1932), who created a form of modern American romanticism that is continuous with English romanticism. They joined what Crane called "the visionary company" ("The Broken Tower," 1932).

SEE ALSO *collage, Dadaism, Enlightenment, futurism, modernismo, romanticism, Surrealism, symbolism.*

modernismo The Nicaraguan poet Rubén Darío (1867–1916) coined the term *modernismo* for Hispanic modernism. He fused Continental symbolism with Latin American themes and subjects, affecting a fresh musical synthesis in Spanish-language poetry. Darío believed in the urgent need for change, in freedom, passion, and the deep renewal of beauty. "He was the beginning," Octavio Paz declared. The movement began in Latin America in the late 1800s and spread to Spain early in the twentieth century. The Cuban poet José Martí was the great forerunner of Darío, who in turn modernized the language and created an important link between two hemispheres. In 1933, García Lorca and Pablo Neruda gave a talk together in Buenos Aires. The two poets — one from the Vega of Granada, the other from a frontier town in rural Southern Chile — used a bullfighting tradition to improvise a speech about Darío and *modernismo,* which they delivered alternately from different sides of the table at the Buenos Aires PEN club. "Ladies . . . ," Neruda began, " . . . and gentlemen," Lorca continued: "In bullfighting there is what is known as 'bullfighting *al alimon,*' in which two toreros, holding one cape between them, outwit the bull together." Darío was a poet both of Spain and of the Americas, the Old and the New World, and Lorca and Neruda, two toreros, were linking themselves through him.

Modernismo burst into Brazil during a raucous three-day series of public events called Modern Art Week in São Paulo in February 1922. The instigators were the multifaceted national cultural leader Mário de Andrade (1893–1945), the polemicist Oswald de Andrade (1890–1954) — his two key manifestoes are "Poesia Pau-Brasil" (Brasil-wood poetry, 1928) and "O manifesto antropófago" (The Cannibalist Manifesto, 1928) — and Manuel Bandeira (1886–1968), nicknamed the "Saint John the Baptist" of *modernismo.* They rejected *passadísmo* (past-ism), advocated for free verse, dreamed of formal liberty, and insisted that Brazilian poetry should be rooted in the search for Brazilian identity.

SEE ALSO *Hallucinism, modernism, Parnassians, symbolism.*

molossus, see *foot.*

Monk's Tale stanza Geoffrey Chaucer employed this stanza in "An A.B.C." (ca. 1370) and in "The Monk's Tale" (*The Canterbury Tales,* ca. 1387–1400), hence its name. It consists of eight iambic pentameter lines that rhyme *ababbcbc.* It looks backward to the French ballade and forward to the Spenserian stanza, which keeps the pattern and adds an alexandrine, a conclusive ninth line. The first letter in his acrostic "A.B.C" sets the pattern:

> ALMIGHTY and al merciable quene,
> To whom that al this world fleeth for socour,
> To have relees of sinne, sorwe and tene [affliction],
> Glorious virgine, of alle floures flour,
> To thee I flee, confounded in errour!
> Help and releve, thou mighty debonaire,
> Have mercy on my perilus languor!
> Venquisshed m'hath my cruel adversaire.

SEE ALSO *ballade, de casibus, huitain, iambic pentameter, octave, Spenserian stanza.*

monody, see *elegy.*

monologue A monologue presents a single person speaking alone—either with an audience, as in a play, or without an audience, as in a prayer or a lament. It is a solo voice. "But a monologue is not the same as talking to oneself," Paul Goodman warns in *Speaking and Language* (1972): "it is more like a daydream." It is the sort of daydream ultimately intended to be overheard.

SEE ALSO *dramatic monologue.*

monometer, see "accentual syllabic meter" in *meter.*

mono no aware Japanese aesthetics refers to *mono no aware,* or "the pathos of things," which derives from their transience. The pathos or "sadness of things" is generally triggered by the plaintive call of birds or other animals in the oldest and greatest anthology of Japanese poetry, the *Man'yōshū* (Collection of Ten Thousand Leaves), which was compiled in the eighth century. *Mono no aware* shows a deep sensitivity to the evanescence of things in time, of life's fragility and therefore its beauty.

SEE ALSO *haiku, pathos, tanka, waka.*

monorhyme, see *rhyme.*

monostich A one-line poem. An example is the Japanese haiku, which is written in a single vertical line. As the *Greek Anthology* (tenth century) illustrates, the monostich can be a proverb, an aphorism, an enigma, a fragment, an image, or an inscription. It is so short that it often has the feeling of a cryptic piece of wisdom literature. A. R. Ammons (1926–2001) wrote monostiches in which the title is so integral to the poem that it becomes a kind of couplet. The contemporary Australian poet Ian McBryde's book *Slivers* (2005) consists entirely of one-line poems. The Scottish poet and artist Ian Hamilton Finlay (1925–2006) reduced the monostich to one-word poems, some of which he painted on tortoise shells or floated on wooden circles in ponds. An exhibit of his neon works was entitled "The Sonnet Is a Sewing-Machine for the Monostich."

A monostich can also be a single or independent line of verse. It is a line that stands alone, as in the first verse of Psalm 23: "The Lord is my shepherd; I shall not want."

SEE ALSO *fragment, image, line, mote, proverb, stanza, stich, tanka, wisdom literature.*

mosaic rhyme, see *rhyme.*

mote The Spanish *mote* is either a monostich (a single line) or a couplet (two lines) that contains a complete thought. It functions as a verse epigram. It is akin to the English motto and has an aphoristic or sententious quality, like the proverb. It often establishes a primary *texte,* which the poet then glosses in verse.

SEE ALSO *couplet, epigram, glose, monostich, proverb.*

mourning songs, see *dirge, elegy, keening.*

the Movement In 1954, J. D. Scott coined the term *the Movement* for a group of English writers that included Philip Larkin, Kingsley Amis, Donald Davie, D. J. Enright, John Wain, Elizabeth Jennings, and Thom Gunn. This skeptical, ironic, antimodernist movement of the 1950s with an unprepossessing name looked back to Thomas Hardy (1840–1928) rather than to W. B. Yeats (1865–1939). The conversion from Yeats to Hardy was a rejection of extreme romanticism, of grand rhetorical gestures, especially the rhapsodic style of Dylan Thomas (1914–1953). Hardy's work gave the Movement confidence in an empirical, antiheroic, anti-transcendental poetic. The poets adhered to traditional forms, celebrated the English countryside, and took a common-sensical approach to daily life. Larkin believed that "the impulse to preserve lies at the bottom of any art" and sought to preserve the memory of a fading England, which was shadowed by grim encroaching modern realities.

SEE ALSO *Georgian poets.*

Mozarabic lyric, see *muwashshah.*

mukàndà, leetrè A relatively recent form of oral heroic Luba-Kasayi poetry. The Luba live in the forests and savannas of the southern Congo. The name *leetrè* or *mukànda* means "letter." The performer is called *nubadi/mwedí wa mukàndà,* or "reader, promoter of mukàndà." And yet as Maalu-Bungi writes, "this literary form is declaimed rather than read, before a participating public, by a male performer, at events that have their origin in the contact of the Luba/Kasayi with the West, especially First Communion, Ordination, graduation, and Holy Matrimony. During the performance, the poet holds a blank sheet of paper that he occasionally looks at in order to simulate a reading." Here oral poetry borrows the status of writing while retaining its spoken character.

SEE ALSO *oral poetry.*

multiple rhyme, polysyllabic rhyme, see *rhyme.*

multum in parvo The Latin term, which means "much in little," summarizes the capacity of a literary work, especially a poem, to express a large theme in a small space.

mundanza, see *zéjel.*

muse, Muses A source of poetic inspiration. Each of the nine Greek goddesses, daughters of Zeus and Mnemosyne (or Memory), traditionally presided over an activity or art: Calliope (epic poetry), Clio (history), Erato (love poetry), Euterpe (lyric poetry), Melpomene (tragedy), Polyhymnia (songs of praise to the gods), Terpsichore (dancing), Thalia (comedy), Urania (astronomy, i.e., cosmological poetry). As Homer calls out in the *Iliad* (ca. eighth century B.C.E.):

> Sing to me now, you Muses who hold the halls of Olympus!
> You are goddesses, you are everywhere, you know all things —
> all we hear is the distant ring of glory, we know nothing —

Homer also alludes to the myth of Thamyris, the Thracian singer, who boasted he could outsing even the Muses. He competed with them, lost, and was punished with the loss of his ability to sing (2, 594–600). Other sources specify that he was also blinded. The Muse gives poetic inspiration and can also take it away.

Hesiod's *Theogony* (ca. 700 B.C.E.) opens with a hymn to the Muses who, while he was keeping his sheep on Helicon, gave him a staff of bay, inspired him to sing ("and they breathed divine song into me"), and then commanded him to sing "of the race of immortals, blessed Gods." The invocation to the Muse ("Sing, goddess . . .") acknowledges the need for an inspiring spirit. "Prophesy (*manteueo*), Muse," Pindar sings, "and I will be your interpreter (*prophateusō*)" (fragment 150, early fifth century B.C.E.). Poetry is never entirely at the dispensation of the poet's conscious will or intellect, and whoever calls out "Help me, O Heavenly Muse" advertises a dependence on a force beyond the intellective powers. Hence this invocation of the chorus at the beginning of Shakespeare's *Henry V* (1600):

> O! for a Muse of fire, that would ascend
> The brightest heaven of invention . . .

The sacred muse (the phrase is Spenser's) is the spirit of creativity, and thus inspires reverence or awe. Such a beloved has uncanny powers. Wallace Stevens invokes her in an essay as "*Inexplicable sister of the Minotaur, enigma and mask*" ("The Figure of the Youth as Virile Poet," 1944), Robert Graves exalted her as the resplendent White Goddess. Louis MacNeice remembers that "the Muse will never / Conform to type" ("Autumn Sequel," 1954). In

"Envoi" (1983), Eavan Boland calls on the muse to do something different than the mythical muse invented by male poets. She seeks a muse who will "bless the ordinary" and "sanctify the common."

SEE ALSO *inspiration, invocation.*

mushaira The Urdu term for a poetic symposium, a collective recitation of poetry. The *mushaira* emphasizes performance and invites the critical participation of the audience. In the golden era of the Moghuls, it was a gathering at the house of a noble to enable poets to recite their work. It typically brought together professional and amateur poets. It is still a beloved part of Pakistani and North Indian culture.

SEE ALSO *ghazal.*

muwashshah An Andalusian Arabic strophic poem that regularly alternates sections with separate rhymes and others with common rhymes (e.g., *aa bbaa ccaa,* etc.). The form thus weaves together two rhyme schemes (and sometimes two complex metrical patterns as well). The *muwashshah* first appeared in Arabic in Muslim Spain during the ninth century. It was apparently a formal inheritance from romance folk poetry. Possibly used for choral recitals, it is closely related to the Arabic form *zéjel.* Whereas the *zéjel* is written in vernacular Spanish, the *muwashshah* is composed in classical Arabic, though it typically closes with an envoi or closing couplet in Arabic or Spanish vernacular (*kharja*), the Mozarab dialect, which is why it is sometimes known as the *Mozarabic lyric.* The word *kharja* means "exit," and the closing couplet was often drawn from folk tradition and spoken by a young woman or a part of nature that has been feminized, like a bird or the wind. Both the *zéjel* and the *muwashshah* are closely associated with music. The poems were sensuous celebrations of love and drink. These types of poems reached their peak between the eleventh and thirteenth centuries in al-Andalus (Muslim Spain) as well as in various other parts of the Arabic-speaking world. The city of Aleppo in northern Syria still has a strong tradition of singers who specialize in the Andalusian *muwashshah.*

The Jewish poets of Andalusia enthusiastically adopted the *muwashshah* in the fourteenth century. There are, for example, fifteen extant secular *muwashshahāt* by Moses ibn Ezra (ca. 1055–1138), sixteen by Joseph ibn Saddiq (d. 1149), and forty-three by Judah ha-Levi (ca. 1075–1141). The term *muwashshah* is often translated as "girdle poems." The Arabic verb *washshaha* means "to dress or adorn," and the noun *wushshaah* is "an ornamented sash or belt — in older times a doubled band with embedded gems worn sash-like over the shoulder." Peter Cole points out that it is useful to think of the *muwashshah* "as a poem in which the rhyming chorus winds about the various strophes of the poem as a gem-studded sash cuts across the body."

The secular *muwashshah* was considered a "non-classical" form in Arabic tradition, but it was soon adapted and favored for the liturgical Hebrew poems called *piyyut.* Some of the most moving medieval liturgical lyrics were written as belted poems.

SEE ALSO *piyyut, zéjel.*

Myōjō Poets, see *tanka.*

mythical method T. S. Eliot invented the phrase *mythical method* to refer to the way that a modern writer, such as James Joyce, employs a myth in a contemporary work, "manipulating a continuous parallel between contemporaneity and antiquity." In his essay on Joyce's *Ulysses,* "Ulysses, Order, and Myth" (1923), Eliot defined the mythical method as "a way of controlling, of ordering, of giving a shape and a significance to the immense panorama of futility and anarchy which is contemporary history." It is telling that Eliot saw his own experience as well as contemporary history as a vast chaos and anarchy. He thus sought a way to shape, order, and tame that chaos. "The Waste Land" (1922) was his own enactment of the mythical method.

naïve and sentimental German: *naive und sentimentalische.* Friedrich Schiller's treatise, *Über naïve und sentimentalische Dichtung* (*On Naïve and Sentimental Poetry,* 1795–1796), distinguishes between two different kinds of poets: one (naïve) is ancient and spontaneous, the other (sentimental), modern and reflective. According to Schiller, the naïve writer, represented by, say, Homer (eighth century B.C.E.), feels part of the natural order (he *is* nature), whereas the sentimental writer, represented by, say, Horace (65–8 B.C.E.), feels banished from it (he *seeks* nature). Naïve poetry is simple, sensuous, and unselfconscious (i.e., unified and whole), whereas sentimental poetry is complex, contemplative, and highly self-conscious (i.e., self-estranged and alienated). Modern poetry is either satirical or elegiac ("every sentimental poet will adhere to one of these two modes of feeling"). Schiller was ambivalent about sentimental poetry. He considered the quest for a lost idyllic world "a beautiful, elevating fiction," but worried that it could be debilitated by nostalgia.

SEE ALSO *pastoral.*

naked poetry *Naked poetry* is a term for the radical modern impulse to strip poetry down to its bare essentials. Lafcadio Hearn coined the phrase *naked poetry* for one of his general lectures at the Imperial University in Tokyo (1896–1903). He said:

> I want to make a little discourse about what we might call Naked Poetry . . . that is, poetry without any dress, without any ornament, the very essence or body of poetry unveiled by artifice of any kind.

The sparseness and classical restraint of Japanese poetry helped lead Hearn to the concept.

The Spanish poet Juan Ramón Jiménez also invented the term *poesía desnuda* (naked poetry) in *Eternidades* (1916–1917). In his poem "At first she came to me pure" he remembers how poetry first came to him in his youth as a naked young girl "dressed only in her innocence," and he loved her. Gradually she dressed up and put on more ornaments and he started to hate her without knowing why. Years later she sheds her clothes and returns as a young girl again: "Naked poetry, always mine, / that I have loved my whole life!"

The impulse to a pure and exposed poetry has had many modern articulations. Charles Baudelaire took the title *My Heart Laid Bare* (1887) for his intimate journals, which were never completed, from Edgar Allan Poe, who said that if any man dared to write such a book with complete frankness it would be a masterpiece. "But to write it — *there* is the rub," Poe said: "No man dare write it. No man ever will dare write it. No man *could* write it, even if he dared. The paper would shrivel and blaze at every touch of the fiery pen" (1848).

W. B. Yeats's 1914 poem "A Coat" personifies his "song" as a coat embroidered with old mythologies, which he then sheds: "For there's more enterprise / In walking naked." In 1921, the Yiddish poet Peretz Ravitch published a collection entitled *Nakete Lider* (*Naked Songs*). The Greek poet Pantelis Prevalakis borrowed Jiménez's phrase and called his second and third books *The Naked Poetry* (1939) and *The Most Naked Poetry* (1941). He wanted a verse free of artifice, sincere and unguarded, bare. Jiménez's naked poetry, which was translated by Robert Bly, had a strong influence on American poets of the 1960s and '70s. In 1969, Stephen Berg and Robert Mezey borrowed Jiménez's phrase for their anthology, *Naked Poetry,* which they followed seven years later with *The New Naked Poetry.* These anthologies of free-verse poetry in open forms reflect their conviction that "the strongest and most alive poetry in America has abandoned or at least broken the grip of traditional meters and had set out, once again, into 'the wilderness of unopened life.' " They suggest that poems "take shape from the shapes of their emotions."

SEE ALSO *free verse, projective verse.*

narodne pesme, see *epic* and *ženske pesme.*

narrative poetry A narrative poem tells a story. It is a poem with a plot and employs many of the devices of prose fiction, such as character and setting. Narrative poems may be short, as in ballads, or long, as in epics, which are the two basic early types of narrative poetry. Both ballads and epics originated in prehistory as forms of oral poetry. They were sung aloud, created — and re-created — by individuals performing with a participating audience. Ballads may originally have been danced and sung by a group of people participating in a ritual action. The epic singer was a singer of tales, a magician who narrated the story of gods and heroes. The vestiges of magical thinking still cling to both ballads and epics. Heroic poetry — the story of heroes rather than gods — secularized the epic by making it the story of a mortal hero. One thinks of the *Epic of Gilgamesh* (ca. 1600–1000 B.C.E.), of the *Iliad* and the *Odyssey* (ca. eighth century B.C.E.), of *La Chanson de Roland* (*Song of Roland,* ca. 1090) and *Beowulf* (ca. eighth to eleventh century).

The first narrative poems were recorded around 2000 B.C.E. in Sumer, Egypt, and generally in the Middle and Near East. This epoch yielded the Creation epic and the *Epic of Gilgamesh,* which were most fully preserved in Akkadian texts. The second major period of narrative poems was the era from around 1000–400 B.C.E. in Babylon, Greece, and Palestine. This gave us parts of the Hebrew Bible, the Homeric poems, the Cyclic epics, and the works of Hesiod. Pindar's choral odes (fifth century B.C.E.) are the first written narrative poems. Callimachus's *Aetia* (*Causes,* ca. 270 B.C.E.), which is a series of narrative poems about the origins of legends and customs, is the precursor to Ovid's *Metamorphoses* (8 C.E.). Virgil's *Aeneid* (29–19 B.C.E.), which narrates the founding of Rome, is a lasting monument from the Augustan period. The Icelandic and early Irish sagas tell gripping stories about legendary heroes. French literature began in the eleventh century with religious narrative poems, such as the "Song of St. Alexis" (ca. 1050). *The Vision of Piers Plowman* (ca. 1360–1387) is an allegorical narrative that stands near the top of English poetry. Chaucer's *Canterbury Tales* (ca. 1387–1400) turned narrative into a central strategy of English poetry.

Each era of English poetry has had its major narratives. To cite a few key examples: think of John Lydgate's *The Fall of Princes* (ca. 1431–1438), a nine-book adaptation of Boccaccio's *De casibus virorum illustrium* (1355–1360), and Spenser's allegorical *The Faerie Queene* (1590–1596), of Michel Drayton's *England's Heroical Epistles* (1597), of the broadsides of *Robin Hood* and *Chevy Chase,* which circulated in England in the sixteenth century, of Christopher Marlowe's *Hero and Leander* (1593), which George Chapman completed (1598), of Milton's *Paradise Lost* (1667), of John Dryden's imitations of Ovid, Virgil, Chaucer, and Boccaccio, and Alexander Pope's translations of Homer, of James Macpherson's Ossian poems (1760, 1761, 1763, 1765) and Thomas Percy's *Reliques of Ancient English Poetry* (1765), which created the vogue for songs and poems of common people, of Byron's satirical narrative *Beppo: A Venetian Story* (1818) and Keats's "The Eve of Saint Agnes" and "Lamia" (1819), of Tennyson's *Idylls of the King* (1856–1885) and William Morris's *The Earthly Paradise* (1868–1870), of Rudyard Kipling's ballads and John Masefield's *The Everlasting Mercy* (1911).

"The secret subject, or subtext, of narrative is time," Stanley Plumly writes: "the subtext of time is mortality, mutability; the subtext of mortality is emotion. Loss is our parent, poetry a parental form." There are a wide variety of lyric poems that take on narrative values, taking time as their underlying subject. They primarily focus on the feelings of a character, but they also tell a foreshortened story, or at least imply one. They have an inferred or compacted plot, which is often signaled by a change in tenses, a suggestion of movement over time. Thus Wordsworth and Coleridge famously named some of their short poems *Lyrical Ballads* (1798). These include Wordsworth's "Goody Blake and Harry Gill: A True Story" and Coleridge's "The Rime of the Ancient Mariner." Rather than lyricizing narrative, the verse novel, a legacy of the nineteenth century, narrativizes verse. It is a novel-length narrative told through poetry. Alexander Pushkin's *Eugene Onegin* (1833) is the classic case of a great poem conscious of the novel as a form.

Narrative poetry was sidelined in the modernist era. Poets employed collage, and they fractured continuous narratives. Imagism, for example, sought to purge modern poetry of narrative altogether. But such poets as Edwin Arlington Robinson, Robert Frost, and Robinson Jeffers continued to write narrative poems of a high order in the early part of the twentieth century. In the 1980s, Mark Jarman and Robert McDowell founded the magazine *The Reaper* (1980–1989) to make a place for narrative poems in contemporary American poetry. They polemically focused on poems that "tell stories *which their imagery serves.*" This helped to launch a return to narrative for a subsection of contemporary poets.

SEE ALSO *ballad, epic, imagism, mock epic, oral poetry, saga, verse novel.*

naturalism Naturalism in literature generally refers to a detailed realism, a literature that anatomizes social conditions and emphasizes the environment as an inescapable force in determining human character. It is almost entirely a fictional and dramatic mode of realism, though the French novelist Émile Zola, the high priest of scientific naturalism or *naturalisme* — "I have simply done on living bodies the work of analysis which surgeons perform on corpses," he said — did try to formulate a naturalistic theory of poetry in his essay *"Les Poètes Contemporains"* (1878). He called for a realistic or "scientific" poetry to express the new age. French poets did not answer the call, but naturalism did take root and become a specific movement, *Naturalismus,* in late nineteenth-century German poetry. The movement included such figures as the brothers Heinrich Hart and Julius Hart; Karl Bleibtreu, who called for a "Neue Poesie"; Bruno Wille; Karl Henckell; and Arno Holz, the leading theorist of the naturalist movement, who laid out the formula "art=nature – x" or art equals nature minus the artist's subjectivity. They were supplanted by the symbolist mode.

Not all critics have used the term *naturalism* as a mode of social realism. The Scandinavian critic Georg Brandes (*Naturalism in Nineteenth-Century English Literature,* 1875) and the Reverend Stopford A. Brooke (*Naturalism in English Poetry,* 1920) used the term to refer to the way that the romantic poets, as Brooke put it, "went back, in order to draw new life into poetry, to simple human nature, and to Nature herself as seen in her wild and uncultivated beauty." What they called "the rise of Naturalism" is what most critics simply call romanticism.

SEE ALSO *Jugendstil, romanticism, symbolism.*

nature poetry, nature in poetry The natural world has been one of the recurring subjects of poetry, frequently the primary one, in every age and every country. Yet we cannot easily define nature, which, as Gary Snyder points out in his preface to *No Nature* (1992), "will not fulfill our conceptions or assumptions" and "will dodge our expectations and theoretical models." Yet the urge to describe the natural world — its various landscapes, its changing seasons, its surrounding phenomena — has been an inescapable part of the history of poetry. Wendell Berry provides a simple useful definition of nature poetry as poetry that "considers nature as subject matter and inspiration."

Our concepts of nature are relative, historically determined. The nature poem is affected by ideology, by literary conventions as well as social and cultural ideas. Raymond Williams contends, "*Nature* is perhaps the most complex word in the language." The term *nature* is itself contested now because it seems to assume an oversimplified relationship between the human and the environment. "Nature" has been the site of so many different naïve symbolisms, such as purity, escape, and savagery. That's why poets and critics often refer to green poetry or environmental poetry, which presupposes a complicated interconnection between nature and humankind.

The idea that the seasons structure the actual rhythms or symbolic passages of life goes back to antiquity. The Canaanite mythical *Poem of Aqhat* (fifteenth century B.C.E.) rotates around seasonal change. Hesiod's *Works and Days* (eighth century B.C.E.) takes special interest in agricultural practices. There is a long tradition of the pastoral, stemming from Theocritus's idylls (third century B.C.E.), which honor the simplicities of rural life and create such memorable figures as Lycidas, the archetypal poet-shepherd who inspired John Milton's pastoral elegy "Lycidas" (1638). Virgil's *Eclogues* (37–30 B.C.E.) define the tradition by characterizing the peaceful serenity of shepherds living in idealized natural settings. The Chinese *Book of Songs* (tenth to fifth century B.C.E.) is rife with seasonal poetry and so is the Japanese haiku, which began as a short associative meditation on the natural world. Think of the Old English "Seafarer" and the Middle English "Cuckoo's Song" ("Sumer is icumen in / Lhude sing, cuccu!"), of the passage of seasons in *Sir Gawain and the Green Knight* (fourteenth century). In the Renaissance, urbane poets apprenticed themselves to poetry by writing pastoral soliloquies or dialogues, which construct and imagine rural life. The tradition is exemplified by Sir Philip Sidney's *Arcadia* (1580) and Edmund Spenser's *The Shepheardes Calender* (1579), which uses the months of the year to trace the changes in a shepherd's life. Rural poetry flourished in seventeenth-century retirement and garden poems, in landscape poems that delivered formal and structured descriptions of topography, such as John Denham's "Cooper's Hill" (1642).

James Thomson, the first important eighteenth-century nature poet, infused his lovingly detailed descriptions in *The Seasons* (1730) with his age's sense of God's sustaining presence in nature. As he writes in "Spring": "Chief, lovely spring, in thee, and thy soft scenes / The SMILING GOD is seen; while water, earth / And air attest his bounty." Alexander Pope leads his "Essay on Criticism" (1711) with the rule, "First follow Nature." For him, "following nature" means honoring classical precedent: "Learn hence for Ancient *Rules* a just Esteem; To copy *Nature* is to copy *Them.*" Pope describes these rules as "*Nature Methodiz'd.*" Writing at a time when English society was being transformed from an agricultural society to an industrial one, the romantic poets treated nature in a groundbreaking way, dwelling in its localities, praising its nurturing powers, spiritualizing it. Think of these summary lines from William Wordsworth's defining nature poem, "Tintern Abbey" (1798):

Therefore am I still
A lover of the meadows and the woods,
And mountains; and of all that we behold
From this green earth; of all the mighty world
Of eye and ear, — both what they half-create,
And what perceive; well pleased to recognize
In nature and the language of the sense,
The anchor of my purest thoughts, the nurse,
The guide, the guardian of my heart, and soul
Of all my moral being.

John Clare was inspired by Thomson's *The Seasons* to become a poet with a rural muse, and his more than thirty-five hundred poems seek out the secret recesses of nature, a hidden, underappreciated, overlooked country, which he detailed with a sharp eye and a naturalist's sensibility. "Poets love nature and themselves are love," he wrote in a late sonnet. His poetry intimately chronicles a world that was rapidly disappearing, systematically divided up into rectangular plots of land, fenced off and restricted, enclosed. There is an ethic of reciprocity that he brought to his encounters with the natural world. Indeed, each of the English romantics had a particular view of that world, a singular way of describing it — they were sometimes solaced, sometimes frightened by its alienating majesty and inhuman force — and yet romantic poetry as a whole inaugurated a new ecological consciousness, a fresh way of treating human beings and nature as interdependent.

Henry David Thoreau is the guiding spirit of American nature writing in general and American nature poetry in particular. "Shall I not have intelligence with the earth? Am I not partly leaves and vegetable mould myself?"

he asks in *Walden* (1854). Ralph Waldo Emerson's *Nature* (1836) is foundational, but *Walden* is a forerunner and a reference point for green writing and reading, green thinking. It would take a volume in itself to track the ways that American poets have envisioned the environment — in *Democratic Vistas* (1871) Walt Whitman calls nature "the only complete, actual poem" — but I would pause over Emily Dickinson's garden poems and Whitman's luminous meditation "Out of the Cradle Endlessly Rocking" (1860), over William Cullen Bryant's celebration of the prairie and Robert Frost's terrifying notion of "design," over Robinson Jeffers's California poems that mourn "the broken balance, the hopeless prostration of the earth / Under men's hands and their minds" ("The Broken Balance," 1928) and Theodore Roethke's horticultural reminiscences, over A. R. Ammons's ecological lyrics ("ecology is my word: tag / me with that"), Wendell Berry's agricultural ideals, and Gary Snyder's lifetime of lyrics, which often turn to Native American models for a sense of right relationship with the earth. W. S. Merwin also invokes native peoples for a reaffirmation of our connection to the natural world. I wish I had time to compare North American nature poems, which are so often sympathetic to natural forces, with those of Canadian poets, who often manifest, as Northrop Frye points out, "a tone of deep terror in regard to nature." There is an eco-feminist pastoralism that includes poetry in Susan Griffin's *Women and Nature: The Roaring Inside Her* (1978) and a recent anthology, *Black Nature* (2010), celebrates the overlooked tradition of African American nature poetry over four centuries. We are not yet done imagining the earth and envisioning the natural world.

SEE ALSO *Arcadia, descriptive poetry, eclogue, georgic, idyll, neoclassicism, pastoral, romanticism, shan-shui, topographical poetry.*

nazm An Urdu/Persian term meaning "verse." In Arabic, *nazm* literally means "the ordering of pearls on a string to form a necklace." In Arabic literature, the term is used metaphorically. One meaning suggests style, a means of connecting words like pearls on a string. The other meaning is "metrical speech" or "versification." It is the opposite of prose, *nathr* ("scattering of pearls"). *Nazm* sometimes refers to didactic verse and thus stands as an alternative or even opposite to *shiʿr*, poetry. The Arabic pun *nazama* means both to string pearls and to compose verse.

SEE ALSO *shiʿr.*

near rhyme Near rhyme is a form of close rhyme. The final consonants of stressed syllables agree but the preceding vowel sounds do not match, as when Emily Dickinson rhymes *room* with *firm* and *storm* (number 465, 1862). It is also called approximate, half, imperfect, oblique, partial, or slant rhyme. Dickinson, Yeats, Wilfred Owen, W. H. Auden, and Dylan Thomas were all masters of half rhyme. Some critics use *pararhyme* as a synonym for *near rhyme;* others reserve it for a type of double consonance, near rhymes in which the consonants are identical but the vowels differ, as when Owen rhymes *hall* and *Hell, grained* and *ground,* and *moan* and *mourn* in three consecutive couplets in "Strange Meeting" (1918). Edmund Blunden pointed out that Owen used pararhyme to create a feeling of "remoteness, darkness, emptiness, shock, echo, the last word." Near rhyme, which offers more possibilities in a rhyme-poor language such as English, often feels modern to us, perhaps because of its slight sense of dissonance and dislocation, but, in fact, it was used in medieval Icelandic, Irish, and Welsh verse. It was probably brought into English poetry in the mid-seventeenth century by Henry Vaughan, who was influenced by Welsh models. Slant rhyme offers the pleasures of novelty and imperfection, of affinity and difference, without the sonic closure of full rhyme.

SEE ALSO *rhyme.*

negative capability John Keats coined this term in a letter to his brothers George and Thomas (December 21, 1817). He wrote:

> several things dove tailed in my mind, and at once it struck me what quality went to form a Man of Achievement, especially in Literature, and which Shakespeare possessed so enormously—I mean *Negative Capability,* that is when man is capable of being in uncertainties, Mysteries, doubts, without any irritable reaching after fact and reason.

The displacement of the poet's protean self into another existence was for Keats a key feature of the artistic imagination. He attended William Hazlitt's Lectures on the English Poets (1818) and was spurred further to his own thinking by Hazlitt's groundbreaking idea that Shakespeare was "the least of an egotist that it was possible to be" and "nothing in himself," that he embodied "all that others were, or that they could become," that he "had in himself the germs of every faculty and feeling," and he "had only to think of anything in order to become that thing, with all the circumstances belonging to it." Keats took to heart the ideal of "disinterestedness," of Shakespeare's essential selflessness, his capacity for anonymous shift-shaping. In a letter to Richard Woodhouse (October 27, 1818), he describes the selfless receptivity he considers necessary for the deepest poetry. He exults in the poetic capacity for total immersion, for empathic release, for entering completely into whatever is being described:

> As to the the poetical Character itself . . . it is not iself—it has no self—it is everything and nothing—It has no character—it enjoys light and shade; it lives in gusto, be it foul or fair, high or low, rich or poor, mean or elevated—It has as much delight in conceiving an Iago as an Imogen. What shocks the virtuous Philosopher, delights the chameleon Poet . . . A Poet is the most unpoetical of any thing in existence; because he has no Identity—he is continually in for—and filling some other Body—The Sun, The Moon, The Sea, and Men and Women who are creatures of impulse are poetical and have about them an unchangeable attribute—the poet has none; no identity—he is certainly the most unpoetical of all God's creatures.

SEE ALSO *egotistical sublime.*

Negishi Tanka Society, see *tanka.*

Négritude Living in Paris in the 1930s, the Martiniquan poet Aimé Césaire (1913–2008) began to think seriously about the ways in which black people were caught between a deep attachment to their African heritage and a need to distance themselves from that heritage, largely because they had internalized the values of colonialism and slavery. He coined the term *Négritude* in an article called "Racial Consciousness and Social Revolution" in *L'étudiant noir* (1935) and widened its usage in his long poem "Cahier d'un retour au pays natal" (*Notebook of a Return to the Native Land,* 1939) to describe an ancient heritage that all blacks shared, the world of an entire continent, but also a heritage of dislocation and dispossession, an experience of diaspora. It was a way of resisting assimilation. Césaire later said: "Négritude is the simple recognition of the fact of being black, and the acceptance of this fact, of our destiny as black people, of our history, and our culture."

The Négritude movement sought to reclaim black identity and restore black consciousness, to free itself of European thinking and political institutions. It was first of all a literary and ideological movement of French-speaking black intellectuals, and Césaire was initially joined by the poet Léon-Gontran Damas (1912–1978) from French Guyana and the Senegalese poet Leópold Senghor (1906–2001), who later became the first president of Senegal. Senghor considered Négritude "the upholding of the cultural patrimony, the values and, above all, the spirit of the Negro African civilization" (1959). His essays in *Libertié 1: Négritude et Humanisme* (1964) are a systematic statement of the principles of Négritude. The Négritude poets were inspired by the lyric affirmations of Africanness that they found in the Haitian journal *La Revue Indigène* (1927–1928), which was headed by the poet and anthropologist Jacques Roumain (1907–1944) and the ethnographer Jean-Price Mars (1876–1969), who also founded l'Institut d'Ethnologie in Haiti.

From the 1940s to the 1960s, the idea of Négritude flourished among black students and writers in France, parts of Africa, and the Caribbean. Négritude became the formal expression of black cultural nationalism. Jean-Paul Sartre treated Négritude as a historical phenomenon in his influential essay "Orphée noir" ("Black Orpheus"), which served as the introduction to Senghor's *Anthology of the New Black and Malagasy Poetry* (1948). Sartre praised the new generation of black writers and argued that Négritude was a necessary stage in the process of black liberation. The French-Algerian writer Frantz Fanon (1925–1961) later challenged Sartre's notion that Négritude would someday be transcended, that it carries "the root of its own destruction," and called instead for a radical rethinking of black identity and political action in *Peau noire, masques blancs* (*Black Skin, White Masks,* 1952). The principles of Négritude have been fiercely debated and reevaluated in postcolonial studies. The movement has been attacked for relying on nativism, for its ahistoricism, its confirmation of white stereotypes, its failure to effect social and economic change. Yet Négritude was a crucial position of resistance, a poetic concept of identity that was essential to the redefinition of black poetry in the twentieth century.

SEE ALSO *Harlem renaissance.*

Neo-Aristotelians, see *Chicago school.*

neoclassicism *Neoclassicism* suggests a new or revived classicism. The term summarizes the turn back toward ancient Greek and Latin models for guidance. In English literature, neoclassicism refers to the period from 1660–1785. The era is sometimes divided into three sub-periods: the Restoration Age (1660–1700), which was presided over by John Milton, John Bunyan, and John Dryden; the Augustan Age (1700–1745), in which Alexander Pope was the central figure; and the Age of Johnson, which was stamped by the sensibility of Samuel Johnson. The movement had a precedent in contemporary French models (see Boileau's "L'Art Poetique," 1674) and neoclassicism in France reached its height in the period from 1660–1700. To give an example of French neoclassic doctrine: the critics of drama adhered to the precept of the dramatic unities. They believed a play should be a unified whole, the scene should be confined to a single place, and the action should unfold over a single day.

Neoclassicism is a retrospective label applied by critics. The *Oxford English Dictionary* lists 1877 as the first recorded use of the term. The neoclassical poets believed in returning to first principles, to the work of the ancients, and turned this into one of the great eras of classical translation. They sought a pragmatic reformation in English language and literature. They placed their faith in reason, which is why the period has frequently been designated the age of reason. This faith has always suggested to me a shadowy fear of unreason or the irrational, of madness. Whoever loves wit, balance, and decorum, whoever values artistic symmetry and proportion, whoever favors conscious craftsmanship and bracing intellect, will turn to this fundamentally social poetry with the greatest pleasure. Many poets have flown the neoclassical banner in different countries at different times, such as the Neoclassic Group in the Ukraine in the 1920s and the neoclassicist trend in Sudan in the 1930s. The revival of classical values, the call for a return to prescribed forms and rules of composition, has been part of the ongoing dialogue in poetry between tradition and innovation.

SEE ALSO *Augustan Age, Battle of the Books, classic.*

neogongorism, see *Generation of '27.*

Neoterici Latin: "the new ones." A neoteric is a modern person, someone who accepts new ideas and practices. Cicero gave the name *Neoterici* to the "new poets" of his age who were inspired by the Greek poets of third-century B.C.E. Alexandria, writers who had purposefully turned away from classical Homeric poetry. Callimachus (ca. 305–ca. 240 B.C.E.), the most famous of the Hellenistic poets, set the standard with his epigrams. Catullus (84–54 B.C.E.), who translated some of Calimachus's poems into Latin, is the most famous of the *Neoterici.* The two most important others are Calvus (82–ca. 47 B.C.E.) and Cinna (d. 84 B.C.E.). Most of the work of the *Neoterici* — the Latin poetry from the late second and early first century — survives only in fragments. Later grammarians also refer to a group of *Neoterici* whose innovative poems flourished during the reign of Hadrian, the period from 119 to 138 C.E. Albrecht Dihle points out, "The most important kinds of Neoteric poetry are short narrative poems in an elegiac metre, short epics, and above all, short poems of a personal content, addressed to the beloved, to friends, or to enemies and written either as epigrams or in one of the Hellenistic short stanza types. But there are also experiments with difficult forms of lyrical verse, taken from poetry that was sung." What sets Catullus apart from the other *Neoterici* — and what makes him closer to Sappho (late seventh century B.C.E.), his primary model — is his passionate temper, the emotional heat of his work.

New Comedy, see *comedy.*

New Criticism New Criticism was a literary movement, a formalist way of reading poetry that dominated American literary criticism from the 1930s to the 1960s. Most of the New Critics were poets. Many were from the American South, including John Crowe Ransom — who named the movement in his book *The New Criticism* (1941) — Allen Tate, Robert Penn Warren, and Cleanth Brooks. The critic William K. Wimsatt and the poet-critics R. P. Blackmur, Kenneth Burke, and Yvor Winters were also associated with the group.

The New Critics proposed that a work of literary art should be treated as autonomous. They were primarily concerned with the techniques of poetry and rejected all extra-literary criteria. They took their lead from T. S. Eliot's critical essays ("It is an artificial simplification, and to be taken only with caution, when I say that the problem appearing in these essays, which gives them what coherence they have, is the problem of the integrity of poetry, with the repeated assertion that when we are considering poetry we must consider it primarily as poetry and not another thing") as well as from I. A. Richards's critical books, *Principles of Literary Criticism* (1924) and *Practical Criticism* (1929). William Empson's *Seven Types of Ambiguity* (1930) was also an influential source.

The New Critics practiced explication, which they called close reading, the detailed textual analysis of poems. The idea was to regard the poem as a unified object. Ransom called this criticism ontological, Brooks considered it formalist. They focused on ambiguities (multiple meanings) and praised symmetry, paradox, irony, and wit. They dismissed trying to determine authorial intent, the so-called intentional fallacy, and rejected biographical and historical information. Poetry was not social commentary or political statement. It was not, as Brooks put it, "a surrogate for religion." Brooks and Warren's textbook, *Understanding Poetry* (1938), made close reading the dominant method in the classroom for a generation.

The New Critics professionalized literary criticism. Their methodology was a pedagogical first step — they taught students to read and interpret what was put before them. They favored certain kinds of poets, such as the metaphysical poets, and devalued other kinds of poets, such as the romantics. They ignored the role of the reader in the creation of poetic meaning. They also severed poetry from history and culture. Yet their own essays, especially those by Warren, often break their tenets and bring all kinds of extra-textual information into their readings of poems. What remains instructive is their resistance to turning poetry into anything but itself.

SEE ALSO *ambiguity, heresy of paraphrase, intentional fallacy, irony, New Historicism, paradox.*

new formalism A very loosely affiliated group of American poets, born after 1940, have returned to formalist values and made a program of writing in rhyme and meter. Some of the poets affiliated with this return to tradition are Timothy Steele, Dana Gioia, Andrew Hudgins, Brad Leithauser, and Mary Jo Salter. There were older American poets who never abandoned traditional forms, such as Richard Wilbur, Anthony Hecht, Howard Nemerov, J. V. Cunningham, and others. The new formalists acknowledge these ancestors and oppose what they perceive as the prevailing contemporary aesthetic of free verse. Frederick Turner and Frederick Feinstein prefer the term *expansive poetry,* which could include a related group of longer narrative poems, many in traditional meters. Mark Jarman and David Mason suggest that the term *new formalism* "best describes this movement and the distinction between free and formal verse. It is understood that a formalist writes primarily in the meters of the English tradition and often in the verse forms associated with those meters." Richard Wilbur provided a dictum for the group when he said that rhyme and meter were necessary to contain the pent-up energy in a poem in the same sense that a genie's power derives from the pressure of its captivity in a bottle.

New Historicism A critical movement that arose in the academy in the 1980s, New Historicism rejects New Critical modes of close reading and emphasizes the dependence of literature on history. Louis Montrose describes the New Historicism as "a reciprocal concern with the historicity of texts and the textuality of history." New Historicism, Catherine Gallagher writes, "entails reading literary and nonliterary texts as constituents of historical discourses that are both inside and outside of texts." New historicists, she says, "generally posit no fixed hierarchy of cause and effect as they trace the connections among texts, discourses, power, and the constitution of subjectivity."

New Historicism has its roots in cultural materialism, the perception that, as Raymond Williams puts it, "we cannot separate literature and art from other kinds of social practice, in such a way as to make them subject to quite special and distinct laws." A Marxist thinker such as Louis Althuser argues that literature is a constitutive part of the way that a society considers and governs itself, an institution that legitimizes state power and ideology. New Historicism also develops from Michel Foucault's theory that the power dynamics and relations in a society at any given time determine the nature of its discourse, its concepts, oppositions, and hierarchies, and therefore what it considers knowledge and truth. Literature is implicated in this system of discourse. Poems, like other kinds of texts, are verbal representations, "cultural constructs," and they can be decoded as such. They are not independent of social, economic, and political considerations. Stephen Greenblatt gave the label *New Historicism* its special currency in the early 1980s, but now prefers to call his own enterprise cultural poetics, which he defines as the "study of the collective making of distinct cultural practices and inquiry into the relations among these practices." One of the great strengths of the new historical method, "a poetics of culture," is to make connections between disparate kinds of texts, to link forms and practices that otherwise seem disconnected. On the other hand, one of the persistent critiques of New Historicism is that it ignores the aesthetic qualities of literary texts, the very qualities that make a poem a distinctive work of art.

SEE ALSO *Marxist criticism, New Criticism.*

New York school of poets Frank O'Hara, James Schuyler, Kenneth Koch, and John Ashbery joined together in New York City in the 1950s, eventually comprising what David Lehman calls "the last authentic avant-garde movement that we have had in American poetry." One of the oddities of the New York school of poets is that none of them came from New York City: O'Hara was born in Baltimore, Maryland, and raised in Grafton, Massachusetts; Schuyler was born in Chicago; Koch in Cincinnati; and Ashbery in Rochester, New York. According to Ashbery, the New York school was the tale of three poetry pals—Koch, O'Hara, and himself—who met at Harvard and united in feeling that "modern French poetry, modern music, and modern painting" seemed "much more congenial to us than the American and English poetry we knew." Later, they came to New York, a convenient crossroads, and met other poets, such as Schuyler. They were deemed the New York school because they were friends, living and writing in New York, often taking the city as their subject matter.

The New York school bears an eerie similarity to the Parisian avant-garde of the early twentieth century. As Lehman puts it, "The poets of the New York School were as heterodox, as belligerent toward the literary establishment and as loyal to each other, as their Parisian predecessors had been. The 1950s and early '60s in New York were their banquet years. It is as though they translated the avant-garde idiom of 'perpetual collaboration' from the argot of turn-of-the-century Paris to the roughhewn vernacular of the American metropolis at midcentury."

The New York school resisted the modernism of T. S. Eliot and favored the more open-ended informality of Walt Whitman and William Carlos Williams. They were at odds with the New Critics and the deep image poets, such as Robert Bly and James Wright, but connected with the Beats and the Black Mountain school. They valued spontaneity and movement, impulse, accident and coincidence, the process-oriented energy of abstract expressionist painting. Their great subject was happiness, and they treated joy as synonymous with the imagination.

A second generation of New York school poets emerged in the 1960s. It was a downtown New York scene that gravitated around the Poetry Project at St. Mark's Church. It included Ted Berrigan and Alice Notley, Ron Padgett, Anne Waldman, and Joe Brainard, among others.

SEE ALSO *Beats, Black Mountain poets, deep image, New Criticism, spontaneity.*

Nine Powers Group, see *Poetism.*

nirat A Thai genre in which a poet describes his separation (the word *nirat* means "separation") from a loved one or a beloved place. It is frequently a love poem. The *nirat* has elements of a travel poem, too, since the poet relates what he sees, the sounds and sights of his journey, to the memories of what he has left behind. These long, reflective poems of separation and movement are often written in the *khlong* form (the word *khlong* means "to rhyme"), one of the five significant Thai verse forms. In his well-known poem *Khlong Nirat Hariphunchai,* the sixteenth-century poet Si Thep describes his journey from Chiang Mai to Hariphunchai. In his masterpiece *Khlong Kamsuan,* the eighteenth-century poet Si Prat describes his journey into exile at Nakhonsithamarat in southern Thailand. He expresses his deep longing both for his loved one and for his beloved city of Ayutthaya. In the nineteenth century — partly due to the influence of the poet Sunthorn Phu (1786–1855), who wrote many *nirats,* partly because of increasing travel abroad — the *nirat* became less of a melancholy poem about separation and more of a full-fledged descriptive poem of travel.

No play, Nō drama The courtly lyrical drama of Japan. The word *No,* which means "accomplishment," "skill," or "talent," was first applied to dancers and actors. The fourteenth and fifteenth centuries were the prime period for the No drama, which draws materials and forms from the folk dances of the countryside and the ritual dances of the temples, from Buddhist scripture and Japanese poetry, legend, and myth. The No play is slow moving, noble, and highly stylized. The actors wear masks, the scenery is stark, and the chorus comments on the action. It is an aristocratic form.

Ezra Pound and W. B. Yeats brought the No theater into modern European and American drama and poetry. Pound built on the pioneering work of Ernest Fenollosa (1853–1908), one of the first scholars to bring Japanese arts to the West. After Fenollosa's death, Pound compiled the drafts of Fenollosa's proposed work on the No into the volume *"Noh" or Accomplishment: A Study of the Classical Stage of Japan* (1916). Yeats introduced *Certain Noble Plays of Japan* (1916), which were chosen and finished by Pound. Yeats's own No plays are compiled in *Four Plays for Dancers* (1921). Yeats revolted against the realistic theater of his time, and the No offered him a drama that was beautiful, lyrical, and highly symbolic. "My blunder has been that I did not discover in my youth that my theatre must be the ancient theatre that can be made by unrolling a carpet or marking out a place with a stick or setting a screen against the wall," he wrote in a "Note on the First Performance of 'At the Hawk's Well' " (1921). "I have found my first model . . . in the Noh stage of aristocratic Japan."

nocturne A night scene. John Donne was the first English poet to employ the term *nocturnal* to designate a genre in "A Nocturnal upon S. Lucy's Day, being the shortest day" (1633). Donne sets his poem at midnight (" 'Tis the year's midnight, and it is the day's") and creates an elegy on the shortest day of the year, the winter solstice, by borrowing from the night Offices of the Roman Catholic canonical hours. In early church writings, the term *nocturnes* (*Nocturni* or *Nocturna*) refers to "night prayer" or night vigil. The notion of associating night with spiritual contemplation goes back at least as far as the Neo-Platonists. "I shall sing of Night, mother of gods and men," one Orphic hymn begins. "The night is often the secret site of initiation, purification, and other threshold activities bridging the relation between what is human and what is not human and providing a context for changed roles and states of being," Susan Stewart writes, pointing to the Japanese tradition of night poems as well as to the Navajo tradition of *yerbichai,* or "night chants," sung during Night Way rituals. The nocturne became a European musical type in the nineteenth century, a pensive, moody instrumental piece especially suitable for playing at night, and thereafter poetic nocturnes frequently evoke the melancholy feelings or tonalities of piano nocturnes.

One could make a good international anthology of the modern poetic nocturne, which is frequently a threshold poem that puts us in the presence of nothingness or God — it returns us to origins — and stirs poets toward song. It often flows from an urban sensibility. Charles Baudelaire considered calling his book of prose poems *Poèmes nocturnes* (Nocturnal poems). Nocturnes are often poems of sleeplessness, the cry of the solitary and bereft ensouled in poetic form (Rubén Dario's "Nocturne," which begins "You who have sounded the heart of the night," 1905; Federico García Lorca's "Sleepless Night [Brooklyn Bridge Nocturne]," 1929; Marina Tsvetaeva's "Insomnia," 1923). Many are elegies, as in Gabriela Mistral's *Tala* (1938), which includes a series of mystical "nocturnos," graveside meditations occasioned by her mother's death, and Léopold Sédar Senghor's book of intimacies, *Nocturnes* (1961).

Midnight is often the witching hour. At this culminating moment in the nocturnal realm, everything must be let go that is associated with day or daylight mind. Rather, the mind is now loosened for reverie and illumination. Walt Whitman's "A Clear Midnight" (1881) is an incantation that delivers a sense of overpowering spiritual immensity:

> Thus is thy hour O Soul, thy free flight into the wordless,
> Away from books, away from art, the day erased, the lesson done,
> Thee fully forth emerging, silent, gazing, pondering the themes thou
> lovest best,
> Night, sleep, death and the stars.

Noigrandes, see *concrete poetry.*

nonce forms Poetic forms invented for a single purpose or occasion, i.e., "for the nonce," meaning "for the occasion." Nonce forms have a discernible pattern, which is seldom (or never) repeated in other poems. They do their work once only. It is a mystery why certain patterns, which began as nonce forms, become fixed for generations, while others do not recur. "As to forms," Robert Pinsky suggests, "I believe that George Herbert invented an interesting one nearly every time he wrote a poem." Thomas Hardy often created metrical nonce forms, such as the odd three-line stanza that he devised for his poem on the loss of the *Titanic,* "The Convergence of the Twain" (1915). In each little stanza, which rhymes *aaa,* the first two lines are strongly indented iambic trimeters, while the third longer line is a hexameter. Each of the eleven stanzas, which look like tiny ships, is also set off by a roman numeral, as in number VIII:

> And as the smart ship grew
> In stature, grace, and hue,
> In shadowy silent distance grew the Iceberg too.

Robert Frost wrote nonce sonnets in which he devised singular rhyme schemes, as in two poems from 1916, "The Oven Bird" (*aabcbdcdeefgfg*) and the fifteen-line "Hyla Brook" (*abbaccaddeefgfg*). The old spelling of "nonce" is "nones." Many of the poems in W. H. Auden's book *Nones* (1951) are nonce poems.

nonsense poetry, nonsense verse The *Oxford English Dictionary* defines nonsense: "That which is not sense; spoken or written words which make no sense or convey absurd ideas; also, absurd or senseless action." The earliest example of the use of the word comes from Ben Jonson's *Bartholomew Fair* (1614): "Here they continue their game of Vapours, which is Nonsense." Nonsense has a long prehistory in oral tradition, in children's nursery rhymes and games, in ancient Greek writing, such as the Old Comedy of Aristophanes where humans behave like birds and birds behave like humans (*The Birds,* 414 B.C.E.) and the normal rules no longer seem applicable. Erasmus (1466?–1536) later praised the wisdom of folly, a wisdom wonderfully demonstrated by Shakespeare's fools.

Nonsense upends the way we normally view things; it disrupts, disorganizes, and then reorganizes common sense. "In every case, nonsense depends upon an assumption of sense. Without sense there is no nonsense," Susan Stewart writes in her definitive study, *Nonsense* (1979). "Nonsense stands in contrast to the reasonable, positive, contextualized, and 'natural' world of sense as the arbitrary, the random, the inconsequential, the merely cultural. While sense is sensory, tangible, real, nonsense is 'a game of vapours,' unrealizable, a temporary illusion." Nonsense operates by turning everyday things inside out, by inversions and reversals, by negations. It has a joyful abandon, an unruly playfulness and anarchic charm, which is why children love it.

Nonsense verse is poetry that doesn't make what we commonly refer to as sense. It rejects ordinary logic and creates its own autonomous world, as in Lewis Carroll's famous opening, "Jabberwocky" (1872):

> 'Twas brillig, and the slithy toves
> Did gyre and gimble in the wabe:

All mimsy were the borogoves
    And the mome raths outgrabe.

Edward Lear (1812–1888), who broadened the scope of nonsense verse, considered nonsense a response to "this ludicrously whirligig life which one suffers from first & laughs at afterwards." He said, "Nonsense is the breath of my nostrils." He initiated *A Book of Nonsense* (1846) with this dedication on the cover and title page:

There was an old Derry down Derry,
Who loved to see little folks merry;
    So he made them a Book,
    And with laughter they shook,
At the fun of that Derry down Derry!

Lear published his first nonsense collections — he called his limericks "Nonsenses" or "Old Persons" — under the pseudonym "Derry down Derry," one of the fools of the traditional English mummers' plays. He sometimes employed what he called his "long nonsense name." Vivien Noakes gives one example in her edition of *The Complete Verse and Other Nonsense* (2001), which he got from *Aldiborontiphoskyphorniostikos: A Round Game, for Merry Parties* by R. Stennett (ca. 1812): "Mr. Abebika Kratoponoko Prizzikalo Kattefello Ablegorabalus Ableborintophashyph or Chakonoton the Cozovex Dossi Fossi Sini Tomentilla Coronilla Polentilla Battledore & Shuttlecock Derry down Derry Dumps, otherwise Edward Lear."

notarikon The Kabbalists used this term for the study of first and last letters. It consists of forming words by combining the initial and terminal letters, or by treating each letter of a word as the initial letter of succeeding words. The new phrase illuminates the meaning of the first word, as when "God" becomes "garden of delight." The *notarikon* has been called a cousin of the acrostic. It is a favored mode of Hebrew mystical poets. Catherine Bowman adapts the technique to contemporary poetry in her book of poems *Notarikon* (2006).

SEE ALSO *acrostic*.

number, numbers I have a fondness for *numbers,* the old term for metrical units, as in Alexander Pope's line, "I lisped in numbers, for the numbers came." In "An Essay on Criticism" (1711), he also declared:

> But most by numbers judge a poet's song:
> And smooth or rough, with them, is right or wrong. . . .

Numbers was also a Renaissance term for poems or poetry in general. It refers to the mathematic harmonies of classical poetry, a way of ordering the universe. George Santayana wrote in "The Elements and Function of Poetry" (1900):

> Although a poem be not made by counting of syllables upon the fingers, yet "numbers" is the most poetical synonym we have for verse, and "measure" the most significant equivalent for beauty, for goodness, and perhaps even for truth. Those early and profound philosophers, the followers of Pythagoras, saw the essence of all things in number, and it was by weight, measure, and number, as we read in the Bible, that the Creator first brought Nature out of the void.

Shakespeare puns and uses the term *fresh numbers* to suggest novel and stimulating verses in "Sonnet 17":

> If I could write the beauty of your eyes,
> And in fresh numbers number all your graces. . . .

SEE ALSO *measure, verse.*

nursery rhymes Traditional rhymes and songs passed on to young children. Nursery rhymes initiate us into poetry, into verbal rhythms and rhymes. These catchy verses, which are also called "Mother Goose Rhymes," are hundreds of years old — records date to the late Middle Ages — and have a surprising persistence. Most adults have a basic repertoire ("Baa Baa Black Sheep," "Little Bo Peep," "Little Jack Horner," "Jack and Jill," "Mary Had a Little Lamb," "Hickory Dickory Dock," etc.) that comes back to them with renewed force as parents.

Many nursery rhymes seem to derive from street cries and songs, proverbs and riddles. Their origins are obscure and their original historical contexts are lost. Most nursery rhymes were not written down until the late eighteenth century. The term *nursery rhyme* came into vogue in the nineteenth century. The earliest known collection of nursery rhymes is *Tommy Thumb's (Pretty) Song Book* (1744), which includes "Little Tom Tucker," "Sing a Song of Sixpence," and "Who Killed Cock Robin?" By far the most influential collection of nursery rhymes was *Mother Goose's Melody* (1781), which included "Jack and Jill," "Ding Dong Bell," and "Hush-a-bye Baby on the Tree Top."

Oberiu *Oberiu,* or "The Association for Real Art," which thrived in the second half of the 1920s, is sometimes characterized as "the last Soviet avant-garde" or "Russia's last avant-garde." The absurdist poets at the core of the group—Alexander Vvedensky, Danil Kharms, and Nikolai Zabolotsky—came of age after the 1917 October Revolution. They are post-futurists. These Leningrad writers became known for their eccentric behavior and riotous public performances. Their work has a wild, comedic, and inventive free spirit. The governmental suppression of these writers in the 1930s was ruthless. Zabolotsky spent eight years in exile, Vvedensky died on a prison train, and Kharms died of starvation in a prison psychiatric hospital. The work of the *Oberiu* poets continues to have an anarchic underground life.

SEE ALSO *avant-garde, futurism.*

objective correlative An external equivalent for an internal state. The term *objective correlative* was coined by the American poet and painter Washington Allston in his *Lectures on Art* (1850). T. S. Eliot famously employed it in his 1919 essay "Hamlet and His Problems": "The only way of expressing emotion is by finding an 'objective correlative'; in other words, a set of objects, a situation, a chain of events which shall be the formula of the *particular* emotion." Eliot's argument that Shakespeare's *Hamlet* (1603) was an artistic failure because the character's emotion does not match the so-called facts of the action was dubious, but the term had a great vogue among the

New Critics. The idea of the objective correlative coincided with the modern critical values of concreteness, impersonality, and objectivity. It was critically deployed as the staging or manifestation of an emotion embodied in action (think of Lady Macbeth's somnambulism). Eliot himself later considered it one of "those notorious phrases" that "have had a truly embarrassing success in the world."

SEE ALSO *impersonality, New Criticism.*

objectivism The short-lived but influential objectivist movement, which was an outgrowth of imagism, treated the poem as an object in and of itself. The four primary objectivist poets were Louis Zukofsky (1904–1978); George Oppen (1908–1984), who founded the Objectivist Press; Carl Rakosi (1903–2004); and Charles Reznikoff (1894–1976). Lorine Niedecker (1903–1970) later became associated with the group. Ezra Pound (1885–1972) and William Carlos Williams (1883–1963) were strong allies. In his *Autobiography* (1948) Williams argued:

> . . . the poem, like every other form of art, is an object, an object that in itself formally presents its case and its meaning by the very form it assumes. Therefore, being an object, it should be so treated and controlled but not as in the past . . . The poem being an object (like a symphony or cubist painting) it must be the purpose of the poet to make of his words a new form: to invent, that is, an object consonant with his day. This is what we wished to imply by Objectivism.

The work of this group, who flourished in the early 1930s, is represented in an "Objectivist" issue of *Poetry* (February 1931), which also included two of Zukofsky's essays ("Program: 'Objectivists' 1931" and "Sincerity and Objectification") and *An "Objectivists" Anthology* (1932). The objectivists paid particular attention to the nature and precision of a poem's structure. They created systems of small words and sought an achieved tranquility, which they considered appropriate to objects.

SEE ALSO *imagism.*

obscurity There are poems that are unclear and hard to perceive, elusive and difficult to understand, which don't express themselves plainly. This obscurity may be involuntary or purposeful. Weak poetry is often unintentionally "obscure" — the poet isn't in control of the material — but strong poems can be authentically difficult, ambiguous, hard to figure out. Over the centuries, critics have invariably leveled the charge of "obscurity" against any truly new poetry, especially any modern poetry, which turns it back on previous standards of clarity. "Obscurity" is a historical construction, and the history of poetry is a history of oscillations between what is clearly discernible and what is uncertain, unfamiliar, artificial, recondite. Often what is difficult for one era is fairly easy for another. "The Waste Land" (1922), for example, once seemed like a poem that was nearly impossible to understand, that could appeal to only the most advanced readers, but it is now widely read by high school students. Poems that treat language materially, such as concrete poetry or sound poetry, "obscure" typical modes of using language for communication. Poems typically seem "obscure" for a variety of discernible reasons — because they employ archaic or ornate language and utilize elaborate figures of speech (Luis de Góngora, John Donne); because they embrace irrationality (Tristan Tzara), rely on subjective images (André Breton), or court nonsense (Wallace Stevens); because they contain "moments of wilderness" (Stanley Kunitz) or seek complex states of consciousness (John Ashbery); because they are riddling (Emily Dickinson), fragmentary (Paul Celan), clotted (Hart Crane), allusive (Ezra Pound), elliptical (T. S. Eliot), hermetic (Eugenio Montale), esoteric (Stéphane Mallarmé). Mystical poetry, like symbolist poetry, is obscure because it is seeking hidden knowledge, pursuing the ineffable, trying to render occult or transcendental states beyond language. These are just a few of the taxonomies of difficulty.

SEE ALSO *allusion, conceit, concrete poetry, elliptical poetry, fragment, Gongorism, Hermeticism, metaphysical poets, the Misty poets, modernism, pure poetry, sound poetry, symbolism.*

occasional poem, occasional verse The occasional poem (French *pièce d'occasion,* German *Gelegenheitsgedicthe*) is written to memorialize a particular occasion, such as a wedding (Edmund Spenser's "Epithalamion," 1595), a death (John Milton's "Lycidas," 1638), or other rites of passage. The poet laureates of England have been obliged to write lyrics to celebrate coronations and royal weddings, to dedicate buildings, etc. They add a ceremonial dimension to the occasion. Some occasional poems are endorsed by political power, others come unsponsored. The tone of an occasional poem can be light or serious, respectful or ironic, the event revered or satirized. Gerard Manley Hopkins entered poetry with an occasional poem, "The Wreck of the Deutschland" (1875–1876). Some of the finest twentieth-century occasional poems have marked large political events, such as W. B. Yeats's "Easter, 1916" and W. H. Auden's "September 1, 1939." In periods of national crisis, occasional poems sometimes still take up the ideological intentions of the epic.

Goethe called occasional poems "the first and most genuine of all kinds of poetry." The great occasional poem represents its specific occasion in time and yet also speaks beyond it, as in Andrew Marvell's "An Horatian Ode Upon Cromwell's Return from Ireland" (1650). The genre represents the public side of poetry — it has a social function — and flourished in the Victorian era. It can sometimes feel rhetorical, as if the voice is being declaimed over a loudspeaker. Robert Frost wrote a somewhat weak poem ("Dedication") for the inauguration of John F. Kennedy in 1961, but the glare of the sun on the snow blinded him at the podium on inauguration day and so he recited from memory a splendid poem that he had written in 1942 ("The Gift Outright"). It was not an occasional poem but a poem that suited the occasion.

SEE ALSO *birthday poems, elegy, epithalamium, frasca, silvae, skald.*

octameter A line of eight measures or feet. This long line is rare in English poetry, though Edgar Allan Poe made a claim for using octameters in "The Raven" ("Once upon a midnight dreary, while I pondered weak and weary," 1845) and Algernon Charles Swinburne managed them in "March: An Ode" ("Ere frost flower and snow-blossom faded and fell, and the splendour of winter had passed out of sight," 1887).

SEE ALSO *huitain,* "accentual syllabic meter" in *meter,* and *octave.*

octastich, see *octave.*

octave, octet The first eight lines of an Italian or Petrarchan sonnet, the octave, or octet, is followed by the last six lines, the sestet. The octave rhymes *abbaabba.* English-language poets have often slightly loosened the Italian rhyme scheme to *abbaacca.* The octave tends to raise an issue, suggest a problem, create a conflict. The first four lines establish the subject; the second four lines complicate it. Think, for example, of how William Wordsworth takes a walk in the first eight lines of his sonnet "It is a beauteous evening, calm and free" (1807), and describes an evening infused with a sense of natural divinity. This octave creates a sense of solitude, a feeling of sacred communion with the night.

It is a beauteous Evening, calm and free;
The holy time is quiet as a Nun
Breathless with adoration; the broad sun
Is sinking down in its tranquility;
The gentleness of heaven is on the Sea:
Listen! The mighty Being is awake,
And doth with his eternal motion make
A sound like thunder — everlastingly.

The octave can also refer to any eight-line poem or stanza (a brace octave), as in W. B. Yeats's "Among School Children" (1928), where he employs ottava rima, an eight-line stanza in iambic pentameter rhyming *abababcc.* A stanza of eight lines can also be called an *octacstich.* The French *huitain* is an octave — well-balanced, symmetrical, a poem in itself.

SEE ALSO *Contrasto, huitain, ottava rima, sestet, sonnet, stanza.*

octavo, see *folio.*

octosyllabic verse Eight-syllable lines. Each tetrameter line (a line with four metrical feet) uses iambs (unstressed syllables followed by stressed ones) or trochees (stressed syllables followed by unstressed ones). The most common type of octosyllabic verse is the octosyllabic couplet, which probably derives from late medieval French poetry, where it was first used for chronicles and romances and then for *lais* and *dits.* The Provençal troubadours brought it to Spain, where it became the primary form of courtly love poetry. It migrated to England via the Anglo-Norman poets and became firmly established by the fourteenth century, when it was employed with great narrative force in longer poems by John Gower (*Confessio Amantis,* ca. 1385) and Geoffrey Chaucer ("The Book of the Duchess" and "The House of Fame"). It was used for satirical verse, such as Samuel Butler's widely imitated Hudibrastics, and for philosophical short poems, such as John Milton's "Il Penseroso" from 1645 ("These pleasures *Melancholy* give, / And I with thee will chose to live"). It worked well for both light and serious lyrical narratives by William Wordsworth ("She was a phantom of delight / When first she gleamed upon my sight") and Samuel Taylor Coleridge ("Christabel," 1797–1800), Robert Burns (*Tam O'Shanter,* 1791), and Lord Byron ("The Corsair," 1814), who warned of "the fatal facility of the octo-syllabic meter." These octosyllabic couplets summarize the plight of the final Harper, the end of a poetic lineage, in the introduction to Walter Scott's *The Lay of the Last Minstrel* (1805):

Old times were changed, old manners gone;
A stranger fill'd the Stuarts' throne;
The bigots of the iron time
Had call'd his harmless art a crime.
A wandering Harper, scorn'd and poor,
He begged his bread from door to door,
And tuned, to please a peasant's ear,
The harp, a king had loved to hear.

SEE ALSO *aleluyas, barzelletta, copla, couplet, decir, dit, Hudibrastic verse, iamb, In Memoriam stanza, lai, ovillejo, quintilla, romances, tetrameter, trochee.*

ode A celebratory poem in an elevated language on an occasion of public importance or on a lofty common theme. Think of Tennyson's ceremonial "Ode on the Death of the Duke of Wellington" (1852) and of Keats's partly rhapsodic, partly forlorn 1819 "Ode to a Nightingale" ("Thou wast not born for death, immortal Bird!"). The word *ode* derives from the Greek *ōidē,* a poem intended to be sung, and this was virtually synonymous with the word *lyric.* It comes to us through its Latin form, *oda.* The young Herder called the ode "the firstborn child of feeling, the origin of poetry, the germ of life" (1765). The modern ode, which freely intermingles Greek and Latin elements, represents the claiming of an obligation, some inner feeling rising up in urgent response to an outer occasion, something owed.

Greek lyrics took either the form of monodies, sung by single persons, or choral odes, sung by groups. Alcaeus ("Ode to Castor and Polydeuces") and Sappho ("Ode to Aphrodite") were unsurpassed monodists, Pindar the key exponent of the choral form. Simultaneously sung and danced, the Pindaric ode consists of three stanzas that mirror a musical dance pattern: strophe, antistrophe, and epode. The strophe and antistrophe share the same metrical pattern and structure (the chorus in movement and countermovement); the epode has a different pattern (the chorus at rest). The Pindaric ode has its roots in religious rites. It called for an ecstatic performance and communally reenacted the ritual of participation in the divine. The movement of the verse is emotionally intense and highly exalted.

Horace (65–8 B.C.E.) perfected the Latin form. He adapted the complex meters of Greek monodists to Latin verse, and replaced the irregular stanzas of the Pindaric ode with symmetrical arrangements. Horace's odes tend to be personal rather than public, general rather than occasional, contemplative rather than frenzied. They take the middle path. "His great gift," Donald Carne-Ross states, "was to make the commonplace notable, even luminous, not to be discarded as part of the small change of existence."

The English ode begins with Ben Jonson's 1629 "To the Imortall Memorie and Friendship of That Noble Paire, Sir Lucius Cary and Sir H. Morison," a self-conscious attempt to create an exact equivalent for Pindar's complicated stanzaic form. The Horatian model was represented by Andrew Marvell's outstanding political poem of the seventeenth century, "An Horatian Ode upon Cromwell's Return from Ireland" (1681). In both English and Continental poetry the ode developed a life of its own with deep roots as a poem on a theme of acknowledged importance. There are odes of speculation, odes *on* (Milton's "On the Morning of Christ's Nativity," 1629; Gray's delightful mock ode "Ode on the Death of a Favourite Cat, Drowned in a Tub of Gold Fishes," 1748) and odes of address, odes *to* (Dryden's "To the Pious Memory of the Accomplished Young Lady, Mrs. Anne Killigrew," 1686; Shelley's rhapsodic "Ode to the West Wind," 1819; Keats's culminating "To Autumn," 1820; and Schiller's magisterial "Ode to Joy," 1785, transformed by Beethoven in the final movement of the Ninth Symphony). The idea of a formal poem of considerable length written in an elevated language has had less currency in modern times, but has sometimes been revitalized, as in Hölderlin's mystical odes or in Pablo Neruda's wildly energetic three books of odes on daily subjects, which praise the dignity and strangeness of ordinary things.

SEE ALSO *antistrophe, epode, lyric, strophe.*

Old Comedy, see *comedy.*

the Old School of Athens, the New School of Athens The Old School of Athens was the first literary group to develop after the formation of the Greek kingdom in 1830. Also called the Old Athens or Athenian School, it lasted for around fifty years and strongly influenced the cultural life of the new Greece. This romantic school combined a feeling for classical Greece with an enthusiasm for contemporary French letters. They loved the lays of Ossian and wrote of love, death, and the home country in the spirit of Victor Hugo, Alphonse de Lamartine, and Lord Byron, their particular hero. The group included the brothers Yeoryios Paraschos (1822–1886) and Achilleus Paraschos (1838–1920), as well as Angelos Vlachos (1838–1920), Alexandros Vyzantios (1841–1898), Dimitrios Paparrigopoulos (1843–1873), and others. Kimon Friar sums them up: "On the whole, their poetry was an exaggerated distortion of European Romanticism expressed in a nostalgic revamping of classical myths, in a rhetorical eulogizing of heroes, in a preoccupation with death and disease, in an unrelieved patriotism, in sentimental love poems and heart-rending threnodies, and in some political satires of power."

The New School of Athens, also known as the Generation of 1880, was a group of young poets who banded together to revolt against the excessive romanticism of the Old School. The group was led by Kostís Palamás (1859–1943), Nikolaos Kombás (1857–1932), Yeoryios Drosinis (1859–1951), and others. The New School of Athens sought to bring greater restraint and objectivity to their art. They embraced the Demotic and based much of their work on village life, folk material, and everyday events. Formally, they were influenced by the French Parnassians, who stressed emotional detachment and technical achievement. The group lasted about fifteen years, until it was displaced by the dominant movement of symbolism.

SEE ALSO *Parnassians, symbolism.*

Omar Khyyám Quatrain, see *rubaiyat stanza.*

Onegin stanza The Russian poet Alexander Pushkin developed a hybrid fourteen-line iambic tetrameter stanza that can work either as an Italian or an English sonnet. His masterpiece, *Eugene Onegin* (1833), a novel in verse, consists of 365 such sonnets with the rhyme scheme *ababccddeffegg.* The form is a shape-shifter. Turn it one way and it looks like the Petrarchan sonnet (*abab ccdd eff egg*). Turn it the other way and it looks like the Shakespearean sonnet (*abab ccdd effe gg*). Pushkin also stressed that the first rhyme in each couplet (*a, c,* and *e*) be unstressed, or feminine, and the others stressed, or masculine. Vladimir Nabokov cleverly "mimics an Onegin stanza" in the last paragraph of his novel *The Gift* (1937–1938), Sir Charles Johnston elegantly employs the Onegin stanza for his verse translation of *Eugene Onegin* (1977), and Vikram Seth uses the Onegin stanza for his verse novel *The Golden Gate* (1986), a tour-de-force that acknowledges Pushkin's model: "Eugene Onegin—like champagne / Its effervescence stirs my brain."

SEE ALSO *feminine rhyme, masculine rhyme, rhyme, sonnet, verse novel.*

onomatopoeia Greek: "name making." The formation and use of words that imitate sound, such as *arf, blare, crash, dip, flare, growl, hum, jeer, knock, lick, murmur, nip, purr, quack, rustle, swish, thud, veer, wallop, yell,* and *zoom.* Listen to what Shakespeare does with animal sounds in this exchange from *The Tempest* (ca. 1611):

> Hark, hark!
>   Bow-wow!
> The watch-dogs bark.
>   Bow-wow!
> Hark, hark, I hear
> The strain of strutting Chanticleer
>   Cry, "cock-a-diddle-dow!"

Onomatopoeia is a form of name making, of phonic symbolism, a poetic device that creates verbal texture by weaving sounds through lines. It differs according to language and operates by convention. It turns the arbitrariness of each language into an intentionality and physicalizes Pope's dictum that "the sound must seem an echo to the sense." Actually, the sound becomes the sense. In poetry, Thomas Lux writes in his poem "Onomatopoeia" (1994), "the sound, the noise of the sound, is / the thing."

SEE ALSO *sound poetry.*

Optophonetics In 1918, the Dadaist Raoul Hausmann developed a system of notating phonetic poetry that he called Optophonetics. He willfully abandoned communication through words, which he broke down into component parts. He declared "the page to be a visual equivalent of acoustic space with placement on the page denoting pitch, type size denoting volume, type overlays denoting multiple voicing, etc." Optophonetics is an open code with multiple interpretations, which is why it still appeals to text-sound composers.

SEE ALSO *Dadaism, Merz, sound poetry.*

oral-formulaic method Milman Parry (1902–1935) and his student Albert Lord (1912–1991) discovered and studied what they called the oral-formulaic method of oral epic singers in the Balkans. Their method has been variously referred to as "oral-traditional theory," "the theory of Oral-Formulaic Composition," and the "Parry-Lord theory." Parry used his study of Balkan singers to address what was then called the "Homeric Question," which circulated around the questions of "Who was Homer?" and "What are the Homeric poems?" Parry's most critical insight was his recognition of the "formula," which he initially defined as "*a group of words which is regularly employed under the same metrical conditions to express a given essential idea.*" The formula revised the standard ideas of "stock epithets," "epic clichés," and "stereotyped phrases." Such often repeated Homeric phrases as "*eos rhododaktylos*" ("rosy-fingered dawn") and "*oinops pontos*" ("wine-dark sea") were mnemonic devices that fitted a certain metrical pattern and aided the epic singer, or *aiodos,* in his extemporaneous composition. Such phrases could be substituted and adapted, serving as place-holders, as a response to the needs of both grammar and narrative. These formulas, which could also be extended, were not particular to individual artists, but a shared traditional inheritance of many singers. Parry's work revolutionized the study of the Homeric poems by treating them as essentially oral texts. For example, Parry and Lord observed the same use of formulas in Serbian oral poetry that they found in the Homeric poems.

Parry and Lord discovered that the epic form was well-suited to the singer's need for fluency and flexibility, for composition as well as memorization. The singers composed poems orally by calling upon a rich storehouse of ready-made building blocks (traditional patterns), which moved well beyond phrasing. Singers could call upon this stock of lines and formulas for describing places, expressing different characters, and narrating action — and thus perform epics of ten thousand lines or more with uninterrupted fluency. Parry and Lord provided us with a generative model of epic performance. F. P. Magoun explains that oral poetry is composed "rapidly in the presence of a live audience by means of ready-made phrases filling just measures of isochronous verse capable of expressing every idea that the singer may wish to express in various metrical situations." The oral-formulaic method has subsequently been applied to a wide variety of texts and genres, such as Babylonian, Hittite, and Anglo-Saxon epic poetry, medieval romances, Russian *byliny,* the corpus of pre-Islamic poetry, Toda ritual songs, Coorg dance songs, English and Spanish ballads, and even African American revivalist sermons. Oral formulas also clearly influenced written poetry. It is now possible, for example, to view Old English poems as transitional texts, written poems that embody oral formulas.

SEE ALSO *aoidos, bylina, epic, oral poetry.*

oral poetry Verbal art presented orally. Oral poetry is a particular mode of communication that is usually transmitted by word of mouth and performed in face-to-face interaction. It is a kind of language-based art characterized by a heightened awareness of the act of expression — how it says what it says — and it is marked, framed, and identified by the community as poetry. Historically, oral poetry ranges across the ancient world and includes the eighth-century B.C.E. Greek Homeric poems the *Iliad* and the *Odyssey,* the Sumerian *Epic of Gilgamesh* (ca. 1600–1000 B.C.E.), and the Sanskrit epic of ancient India *Mahābhārata* (ninth to eighth century B.C.E.). Yet it is not a fossilized survival from the past or the exclusive property of nonliterate peoples. It includes Serbo-Croatian epics (long narrative poems with an emphasis on the heroic) and Anglo-American ballads (sung narrative poems), but also Gond love songs, Malay *pantuns,* Nigerian election songs, South African praise poems, Eskimo meditative poems, Siberian shaman songs, Australian song cycles, West Indian Calypso, Blues songs, Native American chants and spells, children's rhymes and riddles, and different varieties of work songs (sea shanties, the songs of chain gangs), which are timed to physical labor and found all over the world.

There is a fruitful interplay between oral and written poetry, which are like two branches of the same river repeatedly intertwining. Influence flows in both directions. Oral poetry may be composed and transmitted orally. It may be written and then circulated orally, or composed orally and then transmitted orally as well as by written means. Once thought to be entirely spontaneous, oral poetry is often highly self-conscious and regulated by powerful social conventions. One thinks of how praise poems reinforce authority and protest songs upset it, how riddles disturb cognitive categories and proverbs reinforce morays, how wedding songs celebrate joy and mourning songs assuage grief, marking a rite of passage, keeping celebrants and mourners in the social fabric. It was also once thought that all oral poetry was composed anonymously, instinctively, but it turns out that many communities have poets who are studied professionals, such as the Irish School of Bards, or the Maori School of Learning. The role and position of oral poets vary from community to community.

Oral poetry is an emergent art, an art that unfolds in performance. There is usually no fixed text or correct version of a text, and each performance is original. Oral poetry still thrives among rural peoples. For example, regional subdivisions of modern improvised poetry in Spain include Basque *bertsolaritza,* Murican and Alpujarreño *trovos,* the Balearic *glosat,* the Galician *regueifa,* and Canarian *punto cubano.* So, too, in his book *Amharic Oral Poems of the Peasantry in East Gojjam* (2001), Getie Gelaye classifies ten major genres of Amharic oral poetry, which seem typical of peasant communities: war chants, heroic recitals, work songs, wedding poetry, children's and cattle herders' songs, grievance poetry, funeral poetry, religious poetry, praise poetry, and contemporary and historical poetry. He identifies several genres that are now forgotten entirely, or on the verge of being forgotten, along with an old way of life, such as court poetry, hunting poetry, and smallpox poetry.

Drum poetry, which exists in tonal languages, is the most remarkable kind of instrumental poetry. Drummers actually convey the words of the poem through the sounds of the drum. As Ruth Finnegan explains in *Oral Poetry* (1980):

> The same principle of transmission can be used by other instruments: so long as an instrument can conventionally represent different tones it can "speak" the words of a tonal language; even a mono-tone instrument like a gong can convey messages by use of stress and rhythm. Other instruments too are used to convey verbal uttterances, such

> as whistles, horns, bells and flutes. This instrumental mode must be included in any list of the media of poetry.

Poetry changes based on its function, whether it is meant primarily to be spoken or written, heard or read. Oral poetry can't be paused or returned to — it can't be reread — and its effectiveness therefore depends on immediate response, how it affects a live audience.

SEE ALSO *akyn, amoebean verses, aoidos, ashough, aşik, ballad, bertsolaritza, bylina, changga, Contrasto, the dozens, drum poetry, eisteddfod, epic, epithet, ethnopoetics, flyting, gaucho poetry, hain-teny, Kantan Chamorrita, keening, mukàndà, narrative poetry, oral-formulaic method, oríkì, performance poetry, picong, poetic contest, praise poems, puy, qasida, shaman, slam poetry, song, sound poetry, spoken word poetry, voice.*

organic form Since the development of natural history and biology in the eighteenth century, the word *organic* has primarily referred to things living and growing. Machines took on new significance during the Industrial Revolution, and romantic thinkers began to reject eighteenth-century mechanical philosophies of mind, differentiating between organic and inorganic systems, natural and mechanical bodies. Taking a lead from the German critic A. W. Schlegel, Samuel Taylor Coleridge distinguished between mechanic form and organic form in an essay on Shakespeare:

> The form is mechanic when on any given material we impress a predetermined form, not necessarily arising out of the properties of the material — as when to a mass of wet clay we give whatever shape we wish it to retain when hardened. The organic form on the other hand is innate, it shapes as it develops itself from within, and the fullness of its development is one and the same with the perfection of its outward Form. Such is the Life, such is the form. Nature, the prime genial artist, inexhaustible in diverse powers, is equally inexhaustible in forms.

Coleridge made a strong distinction between the mechanical fancy and the living imagination, and suggested that the work of art is like a living organism, especially a plant, which originates in a seed, continues to grow (in Shakespeare, "All is growth, evolution, *genesis,* — each line, each word almost, begets the following"), assimilates and "enters into open communion with all the elements," and evolves spontaneously from within," effectuating "its own secret growth."

The metaphor of organic or appropriate form, something that develops naturally from within, has been crucial to the development of romantic and certain crucial strands of American poetry. The idea that art derives from nature rather than from other art has fueled American ideas of originality. Ralph Waldo Emerson created a credo for American poetry when he adapted Coleridge's botanical metaphor for poetic form and declared in "The Poet" (1844): "For it is not metres, but a metre-making argument, that makes a poem,—a thought so passionate and alive, that, like the spirit of a plant or an animal, it has an architecture of its own, and adorns nature with a new thing." Henry David Thoreau similarly used the language of biology for the genesis of poems: "As naturally as the oak bears an acorn, and the vine a gourd, man bears a poem . . . since his song is a vital function like breathing, and an integral result like weight" (*A Week on the Concord and Merrimack Rivers,* 1849).

The premise of all theories of organic form is that form should not be prescribed or fixed but should emerge from the subject matter at hand. It should, as Emerson said, "ask the fact for the form." Ezra Pound formulated an imagist version when he wrote, "I think there is a 'fluid' as well as a 'solid' content, that some poems may have form as a tree has form, some as water poured into a vase" (1918). In the 1960s, Denise Levertov and Robert Duncan developed a more broadly theological concept of organic form. They believed that the form of the individual poem intuits the divine. Thus Levertov defined organic form as "a method of apperception, i.e., of recognizing what we perceive, and is based on an intuition of an order, a form beyond forms, in which forms partake, and of which man's creative works are analogies, resemblances, natural allegories" ("Some Notes on Organic Form," 1965). Duncan suggested that the poet "seeks to penetrate to that most real where there is no form that is not content, no content that is not form" ("Toward an Open Universe," 1966).

In literary criticism and aesthetics, the word *organic* is commonly used to indicate the interrelationship between the parts of a work. We are employing a metaphor from nature when we say that things have an organic relation or organic connection, meaning that they seem to occur "naturally" rather than being imposed "artificially."

SEE ALSO *fancy, form, free verse, imagination, originality, romanticism, spontaneity.*

originality Something new and unexpected, novel, individual, unprecedented. The word *original* originally referred in Medieval Latin to an original document, a work composed firsthand, the source from which copies were then made. An original was distinguished from a replica, a translation, an imitation. The meaning of the word migrated toward modern usage mainly in the seventeenth century. "In the case of works of art," as Raymond Williams puts it, "there was a transfer from the retrospective sense of original (the first work and not the copy) to what was really a sense close to *new* (not like other works)." *Originality* became a value and term of praise in the second half of the eighteenth century. It was proposed in opposition to the neoclassical idea that poetry should imitate the ancients. "An *Original* may be said to be of a *vegetable* nature; it rises spontaneously from the vital root of Genius; it *grows,* it is not *made: Imitations* are often a sort of *Manufacture* wrought up by those *Mechanics, Art* and *Labour,* out of pre-existent materials not their own," Edward Young wrote in *Conjectures on Original Composition* (1759), thus helping to inaugurate a romantic idea of originality as something natural and organic rather than mechanical, something that grows from within. The metaphor was thus tied to the Industrial Revolution. There has ever after been an ongoing debate about the rival claims of tradition and innovation, the virtue of imitation and the value of invention.

The romantic concept of originality has been especially charged in American poetry, where it seems almost to define the American character. "Why should not we also enjoy an original relation to the universe?" Emerson asked rhetorically at the outset of his essay "Nature" (1836). "Why should not we have a poetry and philosophy of insight and not of tradition, and a religion by revelation to us, and not the history of theirs." Here the New World is opposed to the old one, the freshness of insight contrasted to the staleness of tradition. The question of what constitutes originality has often been worked out at the level of form, the difference between a new poetic of free verse (Whitman) and a fresh remaking of traditional forms (Poe). There is a subsequent dialogue in modern poetry between Ezra Pound's dictum to "make it new" and T. S. Eliot's idea, developed in "Tradition and the Individual Poet" (1919), that the individual poet's originality stands always in relationship to those who have come before. "We dwell with satisfaction upon a poet's difference from his predecessors," Eliot contends. "Whereas if we approach a poet without this prejudice we shall often find that not only the best, but the most individual parts of his work may be those in which the dead poets, his ancestors, assert their immortality most vigorously."

SEE ALSO *imitation, inspiration, invention, organic form, tradition.*

oríkì *Oríkì* is the oral praise poetry of the indigenous Yoruba communities of Western Africa. Similar praise poems turn up throughout much of Africa (Zulu *izíbongo,* Basuto *líthoko,* etc.). The invocation or praise poem starts out as the stringing together of praise names that describe the qualities of a particular man, animal, plant, place, or god. These praise names are handed down from the past and invented by relatives or neighbor or often drummers. The *akewi* are praise-singers at a king's court. The *oríkì* of a plant or an animal is sung by hunters, the *oríkì* of a god is sung by his worshipers. Olatunde Olatunji explains, "Oríkì is the most popular of Yórùbá poetic forms. Every Yórùbá poet therefore strives to know the oríkì of important people in his locality as well as lineage oríkì because every person, common or noble, has his own body of utterances by which he can be addressed." In Yoruba culture, a person's name relates to his or her spiritual essence ("a child's name follows him") and each individual has a series of praise names. The use of one's praise name is a part of daily life as well as of traditional performance. Call people by their *oríkìs* and you inspire them.

Oríkì Esu are the narrative praise poems or panegyrics to Esu, the divine trickster of Yoruba mythology. Here is a traditional *Oríki Esu,* which Leo Frobenius quotes in *The Voice of Africa* (1913):

> Ah yes!
> Edju plays many tricks
> Edju made kindred people go to war;
> Edju pawned the moon and carried off the sun:
> Edju made the Gods strive against themselves.
> But Edju is not evil.
> He brought us the best there is;
> He gave us the Ifa oracle;
> He brought the sun.
> But for Edju, the fields would be barren.

SEE ALSO *drum poetry, epic, epithet, Ifa divination verses, oral poetry, panegyric, praise poems.*

ottava rima An eight-line stanza in iambic pentameter rhyming *abababcc.* The pattern unfolds as six interlocking lines followed by a climactic couplet. The three insistent alternating rhymes propel the narrative forward while also encouraging meditation and commentary. The couplet, on the other hand, is a stopping point, a turn or summation. The Italian poets (Boccaccio, Pulci, Tasso) especially favored the aristocratic and symmetrical eleven-syllable stanza for narrative and epic verse. Ariosto showed that the stanza could be simultaneously lyrical, contemplative, and narrative in *Orlando Furioso* (1516). The ottava rima form was imported to England by Thomas Wyatt (1503–1542), who used it for witty epigrams; it flourished during the Renaissance; and it was brilliantly deployed by Lord Byron in his mock epic *Don Juan* (1819–1824), a poem "meant to be a little quietly facetious upon everything." Here Byron uses the power of the stanza to send up some classic ancestors:

> Ovid's a rake, as half his verses show him,
>   Anacreon's morals are a still worse sample,
> Catullus scarcely has a decent poem,
>   I don't think Sappho's Ode a good example,
> Although Longinus tells us there is no hymn
>   Where the Sublime soars forth on wings more ample;
> But Virgil's songs are pure, except that horrid one
> Beginning with *"Formosum pastor Corydon."*

For W. B. Yeats, ottava rima suggested a Renaissance poise and decorum, an aristocratic ceremoniousness, and he memorably employed the form in a score of meditative lyrics, such as "Sailing to Byzantium" (1927), "Among School Children" (1928), "Coole Park and Ballylee, 1931" (1931), and "The Circus Animals' Desertion" (1939). In central Italy, however, the medieval tradition of ottava rima is a folk way of singing, sometimes called the chant of the *poeti contadini* (peasant poets). The songs are sometimes based on texts by Dante (1265–1321) and Ariosto (1474–1533), sometimes improvised in a competition. Each singer begins a new eight-line stanza with the last rhyme of the previous singer. This is the style of the *Contrasto* ("contrast"), or improvised, poetry in the Tuscan dialect. The oral poets use the verbal art of ottava rima for a dramatic, cooperative form of heated debate.

SEE ALSO *Contrasto, octave, poetic contest.*

Oulipo The **Ou**vroir de **lit**térature **po**tentialle, or Workshop for Potential Literature, is a loosely organized group founded in 1960 in Paris by the writer Raymond Queneau and the mathematician François Le Lionnais. The original OuLiPo group consisted of ten members, which included the poets Jacques Roubaud and Oskar Pastior as well as the novelists Italo Calvino, Georges Perec, and Harry Matthews, the only American. Oulipo characterized "potential literature" as "the seeking of new structures and patterns which may be used by writers in any way they enjoy." The Oulipo writers seek generating devices for creating texts. To invent new work the Oulipo writers rely on rigorous constraints, rules, and formulas, such as n + 7, for which all nouns in a known sentence or line of poetry are exchanged with the seventh noun entry later in a particular dictionary. "In the beginning, God created the heavens and the earth" may become "In the begster, goddard created the heave thigh and the easel." The idea is to create an experimental workshop or laboratory for literary invention and thus investigate the various multiple possibilities of literature. One of the key Oulipo texts is Raymond Queneau's work *Cent mille milliards de poèmes* (One Hundred Million Poems, 1961). It consists of ten sonnets, which can be cut up by every single line and recombined into one hundred million different poems.

SEE ALSO *aleatory, lipogram, tautogram.*

ovillejo The word *ovillego* refers to a spool of thread or wool, and this complicated Spanish stanziac form is "tied in a little knot." Each stanza unravels in ten lines. The first six lines are made up of three rhyming couplets. Each pair consists of a long line followed by a shorter one. The octosyllabic lines (one, three, and five) ask questions, which are answered or echoed in the lines of three or four syllables (two, four, and six). The last four lines form a summarizing quatrain, or *redondilla* (*abba*). The quatrain consists of four octosyllabic lines. The final line consists of the words from the three answers in lines two, four, and six. Miguel Cervantes (1547–1616) first cultivated this maddeningly difficult form, which Sor Juana Inés de la Cruz (1651–1695) later perfected.

SEE ALSO *echo verse, octosyllabic verse.*

oxymoron From the Greek: "pointedly foolish." A figure of speech that combines two seemingly contradictory elements, as when Charles Lamb said, "I like a smuggler. He is the only honest thief." As an apparent contradiction in terms, a condensed paradox, the oxymoron turns on a phrase and seeks a hidden unity of opposites. It draws attention to its way of fusing disparate elements. Thus John Milton describes hell as "darkness visible" (*Paradise Lost,* 1667) and T. S. Eliot hears "the soundless wailing" ("The Dry Salvages," 1941). The oxymoron has a long history in poetry (Horace speaks of "the jarring harmony of things"), but was an especially strong device for the baroque and metaphysical poets, who created elaborate figures to evoke sacred mysteries. It has often been employed both in love poetry ("I see without my eyes, cry with no tongue," Petrarch says), and in religious poetry. Here is how Richard Crashaw describes the infant Jesus in "In the Holy Nativity of Our Lord God" (1646):

> Welcome, all wonders in one sight!
> Eternity shut in a span,
> Summer in winter, day in night,
> Heaven in earth, and God in man!

Working under the influence of the metaphysical poets, modern poets often employed the oxymoron as a compact device. Thus Dylan Thomas writes of "Grave men, near death, who see with blinding sight" ("Do Not Go Gentle into That Good Night," 1951) and Theodore Roethke declares: "I wake to sleep, and take my waking slow" ("The Waking," 1953). In his poem "Oxymorons" (1998), William Matthews lists as further examples "*friendly fire, famous poet, common sense.*" Anne Stevenson suggests that "Poetic language is essentially oxymoronic, a coinage stamped on two sides with logically irreconcilable messages."

SEE ALSO *paradox.*

padam The fifteenth-century Indian poet Annamayya, a Teluga songwriter and Carnatic composer, lived at the Tirupati temple, located in southern Andhra, where he effectively created and popularized a new genre, the short *padam* song. He was said to have written a song daily for Venkatesvara, an incarnation of Vishnu and the "god on the hill." Approximately thirteen thousand of Annamayya's poems were inscribed on some 2,289 copper plates kept in a vaultlike room in the temple, where they were discovered in the 1920s. Colophons on the copper plates divide Annamayya's devotional poems into two major types, erotic and metaphysical. As in so much classical Indian poetry, there is an allegorical blur between the erotic and the divine.

Annamayya's family members continued the *padam* genre, which spread through the Telugu and Tamil regions. The highly performative genre was gradually absorbed into the musical tradition of south India. Velcheru Narayana and David Schulman argue that Annamayya "created Venkatesvara, the god on the hill, as we know him today." They estimate that twenty million people each year make a pilgrimage to pray to the god who resides in the temple on a mountain.

SEE ALSO *bhakti poetry*.

paean A song of joyful praise. In ancient Greece, a paean was originally a hymn used in the worship of Apollo, the god of healing, who was invoked as *Paian* ("healer"). These hymns were later expanded to be sung to other gods and eventually to human beings, thus evolving into choral odes of thanksgiving, which were frequently sung by troops before battles and after victories. The great paeans of antiquity were written by Bacchylides and Pindar. Paeans were Apollonian, dithyrambs Dionysian. The term *paean* can now be used to describe any song of joy or triumph. Thus in *Helen in Egypt,* the poet H. D. calls for chanting "new paeans to the new Sun" (1961).

SEE ALSO *Apollonian/Dionysian, dithyramb.*

paeon In classical Greek prosody, a paeon is a foot of one long and three short syllables. Depending on the position of the long syllable, it is known as the first (— u u u), second (u — u u), third (u u — u), or fourth (u u u —) paeon. This quadruple quantitative measure is generally too long for English-language poetry, though Gerard Manley Hopkins loosely managed to adapt it to accentual use in "The Windhover" (1918) and other poems. Each long line in Alfred, Lord Tennyson's "The Making of Man" (1892) consists of an anapest (u u /) and three paeons, which creates a rhythm of great rapidity. Here is the representative last line:

> Hăllĕú- | ăh tŏ thĕ Má- | kĕr. 'Ĭt ĭs fín- | shĕd. Măn ĭs máde.'

SEE ALSO *foot,* "quantitative meter" in *meter.*

palindrome A palindrome is a word (like "eye") or phrase (like "Able was I ere I saw Elba") that can be read the same way forward or backward. It is a word game, a mirroring device, which invites us to read in a contrary direction, and thus draws attention to our pattern of visual perception. A verse that reads both ways is also called a *cancrine* (Latin: "crab-wise"). In Latin, a verse that has the same meter when the order of words is reversed was called *reciprocus versus.* In the fifth century, Sidonius Apollinaris referred to *versus recurrentes* ("recurrent verses"), lines that have the same meter and order of letters when they are read forward and backward. He illustrated the notion with this palindrome from a medieval legend that plays on the relationship between *Roma* (Rome) and *Amor* (Love): "*Roma tibi subito motibus ibit amor*" ("Rome, to you love will come with sudden passion"). As an example of perhaps misplaced ingenuity, in 1802 an author who called himself Ambrose Hieromonachus Pamperes published a 416-line Greek poem in which every line was a palindrome.

SEE ALSO *acrostic, anagram.*

palinode A poem or song of retraction. The palinode (*palin-ode;* literally, "singing back or over again") is a formal retraction of a view from a previous poem. The term was first given to a poem by Stesichorus (seventh century B.C.E.), who retracted his attack upon Helen as the cause of the Trojan War. As Plato recorded it in *Phaedrus* (ca. 370 B.C.E.):

The story is not true,
She never went in the well-decked ships,
She didn't travel to the towers of Troy.

Ovid created a common theme in love poetry when he wrote *Remedia amoris* (ca. 2 C.E.) supposedly to retract *Ars amatoria* (ca. 1 C.E.). So, too, in "The Legend of Good Women" (1386) Chaucer repudiates his defamatory view of women in *Troilus and Criseyde* (ca. 1380s).

panegyric A public speech or poem in praise of an individual, a group of people, or a public body. Pindar's odes have been loosely characterized as panegyrics. After the third century B.C.E., the panegyric was generally recognized as a specific poetic type (a formal eulogistic composition intended as a public compliment), which persisted until the Renaissance. In English poetry, the panegyric began with the Stuart succession and suggested "praise of great persons," which gives it a strongly political and even propagandistic dimension, as in Samuel Daniel and Ben Jonson's panegyrics to James I, or John Dryden's panegyrics for the restoration of Charles II in 1660. Exaggeration is predictably built into the occasion of the panegyric, a selective form of portraiture. The panegyric may have led to a form of public flattery about which we are now rightly skeptical since it colludes with power, but it most likely has its roots in religious practice, in the Greek and Latin cult hymns. Behind it persists one of the most long-standing and permanent ceremonial impulses in poetry: to praise.

SEE ALSO *Caroline Age, epithet, oríkì, praise poems, qasida, Restoration poetry.*

pangram A pangram is a sentence that uses all the letters of the alphabet. A pangrammatic line or song also contains all the letters of the alphabet, as in Pascasio di San Giovanni's *Poesis artificiosa* (1674): *"Vix Phlegeton Zephiri queres modo glabra Mycillo."* One variation of the pangrammatic method is to have as many successive words as possible begin with the same letter, as in Hucbald of Saint Amand's (ca. 849–930) virtuoso celebration of baldness, "Ecloga de Calvis," which consists of 146 hexameters, each word beginning with the letter C in honor of Charles the Bald.

SEE ALSO *alliteration, lipogram.*

pantoum, pantun The Western pantoum adapts a long-standing form of oral Malayan poetry (*pantun*) that first entered written literature in the fifteenth century. The most basic form of the *pantun* is a quatrain with an *abab* rhyme scheme. Each line contains between eight and twelve syllables. Like the *ghazal,* it is a disjunctive form, since the sentence that makes up the first pair of lines (*ab*) has no immediate logical or narrative connection with the second pair of lines (*ab*). The prefatory couplet is called the *pembayang* and the closing couplet the *maksud.* The rhymes and other verbal associations, such as puns and repeating sounds (assonance, consonance), connect them. But there is also an oblique but necessary relationship, and the first statement often turns out to be a metaphor for the second one. John Hollander summarizes: "*Pantuns* in the original Malay / Are quatrains of two thoughts, but of one mind." The most famous *pantuns* are learned by heart and interconnected by refrains, which serve as an aid to memory for both the oral poet and his audience. The *pantun* is sung very slowly according to a fixed rhythm. As R. J. Wilkinson described it in *Malay Literature* (1924):

> To an English reader the quatrains seem overcrowded with meaning; they force him continually to stop and think. But the *pantun* is not intended to be read. Slowly sung, with a long chorus or refrain after each line, it gains in merit by occupying the mind during the chorus instead of being dismissed as too transparent in its meaning. A verse, written to be read and to carry its meaning on the surface, would not stand the test of *pantun*-singing; it would make the chorus intolerably monotonous. This fact again makes it difficult to reproduce the attractiveness of the Malay quatrain through the medium of a foreign language and in the plain black-and-white of a printed page.

In *Tradition and Change in Contemporary Malay-Indonesian Poetry* (1977), Muhammad Haji Salleh provides an example of a well-known *pantun* "intense and compact":

Tinggi, tinggi simatahari,
Anak kerbau mati tertambat,
Dari dahulu sasya mencari
Baru ini saya mendapat.

Higher and higher climbs the sun,
The young buffalo dies at its peg,
So long have I waited my only one,
Only now are you found.

The Malayan *pantun berkait* is what we know as the pantoum. It is a highly repetitive form of indefinite length that inscribes something of its oral quality. It unfolds in interweaving quatrains and often rhymes *abab.* Lines two and four of each stanza repeat as lines one and three of the following stanza. The reader always takes four steps forward and two back. A pantoum typically begins:

Line 1: A
Line 2: B
Line 3: C
Line 4: D

Line 5: B
Line 6: E
Line 7: D
Line 8: F

Line 9: E
Line 10: G
Line 11: F
Line 12: H

It is customary for the second and fourth lines in the last stanza of the poem to repeat the first and third lines of the initial stanza, so that the whole poem circles back to the beginning, like a snake eating its tail. This slow and highly balanced repetitive form was introduced to Western poetry in the nineteenth century by the French Orientalist Ernest Fouinet (the *malais pantun*) and popularized by Victor Hugo in his book *Les Orientales* (1829). It was a recognizable form in nineteenth-century French poetry (Théodore de Banville, Louisa Siefert, Leconte de Lisle, Charles Baudelaire) and entered English poetry through the vogue for songlike French forms, such as the villanelle and the ballade. As a form, the pantoum is always looking back over its shoulder, and thus it is well-suited to evoke a sense of times past. It is always turning back while moving forward; that's why it works so well for poignant poems of loss, such as Donald Justice's "Pantoum of the Great Depression" (1995), and poems of departure, such as Louis MacNeice's "Leaving Barra" (1937), which calls the sea "A carpet of brilliance taking / My leave for ever of the island."

SEE ALSO *ghazal.*

paradelle Billy Collins invented the *paradelle* to parody strict formal poems, especially the villanelle. In his note to "Paradelle for Susan" (*Picnic, Lightning*, 1998), he claimed that the *paradelle* is "one of the more demanding French fixed forms, first appearing in the *langue d'oc* love poety of the eleventh century. It is a poem of four six-line stanzas in which the first and second lines, as well as the third and fourth lines of the first three stanzas, must be identical. The fifth and sixth lines, which traditionally resolve these stanzas, must use all the words from the preceding lines and only those words. Similarly, the final stanza must use every word from all the preceding stanzas and only those words." Collins set out to write "an intentionally bad formal poem" and created the *paradelle,* a hoax form. Theresa M. Welford subsequently commissioned and compiled the anthology, *The Paradelle* (2006).

paradox The term *paradox* derives from a Greek word meaning "beyond belief." A literary paradox is beyond belief because it brings together two seemingly incongruous or contradictory ideas that turn out to be well-founded or true, as when Oscar Wilde announces, "I can resist anything except temptation." The witty exploration and testing of outrageous paradoxes was one of the strategic devices of seventeenth-century poets, such as John Donne ("The Paradox," 1633), George Herbert ("A Paradox: that the sicke are in a *better case,* then the Whole," first printed 1835), and Andrew Marvell, who writes in "Upon Appleton House" (ca. 1650):

> Let others tell the *Paradox,*
> How Eels now bellow in the Ox;

How Horses at their Tails do kick,
Turn'd as they hang to Leeches quick;
How boats can over Bridges sail;
And fishes do the Stables scale.
How *Salmons* trespassing are found
And Pikes are taken in the Pound.

In twentieth-century literary criticism, *paradox* was a key term for the New Critics. Cleanth Brooks argues that "the language of poetry is the language of paradox" and instances Wordsworth's "Composed upon Westminster Bridge, September 3, 1802," which gets its power from the paradoxical situation, the recognition, that "man-made London is a part of nature, too" (*The Well Wrought Urn,* 1947). In *Paradoxia Epidemica* (1966), her book on paradox in the Renaissance, Rosemary Colie writes that paradoxes exploit "the act of relative, or competing, value systems."

SEE ALSO *ambiguity, analogy, irony, metaphysical poets, New Criticism, oxymoron, tension.*

paragram, see *anagram.*

parallelism Greek: "side by side." Parallelism is the correspondence between two parts of an utterance (a phrase, a line, a verse) through syntactic and rhythmic repetition. It is a constitutive device in oral and archaic poetries. One thinks of the oral-formulaic strategies of the early epics, of chants, charms, and spells, of incantatory prayers. It is the central device of biblical Hebrew poetry, as in these lines from Psalm 96:

Let the heavens rejoice, and let the earth be glad;
let the sea roar, and the fulness thereof.
Let the field be joyful, and all that *is* therein: then
shall all the trees of the wood rejoice.

The buildup of parallel lines often creates a feeling of intense emotion — of incantation, of litany, of exaltation. It instills a reverence. It is also a more complex and estranging device than it might initially seem. It is filled with surprises. The Russian formalist critic Viktor Shklofsky points out in "Art as Technique" (1917), "The perception of disharmony in a harmonious context is important in parallelism. The purpose of parallelism, like the general purpose of imagery, is to transfer the usual perceptions of an object into the sphere of a new perception — that is, to make a unique semantic modification." This complex device of synthesis and accumulation (there are repetitions, for example, based on identity, on antithesis, on complementary meaning) has been wondrously explored in the ecstatic poetry of Christopher Smart (1722–1771) and William Blake (1757–1827). It is at the heart of Walt Whitman's ecstasies and of the work of his free-verse progeny, D. H. Lawrence (1885–1930), Theodore Roethke (1908–1963), and Allen Ginsberg (1926–1997).

SEE ALSO *anaphora, catalog poem, chant, charm, incanation, litany, Russian formalism, spell.*

para-poem Gavin Ewart (1916–1995) coined the term *para-poem* for a poem in which "without any intention of burlesque, you use the form and diction of another poet." His first para-poem, "Audenesque for an Invitation" (1971), emulated Auden's poem "Get there if you can," which borrowed the trochaic meter and couplet rhyme scheme of Tennyson's "Locksley Hall" (1835). The para-poem, an extreme of imitation, does not suffer from anxiety of influence because its connection to a precursor poem is so overt.

SEE ALSO *anxiety of influence.*

paraphrase Greek: "tell in other words." To paraphrase a passage or text is to render it in different language. In particular, to paraphrase a poem is to render it in prose, which raises inevitable problems, since the way a thing is said in poetry cannot be separated from what is being said. Paraphrase thus becomes a mode of translation. We tend to think of paraphrase as a problem taken up by modern literary criticism — the New Critics spoke of "the heresy of paraphrase" — but the issue has a long history in rhetorical studies. Turning poetry into prose became an exercise in the schools of rhetoric sometime around the first century. It was recommended by Quintilian as a model for orators. Statius remembers in *Silvae* (ca. 89–96) how his father bore "the same yoke as Homer" and matched his hexameters in prose "without falling a step behind." Ernst Robert Curtius points out that a significant portion of early Christian poetry continues the practice of paraphrase. The Bible was recast into hexameters. "The Spaniard Juvencus (ca. 330) applies this procedure to the Gospels, the Egyptian Nomus (fifth century) to the

Gospel of John (in Greek), the Ligurian Arator to the Acts of the Apostles." The lives of the saints were also versified, and the versified lives were freshly turned back into prose. Caedmon inherits this tradition with his metrical paraphrase of parts of the Holy Scriptures in Anglo-Saxon. The Middle Ages viewed poetry and prose in reciprocal relationship.

SEE ALSO *explication de texte, heresy of paraphrase, translation.*

pararhyme, see *near rhyme.*

parison, see *isocolon.*

Parnassus A mythological home for poetry and music, Parnassus was a mountain in Greece with two peaks, one sacred to Apollo, the other to Dionysius. It thus represents the two poles of poetry: the cool, rational, and classical as well as the heated, irrational, and romantic. Its Castilian spring was sacred to the Muses.

SEE ALSO *muse, Parnassians.*

Parnassians The Parnassians were a group of late nineteenth-century French poets who stressed detachment and restraint, verbal precision and technical achievement. They reacted against what they perceived as the subjectivism and excess of romanticism in the work of Victor Hugo, Alphonse de Lamartine, and others. The group was initiated by Catulle Mendès and Louis-Xavier de Ricard in the early 1860s. The oracular center was Leconte de Lisle. Other members included Sully Prudhomme, Jean Lehor, José-Maria de Heredia, and Théodore Banville. The Parnassians took their cue from Théophile Gautier's doctrine of *l'art pour l'art* (art for art's sake), which suggested that art was an end in and of itself. They dramatically revived fixed forms and regarded poetry as a religion. They named their anthology *Le Parnasse contemporain,* which came out in three editions (1866–1876), after Mount Parnassus. Banville corresponded with Edmund Gosse, Andrew Lang, and Arthur Dobson, who in turn became English Parnassians. It was these poets (Gerard Manley Hopkins nicknamed them the *Rondeliers*) who largely created the English vogue for French forms, such as the ballade, the sestina, the triolet, and the villanelle.

The French Parnassians influenced such major poets as Stéphane Mallarmé and Paul Verlaine. "If I send you some of these verses," the seventeen-year-old Arthur Rimbaud wrote to Banville, "it is because I love all poets, all good Parnassians — since the poet is a Parnassian — in love with ideal beauty." The Polish poet Atoni Lange was a Parnassian and so was the Russian aesthete Afanasii Fet, whose poems have a high musicality ("I don't know what I will / Sing, but only that a song is maturing"). The international influence of the French Parnassians reached as far as Brazil, where Olavo Bilac became a Parnassian, and Nicaragua, where Rubén Dario transformed it into *modernísmo.* Its most lasting influence was on the symbolist movement itself.

SEE ALSO *aestheticism, ballade, bouts-rimés, modernismo, Parnassus, sestina, symbolism, triolet, villanelle.*

parody Parody is often defined as the exaggerated imitation of a work of art. It distorts for comic effect. The *Oxford English Dictionary* defines parody as "a composition . . . in which characteristic turns of an author . . . are imitated in such a way as to make them appear ridiculous, especially by applying them to ludicrously inapproprópirate subjects." This makes parody close to burlesque, which ridicules a style by exaggerating it, as well as to travesty ("a grotesque or debased imitation or likeness"). Dwight Macdonald proposes the following hierarchy in "Some Notes on Parody" (1960): "*Travesty* (literally 'changing clothes,' as in 'transvestite') is the most primitive form. It raises laughs from the belly rather than the head, by putting high, classic characters into prosaic situations, with a corresponding stepping-down of the language. . . . *Burlesque* (from Italian *burla,* 'ridicule') is a more advanced form since it at least imitates the style of the original. It differs from parody in that the writer is concerned with the original not in itself but merely as a device for topical humor. . . . *Parody,* from the Greek *parodia* (a beside- or against-song), concentrates on the style and thought of the original. If burlesque is pouring new wine into old bottles, parody is making a new wine that tastes like the old but has a slightly lethal effect."

Parody tends to be socially motivated and antiromantic. It feeds equally on the extremes of simplicity and ornateness. In Greek literature, Aristophanes (ca. 450–ca. 388 B.C.E.) first made the leap from burlesque to parody. His satirical imitations of Aeschylus (525–456 B.C.E.), Euripides (480?–406 B.C.E.), and Socrates (470?–399 B.C.E.) in such comedies as *The Frogs* (405 B.C.E.), *The Birds* (414 B.C.E.), and *The Acharnians*

(425 B.C.E.) turned parody into a genuine art. Parody is by its very nature a late, self-conscious, responsive form. Its mockery feeds off something prior, previous. It is a form of gamesmanship that mimics and appropriates the discourse and language of an original text; the form and style become the object of representation. It captures something of an originating spirit while also distancing itself from the original, which it shows up by pointing to its artificiality.

SEE ALSO *burlesque, satire.*

parole in libertà "Words in freedom." The Italian futurist F. T. Marinetti (1876–1944) coined the phrase *parole in libertà.* He sought to abolish such grammatical staples as syntax, adjectives and adverbs, conjunctions. He wanted to free the poem from punctuation and liberate the word from its linear bondage. In such onomatopoetic poems as "Zang Tumb Tuum" (1914), an account of the Battle of Adrianople, he employed a new typography for a sound poem that mimicked the noises produced in battle and mimed the fevers of modern life.

SEE ALSO *futurism, poemetto, sound poetry.*

partimen, see *tenson.*

pastoral From the Latin "pastor," meaning "shepherd." In the third century B.C.E., the Greek poet Theocritus originated the pastoral in his ten poems ("idylls") representing the life of Sicilian shepherds. Virgil deliberately imitated Theocritus in his *Eclogues* (42–39 B.C.E.) and thus created the enduring literary model of the pastoral: a conventional poem that expresses an urban poet's nostalgic image of the simple, peaceful life of shepherds living in idealized natural settings. The term *bucolic,* first introduced by Theocritus in *Idyll* 1 and taken from the Greek word for "herdsman," is generally used as a synonym for *pastoral.* Virgil's ten pastoral poems, which he refers to as *pastorem carmen* (*Georgic* 4), were labeled "bucolics" by grammarians. Virgil believed that a young poet should learn his craft by writing pastorals before proceeding on to the grander form of the epic, an apprenticeship that was followed by English poets from Edmund Spenser (*The Shepheardes Calender,* 1579) to John Keats, who explained in "Sleep and Poetry" (1816):

. . . First the realm I'll pass
Of Flora, and old Pan: sleep in the grass,
Feed upon apples red, and strawberries,
And choose each pleasure that my fancy sees;
Catch the white-handed nymphs in shady places . . .
And can I ever bid these joys farewell?
Yes, I must pass them for a nobler life,
Where I may find the agonies, the strife
Of human hearts — for lo! I see afar,
O'er sailing the blue cragginess, a car
And steeds with streamy manes — . . .

The forms of the pastoral lyric include the complaint, the singing match, the elegy, the blazon, and the palinode. Many bucolic poems end with the setting of the sun, which befits an outdoor conversation. This became one of the conventions of the pastoral. In Garcilaso de la Vega's first eclogue, for example, two shepherds sing through an entire day; one begins at sunrise, the other concludes at sunset. At sixteen, Alexander Pope defined the pastoral as "an imitation of the action of a shepherd; the form of the imitation is dramatic or narrative, or mixed of both, the fable simple, the manners not too polite nor too rustic" ("A Discourse on Pastoral Poetry," 1704). He also believed in concealing the miseries of a shepherd's life and thus revealed one self-imposed limitation of the eighteenth-century form, which he elevated to a work of high artifice in *Pastorals* (1709). In the eighteenth century, poets began to critique the elegant formulas of the pastoral by contrasting them to actual rural life. Thus George Crabbe wrote in *The Village* (1783):

By such examples taught, to paint the Cot,
As Truth will paint it, and as Bards will not.

Crabbe formally rejected the neoclassical pastoral with a type of counter-pastoral:

Fled are those times, when in harmonious strains
The rustic poet praised his native plains:
No shepherds now, in smooth alternate verse,
The country's beauty or the nymphs' rehearse.

In *Some Versions of Pastoral* (1936), William Empson expanded the concept of the pastoral to include any work that contrasts the simple and the complicated life, praising the former at the expense of the latter. The simple life can be represented by a shepherd, a child, a working man, and Empson applies the term to works ranging from Andrew Marvell's seventeenth-century poem "The Garden" to the modern proletarian novel. Writing in the middle of the Depression, Empson considered pastoral a "puzzling form" and "queer business" in which highly educated poets from the city idealized the lives of poor people close to the land. It implies "a beautiful relation between the rich and the poor" by making "simple people express strong feelings . . . in learned and fashionable language." After Empson, no one could read pastorals without being aware of the complex ambiguities and class tensions between cultivated urban authors and their low-born rural subjects. A status difference is always operating in pastoral literature. Raymond Williams has shown that the pastoral is also based on a necessary rhetorical contrast between the country and the city. The United States doesn't have shepherds or shepherdesses, but versions of pastoral have flourished in the cult of the Noble Red Man (Mark Twain derided him as "the Fenimore Cooper Indian" in "Fenimore Cooper's Literary Offenses," 1895) and the heroizing of cowboys, farmers, and miners, especially in the rural South and far West.

SEE ALSO *amoebean verse, blazon, complaint, eclogue, elegy, nature poetry, palinode, pastourelle, poetic contest.*

pastourelle The *pastourelle* (*pastorela* in Provençal) was a medieval French lyric with a pastoral theme. This short narrative poem had no fixed form but a highly determined theme: a passing knight tries to seduce a humble shepherdess, who defends herself against him. The knight tells the story with mock simplicity. At times the pretty shepherdess quickly yields, at times the knight violently takes her, and at times she cunningly outwits him. The encounter, which was often ribald and blasphemous, was more codified than the general pastoral. There is a powerful class difference between the high-ranking knight and the lowly shepherdess that energizes the verbal exchange and seduction. The *pastourelle* was one of the most popular genres created and performed by troubadours and trouvères.

SEE ALSO *pastoral, troubadour, trouvère.*

pathetic fallacy In his book *Modern Painters* (1856), John Ruskin invented the phrase *pathetic fallacy* to describe the attribution of human characteristics to the natural world, or to inanimate objects. To illustrate his point Ruskin quoted from Charles Kingsley's "The Sands of Dee" (1849):

> They rowed her in across the rolling foam—
> The cruel, crawling foam.

"The foam is not cruel, neither does it crawl," Ruskin wrote: "The state of mind which attributes to it these characters of a living creature is one in which the reason is unhinged by grief. All violent feelings . . . produce in us a falseness in all our impressions of external things, which I would characterize as the 'pathetic fallacy.' "

What was for Ruskin a derogatory term, a morbid romantic and Victorian phenomenon, has been a central poetic device of archaic and tribal poetries everywhere, which view the natural world as alive in all its parts. One might alternately think of the pathetic fallacy as empathic feeling for the overlooked world. George Santayana pointed out that "the pathetic fallacy is a return to that early habit of thought by which our ancestors peopled the world with benevolent and malevolent spirits; what they felt in the presence of objects they took to be part of the objects themselves." This projection of feeling has also flourished as a strain in epic poetry from Homer onward, as a feature of prophetic poetry from the major and minor prophets of the Hebrew Bible to Smart and Blake, Coleridge and Shelley, Whitman and Crane. It emerges whenever poets testify to, or dream of, the natural world saturated with psyche.

SEE ALSO *personification.*

pathos Greek: "suffering," "passion." Pathos is the quality in a work of literature that evokes feelings of pity, tenderness, sympathy, or sorrow. Aristotle defines *pathos* in the *Poetics* (350 B.C.E.): "The pathos is a destructive or painful action, for example, deaths in full view, and great pain, and wounds, and things of this kind." It persuades by appealing to the emotions of an audience. "The root idea of pathos is the exclusion of an individual on our own level from a social group to which he is trying to belong," Northrop Frye explains. "Hence the central tradition of sophisticated pathos is the study of the isolated mind, the story of how someone recognizably like ourselves is broken by a conflict between the inner and outer world, between imaginative reality and the sort of reality which is established by a social consensus."

SEE ALSO *mono no aware, tragedy.*

pattern poetry A form of spatial prosody, pattern poetry (or *technopaignia*) offers verses as visual arrangements on the page. The impulse to display poetry in concrete shapes is ancient, and pattern poems have been found in Greek, Latin (*carmen figuratum:* "shaped poem"), Hebrew, Chinese, Sanskrit, ancient Persian, German (*Bildergedict:* "picture poem"), and in most of the other modern European languages. The pattern poem (that is, the poem shaped like an egg or a pair of wings) promotes itself as a hybrid, a combination of verbal and visual art. It concretizes the relationship between content and form, and invites, even challenges, the reader to perceive the relationship between the shape and the theme.

One thinks, for example, of how the shape echoes the meaning in George Herbert's "The Altar" (1633), which presents itself in the shape of an altar table.

A broken ALTAR, Lord thy servant rears,
Made of a heart, and cemented with teares:
Whose parts are as thy hand did frame;
No workman's tool hath touch'd the same.
A HEART alone
Is such a stone,
As nothing but
Thy pow'r doth cut.
Wherefore each part
Of my hard heart
Meets in this frame,
To praise thy Name:
That, if I chance to hold my peace,
These stones to praise thee may not cease.
O let thy blessed SACRIFICE be mine,
And sanctifie this ALTAR to be thine.

George Puttenham characterized pattern poems as "ocular representations" in *The Arte of English Poesie* (1589), where he explains: "Your last proportion is that of figure, so called for that it yields an oracular representation, your meters being by good symmetrie reduced into certain Geometricall figures, whereby the maker is restrained to keepe him within his bounds, and sheweth not onely more art, but serveth also much better for briefenesse and subtitle of device." He says that he discovered such "poem gems" in Italy. Puttenham recognizes the objectlike character of pattern poems, some of which are three-dimensional and appeal first of all to the eye. They objectify poetry. The Turkish and Persian pattern poem traditions, which he calls "Oriental," take poetry into the realm of calligraphy as well as the ornamentation of manuscripts. The pattern poem is part of a visual poetic.

SEE ALSO *calligramme, concrete poetry, emblem.*

payada, payador The *payada* is an Argentine term for a poetic contest of questions and answers among the gauchos, who figure deeply into Argentine national consciousness. The *payadores* were the oral poets of Argentina and have legendary status. There were also *payadores* in Uruguay and Bolivia. In 1945, Mario López de Osornio characterizes the Argentine *payador:*

> The *payador* was something more than a mere improviser, since, in addition to knowing how to improvise, he knew how to sing, how to declaim and strum the guitar. The word *payador* comes from Quecha, *paya/palla* "to pick up from the ground," as if, in metaphorical terms, it was the act of lifting from the ground the gauntlet, the challenge made to a *payador* to answer some question, in verse and with musical accompaniment. Sometimes, versified *contrapunto* dialogues would be struck up, giving each other reciprocal problems and testing the skill and mental agility of each singer, so as to save their respective prestige.

SEE ALSO *gaucho poetry, poetic contest.*

Pegagus The winged horse of Greek mythology. Hesiod (eighth century B.C.E.) thought that Pegasus, a favorite of the Muses, was named for the springs (*pegai*) of Oceanus, and Ovid (43 B.C.E.–18 C.E.) tells how the winged horse produced the spring on Mount Helicon by striking the ground with his hoof. In post-classical times, Pegasus became the traditional symbol of poetic inspiration. "I hope, to ride Pegasus yet," Emerson confided to Thoreau, "and I hope not destined to be thrown." The speaker in C. Day Lewis's poem "Pegasus" (1957) comes across a winged white horse on a hillside: " 'Pegasus,' he called, 'Pegasus,' — with the surprise / Of one for the first time naming his naked lover."

pentastich A stanza or poem of five lines.

SEE ALSO *quintet.*

perfect rhyme, see *rhyme.*

performance poetry Oral poetry is actualized in performance. Poetry itself originated as a performing art. In languages that are not written, such as Yoruba, which has a great poetic tradition, all poetry is by its very nature performance poetry, since it can be experienced only through live performance. The term *performance poetry* specifically came into vogue in the 1980s to refer to a type of contemporary poetry composed either for or during a performance before an audience. Performance poetry is closely akin to performance art (live artistic events) and part of the Spoken Word movement.

In the 1970s and '80s, folklorists also developed a performance-centered approach to verbal art, focusing less on folklore as a body of material and more on folklore as a mode of communication. Accordingly, spoken art is characterized as a way of speaking that emerges in performance, a living context. This is as true for miniature genres, such as proverbs and riddles, as it is for narratives ones, such as the ballad and the epic. As Richard Bauman explains in "Verbal Art as Performance" (1974): "Fundamentally, performance as a mode of spoken verbal communication consists in the assumption of responsibility to an audience for a display of communicative competence."

The idea of performance highlights poetry as something emergent, created for someone else. The poet takes responsibility for the event to an audience. In written poetry, words also perform, but on the page, for the reader. "I look upon a poem as a performance," Robert Frost told an interviewer in 1960. "The whole thing is performance and prowess and feats of association."

SEE ALSO *ballad, epic, oral poetry, proverb, riddle, slam poetry, sound poetry, spoken word poetry.*

periphrasis, see *circumlocution.*

persona The character or voice created by the speaker or narrator in a literary work. In Latin, the term *persona* means "the mask (a false face of clay or bark) worn by actors in the ancient classical theater." The term *dramatis personae,* which refers to the characters in a play, derives from *persona,* as does the word *person.* The concept of persona originates in magical thinking, in archaic rituals where masks are independent beings that possess the ones who assume them. The poetic move into personae has a quality of animism; it embodies the displacement of the poet's self into a second self.

In "A General Introduction for My Work" (1937), W. B. Yeats said that the poet "never speaks directly as to someone at the breakfast table, there is always a phantasmagoria." The term *personae* refers to all forms of this phantasmagoria, from the narrators in Chaucer's *Canterbury Tales* (ca. 1387–1400) to the unidentified autobiographical speakers in Emily Dickinson's lyrics and Stevie Smith's poems to the characters in Robert Browning's dramatic monologues. Writing to Thomas Wentworth Higginson in 1862, Dickinson warned, "When I state myself, as the Representitive of the Verse — it does not mean — me — but a supposed person." Ezra Pound called his selected early poems, one of the key modernist texts, *Personae* (1926), and thus established the masks at the heart of his work. The move into personae brings into psychic range all the historical figures who animated Pound's early poetry, especially the Provençal poets, who served as his primary "masks of the self." Creating a persona is a way of staging an utterance. There is always a difference between the writer who sits down to work and the author who emerges in the text. Selfhood is a constructive process in poetry, which depends on collaboration, something created between writer and reader.

SEE ALSO *dramatic monologue.*

personification The attribution of human qualities to inanimate objects, to animals or ideas, as when Sylvia Plath engenders the moon as female ("The Moon and the Yew Tree," 1961) or Philip Sidney apostrophizes it:

> With how sad steps, O moon, thou climb'st the skies!
> How silently, and with how wan a face!

Native American poets often personify the moon, the sun, and the morning star. Ruth Finnegan points out in *Oral Literature* (1977) that personification is often a prominent feature of African praise poetry, where the warrior hero is personified as a ferocious and brave animal (a lion, a vulture, a buffalo, a spotted hyena, an untamed bull, or a bird of prey) or else as thunder, the sky, or a storm.

We personify poetic terms when we define rhymes as "masculine" or "feminine." Personification has sometimes been thought a quirky or marginal poetic activity, but it may be central to the Orphic function of the poet, who, as Emerson said, "puts eyes and tongues into every dumb and inanimate object."

Prosopopoeia is a form of personification in which an inanimate object gains the capacity to speak. For example, in the Old English poem "The Dream of the Rood," parts of which may date to the early eighth century, the wooden cross describes the death of Christ from its own point of view.

Personification has special purpose as the basis for allegory. Think, for example, of those medieval morality plays in which characters are named "Lust" or "Hope," thus indicating that general ideas, and not individual people, are being dramatized.

SEE ALSO *allegory, pathetic fallacy, praise poems.*

Personism Frank O'Hara mockingly coined this term in "Personism: A Manifesto" (1959). It was a response to Allen Ginsberg's argument, later published in an essay called "Abstraction in Poetry" (1961), that poems such as O'Hara's "Second Avenue" were experiments in writing "long meaningless poems." Ginsburg suggested that O'Hara's "freedom of composition" would help create a new poetry comparable to abstract art. It would avoid everything personal. O'Hara found Ginsberg's argument "intriguing" but not quite accurate:

> Personism, a movement which I recently founded and which nobody knows about, interests me a great deal, being so totally opposed to this kind of abstract removal that it is verging on true abstraction for the first time, really, in the history of poetry . . . Personism has nothing to do with philosophy, it's all art. It does not have to do with personality or intimacy, far from it! But to give you a vague idea, one of its minimal aspects is to address itself to one person (other than the poet himself), thus evoking overtones of love without destroying love's life-giving vulgarity, and sustaining the poet's feeling about the person. That's part of Personism. It was founded by me after lunch with LeRoi Jones on August 27, 1959, a day in which I was in love with someone (not Roi, by the way, a blond). I went back to work and wrote a poem for this person. While I was writing it I was realizing that if I wanted to I could use the telephone instead of writing the poem, and so Personism was born.

The poem that O'Hara refers to is called "Personal Poem" (1959). He jests that he might just as well have used the phone as written the poem, but behind the joke is a genuine idea. The poet doesn't bare his soul, according to O'Hara, but the poem does create a relationship between two people not physically present to each other. It creates an intimacy (or the fiction of an intimacy) between two people, an "I" and a "you." It's as if the reader is overhearing one side of a telephone conversation in progress.

SEE ALSO *New York school of poets.*

Petrarchism Petrarch's *Rerum vulgarium fragmenta* (Fragments of Vernacular Matters), more commonly known as the *Ríma sparse* (Scattered Rhymes) or the *Il Canzonierre* (Song-book), consists of 366 lyrics composed between 1336 and 1374. It comprises what Michael Spiller calls "the single greatest influence on the love poetry of Renaissance Europe until well into the seventeenth century." Petrarchism is the widespread imitation of the conventions of Petrarch's poetry, its themes, motifs, and meters, its conflicts and values, its repertoire of situations, its modes of praise, its idealizations. Some of the *topoi* or commonplaces of Petrarchism: unrequited love; the lover addicted to love even though he is burning in his own passion, in an icy fire; love as pain; love as a passion beyond the will; love as an invisible chain; the lover eternally faithful to his idealized lady. Petrarch created a stylized language of love that became a kind of international Esperanto in Renaissance and baroque poetry. This also gave rise to a demythologizing anti-Petrarchism or counter-discourse. William Shakespeare's early Sonnet 18, "Shall I compare thee to a summer's day?" (1609) develops a Petrarchist conceit. His later Sonnet 130, "My mistress' eyes are nothing like the sun" (1609), rejects what had by then become the convention of flattering a typecast mistress in a clichéd language. It is an anti-Petrarchist poem.

SEE ALSO *baroque, complaint, conceit, courtly love, Elizabethan Age, Renaissance poetry, rhyme royal, songbook, sonnet, topos.*

phanopoeia The imagistic qualities of poetry. In *ABC of Reading* (1934), Ezra Pound described *phanopoeia* as "the throwing of an image on the mind's retina." In *How to Read* (1929), he utilized the term to characterize one of three "kinds of poetry":

> PHANOPOEIA, which is a casting of images upon the visual imagination.

Pound emphasized, "In *Phanoepioeia* we find the greatest drive toward utter precision of word." He also noted that pictorial or revelatory image is the one part of poetry that survives translation. We might say that imagism was a movement that staked everything on *phanopoeia.* Pound found the highest achievement of the visual imagination in classical Chinese poetry. What Pound termed *phanopoeia,* Samuel Taylor Coleridge called "poetry of the eye" ("On the Principles of Genial Criticism," 1814).

SEE ALSO *imagism, logopoeia, melopoeia.*

picong In the West Indies, a light banter, a friendly mockery, a series of sustained taunts is called *picong.* The word may derive from the Spanish adjective *picón,* meaning "mocking" or "huffing," or the French *piquant* (literally, "prickling"), which now means "appealingly provocative," but once also carried the meaning of "stinging" or "causing hurt feelings." Roger Abrahams points out in *Singing the Master* (1992) that this kind of verbal play is found in many places in the West Indies and other parts of the black New World, where it is also called 'busin', cursing, nigger business, *manguyu,* and rhyming. It can tip over into what Trinidadians call *mamaguy,* or putting someone on, deceiving them with flattery. The earliest Trinidadian calypsonians were called chantwells, and in the Francophonic areas the chantwell or praise poet is empowered to aim songs at specific politicians and groups. The name for their songs is *chant pwen* (pointed song).

Picong originated as a verbal duel in song. It is particularly adversarial in Trinidad. At calypso festivals, *picong* takes the form of a spontaneous, combustible, highly competitive verbal contest between two or more performers ("calypsonians"), as in the legendary *Picong Duel* between the Mighty Sparrow and Lord Melody (Smithsonian Folkways Recordings, 2000), who have taken *picong* battle-names. In one common form, verses are sung to the same traditional melody. Each stanza concludes with the patois refrain *sans humanité* ("no pity" or "without humanity"). The singers are pitiless in pillorying each other.

SEE ALSO *poetic contest, praise poems.*

picturesque The word *picturesque* was used as early as 1703 to mean "in the manner of a picture; fit to be made into a picture" (*Oxford English Dictionary*). It came into vogue in the early eighteenth century as an Anglicization of the Italian *pittoresco* or the French *pittoresque.* William Gilpin defined *picturesque* as "a term expressive of that peculiar kind of beauty, which is agreeable in a picture" (*Essay on Prints,* 1768) and introduced it as an English aesthetic ideal in his book with the jaw-breaking title, *Observations on the River Wye, and Several Parts of South Wales, etc. Relative Chiefly to Picturesque Beauty; made in the Summer of the Year 1770* (1782), which instructed travelers to look at "the face of a country by the rules of picturesque beauty." He later explained to Joshua Reynolds, "With regard to the term *picturesque,* I have always used it merely to denote *such objects, as are proper subjects for painting.*"

The picturesque is part of the history of travel and tourism. It reflects a growing eighteenth-century taste for natural scenery and scenic touring. Picturesque poetry aspired to the condition of painting. There is in picturesque or descriptive verse a tension between the spatial dimension of pictorial art and the temporal nature of poetry. Aesthetically, picturesque poetry situated itself between the counter ideals of the beautiful and the sublime. As Angus Fletcher explains in *Allegory* (1964), "Picturesque might best be defined as inverse, or microscopic, sublimity: where the sublime aims at great size and grandeur, the picturesque aims at littleness and a sort of modesty; where the sublime is austere, the picturesque is intricate; where the sublime produces 'terror,' or rather, awed anxiety, the picturesque produces an almost excessive feeling of comfort." The strength of the picturesque is in the landscape poetry of the late eighteenth and early nineteenth centuries, such as Wordsworth's early poetry in *Descriptive Sketches* (1893), which describes his observations during a walking tour through the Alps in 1790. The problem of the picturesque is that it is also a mode of veiling or hiding whatever doesn't suit the prettiness of the picture. David Marshal points out: "The picturesque represents a point of view that frames the world and turns nature into a series of *living tableaux.* It begins as an appreciation of natural beauty, but it ends by turning people into figures in a landscape or figures in a painting."

SEE ALSO *romanticism, the sublime, ut pictura poesis.*

piyyut A Jewish liturgical poem. The medieval *piyyut* was a formal poem, written in Hebrew or Aramaic, intended to be recited, chanted, or sung during religious services. The form developed in Palestine sometime between the second and sixth century. The *piyyut* was a poem with an ornamental purpose, a poetic supplement to the fixed prayers of the traditional liturgy. The major forms followed a strictly observed strophic structure and a rhythm based on a fixed number of words per line. They rhymed in different ways. Many of the poems were also structured around an acrostic that employed all (or some) of the twenty-two letters of the Hebrew alphabet. Often the poet signed the poem with an acrostic of his name. *Paytan* is the term for the liturgical poet who composes *piyyutim.* Both words derive from the Greek word *poietes* (maker).

SEE ALSO *acrostic, parallelism.*

the plain style The plain style originated as an informal rhetorical term to characterize speech or writing that is simple, direct, and unambiguous. Richard Lanham characterizes its three central values as "Clarity, Brevity, and Simplicity." The plain style, which dates to the Latin Stoics, was associated with a "low style" as opposed to a "high style." In "The Sixteenth-Century Lyric in England" (1939), Yvor Winters demonstrated the presence of two styles of poetry in the English Renaissance lyric: one was plain, the other ornate and decorative. Winters used this distinction to suggest an alternative canon of Elizabethan poetry. He excluded the more famous Petrarchan poets, such as Sir Philip Sidney and Edmund Spenser, and proposed elevating anti-Petrarchan poets of a native or plain style, such as George Gascoigne, Barnabe Googe, George Turberville, Sir Walter Raleigh, and Thomas Nashe. He elevated the anti-Petrarchan poems of Sir Thomas Wyatt at the expense of his other Petrachan poems. According to Winters, the plain-style poem has "a theme usually broad, simple, and obvious, even tending toward the proverbial, but usually a theme of some importance, humanly speaking; a feeling restrained to the minimum required by the subject; a rhetoric restrained to a similar minimum, the poet being interested in his rhetoric as a means of stating his matter as economically as possible, and not, as are the Petrarchans, in the pleasures of rhetoric for its own sake."

The two different Renaissance types of poetry grew out of two different traditions, one the "popular" or "vulgar" style, the other the eloquent style. The plain style originated in the idiom of common people as opposed to the eloquent style, which developed out of the traditions of the court, and developed directly out of medieval didactic poetry. Douglas Peterson characterizes its primary characteristics as "direct summary statement tending toward folk aphorism, a predominantly Anglo-Saxon diction, folk proverb and metaphor, a tone of moral severity." The plain style registered as a poetry that was anti-courtly and classically minded. Ben Jonson's classicism, his commitment to a lucid, passionate plainness, has been identified as a model plain style. The Puritans developed a plain style, a spiritual ethic, which was simple, spare, and straightforward. It defined their sermons and informed their poems. Winters himself practiced a formal poetry of the plain style, and so did two of his most gifted protégés, Edgar Bowers (1924–2000) and J. V. Cunningham (1911–1985). Winters describes Cunningham's style in "The Plain Style Reborn" (1967):

> The mature style is what we could call the plain style if we met it in the Renaissance. It is free of ornament, almost without sensory detail, and compact. But it is a highly sophisticated version of the plain style, and is very complex without loss of clarity. It comes closer, perhaps, to Ben Jonson and a few of his immediate contemporaries than to anyone else.

Edward Doughtie notes a strong parallel in sixteenth-century and early seventeenth-century music to the "plain" and "ornate" styles of English Renaissance poetry. The counterparts of the plain style would be the English and Scottish popular ballads, the metrical and homophonic psalms, and native consort songs. The counterparts of the ornate style would be the Italianate madrigals, which were either pastoral or Petrarchan.

SEE ALSO *aureate, ballad, drab and golden poetry, madrigal, pastoral, Petrarchism, psalms, Sons of Ben.*

planh A form of Provençal poetry, the *planh,* a funeral lament, was a specialized type of the sirventes, a didactic genre. It typically mourns the loss of a lover, a friend, or a grand personage. There are forty or so *planhs* that have survived from the years 1137 to 1343. Most of them conventionally bewail the death of a noble, usually the patron or patroness of the poet. These are official poems. The most famous poem of the Italian troubadour Sordello (ca. 1180–1269) was his *planh* "Serventes" on the death of his patron, Blacatz ("Blacatz is dead"), which greatly influenced Dante. The young Ezra Pound borrowed the tone for his "Planh for the Young English King" (1909), which was a translation of a poem written by Bertran de Born on the death of Prince Henry, the "Young King." Pound called the poem "one of the noblest laments or 'planh' in the Provençal" (*The Spirit of Romance,* 1910). He establishes the high tone and subject in the first stanza:

> If all the grief and woe and bitterness,
> All dolour, ill and every evil chance
> That ever came upon this grieving world
> Were set together they would seem but light
> Against the death of the young English King.
> Worth lieth riven and Youth dolorous,
> The world o'ershadowed, soiled and overcast,
> Void of all joy and full of ire and sadness.

W. S. Merwin's mourning poem, "Planh for the Death of Ted Hughes" (1999), imparts the contemporary with a deep sense of poetic lineage.

SEE ALSO *elegy, lament, sirventes, troubadour.*

Platonic love In popular culture, platonic love commonly refers to an affectionate but nonsexual relationship. Plato's ideal of love was not platonic love as we currently understand it. Plato notably discusses love (*erôs*) and friendship (*philia*) in the *Lysis* (ca. 399–ca. 387 B.C.E.), the *Symposium* (ca. 385–380 B.C.E.), and *Phaedrus* (ca. 370 B.C.E.). For Plato, love is a motivating force. The highest love is love of the idea of beauty. He posits that the desire for an individual as well as for physical beauty grows or evolves into the loving contemplation of the spiritual or an ideal beauty. "He who loves the beautiful is called a lover because he partakes of it" (*Phaedrus*). The Greek word *philosophia* means "love of wisdom." But this love of wisdom can also lead to divine madness. Thus Socrates explains "the madness of a man who, on seeing beauty here on earth, and being reminded of true beauty, becomes winged, and fluttering with eagerness to fly upwards, but unable to leave the ground, looks upward like a bird, and takes no heed of things below—and that is what caused him to be regarded as mad" (*Phaedrus*). According to Plato, the love for beauty can never be fully attained on earth.

In the fifteenth century, the Florentine scholar Marsilio Ficino coined the phrase *amor platonicus,* referring to the affection between Socrates and his pupils. It was during the Renaissance that the idea of platonic love was watered down and changed into a notion of chaste friendship—courtly, intellectual—between a man and a woman. The first recorded use of the phrase in English is Sir William Davenant's satirical tragicomedy, *The Platonick Lovers* (1636). Platonic love in this new sense became one of the subjects of Renaissance poetry, as in Abraham Cowley's sexy "Platonic Love" (1656), which begins:

> Indeed I must confess,
> When souls mix 'tis an happiness,
> But not complete till bodies too do join,
> And both our wholes into one whole combine;
> But half of heaven the souls in glory taste
> Till by love in heaven at last
> Their bodies too are placed.

SEE ALSO *courtly love, Renaissance poetry.*

La Pléiade In the third century B.C.E., a group of seven poets in Alexandria named themselves the Pleiad. They took their name from the seven stars of the Pleiad star cluster, which glowed with a single light. Lycophron is the only one whose work survived the destruction of the Great Library of Alexandria. Eighteen hundred years later, Pierre de Ronsard borrowed the name for a group of seven mid-sixteenth-century French poets. The group included Joachim du Bellay, Jean-Antoine de Baïf, Pontus de Tyard, Jacques Pelletier, Remy Belleau, Etienne Jodelle, and Ronsard himself. The members of the group, which was originally called Brigade, sometimes changed (the Hellenist Jean Dorat replaced Pelletier, for example) but the number never exceeded seven.

La Pléiade poets called for a synthesis between French and Greco-Latin literature. They wanted to raise French literature to the stature of the classics. Du Bellay's landmark defense, *The Defense and Ennoblement of the French Language* (1549), became a manifesto for the new Renaissance literature in French. Ronsard's *The First Four Books of Odes* (1550) was one of the high-water marks of a new French poetry that assimilated classical models. The *Pléiade* poets imitated rather than translated classical poetry and helped to inaugurate a new European literature.

SEE ALSO *classic.*

plurisignation A profusion or amplitude of meanings. Philip Wheelright introduced this term to the discussion of poetry as an alternative to William Empson's term *ambiguity.* In *The Burning Fountain* (1954), Wheelwright argues that *ambiguity* connotes doubt and puzzlement and that *plurisignation* would be preferable to suggest the capacity of language to sustain multiple meanings. He writes: "Real plurisignation differs from simply punning or wit-writing. . . . Empson's use of the term 'ambiguity' generally refers to the plurisignative character of poetic language; his word is inappropriate, however, since ambiguity implies an 'either-or' relation, plurisignation a 'both-and.' "

SEE ALSO *ambiguity.*

poem A made thing, a verbal construct, an event in language. In ancient Greek, the word *poiesis* means "making." Plato explains in the *Symposium* (ca. 385–380 B.C.E.), "All production of things is *poiesis.* Producing poetry stands to the general domain of production as part to the whole." The medieval and Renaissance poets used the word *makers,* as in "courtly makers," as a precise equivalent for poets, hence William Dunbar's "Lament for the Makers" (1508). The word *poem* came into English in the sixteenth century and has been with us ever since to denote a form of fabrication, a verbal composition, a humanly created thing of art.

Poems are made out of sounds and, usually, words. The exceptions, such as Zen poetry, which aspires to be soundless and even wordless, prove the rule. The sounds, constituent pieces, are almost always ahead of the words. In *The Wedge* (1944), William Carlos Williams defined the poem as "a small (or large) machine made of words." (He added that there is nothing sentimental or redundant about a machine.) In his useful essay "What Is Poetry?" (1933–1934), the linguist Roman Jakobson declared:

> Poeticity is present when the word is felt as a word and not a mere representation of the object being named or an outburst of emotion, when words and their composition, their meaning, their external and internal form, acquire a weight and value of their own instead of referring indifferently to reality.

The old Irish word *cerd,* meaning "people of the craft," was a designation for artisans, including poets. It is cognate with the Greek *kerdos,* meaning "craft, craftiness." Two basic metaphors for the art of poetry, the making of poems, in the classical world were carpentry and weaving. In many oral cultures, poets are also considered artisans as well as prophets, a dual role. "Whatever else it may be," W. H. Auden said, "a poem is a verbal artifact which must be as skillfully and solidly constructed as a table or a motorcycle."

The true poem has been crafted into a living entity. There is always something mysterious, something inexplicable in a poem. It is an act — an action — beyond paraphrase because what is said is always inseparable from the way it is being said. A poem creates an experience in the reader that cannot be reduced to anything else. Perhaps it exists in order to create that aesthetic experience of happening. Octavio Paz maintained that the poet and the reader are two moments of a single reality.

SEE ALSO *poetry.*

poëme The French poet Alfred de Vigny coined this term for "compositions . . . in which a philosophic thought is staged under an Epic or Dramatic form" (1837). Vigny's *poëmes* were essentially *pensées philosophiques.* He cited the line "I love the majesty of human suffering" ("J'aime la majesté des souffrances humaines") and said, "This verse holds the meaning of all my Poëmes philosophiques."

poemetto, poemetti (pl) Italian: a short longer poem. Two of the defining early twentieth-century *poemetti* are F. T. Marinetti's futurist *Zang Tumb Tuum* (1914) and Eugenio Montale's classical *Mediterranean* (1924), a *poemetto* in nine parts. There is no corresponding name in English for the mid-length poem, such as "The Waste Land" (1922), which is longer than the lyric and shorter than the epic. Frank Bidart's 1983 poems "The War of Vaslav Nijinsky" and "Confessional" could be called *poemetti.*

poesie, see *poetry.*

poète maudit French: "accursed poet." A French term for the poet as outsider, lost, unrecognized, ill-fated, rejected by bourgeois society, damned. Poets who are criminally inclined or socially off-kilter, prone to alcohol or drugs, crazy or suicidal, are often labeled *poètes maudits.* Alfred de Vigny coined the term in 1832 in his philosophical narrative, *Stello,* in which he argues that poets such as André Chénier (1762–1794) and Thomas Chatterton (1752–1770) come to unhappy ends because they belong to "a race always cursed by the powerful of the earth." Paul Verlaine subsequently took *Les poétes maudits* as the title of his 1884 homage to six symbolist poets: Tristan Corbière, Arthur Rimbaud, Stéphane Mallarmé, Marceline Desbordes-Valmore, Villiers de l'Isle-Adam, and Pauvre Lélian (an anagram for Paul Verlaine himself). The fifteenth-century French rascal François Villon is the prototype of the *poète maudit.* The shadow of mental breakdown hangs over such eighteenth-century poets as William Cowper and Christopher Smart, who described his agony: "For in my nature I quested for beauty, but God, God, hath sent me to sea for pearls" (*Jubilate Agno,* 1759–1763). Pierre Seghers redeploys the term in his 1972 anthology, *Poètes maudits d'aujourd'hui* (The Accursed Poets of Today). The curse can be a description, a cliché, a mode of praise, or all three at once. "*Les Maudits,*" Robert Lowell writes in his poem "For John Berryman" (1977), "the compliment / each American generation / pays itself in passing."

poetic closure Textual resolution. The idea of closure, how human beings perceive wholeness, first emerged in the twentieth century in relationship to gestalt psychology. In his book *The Sense of an Ending* (1967), Frank Kermode speaks of the human desire to impose order, the tendency to create endings in both literature and life. Barbara Herrnstein Smith brought the idea of poetic closure into critical discourse in the mid-1960s in her book *Poetic Closure: How Poems End* (1968), a study of the way that texts create structures of coherence, integrity, and completeness. Smith explores the way that poems set up expectations in readers, which are fulfilled or thwarted, thus creating a sense of "appropriate cessation" or open-endedness. Her study recognizes the way that poems operate as formal structures in time, like pieces of music.

Recent poststructuralist theories challenge the idea of textual closure. According to deconstruction, for example, there is no locus of meaning outside of language, and interpretation is without end. Deconstructionists argue that the instability of meaning makes it impossible to resolve a text. The ending doesn't necessarily provide a definitive or unified denouement.

SEE ALSO *deconstruction, poststructrualism, sonnet.*

poetic contest The poetic contest, a verbal duel, is common worldwide. It has been documented in a large number of different poetries as a highly stylized form of male aggression, a model of ritual combat, an agonistic channel, a steam valve, a kind of release through abuse. The poetic contest may be universal because it provides a socially acceptable form of rivalry and battle. It is a forum for insults with a built-in release valve — humor and exaggeration. It also provides a competitive venue for those who are not physically strong but enterprising, intelligent, and quick-witted.

The poetic contest has an ancient origin. There are instances, for example, in Aristophanes's plays *The Clouds* (423 B.C.E.) and *The Frogs* (405 B.C.E.), where he depicts Aeschylus competing against Euripides (after Sophocles declines to compete) and winning the exclusive right as the greatest tragedian to return to life from the underworld. The poetic contest — two speakers going back and forth against each other — played a crucial role in the development of drama, which is driven by agon. The Greek rhapsodes contended for prizes at religious festivals. Indeed, the Greeks created contests out of nearly every form of poetry, from wine songs to high tragedy. The Homeric *Hymn to Apollo,* usually dated to the seventh century B.C.E., depicts competitive singing, which is also mentioned in the *Hymns to Aphrodite* (from the same period). Hesiod claimed that he won a prize for performing a song at the funeral games for Amphidamas in Euboea. Eris, "competition" or "strife," is a god, Hesiod says, and wealth increases when "potter strives against potter, beggar against beggar, and singer against singer" (*Works and Days,* eighth century B.C.E.). Singing competitions in local peasant communities stand behind the literary pastoral, and there are just such contests of wit in the idylls of Theocritus and the eclogues of Virgil (*amoebean verses,* "responsive verses"). In antiquity, the memorization of poetry was frequently turned into a contest, a sort of philological parlor game, to enliven festive gatherings. The sophist Athenaeus (ca. 220) gives a description in "Scholars at a Banquet":

> Clearchus of Soli, a man of the school of Aristotle, also tells us how the ancients went about this. One recited a verse, and another had to go on with the next. One quoted a sentence, and a sentence from some other poet expressing the same idea had to be produced. Verses of such and such a number of syllables were demanded, or the leaders of the Greeks and of the Trojans had to be enumerated, or cities in Asia and Europe beginning with the same letter to be named in turn. They had to remember lines of Homer which begin and end with the same letter, or the first and last syllable taken together must yield a name or an implement or a food. The winner gained a garland, but anyone who blundered had brine poured into his drink and had to drain the whole cup at a draught.

Walter Ong suggests, "In pre-romantic, rhetorical culture, the poet is essentially a contestant." The poetic contest is a way of asserting, establishing, and proving selfhood.

The first professional competition for Welsh bards, an *eisteddfod,* or "session," was held in the twelfth century. The *Sängerkrieg* (minstrel's contest) or *Wartburkrieg* (Wartburg contest) was a legendary competition among the German *Minnesänger* at Thuringia in 1207. The French *débat,* which was especially popular in the twelfth and thirteenth centuries, sets up a contest, a quarrel or debate. The *tenson* (*tenzone, tencon*) was a type of debate poem developed by the troubadours in the twelfth century. From the twelfth to the seventeenth century, musical and literary societies in northern France, which were called *puys,* competed against each other in poetic contests. One of the heirs of the French debate poem is the Brazilian improvised verse dialogues or contests called *desafios* or *pelejas.* In northwestern Brazil, ballad singers with guitars still square off against each other in competitions known as *repentismo.* The audience shouts out themes, and the singers respond by improvising verses in a range of complicated meters. The *pregunta-respuesta* was a form of poetic debate in fourteenth- and fifteenth-century Castialian *cancionero* court poetry. One poet asks a question or a series of questions (the *pregunta* or *requesta*) and the other replies in matching form (the *respuesta*). There is verbal dueling in fifteenth-century Spanish plays. In these poetic contests known as *echarse pullas,* as J. P. Wickerhsam Crawford explained in 1915, "one person wished all sorts of misfortunes, for the most part obscene, upon another, who replied in a similar strain." The golden age scholar Rodgrigo Caro called these contests *darse grita,* or "shouting at one another," and traces Hispanic verbal dueling back to Horace, who in the *Epistolae* (*Epistles,* 2.1.145–146) speaks of the ritual, invented by the Fescennians, of hurling alternate verses at each other, *opprobria rustica,* or rustic taunts (*Días geniales o lúdicos,* ca. 1618). Crawford also describes among the Eskimos "a formal contest . . . which consists of heaping insulting terms upon each other until one of the contestants is exhausted." There are both formal and informal models for poetry contests. The Chamoru natives of the Mariana Islands have an ancient style of improvised rhyming debate known as *Kantan Chamorrita.* In Greenland, song duels were used as a judicial weapon. The offender and the victim faced off in front of a group of spectators, who served as the court.

Hija, or the poetry of invective, was one of the main modes of classical Arabic verse. It was often brutally insulting and frequently obscene. Abū al-Faraj al-Isfahānī's *Kītab al-Aghānī* (Book of Songs, tenth century), the most well-known compendia of medieval Arabic poetry, is filled with anecdotes of pre-Islamic and medieval poets dueling and debating, taking up challenges from their patrons, responding to rivals. There was a form of poetic contest in which one poet completed the lines of another to create a single poem (the *mumālatah*); there were duels in the *rajaz* meter (the *murājazah*) and duels in which poems shared the same rhyme and meter (*mu'āradah*); there were boasting competitions (the *mufākharah*); and there were tribal disputes worked out in a form of boasts and insults (the *munāfarah*). The *Aghānī* refers to the powerful poetry competitions at Sūq 'Ukāz (the market of 'Ukāz), where al-Nābighah al-Dhubyāni (ca. 535–ca. 604), one of the great court poets of Arabic literature, served as the first judge, and where the seventh-century female poet al-Kansā gained fame for her elegies for her brothers, who had died in battle, and dueled with the likes of Hind Bint 'Atabah and Hassān Ibn Thābit. When al-Nābighah suggested that she was the best of poets with a uterus, she responded "and of those with testicles as well!"

There is evidence that the spontaneously composed verbal duel in colloquial Hispano-Arabic dates to the tenth century, which makes it the oldest extant poetry composed in the Hispano-Arabic dialect. In 1161, the poets of the Levantine flocked to Gibraltar for a poetic contest presided over by 'Abd al-Mu'min to celebrate his conquest of al-Andalus. In Japan, in the years between 1087 and 1199, there were approximately two hundred formal poetry competitions held in the imperial palace as well as in temples and shrines. *Utaawase* is the equivalent Japanese form of the poetry match. Poets were often assigned a theme or *dai* ("given subject") for competitions. A *danjo utaawase* pitted men against women in a tanka contest. The topics were handed out well in advance for such major competitions as *Roppyakuban Utawaase* or "Poetry Contest in 600 Rounds" (1193) and the *Sengohyakuban Utaawase* or "Poetry Contest in 1,500 Rounds" (1201). The *utaawise* is a more gentle art than the fifteenth- and sixteenth-century Scottish *flyting,* which consisted of two bards excoriating each other and the chieftains with which they were associated. The word *flyting* derives from the Scots word for "scolding," and indeed, verbal contests are called *scolding* in Scandinavia. The Scottish poet James Hogg made his reputation on a minstrel contest poem, *The Queen's Wake* (1813), which dramatizes a contest of bards held before Mary, Queen of Scots on her arrival in Edinburgh. The poem, as Erik Simpson puts it, "splinters its minstrelsy into a din of competing voices."

There is tremendous energy in the West Indian *picong,* a series of sustained taunts or insults, which originated as a verbal duel in song. It is still a spontaneous competitive art form in calypso festivals. So, too, in the Xinjiang Uighur Autonomous Region of Northwest China, competitive dialogue songs have long been popular, especially at Hua'er festivals. These competitions take place between two singers or two groups of people. There are singing contests in central Asia among the Kirghis and the Kazakhians, among the Telengites in southeastern Altai, where they are known as *chenezh-kozhandar,* among the Shor, among the Yakut of northern Siberia. E. Emsheimer points out that they are a traditional part of the wedding festivities among the Iranian mountain Tajik in the Pamir Mountains. Among the hill-dwelling peoples of Negal, such as the Tamangs, pairs of men and women duel each other in improvised duets. The risk is great, especially for women, since a woman who loses is sometimes offered in marriage to the victor. Oral poetry duels are still an integral part of rural Palestinian weddings in the Galilee. The individual poetic duel, or "wedding *didong*" (*didong ngerjë*), was once the dominant verbal performance form of the Gayo, who live in the mountainous central highlands of the province of Aceh in northern Sumatra, Indonesia. These duels are still performed in the Terangon district of southern Gayoland. They have a strong element of formal oratory and involve two different virtuosi (*céh*) from different villages or units of villages. John R. Bowen points out that group poetic combats (*didong klub*) also emerged in the town of Takèngen in the late 1940s, which involved two teams, each consisting of ten to thirty men and boys, representing their respective villages and enacting a rivalry between two social domains. He writes that between 1900 and 1985, "Gayo poetic duels have shifted from a form that represents dominant sociopolitical relations as fixed and timeless to a form in which social combat, political control, and challenges to that control vie for a voice in the performance setting." The poetic duel is a form of "social modeling."

Improvised verbal confrontations are the center of *bertzolaritza,* oral Basque poetry. In the late nineteenth century, folk poets along the Texas-Mexico border competed to improvise ten-verse *décimas,* a tradition that is still alive in the Canary Islands. The *payada* — the term is Argentine — was a poetic contest of questions and answers among the gauchos, which was made famous in part 2 of José Fernandez's *Martín Fierro* (1879). In Panama, poetic duels and competitions (*duelos y porfías*) continue to take place in formalized public settings. In Madagascar, *hain-teny* ("the knowledge of words") is structured as a competitive verbal exchange between two "opponents" on the subject of love. The Chamula of Southern Mexico have a genre of verbal dueling they call "truly frivolous talk," Gary Gossen points out, "a verbal game in which two players, typically adolescent males, exchange as few as two or as many as 250 verbal challenges." Each opponent tries to marshal a maximum attack with a minimal shift in sound.

The African American verbal game of playing the dozens — an edgy contest of escalating insults — continues to thrive in American cities. The only successful slander and retaliation is a witty one. The poetry contest has been given a vital sociopolitical slant in contemporary American slam poetry, and there are now slam competitions in all fifty states. The beat goes on — fiery, social, engaged, competitive.

SEE ALSO *agon, amoebean verses, bertsolaritza, débat, décima, the dozens, eisteddfod, flyting, gaucho poetry, hain-teny, Kantan Chamorrita, oral poetry, picong, puy, Rhapsode, slam poetry, tenson, utaawase.*

poetic crossing The movement within a poem from one plane of reality to another, as when Dante crosses over from the earthly realm to the infernal regions in *The Inferno* (1304–1309). A poetic crossing, which follows the arc from physical motion to spiritual action, requires the blacking out of the quotidian world and the entrance into another type of consciousness, a more heightened reality. It is a move beyond the temporal, a visionary passage. Harold Bloom explores the consequences of poetic crossing in his study *Wallace Stevens: The Poems of Our Climate* (1976).

SEE ALSO *epiphany, vision.*

poetic diction Poetic diction refers to the operating language of poetry, language employed in a manner that sets poetry apart from other kinds of speech or writing. It involves the vocabulary, the phrasing, and the grammar considered appropriate and inappropriate to poetry at different times. In *Poetic Diction: A Study in Meaning* (1928), Owen Barfield writes, "When words are selected and arranged in such a way that their meaning either arouses, or is obviously intended to arouse, aesthetic imagination, the result may be described as *poetic diction.*"

Aristotle established poetic diction as a subject in the *Poetics* (350 B.C.E.). "Every word is either current, or strange, or metaphorical, or ornamental, or newly-coined, or lengthened, or contracted, or altered," he declared, and he then considered each type of word in turn. His overall concern was "how poetry combines elevation of language with perspicuity." Changes in poetic fashion, reforms in poetry, often have to do with the effectiveness of poetic diction, the magic of language. How, if at all, is poetic speech marked differently than ordinary speech? "The weightiest theoretical legacy which antiquity and the Renaissance passed on to neoclassicism was the ornamental conception of poetic style," Emerson Marks writes. "Till the dawn of Romanticism, writers continued to regard the characteristics of verse as raiment adorning the 'body' of a poet's thought." In *The Life of Dryden* (1779–

1781), Samuel Johnson argued that before the time of Dryden, there was simply

> no poetical diction: no system of words at once refined from the grossness of domestic use and free from the harshness of terms appropriated to particular arts. Words too familiar, or too remote, defeat the purposes of a poet.

In the preface to *Lyrical Ballads* (1802), William Wordsworth argued against the ornate effects of his predecessors and insisted on the essential identity of poetic and nonpoetic language. He argued that poetry should employ "the real language of men in *any situation.*" Wordsworth revolutionized the idea of poetic diction by connecting it to speech. Poetry is linked to speech, to the way that people actually talk at any given time, but it is also framed and marked differently.

poetic justice A literary device in which virtue is rewarded and vice punished. Thomas Rymer coined the term *poetic justice* in *The Tragedies of the Last Age Considered* (1678) to suggest that a work of art should uphold moral principles by rewarding the good and punishing the wicked. It oddly persists as an idea, though it is at odds with reality and was already out of fashion by the late seventeenth century.

poetic license Poetry frees words and disturbs our ordinary usage of language. Sometimes it departs from agreed-upon rules of pronunciation or diction or syntax; it departs from what we usually think of as common sense. "This poeticall license is a shrewde fellow," George Gascoigne wrote in 1575: "it maketh words longer, shorter, of mo sillables, of fewer, newer, older, truer, falser, and, to conclude, it turkeneth [alters] all things at pleasure." John Dryden (1631–1700) defined poetic license as "the liberty which poets have assumed to themselves, in all ages, of speaking things in verse which are beyond the severity of prose."

poetics The systematic doctrine or theory of poetry. The term derives from Aristotle's *Poetics* (350 B.C.E.), where he defined it as dealing with "poetry itself and its kinds and the specific power of each." Poetics investigates the distinguishing features of poetry—its branches, its governing principles, its technical resources, the nature of its forms, etc. The study of the nature of poetry has broadened in modern usage to refer to the general theory of literature, of literariness, which is the sum of features that distinguish literary texts from nonliterary ones. Thus it becomes possible to speak of *The Poetics of Space* (Gaston Bachelard, 1958) or *Structuralist Poetics* (Jonathan Culler, 1975) or *The Poetics of Prose* (Tsvetan Todorov, 1971) or *Everyday Life: A Poetics of Vernacular Practices* (Roger Abrahams, 2005). In *Language as Symbolic Action* (1966), Kenneth Burke came to the conclusion that the desire behind his poetics was to solve this equation: "poem is to poet as Poetics is to critic." Poetics is his testament to the human love of symbols.

Poetism Reacting against the strictures of social realism, a group of Czech poets in the 1920s and '30s set out to create a "pure" poetry. They aimed for lyrics that were playful, sensual, and dissociated from social purposes. Vítězlaw Nezval was its founder. Konstantín Biebl, Joseph Hora, and Jaroslav Seifert all began writing the proletarian poetry of the Nine Powers Group (*Devětsil*), but turned toward the more liberating and fanciful poetics of Poetism. František Halas and Vladimir Holan both developed out of Poetism, lyric poetry for poetry's sake.

poetry An inexplicable (though not incomprehensible) event in language; an experience through words. Jorge Luis Borges believed that "poetry is something that cannot be defined without oversimplifying it. It would be like attempting to define the color yellow, love, the fall of leaves in autumn." Even Samuel Johnson maintained, "To circumscribe poetry by a definition will only show the narrowness of the definer."

Poetry is a human fundamental, like music. It predates literacy and precedes prose in all literatures. There has probably never been a culture without it, yet no one knows precisely what it is. The word *poesie* entered the English language in the fourteenth century and begat *poesy* (as in Sidney's "The Defence of Poesy," ca. 1582) and *posy,* a motto in verse. *Poetrie* (from the Latin *poetria*) entered fourteenth-century English vocabulary and evolved into our *poetry.* The Greek word *poiesis* means "making." The fact that the oldest term for the poet means "maker" suggests that a poem is constructed.

Poets (and others) have made many attempts over the centuries to account for poetry, an ancient and necessary instrument of our humanity:

Dante's treatise on vernacular poetry, *De vulgari eloquentia,* suggests that around 1300, poetry was typically conceived of as a species of eloquence.

Sir Philip Sidney (1554–1586) said that poetry is "a representing, counterfetting, a figuring foorth: to speak metaphorically: a speaking picture: with this end, to teach and delight."

Ben Jonson (1572–1637) referred to the art of poetry as "the craft of making."

The baroque Jesuit poet Tomasso Ceva (1649–1737) said, "Poetry is a dream dreamed in the presence of reason."

Coleridge (1772–1834) claimed that poetry equals "the *best* words in the best order." He characterized it as "that synthetic and magical power, to which we have exclusively appropriated the name of imagination."

Wordsworth (1771–1850) famously called poetry "the spontaneous overflow of powerful feelings . . . recollected in tranquility." John Stuart Mill (1806–1873) followed up Wordsworth's emphasis on overflowing emotion when he wrote that poetry is "feeling confessing itself to itself in moments of solitude."

Shelley (1792–1822) joyfully called poetry "the record of the best and happiest moments of the happiest and best minds." He said that poetry "redeems from decay the visitations of the divinity in man."

Matthew Arnold (1822–1888) narrowed the definition to "a criticism of life." Ezra Pound (1885–1972) later countered, "Poetry is about as much a 'criticism of life' as red-hot iron is a criticism of fire."

Gerard Manley Hopkins (1844–1889) characterized it as "speech framed . . . to be heard for its own sake and interest even over and above its interest of meaning."

W. B. Yeats (1865–1939) loved Gavin Douglas's 1553 definition of poetry as "pleasance and half wonder."

George Santayana (1863–1952) said that "poetry is speech in which the instrument counts as well as the meaning." But he also thought of it as something beyond "verbal expression," as "that subtle fire and inward light which seems at times to shine through the world and to touch the images in our minds with ineffable beauty."

Wallace Stevens (1879–1955) characterized poetry as "a revelation of words by means of the words."

Tolstoy (1828–1910) noted in his diary, "Poetry is verse: prose is not verse. Or else poetry is everything with the exception of business documents and school books." Years later, Marianne Moore (1887–1972) responded "[N]or is it valid/to discriminate against 'business documents and // school books.' " Instead, she called poems "imaginary gardens with real toads in them."

Gertrude Stein (1874–1946) decided, "Poetry is doing nothing but using losing refusing and pleasing and betraying and caressing nouns."

Robert Frost (1874–1963) said wryly, "Poetry provides the one permissible way of saying one thing and meaning another."

Robert Graves (1895–1985) thought of it as a form of "stored magic," André Breton (1896–1966) as a "room of marvels."

Howard Nemerov (1920–1991) said that poetry is simply "getting something right in language."

Joseph Brodsky (1940–1996) described poetry as "accelerated thinking," Seamus Heaney (1939–2013) called it "language in orbit."

Poetry seems at core a verbal transaction. In its oral form, it establishes a relationship between a speaker and a listener; in its written form, it establishes a relationship between a writer and a reader. Yet at times that relationship seems to go beyond words. John Keats (1795–1821) felt that "Poetry should . . . strike the Reader as a wording of his own highest thoughts, and appear almost a Remembrance." The Australian poet Les Murray (b. 1938) argues that "poetry exists to provide the poetic experience." That experience is "a temporary possession." We know it by contact, since it has an intensity that cannot be denied.

Emily Dickinson (1830–1886) wrote in an 1870 letter:

> If I read a book [and] it makes my whole body so cold no fire can ever warm me I know *that* is poetry. If I feel physically as if the top of my head were taken off, I know *that* is poetry. These are the only ways I know it. Is there any other way?

A. E. Housman wrote in *The Name and Nature of Poetry* (1933):

> A year or two ago, in common with others, I received from America a request that I would define poetry. I replied that I could no more define poetry than a terrier can define a rat, but that I thought we both recognized the object by the symptoms which it provokes in us. One of these symptoms was described in connection with another object

> by Eliphaz the Termanite: "A spirit passed before my face: the hair of my flesh stood up." Experience has taught me, when I am shaving of a morning, to keep watch over my thoughts, because, if a line of poetry strays into my memory, my skin bristles so that the razor ceases to act. This particular symptom is accompanied by a shiver down the spine; there is another which consists in a constriction of the throat and a precipitation of water in the eyes; and there is a third which I can only describe by borrowing a phrase from one of Keats' last letters, where he says, speaking of Fanny Brawne, "everything that reminds me of her goes through me like a spear."

political poetry Poetry of social concern and conscience, politically engaged poetry. The feeling often runs high in the social poetry of engagement, especially when it is partisan. Poets write on both sides of any given war, defend the State, attack it. All patriotic and nationalistic poetry is by definition political. Political poetry, ancient and modern, good and bad, frequently responds vehemently to social injustice. Thus the poet is Jeremiah crying out to the assembly to witness the folly, unprecedented in both West (Cyprus) and East (Kedar), of a people who have forsaken the fountain of living waters for the stagnant water at the bottom of a leaky cistern. The Lamentations of Jeremiah, a series of poems mourning the desolation of Jerusalem and the sufferings of her people after the siege and destruction of the city and the burning of the Temple by the Babylonians, is also a political poem.

Strabo came up with the label *stasiotíka* ("stasis-poems") for Alcaeus's partisan songs, political poems, which are propagandistic poems of civil war and exile, accounts of his political commitments. The premise of political poetry is that poetry carries "news" or information crucial to the populace. Political poetry is a poetry self-consciously written inside of history, of politics. It responds to external events. "Mad Ireland hurt you into poetry," W. H. Auden famously decreed in his elegy for W. B. Yeats, and so, too, we might say that the madness of any country's brutality has often wounded its poets into a political response in poetry. "I stand as a witness to the common lot, / survivor of that time, that place," Anna Akhmatova wrote in 1961. Behind the poem in quest of justice, these lines from Shakespeare's *Antony and Cleopatra* (1623): "our size of sorrow, / Proportion'd to our cause, must be as great / As that which makes it."

There is an ephemeral quality to a lot of political poetry — most of it dies with the events it responds to — but a political poem need not be a didactic poem. It can be a poem of testimony and memory. For the best political poems of the twentieth century, I think of Vahan Tekeyan's poems of the Armenian genocide; of the Spanish Civil War poet Miguel Hernandez's haunting prison poems, especially "Lullaby of the Onion" (1939); and the Turkish poet Nazim Hikmet's equally poignant prison poems, especially "On Living" (1948) and "Some Advice to Those Who Will Spend Time in Prison" (1949); of Bertolt Brecht's World War II poems and Nelly Sachs's Holocaust poems. I think of the Italian poet Cesare Pavese's testimonies to ordinary people in trouble, *Hard Labor* (*Lavorare stanca,* 1936), and Pablo Neruda's epic testament, *Canto General* (1950). I think of the many poems of indictment and summons, of land and liberty, collected in the Nigerian writer Wole Soyinka's breakthrough anthology, *Poems of Black Africa* (1975).

There is a strong tradition in England of political poems. Edmund Spenser's *Complaints* (1591) takes aim at social and political targets. John Milton wrote a series of pro-Cromwellian short poems in the 1640s and '50s. Some of John Dryden's greatest poetry was written in response to events, such as his two-part political satire *Absalom and Achitophel* (1681, 1682). William Wordsworth's political poems are among his best, such as his sonnet "To Toussaint L'Ouverture" (1803), though a few of his late patriotic poems are also among his worst. Percy Bysshe Shelley's *The Mask of Anarchy* (1819), which was "Written on the Occasion of the Massacre at Manchester" ("I met Murder on the way — / He had a mask like Castlereagh"), is a frankly political poem that always gives me a chill. Elizabeth Barrett Browning published two striking books of political poetry during her Italian sojourn, *Casa Guidi Windows* (1850) and *Poems Before Congress* (1860). The most popular Victorian poet, Alfred, Lord Tennsyon, never distinguished between the personal and the political, the private and the public.

Political poetry has always seemed somewhat suspect in American literary history. "Our wise men and wise institutions assure us that national political events are beyond the reach of ordinary, or even extraordinary, literary sensitivity," Robert Bly writes. Yet there is a strong underground tradition of the poetry of engagement, which we might also call the poetry of citizenzry. This runs from Walt Whitman's political poems of the 1850s, which prefigure *Leaves of Grass,* and John Greenleaf Whittier's *Anti-Slavery Poems* (1832–1887), to leftist poets of the 1930s (Kenneth Fearing, Edwin

Rolfe, Muriel Rukeyser). The civil rights movement and the Vietnam War enraged poets, and, as Bly points out, some of the most inward poets, such as Robert Duncan, Denise Levertov, and Galway Kinnell, wrote some of the best poems against the Vietnam War. Most poetry of the 1940s and '50s shunned politics, but Thomas McGrath ("Ode for the American Dead in Korea," retitled in the early 1970s "Ode for the American Dead in Asia") and Kenneth Rexroth ("A Christmas Note for Geraldine Udell," 1949) bucked the trend. For forty years, Adrienne Rich was one of the most outspoken political poets in late twentieth-century American poetry, a model for a generation of political and activist poets. She went through several phases in relationship to polemics. She proposed a position that resists didacticism in "Power and Danger: Works of a Common Woman" (1978), her introduction to a collection of poems by Judy Grahn:

> No true political poetry can be written with propaganda as an aim, to persuade others "out there" of some atrocity or injustice (hence the failure, as poetry, of so much anti-Vietnam poetry of the sixties). *As poetry,* it can come only from the poet's need to identify her relationship to atrocities and injustice, the sources of her pain, fear, and anger, the meaning of her resistance.

SEE ALSO *didactic poetry, protest poetry, witness of poetry.*

polyphonic prose John Gould Fletcher coined the term *polyphonic prose* in 1915 for a kind of lyrical writing or prose poetry. The mode was then developed by Amy Lowell, who summarized: "The form is so called because it makes use of all the 'voices' of poetry, viz: metre, *vers libre,* assonance, alliteration, rhyme, and return. It employs every form of rhythm, even prose rhythm at times, but usually holds no particular one for long." Lowell was spurred by the way the French poet Paul Fort broke up the traditional alexandrine in *Ballades* (1886). The editors of her *Selected Poems* (2002) point out that polyphonic prose "combines lyric passages with narrative, rhyme with cadenced verse, and personal perspectives with grand historical events: of all forms, she considered it the most liberating, as it offered a full linguistic and formal spectrum, resembling mixed media in art or a symphony orchestra in music." Lowell most fully realizes her notion of polyphonic prose in her book of four lengthy narrative poems, *Can Grande's Castle* (1918), where she explains, "Metrical verse has one set of laws, cadenced verse another; 'polyphonic prose' can go from one to the other in the same poem with no sense of incongruity."

SEE ALSO *cadence, collage, prose poem.*

polyrhythmic Greek: "of many rhythms." Any poem that combines two or more rhythmic patterns. From Pindar (ca. 522–443 B.C.E.) to Alexander Cowley (1618–1667), from John Donne (1572–1631) to William Blake (1757–1827), from Emily Dickinson (1830–1886) and Gerard Manley Hopkins (1844–1889) to William Carlos Williams (1883–1963) and Langston Hughes (1902–1967), poets have energized their poems by varying and crossing rhythms, by bringing in different patterned energies. Léopold Sédar Senghor states that polyrhythms establish "unity within diversity." Jazz poetry is just one of the kinds of cross or polyrhythmic poetry. Adrienne Rich offers, "What poetry is made of is so old, so familiar, that it's easy to forget that it's not just the words, but polyrhythmic sounds, speech in its first endeavor (every poem breaks a silence that had to be overcome), prismatic meanings lit by each others' light, each others' shadows."

SEE ALSO *counterpoint, free verse, jazz poetry, ode.*

polysyndeton The repetition of connectives or conjunctions in close succession for rhetorical effect. As Elizabeth Bishop puts it, "Everything only connected by 'and' and 'and' " ("The Map," 1935). Polysyndeton is the opposite of asyndeton, the omission of conjunctions. In a poem, the deliberate addition of conjunctions where they do not normally appear often slows the tempo and creates a sense of greater rhetorical insistence, as when John Keats describes the movement of a small boat in *Endymion* (1818):

> And soon it lightly dipped, and rose, and sank,
> And dipped again . . .

SEE ALSO *asyndeton, rhetoric.*

postmodernism Postmodernism is a reaction to modernism, a reappraisal. This wide-ranging term applies to poetry and fiction, art and architecture, literary and cultural criticism, philosophy, and other fields. The *Oxford Eng-*

lish Dictionary calls it "a style and concept in the arts characterized by distrust of theories and ideologies and by the drawing of attention to conventions." Postmodernism follows many of the ideas of modernism, but takes a different and more ironized attitude toward them. It rejects the boundaries between high and low forms of art, shows a decided preference for pastiche, and combines genres and tropes from different historical periods. Mary Klages explains: "Postmodern art (and thought) favors reflexivity and self-consciousness, fragmentation and discontinuity (especially in narrative structures), ambiguity, simultaneity, and an emphasis on the destructured, decentered, dehumanized subject." The postmodernist position: language is the actual author of any work of art; all narratives can be taken apart and deconstructed; what seems determined by nature is actually determined by culture. Reality is a construction, everything is interpreted. Postmodernism is ultimately a skeptical position that denies the existence of all ultimate principles and truths.

Randall Jarrell was probably the first American poet to speak of postmodernity when he characterized Robert Lowell's poetry in 1946 as "post- or anti-modernist." Around the same time, the British historian Arnold Toynbee declared that there was a new "Post-Modern" age of Western history (*A Study of History*, 1946). This was possibly the last phase of Western history, Toynbee suggested. As Matei Calinescu puts it, "such an optimistic-apocalyptic interpretation of the term post-modern made it fit to receive a prominent place in the revolutionary rhetoric of the 1960s."

In midcentury American poetry, the term *postmodernism* was taken up by innovative American poets, such as Charles Olson, who declared in "The Present is Prologue" (1955):

> I am an archaeologist of morning. And the writing and acts which I find bear on the present job are (I) from Homer back, not forward; and (II) from Melville on, particularly himself, Dostoevsky, Rimbaud, and Lawrence. These were the modern men who projected what we are and what we are in, who broke the spell. They put men forward into the post-modern, the post-humanist, the post-historic, the going live present, the "Beautiful Thing."

Postmodernism is an umbrella term that refers to such groups as the Black Mountain poets (Olson, Robert Duncan, Robert Creeley, Denise Levertov), the Beats (Allen Ginsberg, Jack Kerouac, Lawrence Ferlinghetti, Gregory Corso), the San Francisco renaissance poets (Kenneth Rexroth, William Everson, Gary Snyder, Jack Spicer, Robin Blaser), and the New York school (Frank O'Hara, John Ashbery, Kennenth Koch, James Schuyler). Marjorie Perloff considers indeterminacy or undecidabity the chief feature of postmodern work. Umberto Eco points out that postmodernism "consists of recognizing that the past, since it cannot really be destroyed, because its destruction leads to silence, must be revisted: but with irony, not innocently."

SEE ALSO *avant-garde, Beats, Black Mountain poets, deconstruction, fragment, modernism, New York school of poets, San Francisco renaissance.*

poststructuralism An eclectic and loosely defined twentieth-century movement that developed from within and ultimately contested the theoretical assumptions of French structuralism. In philosophy, cultural theory, and literary criticism, poststructuralism rejects the essentialist idea — the totalizing narrative — that there are fundamental structures in language and culture. The term covers the philosophical deconstruction theorized by Jacques Derrida and his followers, the later works of the critic Roland Barthes, the historical critiques offered by the later Michel Foucault, the psychoanalytic theories of the later Jacques Lacan and Julia Kristeva, the postmodernist writings of Jean-François Leotard and Gilles Deleuze. Here is how Barthes summarized his passage from structuralism to poststructuralism:

> In the former text ["Introduction a l'analyse a structural des recits," 1966] I appealed to a general structure from which would derive analyses of contingent texts . . . In S / Z I reversed this perspective: there I refused the idea of a model transcendent in several texts (and, thus, all the more so, of a model transcendent to every text) in order to postulate that each text is in some sort its own model, that each text, in other words, must be treated in its difference, "difference" being understood here precisely in a Nietzschean or a Derridean sense . . . the text is ceaselessly and through and through traversed by codes . . . it is not the *parole* [speech] of a narrative *langue* [language].

Poststructuralist thinkers reject universalizing assumptions and meanings. Rather, they insist on the instability and indeterminacy of texts. In the destabilized readings of poststructuralism, the reader replaces the author as the subject of inquiry. This "destabilizing" or "decentering" of the author (Roland Barthes declared the metaphorical "death" of the author as an authorizing presence in 1968) leads to other sources of meaning. It calls into question the human "subject" or "self" so important to "humanism." There is no origin, no endpoint, and no fixed place outside discourse to establish meaning. Poetry itself becomes unstable "free play," a multiple, often self-contradictory chain of signifiers.

SEE ALSO *deconstruction, postmodernism, structuralism.*

poulter's measure Rhyming couplets that alternate iambic hexameter (twelve-syllable) and iambic heptameter (fourteen-syllable) lines. In a treatise on versification, George Gascoigne coined the term *poulter's measure* based on the poultryman's traditional practice of giving twelve eggs for the first dozen and fourteen for the second (*Certain Notes of Instruction,* 1575). The meter was frequently used by Wyatt (1503–1542), Surrey (1517–1547), and Sidney (1554–1586), among others, but seldom thereafter. It has seemed monotonous and heavy to later practitioners. But if you divide the six-beat and seven-beat couplets into rhyming iambic quatrains, you get the "short meter" or "common time" of the English hymns. Here is the opening of Surrey's "How No Age Is Content" (1557):

> Laid in my quiet bed, in study as I were,
> I saw within my troubled head a heap of thoughts appear.
> And every thought did shew so lively in mine eyes,
> That now I sigh'd, and then I smiled, as cause of thought did rise.

SEE ALSO *hymn, meter, short meter.*

praise poems The praise poem is one of the most highly developed poetic genres in the oral poetry of Oceania and Africa, where it has a long tradition and history. The tradition of praise-singing is cross-cultural. It has a wide variety of overlapping terms, many linked to the word *jamu.* For the Soninké-speaking people, one meaning of *jamu* is *praise song;* in Barnana it is a verb meaning "to praise someone, to express recognition." The Fulbe variant is *jammude.* The Hausa-speaking people use the terms *kirari* (praise-epithets) and *take* (short vocal or drummed praises). The Yoruba have a highly developed form of praise poetry called *oríkì*. The Zulu term for praise poems is *izíbongo,* the Basurto is *lithoko,* and the Kirundi is *amazina,* which literally means "names." The praise poem is a way of naming. "Implicit in the act of praising," Judith Gleason notes, "is the assumption throughout Africa that every person, human group, tutelary spirit, animal, plant, or body of water, as well as certain manufactured things, has a praiseable core that words can elicit, revitalize, and nudge toward behavior beneficial to the human community." The format of praising — the art of assemblage — also implies that everything is interconnected.

A personal praise is a strong empowering name. In her memoir *The Dark Child* (1955), Carmara Laye describes a praise-singer in her father's shop:

> The praise-singer would install himself in our goldsmith shop, tune up his kora, which is our harp, and begin to sing my father's praises [in Malinké]. I would hear recalled the lofty deeds and the names of my father's ancestors from earliest times; as the couplets were reeled off, it was like watching the growth of a great genealogical tree that spread its branches far and wide and flourished its branches before my mind's eye.

There are praise poems for a wide variety of things (animals, clans, hunters, spirits, etc.), but the most significant are the poems directly addressed to people, living or dead, who are celebrated and praised. The praise poem in the second person is part epic, part ode, and exalts power when it is addressed to the king or chief. It solidifies authority, unlike the protest poem, which questions it. In her book *Oral Literature* (1977), Ruth Finnegan explains:

> In the Zulu kingdoms of South Africa, every king or chief with pretension to political power has his own praiser or *imbongi* among his entourage. At the more elaborate courts of West African kingdoms, there were often whole bands of poets, minstrels and musicians, each with his specialized task, and all charged with the duty of supporting the present king with ceremonial praise of his glory and the great deeds of his ancestors.

SEE ALSO *encomium, epithet, griot, oríkì, panegyric.*

préciosité The word *préciosité* ("preciousness") is now generally associated with affectation, with the deliberate pursuit of too much refinement in all things, including dress, manners, and literature. It was not always so. As a literary style, *préciosité* developed out of the playful word games and witty conversations of a group of women in seventeenth-century French salons and polite society. In 1608, the Marquise de Ramboullet retired to her Parisian manor and created a salon, the Chambre bleue, which became the central gathering place for a group of women who valued elegant dress, modest behavior, and clever conversation. This inaugurated the salon movement, which is usually pinpointed to the period 1654–1660.

Molière satirized the affectations of the salon women in his one-act comedy of manners, *Les Précieuses ridicules* (1659), which permanently fixed the connotations of *précieuse* as "affected." Prior to 1650, *précieuse* was a complimentary term for a woman who wished to distinguish herself. The salon women never used the term themselves. The *Dictionnaire Historic de la langue française* (1992) defines *a précieuse* as a "woman with a refined sensibility who adopts a different, uncommon way of living and speaking."

In literary terms, the salon culture valued refinement, elegance, and a purified language that did not yield much lasting poetry. The primary subjects were platonic love and spiritual friendship between women. Ironically, the most consequential poet to emerge from the salon movement was a man, Vincent Voiture (1598–1648), who was one of the first and finest composers of *vers de societé* (society verse).

SEE ALSO *Platonic love, vers de société.*

pregunta, see *poetic contest.*

Pre-Raphaelites The Pre-Raphaelite Brotherhood (P.R.B.) was formed in London in 1848 by a group of three young English artists: William Holman Hunt, a painter; John Everett Millais, a painter; and Dante Gabriel Rossetti, a poet and painter as well as the driving force behind the movement. The Pre-Raphaelites disdained the Royal Academy of Art, whose values were enshrined in the *Discourses* of its president, Sir Joshua Reynolds ("Sir Sloshua," they called him). They set out to re-create a medieval simplicity and purity lost in the High Renaissance, the era of Raphael (1483–1520). Their goal was to paint not like the imitators of Raphael ("the Raphaelites"), but according to nature. The three enlarged to seven by adding William Michael Rossetti, who became the historian of the group; Thomas Woolner, a sculptor; James Collinson, a painter; and F. G. Stephens, an artist and critic. Two others closely associated with the group were the artist Ford Madox Brown and the poet Christina Rossetti. The Rossettis were the essential poets of the movement. The Pre-Raphaelites had a little magazine that lasted for four issues. In the first two issues, it was called *The Germ: Thoughts towards Nature in Poetry, Literature and Art,* and in the second two, *The Germ: Art and Poetry, Being Thoughts towards Nature, Conducted Principally by Artists.* The movement was powerfully influenced by the great art critic John Ruskin, who became an advocate. He predicted the Pre-Raphaelites would "lay in our England the foundations of a school of art nobler than the world has seen for three hundred years."

The Pre-Raphaelites had their detractors, such as Robert Williams Buchanan, who derided Rossetti and his imitators as "the Fleshly School of Poetry" in an 1871 article, an insult that now seems like an honorific. The first stage of the movement was over by 1853. "So now," Dante Gabriel Rossetti wrote to his sister, "the whole Round Table is dissolved." The second flowering of Pre-Raphaelitism was inaugurated when Rossetti met the multitalented William Morris (1834–1896), who essentially created the Arts and Crafts movement, and the artist Edward Burne-Jones (1833–1898), the progenitor of Art Nouveau. George Meredith and Algernon Swinburne were the other primary poets influenced by the Pre-Raphaelite aesthetic.

SEE ALSO *romanticism, Victorian period.*

primitivism The philosophical doctrine that supposedly "primitive" peoples are more noble than civilized peoples. Primitivism was fueled by the nostalgia for a lost Eden or golden age, a time when people were unified and whole. Ever since the first century, when the Roman historian Tacitus praised the German barbarians and contrasted them to the corrupt Gauls, thereby criticizing Roman culture at the root, the primitive was used as a reproach to civilized peoples. Primitive man was praised for living in harmony with nature, for his natural innocence, selflessness, and untutored wisdom. Giambattista Vico first argued that "primitive" man was closer to the sources of poetry and inspiration than "civilized" man (*Scienza nuova,* 1725). The idea that archaic peoples are more "natural" and less influenced by society especially took hold in the eighteenth century and became a key force in the romantic era. Such philosophers as Lord Shaftesbury (1621–1683) and Richard Steele (1672–1729) argued for the "natural" goodness of man uncorrupted by the modern world. The phrase *the noble savage* first appeared in John Dryden's play *The Conquest of Granada* (1672). In his *Discourse on Inequality* (*Discours sur l'origine de l'inégalité,* 1755), Jean-Jacques Rousseau, who is generally considered the most influential primitivist, suggested that our natural freedom had been stifled by the bonds of so-called civilized society. The "Good Savage" or "Wild man" became a romantic fiction.

Throughout the eighteenth century poets praised life in a mythical pre-history. Thus Alexander Pope wrote: "The state of Nature was the reign of God" ("An Essay on Man," 1733–1734). Primitivism expressed itself in literary terms with the idea that the best poetry should be "instinctive" and "natural." This led to the appropriation of folklore genres and helped to create the enthusiasm for "popular poetry," as in Thomas Percy's *The Reliques of Ancient English Poetry* (1765) and the wildly successful "Ossian" poems, which James McPherson purported to have translated from ancient sources in Scots Gaelic (*The Works of Ossian,* 1865). McPherson passed off his Ossian poems as the work of a Celtic Homer. Hugh Blair's *Critical Dissertation on the Poems of Ossian, the Song of Fingal* (1763) described the virtues of primitive poetry exemplified in the Ossian poems, which also inspired, among others, the young Walter Scott, the Sturm und Drang writers Johann Wolfgang von Goethe and Johann Gottfried Herder (*Extract from a Correspondence About Ossian and the Songs of Ancient Peoples,* 1773), and a raft of Hungarian poets, such as Ferenc Kazinczy (1759–1831), János Arany (1817–1882), and Sándor Petöfi (1823–1849), who wrote in his poem "Homer and Ossian":

> All that is light and fair and bright
> Is in thy song, thou beggar-knight,
> Homer! Thou art the world's delight.
> All that is drear, austere, severe
> Is in thy song, thou royal seer,
> Prince Ossian! To mankind dear
> Are ye, Homer and Ossian!
> *(tr. William N. Loew, 1912)*

The Ossian poems also played a part in American primitivism. Thomas Jefferson wrote in a letter to Charles McPherson (Feb. 25, 1773): "I am not ashamed to own that I think this rude bard of the North the greatest poet that has ever existed."

There was also a vogue in England for the unlettered folk or peasant poet, such as John Taylor, the seventeenth-century Water-Poet of London. In the eighteenth century, one thinks of James Woodhouse and John Bennet, the Poetical Shoemakers, Henry Jones, the Poetical Bricklayer; Stephan Duck, the Poetical Thresherman; and Ann Yearsley, the Poetical Washerwoman. Thomas Gray's *The Bard* (1757) and James Beatie's *The Minstrel* (1771–1774) also have a primitivist spirit. This was the zeitgeist that brought to prominence major poets such as Robert Burns (1759–1796), who was called the Poetical Plowboy, and John Clare (1793–1864), who was commonly known as the Northamptonshire Peasant Poet. The fantasy of the untutored genius, the minstrel/bard, fueled eighteenth-century aesthetics. One of the dissenters was Samuel Johnson, who repeatedly opposed "cant in defense of savages."

It is common for critics and theorists to distinguish between chronological primitivism, which looks backward to a golden age and contrasts it to our present decline, and cultural primitivism, which elevates nature over art, the natural over the artificial, spontaneity over self-consciousness, etc. In *The Mirror and the Lamp* (1953), M. H. Abrams points out, for example, that William Wordsworth's critical pronouncements were a highly refined form of cultural primitivism: "Wordsworth's cardinal standard of poetic value is 'nature,' and nature, in his usage, is given a triple and primitivistic connotation: Nature is the common denominator of human nature; it is most reliably exhibited among men living 'according to nature' (that is to say, in a culturally simple, and especially a rural environment); and it consists primarily in an elemental simplicity of thought and feeling and a spontaneous and 'unartificial' mode of expressing feeling in words."

The newest art often turns to the oldest sources and there is a strong primitivist current within modernism. Sir James George Frazer's *The Golden Bough* (1890) stimulated interest in folklore and myth and famously influenced T. S. Eliot's "The Waste Land" (1922). One thinks of the primitivisms of Paul Gauguin and Pablo Picasso in art, of Igor Stravinsky in music, of D. H. Lawrence in prose and poetry. There is a strong primitivist spirit in a movement such as ethnopoetics, which finds models for contemporary practice in native poetries.

SEE ALSO *ethnopoetics, modernism, nature poetry, romanticism, spontaneity, Sturm und Drang.*

proceleusmatic, see *foot.*

proem From the Greek: "prelude." A proem is a preface or preamble; an introductory passage, either in poetry or prose, to a longer work. It sets the terms for what follows. One of the finest early examples is the 104-line proem to Hesiod's *Theogyny* (late eighth to early seventh century B.C.E.): "From the Muses of Helicon let us begin to sing. . . ." Hesiod's proem praises the Muses — it is sometimes called "Hymn to the Muses" — but it also enables him to praise and name himself. The poet can commence by using "I" (or the royal "we"), a liberty not allowed in the epic proper. As Andrew Ford puts it in a book on Homer: "The difference between the "*I* will sing" of the proem and the "Sing, Muse" of the invocation summarizes a great difference in the way the poet is allowed to present himself in different stages of the performance. In fact, the function of the proem seems to have been to allow the poet to say "I" and to refer to himself as a particular poet about to perform on a particular occasion." It creates a space for the personal voice in the epic tradition.

The proem takes on a different function outside the Greek epic tradition. In his proem to *The Prelude* (1805, 1850), Wordsworth uses the prefatory lines to describe the origins of the work itself; in his "Proem" to *In Memoriam* (1849), Tennyson summarizes his feelings about the mysteries of grief. The proem has seldom been used in modern and contemporary poetry, though Hart Crane's "Proem: To Brooklyn Bridge" serves as a prelude to his modernist epic poem, *The Bridge* (1930). Mark Strand includes "Proem" in *Dark Harbor* (1993).

SEE ALSO *invocation.*

projective verse Charles Olson coined this term for an organic composition process, a type of free verse that he also called "composition by field." His 1950 essay "Projective Verse" treated the composition of poetry as a kinetic process, "a high-energy construct." He opposed projective verse to so-called closed or nonprojective verse ("inherited line, stanza, over-all form"), praised immediacy and spontaneity, emphasized the importance of breath in the creative process, argued that "one perception must immediately and directly lead to a further perception," and quoted Robert Creeley to the effect that "form is never more than an extension of content." It is hard to fasten down the idea of the breath line in projective verse, which is all about movement, the activity of making itself. The three major practitioners of projective verse — Charles Olson, Robert Creeley, and Robert Duncan — taught at Black Mountain College in North Carolina in the early 1950s, and are therefore sometimes called the Black Mountain school. Some poets also affiliated with the movement: Denise Levertov, Paul Blackburn, Joel Oppenheimer, and Edward Dorn. Projective verse emphasizes process over product and inspires a quick, high-octane, idiomatic poetry.

SEE ALSO *Black Mountain poets, free verse.*

proode In Greek tragedy, "the ode that precedes the ode" is a single stanza of a lyric poem that comes before the strophic structure or poem proper (Euripides, *Bacchae,* 405 B.C.E.). A *mesode* ("the ode in the middle of an ode") is a nonrepeating lyric section that appears between the strophe and antistrophe (Aeschylus, *The Libation Bearers,* 458 B.C.E.). An *ephymnion* ("what is sung afterwards, refrain") is a lyric refrain after a lyric section (Aeschylus, *Suppliants,* ca. 463 B.C.E.).

SEE ALSO *antistrophe, ode, strophe.*

prose poem A composition printed as prose that names itself poetry. The prose poem takes advantage of its hybrid nature — it avails itself of the elements of prose (what Dryden called "the other harmony of prose") while foregrounding the devices of poetry. The French writer Aloysius Bertrand established the prose poem as a minor genre in *Gaspard de la nuit* (1842), a book that influenced Baudelaire's *Petits poèmes en prose* (1869). Baudelaire used prose poems to rebel against the straitjacket of classical French versification. He dreamed of creating "a poetic prose, musical without rhyme or rhythm, supple and jerky enough to adapt to the lyric movements of the soul, to the undulations of reverie, to the somersaults of conscience." Baudelaire's prose poems — along with Rimbaud's *Les Illuminations* (1886) and Mallarmé's *Divagations* (1897) — created a mixed musical form (part social, part transcendental) that has been widely and internationally practiced in the twentieth century. "There is no such thing as prose," Mallarmé insisted in 1891. "There is the alphabet, and then there are verses which are more or less closely knit, more or less diffuse. So long as there is a straining toward style, there is versification."

The prose poem, which often seems like a French import, has had a strong underground American life. It is often treated as kin to the parable. David Lehman's anthology *Great American Prose Poems* (2003) begins with Emerson ("Woods, A Prose Sonnet," 1839) and Poe ("Shadow—A Parable," 1835), picks up speed with the experimental moderns, such as Gertrude Stein (*Tender Buttons,* 1914) and William Carlos Williams (*Kora in Hell,* 1920), and hits a high mark in the 1960s, 1970s, and 1980s with quasi-surrealist work by W. S. Merwin, John Ashbery, James Wright, Mark Strand, and James Tate, among others. "The prose poem is the result of two contradictory impulses, prose and poetry, and therefore cannot exist," as Charles Simic puts it: "This is the sole instance we have of squaring the circle."

Here is a parable-like prose poem by Russell Edson, which works by crossing the boundaries between human beings and animals. Edson has always sought what he calls "a poetry freed from the definition of poetry, and a prose free of the necessities of fiction."

A Performance at Hog Theater (1973)

There was once a hog theater where hogs performed as men, had men been hogs.

One hog said, I will be a hog in the field which has found a mouse which is being eaten by the same hog which is in the field and which has found the mouse, which I am performing as my contribution to the performer's art.

Oh let's just be hogs, cried an old hog.

And so the hogs streamed out of the theater crying, only hogs, only hogs . . .

SEE ALSO *alexandrine, free verse, vers libre.*

prosody The word *prosody* is the anglicized form of the Latin word *prosodia* (accent of a syllable), which derives from the Greek *prosōidia* (a song sung to instrumental music). Prosody is the systematic art or study—the notation, principles, and theory—of versification. It especially refers to aspects of musicality, such as rhythm and sound (alliteration, assonance, euphony, onomatopoeia, and so forth), but can also include the study of such things as structure and rhetoric. Linguistic prosody is the study of these elements in ordinary language. Literary prosody, which is also known as metrics, is the study of them in the literary arts.

SEE ALSO *meter, scansion, verse, versification.*

prosopopoeia, see *personification.*

protest poetry Poetry of dissent, of social criticism. It protests the status quo and tries to undermine established values and ideals. The protest poet is a rebellious citizen, speaking out, expressing disapproval of a political policy or social action. Protest poetry, the most earnest of genres, is timely, oppositional, reactive, urgent. It is an activist type of political poetry born from outrage and linked to social action. It turns poetry into a medium for polemics.

The reprehensible policy of apartheid in South Africa, which legislated racism, also stimulated a powerful tradition of protest poetry. The Zulu poet Herbert I. E. Dhlomo's long poem *Valley of a Thousand Hills* (1941) is the most extended work of South African protest poetry. One thinks of the contributions of Dennis Brutus (1924–2009), whose work is brought together in *Poetry and Protest: A Dennis Brutus Reader* (2006); Arthur Nortje (1942–1970), whose work is published posthumously in *Dead Roots* (1973) and *Lonely Against the Light* (1973); and Mazisi Kunene (1930–2006), who first sounded his aggressive, telegraphic note in *Zulu Poems* (1970). The New Black poetry of the 1970s, or Soweto poetry, was a protest poetry of black consciousness. In the United States, there is also a strong tradition of African American poetry that protests racism. It extends from the Harlem renaissance to the Black Arts movement. Most antiwar poetry is protest poetry. The combatant antiwar poetry of Wilfred Owen (1893–1918) and Siegfried Sassoon (1886–1967) protested the technological horrors of modern warfare. The Spanish Civil War generated both local and global protest poetry. The Vietnam War galvanized a tremendous amount of protest poetry by such poets as Robert Lowell, Allen Ginsberg, Adrienne Rich, and Robert Bly. These poets felt a cultural imperative to speak out against the war. The repression and disintegration of the American imagination is one of the persistent themes of Vietnam-era protest poetry. Much of the feminist poetry of the 1960s and '70s is protest poetry. "A patriot is not a weapon," Adrienne Rich writes in her long poem *An Atlas of the Difficult World* (1981). "A patriot is one who wrestles for the soul of her country / as she wrestles for her own being." Sam Hamill's anthology *Poets Against the War* (2003) was a hastily gathered book of protest poems against the war in Iraq. The strength of protest poetry is its sense of immediacy and outrage. However, most of these politically motivated poems, which are often made in outrage against a specific atrocity, don't outlive their historical moment.

SEE ALSO *Black Arts movement, didactic poetry, Harlem renaissance, Marxist criticism.*

prothalamion, see *epithalamium.*

proverb A terse didactic statement that embodies a general truth, the proverb is short and pithy, akin to the aphorism and the maxim, and draws attention to itself as a formal artistic entity. Folk and traditional proverbs are well-known expressions, usually the length of a simple sentence, that function in conversation. They are part of daily discourse. They also operate in educational situations and judicial proceedings. Proverbs take personal circumstances and embody them in impersonal form. Their meanings seem fixed, but depend on context, since texts are adapted to different situations. Proverbs are normative, consensual. The proverb simplifies a problem by naming and solving it with a traditional solution.

The linguist Roman Jakobson called the proverb "the largest coded unit occurring in our speech and at the same time the shortest poetic composition." Proverbs frequently employ traditional devices of poetry, such as balanced phrasing ("Out of sight, out of mind") and binary construction ("A stitch in time / saves nine"), rhyme ("Haste makes waste"), alliteration ("Live and learn"), and repetition ("Live and let live"). They often apply a metaphor to a situation ("Don't change horses in midstream"). By definition, proverbs must be memorable. Expressions become proverbial through quotation. In "Literature as Equipment for Living" (1938), Kenneth Burke pointed out that "social structures give rise to 'type' situations . . . many proverbs seek to chart, in more or less homey and picturesque ways, these 'type' situations." Proverbs are a fundamental way that literature provides "equipment for living." He then extended the analysis of proverbs to the whole field of literature in *Philosophy of Literary Forms: Studies in Symbolic Action* (1941). "Could the most complex and sophisticated works of art legitimately be considered somewhat as 'proverbs writ large'?"

The humble proverb has an ancient and generally overlooked literary provenance. Proverbs are amongst the oldest works in Sansrkit. Daniel Ingalls writes: "a collection of Sanskrit proverbs would soon attain a size that no book could hold, for it is consonant with the Sanskrit preference for the general over the particular, for the type over the individual, that it should use proverbs very widely." Proverbs also animated early Germanic, Scandinavian, and especially Hebrew literature, as in the book of Proverbs, a form of wisdom literature whose principle is encapsulated in the following example:

Treasures of wickedness profit nothing:
    but righteousness deliverith from death. (10:2)

The binary proverb is the literary foundation of wisdom poetry. It consists of two units brought together in a type of parallelism:

Pride goeth before destruction,
    and an haughty spirit before a fall. (16:18)

A soft answer turneth away wrath:
    but grievous words stir up anger. (15:1)

Proverbs entered European literature through the Bible, the Church fathers, and classical Greek writers, such as Aristophanes (ca. 450–ca. 388 B.C.E.), Plautus (ca. 254–184 B.C.E.), and Lucian (ca. 125–after 180). Erasmus's enormously popular *Adagia* (1500) was crucial in spreading classical proverbs into vernacular European languages. John Heywood's *A Dialogue contening. . . . all the proverbs in the English tongue* (1546) was the first English collection. There is an intermittent tradition of creating poems and songs from proverbs that extends from François Villon's virtuoso display "Ballade des proverbes" (1458) to works by Gilbert and Sullivan, such as the the Pinafore duet (1878), which has sixteen identifiable proverbs. The proverb contributed to the development of the epigram, an occasional short verse with a moral point. Proverbs are employed in face-to-face situations, and the literary epigram compensates by pointing to the situation, either as a title or within the poem itself. The proverb also had a direct influence on the heroic couplet, which in turn provided proverbs that became part of conventional wisdom, such as Alexander Pope's "To err is human, to forgive divine." Proverbs are embedded in poems from Geoffrey Chaucer, especially in *Troilus and Criseyde* (ca. 1380s), to Carl Sandburg ("Good Morning, America") and Robert Frost ("Good fences make good neighbors"). William Blake's provocative "Proverbs of Hell" (1790–1793) teach us that "Exuberance is Beauty."

SEE ALSO *epigram, gnome, parallelism, riddle.*

psalm A sacred song or hymn. The term *psalm* generally refers to the Hebrew poems in the biblical book of Psalms, which *The Oxford Companion to Music* (2002) calls "the oldest and the greatest book of songs now in use anywhere in the world." The psalms have been traditionally ascribed to King David, but David seems to be a composite author ensuring the formal integrity of poems composed over a period of more than five hundred years. Some seem to go as far back as the ninth and tenth centuries B.C.E. The earliest manuscripts date from the ninth century B.C.E. in Hebrew, from the fourth century B.C.E. in Latin, and from the second century B.C.E. in Greek when the book of Psalms, spliced together from at least four previous collections, took final form. The Hebrew heading of the complete psalter (collection of psalms) found in several early manuscripts is a word meaning "the book of praises," and the psalms are ancient liturgical praise poems with terrific performative power.

> MAKE a joyful noise unto the LORD, all ye lands.
> Serve the LORD with gladness: come before his presence with
> singing.
> Know ye that the LORD he *is* God: *it is* he *that* hath made us,
> and not we ourselves; *we are* his people, and the sheep of
> his pasture. (Psalm 100:1–3)

In his talk "A Folk Inferno" (1988), the Australian poet Les Murray describes the psalms when he says, "Unlike poetries of formula and definition, the celebratory doesn't presume to understand the world . . . and so leaves it open and expansive, with unforeclosed potentials."

The psalms have been a tremendous sourcebook for Western poets. As Donald Davie writes in the introduction to his anthology *The Psalms in English* (1966), "Through four centuries there is hardly a poet of even modest ambition who does not feel the need to try his hand at paraphrasing some part of Scripture, most often the psalms." One legacy of the psalms is what Coburn Freer calls "joyful religious play."

> All people that on earth do dwell,
>   Sing to the Lord with cheerful voice:
> Him serve with mirth, his praise forth tell,
>   Come ye before him, and rejoice.
> *(tr., William Kethe, 1561)*

pseudo-statement In *Science and Poetry* (1926), I. A. Richards coined the term *pseudo-statement* to explain the special kind of statements made in poetry. He distinguishes between the scientific statement, which is verifiable in the laboratory, and the emotive utterance, which is evocative of attitudes. He characterizes a pseudo-statement as "a form of words which is justified entirely by its effect in releasing or organizing our impulses and attitudes; a statement, on the other hand, is justified by its truth, *i.e.* its correspondence, in a highly technical sense, with the fact to which it points." Richards was trying to distinguish between different kinds of "truth," different forms of verification, but his coinage has frequently been taken to suggest something derogatory about poetry and its special kind of knowledge. W.H.N. Hotoph suggests, "Richards would have been better advised to call them pseudo-assertions or to have dropped the word 'pseudo' altogether since, by reason of its frequently pejorative connotation, this has led many who were unable to use Richards' contextual guidance, to think he was saying something derogatory about statement in poetry." Richards was pointing to the fictive status of poetic statements, which is what Sir Philip Sidney does in his *Apology for Poetry* (1595), when he asserts, "The poet he nothing affirms, and therefore never lieth."

SEE ALSO *New Criticism.*

psychoanalytic criticism, psychological criticism Psychoanalytic criticism brings the terms and insights of psychoanalysis, which is both a theory of mind and an interpretive practice, to the study of literary texts. Sigmund Freud (1856–1939), the founder of psychoanalysis, theorized the unconscious mind as a source that reveals itself through words, mental images, and actions, which the conscious mind deflects and bars from understanding through a process of psychic censorship called repression. Freud argued that we are all shaped and driven by our sexual bodies, sexual histories, the contents of our unconscious, and there is a dynamic psychic battle between unconscious drives, which seek release, and forces of repression, which keep them from surfacing. Unconscious material expresses itself through everyday disguises, such as physical symptoms, accidental gestures, parapraxis, mainly slips of the tongue ("Freudian slips"), dreams and jokes, as well as through free association, which is the main tool of clinical psychoanalysis. The unconscious also wells up through works of art, through poems and plays, short stories and novels. Freud's metapsychology gives privileged status to dreams: "the interpretation of dreams is the royal road to a knowledge of unconscious activities of the mind." He also found a strong kinship between dreams and poetry, and this association proved to be especially stimulating for surrealist and other poets drawing from the deeps of the unconscious: "The dream-thoughts which we first come across as we proceed with our analysis often strike us by the unusual form in which they are expressed; they are not clothed in the prosaic language usually employed by our thoughts, but are on the contrary represented symbolically by means of similes and metaphors, in images resembling those of poetic speech" (*The Interpretation of Dreams,* 1900). Freud argued that literature, like the other arts, like dreams and neuroses, is driven by desires and fantasies, "libidinal" wishes, repressed by the conscious mind, denied by reality, and/or prohibited by society. More humanistic than many of his followers, Freud recognized that poets and fiction writers often anticipated his psychological research into the self. Lionel Trilling points out that when Freud was hailed on his seventieth birthday as the "discoverer of the unconscious," he corrected the speaker: "The poets and philosophers before me discovered the unconscious. What I discovered was the scientific method by which the unconscious can be studied."

Freud employed that method — the question of whether or not it was actually "scientific" has been fiercely debated — to interpret Sophocles's *Oedipus Rex* (ca. 430 B.C.E.), which he took as the basis of his theory of the Oedipus complex (*Three Essays on the Theory of Sexuality,* 1905) and E.T.A. Hoffman's story "The Sandman" (1816), which helped him understand uncanny experiences ("The Uncanny," 1919). He linked fiction-making to daydreaming ("Creative Writers and Daydreaming," 1908) and drew on a range of literary examples for his study of *Jokes and Their Relation to the Unconscious* (1905). Freud used a poetic metaphor to compare the unconscious to an ancient city in which all the previous versions of that city are superimposed on one another (*Civilization and Its Discontents,* 1930). He taught us to listen to the unsaid or half-said in literary texts, to look for unresolved conflicts and unconscious motives in writers and equally unconscious responses in readers, to recognize the return of the repressed in literary texts. But his own studies of literature as well as those of his followers were often reductive, treating artists as neurotics and art as a form of pathology. In 1910, Ernest Jones, Freud's British disciple, pioneered the psychoanalytic "school" of literary criticism with "A Psychoanalytic Study of *Hamlet,*" which he then expanded into *Hamlet and Oedipus* (1949), a work that obsessively pins the Oedipus complex on Shakespeare's complicated hero, whose conflict "is an echo of a similar one in Shakespeare himself." Marie Bonaparte, Freud's French disciple, entered the field with a seven-hundred-page psychobiography, *Edgar Poe: Etude psychoanalytique* (1933), which links the American writer's recurring literary themes, especially his obsession with death, to events in his early childhood. These works established the early explicit mode of psychoanalytic criticism, but Freud's controversial legacy to literature stretches far beyond these first-generation studies concerned with the psyche of the artistic creator and his characters. "One is always aware in reading Freud how little cynicism there is in his thought," Trilling said:

> His desire for man is only that he should be human, and to this end his science is devoted. No view of life to which the artist responds can insure the quality of his work, but the poetic qualities of Freud's own principles, which are so clearly in the line of the classic tragic realism, suggest that this is a view which does not narrow and simplify the human world for the artist but on the contrary opens and complicates it.

Freud, a conflict theorist, proposed a tripartite topographical structure of the psyche: the id, which is unconscious and driven by libidinal and other desires; the superego, the conscience; that internalizes social injunctions and morays; and the ego, which negotiates between the insatiable desires of the id and the overly stringent demands of the superego. The ego and the superego are both partly conscious. Freud believed that "Where id was, there ego shall be." Some of Freud's followers, especially Heinz Hartmann (1894–1970), the American analyst Erik Erikson (1902–1994), and Ernest Kris (1900–1957), author of *Psychoanalytic Explorations in Art* (1952), developed a theory of ego-psychology, a vision of the "autonomous ego" functioning separately from the id. Anna Freud (1895–1982), Freud's daughter, developed an innovative theory of defense mechanisms (ego defenses) that talked about a whole range of defenses, not just repression, which people use to deal with frustration, conflict, and reality. She considers sublimation one of the higher and more sophisticated defense mechanisms used by writers and artists who sublimate sexual and aggressive impulses into their work. According to ego-psychology, creative activity derives from the energy of the mastering ego. The artist is not so much controlled by his material as in control of it. This changes the focus from the pathology of the creator to the formal features of the work itself. Ego-psychology provided insights for other forms of literary criticism and influenced such works as William Empson's New Critical treatise, *Seven Types of Ambiguity* (1945), Edmund Wilson's *The Wound and the Bow* (1941), and Trilling's essays, "Art and Neurosis" (1945) and "Freud and Literature" (1947). In such works as *The Dynamics of Literary Response* (1968) and *Five Readers Reading* (1975), Norman Holland systematized the role of the reader in relationship to the literary work, studying how readers transform literary works to their own psychological ends. His focus turns psychoanalytic criticism into a mode of reader-response criticism. Harold Bloom, on the other hand, employs Freudian ego-psychology to establish a difficult rivalry between readers and poets. He views the reading of poetry as a particularly contested space. He argues in *The Anxiety of Influence* (1975) and elsewhere that poets themselves are enmeshed in an ongoing Oedipal battle with their predecessors, a war that enables sons to engage and try to surpass their fathers. All reading for Bloom is a "transferential" misreading based on psychological strife and sublimation (*A Map of Misreading*, 1975).

Carl Gustave Jung (1875–1961) developed a theory of "universal symbols," which he called "analytical psychology." Jung had a more optimistic view of the unconscious than Freud. He was less concerned with infantile sexuality and more interested in creativity, especially midlife development and spirituality. He viewed the unconscious as a powerful force for creativity, to be mined and harvested. Diverging from Freud's focus on the individual psyche in a cultural matrix, he proposed that the individual unconscious participates in a trans-individual "collective unconscious," the repository of "racial memories" that cuts across all cultures and times. Every psyche carries certain primordial images or motifs, which Jung identifies as archetypes because they derive from the collective unconscious. Jung's postulations led to a form of archetypal criticism that focused on common and "universal" psychic forms and patterns present in poems and fictions, dreams and myths. Maud Bodkin's *Archetypal Patterns in Poetry* (1934) represents the first generation of archetypal criticism, which Northrop Frye developed into an influential mode of myth criticism in the 1950s and '60s. Jungian criticism has been criticized for ignoring history, for turning recurrent cultural patterns into absolute realities, symbols of natural unity. Yet Jung's books *Man and His Symbols* (1964) and *Memories, Dreams, Reflections* (1963) have continued to resonate for some contemporary poets and critics, such as Ted Hughes and Robert Bly, who try to tap the primal energies of the image.

Literary theorists have more recently drawn on object-relations theory, which focuses on the dynamic relationship between the "self" and its related "objects." A subject is constituted by the objects around him and uses those objects to constitute an external world. Object-relations theory shifts the Freudian emphasis to the intrapersonal and interpersonal realm, how people change and are changed by the culture and environment in which we live. Such influential psychoanalysts as Melanie Klein (1882–1960) and D. W. Winnicott (1896–1971) stress the interrelationship between the "Self" and the "Other," especially the critical role of the mother-infant dyad in human development. Winnicott's emphasis on the "transitional object" in infant development, an "intermediate area of experience" — an infant transfers its oral dependence on the mother to a transitional material object — has been fruitful because it focuses on the space of playfulness, illusion, and fantasy in adult creativity. Poetry, then, like the other arts, exists in an intermediate space between the inner or subjective and the outer or objective worlds, between fantasy and reality.

Jacques Lacan (1901–1981) famously proposed that "the unconscious is structured like a language." This is the central, invariant thesis of his complex structural psychoanalytic theory, a reformulation of what he calls "the Freudian field." Lacan argues that language is the major force in which the individual is constituted as a structured, gendered subject. Nothing is beyond the reach of language. There is no stable "self" — we are not fixed entities — and human identity is fragmented, de-centered. This is one of the central propositions of poststructuralism. Human subjects, Lacan argues, are always split off from themselves, divided by the conscious mind, which is accessible, and the unconscious, which consists of drives and forces that are inaccessible. We recognize something missing in ourselves, something unfulfilled and unfulfillable, a lack, which Lacan characterizes as desire.

Lacan theorizes that the psyche is divided into three major controlling structures or "orders": the Real, the Imaginary, and the Symbolic. The Real is an originating state of nature, a time of fullness and completeness, from which we are all permanently severed by our entrance into language. For human beings, the Real is an impossible plenitude, an unattainable state, which continues to influence us as adults but cannot be made conscious or symbolized through language. Lacan reformulates Freud's idea of psychological development into two stages: the pre-linguistic, pre-Oedipal stage, which he terms the Imaginary, and the stage after the acquisition of language, which he calls the Symbolic. Lacan commences with the infant in an amorphous or boundless state. He identifies a key mythical moment, sometimes literal, in which the infant misidentifies itself as continuous with the mother. Here the child looks in the mirror and experiences a gratifying sense of wholeness, a feeling of completeness. The infant models itself on the mother, who seems to respond to its every need, but this identification is an illusion, which is why the mirror stage is "a homologue for the Mother/Child symbolic relation." There is no distinction between the self and others, the subject and the object, in the Imaginary stage, but in the Symbolic stage the infant assimilates a system of inherited differences and oppositions, such as the assigning of gender roles, which constitutes a simultaneous submission to social authority, especially "the law of the father." The "Desire of the Mother" (the child's desire for the mother and the mother's own desire) is replaced by the "Name-of-the-Father." Thus the desire of the human being, a speaking animal, becomes "inmixed" with the "phallic order," the rules and prohibitions of law.

Lacanian literary analysis shifts the focus away from the psychology of the author, the literary character, or the audience, and onto the linguistic structure of the text itself, which is akin to a psyche. There are no primordial "archetypes," no "object-relations." By examining the process of signification, the theorist collapses the distinction between the reader and the writer. The goal is to find the laws of desire operating in literary texts.

Contemporary French feminists such as Julia Kristeva and Hélène Cixous have probed the distinction between the pre-Oedipal maternal stage of the Imaginary and the "phallocentric" stage of the Symbolic, the entry and fall into language. The feminists Juliet Mitchell and Jacqueline Rose have also reconsidered Freud's insights into the unconscious in light of Lacan's theory of signification in order to critique the phallocentric order and reconsider the nature of gendered subjects. Jacques Derrida argues that the unconscious is not so much structured as a language as it is a weave of traces that are forever operating in language. Deconstructive literary critics, such as Paul de Man (1919–1983), focus on the ways that texts misspeak or contradict themselves, giving themselves away. Michel Foucault (1926–1984), who views psychoanalysis itself as a discourse of power, nonetheless draws on psychoanalytic concepts to critique the power relations that are inextricably part of society and history. Influenced by Foucault, psychoanalytically minded literary critics, such as Edward Said (1935–2003), set out to unearth how these relations inevitably operate, often unconsciously, in literary texts. Poems are bodily experiences driven by conscious and unconscious motives. The contested self, the struggle between the body and the social order, the unconscious and conscious minds, continues to fuel different kinds of psychoanalytic criticism.

SEE ALSO *agon, anxiety of influence, archetype, deconstruction, deep image, New Criticism, poststructuralism, reader-response criticism, structuralism, Surrealism, the uncanny.*

pun A form of wordplay, the pun is a figure of speech that depends upon a similar sound or spelling and disparate meaning. Joseph Addison called the pun "A Sound, and nothing but a Sound." Charles Lamb pointed out that a pun "is a pistol let off at the ear." It has, he said, "an ear-kissing smack with it." Since the early eighteenth century, the pun has sometimes been condescended to as a "low species of wit" (Noah Webster), but the device has appeared in all literatures and seems to be as old as language itself. A good pun releases the multiple energies in words. It can be a kind of holy fooling, as in Christopher Smart, who was obsessively fond of the strategy. The punning used as a literary device in the Hebrew Bible is called *paronomasia.*

The homographic pun consists of words that are spelled the same but have different meanings. In *Romeo and Juliet* (1597), the dying Mercutio declares, "Ask for me to-morrow, you shall find me a grave man." He thus combines two meanings of the word *grave* (somber or reflective, a place of burial). A homophonic pun consists of words that sound alike but have different meanings. In this stanza from "A Hymne to God the Father" (1633), John Donne puns both on his own name (done, Donne) and on the word *Son* (meaning both Christ and the sun):

> I have a sin of fear, that when I have spun
> My last thread, I shall perish on the shore;
> Swear by Thyself that at my death Thy Sun
> Shall shine as it shines now, and heretofore;
> And, having done that, Thou hast done,
> I have no more.

pure poetry and ***impure poetry*** In 1925, the Abbé Henri Bremond delivered a lecture entitled "Pure Poetry" (or in French, *Poésie Pure*), which he followed up the next year with *Prayer and Poetry*. Two years later, Paul Valéry clarified the idea that poetry aims "to give the impression of a complete system of reciprocal relations between our ideas and images on the one hand and our means of expression on the other—a system which would correspond particularly to the creation of an emotive state in the mind" ("Pure Poetry"). It was crucial, he argued, that the poetic system should be "unconnected with the practical order." Valéry was particularly influenced by Edgar Allan Poe, who had argued that the sole purpose of poetry is the creation of beauty and that poems should be free of didactic content ("The Poetic Principle," 1850).

Robert Penn Warren took up the argument in his 1942 essay "Pure and Impure Poetry," where he argues, "Poetry wants to be pure, but poems do not." Poetry creates its own systematic structures, but poems must be open to impurities and contradictions, to ideas, "to the fires of irony." He said: "nothing that is available in human experience should be legislated out of poetry." He also noted that "a good poem involves the participation of the reader."

Pure poetry and impure poetry represent two sides of a spectrum. One emphasizes poetry's difference from the actual world; the other emphazies poetry's immersion in that world. One denies the importance of subject matter, the other insists on it. On one side, pure poetry is represented by the nineteenth-century French symbolist Stéphane Mallarmé, who characterized the poet's role as "to purify the language of the tribe." Mallarmé wanted to compose a poem of complete connotation without any denotative reference, "le poème tu, aux blancs" ("Crise de vers," 1895). On the other side, impure poetry is represented by the twentieth-century Chilean Pablo Neruda, who sought "A poetry impure as the clothing we wear, or our bodies, soup-stained, soiled with our shameful behavior, our wrinkles and vigils and dreams, observations and prophecies, declarations of loathing and love, idylls and beasts, the shocks of encounter, political loyalties, denials and doubts, affirmations and taxes" ("Toward an Impure Poetry," 1974).

SEE ALSO *didactic poetry.*

purple patch In his *Ars Poetica* (ca. 19–18 B.C.E.), Horace famously refers to the purple piece of cloth (*purpureus . . . pannus*) or irrelevant insertion of a grandiloquent descriptive passage into an art work: "Serious and ambitious designs often have a purple patch or two sewn into them just to make a good show at a distance — a description of a grove and altar of Diana, the meanderings of a stream running through pleasant fields, the River Rhine, a rainbow: but now there is no place for them." Today the term *purple patch* or *purple prose* generally means an overly florid or gaudy passage that stands out from the rest of the work, a defect of overwriting.

SEE ALSO *bombast, ekphrasis.*

puy The *puys* were literary and musical societies, primarily in the north of France, which survived from the twelfth to the seventeenth century. These societies, associations of notables gathered around the same spiritual or cultural values, competed against each other in poetic contests. The name *puy* comes from the Old French *pui,* "a hill," which is found in *La Chanson de Roland* (*The Song of Roland,* ca. 1090), and derives from the Latin *podium,* which in turn derives from a Greek word meaning "base, height, balcony." The societies seem to have taken their name from the raised platform where poets in competition delivered their *chansons,* or songs. Charles Newcomer contends that the *puy* as a literary court derives from the ancient judicial custom of bringing the accused to the top of a hill, where they were heard and judged by a jury of peers. The *puys* were initially more religious societies than literary ones — most of them were dedicated to the cult of the Virgin Mary — but later became secular. The trouvère Adam de la Halle (1237?–1288), who was affiliated with the Puy d'Arras, was the first poet to describe a literary society that holds poetic contests. The poets of the *puy,* which peaked in the Late Middle Ages, especially favored the *formes fixes* or French fixed forms, the ballade, the chant royal, the sirventes, and the *tenson.* The poetry society Puy Sainta Maria sponsored contests among the troubadours at Le-Puy-en-Velay, where the Monge de Montaudon famously received a sparrow hawk as a first prize. Something akin to the *puys* may have existed in medieval Germany as well. In London, the Puy, a cultural organization that resembled a devotional guild, flourished in the last quarter of the thirteenth century. Chaucer may have encountered or invented his patented seven-line stanza, the rhyme royal, through his contact with the ballades presented at the Puy.

SEE ALSO *ballade, chansons de geste, chant royal, formes fixes, poetic contest, rhyme royal, sirventes, tenson, trouvère.*

pyrrhic, also called *dibrach.* From the Greek: "war dance." A metrical foot of two unstressed beats (u u), the pyrrhic is the shortest foot in classical poetry. In English, however, an accentual-syllabic language, the pyrrhic is a hypothetical metrical unit. The unstressed syllables are usually treated as a substitution or associated with adjacent feet. In "The Rationale of Verse" (1848), Edgar Allan Poe contemptuously dismissed the pyrrhic in English:

> Its existence in either ancient or modern rhythm is purely chimerical, and the insisting on so perplexing a nonentity as a foot of *two short* syllables, affords, perhaps, the best evidence of the gross irrationality and subservience to authority which characterize our Prosody.

SEE ALSO *foot, meter.*

qasida The term *qasida* derives from a word meaning "to aim for, to intend." It was at times employed in early Arabic poetry for any poem, more commonly for a poem with a minimum length — sometimes that length was ten, sometimes sixty, sometimes one hundred or more lines, depending on the particular era and place. It began as a form of oral poetry, an ode with varied themes (eulogy, panegyric, satire), some of which was improvised, some inherited. The meters vary. The poem establishes a rhyme word at the end of the first hemistich (half-line). This becomes the single end-rhyme that carries through the entire composition. The earliest specimens date to the fifth century. It was a primary genre of pre-Islamic Bedouin poetry and called on the tribal loyalties of the poet. Indeed, it continues to be crucial to Bedouin poetry. It was also employed by Persian, Turkish, and Urdu poets.

In the ninth century, the Arabic writer Ibn Qutaybah (d. 889) codified a tripartite structure for the *qasida* (*Book of Poetry and Poets*), which scholars sometimes divide into "remembrance poems," "message poems," and "laudatory poems." The medieval *qasida* begins with a prelude, usually erotic and nostalgic — the poet rediscovering a place and recalling his lost beloved (*nasib*). It then moves on to recount various journeys (*rahill*) and concludes with a summary, the poet praising himself, his patron, or his tribe (*fakhr*).

The *qasida* was traditionally revered as the highest form of poetry. It was maintained by poets with a classical bent until the nineteenth century, when it began to lose its luster. The first Egyptian neoclassical poet, Mahmūd Sāmī al-Bārūdī (1839–1904), started the trend of the nineteenth- and twentieth-century traditional *qasida* (*al qasīda al-taqlīdiyya*), which conforms to the conventions established by classical Arabic poets and critics. This became known as the school of al-Bārūdī. The *qasida* form retains its advocates. But it is the pre-Islamic *qasidas* that continue to shine.

SEE ALSO *adab, fakhr.*

qene An Ethiopian genre of short religious poems with a single rhyme. This form of sacred poetry is traditionally attributed to Saint Yared, an Ethiopian saint of the sixth century, though it probably dates to an earlier time, and it comprises a significant portion of the Ethiopian liturgy. The *mawades qene* is a form of praise poetry. At one time there were schools of rhetoric that trained Ethiopian poets in the art of composing *qene.* A central stylistic feature of *qene* is called *samenna warq,* or "wax and gold," an analogy borrowed from the craft of the goldsmith in the making of jewelry. Each *qene* contains words with both a literal and an encrypted or hidden sense. The wax is the surface meaning; the gold is the underlying or esoteric one. Thus the *qene* becomes an occult art. It is beloved for its philosophical value and extolled as a unique creation of Ethiopian spiritual culture.

qit'a In classical or pre-Islamic Arabic poetry, the *qit'a* was a short, occasional poem. The word *qit'a* means "fragment" or "piece," and this secular lyric, which ranges from three to twenty lines, can either be "broken off" from a larger composition, as in the *qasida,* or comprise a discrete poem unto itself. It was generally related to a specific event or focused on a single theme.

SEE ALSO *fragment, qasida.*

quantity, see "quantitative meter" in *meter.*

quarto, see *folio.*

quatorzain Derived from the French *quatorze,* "fourteen," the *quatorzain* is a fourteen-line poem that deviates from the patterns of a sonnet. Strictly speaking, it is sonnetlike. It has the feeling of a sonnet but eschews the ruling structure, usually by avoiding or missing the turn, or *volta.* The *quatorzain* especially flourished during the Elizabethan era. Spenser first translated the French poet Joachin du Bellay into *quatorzains* in blank verse ("The Visions of Bellay," 1591). Sir Thomas Wyatt wrote a *quatorzain* in octosyllabics, which was otherwise a sonnet, a form mimicked by Shakespeare in Sonnet 20. Sidney wrote *quatorzains* in alexandrines, the twelve-syllable line of French poetry (*Astrophel and Stella,* Sonnets I, LXXVI, LXXVII, CII). Sir Walter Raleigh's "A Vision Upon the Fairy Queen" (1590) is an expansive *quatorzain* of seven poulter's measures:

Methought I saw the grave where Laura lay,
    Within that temple where the vestal flame
    Was wont to burn; and, passing by that way,
    To see that buried dust of living fame,
Whose tomb fair Love and fairer Virtue kept:
    All suddenly I saw the Fairy Queen;
    At whose approach the soul of Petrarch wept,
    And, from thenceforth, those Graces were not seen:
For they this queen attended; in whose stead
    Oblivion laid him down on Laura's hearse:
    Hereat the hardest stones were seen to bleed,
And groans of buried ghosts the heavens did pierce:
    Where Homer's spright did tremble all for grief,
    And cursed the access of that celestial thief!

Thomas Campion railed against the fourteen-line poem in his polemic against rhymed verse, *Observations in the Arte of English Poesy* (1602): "in Quatorzens, methinks, the poet handles his subject as tyrnically as *Procustes* the thiefe his prisoners, whom, when he had taken, he used to cast upon a bed, which if they were too short to fill, he would stretch them longer, if too long, he would cut them shorter." He was not a sonneteer and considered fourteen lines too long to make a simple point and too short to develop an argument or tell a story. The long history of the sonnet suggests otherwise. The term *quatorzain* now sounds old-fashioned, and most critics simply refer to all fourteen-line poems as sonnets.

SEE ALSO *Elizabethan Age, poulter's measure, sonnet.*

quatrain A four-line stanza. The quatrain—used as a unit of composition in longer poems and as a complete utterance unto itself—is probably the most common stanzaic form in the world. It has the power of heavy stone, of sturdy buildings and rooted trees. It has the adaptability of workers everywhere. It has great antiquity and travels well between languages and countries. Thus it is the staple of the English ballad and the Latin hymn, the Malay *pantun,* the Russian *chastushka.* It exists in a variety of rhyme schemes and meters, formal variations. One thinks of Alcaics and Sapphics (named after two of the greatest early Greek lyricists), of the heroic quatrain (also known as the elegiac stanza and Hammond's meter because it is used in Thomas Gray's "Elegy Written in a Country Churchyard," 1751, and James Hammond's *Love Elegies,* 1732), of the In Memoriam stanza (so-called for its adept use in Tennyson's *In Memoriam,* 1849), and the Omar Khayyám quatrain or rubaiyat stanza (from Edward Fitzgerald's loose adaptation of the Persian original).

Each form of the quatrain has its own way of treating the stanza as a solid block of meaning, a rectangular place of indwelling. Each has its own distinctive measure, distinctive music. Here is a famous anonymous poem that was found, along with its music, in an early sixteenth-century manuscript:

> Western wind, when wilt thou blow,
>   The small rain down can rain?
> Christ, if my love were in my arms
>   And I in my bed again!

SEE ALSO *Alcaic, ballad, chastushka, heroic quatrain, hymn, In Memoriam stanza, pantoum, rann, rubaiyat stanza, Sapphic stanza, stanza.*

quest-romance The quest-romance tells the story of how a hero moves from weakness to strength, ignorance to knowledge, obscurity to glory. The protagonist typically progresses through three main stages. In the first stage, he undertakes a perilous journey and goes through various minor adventures. In the second stage, he faces the ultimate test, usually a battle that leads either to his own death or the death of his foe (or both). In the third stage, his achievement is recognized and he is exalted as a hero. Northrop Frye borrows Greek terms to name these three stages: the *agon,* or conflict, the *pathos,* or death struggle, and the *anagnorisis,* or discovery, which involves the recognition of the hero.

The archetypal quest-romance is the folk tale type known as the "dragon-slayer." A monster has kidnapped the king's daughter and laid waste to the kingdom. One fighter after another is devoured by the creature until it falls to the hero to go off and fight the dragon, which he defeats, thereby freeing the young princess, whom he marries. He is guided and aided along the way by supernatural actors, who help him defeat his enemies and gain recognition. This basic story, exemplified in the tales of St. George and Perseus, has been an immensely productive schema for the human imagination.

The *Odyssey* (ca. eighth century B.C.E.) stands as the epic progenitor of the quest-romance as a journey. The medieval romances often recounted the marvelous adventures of a chivalrous knight, who goes on a quest to win the favor of a beloved lady. The story of the search for the Holy Grail has been foundational for Western literature. Frye argues that the quest-romance has analogies both to rituals and to dreams. Translated into dream terms, it represents "the search of the libido or desiring self for a fulfillment that will deliver it from the anxieties of reality but will still contain that reality." Translated into ritual terms, it represents "the victory of fertility over the waste land." The romantic poets internalized the structure of the quest-romance. Harold Bloom explains: "The poet takes the patterns of quest-romance and transposes them into his own imaginative life, so that the entire rhythm of the quest is heard again in the movement of the poet himself from poem to poem." From Shelley's *Alastor* (1815) to Yeats's *The Wanderings of Oisin* (1889), the internalized quest-romance is enacted in poems of symbolic voyaging.

SEE ALSO *agon, chivalric romance, epic, pathos, romance.*

quintain, see *quintet.*

quintet A stanza of five lines. Also called a quintain, it appears in various forms, from the clever English limerick (which rhymes *aabba* and thus relies on a principle of return) and the classical Japanese tanka (composed in lines containing 5, 7, 5, 7, 7 syllables). A wildly inventive mask of insanity energizes the conventional "mad song," as in this anonymous example from a sixteenth-century "Tom o' Bedlam" song:

I know more than Apollo,
  For, oft when he lies sleeping,
    I behold the stars
    At bloody wars
And the wounded welkin weeping.

There seems to be something a little beyond reason, something emotionally excessive in punching past the symmetrical quatrain. Thus the possibilities of five unfold: Edmund Waller joins a three-line stanza to a couplet (*ababb*) in "Song: Go, lovely Rose" (1645); Sidney employs the Sicilian quintet (an iambic pentameter stanza that rhymes *ababa*) in his enjoyable "Eleventh Song" (1591); Wyatt utilizes an interlocking tetrameter pattern (*aabab*) in "The Lover Complaineth the Unkindness of His Love" (1557), the last stanza of which concludes:

> Now cease, my lute, this is the last
> Labour that thou and I shall waste,
> And ended is that we begun.
> Now is this song both sung and past,
> My lute, be still, for I have done.

SEE ALSO *cinquain, limerick, quatrain, quintilla, stanza, tanka.*

quintilla In Spanish poetry, the *quintilla* is a five-line stanza with eight-syllable lines. The whole poem turns on two rhymes and cannot end in a couplet. There are five possible rhyme schemes: *abaab; ababa; abbab; aabab; aabba.* The *quintilla* was especially popular in the fifteenth century. Lope de Vega's *Isidro* (1599), which tells the story of Isidore, the patron saint of Madrid, has a balladlike feeling, which, as one critic puts it, "is reinforced by the easy rhythms of the *quintilla.*" Mexican oral poets continue to improvise *quintillas.*

SEE ALSO *octosyllabic verse, quintet.*

rajaz In Arabic poetry, *rajaz* is the meter of a camel's hooves on sand. It is a short verse line with a fixed number of feet (usually three). Each line is composed of four syllables: the first two are either short or long, the third short, the fourth long. The nomadic Bedouins used this meter, one of the most basic, for *al-Huda,* the caravan song. There is a legend that the song was so effective at distracting camels from their heavy load that they often arrived after a long journey still moving friskily to the beat of a drum, and then immediately dropped dead from fatigue.

rann A four-line stanza in Irish verse. The early Irish poets had rigorous rules for creating stanzas. One primary type divided the quatrain into two parts. The initial couplet was called the *Seoladh,* or the leading couplet, the second the *Comhad,* or the closing couplet. Each *rann* was a self-contained unit. The "Saltair na Rann" or "Psalter of the Verses," composed in the tenth century, consists of 162 poems, all written in two meters, which versify biblical history. In *Irish Poetry* (1902), Douglas Hyde presents a *rann* created by Malachy O'Higgin "of the Romances":

> Though there were only Art's single hand
> in the day of battle protecting it
> without doing a grief to them
> he would make a plundering of Ulster.

In "To Ireland in the Coming Times" (1893), W. B. Yeats flashed his credentials and declared that he wanted to be counted one of those who sang "to sweeten Ireland's wrong, / Ballad and story, rann and song."

SEE ALSO *quatrain.*

rasa This multidimensional Sanskrit word may mean "sap," "essence," "juice," "semen," "nectar," "intoxicating drink of Soma," "taste," "flavor," "mystic ecstasy." In the *Ríg-Veda* (1700–1100 B.C.E.), it meant the ecstatic taste of a drink. *Rasa* is the most important term in Sanskrit poetics. The aesthetician Bharata defined *rasa* as "a realization of one's own consciousness as colored by emotions" in the Sanskrit treatise *Nāṭyaśāstra,* which consists of six thousand *sutras,* or verse stanzas, and loosely translates as *A Manual of Dramatic Arts.* Probably composed in the second century B.C.E., this encyclopedia work is the first Sanskrit discourse on drama, dance, and music. The term *rasa* was first formulated for drama, but was soon adapted to poetry. Abhinavagupta later interprets the term in *Locana* (ca. 1000):

> On the other hand rasa is something that one cannot dream of expressing by the literal sense. It does not fall within workaday expression. It is, rather, of a form that must be tasted by an act of blissful relishing on the part of a delicate mind through the stimulation of previously deposited memory elements which are in keeping with the vibhavaas and anubhavas, beautiful because of their appeal to the heart, which are transmitted by [suggestive] words [of the poet]. The suggesting of such a sense is called rasadhvani and is found to operate only in poetry.
>
> This, in the strict sense of the word, is the soul of poetry.

The early Sanskrit theorists identified eight primordial passions or *rasas:* 1) the erotic, 2) the heroic, 3) the pathetic, 4) the wondrous, 5) the comic, 6) the terrible, 7) the frightful, 8) the noxious. In poetry, *Shanta,* the tranquil, also ranked as a *rasa.*

Rasa is something experienced by the audience. It links the performer and the listener, the poet and the reader. As the French critic René Daumal explains in *Rasa, or Knowledge of the Self* (1982), *rasa* "is neither an object, nor an emotion, nor a concept; it is an immediate experience, a gestation of life, a pure joy, which relishes its own essence as it communes with the 'other' — the actor or poet." *Rasa* can transport one to a transcendental level, a merging with the absolute.

There is no Western equivalent for this widely discussed and debated Sanskrit term.

SEE ALSO *the sublime, sutra.*

reader-response criticism In the late 1960s and 1970s a disparate group of North American literary theorists emphasized the role of the reader or the act of reading in interpreting literary texts. Reader-response criticism developed as a reaction against the way that New Criticism treated the literary text as an isolated object dissociated from the reader's experience. Some of the theorists associated with reader-response criticism include Stanley Fish, who developed a rhetorical approach; David Bleich, who argued that the meaning of a literary work is a function of the reader's personality; Norman Holland, who created a psychodynamic model of reader response; and Wolfgang Iser, who developed a phenomenology of reception. Reader-response criticism came under fire in the 1980s for its revisionary formalism and binary opposition of the text and the reader. It has been displaced by other theoretical models, such as deconstruction, and yet it brought a useful focus to reading as an interpretive activity.

One of the insights of reader-response criticism is that written poetry depends on the mutuality of writer and reader. Writing is embodiment, reading is contact. In the preface to *Obra poética* (1964), Jorge Luis Borges writes,

> The taste of the apple (states Berkeley) lies in the contact of the fruit with the palate, not in the fruit itself; in a similar way (I would say), poetry lies in the meeting of poem and reader, not in the lines of symbols printed on the pages of a book. What is essential is the aesthetic act, the thrill, the almost physical sensation that comes with each reading.

SEE ALSO *affective stylistics, deconstruction, New Criticism, poststructuralism, structuralism.*

reciprocus versus, see *palindrome.*

Rederijkers Dutch: "Chambers of Rhetoric." Amateur guilds devoted to writing poetry and performing plays in the Low Countries. These rigidly hierarchical middle-class guilds formed in the early fifteenth century, flourished in the sixteenth century, and faded out in the seventeenth century. They devoted themselves to elaborate dramatic spectacles and complicated poetic forms, such as the "chessboard," an eight-line poem that could be read thirty-eight different ways. The *refrein* (Dutch: "refrain"), the favored form of the Rhetoricians, usually consisted of five to ten stanzas. Each stanza contained between eight and twenty lines and concluded with the same verse line or *stockregal.* The guilds often took metaphorical names for themselves, such as De Fontein (the fountain) of Ghent, De Helighe Gheest (the Holy Ghost) of Bruges, De Pellicanisten (the Pelicanists) of Haarlem, and De Englantier (the Eglantine) of Amsterdam. Some guilds had only ten or twelve members, others numbered in the hundreds. Each guild had an individual coat of arms emblazoned with an illustrative drawing and motto. Their gatherings were sumptuous, but their poems are generally mediocre. The Dutch *Elckerlijc* (1485), or *Everyman,* the quintessential morality play, stands at the top of their hundreds of surviving plays. The *Rederijkers* are similar to the *Rhétoriqueurs* in northern France and the *meistersingers* in Germany.

SEE ALSO *meistersinger, poetic contest, Rhétoriqueurs.*

refrain A phrase, a line, or a group of lines recurring at intervals during a poem, often at the ends of stanzas (as in Shakespeare's nonsense refrain from act 2 of *Much Ado about Nothing,* "hey nonny, nonny"). A refrain can be as short as a single word; it can appear irregularly or as a partial rather than a complete repetition (when it tends to be called a repetend); it can be as long as an entire stanza (when it is called a burden). The refrain is a universal device of archaic and tribal poetries, and indeed, reiterated words and phrases may stand at the origin of poetic practice. The refrain functionally accompanies communal labor, dance, and song (it is called a chorus because it allows everyone to join in) and perhaps evokes its distant ancestry in collective life. Refrains can be found in *The Egyptian Book of the Dead,* some of which dates to 3000 B.C.E., and the Hebrew Bible, in Greek and Latin poetry, in Provençal and Renaissance verse, in English and Scottish ballads ("hey nonny, nonny").

The refrain can build and accrue meaning, whether by exact repetitions that change meaning in each new context ("nevermore" in Poe's "The Raven," 1845) or by undergoing slight modulations in a process called incremental repetition (as in Trumbull Stickney's poem "Mnemosyne," 1902).

As John Hollander puts it in *Melodious Guile* (1990), "Refrains are, and have, memories — of their prior strophes or stretches of text, of their own preoccurrences, and of their own genealogies in earlier texts as well." Refrains are haunted by circularity, by turnings and recurrences ("hey nonny, nonny").

SEE ALSO *burden, chorus, incremental repetition, repetend, work song.*

refrán, refranes (pl) The generic word in Spanish for proverbs. The popular *refranes* are often pithy and pointed little rhythmic expressions that rhyme. The book-length collections of *refranes* (*refranero*) were exceedingly popular in the Spanish golden age. Miguel de Cervantes was especially fond of using proverbs in *Don Quixote* (1605, 1615). Henry Edward Watts points out, "in *refranes,* or currently repeated sayings, as used by Cervantes, are included *adagios,* which are didactic, and contain rules of conduct, or philosophic counsels or abstract maxims; *proverbios,* which are historical and relate to facts and occurrences; and *refranes* simple, which are common sayings (Fr. *dicton*), familiar allusions, relics of personal sarcasm, remains of old jokes, mere bits of humour."

SEE ALSO *envoi, the golden age, proverb.*

Regency period, see *romanticism.*

remáte In Spanish, the word *remáte* means "end, conclusion, expiration." In poetry, the *remáte* is a metric term for a shorter stanza that concludes a lyric. It frequently repeats the final rhymes of the previous full-length stanza. Somewhat confusingly, it has also been referred to as *commiato, contera, despido, envoi, ripressa, ritornelo* (*retornelo*), and *vuelta.* Each term is another way of pointing to it as a final envoy or turning point. In bullfighting, a *remáte* is a finishing pass to a series of passes, which also applies to this final flourish in a *canción* (song), when the poet addresses himself to the poem itself, asking it to carry a special message to a particular person. It is a way of recognizing, as Juan Diáz Rengifo put it in his sixteenth-century treatise *Arte poética espanola* (Spanish Art of Poetry), "some flaw in the *canción,* or making an excuse for it, or telling it what it might answer if it should be found wanting in some respect."

SEE ALSO *canciones, envoi.*

Renaissance poetry The Renaissance ("rebirth"), which commonly refers to the period of European history following the Middle Ages, saw a vital revival of interest in the pagan classical world as well as a vibrant renewal of artistic and intellectual energies. The study of Greek and Latin classics was a touchstone for a new humanism. The Renaissance is usually thought to have begun in Italy in the late fourteenth century and spread to the rest of Europe through the fifteenth and sixteenth centuries. This period is now commonly referred to as Early Modern. The English Renaissance is usually dated from the accession of Henry VIII in 1509 to the restoration of the monarchy in 1660. One of the problems with the periodization of the Renaissance — was there really such a thing as *the Renaissance?* — is that it suggests the previous centuries experienced little cultural and academic achievement. Jacob Burkhardt pointed out in *The Civilization of the Renaissance in Italy* (1860) that the Renaissance first marked the birth of the modern individual. And yet modern people did not suddenly wake up around 1450 and conceive of themselves as individuals. Humanistic development was a long and complex process. As early as 1603, Samuel Daniel was complaining about the humanist habit of describing the previous age: "Nor can it be but a touch of arrogant ignorance, to hold this or that nation as Barbarous, these or those times grosse, considering how this manifold creature man, wheresoever hee stand in the world, hath alwayes some disposition of worth" (*A Defence of Ryme*).

Nonetheless, the Renaissance was a period of an extraordinary new poetry and poetics. It marks the transition from an oral culture to a print culture. The imitation of classical styles and genres was balanced by a new interest in the vernacular. One thinks of Francesco Pertrarca, known in English as Petrarch (1304–1377), Matteo Maria Boiardo (1441–1494), Ludovico Ariosto (1474–1533), and Torquato Tasso (1544–1595) in Italy; of Pierre de Ronsard (1524–1585) and the poets of the Pléiades in France; of Lope de Vega (1562–1635) and Pedro Calderón de la Barca (1600–1681) in Spain; and of such poets and playwrights as Edmund Spenser (1552?–1599), Christopher Marlowe (1564–1593), William Shakespeare (1564–1616), Ben Jonson (1572–1637), and John Donne (1572–1631) in England. There was a sense of conquering poetic worlds, of thinking newly through the problems of poetry from the smallest technical detail to the largest spiritual vision. Thus Sir Philip Sidney argued in his *Apology for Poetry* (ca. 1579), the first work of literary criticism in English, that poets outdo nature and put us in touch with a golden age before the Fall, an originary time:

> Nature never set forth the earth in such rich tapestry as divers poets have done, neither with pleasant rivers, fruitful trees, sweet-smelling flowers, nor whatsoever else may make the too much loved earth more lovely. Her world is brazen; the poets only deliver a golden.

SEE ALSO *baroque, Cavalier poets, the golden age, Gongorism, metaphysical poets, Sons of Ben.*

renga This Japanese verse form, meaning "linked poem," is a collaborative venture, which originated in Japan as a party game around a thousand years ago. Poets took turns composing alternate three-line and two-line stanzas. Each stanza links to the one before it. The *renga,* which follows the prescribed thirty-one-syllable count of the tanka (5–7–5, 7–7), enabled poets to test their skills at creating images and linking dissimilar elements. The *hokku,* or opening verse of a *renga* sequence, consisted of seventeen syllables and included a season word. It was eventually singled out, especially during the late Edo period (1600–1868), and appreciated for its own beauty. Thus, the seventeen-syllable haiku (5, 7, 5) originated in the *renga* form.

Renga started as a somewhat frivolous kind of poetry (an alternative to the rigors of creating tanka), but later evolved into playful (*mushin*) and serious (*ushin*) forms. One hundred stanzas was the standard length, though the master Matsuo Bashō (1644–1694) preferred a thirty-six verse form that he called a *kasen,* a word that previously had referred to the thirty-six immortal poets of Japan. A fifty-link *renga* is called a *gojuin.* The traditional *renga* had highly elaborated rules of progression and association. The team leader, usually the honored guest, would write an opening verse (a *hokku*), which the host would follow with a *wakiku* ("accompanying verse") consisting of two phrases with seven syllables in each. This was followed by a third poet's three-phrase, seventeen-syllable verse, then by a fourth poet's two-phrase, fourteen-syllable verse, and so forth until the sequence reached its final thirty-sixth, or one-hundredth verse. The last stanza was called the "completing verse," or *ageku.* It attempted to summarize the work by referring back to the opening stanza.

The *haikai de renga* or *haikai* (literally "playful style") was a lighthearted kind of linked poetry that emerged from the traditional *renga* and gradually included people of all classes. The *haikai* democratized Japanese poetry. Bashō was the first poet to transform the *haikai* from an entertaining game into a serious poetic form.

In recent times poets have eased the terms and opened up the structure of the traditional *renga.* In *Renga* (1971), for example, four international poets (Octavio Paz from Mexico, Jacques Roubaud from France, Edoardo Sanguineti from Italy, and Charles Tomlinson from England) westernized the form by creating a chain of poems, a sequence of sonnets, in four languages.

SEE ALSO *haikai, haiku, tanka.*

repetend A repeated sound, word, or phrase, often defined as a refrain. The repetend differs from most refrains, however, because it tends to occur irregularly or in a partial rather than a complete repetition. It has a strong emphatic quality, but is less circular and more unpredictable than a refrain. Think, for example, of how in Edgar Allan Poe's "Ulalume" (1847), the phrase "the ghoul-haunted woodland of Weir" is repeated at the conclusion of three of the ten stanzas. In T. S. Eliot's "The Love Song of J. Alfred Prufrock" (1920), the main character reveals his timidity by repeatedly rephrasing the question "And how should I presume?"

SEE ALSO *refrain.*

repetition Repetition — the use of the same term several times — is one of the crucial elements in poetry. "Repetition in word and phrase and in idea is the very essence of poetry," Theodore Roethke writes in "Some Remarks on Rhythm" (1960). It is one of the most marked features of all poetry, oral and written, one of the primary ways we distinguish poetry itself. Repetition, as in rhyme, is a strong mnemonic device. Oral poets especially use it for remembering structures. The incantatory magic of poetry — think of spells and chants, of children's rhymes and lullabies — has something to do with recurrence, with things coming back to us in time, sometimes in the same way, sometimes differently. Repetition is the primary way of creating a pattern through rhythm. Meaning accrues through repetition. One of the deep fundamentals of poetry is the recurrence of sounds, syllables, words, phrases, lines, and stanzas.

Repetition can be one of the most intoxicating features of poetry. It creates expectations, which can be fulfilled or frustrated. It can create a sense of boredom and complacency, but it can also incite enchantment and inspire bliss.

Many of the sound devices of poetry (alliteration, assonance, consonance) depend on recurrence. Metrical patterns are established by recurrences, and so are poetic forms (the canzone, the sestina), some with repetends and refrains. The repeating structure of the catalog is one of the legacies of the Hebrew Bible to later poets, and some of the key devices of free verse (anaphora, parallelism) are structures of repetition. This glossary contains a wide repertoire of poetic modes of repetition in poetries around the world. One could be forgiven for thinking that our brains are hardwired for repetition. Peter Sacks writes in *The English Elegy* (1987), "Repetition creates a sense of continuity, of an unbroken pattern such as one may oppose to the extreme discontinuity of death."

Repetition can be so insistent that it spills over into obsessiveness, as in the defiant title of Daniel Hoffman's book *Poe Poe Poe Poe Poe Poe Poe* (1972), which borrows its signal rhythm from Edgar Allan Poe's poem "The Bells" (1849). Poe uses different kinds of repetition (internal and end rhyme, meter, words, lines) to create a hypnotic effect. He concludes with a man in a belfry dancing, yelling and

> Keeping time, time, time,
> In a sort of Runic rhyme,
>   To the Pæan of the bells —
>   Of the bells: —
> Keeping time, time, time,
> In a sort of Runic rhyme,
>   To the throbbing of the bells —
> Of the bells, bells, bells —
>   To the sobbing of the bells: —
> Keeping time, time, time,
>   As he knells, knells, knells,
> In a happy Runic rhyme,
>   To the rolling of the bells —
> Of the bells, bells, bells: —
>   To the tolling of the bells —

Of the bells, bells, bells, bells,
    Bells, bells, bells —
To the moaning and the groaning of the bells.

SEE ALSO *alliteration, assonance, catalog poem, consonance, incantation, incremental repetition, litany, meter, parallelism, refrain, repetend, rhythm.*

respuesta, see *poetic contest.*

Restoration poetry Poetry written during the period from the coronation of Charles II in 1660, which restored the English monarchy after the civil war, until 1700 or so. In "To My Lord Chancellor," John Dryden expressed the commonplace that in 1660 art was restored along with the Stuart monarchy:

When our great monarch into exile went,
Wit and religion suffered banishment . . .
At length the Muses stand restored again
To that great charge which Nature did ordain.

The Restoration was an era of facts and reason. The focus was on middle-class Protestant values, on commerce and respectability, on important institutions, such as the founding of the Royal Society and the Bank of England. There was a return to traditional values and beliefs, which was reflected in literary texts. Thus the neatly balanced heroic couplet, which had five beats per line, was the predominant and normative instrument of late seventeenth-century English poetry.

The literary extremes of this period include Dryden's witty public satires, such as *Mac Flecknoe* (1682–1684) and *Absalom and Achitophel* (1681–1682), which were directed at contemporary targets while returning poetry to its classical Roman precedents in Horace (65–8 B.C.E.) and Juvenal (ca. 55–130); John Bunyan's *The Pilgrim's Progress from This World to That Which is to Come* (1678), a pious Christian allegory; and John Milton's Protestant epic *Paradise Lost* (1667), at once a sublime prophecy and an act of political protest. It was read during this period as a commentary on God's supremacy.

This was also the era of the courtier poets, such as the fluent Edmund Waller ("Go, lovely Rose," 1645) and the outlandish rake, John Wilmot, Earl of Rochester ("Whoring and Drinking, but with good Intent"), whose erotic lyrics and graphic satires circulated in manuscript until after his death. He writes in his long poem "A Satire against Reason and Mankind" (1674):

> Were I (who to my cost already am
> One of those strange prodigious Creatures *Man*)
> A Spirit free, to choose for my own share,
> What Case of Flesh, and Blood, I pleased to wear,
> I'd be a *Dog*, a *Monkey*, or a *Bear*.
> Or any thing but that vain *Animal*
> Who is so proud of being rational.

SEE ALSO *Caroline Age, Cavalier poets, couplet, neoclassicism, Renaissance poetry, satire.*

retroencha, see *chanso.*

Retrogardism In 1995, the Swedish poets Hokan Sandell and Clemens Altgard published a book, *On Retrogardism* (*Om Retrogardismen*), and founded their own movement. They argued that poetry had become too self-regarding and insular to communicate with general readers, a larger public. They especially took aim at L=A=N=G=U=A=G=E poetry, which they considered too critical and even contemptuous of language. They proposed a return to the genres and techniques that had been displaced and rejected by modernism. Retrogardism is a renewed traditionalism.

SEE ALSO *L=A=N=G=U=A=G=E poetry, modernism, tradition.*

reverdie An Old French dance poem that celebrates the arrival of spring. The type originated in troubadour ballads of the Middle Ages — the word *reverdie* means "re-greening" — and spring is often symbolized as a beautiful woman, as in other troubadour lyrics. The Middle English song "Sumer is icumen in, / Lhude sing cuccu!" is a *reverdie,* which Ezra Pound parodied as "Winter is icumen in, / Lhude sing Goddamm" ("Ancient Music," 1915). William Carlos Williams's poem "Spring and All" (1923) inherits and inverts the tradition of the *reverdie.* It is set in New Jersey in March and enacts the difficult struggle of everything to get born, to "enter the new world naked."

SEE ALSO *aisling, troubadour.*

rhapsode (or ***rhapsodist***), ***rhapsody*** In ancient Greece a rhapsode was an itinerant minstrel who composed and recited epic poetry aloud. Some material was memorized, some improvised by these professional performers. The word *rhapsody* means "stitch song" in Greek, and a rhapsode orally "stitched together" various strands of heroic material. The Homëridai (literally "children of Homer") were a group of rhapsodists who traced themselves back to an ancestor called "Homëros." Rhapsodes competed at religious festivals, and Plato's dialogue *Ion* (ca. 399–ca. 387 B.C.E.) concerns a formal competition among rhapsodes. In ancient Mesopotamia, Sumerian myths and epics were probably recited by rhapsodes, who were called *nar* and played the lyre, *zag-mí,* which developed into a term for *praise.*

A rhapsody originally referred to the section of epic literature sung by a rhapsode, but later it came to mean an intensely emotional literary work, an ecstatic poetic utterance, as in Sir William Watson's "Hymn to the Sea" (1895):

> While, with throes, with raptures, with loosing of bonds, with unseal-
> ings,
> Arrowy pangs of delight, piercing the core of the world,
> Tremors and coy unfoldings, reluctances, sweet agitations,
> Youth, irrepressibly fair, wakes like a wondering rose.

SEE ALSO *aoidos, epic, minstrel, poetic contest.*

rhetoric The art of speaking well or "the art of discourse." Plato refers to rhetoric as "the art or science (*technē*) of speech." Rhetoric has meant two things since the ancients: ornamental speech (the study of tropes and figures), and persuasive speech (the study of argumentation, eloquence in action). One frequently bleeds into the other, and rhetoric now generally refers to the technique of persuading an audience through the artful use of language. The words *rhetoric, oratory,* and *eloquence* all derive from the same root, meaning "to speak." The Sophist Gorgias of Leontini (ca. 483–ca. 376 B.C.E.), the first great rhetorician, said: "I hold all poetry to be speech with metre, and that is how I use the word. Those who hear poetry feel the shudders of fear, the tears of pity, the longings of grief." The scholar Ernst Robert Curtius explains:

Rhetoric signifies "the craft of speech"; hence, according to its basic meaning, it teaches how to construct a discourse artistically. In the course of time, this seminal idea became a science, an art, an ideal of life, and indeed a pillar of antique culture.

Rhetoric, which has influenced Western culture for more than two thousand years, was recognized in literature long before it was codified as an art in its own right. Reading the great speeches by the characters in the Homeric epics, we can still see why in antiquity Homer earned the epithet "the father of rhetoric." Rhetoric was first established as an art because of its practical utility in civic life. As Plato has Gorgias say in the dialogue of that name: "[rhetoric] is in truth the greatest boon, for it brings freedom to mankind in general and to each man dominion over others in his own country. . . . I mean the power to convince by your words the judges in court, the senators in Council, the people in the Assembly, or in any other gathering of a citizen body." A powerful orator, Gorgias appropriated for prose the symmetries of poetry, which became known as the Gorgianic figures, some of the first staples of rhetoric: antithesis ("setting opposite," a counter proposition, the juxtaposition of contrasting words or ideas), *isocolon* and *parison* ("equal list," a sequence of clauses or sentences of identical length), and *homoeoteleuton* (when several words or utterances end in a similar fashion). Plato shows a great animus to rhetoric in his dialogue *Gorgias* (ca. 399–387 B.C.E.), where Socrates argues against the moral relativism of rhetoric, which has no subject matter of its own and can be manipulated for evil ends. In his foundational treatise, *Rhetoric* (ca. 335–330 B.C.E.), Aristotle defines rhetoric as "the faculty of discovering all the available means of persuasion in any given situation" and counters Plato's arguments, establishing the universal scope of rhetoric as a tool:

> And if it be objected that one who uses such power of speech unjustly might do great harm, *that* is a charge which may be made in common against all good things except virtue, and above all against all things that are most useful, as strength, health, wealth, generalship. A man can confer the greatest of benefits by a right use of these, and inflict the greatest of injuries by using them wrongly.

Aristotle also identified persuasion as a characteristic of rhetoric and imitation as a characteristic of poetry. Since Aristotle, rhetoric has been intertwined with poetics. Aristotle's treatise was followed by a long string of rhetorical textbooks in Greek and Latin, which focused on the means and devices that orators used to persuade audiences to think or act in certain ways. Cicero sharpened the precepts of rhetoric in seven Latin treatises, especially *De Oratore* (55 B.C.E.) and *Orator* (46 B.C.E.), where he argues that both oratory and poetry depend on the same five parts: *inventio* (invention), *dispositio* (arrangement), *elocutio* (style), *memoria* (memory), and *actio* (delivery): "All the activity and ability of an orator falls into five divisions . . . He must first hit upon what to say; then manage and marshal his discoveries, not merely in orderly fashion, but with a discriminating eye for the exact weight as it were of each argument; next go on to array them in the adornments of style; after that keep them guarded in his memory; and in the end deliver them with effect and charm." Quintilian's *Institutio oratorio* (ca. 95) refashioned the subject of rhetoric into something altogether different, a humanistic recognition of the importance of literature to life: "The love of literature and the reading of the poets are not confined to school days, but end only with life itself." In his first-century treatise *On the Sublime,* Longinus demonstrated how rhetoric served as a method of transport to deliver sublimity in poetry.

Curtius identifies Ovid (43 B.C.E.–18 C.E.) as the poet who first brought the principles of rhetoric into the service of a charming, witty, written poetry that revels in sound and sense. Horace's notion in his *Ars Poetica* (Art of Poetry, first century B.C.E.) that poetry should instruct or delight, or preferably both, opened the gateway to rhetorical criticism, which studies the means through which a work achieves its effect upon a listener or reader. George Puttenham applied rhetoric to the consideration of English poetry in *The Arte of English Poesie* (1589), which takes 107 figures adapted from classical sources and divides them into three categories according to their appeal: the auricular (the ear), the sensable (the mind), and the sententious (the mind and ear). Puttenham's telling descriptions, examples, and nicknames for the figures have their own pleasurable rhetoric: eliminate conjunctions (*I saw it, I said it, I will swear it*) and you have "*Asyndeton,* or the Loose Language"; put them in (*And I saw it, and I say it and I / Swear it to be true*) and you have "*Polysendeton,* or the Couple Clause"; deliberately understate a case and treat the more dignified in terms of the less dignified (*A great mountaine as bigge as a molehill, / A beauy burthen purdy, as a pound of feathers*) and you have *"Meiosis,* or the Disabler"; deliberately overstate and exaggerate a case (*What should I go about to recite your Maiestees innumerable vertues, euen as much as I took vpon me to number the stares of the sky, or to tell the sands of the sea*) and you have *"Hiperbole,* or the Ouer reacher, otherwise called the loud lyer."

There is no speech or poetry without a rhetorical dimension, which can be studied and analyzed, and yet ever since the Renaissance the relationship between poetry and rhetoric has been a conflicted terrain. Didactic poetry is intentionally rhetorical, but what about nondidactic poetry? Many of the romantic objections to rhetoric, for example, seem actually to be objections to a particular kind of rhetoric, to oratory and didactic literature. Rhetoric depends on the relationship established between (or among) the speaker, the oral text, and the audience, or the writer, the written text, and the reader. The relationship changes according to genre. An oral poet is not an orator but a poet. The speaker in a lyric is in a different relationship to the audience than the narrator of either an oral or a written epic, who in turn stands in a different relationship to a live audience than the actors who portray characters in a play, who speak differently than the characters in a short story or novel. There is a difference between the two primary senses of rhetoric as 1) didactic persuasive language, which can be negative, and 2) the means of communicating anything, which is neutral. Every poet uses a sort of rhetoric to communicate—the relationship between the poet and reader always includes some sort of persuasion, even if it is ambiguity and open-endedness. Rhetorical criticism inevitably addresses the similarities and differences between poetry, a noninstrumental art, and rhetoric, a practical one. Poets themselves have frequently divided on the usefulness of rhetoric in thinking about poetry. On one hand, the young Wallace Stevens wrote in a journal: "The best poetry will be rhetorical criticism." On the other hand, W. B. Yeats, one of the most persuasive modern poets, said, "We make out of the quarrel with others, rhetoric, but out of the quarrel with ourselves, poetry."

SEE ALSO *adynaton, anastrophe, antithesis, asyndeton, catachresis, Chicago school, circumlocution, deconstruction, didactic poetry, dulce et utile, epideictic poetry, figures of speech, genre, hendiadys, hypallage, hyperbole, hysteron proteron, imitation, inversion, isocolon, litotes, meiosis, metaphor, metonymy, New Criticism, polysyndeton, simile, the sublime, syllepsis, tapinosis, trope, zeugma.*

rhetorical question A question that doesn't need an answer because its answer is so obvious that it doesn't need to be stated. In his treatise *On the Sublime* (100 C.E.), Longinus views the rhetorical question as a way to arrest a listener, and cleverly casts his remarks as rhetorical questions: "What are we to say of inquiries and questions? Should we not say that they increase the realism and vigour of the writing by the actual form of the figure?"

Rhetorical questions are one of the recurrent devices in biblical poetry, where they often come in pairs or sequences. They have their origins in oral poetry and public oratory, in wisdom literature, which stands behind a work like the book of Job, which uses them extensively. In 38 Job, for example, the Lord speaks to Job out of the whirlwind almost entirely in rhetorical questions, such as

> (28) Hath the rain a father? or who hath begotten the drops of dew?
> (29) Out of whose womb came the ice? and the hoary frost of heaven,
> who hath gendered it?

John Suckling begins his seventeenth-century song of unrequited love, "Why so pale and wan, fond lover?" with two stanzas of rhetorical questions, and Percy Bysshe Shelley closes his nineteenth-century "Ode to the West Wind" with one of the most well-known rhetorical questions in English literature: "O, Wind, / If Winter comes, can Spring be far behind?" In modern poetry, W. B. Yeats was especially fond of the strategic device. The twelve-line poem "No Second Troy" (1910) consists mostly of rhetorical questions, and concludes with two:

> Why, what could she have done, being what she is?
> Was there another Troy for her to burn?

SEE ALSO *didactic poetry, figures of speech, rhetoric, the sublime, trope.*

Rhétoriqueurs, Grand Rhétoriqueurs The *Rhétoriqueurs* or the *Grand Rhétoriqueurs,* as they are sometimes called, refer to three closely linked generations of rhetorically self-conscious, late medieval French poets working in northern France, Flanders, and the Duchy of Burgandy between 1460 and 1520. The group includes six significant poets: Jean Meschinot, Jean Robertet, Jean Molinet, Jean Marot, Jean Lemaire de Belges, and Guillaume

Crétin. For centuries these court poets, who are now viewed as a crucial link between medieval and Renaissance culture, were mostly erased from the literary canon as propagandists, as part of what Johan Huizinga called "the waning of the Middle Ages." They were in politically subservient roles, they had a penchant for moralizing, and they relied on fixed, highly oratorical forms. They loved verbal play and valued complexity, experimenting with difficult meters and intricate rhyme schemes (their favorite kind of rhyme was *rimes equivoques* or rhymes that extend across words), typography and the graphic use of letters, convoluted allegories. They excelled at such forms as the ballade and the rondeau, acrostics and pattern poems. The name *rhétoriqueurs* derives from French treatises on versification known as *arts de second rhétorique* (arts of second rhetoric), such as Eustache Deschamps's *L'art de dictier* (1392), Jacques Legrand's *Des rimes* (1405), Baudet Harenc's *Le doctrinal de la seconde rhétorique* (1432), and Jean Molinet's *L'art de rhétorique* (1493). The first rhetoric was prose, the second verse. The verbal ingenuity of the *Rhétoriquers* anticipates the experimental games of some late modernist poetry, such as the Oulipo movement.

SEE ALSO *acrostic, ballade, Oulipo, pattern poetry, Rederijkers, Renaissance poetry, rhetoric, rhyme, rondeau.*

rhopalic verse Also known as wedge verse or snowball verse. The word *rhopalic* comes from the Greek *rhopalos,* meaning "clublike" or "cudgel," something that expands or thickens toward the end. Each word or group of words in a line of *rhopalic* verse is one syllable longer than the one that precedes it. A verse can also be *rhopalic* when each line in a stanza increases by a foot or so. The technique of accruing weight seldom occurs more than once in a passage of verse. Both Homer and Virgil employed it to create a single line that thickens like a club as it moves toward the end. Here are the three opening lines of *rhopalic* verse in the metaphysical poet Richard Crashaw's poem "Wishes to His Supposed Mistress" (1641). The first line is dimeter, the second trimeter, the third tetrameter in a poem that progresses over forty-two stanzas.

Whoe'er she be,
That not impossible she
That shall command my heart and me

rhyme Rainer Maria Rilke called rhyme "a goddess of secret and ancient coincidences." He said that "she comes as happiness comes, hands filled with an achievement that is already in flower." Rhyme has the joyousness of discovery, of hidden relations uncovered, as if by accident. Rhyme occurs, Joseph Brodsky said, "when two things sound the same but their meanings diverge." It creates a partnership between words, lines of poetry, feelings, ideas. Gerard Manley Hopkins called rhyming words "rhyme fellows." He also said, "All beauty may by a metaphor be called rhyme" (1865).

The *Oxford English Dictionary* defines *rhyme* as "Agreement in the terminal sounds of two or more words or metrical lines, such that (in English prosody) the last stressed vowel and any sounds following it are the same, while the sound or sounds preceding it are different." There is something charged and magnetic about a good rhyme, something both unsuspected and inevitable, something utterly surprising and unforeseen and yet also binding and necessary. It is as if the poet had called up the inner yearning of words to find each other.

Rhyme foregrounds the sounds of words as words. It also functions as a marker signaling the end of a rhythmic unit. It is mnemonic:

> Red sky at night, sailor's delight.
> Red sky in morning, sailor's warning.

Two different kinds of rhyme capture two different portents here: one about safety, the other about danger.

There is a pleasure in the sound of words coming together, in the pulse and beat, the rhythm of their conjoining. ("The chances of rhyme are like the chances of meeting— / In the finding fortuitous, but once found, binding," Charles Tomlinson writes in his poem "The Chances of Rhyme," 1969.) There was systematic rhyming in ancient Chinese, Sanskrit, Arabic, Norse, Provençal, and Celtic languages, but the origins of rhyme in English are mysterious since, as George Saintsbury once declared, no one really knows quite how or why or when rhyme actually entered our language. The word *rhyme* was spelled *rime* until the seventeenth century.

Rhyme is a device based on the sound identities of words. It is repetition with a difference. It involves the inner correspondence of end sounds in words or in lines of verse. W. N. Ewer writes in "The Chosen People" (1924):

How odd
Of God
To choose
The Jews.

This is an example of exact rhyme (also called complete, full, perfect, true, or whole rhyme) since the initial sounds are different, but all succeeding sounds are identical (How *odd* / of *God* / To *choose* / The *Jews*). It is called a near rhyme when the final consonants are identical but the preceding vowels or consonants differ (as when W. B. Yeats rhymes *houses* and *faces* at the opening of "Easter, 1916"). Near rhyme is also called approximate, half, imperfect, oblique, partial, or slant rhyme. A pararhyme is a form of near rhyme in which all the consonants are the same but the vowels are different (as when Wilfred Owen pairs *blade* with *blood, flash* with *flesh,* and *leads* with *lads* in "Arms and the Boy," 1918). A rhyme that concludes a line is called an end rhyme. Rarer is the rhyme that starts a line, which is called an initial rhyme, a head rhyme, or a beginning rhyme, as when Thomas Hood writes in "The Bridge of Sighs" (1844): "*Mad* for life's history, / *Glad* for death's mystery." A rhyme that occurs within a line is called an internal rhyme ("Red sky at *night,* sailor's de*light*"). An internal rhyme is considered a leonine rhyme when a word near the middle of the line rhymes with a word at the end, as when Edgar Allan Poe summarizes in "Annabel Lee" (1849): "For the moon never *beams* without bringing me *dreams.*" An interlinear internal rhyme rhymes two words that are not in end positions, as in Shelley's "Stanzas Written in Dejection" (1818): "Till death like sleep might *steal* on me, / And I might *feel* in the warm air." An interlaced rhyme, also known as a cross-rhyme, is a more elaborate form of medial rhyme that occurs in long rhyming couplets, especially the hexameter. Words in the middle of each line rhyme with each other, as in Swinburne's "Hymn to Proserpine" (1866):

Thou hast conquered, O pale *Galilean;* the world has grown grey from
  Thy breath;
We have drunken of things *Lethean,* and fed on the fullness of death.
Laurel is green for a *season,* and love is sweet for a day;
But love grows bitter with *treason,* and laurel outlives not May.

A one-syllable rhyme is called masculine (*Oh*/*no*), a two-syllable rhyme feminine, as when Stevie Smith rhymes *epileptic* and *skeptic* and John Crowe

Ransom *Plato* and *potato.* (The rules regulating the alternation of masculine and feminine rhymes in French prosody are called *alternance des rimes*). A three-syllable rhyme (*wittily/prettily*) is called triple rhyme (or *sdrucciola,* an Italian word meaning "sliding" or "slippery"), a four-syllable rhyme (*magically/tragically*) a quadruple rhyme. It is called a mosaic rhyme when one of the rhymes is made out of more than one word, as when Robert Browning rhymes *failure* and *pale lure* and *soon hit* and *unit* ("A Grammarian's Funeral," ca. 1854). When rhymes are based on a similarity of spelling rather than sound, it is called eye rhyme (*prove/love*). Homographs are spelled the same, as in *well,* an adverb meaning doing excellently, and *well,* a noun meaning a hole dug in the ground. Homophones are spelled differently but sound alike (*blue/blew*). When the same words line up as a rhyme two or more times it is called identical rhyme:

> And when we lay naked among the books,
> the books enclosed a sacred garden
> for Adam and Eve safely restored to Eden,
> ourselves immersed in a paradise of books.

Rhyming every other line, as in the ballad, is called an intermittent rhyme. Rhyming *abba,* as Tennyson does in the "In Memoriam" (1849) stanza, is called an envelope rhyme. Rhyming that doesn't follow a fixed pattern is called an irregular rhyme, as in the pseudo-Pindaric, and rhyming that occurs in an otherwise unrhymed poem is called sporadic rhyme or occasional rhyme. A thorn line is a line that doesn't rhyme in an otherwise rhyming passage. It breaks expectation.

A few other types: Monorhyme, which is common in Arabic, Latin, and Welsh poetry, is a poem or section of a poem in which all the lines have the same end rhyme. There is a monorhyme in the tiny anonymous poem "Fleas": "Adam / Had 'em." One poem in the Middle Ages rhymed forty-eight lines on the letter *a,* which was called tirade rhyme. Macaronic rhymes use more than one language, as in medieval lyrics with Latin refrains. Linked rhyme, which was widely used in Welsh poetry, connects the last syllable of one line with the first syllable of the next one. An apocopated rhyme rhymes a line end with a penultimate syllable. A so-called backward rhyme or amphisbaenic rhyme is a reversed rhyme (*tort* and *trot*). It can consist of words that are spelled backward (*rail/liar*) or pronounced backward (*later/retail*). Thus Edmund Wilson subtitled his 1948 poem "The Pickerel Pond—a Double Pastoral" "*Elegaics, with Amphisbaenics (backward rhymes)*." (The word *ripple* is paired with *leper* and *air* with *ray*, and so on.) A synthetic rhyme deletes, expands, or otherwise wrenches letters, which is why it is also called wrenched rhyme, in order to create a false rhyme, often for comic effect, as in this couplet from Ogden Nash's "Kindly Unhitch That Star, Buddy" (1929):

> Some people think they will eventually wear diamonds instead of *rhinestones*
> Only by everlastingly keeping their noses to the *ghrinestones.*

Tail rhymes are rhymes that answer each other across intervening stanzas. A word split across the end of a line is called a broken rhyme (or rhyme-breaking), as when Alexander Pope rhymes "for*get*- / Ful" and *debt*" ("Fourth Satire of Dr. John Donne, Dean of St. Paul's, Versified," 1733) or Marianne Moore rhymes "*ac* / ccident" and "*lack*" ("The Fish," 1918).

Rhyme creates in the reader a sense of interaction between words and lines. In "One Relation of Rhyme to Reason" (1954), W. K. Wimsatt suggests that every rhyme invites the reader to consider semantic as well as sound similarities. The reader participates by feeling the weight of the rhyming words, by forging the meaning of their connections, by teasing out the implications of words coming together and identifying each other as partners. Emerson gives a wonderful sense of the boldness of rhyme in a notebook entry from June 27, 1839:

> *Rhyme*—Rhyme; not tinkling rhyme, but grand Pindaric strokes, as firm as the tread of a horse. Rhyme that vindicates itself as an art, the stroke of the bell of a cathedral. Rhyme which knocks at prose and dullness with the stroke of a cannon ball. Rhyme which builds out into Chaos and old night a splendid architecture to bridge the impassable, and call aloud on all the children of morning that Creation is recommencing. I wish to write such rhymes as shall not suggest a restraint, but contrariwise the wildest freedom.

SEE ALSO *assonance, consonance, feminine rhyme, interlaced rhyme, leonine rhyme, masculine rhyme, near rhyme, Rhétoriqueurs, tail rhyme.*

rhymed prose Many cultures have the category rhymed prose for nonmetrical speech. When poetry is defined as "metrical speech," rhymed prose becomes an alternative category regulated not by meter but by rhythm. It adapts the devices of poetry to rhythmical prose. Rhyme in this general sense is used to mean repetition, not matching vowel or consonant sounds. It sometimes consists of free and irregular rhythms, as in the Divine Offices of the medieval church, which were gradually replaced by more regular rhythmical offices. Thomas of Capua (ca. 1230) defined rhymed prose as "ordinary prose, whose members or cola, as delimited by pauses in delivery, are rhymed at the ends of the colon." Rhymed prose also sometimes consists of well-balanced, strongly cadenced rhythms, which dignify speech. In Arabic literature, *saj'* is an artificial, rhythmical form of rhymed prose, a powerful stylistic tool used both in sacred literature, such as the Koran, and in secular literature, such as the *One Thousand and One Nights*. *Maqāma* is an elaborate form of picaresque stories in rhymed prose. In Chinese poetry, *fu* (rhyme-prose) is a hybrid genre that combines narrative passages with descriptions in verse. Rhymed prose was common in early nineteenth-century Urdu/Hindi literature, such as Lallu Lal's popular *Prem Sagar* (Ocean of Love, 1867).

SEE ALSO *cadence, free verse, fu, maqāma, meter, prose poetry, rhythm.*

rhyme royal, rime royal A seven-line stanza, usually written in iambic pentameter, rhyming *ababbcc*. The most regal of all seven-line stanzas, the rhyme royal was introduced into English poetry by Geoffrey Chaucer in his long poems "Parlement of Foules" (ca. 1381–1382) and *Troilus and Criseyde* (ca. 1380s), which is why it is sometimes also called the Troilus stanza:

> The double sorwe of Troilus to tellen,
> That was the kyng Priamus sone of Troye,
> In lovynge, how his aventures fellen
> Fro wo to wele, and after out of joie,
> My purpos is, ere that I parte fro ye.
> Thesiphone, thow help me for t'endite
> Thise woful vers, that wepen as I write.

Chaucer also used it for four of *The Canterbury Tales* (ca. 1387–1400) and for a number of short poems, including "Fortune," "Truth," "Complaint unto

Pity," "Complaint to His Purse," "Gentilesse," "Complaint to His Lady," "Lak of Steadfastness," and "Against Women Unconstant." It was thus sometimes referred to as the Chaucerian stanza. Chaucer's friend John Gower also used the stanza effectively in both French and English for occasional poetry (*In Praise of Peace*) as well as for philosophical love poetry (*Cinkantes balades, Traités pour essampler les amantz marietz,* Aman's "supplicacioun" from *Confessio Amantis*).

Chaucer probably borrowed this favored stanza from Guillaume de Machaut (ca. 1300–1377), who either invented it or developed it from earlier Provençal or French models. He may have adapted it from the French ballade stanza or the Italian ottava rima, omitting the fifth line. It is an ambidextrous stanza that can be balanced as a tercet and two couplets (*aba, bb, cc*) or as a quatrain and a tercet (*abab, bcc*). Some scholars think that the rhyme royal derives its name from the chant royal, while others believe that it comes from one of its disciples, James I of Scotland, who employed it in his fifteenth-century poem "The Kingis Quair." James himself refers to the stanza within the poem as "thir versis sevin." Georges Gascoigne justified the name "rithhme royall" because he found it "a royall kinde of verse" in his treatise, *Certayn Notes of Instruction concerning the Making of Verse or Rime in English* (1575).

Some key examples: Thomas Wyatt, "They Flee From Me" (1557); William Shakespeare, "The Rape of Lucrece" (1594); William Wordsworth, "Resolution and Independence" (1802); William Morris, *The Earthly Paradise* (1868); John Masefield, "The Widow in the Bye Street" (1912); and Theodore Roethke, "I Knew a Woman" (1958). W. H. Auden uses it with great panache in "Letter to Lord Byron" (1936).

SEE ALSO *ballade, chant royal, ottava rima, puy, septet.*

rhyme scheme A characteristic pattern of rhymes. As a shorthand for representing a rhyme scheme, each different rhyme is assigned a different letter. Thus a pair of couplets is designated *aabb,* a quatrain alternating rhymes is represented *abab* and called alternate rhyme. The French use the term *rimes croisées* (crossed rhyme) for an *abab* rhyme scheme that alternates masculine and feminine rhymes. A rhyme scheme with mirror symmetry, as *abba,* is called arch-rhyme.

The rhyme scheme, an abstraction blooded, is a way of advancing meaning in a poem. Think of the winding staircase of Dante's terza rima, which rhymes *aba, bcb, cdc,* etc. (you are always going forward while glancing backward), or the logical development of the Shakespearean sonnet, which rhymes *abab, cdcd, efef, gg,* and carries in its body the rhetorical argument of love. Some rhyme schemes repeat the same end words in complex arrangements, as in the sestina. The term *rhyme scheme* suggests that the rhyme is one way to organize the structure of a poem. It simultaneously opens up and concludes the sense. It is a binding together, a test of prowess. Robert Frost said that whenever he read a poem that rhymed, he scanned the right side of the page to decide who had won, the poet or the rhyme scheme.

SEE ALSO *couplet, quatrain, rhyme, sestina, sonnet, terza rima, villanelle.*

rhythm The word *rhythm* comes from the Greek word *rhythmos,* "measured motion," which in turn derives from a Greek verb meaning "to flow." Rhythm is sound in motion. It is related to the pulse, the heartbeat, the way we breathe. It rises and falls. It takes us into ourselves; it takes us out of ourselves. Rhythm is the combination in English of stressed and unstressed syllables that creates a feeling of fixity and flux, of surprise and inevitability. Rhythm creates a pattern of yearning and expectation, of recurrence and change. It is repetition with a difference. Renewal is "the pivot of lyricism," as Marina Tsvetaeva puts it, comparing the lyrical element to the waves of the sea: "The wave always returns, and always returns as a different wave," she writes in her essay "Poets with History and Poets without History" (1934):

> The same water — a different wave.
> What matters is that it is a *wave.*
> What matters is that the wave *will return.*
> What matters is that it will *always* return *different.*
> What matters most of all: however different the returning wave,
> it will always return as a wave of the *sea.*
> What is a wave? Composition and muscle. The same goes for lyric
> poetry.

I would say with Robert Graves that there is a rhythm of emotion in poetry that conditions the musical rhythm, the patterned energy, the mental bracing and relaxing that comes to us through our sensuous impressions. Rhythm is poetry's way of charging the depths, hitting the fathomless. It is oceanic.

Les Murray points out that "there is a trance-like pleasure bordering on epileptic seizure to be had from certain regular rhythms" ("Poems and the Mystery of Embodiment," 1988). So, too, "rhythm is not measure, or something that is outside us," Octavio Paz writes in *The Bow and the Lyre* (1956), "but we ourselves are the ones who flow in the rhythm and rush headlong toward 'something.' " That "something" is a place where we are always arriving, an immanent revelation. In "The Symbolism of Poetry" (1900), W. B. Yeats declares unequivocally that the "purpose of rhythm is to prolong the moment of contemplation, the moment when we are both asleep and awake, which is the one moment of creation."

SEE ALSO *meter.*

riddle "A mystifying, misleading, or puzzling question posed as a problem to be solved or guessed often as a game" (*Webster's Third New International Dictionary*). Though the dictionary definition focuses on the riddle as a question and describes it as a game, the riddle is more than a puzzle. It is both an interrogative and an expressive form, possibly the earliest form of oral literature — a formulation of thought, a mode of association, a metaphor.

The comparative work of folklorists suggests that riddle-making is virtually a universal activity, a lyric root, a contest of wit, a process of naming. The earliest riddles on record are preserved on a clay tablet from ancient Babylon. They are inscribed in Sumerian along with Assyrian translations. Here is one that Archer Taylor, the premier scholar of riddles, presents in *The Literary Riddle before 1600* (1948):

Who becomes pregnant without conceiving,
who becomes fat without eating?

The answer: *a raincloud.*

The riddle, a short form with a long history, uses the sentence as its frame. It is often employed for educational purposes, but there are cases — whole cultures — where the riddle is more than child's play. The oldest Sanskrit riddles (ca. 1000 B.C.E.) appear in the riddle hymn of Dirhatamas (Hymn 164) in book 1 of the *Rig-Veda* (1700–1100 B.C.E.). The Hebrew Bible refers to riddling and riddling contests. Thus the prophet Daniel was "known to have a notable spirit, with knowledge and understanding, and the gift of interpreting dreams, explaining riddles and unbinding spells" (Daniel 5:12). In the first book of Kings (1:10), Queen Sheba travels to the court of King Solomon to test his prodigious wisdom with "hard questions" or riddles. The judge Samson is known for the riddle he proposes to the Philistines at his wedding reception (Judges 14:14):

> Out of the eater came something to eat,
> Out of the strong came something sweet?

In the desert, Samson had chanced upon a lion's carcass in which bees had made a hive. With the help of his bride who tells the riddle to her countrymen, the Philistines answer the riddle with another riddle: "What is sweeter than honey? What is stronger than a lion?" Samson replies to them with a startling metaphor: "If you had not ploughed my heifer, / you would not have solved my riddle."

The Greeks were great riddlers. Pindar (ca. 522–443 B.C.E.) was first to use the term *riddle* in a way that we still recognize. Everyone remembers the riddle at the heart of the narrative in Sophocles's *Oedipus Tyrannus* (ca. 430 B.C.E.), which has also been found in various parts of the world: "What has four legs in the morning, two legs in the afternoon, and three legs in the evening?" This is the riddle of the Sphinx, a monster with the head of a woman and the winged body of a lion, who threatened anyone who wanted to enter Thebes. Oedipus solved the riddle with the word "man" and thus proved his cleverness, a quality that would lead to his destruction. Plato refers to riddling in *The Republic* (ca. 380 B.C.E.) and quotes a variant of Panarces's riddle: a man who is not a man [a eunuch] threw a stone that was not a stone [a pumice stone] at a bird that was not a bird [a bat] sitting on a twig that was not a twig [a reed]. Heraclitus's remarks about the universe were so cryptic that Cicero and Diogenes Laertius referred to him as "the Riddler" and "the Obscure." It was Heraclitus who reported:

> All men are deceived by the appearances of things, even Homer himself, who was the wisest man in Greece; for he was deceived by boys catching lice; they said to him, "What we have caught and what we have killed we have left behind, but what has escaped us we bring with us."

A riddle is first of all a way of describing one thing in terms of another, as in "Humpty Dumpty," which describes an egg in terms of a man. In *English Riddles from Oral Tradition* (1951), Archer Taylor classifies descriptive riddles according to whether the object — "the answer" — is compared to a person, to several persons, to animals, to several animals, to plants, to things, or to a generalized living creature. Aristotle first pointed out in the *Rhetoric* (335–330 B.C.E.), "Good riddles do, in general, provide us with satisfactory metaphors: for metaphors imply riddles, and therefore a good riddle can furnish a good metaphor." He also stated in the *Poetics* (350 B.C.E.) that "the essence of a riddle is to express true facts under impossible combinations."

True riddles, as they are sometimes called, are enigmatic questions in descriptive form. They are meant to confuse or test the wits of those who don't know the answer. The riddle arrests our attention by establishing some paradox or internal contradiction, an opposition or blocking element, which makes it hard to solve. The folk riddle is staged, fundamentally aggressive, antisocial. It is vexing and socially disruptive unlike, say, the proverb, which is reassuring and meant to reinforce social wisdom.

The folklorist Roger Abrahams demonstrates that opposition is the most salient of four techniques by which the image (or *Gestalt*) of the riddle-question is impaired, making it indecipherable. These techniques consist of:

1. opposition — *Gestalt* is impaired because the opponent parts of the presented image do not harmonize.
2. incomplete detail — not enough information is given for proper *Gestalt* to be made (i.e., for the parts to fit together).
3. too much detail — the important traits are buried in the midst of inconsequential detail, thus "scrambling" *Gestalt.*
4. false *Gestalt* — details are provided that lead to an ability to discern a referent, and thus call for an answer, but the answer is wrong. The answer is often an embarrassing, obscene reference. This technique is most common in catch riddles.

The techniques of impairment establish the conventions by which riddles are recognized and remembered. Modes of impairment also provide literary strategies. The medieval Hebrew and Arabic poets of Spain, for example, wrote deliberately misleading riddles in verse. There are forty-nine such riddles in the work of the master of Hebrew poetry, Yehuda Halevi (ca.

1075–1141). So, too, the Arabic poet Al-Harari (1054–1122) filled his masterpiece known as the *Maqamat* ("Assemblies") with a wealth of classical lore, including riddles. In Western Europe, the literary riddle begins with the 100 Latin riddles of Symposius (fifth century). The oldest European vernacular riddles are the poetic riddles of the Old English *Exeter Book* (eighth century). In *Enigmas and Riddles in Literature* (2006), Eleanor Cook suggests that "riddling illuminates the greatest mysteries through the smallest things."

Here is a Persian riddle that gives a feeling of sudden liberation, like a Japanese haiku:

> A blue napkin full of pears —
>
> Sky

SEE ALSO *metaphor, oral poetry, proverb.*

riding rhyme, see *couplet.*

ríma, rímur (pl) These versified sagas (narrative poems of any length in rhyming verse) were the most popular form of Icelandic poetry from the fourteenth to the nineteenth century. The *rímur* were adapted into Icelandic poetry under French influences (*ríma* is cognate with the French word *rime*). There are more than one thousand extant narratives, most of which are based on heroic tales and chivalric romances. There was a special way of chanting or intoning *rímur* to tunes called *stemmur.* The fundamental form was the alliterative four-line stanza, but there have been a dizzying number of intricate metrical and stanzaic forms. The Icelandic novelist Halldór Laxness's epic novel *Independent People* (1934, 1935) recounts the story of a doomed farmer, Bjatur of Summerhouses, who has a taste for composing *rímur,* a form "technically so complex that it could never attain any noteworthy content."

SEE ALSO *ballad, kenning, narrative poetry, saga, skald.*

rimas dissolutas A Provençal syllabic form. Each line in an unrhymed stanza rhymes with its corresponding line in a subsequent stanza. For example, James Merrill's two-stanza poem "A Renewal" (1959) rhymes *abcd abcd.* The *rimas dissolutas* is a way of isolating rhyme and welding stanzas together.

The form was wonderfully employed by Provençal poets, such as Arnaut Daniel (ca. 1150–ca. 1200), who treated it as kin to the canzone and the sestina. Ezra Pound demonstrates the pattern in his adaptation of Daniel's "Canzon: Of the Trades and Love," which begins:

> Though this measure quaint confine me,
> And I chip out words and plane them,
>   They shall yet be true and clear
> When I finally have filed them.
> Love glosses and gilds them knowing
>   That my song has for its start
> One who is worth's hold and warrant.
>
>   Each day finer I refine me
>   And my cult and service strain them
>   Toward the world's best, as ye hear,
>   "Hers" my root and tip have styled them.
> And though bitter winds come blowing,
>   The love that rains down in my heart
> Warmeth me when frost's abhorrent.

My shortlist of American poems that use *rimas dissolutas* would include Frank O'Hara's "To the Poem" (ca. 1952), Sylvia Plath's "Black Rook in Rainy Weather" (1956), Mona Van Duyn's "Causes" (1970), David Wagoner's "Staying Alive" (1966), and Jon Anderson's "The Blue Animals" (1968).

SEE ALSO *canzone, sestina.*

rising rhythm, ascending rhythm Rhythm that moves from an unstressed syllable to a stressed syllable. Iambic and anapestic meters, which constitute most meters in English, are rising rhythms, though the technical term can be misleading because it doesn't imply anything about the emotional movement or impact of the verse.

SEE ALSO *anapest, iamb, rocking feet and rhythms.*

rispetto This Italian form is generally an amorous poem, hence the name *respect.* It respects the beloved with a six- or (more commonly) eight-line stanza (octave), written in eleven-syllable lines (hendecasyllabics). It consists of two quatrains, usually rhyming *abababcc.* It may have originated as a form of Tuscan folk poetry. The *rispetto* is special kin to the Sicilian *strambotto.* There is a telling moment in Roberto Bolaño's novel *The Savage Detectives* (2007) when the young Argentine poet accuses his poetry workshop teacher in Mexico City of not knowing the meaning of a *rispetto.* The young poet explains:

> A rispetto, professor, is a kind of lyrical verse, romantic to be precise, similar to the strambotto, with six or eight hendecasyllabic lines, the first four in the form of a serventesio and the following composed in rhyming couplets . . .

SEE ALSO *hendecasyllabics, octave, strambotto.*

ritornello "Little return." The ritornello, which is also called *stornello, fiore,* or *motteto,* consists of a group of two lines repeated at the end, sometimes at the beginning, of each stanza of a poem. It sometimes consists of three lines. The last two lines of the ritornello form a couplet. The first line either combines with them to combine a three-line stanza or rhymes with a line from the preceding stanza. *The Harvard Dictionary of Music* (4th ed., 2003) notes that the ritornello is not a refrain: "The name ('little return') may indicate that the ritornello restates the content of the main stanza in modified form." The fourteenth-century Italian verse forms of the *caccia* and the madrigal concluded with a ritornello, a summary rhyming couplet, which is stated only once. "Where did the words arise?" Charles Tomlinson asks in his poem "Ritornello" (1981): "Human they sublimed out of the humus."

SEE ALSO *caccia, madrigal.*

rocking feet and rhythms Gerard Manley Hopkins coined this term for a trisyllabic meter in which two unstressed syllables surround a stressed one. He explained in his "Author's Preface" (1883):

> Every foot has one principal stress or accent, and this or the syllable it falls on may be called the Stress of the foot and the other part, the one or two unaccented syllables, the Slack. Feet (and the rhythms made

> out of them) in which the Stress comes first are called Falling Feet and Falling Rhythms, feet and rhythm in which the Slack comes first are called Rising Feet and Rhythms, and if the Stress is between two Slacks there will be Rocking Feet and Rhythms.

SEE ALSO *falling rhythm.*

romance The word *romance* originated in the Old French word *romanz,* meaning simply literature written in the vernacular, the Romance language of French. In Old French, the *roman* or *romant* was a "courtly romance in verse," a "popular book." The chivalric romance developed as a literary genre in the twelfth century. The stories of legendary knights celebrating an ideal code of behavior established the romance as an adventure story, a sequential form, which is why it has historically been so well-suited to long verse narratives and prose fictions. The pursuit of love was one of the specialties of the early romances, though the genre was so diverse in the Middle Ages that it is nearly impossible to define. Certain recurrent motifs characterize what Corinne Saunders identifies as the backbone of romance: "exile and return, love, quest and adventure, family, name and identity, the opposition between pagan and Christian." Romances require handsome heroes and beautiful heroines, such as Tristan and Isolde, who stand above the ordinary, though they are human and not divine, as in mythological stories. In *Memesis* (1946), Erich Auerbach identified the archetypal pattern of medieval romance as the movement from court to forest, "setting forth" in search of adventure. The quest romance, the story of a hero's progressive journey — his tests, his struggle to the death with a supernatural enemy, his ultimate triumph — is the most complete and thus satisfactory form of literary romance.

Romance literature was originally written in Old French, Anglo-Norman, and Occitan, the language of the troubadours, and later in English and German. Northrop Frye argues in *The Anatomy of Criticism* (1957) that romance is both a historical mode and a mythos, or generic narrative form, which reflects a "tendency . . . to displace myth in a human direction and yet, in contrast to 'realism,' to conventionalize content in an ideal direction." The literature that stems from this romance impulse suggests "implicit mythical patterns in a world more closely associated with human experience." Romance, then, is not a genre but a generic plot, a dramatic structure found in poetry, drama, and fiction. As a mythos of summer, romance leads from a state of order through winter, darkness, and death, to rebirth, a fresh order, full maturity. Romance literature has many forerunners in biblical narratives, such as the story of Joseph in Genesis, and in classical Greek epics, such as Homer's *Odyssey* (ca. eighth century B.C.E.). It develops into a wide variety of genres with different formats and functions, such as Shakespeare's plays, pastoral romances, Gothic novels, romantic poetry, modern fantasies, and science fiction movies.

SEE ALSO *archetype, chivalric romance, courtly love, pastoral, quest-romance, romanticism, troubadour, trouvère, universality.*

romances The *romances,* or Spanish ballads, are an essential part of Hispanic culture and heritage. These short episodic poems are concise and dramatic. Many of the early medieval *romances* adapted episodes and lines from the *cantares de gesta* (heroic epic poems) or epic cycles, and sound like fragments of lost epics. The *romances* were shaped by hundreds and even thousands of different voices and imaginations, and have had an incalculable influence on Spanish poets and prose writers. The poets of the Spanish golden age knew and loved the *romances,* as did the author of *Don Quixote* (1605, 1615).

The epic poems were sung at court, but the *romances* were ideal for the *juglares,* the popular entertainers who performed in marketplaces. The early *romances* consist of long sixteen-syllable lines (written down, the verses are divided into two eight-syllable lines). The even-numbered lines rhyme. The heavy caesura or pause in the middle of the sixteen-syllable line grew fainter as the *romances* moved further and further from their epic origins, but it has never been entirely lost. It is still there in the *romances* collected in Spain and South America in the twentieth century. As W. S. Merwin puts it in his translation *Spanish Ballads* (1961), "this unbroken connection with the indigenous popular epics of the Middle Ages is one thing which makes the Spanish *romances* unique among the ballad literatures of the rest of Europe."

The *romances* especially influenced modernist poets, who wanted to bring traditional folkloric elements into their written work. Federico García Lorca created a stylized version of the *romances* in his immensely popular *Primer Romancero Gitano,* or *The Gypsy Ballads* (1928), the supreme achievement of his early style.

SEE ALSO *ballad, cantar de gesta, epic, the golden age, juglar, octosyllabic verse.*

romancillo, see *endecha.*

romanticism *Romanticism* describes both an ongoing sensibility and a particular historical period, the age of wonder, which spanned the sixty-year period between 1770 and 1830. A widespread cultural movement, romanticism was characterized by new modes of thinking and feeling. The term *romantic* originally referred to the characteristics of the romances of the Middle Ages, i.e., something "that could happen in a romance," and suggested, somewhat pejoratively, something fanciful, an extravagant idealization of reality. In the early nineteenth century, the German critic Karl Wilhelm Friedrich von Schlegel used romantic literature to designate a new school opposed to classic literature. In 1798, he defined romantic poetry in a fragment as "a progressive universal poetry." The idea spread to France and England, as did the polar opposition. The controversy over romanticism and classicism is essentially a continuation of the battle between the moderns and the ancients.

Romanticism is a retrospective label for a diverse group of poets. David Perkins identifies Hippolyte Taine in 1863 as the first critic to describe the early nineteenth-century English poets, especially the Lake poets, as a "romantic school." We now recognize three major English poets at the start of the era — William Blake, William Wordsworth, and Samuel Taylor Coleridge — and three others at the end of it — Percy Bysshe Shelley, George Gordon, Lord Byron, and John Keats. The first generation outlived the second one. The romantic poets are darker and wilder than the classical poets of the Augustan Age who preceded them (John Dryden, Alexander Pope) and the Victorian poets who followed (Alfred, Lord Tennyson, Robert Browning). The period was a counter-Enlightenment shaped by the historical experience of the French Revolution, which opened new doorways, endless possibilities. "Old things seemed passing away, and nothing was dreamt of but the regeneration of the human race," Robert Southey said. Socially, as Jacques Barzun puts it, "romanticism has to do with creating a new society different from its immediate predecessor."

One of the fundamentals of the romantic era is faith in the natural goodness of man. Human beings are naturally pure but hindered by urban life, civilization itself. "Man is born free and everywhere he is in chains," Jean Jacques Rousseau claimed in *The Social Contract* (1762). A constellation of ideas came together around the greatness of the "Noble Savage," the sacred innocence of childhood, and the sublimity of the natural world. Nature was for romantic thinkers not just a place of inviolable physical beauty, local and concrete, but also the manifestation of a spiritual force that operated in, to use Wordsworth's phrase, "the Mind of Man" ("The Recluse," 1800). The passion for nature and "natural man" was accompanied by a vogue for "primitive" poetry, hence the popularity of Thomas Percy's *Reliques of Ancient English Poetry* (1765) and Charlotte Brooke's *Reliques of Irish Poetry* (1789). In general, the romantic poets emphasized the primacy of feeling over reason and sought new means of artistic expression. They had an unhampered faith in the imagination. "I am certain of nothing but of the holiness of the Heart's affections, and the truth of Imagination," Keats wrote in 1817. "What the imagination seizes as Beauty must be truth."

The romantic poets demonstrated a commitment to locale, a poetics of process, and skepticism toward closure, wholeness, and totalizing forms, which is why the greater romantic lyric, a descriptive-meditative poem, and the romantic fragment are two of the prototypes of romantic poetry. They opposed imaginative inhibitions of all kinds. They were subjective idealists with what Lascelle Abercombrie called "*a tendency away from actuality*," and yet their belief in freedom extended to politics, and they demonstrated a strong commitment to political liberty. Romanticism continues to refer to a time-bound era, a particular achievement, and to a permanent human impulse toward the limitless or infinite. "When I say I'm a romantic poet," Philip Levine once said, "it seems to me that I feel the human is boundless, and that seems to me the essential fact of Romanticism."

SEE ALSO *Augustan Age, the Battle of the Books, chivalric romance, classic, conversation poems, Enlightenment, fragment, greater romantic lyric, imagination, Lake poets, nature poetry, picturesque, primitivism, romance, romances, the sublime.*

rondeau The word *rondeau* derives from the French *rond,* meaning "round," and, indeed, it is a form that turns round and round. The rondeau originated in Provençal poetry in the thirteenth and fourteenth centuries. The term originally included various short poetic forms. The current form was fixed toward the end of the fifteenth century and became especially popular in French poetry. Théodore de Banville codified it in *Petit traité de poesie française* (1872). The whole poem consists of fifteen lines, which divide into three groups: 1) lines 1–5; 2) lines 6–9; 3) lines 10–15. It is common but not necessary to have a stanza break after the first five lines. The refrain, which is the first half of the opening line, repeats at the ends of the second and third groups. It is a half-line, a tail. The whole poem turns on two rhymes. The meter of the thirteen longer lines usually consists of four or five iambic feet.

Thomas Wyatt introduced the rondeau into English poetry in the first half of the sixteenth century. Here is his illustrative use of the form:

Helpe me to seke for I lost it there,	R (refrain) A
And if that ye have founde it ye that be here,	A
And seke to convaye it secretely,	B
Handell it soft and trete it tenderly,	B
Or els it will plain and then appere.	A
But rather restore it mannerly,	B
Syns that I do aske it thus honestly;	B
For to lese it, it sitteth me to nere	A
Helpe me to seek.	R
Alas, and is there no remedy,	B
But have I thus lost it wilfully?	B
I wis it was a thing all to dere	A
To be bestowed and wist not where.	A
It was myn hert: I pray you hertely	B
Helpe me to seke.	R

The most iconic twentieth-century rondeau is the Canadian John McCrae's war poem "In Flanders Field" (1915). The most well-known American rondeau is Paul Laurence Dunbar's "We Wear the Mask" (1896). W. H. Auden's "The Hidden Law" (1940) may be the high point of the form in English.

SEE ALSO *rondellus.*

rondeau redoublé This rare and twisted poetic form consists of twenty-four lines plus a coda line, a refrain comprised of the first half of the first line. It has five quatrains and one quintet. The whole poem turns on two rhymes, as the rondeau and the rondel, and has five refrains modeled on the lines of the first stanza. The entire first line reappears as line eight in the second stanza, the third line as line sixteen in the fourth stanza, and the fourth line as line twenty in the fifth stanza. Jean de la Fontaine (1621–1695), who may have devised it, and Théodore Banville (1823–1891) both experimented with this complex form. It has been used for light verse by such poets as Dorothy Parker (1893–1967) and Louis Untermeyer (1885–1977). Wendy Cope provides a witty contemporary example, "Rondeau Redoublé," in *Making Cocoa for Kingsley Amis* (1986):

There are so many kinds of awful men —	A
One can't avoid them all. She often said	B
She'd never make the same mistake again:	A
She always made a new mistake instead.	B
The chinless type who made her feel ill-bred;	B
The practiced charmer, less than charming when	A
He talked about the wife and kids and fled —	B
There are so many kinds of awful men.	A (refrain entire first line)
The half-crazed hippy, deeply into Zen,	A
Whose cryptic homilies she came to dread;	B
The fervent youth who worshipped Tony Benn —	A
'One can't avoid them all,' she often said.	B
The ageing banker, rich and overfed,	B
Who held forth on the dollar and the yen —	A
Though there were many more mistakes ahead,	B
She'd never make the same mistake again.	A (refrain entire third line)
The budding poet, scribbling in his den	A
Odes not to her but to his pussy, Fred;	B
The drunk who fell asleep at nine or ten —	A
She always made a new mistake instead.	B (refrain entire fourth line)
And so the gambler was at least unwed	B
And didn't preach or sneer or wield a pen	A

Or hoard his wealth or take the Scotch to bed.	B
She'd lived and learned and lived and learned but then	A
There are so many kinds.	R (refrain of first half-line)

SEE ALSO *rondeau, rondel.*

rondel This French form consists of thirteen lines turning on two rhymes. It has three stanzas of four, four, and five lines that rhyme *abba, abab, abbaa.* Lines seven and thirteen repeat the first line. Line eight repeats line two. It is often confused with the rondeau. For example, Charles d'Orleans entitled his fifteenth-century rondel a "Rondeau" ("Le temps a laissé son manteau"), which has been beautifully translated by Richard Wilbur:

The year has cast its cloak away	A (refrain)
That was of driving rains and snows,	B (refrain 2)
And now in flowered arras goes,	B
And wears the clear sun's glossy ray.	A
No bird or beast but seems to say	A
In cries or chipper tremolos:	B
The year has cast its cloak away	A (refrain, first line)
That was of driving rains and snows.	B (refrain, second line)
Stream, brook and silver fountain play,	A
And each upon itself bestows	B
A spangled livery as it flows.	B
All creatures are in fresh array.	A
The year has cast its cloak away.	A (refrain, first line)

The Italian poet Eugenio Montale used the term *rondel* to refer to a series of short songlike lyrics and called the title section of his first book *Cuttlefish Bones* (1925) "my rondels."

SEE ALSO *rondeau.*

rondelet A shorter form of the rondeau, the rondelet consists of one seven-line stanza. The first line is a refrain that reappears as lines three and seven.

The refrain is four syllables long. The rest of the lines have eight syllables each. The poem turns on two rhymes: *abaabba.* Here is a rondelet that the English Victorian poet May Probyn published in 1883:

> Say what you please,
> But know, I shall not change my mind!
> Say what you please,
> Even, if you wish it, on your knees—
> And, when you hear me next defined
> As something lighter than the wind,
> Say what you please!

SEE ALSO *rondeau, septet.*

rondellus A late Latin variant of the French rondeau. It is a poetic form that includes an initial and/or end refrain with a corresponding musical form. It may have been an ecclesiastical ring-dance within the Christian Church. The singers and dancers used refrains to conclude their psalms. It was not a fixed but a flexible form. The anonymous early English lyric of the moor-maiden, "Maiden in the mor lay," was probably a Latin dance song. John Stevens calls it " 'refrain-*like*' because, surprisingly, no material is repeated from one stanza to the next, though the incantatory pattern of apparently incomplete lines continues and is intensified." It seems to be a song for several dancers, several voices, and almost sings itself. It has the quality of a trance.

> Maiden in the mor lay—
> in the mor lay—
> sevenyst fulle, sevenist fulle.
> Maiden in the mor lay—
> in the mor lay—
> sevenistes fulle ant a day.
>
> Welle was hire mete—
> wat was hire mete?
> the primerole ant the—the primerole ant the—
> Welle was hire mete.—
> wat was hire mete?
> the primerole ant the violet.

Welle was hire drying —
wat was hire drying?
The chelde water of the, the chelde water of the —
Welle was hire drying —
wat was hire drying?
The chelde water of the welle-spring.

Welle was hire bour —
wat was hire bour?
The rede rose an te, the rede rose an te —
Welle was hire bour —
wat was hire bour?
The rede rose an te lilie flour.

SEE ALSO *rondeau.*

roundel Algernon Charles Swinburne (1837–1909) invented this song-like variation of the French rondeau form. Chaucer used the term *roundel* interchangeably with *rondel,* as in his poem "Merciles Beaute: A Triple Roundel" (late fourteenth century). Swinburne's refashioned roundel consists of eleven lines that employ two rhymes in three stanzas (4, 3, 4). There is an identical refrain after the third and tenth lines. The refrain, which can be a half-line, rhymes with the second line. The short refrain has only one or two stresses. The longer lines contain four or five stresses. Here is Swinburne's self-describing roundel from his collection *A Century of Roundels* (1883):

The Roundel

A roundel is wrought as a ring or a starbright sphere, A
(refrain, first phrase)
With craft of delight and with cunning of sound unsought, B
That the heart of the hearer may smile if to pleasure his ear A
A roundel is wrought. B
(refrain)

Its jewel of music is carven of all or of aught — B
Love, laughter or mourning — remembrance of rapture or fear — A
That fancy may fashion to hang in the ear of thought. B

As a bird's quick song runs round, and the hearts in us hear A
Pause answer to pause, and again the same strain caught, B
So moves the device whence, round as a pearl or tear, A
A roundel is wrought. B
(refrain)

SEE ALSO *rondeau, rondel.*

roundelay A simple song with a refrain. The term can also be used to cover the other highly repetitive fixed forms with refrains, such as the rondeau, the rondel, and the villanelle. In England, the Elizabethan poets used it for a wide range of songs without any fixed form. Thomas Chatterton's "Minstrel's Roundelay" (1770) begins:

O sing unto my roundelay,
O drop the briny tear with me,
Dance no more at holy-day,
Like a running river be.
My love is dead,
Gone to his death-bed,
All under the willow-tree.

Samuel Beckett's thirteen-line "Roundelay" (1976) obsessively turns on the words *sound* and *strand.*

SEE ALSO *rondeau, rondel, villanelle.*

rubái, see *rubaiyat stanza.*

rubaiyat stanza, Omar Khyyám Quatrain The rubaiyat stanza (*rubái* is the Persian word for "quatrain") consists of four ten-syllable lines that rhyme *aaba.* It occasionally rhymes *aaaa.* The rubaiyat stanza is also called the Omar Stanza or Omar Khyyám Quatrain. The rubaiyat, a collection of quatrains, was a particular strength of medieval Persian verse. The form was popularized in the English-speaking world by Edward Fitzgerald's 1859 translation, a loose adaptation, of *The Rubáiyát* by the Persian astronomer-poet Omar Khayyám (1048–1131). Fitzgerald arranged the iambic pentameter stanzas in a cohesive order, but each quatrain in a

Persian rubaiyat is a distinct unit independent of its neighbors. Here is Fitzgerald's beloved opening:

A book of Verses underneath the Bough,
A Jug of Wine, a Loaf of Bread — and Thou
  Beside me singing in the Wilderness —
O, Wilderness were Paradise enow!

It is called an interlocking rubaiyat when the unrhymed line of a stanza becomes the rhyme for the following stanza, as in Robert Frost's "Stopping by Woods on a Snowy Evening" (1923). Some excellent examples of the rubáiyat stanza in twentieth-century American poetry: Robert Frost's "Desert Places" (1936), Ezra Pound's "Canto LXXX" (1946), a section of James Merrill's "Lost in Translation" (1976), Brad Leithauser's "Law Clerk, 1979" (1982), and Dick Davis's "A Letter to Omar" (1989). The Turkish poet Nazim Hikmet wrote a series of quatrains in 1945 and 1946 that "put dialectical materialism into the rubaiyat form."

SEE ALSO *chain rhyme, quatrain.*

rune A letter or character of the Old Germanic alphabet. The word *rune* meant "whisper, mystery, secret counsel," and from the earliest times runes were associated with magical incantations and practices. The Runic alphabet was eclipsed by the Latin alphabet during the spread of Christianity in the fourteenth century, but runes survived, often carved on coins, weapons, amulets, and memorial stones. The three extant "Rune Poems" (the "Anglo-Saxon Rune Poem," the "Norwegian Rune Poem," and the "Icelandic Rune Poem") list the letters of the Runic alphabets while presenting an explanatory stanza for each letter. Runes may have served as mnemonic devices that enabled speakers to remember and recite the order and names of each letter of the alphabet. They may also have been a way of transmitting secret or mystical knowledge. The Anglo-Saxon poet Cynewulf (ca. ninth century) signed his poems by weaving the runes for his name into his verses "to seek the prayers of others for the safety of his soul."

A rune now suggests a magical formula, incantation, or poem. Thus, Edgar Allan Poe hears the bells keeping "in a sort of Runic rhyme" ("The Bells," 1849). And Robert Graves portrays an anonymous early Finnish poet hurling his "rough rune / at the wintry moon" and stamping "to mark the tune" ("Finland," 1918).

SEE ALSO *incantation, spell.*

running rhythm Also called common rhythm and standard rhythm. Gerard Manley Hopkins (1844–1889) coined this term for the standard rhythm of English verse "measured by feet of two or three syllables." The rhythm is said to be falling if the stress occurs at the beginning of the foot, rising if the stress occurs at its end. He opposed running rhythm to sprung rhythm.

SEE ALSO *sprung rhythm.*

Russian formalism Russian formalism was born out of the heady mix of modern linguistics, investigative poetics, and futurist poetry. The Society for the Study of Poetic Language (OPOIAZ), which was founded in Petrogad in 1916 and led by the literary scholars Viktor Shklovsky (generally considered its first president), Boris Eikhenbaum, Osip Brik, Boris V. Tomasevskij, and others, joined forces with the Moscow Linguistic Circle (MLK), which was formed in Moscow in 1915 by the linguists Roman Jakobson (its first president), Petr Bogotyrev, and Grigorii O. Vinokur. The society was linked, too, with the futurist poets Velimir Khlebnikov, Aleksei Kruchenykh, and Vladimir Mayakovsky. *Formalism* was at first a derogatory term for a method that refused to consider literature as a reflection of social reality or to study it in conjunction with biography, sociology, or psychoanalysis. Rather, the formalists were intent on placing the study of literature on scientific grounds by defining its object and establishing its methods and procedures. They sought to distinguish the features of a specialized mode of discourse governed by its own internal laws. The formalist doctrine was defined in three early collections of articles, *Studies in the Theory of Poetic Language* (1916 and 1917) and *Poetics: Studies in the Theory of Poetic Language* (1919).

The formalists initially focused their attention on poetry, especially the use of sounds and words, structure and style, and they proposed a simple, categorical opposition between poetic language, which they considered self-focused and self-sufficient, and practical or ordinary language, which they considered instrumental. "Poetry is language in its aesthetic function," Jakobson claimed in "The Newest Russian Poetry" (1921). "Thus the subject of literary scholarship is not literature but literariness (*literaturnost*), that is, that which makes a given work a work of literature."

> Poetry is *an utterance with a set toward expression.* . . . If the plastic arts involve the shaping of the autonomous material of visual representations, music the shaping of autonomous sound material, choreography of the material of autonomous gesture, then poetry is the shaping of the autonomous word, of what Khlebnikov calls the "selfsome word." . . . This set toward expression, toward the verbal mass, which I qualify as the sole essential feature of poetry.

The most extreme example of autonomous or autotelic language, the word itself, was the sound poetry the Russian futurists called *zaum* — "transrational" or "supraconsious language." "The Futurists' trend toward a 'transrational language' (*zaumnyi jazyk*) [is] the utmost baring of autonomous value," Eikhenbaum states ("The Theory of the 'Formal Method,' " 1926). Shklovsky considered poetry "a difficult, roughed, impeded language"; he defined it as "*attenuated, tortured* speech" ("Art as Technique," 1917). It was in considering prose, however, that he came up with his most influential concept, the idea of defamiliarization, the estrangement of reality:

> Art exists that one may recover the sensation of life; it exists to make one feel things, to make the stone *stony*. The purpose of art is to impart the sensation of things as they are perceived and not as they are known. The technique of art is to make objects "unfamiliar," to make forms difficult, to increase the difficulty of and length of perception because the process of perception is an aesthetic end in itself and must be prolonged. *Art is a way of experiencing the artfulness of an object; the object is not important.*

The formalists, who elevated the study of poetic language or poeticity, were brutally silenced by the Soviets toward the end of the 1920s.

SEE ALSO *deconstruction, futurism, New Criticism, structuralism, zaum.*

saga Old Norse and Icelandic for "narrative," "story," "history." The noun *saga* derives from the verb *sagja* ("to say") and means a tale or report. Saga was the goddess of poetry in Old Norse mythology, but the medieval sagas are tales in prose. They were written down between the twelfth and fourteenth centuries, but are based on older oral traditions. They tell stories, often legendary, about heroes and historical events. The Icelandic sagas and the early Irish sagas are the pinnacles of this narrative oral literature. Sometimes embedded with alliterative verses, the sagas prefigure the historical novel.

SEE ALSO *epic, narrative poetry.*

San Francisco renaissance A group of writers and artists emerged in the Bay Area after World War II, including the poets Kenneth Rexroth, William Everson (later Brother Antoninus), Jack Spicer, Robin Blaser, and Michael McClure. Robert Duncan, who was closely associated with the Black Mountain movement, was a key figure, as was Gary Snyder. In 1957, Rexroth summarized what he felt they were up against: "This is the world in which over every door is written the slogan: 'The generation of experiment and revolt is over. Bohemia died in the Twenties. There are no more little magazines.' "

The San Francisco poets believed that American poetry had turned its back on the breakthroughs of modern poetry and art. The poets constituted overlapping bohemian circles and were often aesthetically and politically at odds with each other. They shared a commitment to the Pacific Coast and a determination to carry on the innovative traditions of modernism. Their work was bracketed by the human devastations of World War II on one side and the debacle of Vietnam on the other. Duncan believed the elegiac mode was the single unifying principle of the local poets. They sought to replace a lost world by turning to sacramental nature (Everson) or to Eastern cultures and religion (Snyder).

Two formal poets working inside the academy in the San Francisco area were Yvor Winters (Stanford), who developed his own school of plain-style poetry, and Josephine Miles (University of California–Berkeley), who had a strong relationship with the poets of the so-called "Berkeley renaissance," a Robert Duncan–Jack Spicer–Robin Blaser axis that also included Landis Everson. "What have I lost?" Spicer asked in "A Postscript to the Berkeley Renaissance" (1974): "I sing a newer song no ghost-bird sings."

The Beat movement grew out of the San Francisco renaissance. On October 13, 1955, Kenneth Rexroth, the reluctant godfather of the movement, curated a reading that featured Michael McClure, Gary Snyder, Philip Whalen, Philip Lamantia, and Allen Ginsberg, who captivated the crowd with his reading of "Howl." Jack Kerouac was in the audience and later described the scene in *The Dharma Bums* (1958):

> I followed the whole gang of howling poets to the reading at Gallery Six that night, which was, among other important things, the night of the birth of the San Francisco Poetry Renaissance. Everyone was there. It was a mad night. And I was the one who got things jumping by going around collecting dimes and quarters from the rather stiff audience standing around in the gallery and coming back with three huge gallon jugs of California Burgundy and getting them all piffed so that by eleven o'clock when Alvah Goldbook [Ginsberg] was reading his, wailing his poem "Wail" drunk with arms outspread everyone was yelling "Go! Go! Go!" (like a jam session) and old Rheinhold Cacoethes [Rexroth] the father of the Frisco poetry scene was wiping his tears in gladness.

SEE ALSO *Beats, Black Mountain poets, jazz poetry.*

Sapphic stanza, Sapphics This stanza pattern is named after Sappho (late seventh century B.C.E.), the ancient Greek poet born on the isle of Lesbos, known in the Palatine Anthology (tenth century) as the Tenth Muse. The Sapphic stanza may have been invented by Sappho's contemporary, Alcaeus of Mytilene, but it was favored by Sappho, who used it for a significant portion of her work. The Sapphic stanza consists of four lines. It was written in quantitative meter and later adapted into qualitative meter or accentual syllabics. Each of the first three lines has eleven syllables (hendecasyllabics) and five verse feet (two trochees, a dactyl, two trochees). There are sometimes substitutions in the fourth and final syllables of each line. The final short line, which is called an adonic, has five syllables and two verse feet (a dactyl and a trochee):

/ u | / u | / u u | / u | / u
/ u | / u | / u u | / u | / u
/ u | / u | / u u | / u | / u
/ u u | / u

Six centuries later, Catullus adapted Sappho's haunting poem "Phanetai moi" into Latin in his poem #51 ("Ille mi par . . ."), which has been finely translated into English by both W. S. Merwin ("Like a god he seems to me") and Rosanna Warren ("He's like a god, that man"). Horace transformed the form in his *Odes* (23–13 B.C.E.) — it was one of his two favorite meters — and provided a model for future poets. For example, William Cowper follows the Horatian model in his desolate poem, "Lines Written During a Period of Insanity" (ca. 1774), which I have loved since I was a teenager.

Hatred and vengeance, my eternal portion,
Scarce can endure delay of execution,
Wait, with impatient readiness, to seize my
    Soul in a moment.

Dam'd below Judas: more adhorr'd than he was,
Who for a few pence sold his holy Master.
Twice betrayed Jesus me, the last delinquent,
    Deems the profanest.

Man disavows, and Deity disowns me:
Hell might afford my miseries a shelter;
Therefore hell keeps her ever-hungry mouths all
    Bolted against me.

Hard lot! encompass'd with a thousand dangers;
Weary, faint, trembling with a thousand terrors;
I'm call'd, if vanquish'd, to receive a sentence
    Worse than Abiram's.

Him the vindictive rod of angry justice
Sent quick and howling to the centre headlong;
I, fed with judgment, in a fleshly tomb, am
    Buried above ground.

The Sapphic pattern has its own history in English. There were attempts in the Renaissance to approximate syllable length as opposed to stress (Richard Stanyhurst, Mary Herbert, Countess of Pembroke), but most adapted the form to accentual-syllabics, which are native to English, such as Thomas Campion's "Rose-Cheeked Laura" (1602), which he "offered as an example of the English Sapphick." Swinburne uses the pattern to depict Sappho herself. The final stanza of his poem "Sapphics" (1866) envisions the ghosts of Sappho's followers:

Clothed about with flame and with tears, and singing
Songs that move the heart of the shaken heaven,
Songs that break the heart of the earth with pity,
    Hearing, to hear them.

In 1919, William Faulkner adapted and condensed Swinburne's twenty-stanza poem into six stanzas of his own devising, an imitation that he also called "Sapphics." My anthology of Sapphics in English would include: Isaac Watts, "The Day of Judgment" (1706); Fulke Greville, *Caelica* VI (ca. 1580); Thomas Hardy, "The Temporary the All" (1898); Louis MacNeice, "June Thunder" (1938); Louis Bogan, "Portrait" (1923); Hyam Plutzik, "I Am Disquieted When I See Many Hills" (1959); William Meredith, "Effort at Speech" (1970); James Merrill, "Farewell Performance," 1988 ("Art. It cures affliction"); James Wright, "Erinna to Sappho" (1957); John Hollander, "After an Old Text" (1978); Timothy Steele, "Sapphics Against Anger" (1986); Rachel Hadas, "Mars and Venus" (1995); Marilyn Hacker, "Cleis" (1991; named after Sappho's daughter); and Alfred Corn, "Sapphics at a Trot" (1997).

SEE ALSO *adonic, dactyl, foot, hendecasyllabics, quatrain, trochee.*

Satanic school In his preface to *The Vision of Judgment* (1821), an official tribute to the late King George III, Robert Southey attacked "the Satanic School," Byron and Shelley, for the immorality of their lives and work: "for though their productions breathe the spirit of Belial in their lascivious parts, and the spirit of Moloch in those loathsome images of atrocities and horrors which they delight to represent, they are more especially characterized by a satanic spirit of pride and audacious impiety, which still betrays the wretched feeling of hopelessness wherewith it is allied." Byron's satirical reply, his own *Vision of Judgment* (1822), devastated the reputation of the poet laureate, who is today best known for "The Story of the Three Bears" (1837).

SEE ALSO *the Cockney school of poetry, romanticism.*

satire A literary composition, either in poetry or prose, that scorns, derides, or ridicules human weakness, stupidity, or vice. Satire was the only literary form invented by the Roman poets — Quintilian boasted, "Satire is altogether ours" in the first century (*Institutio Oratoria*) — though it has antecedents in Athenian Old Comedy, represented by Aristophanes (ca. 450–ca. 388 B.C.E.). The word *satire* derives from the Latin *satura lanx,* meaning "medley, dish of colorful fruits." Rich and various, it consists of loosely related scenes that treat a wide range of issues. It is a sarcastic, sometimes scathing genre, not for the faint-hearted.

There were two main lines of Roman satire. The Syrian Cynic philosopher, Menippus of Gadara (fl. 290 B.C.E.), invented the Menippean satire, a parody form that blended prose with short verse interludes, which he used to skewer his philosophical opponents. His work is lost. The Menippean satire was brought into Latin by Varro (16–67 B.C.E.), whose work also did not survive. The only extant Menippean satire is *The Apocolocyntosis* (*Joke on the Death of Claudius* or *Pumpkinification of Claudius*), attributed to Seneca (ca. 4 B.C.E.–65 C.E.), which parodies the deification of the drooling emperor.

The verse satirists, who represent the second line of Roman satire, specialized in invective against identifiable, often thinly disguised personalities. Gaius Lucilius (ca. 160s–103 B.C.E.) was the earliest Roman satirist, though his thirty books of satires survive in only about eleven hundred unconnected lines. Horace wrote that Lucilius "first had the courage / to write this kind of poetry and remove the glossy skin / in which people were parading before the world and concealing / their ugliness" (*Satires,* 2.1). Lucilius and Horace called their satires *Sermones* ("conversations"). As a term, *satire* was only later applied to their works. Horace's two books of *Satires* are dedicated to his *pedestris* — a pedestrian muse, a muse who goes afoot, rather than one who looks down from afar. *Satires* 1, which consists of ten poems, was completed near 35 B.C.E.; *Satires* 2, which comprises eight poems, toward 30 B.C.E. The satires are conversational moral tales, preachy anecdotes written in prosy hexameters ("There are those who judge me too ferocious," Horace begins book 2, "one who goes beyond the limits conceded / to the genre"). Nonetheless, Horace's humor was playful and urbane. His nature was more to laugh than to lacerate. The bitterly eloquent Juvenal (ca. 55–130) wrote sixteen poems in five books of *Satires:* "It is hard not to write Satire. For who is so tolerant / of the monstrous city, so steeled, that he can restrain his wrath," he rhetorically asks in his so-called Programmatic Satire (*Satire* 1). He said, "Indignation will drive me to verse," and understood that the satirist is interested in "all human endeavors."

The Romans bequeathed satire to other literatures. A satiric comedy became a poem or play that uses humor as its primary means of attack. The medieval Arab poets developed a genre of satirical poetry called *hija.* The Scottish *flyting* is a form of satirical name-calling. The French verse satirist Mathurin Régnier (1573–1613) boasted that satire had felt the tread of many poets, but was unvisited by French rhymers: "I enter it, following Horace close behind, / to trace the various humours of mankind" (*Satire* 14). He was followed by the strongest of all French satirists, Nicolas Boileau, called Despréaux (1636–1711).

The great era of satire in English literature was the age roughly from 1660 to 1800. One thinks especially of John Dryden, who provided the finest English version of Juvenal (1693) and created the mock epics *Absalom and Architophel* (1681, 1682) and *Mac Flecknoe* (1682), as well as of Alexander Pope, who notoriously penned *The Rape of the Lock* (1712–1714) and *The Dunciad* (1728, 1729, 1743). Jonathan Swift's enraged indignation often acts as a kind of experimental laboratory — think of the weird, oppressive plausibility of his satirical essay "A Modest Proposal" (1729) and the shifting perspectives of his satirical novel *Gulliver's Travels* (1726, 1735) that, as Northrop Frye points out, "shows us man as a venomous rodent, man as a noisome and clumsy pachyderm, the mind of man as a bear-pit, and the body of man as a compound of filth and ferocity." Swift said, "Satire is a sort of glass, wherein beholders do generally discover everybody's face but their own." Lord Byron announced, "Fools are my theme, let satire be my song." In "An Essay on Comedy" (1877), George Meredith recognized that "the satirist is a moral agent, often a social scavenger, working on a storage of bile."

Satire is essentially moral. Its fundamental mode is earnest joking, kidding on the square, improving society by attacking villains and fools. The editor of *The Oxford Book of Satirical Verse* (1980) notes, "One can say gravely that satire postulates an ideal condition of man or decency, and then despairs of it; and enjoys the despair, masochistically. But the joke must not be lost — the joke of statement, of sound, rhythm, form, vocabulary, rhyme, and surprise. Without the joke everything goes; and we may be left only with complaint, invective, or denunciation; all of which may be poetry, but of another kind."

SEE ALSO *Battle of the Books, flyting, hija, irony, mock epic.*

saudade, saudades (pl) A Portuguese and Galician term that suggests a profoundly bittersweet nostalgia. Aubrey F. G. Bell described *saudade* as a "vague and constant desire for something that does not and probably cannot exist, for something other than the present, a turning towards the past or towards the future" (*In Portugal,* 1912). It is not just a nostalgia for something that was lost; it can also be a yearning for something that might have been. The feeling can be overwhelming, and the Portuguese also speak of the desire to *matar as saudades* ("kill the saudades"). The word *saudade* is found in the *Cancioneiro de Ajuda* (*Ajuda Songbook*), a collection of poems written in Galician-Portuguese and dating from the end of the thirteenth century, and in the *Cancioneiro da Vaticana* (*Vatican Songbook*), a compilation of troubadour lyrics in Galician-Portuguese from the thirteenth and fourteenth centuries. One especially hears *saudade* in the Portuguese fado and in Brazillian music. Tom Jobim's "Chega de Saudade" ("No More Saudade," 1959) was the first bossa nova song. Whereas we tend to consign nostalgia to the all-encompassing dustbin of sentimentality, the Hispanic sensibility has saved it as a poignant and durable feeling relating to the transitoriness of life.

scansion Metrical analysis. The word *scansion* derives from the Latin *scandere,* "to climb" or "a climbing." Scansion, the study of metrical patterns, refers to the division of verse lines into feet as well as to the organization of syllables within a foot. Metrical analysis documents the arrangement of accented and unaccented syllables in different lines; it groups those lines according to the number of feet within them, classifies stanzas by rhyme schemes and the number of lines per stanza, etc. Scansion doesn't create rhythm; it reveals and visually represents it.

SEE ALSO *foot, meter.*

School of Night In *Shakespeare and the Rival Poet* (1903), the scholar Arthur Acheson posited a secret literary and philosophical society that, he theorized, existed in England in the last years of the sixteenth century. The society was purportedly founded by Sir Walter Raleigh and included Christopher Marlowe and George Chapman, whose dual obscure poems "The Shadow of Night" (1594) and "Ovid's Banquet of Sense" (1595) expressed its philosophical interests, especially in their use of "night" as an esoteric and divine symbol. Acheson's theory relies heavily on some evidentiary lines in Shakespeare's *Love's Labour's Lost* (ca. mid-1590s): "O paradox! Black is the badge of hell, / The hue of dungeons, and the school of night." The existence of the group has never been definitively proved.

scop An Anglo-Saxon minstrel-poet, attached to the court of a chieftain or king, who both composed his own poems and sang or recited the traditional compositions of others. The earliest records of scops, who worked in preliterate societies, date to the fourth century, where they are referred to in early English poems. The scop was traditionally a harpist and poet-singer who commanded the full mastery of the complex oral-formulaic materials of old Germanic prosody. Only one poem definitely attributed to a specific scop has come down to us. This forty-two-line poem is recorded in the *Exeter Book,* a tenth-century compilation of Old English poetry, and traditionally called "Déor" after its reputed author.

> Then I of myself   will make this known
> That awhile I was held   the Héodenings' scop,
> To my duke most dear   and Déor was my name. (lines 35–37)

Robert Graves believed that the rhythm of Anglo-Saxon poetry was based on the slow pull and push of the oar, and thus concluded that the function of the Nordic scop was twofold: the poet's first task was as a "shaper" of charms to protect the king and thus ensure prosperity for the kingdom, but, secondarily, to persuade "a ship's crew to pull rhythmically and uncomplainingly on their oars against the rough waves of the North Sea, by singing them ballads in time to the beat." The scop is akin to the Celtic (Welsh) bard, the Gaelic (Irish) *fili,* and the Scandinavian skald.

SEE ALSO *ballad, bard, fili, oral-formulaic method, skald.*

Scottish Chaucerians This name applies to a group of fifteenth- and sixteenth-century Scottish poets indebted to Chaucer (1340?–1400). They were especially adroit at the seven-line stanza that Chaucer had introduced into English poetry. The cast included James I of Scotland, whose fifteenth-century poem "The Kingis Quiar" may have given the name to the form "rhyme royal"; Gavin Douglas, who is known for his translation of Virgil's *Aeneid* into Scots (the *Eneados,* 1513); Sir David Lindsay, who was closest to Chaucer in "The Historie and Testament of Squyer Meldrum" (ca. 1550); and, most important of all, Robert Henryson, whose late fifteenth-century poem "The Testament of Cresseid" picks up a classical myth where Chaucer left it and conducts his heroine ("sumtyme countit the flour of Womanheid") to her grave, and William Dunbar, the most gifted of Scottish makers, whose mournful poem "Lament for the Makers" (1508) is possibly the greatest collective elegy for poets.

> I see that makaris amang the laif [remainder]
> Playis heir ther pageant, syne [then] gois to grave;
> Sparit [spared] is nought [not] ther faculte;
>   *Timor Mortis conturbat me.*

The term *Scottish Chaucerians* is disparaged in Scotland because it appears to diminish the originality of these golden poets.

SEE ALSO *aureate, rhyme royal.*

Scottish renaissance Hugh MacDiarmid (the pseudonym of Christopher Murray Grieve, 1892–1978) led the so-called Scottish renaissance, a revitalization of Scottish poetry in the twentieth century. He wrote his first three books—*Sangchaw* (1925), *Penny Wheep* (1926), and his masterpiece, *A Drunk Man Looks at the Thistle* (1926)—in what he first called vernacular and then braid Scots and finally Lallans. It was a synthetic Scots, an artificial language that blended and integrated several Lowland dialects, which were supplemented by archaic Scots words and phrases, mostly rescued from John Jamieson's *Etymological Dictionary of the Scottish Language* (1808). MacDiarmid turned to something old in Scottish poetry—his motto was "back to Dunbar"—in order to create something new for modern Scottish literature. Synthetic Scots was derided by MacDiarmid's detractors as plastic Scots. Sydney Goodsir Smith (1915–1975) responded to the criticism in "Epistle to John Guthrie" (1941):

> We've come until a gey queer time
> When scrievin Scots is near a crime.
> "There's no one speaks like that," they fleer,
> —But wha the deil spoke like King Lear?

Scottish stanza, see *sestet.*

sea shanties (chanteys, chanties) Sea shanties are the strongly rhythmical work songs of sailors. The word *shantie* probably derives from the French *chantez,* to sing. The imperative is evident: singing enables, paces, and transforms work. These songs generally alternate between a solo passage sung by the leader, or chanteyman, and a refrain roared back in chorus. As Louise Bogan explains in "The Pleasures of Formal Poetry" (1953):

> The variety of rhythm in sea chanties depends upon the variety of tasks on board a sailing ship, with the doing of which a sailor was confronted. Hauling up sail or pulling it down, coiling rope, pulling and pushing and climbing and lifting, all went to different rhythms; and these rhythms are preserved for us, fast or slow, smooth or rough, in sailors' songs.

The *Standard Dictionary of Folklore, Mythology and Legend* (1972) points out that there are three main types of shanties that correspond to the three main types of labor: 1) Short-haul or short-drag shanties, which are used when only a few strong pulls are required. The earliest short-drag shantie known is "Haul on the Bowline," which goes at least as far back as the early sixteenth century; 2) Halyard shanties, which are timed to the massed pull and relaxed interval of long hauls (hoisting sail, catting the anchor, etc.). Such songs as "Wild Goose Shanty," "Whiskey, Johnny," "Blow, Boys, Blow," and

"Blow the Man Down," which is still sung in the Bahamas, are halyard shanties; 3) Windlass or capstan shanties, which are sung to the processional beat of sea boots around the capstan (hoisting anchor, warping the ship into the dock, etc.). Some well-known capstan shanties are "Sally Brown," "Shenandoah," "A-Rovin'," and "Rio Grande," which is most commonly sung on outbound ships ("we are bound for the Rio Grande").

SEE ALSO *oral poetry, work song.*

secentismo, see *Marinism.*

seguidilla The seguidilla, a Spanish poetic form, probably originated as a triple-time folk and dance song. It seems to have begun as a quatrain of alternating long (usually seven or eight syllables) and short lines (usually five or six syllables). The short lines assonated. These songs were called *seguidilla simple* (simple seguidilla) or *seguidilla para cantar* (seguidilla for singing). The folk lyric was the basis for the form, which was established in the sixteenth century and practiced by such poets as Sebastián de Horozco, Lope de Vega, and Sor Juana Inés de la Cruz. Later, a second set of three quasi-independent lines (short, long, short) — an *estrabillo* — were added to the end. This became regularized as a literary form, which consists of 7, 5, 7, 5 pause 5, 7, 5. Lines two and four have one assonance, lines five and seven another. This form is called the *seguidilla compuesta* (composed seguidilla) or *seguidilla para bailar* (seguidilla for dancing). The *seguidilla gitana* or Gypsy seguidilla, also known as the *sequiriya,* is used in flamenco music. In his lecture "Deep Song" (1922), Federico García Lorca states:

> The Gypsy siguiriya begins with a terrible scream that divides the landscape into two ideal hemispheres. It is the scream of dead generations, a poignant elegy for lost centuries, the pathetic evocation of love under other moons and other winds. Then the melodic phrase begins to pry open the mystery of the tones and remove the precious stone of the sob, a resonant tear on the river of the voice. No Andalusian can help but shudder on hearing that scream. No regional song has comparable poetic greatness. Seldom — very seldom — has the human spirit been able to create works of that sort.

SEE ALSO *assonance, folía.*

senryū, see *haiku.*

sensibility Sensibility became a cultural phenomenon in the eighteenth century, a popular term and doctrine with aesthetic and moral overtones. It suggested both a capacity for sympathy, what Rousseau identified as his "susceptibility to tender feelings" (*The Confessions,* 1781), and an intense emotional response to beauty and sublimity, whether in art or nature. In moral philosophy, it was a particular reaction against Thomas Hobbes's claim in *Leviathan* (1651) that human nature is innately selfish and human behavior driven by self-interest. The third Earl of Shaftesbury and others countered that human beings have an innate "benevolence" and sympathy for others. They placed a premium upon warm emotional responsiveness: "Dear Sensibility!" Laurence Sterne exclaims in *A Sentimental Journey* (1768), "Source unexhausted of all that's precious in our joys, or costly in our sorrows." Sensibility was valuable in the development of late eighteenth-century social consciousness during a time of burgeoning, self-interested commercialism, but over time it evolved from suggesting sensitiveness, "the ability to receive sensations," into "refined or excessive sensitiveness in emotion and taste." "It was, essentially, a social generalization of certain personal qualities," Raymond Williams summarizes, "or, to put it another way, a personal appropriation of certain social qualities." The idea overflowed into the realm of manners and the so-called cult of sensibility, highly exaggerated forms of sympathy, an emotional bodily language, the shedding of compassionate tears. It became associated with virtue and breeding, cultivated taste and upper-class status. At its most self-indulgent extreme, sensibility overlapped strongly with what we would now call sentimentality, hence Jane Austen's critique in *Sense and Sensibility* (1811), though the word has never had quite the same negative taint.

The age of sensibility is a name for the literature of the latter part of the eighteenth century, a forerunner to romanticism and a period of flux particularly centered in the 1760s and 1770s. This is the era of sentimental novels (the novel of sensibility) and sentimental comedies (the drama of sensibility) characterized by the pathos of sensitivity, overly refined emotions, acute perceptions and responses. There is a turn from the restraints of neoclassicism and a new sympathy for the Middle Ages, for Spenser, Shakespeare, and Milton, for archaic or "primitive" poetry, manifested in an awakened interest in ballads and other folk poetry, hence the vogue for the Ossianic poems and Thomas Percy's *Reliques of Ancient English Poetry* (1765). Northrop Frye finds a new attention to the psychological view of literature as process rather than product, something more fragmentary, irregular, and unpredictable than the finished works of the Augustans, which helps to account for the sudden emergence of a lyrical impulse in the age of sensibility, the era of Christopher Smart's "A Song to David," Thomas Chatterton's elegies, Robert Burns's songs, and William Blake's lyrics. "The poetry of process is oracular, and the medium of the oracle is often in an ecstatic or trance-like state," Frye writes. "Autonomous voices seem to speak through him, and as he is concerned to utter rather than to address, he is turned away from his listener, so to speak, in a state of rapt self-communion. The free association of words, in which sound is prior to sense, is often a literary way of representing insanity."

The excess of feeling in this lyrical poetry can be dizzying. In the age of sensibility, Marshall Brown remarks, "Intense feelings for nature and humanity were accompanied by . . . intense anxieties about the integrity of the self," including the melancholy we find in Samuel Johnson and Thomas Gray, and the fear of madness — and the madness itself — we encounter in Smart, William Collins, and William Cowper, whose instabilities of selfhood vibrate into splendid torrents of sorrow or rapture. In Collins's "Ode on the Poetical Character" (1747), Smart's *Jubilate Agno* (1759–1763), and Blake's *The Four Zoas* (1807), the soul, God, and nature are brought into what Frye calls "a white-hot fusion of identity, an imaginative fiery furnace in which the reader may, if he chooses, make a fourth."

In the twentieth century, T. S. Eliot formulated a doctrine of what he called dissociation of sensibility, a supposed split between thinking and feeling that he traced to the seventeenth century. The task of modern poetry, Eliot thought, was to reunify sensibility, to make it a whole activity. As a critical term, *sensibility* now has a more limited usefulness. When we speak of a poet's sensibility, we generally mean his or her characteristic way of responding, both intellectually and emotionally, to experience.

SEE ALSO *Augustan Age, dissociation of sensibility, empathy, Enlightenment, Graveyard poets, neoclassicism, pathos, primitivism, romanticism, sentimentality, the sublime, taste.*

sentimentality The word *sentiment* derives from the Medieval Latin *sentimentum,* from the Latin *sentire,* "to feel." It was employed in a variety of ways to refer to an attitude, thought, or judgment prompted by feeling, and thus was used for both emotion and opinion. The adjective *sentimental* began to be popularly used in the eighteenth century. Raymond Williams quotes Lady Bradshaugh (1749) — "*sentimental,* so much in vogue among the polite . . . Everything clever and agreeable is comprehended in that word . . . a *sentimental* man . . . a *sentimental* party . . . a *sentimental* walk" — and recognizes that the term encompasses both "a conscious openness to feelings" and "a conscious consumption of feelings." It was the latter that made the word *sentimental* especially vulnerable to criticism.

In the nineteenth century, *sentimentality* took on decidedly negative connotations from which it never recovered. It is a deliberately modern, self-reflexive term, and generally suggests a disproportionate emotional response. George Meredith defined sentimentalists as those who "seek to enjoy Reality without incurring the Immense Debtorship for a thing done" (*The Ordeal of Richard Feverel,* 1859), and Oscar Wilde said that "a sentimentalist is simply one who desires to have the luxury of an emotion without paying for it" (*De Profundis,* 1905). I. A. Richards brought the term into the twentieth-century critical discourse about poetry when he argued that "a response is sentimental if it is too great for the occasion," adding: "We cannot, obviously, judge that any response is sentimental in this sense unless we take careful account of the situation" (*Practical Criticism,* 1929). Brian Wilke surveys ten basic handbooks on literature in his 1967 essay "What Is Sentimentality?" and concludes that all ten agree that the common keynote is the idea of disproportion or excess.

Sentimentality is frequently used as a term of condescension. For example, it was used by the New Critics and others as a common judgment against the high-feeling, traditionally minded female lyricists of the 1920s and '30s, such as Edna St. Vincent Millay, Sara Teasdale, and Elinor Wylie. "In some poems you're taking the risk of sentiment brimming over into sentimentality," an interviewer once told Philip Larkin, who replied: "Am I? I don't understand the word sentimentality. It reminds me of Dylan Thomas's definition of an alcoholic: 'A man you don't like who drinks as much as you do.' I think sentimentality is someone you don't like feeling as much as you do."

SEE ALSO *naïve and sentimental, pathos, sensibility, taste.*

septenary, see "accentual syllabic meter" in *meter.*

septet The seven-line stanza, of varying meter and rhyme, has been utilized by a large number of English poets from Chaucer (1340?–1400) and Lydgate (ca. 1370–ca. 1451) to William Morris (1834–1896) and John Masefield (1878–1967). The septet has an odd extra punch, a piercing last line, which moves past the symmetry of any even-numbered stanza. Here is a breathtaking stanza from Thomas Nashe's "A Litany in Time of Plague" (1600):

> Beauty is but a flower
> Which wrinkles will devour;
> Brightness falls from the air;
> Queens have died young and fair;
> Dust hath closed Helen's eye.
> I am sick, I must die.
>   Lord, have mercy on us!

The most historically interesting fixed form of the seven-line stanza is rhyme royal, an iambic pentameter stanza rhyming *ababbcc,* which was employed with great dignity by Chaucer in *Troilus and Criseyde* (ca. 1380s) and by Shakespeare in "The Rape of Lucrece" (1594). Something in the lucky number seven seems to lead to desperation or comedy.

SEE ALSO *rhyme royal, rondelet.*

serranilla A type of medieval Spanish poetry, the *serranilla* is a subgenre of the pastoral. It is narrated by a courtier, who tells the story of his chance meeting in the countryside with a rustic girl, and his attempt to seduce her. The *serranilla* almost certainly has its origins in the Provençal *pastourelle* and operates as an alternative to the courtly love poem. The genre underlines and exploits the encounter of contrasting social classes. Marqués de Santillana (1398–1458) first introduced the term *serranilla,* and his best work exemplifies the genre. There is a parody type of the *serranilla,* most notably in the *Libro de buen amor* (*The Book of Good Love,* 1330, 1343), in which the shepherdess initiates the amorous contact with the gentleman. Unlike the hypocritical courtier, she doesn't pretend to be seeking anything more than a lascivious encounter.

SEE ALSO *courtly love, pastoral, pastourelle.*

sestet The subdivision or last six lines of an Italian sonnet, following the first eight lines, the octave. It is also applied (along with the terms *sexain, sixain, sextain, sextet,* and *hexastich*) to the different varieties of the six-line stanza, such as the sestina and the so-called Venus and Adonis stanza (iambic pentameter: rhyming *ababcc*) named after Shakespeare's poem. The sestet, which was first developed by Italian poets, is also called the *sesta rima.* It has an American lineage that runs from Anne Bradstreet's 1650 "The Prologue" ("To sing of wars, of captains, and of kings") to Edward Taylor's *Prepatory Meditations* (1682–1725) to Richard Wilbur's "A Wood" (1969). Charles Wright's *Sestets* (2009) is a collection of terse, open-ended six-line poems.

The Spanish *sextilla* usually has eight syllables, though there are also examples that use tetrameter and pentameter. It options two rhyme schemes: *aabccb* or *abbacc.* Robert Burns mastered the Scottish stanza, or Habbie stanza, a form found in medieval Provençal poems and in miracle plays of the Middle Ages, to such a degree that it came to be called the Burns stanza, or Burns meter. The Burns stanza intermingles two rhymes and meters: it rhymes *aaabab;* lines 1, 2, 3, and 5 are tetrameter, lines 4 and 6 are dimeter. Here are three central stanzas from "Epistle to John Lapraik, an Old Scottish Bard" (1785). Notice how the first three lines build to a crescendo, which is then punctuated by the punch of the fourth line and the epigrammatic cut of the sixth one.

What's a' your jargon o' your schools,
Your Latin names for horns an' stools;
If honest Nature made you fools,
What sairs your Grammars?
Ye'd better taen up spades and shools,
Or knappin-hammers.

A set o' dull, conceited hashes,
Confuse their brains in colledge-classes!
They *gang in* stirks, and *come out* asses,
Plain truth to speak;
An' syne they think to climb Parnassus
By dint o' Greek!

Gie me ae spark o' Nature's fire,
That's a' the learning I desire;
Then tho' I drudge thro' dub an' mire

At pleugh or cart,
My Muse, tho' hamely in attire,
May touch the heart.

SEE ALSO *sestina, sonnet, stanza.*

sestina The sestina, an intricate verse form created and mastered by the Provençal poets, is a thirty-nine-line poem consisting of half a dozen six-line stanzas and one three-line envoi (or "send-off"). The six end words are repeated in a prescribed order, as end words in each of the subsequent stanzas. The concluding tercet brings together all the end words; each line contains two of them, one in the middle and one at the end.

The twelfth-century Provençal poet Arnaut Daniel is credited with inventing the sestina, a form widely practiced by Dante (1265–1321) and Petrarch (1304–1377), who followed the troubadours. Sir Philip Sidney put the form to good use in *Arcadia* (1590). The sestina has had particular fascination for Victorian and modern poets, perhaps because it generates a narrative even as it circles back on itself and recurs like a song. Ezra Pound compared it in *The Spirit of Romance* (1910) to "a thin sheet of flame folding and infolding upon itself."

The numerological scheme, which once may have had magical significance, has the precision and elegance of musical (or mathematical) form:

Stanza one:	1, 2, 3, 4, 5, 6
Two:	6, 1, 5, 2, 4, 3
Three:	3, 6, 4, 1, 2, 5
Four:	5, 3, 2, 6, 1, 4
Five:	4, 5, 1, 3, 6, 2
Six:	2, 4, 6, 5, 3, 1
Envoi:	1 — 2, 3 — 4, 5 — 6

There are often variations on how the six words recur in the final tercet, such as 2 — 5, 4 — 3, 6 — 1.

In this late nineteenth-century sestina, Edmund Gosse pays homage to Arnaut Daniel, who is cited in the epigraph as "the first among all others, great master of love [poetry]":

Sestina

> Fra tutti il primo Arnaldo Daniello
> Gran maestro d'amor — *Petrarch*

In fair Provence, the land of lute and rose,
Arnaut, great master of the lore of love,
First wrought sestinas to win his lady's heart,
Since she was deaf when simpler staves he sang,
And for her sake he broke the bonds of rhyme,
And in this subtler measure hid his woe.

"Harsh be my lines," cried Arnaut, "harsh the woe
My lady, that enthorn'd and cruel rose,
Inflicts on him that made her live in rhyme!"
But through the metre spake the voice of Love,
And like a wild-wood nightingale he sang
Who thought in crabbed lays to ease his heart.

It is not told if her untoward heart
Was melted by her poet's lyric woe,
Or if in vain so amorously he sang;
Perchance through cloud of dark conceits he rose
To nobler heights of philosophic love,
And crowned his later years with sterner rhyme.

This thing alone we know: the triple rhyme
Of him who bared his vast and passionate heart
To all the crossing flames of hate and love,
Wears in the midst of all its storms of woe, —
As some loud morn of March may bear a rose, —
The impress of a song that Arnaut sang.

"Smith of his mother-tongue," the Frenchman sang
Of Lancelot and of Galahad, the rhyme
That beat so bloodlike at this core of rose,
It stirred the sweet Francesca's gentle heart
To take that kiss that brought her so much woe
And sealed in fire her martyrdom of love.

And Dante, full of her immortal love,
Stayed his drear song, and softly, fondly sang
As though his voice broke with that weight of woe;
And to this day we think of Arnaut's rhyme
Whenever pity at the laboring heart
On fair Francesca's memory drops the rose.

Ah! sovereign Love, forgive this weaker rhyme!
The men of old who sang were great at heart,
Yet have we too known woe, and worn thy rose.

An anthology of late nineteenth- and twentieth-century examples might begin with Swinburne's remarkable feat, "The Complaint of Lisa," a rhyming double sestina with twelve twelve-line stanzas and a six-line envoi. It would include examples by Rudyard Kipling, Ezra Pound, and W. H. Auden; by Elizabeth Bishop ("Sestina"), John Ashbery ("Farm Implements and Rutabagas in a Landscape"), Alan Ansen ("A Fit of Something Against Something"), Donald Justice ("Here in Katmandu"), Donald Hall ("Sestina"), Anthony Hecht ("The Book of Yolek"), Marilyn Hacker ("Untoward Occurrence at Embassy Poetry Reading"), Donald Revell ("Near Rhinebeck"), and Deborah Digges ("Hall of Souls"). James Cummins adapts the form to American popular culture in his first book, *The Whole Truth* (1986), which consists entirely of twenty-five sestinas revolving around the characters in the Perry Mason television series. Here the Provençal form indecorously meets the hackneyed detective story and shimmers with comic life.

sexain, see *sestet.*

sextilla, see *sestet.*

shaman, shamanism In tribal societies, a shaman is a medium between the visible and invisible worlds, an intermediary between the human and spirit worlds. Shamans practice magic or sorcery for purposes of healing, divination, and control over natural events. They often have close associations with poetry. Marcea Eliade views the shaman as a "proto-poet" and "specialist of the sacred" who masters "techniques of ecstasy." In shamanic séances, the shaman goes into a trance and becomes possessed by a god or gods who speak through him or her. The shaman, who travels in supernatural worlds and speaks in an exalted or trancelike manner, embodies and enacts the idea of the poet as a prophet or seer. "It is likewise possible that the pre-ecstatic euphoria constituted one of the universal sources of lyric poetry," Eliade speculates. "In preparing his trance, the shaman drums, summons his spirit helpers, speaks a 'secret language' or the 'animal language,' imitating the cries of beasts and especially the songs of birds. He ends by obtaining a 'second state' that provides the impetus for linguistic creation and the rhythms of lyric poetry."

Nora Chadwick makes the case in *Poetry and Prophecy* (1942) that the fundamental elements of the prophetic function of poetry operate the same all over the world:

> Everywhere the gift of poetry is inseparable from divine inspiration. Everywhere this inspiration carries with it knowledge — whether of the past, in the form of history and genealogy; of the hidden present, in the form commonly of scientific information; and of the future, in the prophetic utterance in the narrower sense. Always this knowledge is uttered in poetry which is accompanied by music, whether of song or instrument. Music is everywhere the medium of communication with spirits. Invariably we find that the poet and seer attributes his inspiration to contact with supernatural powers, and his mood during prophetic utterance is exalted and remote from that of his normal existence. Generally we find that a recognized process is in vogue by which the prophetic mood can be induced at will. The lofty claims of the poet and seer are universally admitted, and he himself holds a high status wherever he is found.

Some researchers have believed that the traditional shamans of northern and central Asia were the predecessors of the epic singers of ancient Greece. Ted Hughes called the shamanic flight "one of the main regeneration dramas of the human psyche: the fundamental poetic event."

SEE ALSO *ethnopoetics, inspiration, the language of the birds, oral poetry, vatic.*

shan-shui Rivers-and-mountains poetry. Originating in the early fifth century, this Chinese tradition represents, as David Hinton puts it in his anthology *Mountain Home* (2002), "the earliest and most extensive literary engagement with wilderness in human history." The poetry embodies a deep physical and spritiual sense of belonging to the wilderness. The poet Hsieh Ling-yün (385–433) is the founder of the rivers-and-mountains tradition, whereas the poet T'ao Ch'ien (365–427) is the founder of the fields-and-garden tradition. Yet T'ao Ch'ien wrote: "Vast and majestic, mountains embrace your shadow; / broad and deep, rivers harbor your voice." The great T'ang Dynasty poets all wove their consciousness into the wilderness. One thinks of Meng Hao-jan (689–740), Wang Wei (701–761), Li Po (701–762), who is called the "Banished Immortal," and Tu Fu (712–770), who wrote: "The nation falls into ruins; rivers and mountains continue." Gary Snyder summons up the ancient tradition, which suggests the eternal dialectic of water and rock, in his long poem, *Mountains and Rivers Without End* (1996).

SEE ALSO *nature poetry.*

shibbus, shibbutz Hebrew: "setting" or "inlay." The medieval Hebrew poets lived in a bibliocentric poetic world. They commonly ornamented their poems with recognizable scriptural verses, or fragments of verses, which are called *shibbus,* a term borrowed from the art of the jeweler. This way of implanting one poem into another, of interpenetrating verses, is closely akin to, and partially derived from, the Arabic practice of weaving the Koran into poems, which is called *iqtibas.* It is an allusive method, a way of transferring energy. The art of inlay for this skillful activity, this pliable action, is somewhat misleading. Neal Kozodoy explains: "With greater accuracy we might think of the poem as a garment, woven with great skill from costly and colorful material. Into this fabric have been twined threads of pure gold, beaten down from a single golden bar, the Bible . . . [These golden threads] call attention to themselves, first, inviting us to hold up the work, tilting it at a variety of angles and planes in an attempt to perceive whether they might not form some hidden pattern. At the same time, they impart real depth and brilliance to the surfaces surrounding them, and as we study those surfaces we become struck by the impression of motion, as the presence of the pure gold subtly alters the values and intensities of the surrounding hues."

SEE ALSO *iqtibas.*

shih In Chinese, the word *shih* means "song-words." It can be used as a general name for poetry, for a poem or poems, or for a collection of poems. It may also designate a specific type of poetry. It is noteworthy that the word *shih* consists of two elements meaning "spoken word" and "temple." The sense of words recited at the earth-altar indicates the sacred mission of poetry. The *shih,* or lyric form, traces its origins to the 305 anonymous poems, mostly hymns and folk songs, in the Confucian classic, the *Shih Ching,* or *The Book of Songs* (tenth to sixth century B.C.E.), which inaugurates the Chinese poetic tradition. These poems generally employ a meter of four-character lines. The preface states: "Poetry is the product of earnest thought. Thought cherished in the mind becomes earnest, then expressed in words, it becomes poetry."

In the second century, the *shih* form expanded to a line of five characters, one of the fundamental prosodic units of traditional Chinese poetry. During the Han Dynasty (206 B.C.E.–220 C.E.), there developed many subgenres and themes of *shih* that lasted through much of Chinese literary history, such as *yung-wu shih* (object poems), *yung-shih* (historical poems), *yen-hui shih* (feast poems), *yu-lan shi* (sightseeing poems), *yu-hsien shih* (poems on roaming amid the immortals), *yüan-nü shih* (poems on lonely women), and so forth.

Shih poetry reached one of its apogees in the five-word line (and a corresponding seven-word line) during the T'ang Dynasty (618–907), the golden age of Chinese poetry. The prosodic features became formalized as *lü-shih* ("regulated verses"). A prominent feature of these regulated verses was the tonal contrast between the two lines of each couplet. Each poem employed a complex pattern of tones, of syntactical parallels, of rhyming alternate lines. The standard length was twelve or, primarily, eight lines. The poet who worked outside these rules was writing *ku-shih* ("old-style poems"). Such poets as Wang Wei (701–761), Li Po (701–762), and Tu Fu (712–770) employed these highly regulated verses to write their compact, spacious poems of companionship and isolation, being and nonbeing, mountains and rivers, time and space.

SEE ALSO *shan-shui, yüeh-fu.*

shinch'eshi (New Poetry) The New Poetry movement introduced modern poetry to Korea. Ch'oe Nam-son (1890–1957), who edited the first modern Korean literary magazine, was the key figure, importing Western influences and creating a freer, more experimental style than traditional Korean poetry, which consists of such forms as the *sijo* (a short suggestive poem of three lines). His poem "From the Sea to Children" (1908), which was inspired by Lord Byron's *Childe Harold's Pilgrimage* (1812–1818), initiated the movement by celebrating the power of the young to embrace and carry out revolutionary change. Peter H. Lee points out: "The poem's inventions include the copious use of punctuation marks (a convention borrowed from the West), stanzas of unequal length, a string of onomatopoeia in the first and seventh lines of each stanza, and the dominant image of the sea and children, which has been little mentioned in classical Korean poetry." New Poetry is not free verse — it held on to the constraints of traditional Korean prosody — but it is the forerunner of all modern Korean poetry.

SEE ALSO *sijo.*

shi^{c}r The Arabic word for poetry derives from the verb *sha^{c}ara,* which means "to know," "to understand," and "to perceive." In *An Introduction to Arab Poetics* (1985), the poet Adonis explains: "We call the poet *shā^{c}ir* (literally, 'one who knows, understands, perceives') in Arabic because he perceives and understands (*yash^{c}uru*) that which others do not perceive and understand, that is he knows (*ya^{c}lamu*) what others do not know." In general, the term *poetry* refers to a special kind of speech regulated by rhyme and meter. The verb *sha^{c}ara* has also come to have an additional meaning: "to feel."

SEE ALSO *nazm.*

shloka, sloka The Sanskrit word *shloka* derives from the verbal root *shru* ("to hear") and is sometimes translated as "poetry." In the *Upanishads,* the word is employed to mean "union." In classical Sanskrit literature, it is used for both "poem" (verse in any meter) and "fame." Tradition has it that in post-Vedic literature, which comes after the most sacred writings of Hinduism in early Sanskrit (the *Samhitas,* the *Brahmanas,* the *Aranyakas,* the *Upanishads*), Valmiki uttered the first *shloka,* the famous opening section in the *Ramayana* (fifth to fourth century B.C.E.). This stanza, two sixteen-syllable lines, was composed in the common epic meter called *anushtup* (four *padas* or feet, each eight syllables long), which in turn came to be called the *shloka* meter.

The story tells how the sage walked along the banks of the River Tamasa, where he heard "the sweetest song" of two krauncha birds mating in spring.

Suddenly, there was a vicious whistling and the male bird crashed to the ground, an arrow stuck in him "like a monstrous curse." Valmiki saw a pale-faced hunter and heard the female bird screaming in grief. And then out of a raging sorrow, a tremendous curse erupted from him. It came out in perfect meter. He relived the strange experience many times. And then one dazzling morning Brahma himself came to him:

> In his voice of ages, Brahma said, "Valmiki, I put the sloka on your tongue with which you cursed the hunter. I sent Narada to you, so you could hear the legend of the perfect man from him. I want you to compose the life of Rama in the meter of the curse. You will see clearly not only into the prince's life, but into his heart; and Lakshmana's, Sita's, and Ravana's. No secret will be kept from you and not a false word will enter your epic. It shall be known as the Adi Kavya, the first poem of the earth. As long as Rama is remembered in the world of men, so shall you be. The epic you are going to compose will make you immortal." His hand raised in a blessing, Brahma faded from their midst. The dazed Valmiki found himself helplessly murmuring his curse again, "*Ma Nisada pratishtam tvamagamah,*" ["Oh Hunter! Since you killed one of the pair of Krauncha birds in love, you shall never attain fame!"] in the meter called *anushtup.*
> *(tr. Ramesh Menon)*

Shloka is equated with Hindu prayer, where it is heard as a kind of hymn chanted or sung in liturgy. It can also have a proverbial sense. The Kashmiri offshoot of *shloka* is *shrukh* or "wise sayings of a great man."

SEE ALSO *kávya.*

short meter, short measure A variation of the common meter found in hymns. Whereas the ballad meter follows a pattern of alternating stresses (4, 3, 4, 3), the short meter foreshortens the first tetrameter line (3, 3, 4, 3). It is usually iambic. The stanza rhymes *abcb* or *abab.* The form is similar to poulter's measure, which consists of rhyming couplets that alternate iambic hexameter (twelve-syllable) and iambic heptameter (fourteen-syllable) lines. Emerson purposefully employs the short measure of the hymnal in his quatrain "Poet" (1867):

Tŏ clóthe thĕ fíerȳ thóught
Ĭn símplĕ wórds sŭccéeds,
Fŏr stíll thĕ cráft ŏf génĭus ís
Tŏ másk ă kíng ĭn wéeds.

SEE ALSO *ballad, hymn, long meter, poulter's measure.*

Sicilian octave, see *strambotto.*

Sicilian school The Sicilian school consisted primarily of Sicilian but also of some Tuscan and southern Italian poets gathered around the court of the emperor Frederick II (1194–1250) and then his son Manfred (d. 1266). Dante termed the group "Sicilian" in *De vulgari eloquentia* (*Eloquence of the Vernacular,* ca. 1302–1305) and recognized that they established the vernacular as the standard language of Italian love poetry. These logically minded poets, many of them notaries, invented the sonnet and the canzone, two major Italian poetic forms, and established the fundamental subject of courtly love. The Italian lyric was thus born in Sicily. Three of the most significant poets were Giocomo da Lentino, who is usually credited with inventing the sonnet, Giacomino Pugliese, and Rinaldo d'Aquino. The poets of the Sicilian school were great readers and translators, not musicians, and they transformed oral forms into written ones. They were influenced by the Provençal troubadours, the French jongleurs, and the German minnesingers, and most likely the Arabic poets of southern Spain. There are about 125 surviving poems from the group, some 85 canzones, and the rest mostly sonnets. The Sicilian school created a legacy for Guido Cavalcanti (ca. 1250–1300), Dante (1265–1321), and Petrarch (1304–1377), and helped to set the course for future European and English poetry.

SEE ALSO *canzone, dolce stil nuovo, jongleur, minnesinger, sonnet, strambotto, troubadour.*

siday The word *siday* generally means all forms of poetry (moralistic, humorous, satirical) in the Waray language, which is spoken in the northern parts of Leyte and on the island of Samar in the Philippines. The Spanish Jesuit Father Ignatio Francisco Alizina mentioned the *sidai* as a specific poetic type in his *Historia de las Islas Bisayas* (1668): "They use it in order to praise others or to relate accomplishments of their ancestors or to extol the beauty of some woman or brave man." The *siday* subsequently turned into a Bisayan generic term for any kind of poetry.

In the 1990s, however, the word *siday* became localized to a particular form of rhyming didactic poetry that is broadcast daily on the radio station DYVL. "The *Waray siday* has become the DYVL siday," Jose Duke S. Bagulaya explains. "The DYVL siday is now the poetry of Leyte and Samar." The *siday* follows the same basic rhyming as the satirical poetry or *durogas* that flourished in the forty-year period from 1920 to 1960, but tend to be less ironic, more oratorical. The audience loves these simple poems of social commentary, which are made up by local people — farmers, clerks, housewives, teachers — and read after the morning news.

SEE ALSO *bical, ode.*

signifying, signifyin(g) Signifying is a fundamentally black rhetorical practice, a type of verbal play, a means of saying one thing and meaning another, a way of getting around a subject. It is a type of verbal trickery, an improvisatory mode of troping. Roger Abrahams suggests in *Deep Down in the Jungle* (1964) that signifying refers to "an ability to talk with great innuendo, to carp, cajole, wheedle and lie . . . in other instances to talk around a subject . . . making fun of a person or situation." It is "a language of implication." The system of verbal insults known as the dozens is sometimes called signifying. Signifying includes fooling around with rhymes, joking and jiving, talking bad and talking sweet. In *The Signifying Monkey* (1988), Henry Louis Gates Jr. reconfigures *signifying* as *signifyin(g)* and enlarges this vernacular verbal strategy — a rhetorical way of "showing off" — which derives from the trickster story of the Signifying Monkey, into a trope for black discourse itself, a figure of double-voiced repetition and reversal that distinguishes African American literary discourse, "a trope of tropes." He argues that the dozens are "an especially compelling subset of Signifyin(g)."

SEE ALSO *the dozens, trope.*

sijo The *sijo,* one of the earliest forms of Korean poetry, is a short suggestive poem, which was originally chanted or sung (the word means "current tune" or "melody of the times") to fixed tunes. It is comparable to the Japanese haiku. *Sijo* has three lines each with fifteen syllables. The last line can vary in length. Each line is divided into two parts with a medial pause. The first line presents the theme of the poem, while the second reinforces or elaborates it, and the third turns, twists, or counters it. The *sijo* is the most mnemonic and beloved of all traditional Korean forms. Yun Sŏn-do (1587–1671) is regarded as the great master of *sijo*.

SEE ALSO *haiku, kasa.*

Silesian school The Silesian school refers to two groups of seventeenth-century German poets. Martin Opitz was the leader of the so-called first Silesian school, which originated in Liegnitz. His *Buch von der deutschen Poeterey* (1624) recommended using strict romance forms in German while replacing the common "neo-Latin style" with "a pattern of alternating stressed and unstressed syllables which coincided with the natural stress patterns of German words." He thus introduced the vernacular into German poetry. His book served as a kind of poetic manual for the group, mostly from Silesia, which included Simon Dach, Philipp von Zesen, Johann Rist, and Paul Fleming. Influenced by Ronsard and the French La Pléiade, these poets rejected the nativist tradition of the meistersingers and replaced the native *Knittelvers,* which they considered doggerel, with the imported, classically balanced alexandrine. The resulting work from these baroque poets, however, was a curiously stilted, didactic, and descriptive poetry.

Christian Hofmann von Hofmannswaldau and Daniel Casper von Lohenstein were the leading representatives of the so-called second Silesian school, which originated in Breslau. Their work is a kind of culmination of German baroque poetry, which has marked affinities with the extremities of Marinism (Italy), Gongorism (Spain), and metaphysical poetry (England). The pronounced excesses of German baroque poetry were later labeled *Schwulst,* or bombast, the "swollen style."

SEE ALSO *alexandrine, baroque, bombast, didactic poetry, Gongorism, Knittelvers, La Pléiade, Marinism, meistersinger, metaphysical poetry.*

silva A traditional Spanish stanza or strophe that consists of a random combination of eleven-syllable lines (*hendecasyllables*), alone or combined with seven-syllable lines (*heptasyllables*). There is no specific pattern of rhyme in this somewhat free form. Luis de Góngora wrote the *Las Soledades,* or *The Solitudes* (1613–1618), which consists of approximately two thousand lines, in the silva, alternating seven- and eleven-syllable lines. One critic claims that the silva of the poetic form — the word means "forest" in Latin — mirrors the jungle *soledad* of the poem itself. Sor Juana Inés de la Cruz's intellectual autobiography in verse, "Primero sueño," also known as "El Sueño" (First Dream, 1692), which is a 950-line imitation of Góngora, is also written in the form of the silva.

SEE ALSO *Gongorism, hendecasyllabics, versi sciolti.*

sílvae, sílva A collection of encomiastic odes, epigrams, and other kinds of short verse. *Sílvae* means woods or forest but also raw material and, metaphorically, a miscellaneous collection. Statius's *Sílvae* (ca. 89–96 C.E.), which set the model — he may have invented the genre — consists of thirty-two occasional poems that congratulate and thank friends, console mourners, admire monuments, describe memorable scenes. These rapid impromptu poems or "bits of raw material" created a vogue for deliberately rough, extemporaneous poems. Statius's contemporary Quintilian considered it a fault that certain writers "run over the material first with as rapid a pen as possible, extempore, following the inspiration of the moment: this they call *sílva*" (*Institutio Oratoria,* first century). The improvisatory sketch appealed to Renaissance writers, such as Poliziano (Angelo Ambrogini), who entitled his verse lectures *Sílvae* (1480–1490), and Ben Jonson, whose note "To the Reader" before *The Underwood* (1640) explains:

> With the same leave, the ancients called that kind of body *Sylva,* or *Hylë,* in which there were works of divers nature, and matter congested; as the multitude call Timber-trees, promiscuously growing, a *Wood,* or *Forest:* so am I bold to entitle these lesser Poems, of later growth, by this of *Under-wood,* out of the Analogy they hold to the *Forest:* in my former book, and no otherwise.

Julius Caesar Scaliger postulated in his *Poetics* (1561) that the term derived "either from the multifarious matter, from the crowd of things crammed in, or from their roughness [*ipsis rudimentis*]. For they used to pour out unpolished effusions and correct them afterwards." Some examples of the poetical *sílvae* as a collection of occasional poetry: Pierre de Ronsard's *Bocages* (1554), Phineas Fletcher's *Sílva Poetica* (1633), Abraham Cowley's *Sylva, or divers copies* (1636), Robert Herrick's *Hesperides* (1648), and John Dryden's

Silvae: or, the second Part of Poetical Miscellanies (1693). Alastair Fowler points out that the silva has maintained a tenuous tradition in such works as Samuel Taylor Coleridge's *Sibylline Leaves* (1817), Leigh Hunt's *Foliage; or Poems Original and Translated* (1818), Walt Whitman's *Leaves of Grass* (1855), Robert Louis Stevenson's *Underwoods* (1887), Robert Lowell's *Notebook* (1967–1968), and Edwin Morgan's *New Divan* (1977). "We tend to take for granted the idea of a collection of poems on various subjects and in different forms, without reflecting that such collections constitute a specific genre. It seems almost as if the genre were too dominant, too nonpareil, to have a name."

SEE ALSO *occasional poem.*

Silver Age Silver is a valuable metal, but less valuable than gold, and the Silver Age tends to refer to a particular period of important but secondary achievement. In *Works and Days,* the eighth-century B.C.E. Greek poet Hesiod described the Silver Age as the second of the five "Ages of Man." The Olympian gods created a race of men who were less noble than the race of the golden age. There is something slightly condescending and perhaps fallacious in the retrospective term *Silver Age.* Scholars refer to the Silver Age of Latin Literature, which covers the poetry and prose of the early empire, the first two centuries of the Common Era. The period runs from Seneca (4 B.C.E.–65 C.E.) to the Roman emperor and Stoic philosopher Marcus Aurelius (121–180). The work was considered good but not quite equal to the high standards of the Augustan "golden age" (70 B.C.E.–14 C.E.). My favorite poets of the Latin Silver Age are Juvenal (ca. 55–130), a poet of great satirical indignation, and Martial (40–104), a poet whose scathing wit sparkles in polished epigrams. Their work is shadowed by a strong feeling that they live in a period of cultural decadence.

The term *Silver Age (serebrianyi vek)* is also traditionally applied to Russian poetry in the first two decades of the twentieth century. Omry Ronen points out that Ivanov-Razumnik (the pseudonym of Razumnik Vasil'evich Ivanov) was the first writer to employ the opposition of the Golden and Silver Age in relation to modern Russian literature. The period commences with Aleksandr Blok's *Verses on the Beautiful Lady* (1904) and concludes with Boris Pasternak's *My Sister — Life* (1922). This is the era of upheaval and crisis that encompassed Russian symbolism, Acmeism, and Russian futurism, the period that launched Anna Akhmatova, Marina

Tsvetaeva, and Osip Mandelstam. It was one of the golden ages of twentieth-century poetry.

SEE ALSO *Acmeism, Augustan Age, Four Ages of Poetry, futurism, golden age, symbolism.*

simile The explicit comparison of one thing to another, using the word *as* or *like* — as when Robert Burns writes:

> My love is like a red, red rose
>   That's newly sprung in June:
> My love is like the melodie
>   That's sweetly play'd in tune.

The essence of simile is similitude; it is likeness and unlikeness, urging a comparison of two different things. A good simile depends on a kind of heterogeneity between the elements being compared. "You smell of time as a Bible smells of thumbs," the Irish poet Mebdh McGuckian writes in her poem "The War Degree" (1995), thus comparing the odor that clings to someone aging to the smell imprinted on a holy book that has been paged through by hundreds of people over the years.

Similes are comparable to metaphors, but the difference between them is not merely grammatical, depending on the explicit use of *as* or *like*. It is a difference in significance. Metaphor asserts an identity. It says, "A poem is a meteor" (Wallace Stevens); it says A equals B and in doing so relies on condensation and compression. By contrast, the simile is a form of analogical thinking. It says: "Poetry is made in a bed like love" (André Breton); it says A is like B and thereby works by opening outward. There is a digressive impulse in similes that keeps extending out to take in new things. Breton recognizes, "The embrace of poetry like the embrace of the naked body."

The simile asserts a likeness between unlike things, it maintains their comparability, but it also draws attention to their differences, thus affirming a state of division. When Shakespeare asks, "Shall I compare thee to a summer's day?" (Sonnet 18, 1609), he is drawing attention to the artificial process of figuration. So is the Hebraist when he asserts in the Song of Songs (1:9): "I have compared thee, O my love, to a company / of horses in Pharaoh's chariots." The reader participates in making meaning through simile, in establishing the nature of an unforeseen analogy, in evaluating the aptness of unexpected resemblance.

SEE ALSO *analogy, figures of speech, metaphor, rhetoric, trope.*

Simultaneism or ***Simultanism*** Guillaume Apollinaire (1880–1918) invented the term *Orphism* for an artistic mode in which everything is happening at once. It seeks to destroy the sequentiality of time with its presentness. Apollinaire first applied *Orphism* to the art of Robert Delaunay (1885–1941) and his associates, and the term spread to the other arts. *Dramatism* appeared in Paris in 1911 and was later called *simultaneism.* Delaunay invented the term *simultanism* to describe the abstract work that he and his wife, Sonia Delaunay, developed from around 1910. They were simultanist artists.

All of these terms committed art to the present moment. In 1912, Henry Martin Barzun argued that simultaneism was the most suitable poetic solution to the tumultuousness realities of modern life. He treated poetry as sound-noise in "Orphéide" (1914–1923). Pierre Albert-Birot propagandized for *nunism* or *nowism,* which he called "an 'ism' to outlast the others" (1916), and Blaise Cendrars advocated for a poetic of "Simultaneous Contrast" (1919):

> The word "simultaneous" is a term of professional jargon, like "reinforced concrete" in construction, or "sublimation" in medicine. Delaunay uses it when he works with tower, port, house, man, woman, toy, eye, window, book, when he is in Paris, New York, Moscow, in bed or in the sky. The "simultaneous" is a technique. The technique shapes primary matter, universal matter, the world.

Cendrars used cinematic techniques, such as flashback and montage, to shatter the linearity of traditional poetry. So, too, Apollinaire cut out connectives and tried to fuse time and space on the page. Octavio Paz argues that "Pound and Eliot adopted Simultaneism" and links the movement to poetic cubism. The futurists called it *simultaneism* when they read different parts of a poem aloud at the same time.

Early modern poetry celebrated the present, the instantaneous moment, and tried to harness some of the same simultaneous energies as modern painting. Bram Dijkstra points out that "in New York, in the first issue of 291, an anonymous writer (probably Marius de Zayas) defined Simultaneism in painting as 'the simultaneous representation of the different figures of a form seen from different points of view, as Picasso or Braque did some time ago; or — the simultaneous representation of the figure of several forms, as the futurists are doing.' " Simultaneism challenged William Carlos Williams to a poetic of intensified perceptions and quick, almost automatic writing, which resulted in *Kora in Hell* (1920). Dean Young is as close to a simultaneist poet as we now have.

SEE ALSO *automatic writing, collage, Cubist poetry, futurism, sound poetry, spontaneity.*

sincerity *Sincerity,* which Lionel Trilling defines as "a congruence between avowal and actual feeling," was a negligible term in criticism until the second half of the eighteenth century, when it came into vogue with Jean-Jacques Rousseau's *Confessions,* an autobiography of unprecedented frankness completed in 1769, and Goethe's *The Sorrows of Young Werther* (1774), an early novel that passionately exalted feeling and attacked rationalism in the name of sincerity. The romantic poets placed a high value on the uniqueness of individual experience. They made the expression of powerful emotion, what Keats calls "the true voice of feeling," a crucial touchstone, a raison d'être for poetry itself. Romantic sincerity, like romantic spontaneity, was an artful construction that gave the feeling of an utterly authentic relationship between the poet and his subject without any intervening artifice. "There is nothing of the conventional craft of artificial writers," Leigh Hunt said about Keats's luxurious poem "The Eve of St. Agnes" (1819): "All flows out of sincerity and passion."

There are two countermovements related to sincerity in the second half of the nineteenth century. On one hand, Victorian poets and critics gave greater moral weight to the idea of sincerity. Writing from the heart, the appearance of sincerity, became a measure of poetic integrity. The most genuine poetry corresponded to the poet's deepest state of mind. Matthew Arnold spoke of "the high seriousness which comes from absolute sincerity." On the other hand, as Nietzsche said, "Every profound spirit needs a mask," and insincerity, the idea of a dramatic pose, also gained traction. Charles Baudelaire enshrined the idea of the dandy, a cultivated figure, and Robert Browning created the fictive speakers of the dramatic monologue, a type of poem that marginalizes the idea of poetic sincerity. The advantage of posing would culminate in Oscar Wilde's aphorism, "Man is least himself when he talks in his own person. Give him a mask and he will tell you the truth."

The true voice of feeling speaks in many registers. The modernist poets entered poetry by taking on different personas, which they made a central feature of their work. They also shifted the idea of sincerity away from self-expression, the honest transcription of feeling, toward verbal accuracy, artistic precision. Sincerity is reflected in making. Ezra Pound said, "I believe in technique as the test of a man's sincerity."

SEE ALSO *decadence, dramatic monologue, impersonality, neoclassicism, persona, romanticism, sensibility, spontaneity, Sturm und Drang.*

sīra, siyar (pl) The *sīra* is an indigenous Arabic genre of oral folk epic. It has no exact equivalent in European literatures. The word literally means a traveling, a journeying, or a path. It can designate a history, a biography, a mode of behavior. Within written Arabic literature, Ibn Ishāq (d. 768) first applied the term to the biography of the prophet Muhammad, and thereafter the literary genre became more and more closely associated with biography. The earliest surviving fragments of the folk *siyar* date to the late medieval period. They are long narratives told in alternating sequences of poetry and prose. There was a complex interplay between the oral and written traditions of the folk *siyar.* Two favorite examples are *Sīrat 'Antar ibn Shaddād* (the *sīra* of the pre-Islamic black poet-knight, 'Antara son of Shaddād, eleventh or twelfth century) and *Sīrat Banī Hilāl* (the epic history of the Banī Hilāl Bedouin tribe, ca. eleventh century), which is the last of the folk *siyar* to survive in oral tradition.

SEE ALSO *epic.*

sirventes, serventes A type of satirical poem in Provençal poetry. This partisan genre, filled with praise and blame, was usually employed to satirize the vices and follies of the age. It was common for a troubadour to borrow the tune for a sirventes from a more popular *chanso* (love song), which was considered the superior genre. The poems were usually topical, often exhorting, and they attacked any subject but love. Bertran de Born (ca. 1140s–1215) was widely recognized as the master of the sirventes, or political song.

The double sirventes consists of a pair of formally matching antithetical lyrics. It takes the strophic back and forth of the *tenson,* a debate poem, and develops it into whole lyrics. The most celebrated example of the sirventes-*tenson* is the series of six exchanges, thrusts and parries, between Sordello and Pierre Bremon between 1234 and 1240.

SEE ALSO *chanso, planh, poetic contest, satire, tenson, troubadour.*

sixain, see *sestet.*

skald, scald This Old Norse word for a poet is generally applied to Norwegian or Icelandic court poets from the ninth to the thirteenth century. The most credible etymology suggests that the word *skald* derives from a lost Germanic verb, *skeldan,* "to abuse verbally." Thus a *skald* may originally have meant "poet who abuses someone verbally." The skalds, or "verse smiths," were proud of their craft and often compared themselves to artisans. They were experts at kennings (metaphoric compounds) and mastered complicated alliterative verse forms, such as the *dróttkvætt,* meaning "lordly meter." "Skaldic poetry was in the main occasional poetry," James Graham-Campbell explains in *The Viking World* (2001). "It showed the poet's reaction to current events, to something that had just happened to him, or a prince he was visiting." Skaldic poets were well-rewarded historians of their patrons, and much of their work had to do with praising their lords. Here Henry Wadsworth Longfellow introduces "The Saga of King Olaf" (1863):

> Legends that once were told or sung
> In many a smoky fireside nook
> Of Iceland, in the ancient day,
> By wandering Saga-man or Scald . . .

The Scottish poet Hugh MacDiarmid identified with the passionate social role of the skald: "I have been a singer after the fashion / Of my people — a poet of passion," he wrote in his poem "Skald's Death" (1934), which is engraved on the caird beside his memorial.

SEE ALSO *drápa, dróttkvætt, kenning.*

Skamander The exuberant group of Polish poets who clustered around the magazine *Skamander* after World War I. The title of the magazine — and the group — comes from the river of Troy, which "glittered with a Vistula wave" in Stanislaw Wyspiański's 1904 play *Akropolis.* The main members of the group were Jaroslaw Iwaskiewicz, Jan Lechoń, Antoni Slonimski, Julian Tuwim, and Kazimierz Wierzyński. The Skamanderites were vital Bergsonian traditionalists — lyric, tender, cosmopolitan — who declared, "We want to be poets of the present and this is our faith and our whole 'program.' " Formally, they believed "unshakably in the sanctity of a good rhyme, in the divine origin of rhythm, in revelation through images born in ecstasy and through shapes chiseled by work."

skazitel, skaziteli (pl) Professional minstrel-entertainers of the lower class in Russia. Some scholars think that these popular entertainers (musicians, acrobats, magicians, clowns), who flourished from the fifteenth to the early seventeenth century, were the surviving remnant of a class of pagan priests. The *skaziteli* were crucial in disseminating the Russian oral heroic poems.

SEE ALSO *bylina, epic.*

Skeltonics, Skeltonic verse A rough-and-tumble verse form named after its originator, John Skelton (1460–1529), who wrote in jumpy short lines with irregular rhythms. Skelton's lines had two or three stresses and any number of syllables, and his lyrics rhymed in irregular groups. He liked wordplay, alliterating couplets, and parallel constructions. Here is how he described his own verse in "Colin Clout" (1522):

> And if ye stand in doubt
> Who brought this rhyme about,
> My name is Colin Clout.
> I purpose to shake out
> All my connying bag.
> Like a clerkly hag;
> For though my rhyme be ragged,
> Tattered and jagged,
> Rudely rain beaten,
> Rusty and moth-eaten,
> If ye take well therewith,
> It hath in it some pith.

James VI called Skelton's lively, funny, doggerel-like poems Tumbling verse, and, indeed, his energetic short lines and fast, frequent rhymes do tumble down the page. Skelton's "rude rayling" was praised by Wordsworth and Coleridge, and championed by such poets as W. H. Auden, who said that Skeltonics "have the natural ease of speech rhythm," and Robert Graves, who asked: "What could be dafter / Than John Skelton's laughter?" ("John Skelton," 1918).

SEE ALSO *doggerel, light verse, tumbling verse.*

skolion, skolia (pl), also ***scolion, scolia*** (pl) A banquet song accompanied by the lyre. *Skolia* were convivial songs sung by invited guests at banquets in ancient Greece. They were often improvised and connected to drinking. Terpender is credited with having invented the form in the seventh century B.C.E. By the fifth century, *skolia* were being recorded and collected into editions, presumably for circulation at symposia. The term thus came to suggest the occasion for the poem, though the form retained something of its spontaneity. There are surviving examples by Alcaeus (late seventh to early sixth century B.C.E.), Anacreon (ca. 570–485 B.C.E.), Praxilla (fifth century B.C.E.), Simonides (ca. 556–468 B.C.E.), Sappho (late seventh century B.C.E.), and Pindar (ca. 522–443 B.C.E.), whose fragmentary *skolion* addressed to the boy Theoxenus of Tenedos has been called "one of the most perfect love songs in the Greek language." Pindar proclaims that "any man who glances / The bright rays flashing from Theoxenus's eyes / And is not tossed on the waves of desire / Has a black heart."

slam poetry A poetry slam is a form of poetic boxing, a competition in which poets perform original work before an audience. Slam poetry returns poetry to its oral roots, though its subject matter is radically current and often focuses on social, racial, economic, and gender injustices. The poems are almost always memorized in advance. They aren't meant to be read on the page, but performed. The judges are selected from the audience, which tends to be highly vocal. The competitors perform alone or in teams. Poetic contests are ancient, but the structure of the contemporary slam was started by Marc Smith at the Blue Mill Cocktail Lounge in Chicago, Illinois, in 1986. He called his series "The Uptown Poetry Slam," and subsequently explained:

> When I started, nobody wanted to go to poetry readings. Slam gave it life . . . a community where you didn't have to be a special something, feel bad that you weren't educated a special way . . . I think slam gets poetry back to its roots, breathing life into the words.

The poetry slam quickly spread all across the country. One of its liveliest homes has been the Nuyorican Poets Café in New York City, which Bob Holman calls "a safe place full of risk." "Each Slam / a finality," Bob Kaufman said, which Holman expanded: "Every slam an event, a trial, a roller coaster, a poetry mixer, a crossover dream." Since 1997, the group Poetry Slam Incorporated, or PSI, has promoted "the performance and creation of poetry," and now has venues in all fifty states and seven different countries. But as Allan Wolf, the "slam-master" of the 1994 National Poetry Slam in Asheville, North Carolina, said: "The points are not the point; the point is poetry."

SEE ALSO *poetic contests, spoken word poetry.*

slant rhyme, see *near rhyme.*

snowball verse, see *rhopalic verse.*

sNyan ngag "Ornate poetry." *sNyan ngag,* or "speech to the ear," originated in Tibetan literature in the thirteenth century as a stylized, written type of Buddhist poetry inspired by Indian examples. It first appeared as a translation of the ornate Sanskrit poetry known as *kāvya.* In principle, as Roger Jackson suggests, "*snyan ngag* are supposed to evoke one or more of the traditional affect-states (*bhāva, nyams 'gyur*) of Sanskrit aesthetics: charm, heroism, disgust, merriment, wrath, fear, pity, wonderment and peace, and to display the formal and verbal ornaments (*alamkāra, rgyan*) that help to produce those states." The idea of "ornate language" suggests that poetry moves above and beyond speech, which it ornaments with rhetoric and sound, the various devices of verse.

Here is an example from Tsong kha pa's "Praise of Dependent Origination" (ca. 1400), a short verse text in praise of the Buddha, which suggests that "the night-lily garden of the treatises of Nāgārjuna"

> Is lit by the white-light rosary
> Of the sayings of the glorious moon [Candrakīrti],

Whose expanding circle of stainless wisdom
Moves unimpeded through the sky of scripture,
Clearing the darkness of the heart that graps extremes,
Its brilliance obscuring the stars produced by falsehood.
(Tr. Gyaltsen Namdol and Ngagwang Samten)

SEE ALSO *glu, kāvya, mGur.*

the Society of Fireflies The Sosyete Koukouy (the Society of Fireflies) is a Haitian literary movement of poets who write in Creole, a language that originated as a mixture of French, spoken by white masters, and of the African languages and dialects of Black slaves. As Paul Laraque says, "It is a beautiful language with the rhythm of the drum and the images of a dream, especially in poetry, and a powerful weapon in the struggle of our people for national and social liberation." The Society of Fireflies was founded in 1965 by Pyè Banbou (Ernst Mirville), who was joined in Haiti by Togiram (Emile Célestin-Mégie), Jan Mapou (Jean-Marie Willer-Denis), and others, some of whom were jailed and exiled by the Duvalier dictatorship. Mapou extended the reach of the group to New York and Miami, Kaptenn Koukouwouj (Michel-Ange Hyppolite) to Ottawa. It includes Deita (Mercedès F. Guignard), one of the first Haitian women to have written and published poems in Creole, and Manno Ejèn, cofounder of the Haitian newspaper *Libète.* The group often wrote *wongòl,* a form invented in the sixties. It is a poem of two to six lines that contains a pointed (and often politically dissident) message. Thus Banbou writes:

In the land of Haiti
if you want to be rich
open a mortuary business.
(tr. Jack Hirschman and Boadiba)

somonka, see *tanka.*

song A musical composition intended or adapted for singing. Song was originally inseparable from poetry—they were one and the same—and poems were meant to be chanted and sung, sustained by oral tradition. Poetry is still considered song in many parts of the world, whether it is presented with or without musical accompaniment. The word *lyric* derives from the Greek *lyra,* or "musical instrument," and the Greeks spoke of lyrics as *ta mele,* "poems to be sung." Greek lyrics, poems to be sung to the lyre, took the form of either monodies, sung by a single person, or choral odes, sung by choirs. Sappho (late seventh century B.C.E.) was a monodist, Pindar (ca. 522–443 B.C.E.) an exponent of the choral form. His poems were simultaneously sung and danced. Epic poems were considered *aoidê,* or "singing." They were performative. The musical element is so intrinsic to poetry that one never forgets its origin in musical expression — in singing, chanting, and recitation to musical accompaniment.

Until the sixteenth century in Europe, poets were also composers and musicians. The poet was a performer — a bard, a skald, a scop, a troubadour. Heroic poems were sung (or chanted) and so were courtly love poems. There were professional and nonprofessional poets. One sang or listened to ballads, one shared hymns in church. Before the eighteenth century, writers or critics seemed to make little or no distinction between melodic lyrics, such as Thomas Campion's ayres ("Whoever dreams of a poem where language begins to resemble music, thinks of him," Charles Simic writes) or the songs of William Shakespeare's plays, and nonmusical written lyrics, such as Shakespeare's sonnets. Horace (65–8 B.C.E.) called the language of his satires, which are often close to daily speech, "singing." During the Renaissance, English writers first began to write their lyrics for readers rather than composing them for musical performance. The word *song* increasingly came to suggest a literary composition in verse form. Songs were still written for music, but the term *song* was also used metaphorically, as in Christopher Smart's "A Song to David" (1763) or William Blake's *Songs of Innocence and Experience* (1789), which are meant to be read.

SEE ALSO *air, aoidos, ballad, bard, canciones, chanson, epic, folk song, lyric, oral poetry, scop, skald, troubadour.*

songbook A collection of verses set to music. The "Great American Songbook," for example, refers to the vast repertoire of pre–World War II pop music, which includes such standards as "Alexander's Ragtime Band" (1911, Irving Berlin), "Someone to Watch Over Me" (1926, George and Ira Gershwin), "Ain't Misbehavin" (1929, Fats Waller), "I've Got You Under My Skin"

(1936, Cole Porter), and "My Funny Valentine" (1937, Richard Rodgers and Lorenz Hart).

There were various anthological *canzonierei,* or songbooks, in late medieval and Renaissance Italian poetry. These provided a lyrical prototype for Petrarch's *Il Canzoniere,* or *Songbook* (1374), which is also called in Latin *Rerum vulgarium fragmenta* (Fragments of Vernacular Poetry), his own nickname for the collection, and in Italian *Rime Sparse* (Scattered Rhymes). It includes 317 sonnets, twenty-nine *canzoni* or "songs," nine sestinas (one double), seven ballads, and four madrigals. Ever since Petrarch, the songbook has been used metaphorically to capture the oral power of "song" for the written lyric. Thus Unberto Saba evokes his great predecessor in his *Il Canzoniere* or *Songbook* (1900–1954), which he continued to update throughout his life.

SEE ALSO *ballad, canzone, chanson, madrigal, sestina, song, sonnet.*

sonnet The fourteen-line rhyming poem was invented in southern Italy around 1235 or so ("Eternal glory to the inventor of the sonnet," Paul Valéry declared) and has had a durable life ever since. The word *sonnet* derives from the Italian *sonetto,* meaning "a little sound" or "a little song," but the stateliness of the form belies the modesty of the word's derivation. The sonnet is a small vessel capable of plunging tremendous depths.

Something about the spaciousness and brevity of the fourteen-line poem seems to suit the contours of rhetorical argument, especially when the subject is erotic love. The form becomes a medium for the poet to explore his or her capacity to bring together feeling and thought, the lyrical and the discursive. The meter of the sonnet tends to follow the prevalent meter of the language in which it is written: in English, iambic pentameter; in French, the alexandrine; in Italian, the hendecasyllable. The two main types of sonnet form in English are the English, or Shakespearean sonnet (so-called because Shakespeare was its greatest practitioner), which consists of three quatrains and a couplet usually rhyming *abab, cdcd, efef, gg,* and the Italian, or Petrarchan sonnet (so-called because Petrarch was its greatest practitioner), which consists of an octave (eight lines rhyming *abbaabba*) and a sestet (six lines rhyming *cdecde*). The *volta,* or "turn," refers to the rhetorical division and shift between the opening eight lines and the concluding six.

The Petrarchan sonnet probably developed out of the Sicilian *strambotto,* a popular song form consisting of two quatrains and two tercets. The sonnet was widely practiced throughout the later Middle Ages by all the Italian lyric poets, especially the *stilnovisti*—Guinizelli, Cavalcanti, and Dante—who used it to reinvent the love poem as a medium of quasi-religious devotion to a beloved lady, a *donna.* (Giosuè Carducci wrote that Dante gave the sonnet "the movement of cherubim, and surrounded it with gold and azure air.") Petrarch's 317 sonnets to Laura are a kind of encyclopedia of passion. (Shelley called them "spells which unseal the inmost enchanted fountains of the delight which is the grief of love.") The Petrarchan sonnet invites an asymmetrical two-part division of the argument. Its rhyming is impacted and it tends to build an obsessive feeling in the octave that is let loose in the sestet. "One of the emotional archetypes of the Petrarchan sonnet structure," Paul Fussell says, "is the pattern of sexual pressure and release."

Sir Thomas Wyatt and the Earl of Surrey imported the Petrarchan form to England early in the sixteenth century. Surrey later established the rhyme scheme *abab, cdcd, efef, gg.* George Gascoigne described this new version of the sonnet in 1575:

> Sonnets are of fourteene lynes, every lyne conteyning tenne syllables. The first twelve do ryme in staves of foure lynes by crosse metre, and the last two ryming together do conclude the whole.

"SHAKE-SPEARE'S SONNETS. Neuer before imprinted" appeared in 1609, and these 154 sonnets comprise one of the high-water marks of English poetry. The Shakespearean sonnet invites a more symmetrical division of thought into three equal quatrains and a summarizing couplet. It is well-balanced, well-suited to what Rosalie Colie calls Shakespeare's "particularly brainy, calculated incisiveness." The form enables a precision of utterance and freedom of forensic argument. "The sonnet of Shakespeare is not merely such and such a pattern, but a precise way of thinking and feeling," T. S. Eliot notes. It also offers more flexibility in rhyming, which is crucial since Italian is so much richer in rhyme than English. (Nonetheless, "Ryme is no impediment to his conceit," Samuel Daniel wrote in a 1603 defense of rhyme, "but rather giues him wings to mount and carries him, not out of his course, but as it were beyond his power to a farre happier flight.") The poet using this logical structure can also create wild disturbances within the prescribed form. This seems to work especially well for closely reasoned and ultimately highly unreasonable and even obsessive subjects, like erotic love.

Over the centuries poets have proved ingenious at reinventing the formal chamber of the sonnet. The Elizabethan poet Edmund Spenser developed an interlacing version of the sonnet called the link or Spenserian sonnet. It interlinks rhymes and concludes with a binding couplet (*abab, bcbc, cdcd, ee*). The Miltonic sonnet retains the octave rhyme scheme of the Petrarchan sonnet, but doesn't turn at the sestet and varies its rhyme scheme, thus opening up the form. Milton further extended the form in a tailed sonnet, composed of twenty lines. He turned the sonnet away from love to occasional and political subjects ("When the Assault Was Intended to the City," 1642, "On the Late Massacre in Piedmont," 1655).

The sonnet was virtually extinct after 1650 until the romantic poets revitalized it. Leigh Hunts said, "Every mood of mind can be indulged in a sonnet; every kind of reader appealed to. You can make love in a sonnet, you can laugh in a sonnet, can narrate or describe, can rebuke, can admire, can pray." How much poorer English poetry would be without Wordsworth's "Composed upon Westminster Bridge, September 3, 1802," Keats's "On First Looking into Chapman's Homer" (1816), and Shelley's "Ozymandias" (1818). So, too, in France the sonnet was revived by Gautier (1811–1872) and Baudelaire (1821–1867) and further developed by Mallarmé (1842–1898), Rimbaud (1854–1891), and Valéry (1871–1945). George Meredith lengthened the traditional sonnet to sixteen lines in his fifty-poem sequence about the breakup of his marriage, *Modern Love* (1862). Gerard Manley Hopkins, whose so-called terrible sonnets are masterpieces of despair, also invented a form he called a curtal sonnet — literally, a sonnet cut short to ten and a half lines, such as "Pied Beauty" (1877), which ends with a simple directive: "Praise him." Hopkins also experimented with metrics in "Spelt from Sibyl's Leaves" (1886) ("the longest sonnet ever made"), which employs eight-stress lines and begins:

> Earnest, earthless, equal, attuneable, vaulty, voluminous, . . . stupendous
> Evening strains to be time's vast, womb-of-all, home-of-all, hearse-of-
> all night.

One thinks of Verlaine's "inverted" sonnets and Rupert Brooke's "Sonnet Reversed" (1911), which send up the tradition of idealized love, of Robert Frost's one-sentence sonnet "The Silken Tent" (1942) and W. H. Auden's sonnets about A. E. Housman, Arthur Rimbaud, and Edward Lear, a form used equally well by Jorge Luis Borges, who wrote sonnets about Ralph Waldo Emerson and Walt Whitman ("Emerson," "Camden 1892," 1964), among others. There are five edgy, almost hallucinatory one- and two-sentence sonnets in Denis Johnson's *The Incognito Lounge* (1982). John Hollander's *Powers of Thirteen* (1983) employs a variety of the sonnet form that consists of thirteen unrhymed lines of thirteen syllables each ("a thirteen by thirteen," he calls it, in which "the final line, uncoupled, can have the last word"). Mark Jarman has a series of seven-line poems he terms *half sonnets:* "My sense was and is that the seven-line half sonnet occurs either before or after the turn in the traditional sonnet; it might also include its own turn." Mona Van Duyn's *Firefall* (1983) includes a series of short poems she calls "minimalist sonnets" along with a few she baptizes (oxymoronically) "extended minimalist sonnets." "Of all the forms," she writes, "the sonnet seems most available to poets for deconstruction." In his poem "Post-Coitum Tristesse: A Sonnet" (1986), Brad Leithauser strips down the form to fourteen rhyming syllables (one per line) and, in so doing, takes the love poem all the way back to a sigh ("Hm . . ."). Edwin Morgan took a fourteen-word quote by John Cage, "I have nothing to say and I am saying it and that is poetry," and rearranged it fourteen times to create a fourteen-line sonnet called "Opening the Cage" (1968).

There is a sense of permanence and fragility, of spaciousness and constriction, about the sonnet form that has always had poets brooding over it, as in John Donne's well-known lines from "The Canonization" (1633):

> We'll build in sonnets pretty roomes;
> As well a well wrought urne becomes
> The greatest ashes, as halfe-acre tombes . . .

Poets have written a number of stylish sonnets about the sonnet itself. Eavan Boland and I begin our anthology on the sonnet with a section of twenty-seven poems called "The Sonnet in the Mirror" (2008). The form becomes the muse of these poems, which include Wordsworth's "Nuns fret not at their Convent's narrow room" (1806) and "Scorn not the Sonnet; Critic, you have frowned" (1827); Keats's "If by dull rhymes our English must be chain'd" (1819) ("Let us find out, if we must be constrain'd / Sandals more interwoven and complete / To fit the naked foot of poesy"); Edwin Arlington Robinson's "Sonnet" (1897), which begins "the master and the slave go hand in hand"; Robert Burns's joyous meditation on the quintessential *fourteen-ness* of the sonnet form, "A Sonnet upon Sonnets" (1788) ("Fourteen, a sonateer thy praises sings / What magic mys'tries in that number lie!"); and Dante Gabriel Rossetti's prefatory sonnet to *The House of Life* (1881), which begins

> A Sonnet is a moment's monument,—
> Memorial from the Soul's eternity
> To one dead deathless hour . . .

Every great sonnet is itself a moment's monument to the form itself. As Northrop Frye wrote about the Shakespearean sonnet, "The true father or shaping spirit of the poem is the form of the poem itself, and this form is a manifestation of the universal spirit of poetry."

SEE ALSO *alexandrine, courtly love, dolce stil novo, hendecasyllable, iambic pentameter, Petrarchism, Sicilian school, sonnet cycle.*

sonnet cycle The sonnet tends to be a compulsive form. As John Donne wryly put it, "The Spanish proverb informs me, that he is a fool which cannot make one sonnet, and he is mad which makes two." The sonnet cycle (or sonnet sequence) consists of a series of sonnets on a particular theme to a particular person. Love is often the obsessive theme of this petition for emotional recognition. The great advantage of the cycle is that it allows the poet to record every aspect and mood of the experience, to explore feeling in detail, and to analyze the progress of attachment, the ups and downs of the affair. Yet each individual sonnet maintains its energy and integrity. Thus the cycle combines the rhetorical intensity of the short poem with the thematic scope of the long poem or story.

Some key early examples: Dante's *Vita nuova* (1293), which has extensive prose links; Petrarch's *Canzoniere* or *Rime* (1360), a sequence of 317 sonnets and forty other poems in praise of one woman, Laura; Ronsard's *Amours* (1552–1584); Sidney's quasi-narrative *Astrophel and Stella* (1591): "My Muse may well grudge at my heav'nly joy"; Spenser's *Amoretti* (1595); and Shakespeare's *Sonnets* (1609): "Who will believe my verse in time to come?" There were no British sonnets before about 1530 and very few after 1650 until the romantic revival of the form. Some key romantic and postromantic examples of the sequence: Wordsworth's *Ecclesiastical Sonnets* (1822); Rossetti's *The*

House of Life (1881): "A sonnet is a coin: its face reveals / The soul, — its converse, to what Power 'tis due"; Elizabeth Barrett Browning's popular *Sonnets from the Portuguese* (1850); Dylan Thomas's ten-part "Altarwise by Owl-Light" (1936); W. H. Auden's "Sonnets from China" (1938); Geoffrey Hill's "Funeral Music" (1968); and Seamus Heaney's "Glanmore Sonnets" (1979).

One specialized version of the sonnet sequence is the corona, or crown of sonnets, which consists of seven interlocked poems. The final line of each lyric becomes the first line of the succeeding one, and the last line of the seventh sonnet becomes the first line of the opening poem. The whole is offered as a crown (a panegyric) to the one addressed. The repetitions and linkages within the larger circular structure are well-suited to obsessive reiterations of supplication and praise. A crowning fervent example is the opening sequence of Donne's *Holy Sonnets* (1633), which begins and ends with the line "*Deigne at my hands this crown of prayer and praise.*"

In our century, poets have also revitalized the sonnet sequence by revising and inverting some of its key generic conventions regarding gender. One thinks of the eleven explicitly homoerotic *Sonnets of Dark Love* that García Lorca composed in 1935, or of how the American female lyricists of the 1920s (Elinor Wylie, Edna St. Vincent Millay, and others) radicalized the traditional subject of the sonnet and the sonnet sequence by making the female speaker a ravenous lover — the authorizing presence — in quest of the beloved. So, too, such poets as Edwin Morgan (*Glasgow Sonnets,* 1972) and Tony Harrison (*From the School of Eloquence,* 1978) have used a tough-minded vernacular to deploy the sonnet as a site of class conflict. In our time many poets have also used the sonnet sequence as a vehicle to regain some of the scope and territory of prose fiction. One thinks of Gwendolyn Brooks's "The Womanhood" (1949), which intermingles sonnets with ballads and other poems, and James Merrill's witty masterpiece of childhood, "The Broken Home" (1966), of John Berryman's "Sonnets to Chris" (1947, 1966), which trace an adulterous affair ("The original fault was whether wickedness / was soluble in art"), and Robert Lowell's three books of highly personal unrhymed sonnets, *Notebook* (1969), *For Lizzie and Harriet* (1973), and *The Dolphin* (1973). "Even with this license, I fear I have failed to avoid the themes and gigantism of the sonnet," Lowell wrote. Thus the intensity and spaciousness of the form continues to incite poets.

SEE ALSO *sonnet.*

Sons of Ben, Tribe of Ben In the 1620s, Ben Jonson presided over a coterie of friends and admirers who met in the Apollo Room of the Devil and St. Dunstan Tavern in London. Jonson devised a set of *Leges Convivales,* which Alexander Brome translated as *Ben Jonson's Sociable Rules for the Apollo,* and wrote a welcoming poem inscribed next to the Bust of Apollo above the door: "Welcome all, who lead or follow, / To the Oracle of Apollo . . ."

Jonson established an ideal of friendship for a circle that included both poets and playwrights. The young writers, who called themselves Sons of Ben, were either directly associated with him or dedicated to his memory. They also styled themselves the Tribe of Ben. The poets included Robert Herrick, William Cartwright, Richard Corbet, and Thomas Randolph, who named him "the divine Ben, the Immortall Jonsön." Randolph's poem "A Gratulatory to Mr. Ben Jonson for His Adopting of Him to Be His Son" (ca. 1632) indicates that Jonson presided over rites to initiate his adopted "sons" into the ancient tribe of poets. Jonson's own poem "An Epistle Answering to One That Asked to Be Sealed of the Tribe of Ben" (1623) conducts an initiate to the center of the poet's central self.

Here is Herrick's poem "His Prayer to Ben Jonson" (*Hesperides,* 1648):

When I a verse shall make,
Know I have prayed thee,
For old religion's sake,
Saint Ben, to aid me.

Make the way smooth for me,
When I, thy Herrick,
Honoring thee, on my knee
Offer my lyric.

Candles I'll give to thee,
And a new altar;
And thou, Saint Ben, shalt be
Writ in my psalter.

SEE ALSO *Cavalier poets.*

sound poetry Sound is crucial to poetry and thus, in one sense, all poetry is sound poetry, except, perhaps, deaf poetry. Sidney Lanier emphasized the idea of sound in poetry when he commenced his treatise *The Science of English Verse* (1880) with an "Investigation of Sound as Artistic Material": "When formal poetry, or verse . . . is repeated aloud, it impresses itself upon the ear as verse only by means of certain relations existing among its component words considered purely as sounds, without reference to their associated ideas."

Sound poetry generally refers to a type of poetry that aggressively foregrounds the sounds of words. It is performance oriented and seeks to override conventional denotative and syntatical values. It goes beyond the page, beyond logocentrism, so that sound alone dominates. Sound poetry has its roots in preliterate oral traditions, in tribal chants and magic spells. The more extreme that nonsense poetry becomes, repressing sense, the more it tends toward sound poetry. There is a mode of tribal poetry that uses instruments to mimic the human voice. Thus the media of poetry in tonal languages includes drums, whistles, flutes, and horns. Whereas in American jazz, scat singers use their voices to create the equivalent of instrumental solos ("bap ba dee dot bwee dee"), in tribal poetries, musicians use their instruments to create the equivalent of human voices.

As a self-conscious avant-garde phenomenon, sound poetry dates to the early years of the twentieth century. The Russian futurists Aleksei Kruchenykh and Velimir Khlebnikov isolated the phonic aspects of language in their manifesto "The Word as Such" (1913), which insists that "the element of sound lives a self-oriented life." The Italian futurist F. T. Marinetti developed a poetic technique he called *parole in libertà,* or "words in freedom," which he used for his onomatopoetic *Bombardamento di Adrianapoli* (1913), to re-create the 1912 siege of Adrianopole. Sound poetry was explicitly a Dadaist creation, and the movement radiated outward from Zurich and Berlin. Hugo Ball claimed to have invented it at the Cabaret Voltaire in 1916. The spontaneous desire to rescue language and return it to its origins, to release its magical powers, helped motivate his "destruction of language." He said: "I invented a new genre of poems, verse without words, or sound poems. I recited the following: 'gadji beri bimba / glandridi lauli lonni cadori . . .' "

> In these phonetic poems we totally renounce the language that journalism has abused and corrupted. We return to the innermost alchemy of the word, we must even give up the word, too, to keep for

> poetry its last and holiest refuge. We must give up writing second-hand: that is, accepting words (to say nothing of sentences) that are not newly invented for our own use. Poetic effects can no longer be obtained in ways that are merely reflected ideas or arrangements of furtively offered witticisms and images.

Ball called these hypnotic nonce words *grammologues* or "magical floating words." There is a strong element of shock in the way the Dadaists used sound poetry to attack notions of reason, order, and control. For example, Ball joined Richard Huelsenbeck (1892–1974), Tristan Tzara (1896–1963), and Marcel Janco (1895–1984) in a simultaneist group poem in which all the participants were whistling, singing, speaking, and making noises at the same time. The Dadaists Raoul Hausmann (1861–1971) and Kurt Schwitters (1887–1948) both created their own versions of sound poems.

In 1921, Theo Van Doesburg, the founder of the Dutch avant-garde movement De Stijl, published three "letter-sound images" and asserted: "To take away its past it is necessary to renew the alphabet according to its abstract sound values. This means at the same time the healing of our poetic auditory membranes, which are so weakened, that a long term phono-gymnastics is necessary!" As early as 1919, Arthur Pétronio (1897–1983) invented something he called *verbophonie,* which harmonized phonetic rhythms with instrumental sounds, and the French Lettrists of the 1940s created full-scale sonic texts, a "New Alphabet." Since the 1950s, poets around the world have continued to experiment with sound compositions and soundscapes, often relying on technology to create startling new effects. Some examples: Henry Chopin's *audiopoems,* which Steve McCaffery calls a "technological attack upon the word," Bernard Heidsieck's *poempartitions* and *biopsies,* the text-sound compositions of the Swedish Fylkingen's Group for Linguistic Arts, Bob Cobbing's *Concrete Sound* ("a return to an emphasis on the physical structure of language"), Herman Damen's sonic genres *verbosony* and *verbophony,* Tera de Marez Oyens's *vocaphonies,* Jacson Mac Low's systematic chance operations. The Four Horsemen, a group of Canadian poets in the 1970s, started using their voices as instruments to celebrate vocal sound. Sound poetry is performance poetry. "When did you start writing sound-poetry?" the interviewer asks in Edwin Morgan's poem "Interview" (ca. 1981). The answer comically enacts sound poetry itself:

— Vindaberry am hookshma tintol ensa ar'er.
Vindashton hama haz temmi-bloozma töntek.

SEE ALSO *abstract poetry, Dadaism, De Stijl, drum poetry, futurism, Lettrisme, Merz, nonsense poetry, onomatopoeia, Optophonetics, oral poetry, parole in libertà, performance poetry, simultaneism, zaum.*

Spasmodic school W. E. Aytoun borrowed the term *spasmodic,* which was coined by Charles Kingsley (1853), to describe a group of popular neoromantic poets of the 1840s and '50s, who wrote inordinately long and turgid verse plays. The group included Alexander Smith (*A Life Drama,* 1853), Sydney Thompson Dobell (*Balder,* 1854), Philip James Bailey (*Festus,* 1839), and others. Aytoun's parody, *Firmilian: A Spasmodic Tragedy* (1854), mercilessly satirized the verse dramas and forced conceits of the group. Aytoun's hero hoped to "utter such tremendous cadences / That the mere babe who hears them at the breast . . . / Shall be an idiot to its dying hour!"

Critics and poets both (save I who cling
To older canons) have discarded sense,
And meaning's at a discount. Our young spirits,
Who call themselves the masters of the age,
Are either robed in philosophic mist,
And, with an air of grand profundity,
Talk metaphysics — which, sweet cousin, means
Nothing but aimless jargon — or they come
Before us in the broad bombastic vein,
With spasms, and throes, and transcendental flights,
And heap hyperbole on metaphor.

spectrism In 1916, Witter Bynner and Arthur Davison Ficke, two classically minded poets fed up with the proliferating movements of cubism, imagism, futurism, and vorticism, among others (Mary Ann Caws calls the twentieth century "a century of *isms*"), decided to launch their own fake group called the spectrists. Bynner (a.k.a. Emanuel Morgan), Ficke (a.k.a. Anne Knish), and later Marjorie Allen Seiffert (a.k.a. Elijah Hay) penned some deliberately bizarre poems, created a manifesto, and invented enigmatic personas for themselves. The result, *Spectra: A Book of Poetic Experiments* (1916), made a splash among the literati of the time. The magazine *Others,* for example, devoted a special issue to the movement. "The Spectric School of Poetry" fooled Harriet Monroe, Amy Lowell, William Carlos Williams, and others. The hoax lasted for two years. Morgan and Knish wrote:

> Laughter, dear friends, will do for kindling;
> And we shall wear ridiculous beads of flame
> To tinkle toward the corners of the world,
> Slapping with light the faces of old fools.

spell An incantation or charm designed to produce magical effects. "It is exceedingly well / To give a common word the spell," the eighteenth-century poet Christopher Smart writes, punning on the word *spell.* Tribal peoples everywhere have believed that the act of putting words in a certain rhythmic order has magical potency, a power released when the words are chanted aloud.

SEE ALSO *chant, charm, incantation, oral poetry.*

Spenserian stanza Edmund Spenser invented a nine-line pattern for his epic romance *The Faerie Queene* (1590–1596). The Spenserian stanza consists of eight iambic pentameter lines with a hexameter (alexandrine) at the end. It rhymes: *ababbcbcc.* The interweaving rhymes seem influenced by Chaucer's use of rhyme royal (seven-line stanzas rhyming *ababbcc*) and the Monk's Tale stanza (eight lines rhyming *ababbcbc*). It is also related to the eight-line or ottava rima stanza, which Ludovico Ariosto mastered in *Orlando Furioso* (1516), but it goes one step further, since the last line has a conclusive or epigrammatic power. It is a stanza of great versatility and enables Spenser to be lusciously dreamy and vividly narrative, brisk enough for quickly sketched vignettes, slow enough for visual description and philosophic speculation.

> Help then, O holy virgin, chief of nine,
> Thy weaker novice to perform thy will;
> Lay forth out of thine everlasting scrine [chest for records]
> The antique rolls [records], which there lie hidden still,
> Of faery knights and fairest Tanaquill,
> Whom that most noble Briton prince so long

Sought through the world and suffered so much ill
That I must rue his undeservèd wrong.
O help thou my weak wit, and sharpen my dull tongue.

The Spenserian stanza was dropped in the eighteenth century, but revived by the romantic poets. A good short list of the second flowering would include Wordsworth's "The Female Vagrant" (1798), Burns's "The Cotter's Saturday Night" (1785–1786), Scott's "The Vision of Don Roderick" (1811), Byron's *Childe Harold's Pilgrimage* (1812–1818), Keats's "The Eve of St. Agnes" (1819), and Shelley's "The Revolt of Islam" (1817) and "Adonais" (1821). Shelley declared that he adopted it for "The Revolt of Islam" not because he considered it a "finer model of poetical harmony than the blank verse of Shakespeare and Milton, but because in the latter there is no shelter for mediocrity; you must either succeed or fail."

SEE ALSO *Monk's Tale stanza, ottava rima, rhyme royal, terza rima.*

Spielmannsepen, see *epic.*

spirituals Sacred songs. The word *spiritual,* applied to religious songs, was initially used to distinguish "godly" songs from secular or "profane" ones. The spiritual developed from the folk hymns of dissenters in America. It generally refers to two closely connected bodies of music: white spirituals and African American spirituals. It was around the time of the Great Revival (1800) that *spiritual* became the name for revival hymns or camp-meeting songs. The *Standard Dictionary of Folklore, Mythology and Legend* (1972) points out that "its special application to Negro religious song is of fairly recent date as a catch-all term for the 'hallies,' shouts, jubilees, carols, gospel songs, and hymns for regular services, prayer meetings, watches, and 'rock' services."

White spirituals began with the doleful psalm-singing of the Puritans. The tradition was later enlivened by many splinter sects of Baptists and Methodists, who added marching and dancing rhythms, ballad tunes, and simple colorful lines suitable to frontier camp meetings. The Holiness Revival, which started around 1890 and still continues, added jazzy, syncopated rhythms. The songs are accompanied by instruments, such as the banjo and the guitar, once considered profane.

African American spirituals developed as the music of American slaves of African descent. They are formally an example of Afro-American hybridity, spiritually the substance of African American Christianity. They tell a story of suffering, endurance, and triumph, history and eternity. They seek absolute or ultimate justice. They use biblical stories to express the longing for delivery out of slavery:

> Go down Moses,
> Way down in Egypt land,
> Tell ole Pharaoh,
> To let my people go.

African American spirituals were not collected until after the Civil War. Three northerners, William F. Allen, Charles P. Ware, and Lucy McKim Garrison, made the first systematic collection, *Slave Songs of the United States* (1867), which included some of the spirituals that are still best known, such as "Old ship of Zion," "Lay this body down," "Michael, row the boat ashore," and "We will march through the valley." The songs were more widely introduced to the world by the Fisk University students, who toured the United States under the leadership of George White in 1871, singing the songs handed down from their slave parents. Cornell West states that "the spirituals of American slaves of African descent constitute the first expression of American modern music. How ironic that a people on the dark side of modernity — dishonored, devalued and dehumanized by the practices of modern Europeans and Americans — created the fundamental music of American modernity."

SEE ALSO *blues*.

spoken word poetry Poetry is an ancient oral art, but the spoken word movement developed in the late 1980s and early 1990s as a particular phenomenon. The term *spoken word* is a catch-all that includes any kind of oral art, including comedy routines and prose monologues, such as those by Spalding Gray. Spoken word poetry refers to any kind of poetry recited aloud: hip-hop, jazz poetry, poetry slams, traditional poetry readings. Perhaps its Ur form is performance poetry, which is kindred to performance art. Performance poems are explicitly written to be performed aloud; they tend to have a visceral spontaneity, a highly vocal, in-your-face quality. They are not meant to be read on the page, or sung. They are decidedly spoken.

The spoken word movement was inspired by the countercultural vitality of the Beat poetry of the 1950s. Allen Ginsberg stated categorically, "The spoken-word movement comes out of the Beats, but with rhyme added." Both movements disdain the academy. Spoken word poetry often carries a strong social critique, aggressive political commentary. It speaks up for those who are mostly unheard in society. Spoken word, as Bob Holman says, "has a rough-edged populist attitude, is intent on spreading the word of all poetry, and carries a democratizing energy." The setting is a key part of the experience, which has an element of the carnivalesque. Its great strength is that it is driven by the human voice.

SEE ALSO *dub poetry, jazz poetry, oral poetry, performance poetry, poetry contest, slam poetry, spontaneity, talk poem.*

spondee A poetic foot consisting of two equally accented syllables, as in the words *dáylíght* and *níghtfáll.* The Greek term for two spondees is *díspondee,* which we recognize in the words *hómemáde ártwórk.* The word *spondee* derives from *sponde* ("solemn libation"), and the Greek meter (two equally long syllables) was originally used in chants accompanying libations. It was a meter for making an offering, performing a rite. In accentual-syllabic poetry, spondees create an emphatic stress, a hammer beat, but seldom control an entire rhythm in English. The first, third, and fifth lines are spondaic in this anonymous nursery rhyme:

> Óne, twó
> Buckle my shoe;
> Thrée, fóur,
> Shut the door;
> Fíve, síx,
> Pick up sticks . . .

Since stress is always relative in English, there may be no perfect spondee.

SEE ALSO *foot, meter.*

spontaneity *Spontaneity* was originally a negative term, which was used against art that wasn't created by conscious design, but it was redeployed in the nineteenth century by the romantic poets. For them, spontaneity was a positive attribute, which suggested the self-generating quality of the poetic imagination, something impulsive, involuntary, unconstrained, inspired. Wordsworth defined poetry as the "spontaneous overflow of powerful feelings"; Keats maintained that "if Poetry comes not as naturally as the Leaves to a tree it had better not come at all"; Shelley rejected the idea that "the finest passages of poetry are produced by labor and study" and sought inspiration from the skylark's "unpremeditated art." Spontaneity, which has now become a somewhat old-fashioned term, was actually a rhetorical strategy of romantic poetry, a series of stylistic devices and conventions, to give the sensation of immediacy, the feeling of directness, the illusion of "spontaneous overflow." Nonetheless, it points to the uncontrollable aspect of writing poetry, the part connected to trances and charms, unconscious invention and free association, nonconsecutive reasoning, chance, imaginative power. It suggests that poetry is never entirely willed. The role of spontaneous creation tends to be discredited by those who concentrate entirely on the conscious, craftsmanlike aspects of writing poetry, extreme formalists, neoclassicists of all kinds, and endorsed as a doctrine by romantic and postromantic, modern (the Russian futurists, the French Surrealists), and postmodern poets (the New York school of poets) who invoke the magical potency of poetry, the wayward mystery of creativity.

SEE ALSO *afflatus, automatic writing, awen, Beats, charm, Dadaism, futurism, imagination, inspiration, invention, muse, neoclassicism, New York school of poets, primitivism, romanticism, simultaneism, Surrealism, zaum.*

Sprüche, see *minnesinger.*

sprung rhythm Gerard Manley Hopkins's term for a type of rhythm that depends solely on the number of stresses in a line. Sprung rhythm scans by counting accents and not syllables, like the accentual beat in Anglo-Saxon verse. It is a particular method of timing. Hopkins objected to the way that in most post-Renaissance English poetry a stressed syllable is accompanied by a uniform number of unstressed ones. He thought this was musically deadening. "Why do I employ sprung rhythm at all?" Hopkins wrote to Robert Bridges. "Because it is the nearest to the rhythm of prose, that is the native and natural rhythm of speech, the least forced, the most rhetorical and emphatic of all possible rhythms . . . combining . . . opposite and . . . incompatible excellences, markedness of rhythm — that is rhythm's self — and, naturalness of expression."

Here is an example of four lines in sprung rhythm from Hopkins's poem "The May-Magnificat" (1878). The first two lines have four streses each; the next two lines have three stresses each.

> Máy is Máry's mónth, and Í
> Múse at thát and wónder whý:
>   Her féasts fóllow réason,
>   Dáted dúe to séason — .

Hopkins thought of the rhythm of his poems as orally driven — "My verse is less to be read than heard," he said — and he believed that sprung rhythm could better capture the musical rhythms of speech than traditional meters. "The sense of pressure or stress is the sixth and radical sense in the experience of Hopkins," Geoffrey Hartman asserts. "It is evident to the tongue in reading his poetry."

SEE ALSO *counterpoint*, "pure accentual meter" in *meter, running rhythm.*

Stand Up poetry Taking a phrase from Edward Field's book, *Stand Up, Friend with Me* (1962), Charles Webb characterizes a kind of highly verbal poetry as Stand Up poetry. This type of poetry prizes clarity, the use of vernacular language ("Stand Up poetry embodies Wordsworth's famous dictum that poetry should be written in the language people actually use"), and a wide-open subject matter. It is a written, not an oral, poetry, but, like stand-up comedy, it prizes spontaneity, humor, and performability.

SEE ALSO *performance poetry, spoken word poetry, spontaneity, talk poem.*

stanza The natural unit of the lyric: a group or sequence of lines arranged in a pattern. A stanzaic pattern is traditionally defined by the meter and rhyme scheme, considered repeatable throughout a work. A stanzaic poem uses white space to create temporal and visual pauses. The word *stanza* means "room" in Italian — "a station," "a stopping place" — and each stanza in a poem is like a room in a house, a lyric dwelling place. "The Italian etymology," Ernst Häublein points out in his study of the stanza, "implies that stanzas are subordinate units within the more comprehensive unity of the whole poem." Each stanza has an identity, a structural place in the whole. As the line is a single unit of meaning, so the stanza comprises a larger rhythmic and thematic sequence. It is a basic division comparable to the paragraph in prose, but more discontinuous, more insistent as a separate melodic and rhetorical unit. In written poems stanzas are separated by white space, and this division on the printed page gives the poem a particular visual reality. The reader has to cross a space to get from one stanza to another. Stave is another name for stanza, which suggests an early association with song.

A stanza that consists of lines of the same length is called an isometric stanza. A stanza that consists of lines of varying length is called a heterometric stanza.

A stanza of uneven length and irregular pattern—of fluid form—is sometimes called quasi-stanzaic or a verse paragraph.

The monostich is a stanza—a whole poem—consisting of just one line. After that, there is the couplet (two-line stanza), tercet (three-line stanza), quatrain (four-line), quintet (five-line), sestet (six-line), septet (seven-line), and octave (eight-line). There are stanzas named after individual poets, such as the Spenserian stanza (the nine-line pattern Spenser invented for *The Faerie Queene,* 1590–1596) and the Omar Khyyám quatrain (the four-line stanza the Persian poet employed in the eleventh century for *The Rubáiyát*). Each stanza has its own distinctive features, its own music, and its own internal history that informs and haunts later usage.

SEE ALSO *couplet, heterometric stanza, isometric stanza, meter, monostich, octave, quatrain, quintet, rhyme, rubaiyat stanza, septet, sestet, Spenserian stanza, stave, stichic, strophe, tercet, verse paragraph.*

stasiotika, see *political poetry.*

stave A synonym for *stanza,* the stave, a set of verses, may once have been limited to poems that were sung, such as hymns.

A stave in music is a staff, a set of horizontal lines and intermediate spaces used in notation to represent a sequence of pitches. It normally consists of five lines and four spaces in modern notation.

SEE ALSO *stanza.*

stich, stichos The Greek word *stichos* means a "row" or "line," and a stich is a line of Greek or Latin verse. Half of a line is called a hemistich, a sole line (or a one-line poem) is called a monostich, and a couplet is called a distich.

SEE ALSO *couplet, hemistich, line, monostich, stichic.*

stichic A stichic poem is composed as a continuous sequence of lines without any division of those lines into regular stanzas. Contrasted to strophic organization, where the lines are patterned in stanzas, it is thus astrophic. *Paradise Lost* (1667), *The Prelude* (1805, 1850), and *Four Quartets* (1943) are stichic; *The Faerie Queene* (1590–1596), "Ode to a Nightingale" (1819), and "Asphodel, That Greeny Flower" (1955) are strophic. If subdivided at all, the blocks of a stichic poem are called stanzas of uneven length, or verse paragraphs. The tendency toward stichic verse is particularly strong in narrative and descriptive poetry, in long poems with the wide sweep of prose, such as A. R. Ammons's *Tape for the Turn of the Year* (1994), John Ashbery's *Flow Chart* (1991), and W. S. Merwin's *The Folding Cliffs: A Narrative* (1998).

SEE ALSO *descriptive poetry, narrative poetry, stanza, strophe, verse paragraph.*

stichomythia Greek: "line-speech," or speaking in alternating lines. *Stichomythia* is a term that derives from classical Greek drama. There are alternating exchanges in Euripides (480?–406 B.C.E.), for example, which continue for more than one hundred lines. Stichomythia is often formally employed, in drama and poetry, for rapid dialogue, witty repartee, and fierce dispute, as in the furious exchange between Hamlet and his mother at the outset of the closet scene in *Hamlet* (1603):

> QUEEN. Hamlet, thou hast thy father much offended.
> HAM. Mother, you have my father much offended.
> QUEEN. Come, come, you answer with an idle tongue.
> HAM. Go, go, you question with a wicked tongue.

Hemistichomythia is the name for a dialogue when characters exchange short utterances of half a line each, as in Eurpides's *Bacchae* (966–970). It is often used for cutting arguments. The alternation of two-line speeches is called distichomythia. The abrupt breaking of a line between two speakers is called *antilabé.* Sophocles employs *antilabé* in *Oedipus the King* (626–29) when Oedipus and the herdsmen share a series of lines as he puts together the final terrible clues to his identity.

SEE ALSO *dialogue, hemistich.*

De Stijl The avant-garde artistic movement De Stijl ("The Style") flourished in the Netherlands from 1927 to 1931. It is also known as neoplasticism. The artists sought "ideal" geometric forms. The founder of the group, Theo van Doesburg, wanted to renovate modern literature as well as art. The group, which included the painter Piet Mondrian and the architect J.J.P. Oud, published a manifesto that called for a new poetry to overcome rationality and engender "the spiritual renovation of the word." The devices would be syntax, prosody, topography, arithmetic, and orthography. Much of the actual poetry of De Stijl is a form of either concrete or sound poetry.

SEE ALSO *concrete poetry, sound poetry.*

stilnovismo, stilnovisti, see *dolce stil novo.*

stock response A predictable, habitual, or stereotyped reaction to a literary text. I. A. Richards gave currency to this usually pejorative term for ready-made responses, an "important, neglected, and curious topic," in *Practical Criticism* (1929), where he regards stock responses as "energy systems which have the right of entry, unless some other system of greater energy can bar them out or perhaps drain their energy away from them." Poets themselves can import stock rhythms and stock ideas into their poems, and Richards calls Thomas Gray's "Elegy in a Country Churchyard" (1750) "perhaps the best example in English of a good poem built upon a foundation of stock responses."

SEE ALSO *convention.*

stornello, see *ritornello.*

stress, see *beat.*

strambotto One of the oldest Italian verse forms, the *strambotto* was a rustic song commonly set to music, which consists of a single six- or eight-line stanza in eleven-syllable lines (hendecasyllabics). It was a self-contained unit that could rhyme in various ways: *ababab; ababcc; aabbcc; abababab; ababccdd; abababcc; aabbccdd.*

The *ottava siciliana* (Sicilian octave) or *strambotto popolare,* which rhymed alternately *abababab,* was especially popular in the south, whereas the *strambotto toscano* or ottava rima form, which rhymed alternately with a concluding couplet (*abababcc*), flourished in Tuscany. The Sicilian octave, which dates to the thirteenth century, did not survive, but the Tuscan form, which flourished during the Renaissance, became the staple of Italian narrative poetry. It migrated to Spanish, Portuguese, and English poetry, and became part of German and Slavic poetry. It is likely that the *strambotto* was incorporated into the Italian sonnet, which was created at the Sicilian court. Create a hybrid out of the eight- and six-line stanza, and you get the sonnet form.

SEE ALSO *hendecasyllabics, octave, ottava rima, rispetto, Sicilian school, sonnet.*

strategy The word *strategy,* which derives from the Greek for "office or command of a general," refers to the tactical plan of a poem, its method of attack, its craft. The military term first started to be deployed by literary critics in the 1930s. Kenneth Burke argues in "Literature as Equipment for Living" (1941) that poetry is basically a strategy for dealing with a situation, "handling" and "encompassing" it:

> For surely, the most alembicated and sophisticated work of art, arising in complex civilizations, could be considered as designed to organize and command the army of one's thoughts and images, and so to organize them that one "imposes upon the enemy the time and place and condition for fighting preferred by oneself." One seeks to "direct the larger movements and operations" in one's campaign of living. One "maneuvers" and the maneuvering is an "art."

SEE ALSO *New Criticism, symbolic action.*

strict-meter poetry, free-meter poetry In the first half of the fourteenth century, Einion the Priest divided all Welsh meters into three categories: *awdl, cwydd,* and *englyn.* Revised by Dafydd ab Edmwnd in 1450, this arrangement of the "twenty-four metres" into three classes has defined "strict-metre" poetry. All other forms that fell outside the twenty-four meters were considered free-meter poetry. The breakdown of the Bardic orders also led to the rise of the free meters. The resurgence of strict-meter poetry in modern Welsh poetry is a striking development. "At no time since the Middle Ages has such poetry ceased to be composed, but it certainly fell out of fashion amongst the leading poets of the mid-twentieth century," D. R. Johnson explains. "Its revival since the 1960s is part of a new interest in traditional culture, and a prominent role has been played by folk poets such as Dic Jones, whose talent has been nurtured by association with a remarkable circle of poets in south Cardiganshire extending back into the nineteenth century." There is a strong nationalistic dimension to the metrical revival.

SEE ALSO *awdl, bard, cwydd, eisteddfod, englyn.*

strophe A term for stanza or verse paragraph. A poem is traditionally considered strophic when its lines are arranged into stanzaic patterns, and astrophic or stichic when not. There is a strong tendency in some poetries to arrange poems into recognizable units of two, three, four, five, six, or more lines. European folk songs, for example, are strophic. The word *strophe* (from the Greek for "turning") originally applied to the opening section (and every third succeeding section) of the Greek choral ode, which the chorus chanted while moving across the stage. This movement was followed by the antistrophe, an identical countermovement, and an epode, recited while the chorus was standing still.

SEE ALSO *antistrophe, epode, ode, stanza, stichic, verse paragraph.*

structuralism Structuralism is a mode of analysis that originated in linguistics. In his *Cours de linguistic générale* (Course in General Linguistics), given between 1906 and 1911, Ferdinand de Saussure distinguished between synchronic analysis (the study of language as a functioning totality at any given moment) and diachronic analysis (the study of changes in language through historical periods). He also made a crucial distinction between *langue* (language), which represents the system of any particular language, its particular set of interpersonal norms and rules, and *parole* (speech or utterance), which embodies the particular utilizations of the system, its actual manifestations in speech and writing. Language exists apart from speech. It is thus "outside the individual who can never create nor modify it by himself."

The material of linguistics is the sign, which consists of a sound image, which he called the signifier, such as D-O-G, and the concept, which he named the signified, such as the animal that comes to mind when we think of dog. The connection between them is arbitrary. Saussure's theory of the sign is not concerned with a sign's ultimate referent in the world. "In language, there are only differences," he claimed:

> Even more important: a difference generally implies positive terms between which the difference is set up; but in language there are only differences *without positive terms.* Whether we take the signified or the signifier, language has neither ideas nor sounds that existed before the linguistic system, but only conceptual and phonic differences that have issued from the system.

Signs are not "positive terms" because they don't have meanings of their own. They take on meaning only in relationship to other signs.

Saussure and his followers also considered two relationships between linguistic terms, two axes of language: *syntagmatic* refers to the rules that govern the order of words (it specifies the relationship that a word has with other words in a sequence), whereas *paradigmatic* refers to distinctions among a category of words (it concerns the possible substitution for any particular word or set of words).

Saussure's theories were later developed into the structuralist systematizations of different human sciences, including folklore, anthropology, and literature. "Although they belong to *another order of reality,* kinship phenomena are *of the same type* as linguistic phenomena," Claude Lévi-Strauss argued. Structuralism became a method of analysis, a way of studying relations among terms. It posited itself as a science, hence Tvetan Todorov's claim: "The structural analysis of literature is nothing more than an attempt to transform literary studies into a scientific discipline . . . a coherent body of concepts and methods aiming at the knowledge of underlying laws." Roland Barthes spoke of structuralism as "essentially an *activity,* that is to say the ordered sequence of a certain number of mental operations."

The first premise of the structuralist approach to poetry is that a poem is a linguistic product, which can be analyzed only when its constituent parts are studied in relationship to each other. Poems are primarily self-referential. "Focus on the message for its own sake is the poetic function of language," the linguist Roman Jakobson writes. Or as J. Mukarovsky puts it: "the function of poetic language consists in the maximum foregrounding of the utterance." The relations that are most important for structural analysis are binary oppositions, a pair of terms or concepts that are theoretical opposites. Poems are examined through the lens of such binary oppositions as love versus hatred, absence versus presence, reason versus instinct, and mortality versus eternity. Jakobson considered binary oppositions inherent in languages, and structuralists have generally considered binary systems as a fundamental operation of the human mind.

The structuralist critic tries to unearth the underlying system of relationships that makes possible a literary work. Robert Scholes adds in *Structuralism in Literature* (1974) that "poetry has also proved . . . less amenable to structuralist criticism than fiction."

SEE ALSO *deconstructon, intertextuality, New Criticism, Russian formalism.*

structure A structure is something built or constructed—a building, a bridge, a dam. Poetry borrows a term from architecture to account for the system of relations in a literary work. Structure is the developing or organizational means of a patterned work of art. The New Critics made the term one of the cornerstones of the attempt to differentiate the individual poem from a prose statement. Thus John Crowe Ransom advocated for a "structural understanding of poetry" and divided a poem into two constituent parts: "a central logic or understanding" and a "local texture" ("Criticism as Pure Speculation," 1941). The logical core of a poem constitutes its structure.

The term *structure* is sometimes misconstrued as form and often wavers in meaning because it takes a spatial metaphor and applies it to temporal work. Ellen Bryant Voigt argues that "structure is the way all the poem's materials are organized, whether they are abstract or concrete, precise or suggestive, denoted or connoted, sensory or referential, singular or recurring." She calls structure "the purposeful order in which materials are released to the reader." Michael Theune defines structure as "*the pattern of a poem's turning*" and thus focuses on the skeletal part of a poem's structure. For example, the structure of the Petrarchan sonnet would hinge on the *volta,* or turn, the movement between the opening eight lines (octave) and the concluding six (sestet), the two constituent parts.

A dramatic structure refers to the way that a play is organized, its unfolding plot. It has temporal divisions, a beginning, middle, and end. The New Critics applied the idea of dramatic structure to lyric poetry. Thus Robert Penn Warren describes dramatic structure as "a movement through action toward rest, through complication toward simplicity of effect" ("Pure and Impure Poetry," 1942). This involves, as Warren himself recognized, the active participation of the reader. In his book *Frame Analysis* (1974), the sociologist Erving Goffman took the idea of dramatic structure and applied it to social situations in everyday life.

SEE ALSO *form, New Criticism, sonnet, texture.*

Sturm und Drang "Storm and Stress." In English, the phrase *Sturm und Drang* is used in a general way to refer to an exuberant outburst of youthful emotion. It refers more specifically and originally to a group of young German writers who flourished in the 1770s. The Stürmer und Dränger revolted against the neoclassical values of objectivity and rationalism with a revolutionary commitment to passion. They were driven by the urge for self-realization and created an intensely personal literature. The name Sturm und Drang is taken from the title that Christoph Kaufmann, who called himself "God's Bloodhound," proposed in 1776 for a play by his friend F. M. Klinger, which was instead called *Wirrwarr* (Confusion). The older name for the period, *Geniezeit* (Age of Geniuses), was thus recast as Sturm und Drang, an era that valued creative confusion over settled orderliness. Johann Wolfgang von Goethe (1749–1832), the central figure of the group, gives a vivid account of it in his unfinished autobiography, *From My Life: Poetry and Truth, 1811–1833.* The Sturm und Drang movement was largely characterized by Goethe's emotional lyrics, which express a deep longing to merge with nature; his plays, especially *Götz von Berlichingen Ironhand* (1771, 1773); and his novel *The Sorrows of Young Werther* (1774), which set off a furor because of its insights into a young man who commits suicide over a hopeless love affair. The group included Johann Heinrich Merck, "a singular man," Goethe said in his autobiography, "who had the greatest influence on my life"; the playwright Jakob Michael Reinhold Lenz, who influentially argued against the dramatic unities of time, place, and action; and Friedrich Maximilian Klinger himself, who was nicknamed the "lion's-blood-drinker." The young Friedrich Schiller had no personal links to the group, but his early work shows some of the same stylistic and thematic concerns. The movement was in large part propelled by the intellectual energy of Johann Gottfried Herder, who was in turn inspired by the ideas of Johann Georg Hamann and Jean-Jacques Rousseau. Herder argued that the advance of civilization had alienated humankind from nature and proposed turning for inspiration to the folk arts of people most closely in touch with the natural world, the *Volk.* Herder and Goethe made poetry central to the Sturm und Drang enterprise. They attacked the eighteenth-century idea of poetry as "the handmaiden of polite society" and sought to restore its ancient archaic power, a robust vitality they found in folk songs and primitive poetry, in Ossian, whom Goethe translated, Homer, and Shakespeare.

SEE ALSO *Enlightenment, folk song, neoclassicism, oral poetry, romanticism, sensibility, sentimentality.*

style The manner of linguistic expression in a work of literature, the way in which something is said or done, expressed, written. Style is a quality of distinctive features — the choice of words, the figures of speech, the rhetorical devices, etc. — that belong to an individual, a group, a school, or an era. In classical theories of rhetoric, styles were traditionally classified into three main types: high (or grand), middle (or mean), low (or plain). The level of style was matched to the speaker and the occasion. In poetry, styles are often classified according to the distinctive features of an individual writer (Chaucerian, Miltonic), an influential text (biblical style), or a literary period or tradition (metaphysical, Georgian). In the end, style cannot be separated from meaning. It is a way a work carries itself.

SEE ALSO *decorum, figures of speech, poetic diction, rhetoric.*

stylistics A twentieth-century invention, stylistics has its roots in the classical study of rhetoric. It derives its name from the Greek *techne rhetorike,* the art of speech, which was concerned with the art of speech as a means of persuasion. "Stylistics," to quote one textbook on the subject, "is the study of the ways in which meaning is created through language in literature as well as in other types of text." Stylistics as an approach, which began to flourish in the 1960s, was spurred by the work of the Russian formalists and the New Critics to make literary inquiry more "scientific." A key text was Roman

Jakobson's "Linguistics and Poetics" (1960). Stylistics proposes itself as an analytical science, which uses linguistic models to describe how texts work the way they do. It tries to take into account all the expressive aspects of language: phonology, prosody, morphology, syntax, and lexicology.

SEE ALSO *affective stylistics, rhetoric, Russian formalism, structuralism.*

the sublime The *Oxford English Dictionary* defines the *sublime* as "Set or raised aloft, high up." The word derives from the Latin *sublimis,* a combination of *sub* (up to) and *limen* (lintel, the top piece of a door) and suggests nobility and majesty, the ultimate height, a soaring grandeur, as in a skyscraper or a mountain, or as in a dizzying feeling, a heroic deed, a spiritual attainment, a poetic expression — something that takes us beyond ourselves, something boundless, the transporting blow. "The essential claim of the sublime," Thomas Weiskel asserts in *The Romantic Sublime* (1986), "is that man can, in feeling and in speech, transcend the human." The sublime instills a feeling of awe in us, which can be terrifying. The *Oxford English Dictionary* also describes the effects of the sublime as crushing or engulfing, something that cannot be resisted. The sublime is one of our large metaphors. As Weiskel puts it, "We cannot conceive of a literal sublime."

In the third century, Longinus inaugurated the literary idea and tradition of the sublime in his treatise *Peri Hypsous* (*On the Sublime*). For him, the sublime describes the heights in language and thought. It is accessed through rhetoric, the devices of speech and poetry. It is a style of "loftiness," something we experience through words. "Sublimity is always an eminence and excellence in language," he claims. "It is our nature to be elevated and exalted by true sublimity. Filled with joy and pride, we come to believe we have created what we have only heard." The sublime is our "joining" with the great. Longinus raised the rhetorical and psychological issues that haunt the idea of the sublime, ancient and modern. As Mary Arensberg summarizes them in *The American Sublime* (1986):

1. The experience of the sublime is an affective or emotional response (joy and ecstasy) to power, authenticity or authority.
2. This power is perceived in a moment (like a "lightning-flash") through the effects of speech and language.
3. The sublime moment is preceded by a disruption in normal con-

sciousness ("parts all matter this way and that") whose equilibrium must be restored.

4. Equilibrium is seemingly restored through an identification with that power or authority ("exalts our soul as though we had created what we merely heard") and a repression of that power.
5. The repression takes the form of a defense (in this case mimesis) in which the reader makes the sublime her own.

Longinus's treatise was translated into French by Boileau (1674) and passed quickly into English. Alexander Pope claimed that Longinus "is himself the great Sublime he draws" ("An Essay on Criticism," 1711). Edmund Burke took up the effects of the sublime in language in *A Philosophical Inquiry into the Origin of Our Ideas of the Sublime and Beautiful* (1756), where he argues that the sublime and the beautiful are mutually exclusive. He adds terror as a crucial component. "Whatever is fitted in any sort to excite the ideas of pain and danger, that is to say, whatever is in any sort terrible, or is conversant about terrible objects, or operates in a manner analogous to terror, is a source of the *sublime;* that is, it is productive of the strongest emotion which the mind is capable of feeling." There are subsequent philosophical investigations of the sublime in Kant, who says "We call that sublime which is absolutely great" (*Critique of Judgment,* 1790), Schopenhauer (the first volume of *The World as Will and Representation,* 1819), and Hegel (*Aesthetics: Lectures on Fine Art,* 1835). "In the European Enlightenment," Harold Bloom explains, the literary idea of the sublime "was strangely transformed into a vision of the terror that could be perceived both in nature and in art, a terror uneasily allied with pleasurable sensations of augmented power, and even of narcissistic freedom, freedom in the shape of that wildness that Freud dubbed 'the omnipotence of thought,' the greatest of all narcissistic illusions."

The romantic poets were obsessed with sublimity; that is, with the idea of transcendence, with possible crossings between the self and nature, with the boundlessness of the universe. Each had a different idea of transcendence, as when Keats distinguished the true poetical character, which is selfless, from "the Wordsworthian or egotistical sublime," a sublime suffused with the self. Wordsworth himself called the elevation of the sublime a "visionary gleam." The romantics transformed the sublime into a naturalistic key, internalizing it, which opened a space later entered by Freud, who was preoccupied with powerfully disruptive and uncanny moments.

In America, the sublime has its own genealogy and history, its own recurring questions and immensities. "How does one stand / To behold the sublime?" Wallace Stevens asks in his poem "The American Sublime" (1936). In "Self-Reliance" (1841), Emerson takes up Longinus's idea of the reader's sublime when he declares that "in every work of genius we recognize our own rejected thoughts; they come back to us with a certain alienated majesty."

Ever since Whitman (1819–1892), our poets have been magnetized by the power of the American sublime, the engulfing space that Emerson delineates as "*I and the Abyss,*" the intractable sea that Stevens confronts in "The Idea of Order at Key West" (1936), which contains a direct echo of Whitman's poem "Out of the Cradle Endlessly Rocking" (1860). The strip of land at the boundary of the fathomless sea is comparable to the liminal space that Robert Frost repeatedly encounters at the edge of a dark wood, the majestic space where, as Emily Dickinson says memorably, "The Soul should stand in Awe." The feeling of awe bears traces of a holiness galvanized and deepened by the mysterious presence of death. Irving Howe spoke of "a democratized sublime," a space for schooling the spirit.

SEE ALSO *picturesque, rhetoric, the uncanny.*

surah, sura The Koran is organized by surahs (chapters) and verses. There are 114 individually named surahs. Each surah consists of any number of verses and, except for surah 9, begins with the invocation "In the name of God, the merciful, the beneficent." The word *surah* is used exclusively to describe the Koran's divisions.

the Surprised Poetry The Surprised Poetry movement was launched in 1943 in the Dominican Republic with the publication of the journal *La Poesía sorprendida.* The Surprised Poets, who were influenced by the late Surrealists, were internationalists committed to taking Dominican poetry away from regional writing and expanding its reach: "We are for a national poetry nourished in the universal, the only proper form of being." They created a more inclusive and outward-looking poetry than the preceding movements, such as Indianismo, Costumbrismo, and Posthumanismo, which they considered provincial. The group, which reveled in free creativity and took "the path of evasion" to avoid censorship, included Franklin Mieses Burgos, Freddy Gatón Arce, Manuel Rueda, and especially Aída Cartagena Portalatín.

SEE ALSO *Surrealism, universality.*

Surrealism The convulsive phenomenon known as Dadaism was revitalized and transformed into the more durable movement of Surrealism in France in the 1920s. The term *surréaliste* was coined by Guillaume Apollinaire in 1917 to suggest a dramatic attempt to go beyond the limits of an agreed-upon "reality." André Breton used the term *Surrealism* ("superrealism," or "above reality") in 1924 in the first of three manifestoes. ("I believe in the future resolution of these two states, dream and reality, which are seemingly so contradictory, into a kind of absolute reality, a *surreality.*") The Surrealists were apostles of what Breton called "beloved imagination." They hungered for the marvelous and believed in the revolutionary power of erotic desire and "mad love," of dreams, fantasies, and hallucinations. They freed the mind from the shackles of rational logic and explored the subterranean depths, the deeper reality, of the unconscious, the night mind. They cultivated a condition of lucid trance or delirium and experimented with automatic writing or automatism — that is, writing attempted without any conscious control, as under hypnosis. The Surrealists courted disorder and believed in the possibilities of chance, of emotion induced by free association and surprising juxtapositions, as when Lautréamont had called something "Beautiful as the chance meeting, on a dissection table, of a sewing machine and an umbrella."

The Surrealists were scandalized by the repressiveness of society, and they scandalized society in return. They wanted to change the human condition. A practical, political dimension entered the movement in 1925, linking economic revolution with mental liberation (priority was always given to mental experiments), and a problematic relationship developed with the Communist party, which never quite flowered into a full-scale alliance.

The Surrealists' true goal was inner freedom. André Breton states in the second manifesto (1929):

> The idea of Surrealism tends simply to the total recuperation of our psychic forces by a means which is no other than a vertiginous descent within ourselves, the systematic illumination of hidden places, the

> progressive darkening of all other places, the perpetual rambling in the depths of the forbidden zone.

The Surrealists reiterated their faith in love, liberty, and the arts. (Robert Desnos called one work *La liberté ou l'amour!,* 1927; Paul Éluard entitled another *L'amour la poésie,* 1929.)

The major Surrealists in poetry: André Breton, Louis Aragon, Robert Desnos, Paul Éluard, Philippe Soupault, Benjamin Peret. In the visual arts: Man Ray, Picabia, de Chirico, Masson, Tanguy, Ernst, Dali. In film: Luis Buñuel. In theater: Antonin Artaud. Breton acknowledged that Surrealism was the "prehensile tail" of romanticism. The Surrealists recognized their ongoing debts to the Marquis de Sade (1740–1814) and Gérard de Nerval (1808–1855), who first used the term *supernaturalism,* to Charles Baudelaire (1821–1867) and Stéphane Mallarmé (1842–1898), who considered the poet a magician, to Rimbaud (1854–1891), Apollinaire (1880–1918), and Freud (1856–1939).

Surrealism dissolved as a cohesive movement in the late 1930s, but the United States benefited from the wartime presence of some of the leading Surrealist figures, such as Breton and Ernst. In a broad sense, Surrealism means a love of dreams and fantasies, a taste for strange marvels and black humor, an eagerness to take the vertiginous descent into the self in quest of the secret forces of the psyche, a faith in the value of chance encounters and free play, a belief in the liberating powers of eros, of beloved imagination.

SEE ALSO *aleatory, automatic writing, Dadaism, imagination, metagram, romanticism.*

sutra In Sanskrit, a *sutra* is literally a "thread" (the word derives from a verbal root meaning "to sew") or line that holds things together. It generally refers to an aphorism or a collection of aphorisims in the form of a manual. In Hinduism, the sutras (500–200 B.C.E.) are treatises that deal with Vedic rituals and customary laws. They provide concise surveys of past literature in mnemonic, aphoristic form. It is as if the book of Leviticus were written in verse that could be easily memorized. In Buddhism, the term *sutra* generally refers to the oral teachings of the Buddha.

The Beat poets very loosely adapted the word *sutra* to refer to rules that hold an idea together, as in Jack Kerouac's sutra on Buddhist philosophy, *The Scripture of the Golden Eternity* (1960), a book of sixty-six prose poems, or Allen

Ginsberg's "Wichita Vortex Sutra" (1966), his long poem against the Vietnam War that he spoke into a tape recorder while traveling across the American heartland. Ginsberg's "Sunflower Sutra" (1955) "reflects the Buddhist idea that life and death are inseperable," Amanda Porterfield explains: "Seeing the beauty of a sunflower in its dead and dusty manifestation beside the railroad tracks is like seeing the Buddha in a corpse, or like finding enlightenment, as the Buddha did, simply by sitting down under a tree and becoming completely attuned to the mind-stream of reality." Gary Snyder's "Smokey the Bear Sutra" (1969) follows the structure of a Mahayana Buddhist sutra. "Now those who recite this Sutra and then try to put it in practice," Snyder declares, "[w]ill win the tender love and caresses of men, women, and beasts."

SEE ALSO *Beats, rasa.*

the sweatshop poets Appalled by the working conditions in New York sweatshops, four politically engaged Yiddish poets, all immigrants — Morris Rosenfeld, Morris Winchevsky, David Edelshtadt, and Joseph Bovshover — bonded together to create the "sweatshop" or "labor" poets, a school of Yiddish poetry. In the 1890s and early 1900s, these worker-poets employed poetry to enlighten Jewish workers. Unlike the later socially minded Jewish poets of the 1930s, the sweatshop poets wrote protest poetry out of their own working experiences. "The bloody dramas of these times," as Edelshtadt put it in "To the Muse" (ca. 1882–1892), "were staged within my breast." Rosenfeld, who sang his poems and was often scorned by fellow writers, was especially beloved by workers and achieved a fleeting fame outside the Yiddish-speaking world when Leo Wiener, a Harvard professor of Slavic languages, translated *Songs from the Ghetto* (1899). "The nightingale sings even in the sweat-shop," William Dean Howells wrote in a review. "Here is 'The Song of the Shirt' from one who made the shirt."

SEE ALSO *the Introspectivists, the Young Ones.*

syllable The syllable is the smallest measurable unit of poetic sound. *Verse* is a monosyllabic word (composed of one syllable), *poetry* is a polysyllabic one (composed of multiple syllables). "English speech is carried on a stream of *syllables,* each one a little articulation of energy produced by the muscles that expel air out of the mouth, shaped by the vocal cords and the organs of the mouth," Derek Altridge writes in *Poetic Rhythm* (1995).

The syllable is the sole constituent in pure syllabic meter. Syllabic verse is common in languages that are syllable-timed, such as Japanese. It is less common in English, which is a stress-based language. Most traditional English poetry is thus accentual-syllabic; it counts both stresses and syllables. Pure syllabics, which counts only syllables, is rarer in English-language verse.

In English, syllabics is a numerical system the poet uses to structure the poem. It is a method of organization, a sort of game or puzzle, which has to do with counting. It is imposed but it doesn't necessarily *feel* imposed. Elizabeth Daryush (1887–1977) in England and Marianne Moore (1887–1972) in America pioneered the use of syllabic verse in modern poetry. They played with — and defied — the expectations of iambic verse. In our era, such poets as Thom Gunn and Richard Howard have been able to create a feeling of ease and flexibility, a natural-sounding verse in syllabics.

SEE ALSO *beat*, "pure syllabic meter" in *meter*.

syllepsis Syllepsis ("taking together") is a figure of speech in which one word syntactically applies to two or more others, but has a different meaning in relation to each of the words. For example, in Ovid's *Metamorphoses* (8 C.E.), Alcmaeon, who is persecuted by the Furies, is described as *exul mentisque domusque*, "an exile from his wits and from his home." This is something we understand both metaphorically ("an exile from his wits" is a clever way of saying that someone has lost his mental capacities, his sanity) as well as literally ("an exile from his home" suggests that someone can no longer return to the place where he once lived). The syllepsis is a form of witty surprise in poetry when the same word is taken in both a literal and a figurative sense within a single phrase. It is a mixed trope, a coin with two sides. Ovid glides so fluently between the literal and the figurative, or supposedly figurative, the asserted and the implied, that he has a "sylleptic imagination."

SEE ALSO *rhetoric*, *zeugma*.

symbol The word *symbol* derives from the Greek verb *symballein*, meaning "to put together," and the noun *symbolon*, meaning "mark," "emblem," "token," or "sign." In the classical world the *symbolon* was a half coin or half of a knucklebone carried by one person as a token of identity or a mark of obligation to someone holding the other half. It was a sign of agreement, a concrete object that represented a pledge. Each represented a whole.

When the two halves were rejoined they composed one knucklebone, a complete meaning.

Broadly speaking, a symbol is anything that signifies, or stands for, something else. Dr. Johnson defines it as "that which comprehends in its figure a representation of something else." Thus a dove is both a graceful bird *and* a universal symbol of peace. A rose is both a literal flower ("A rose is a rose is a rose," Gertrude Stein reminds us in a famous tautology) *and* the most commonly used floral symbol in the West. "It is the paragon of flowers in Western tradition," as one dictionary of symbols explains — "a symbol of the heart, the centre and the cosmic wheel, and also of sacred, romantic, and sensual love."

Words are arbitrary symbols of meaning. They are also textured entities. Specific words are symbols that go beyond the literal. In poetry, it is critical to remember that *rose* is first of all a one-syllable, four-letter noun with a specific sound that ovals the mouth when you say it aloud. It has an acoustic impact, as when Wordsworth seals it as a rhyme in his "Intimations" (1807) ode:

The Rainbow comes and goes,
And lovely is the Rose . . .

The rose here is a word that stands for a literal flower, but it is also something more, something else, like the transient rainbow. (The loveliness of Wordsworth's rose also alludes to the emblematic nature of the flower in Waller's well-known seventeenth-century poem "Go, lovely Rose" and echoes the anonymous fourteenth-century lyric "Of a rose, a louely rose, of a rose is al myn song.") In a poem, the literal meaning and the literary symbolic work together. ("The greatness of a poem does not depend on the magnitude of its theme," García Lorca explained in a lecture on Góngora: "The form and fragrance of just one rose can be made to render an impression of eternity.") We bring to our reading of a poem all the symbolic connotations and meanings available to us, but the symbol should first be understood in terms of how it works as a device within a poem itself. Then we can see, for example, how in a series of symbolist poems in the 1890s, Yeats was writing about the scent, shape, and petaled beauty of a rose even as he employed it as a major Rosicrucian and alchemical symbol, a sign of the eternal purity of love.

The *Princeton Encyclopedia of Poetry and Poetics* (1974) summarizes that in literary usage, a symbol refers to "a manner of representation in which what is shown (normally referring to something material) means, by virtue of association, something more or something else (normally referring to something immaterial)." How a thing can be both itself and something else is one of the great mysteries of poetry. In poetry, a symbol offers a surplus of resonance, of significance, since a poem can have great suggestive power, like a dream. It can also have the strange precision of a dream, what Baudelaire termed "evocative bewitchment" and Yeats called "indefinable and yet precise emotions." In "The Symbolism of Poetry" (1900), Yeats called these lines by Burns, which he altered slightly in memory, "perfectly symbolical":

> The white moon is setting behind the white wave,
> And Time is setting with me, O!

Yeats said:

> Take from them the whiteness of the moon and of the wave, whose relation to the setting of Time is too subtle for the intellect, and you take from them their beauty. But, when they are together, moon and wave and whiteness and setting Time and the last melancholy cry, they evoke an emotion which cannot be evoked by any other arrangement of colours and sounds and forms. We may call this metaphorical writing, but it is better to call it symbolical writing.

SEE ALSO *allegory, symbolism.*

symbolism Symbolism was a central literary movement that thrived in France between the 1870s and the 1890s. It was initially called idealism. The leading symbolist poets, Paul Verlaine, Arthur Rimbaud, and Stéphane Mallarmé, along with the key figures Jules Laforgue and Tristan Corbière, were at the forefront of the modern poetic tradition. The symbolist poets opposed all forms of naturalism and realism. They craved a poetry of suggestion rather than direct statement and treated everything in the external world as a condition of soul. They sought to repress or obfuscate one kind of reality, the quotidian world, in order to attain a more permanent reality, a world of ideal forms and essences. They believed that a magical suggestiveness (what Rimbaud termed "l'alchimie du verbe") could best be achieved by synaesthesia, fusing images and senses, and bringing poetry as close as possible to music.

Thus Verlaine's poem "Art poétique" (1874) advocates "music before everything." Walter Pater formulated a parallel doctrine in 1873 when he asserted, "All art constantly aspires towards the condition of music."

Baudelaire was one of the chief progenitors of the movement. His sonnet *"Correspondances"* (1857) envisioned nature as a "forest of symbols" and suggested a correspondence between the phenomenal world and the ideal one. He asserted in a prose piece that "everything, form, movement, number, color, perfume, in the *spiritual* as in the *natural* domain, is significant, reciprocal, converse, *corresponding*." Rimbaud followed Baudelaire and anticipated the Surrealists when he posited, "The poet makes himself a *seer* by a long, immense, and reasoned *derangement* of the senses." Correspondence was achieved through heightened concentration on the symbol, which had what Maeterlinck called a "*force occulte.*"

In 1891, Mallarmé defined symbolism:

> To name an object is to suppress three-quarters of the delight of the poem, which consists in the pleasure of guessing little by little; to *suggest* it, that is the dream. It is the perfect use of this mystery that constitutes the symbol: to evoke an object, gradually in order to reveal a state of the soul, or, inversely, to choose an object and from it identify a state of the soul, by a series of deciphering operations. . . . There must always be enigma in poetry.

Enigma widens the space for daydreaming. It loosens the intellect and invites poetic reverie, readerly imagination.

The symbolist movement reverberated around the globe. Everywhere it initiated poets into its mysteries. Some of the key figures it influenced: W. B. Yeats, Arthur Symons, Oscar Wilde, Ernest Dowson, and George Russell (Æ) in the British Isles; Stefan George and Rainer Maria Rilke in Germany; Hugo von Hofmannsthal in Austria; Innokenty Annensky, Alexander Blok, and Andrey Bely in Russia; Antonio Machado, Juan Ramón Jiménez, and Jorge Guillén in Spain; Rubén Darío in Nicaragua; T. S. Eliot, Ezra Pound, Amy Lowell, Hilda Doolittle (H. D.), Hart Crane, e. e. cummings, and Wallace Stevens in the United States. Whoever believes in the occult or spiritual power of the poetic word is an heir to the symbolists.

SEE ALSO *aestheticism, decadence, fin-de-siècle, Hermeticism, modernism, modernismo, naturalism, Parnassians, Silver Age, symbol, synaesthesia.*

sympathy, see *empathy.*

synaesthesia A blending of sensations; the phenomenon of describing one sense in terms of another. The specific term *synaesthesia* dates to only the late nineteenth century, but the device may be as old as literature itself. The *Iliad* (ca. eighth century B.C.E.) compares the voices of aged Trojans to the "lily-like" voices of cicadas; the *Odyssey* (ca. eighth century B.C.E.) evokes the "honey voice" of the Siren; the Bible refers to "seeing" a voice and "tasting" the word of God. Baudelaire popularized the notion of synaesthesia with his compelling idea that "the sounds, the scents, the colors correspond" ("Correspondances," 1857). In his poem "Voyelles" ("Vowells," 1872), Rimbaud famously assigned colors to each of the vowels:

> Black A, white E, red I, green U, blue O — vowels,
> Some day I will open your silent pregnancies . . .

Rimbaud's lines exemplify the type of synaesthesia known as *audition colorée,* wherein sounds are described as colors. Coleridge declares in the *Biographia Literaria* (1817) that "the poet must . . . understand and command what Bacon called the *vestigia communia* of the senses, the latency of all in each, and more especially . . . the excitement of vision by sound and the exponents of sound."

SEE ALSO *symbolism.*

synecdoche, see *trope.*

synthetic rhyme A rhyme that distorts a word, deleting, contracting, protracting, or otherwise wrenching letters into place to create a rhyme. This false rhyming, a weakness of bad poetry, is turned into a comic strength in light verse, as when Ogden Nash writes in "Spring Comes to Murray Hill" (1930):

> I sit in an office at 244 Madison Avenue
> And say to myself you have a responsible job, havenue?

SEE ALSO *light verse, rhyme.*

Tachtigers "Generation of the 1880s." In Amsterdam in the 1880s, a group of iconoclastic young Dutch poets revitalized Dutch poetry, which had been stagnant for more than a century.

The Tachtigers were inspired by the individualism and aesthetic principles of the English romantics, especially Keats and Shelley. Jacques Perk, who died at the age of twenty-one, was the first voice of the movement, and his posthumously published idealizations of beauty helped to galvanize the rebellion, the creation of a subjective, impressionistic poetry. "The 80ers" challenged the old guard, whose periodical was called *De Gids* (*The Guide*), with a new vision and a fresh revisionary review, *De Nieuwe Gids* (*The New Guide*), which was organized by William Koos ("I am a God in the depths of my mind"), Albert Verwey ("I am a poet and son of Beauty"), and Frederik van Eeden, who became a psychiatrist and coined the term *lucid dream,* a type of dream in which the dreamer recognizes that he or she is dreaming, a forerunner to Surrealism. The group also included Herman Gorter, whose long lyrical poem *Mei* (*May,* 1889), reminiscent of Keats's *Endymion* (1818), is the high-water mark of the movement.

SEE ALSO *romanticism.*

Tagelied, see *aubade, Surrealism.*

tail rhyme Rhymes that answer each other across intervening stanzas. The form consists of a rhyming stanza, often a couplet or a triplet, followed by a line of a different length, usually shorter. The shorter lines (or tails) frequently rhyme with each other. At times, however, they rhyme with a line or lines in the preceding stanza; at times they don't rhyme at all; and at times they serve as refrains. Some refrains have the same formula (Tennyson's "Ask me no more"), while others vary it (Burns's "The Holy Fair").

In Medieval Latin, tail-rhyme stanzas were called *rhythmus caudatus* or *versus caudati,* in French *rime couée,* in Middle English *rime couwee.* The most popular medieval types were the six-line form, which George Saintsbury named Romance Sixes, and the twelve-line form, which predominated in romances. The tail-rhyme stanza was the favorite stanzaic form in thirteenth- and fourteenth-century poetry. Robert Herrick cleverly employs a tail rhyme to succeed and punctuate the triplets in "The White Island or Place of the Blest" (1648):

There in calm and cooling sleep
We our eyes shall never steep,
But eternal watch shall keep,
    Attending

Pleasures such as shall pursue
Me immortalz'd, and you,
And fresh joy, as never to
    Have ending.

SEE ALSO *rhyme.*

talk poem In the 1970s, David Antin combined the genres of poetry, storytelling, stand-up comedy, and lecture in his improvised talk-pieces or talk poems, a form of thinking aloud that blends personal narration with philosophical reflection. He states in *Talking at the Boundaries* (1976): "if thinking was a kind of talking and it had to be if there was no writing then a poet was someone who could talk when the time came could remember other talking and could tell the important things how they had happened in the way they happen to have happened." There is precedent for Antin's poetics of process in John Cage's talks and lectures collected in *Silence* (1961), *A Year from Monday* (1967) and *M* (1973). "I don't give these lectures to surprise people," Cage said, "but out of a need for poetry." Such key talks as "Composition as Process" (1958) stand behind Antin's treatment of speech as a site of creation, which in turn inaugurated an avant-garde tradition of talk pieces. "Talk has its charm, evanescent but persistent," Bob Perelman asserts in "Speech Effects: The Talk as a Genre" (1998): "The talk is very much a middling genre. Made out of speech but often later constituted by writing, the talk's amorphous territory is bounded by poetry readings, performance art, teaching and other academic procedures, interviews, and entertainment."

Mark Halliday has also coined the term *ultra-talk* for the loose-limbed, highly discursive contemporary poems of David Kirby, Barbara Hamby, Albert Goldbarth, and others. These free-wheeling, often garrulous poems mimic a kind of hyper-speech (Halliday calls them "hyperjunctive"), though they are not spoken but written. The oral art of talk poetry and the written art of ultra-talk both try to break down the traditional distinction between lyric poetry and ordinary speech. Yet they also frame speech in a way that marks it not as talk but as poetry.

SEE ALSO *Stand Up poetry.*

tanka Also called *uta* or *waka.* The character for *ka* means "poem." *Wa* means "Japanese." Thus a *waka* is a Japanese poem. *Tan* means "short" and so a *tanka* is a short poem, thirty-one syllables long. It is unrhymed and has units of five, seven, five, seven, and seven syllables, which were traditionally printed as one unbroken line. In English translation, the tanka is customarily divided into a five-line form. The tanka is sometimes separated by the three "upper lines" (*kami no ku*) and the two "lower ones" (*shimo no ku*). The upper unit is the origin of the haiku. The brevity of the poem, and the turn from the upper to the lower lines, which often signals a shift or expansion of subject matter, is one of the reasons the tanka has been compared to the sonnet. There is a range of words, or *engo* (verbal associations), that traditionally associate or bridge the sections. Like the sonnet, tanka is also conducive to sequences, such as the *hyakushuuta,* which consists of one hundred tankas.

The tanka, which comprised the majority of Japanese poetry from the ninth to the nineteenth century, is possibly the central genre of Japanese literature. It has prototypes in communal song, in oral literature dating back to the seventh century, or earlier. The earliest anthology of Japanese poetry, *Man'yōshū* (*Collection of Ten Thousand Leaves,* ca. 759), contains more than forty-two hundred poems in the tanka form. The form gradually developed into court poetry and became so popular that it marginalized all other forms. The *renga* developed out of the tanka as a kind of court amusement or game. The *somonka* form consists of two tankas. They are relationship poems, exchange songs. In the first stanza, a lover conventionally addresses the beloved. In the second stanza, the beloved replies.

Tankas often appear inside or alongside longer prose or narrative works. Lady Murasaki Shikibu's foundational prose work *The Tale of Genji,* which dates to the early eleventh century and is sometimes called the world's first novel, contains more than four hundred tankas. Many of the great tanka court poets were women, such as Akazome Emon (956–1041), Ono no Komachi (ca. 825–ca. 900), and Izumi Shikibu (ca. 970–1030). Here is one of Princess Nukata's (ca. 630–690) tankas, "Yearning for the Emperor Tenji," collected in the *Man'yōshū:*

While, waiting for you,
My heart is filled with longing,
The autumn wind blows —
As if it were you —
Swaying the bamboo blinds of my door.

Starting in the nineteenth century, poets began to reconsider, reconfigure, and modernize the highly codified tanka form. This is especially evident in the work of the tanka poet Ishikawa Takuboku (1886–1912). The New Poetry Society, or *Myōjō Poets* (Morning Star Poets), and their chief rivals, the Negishi Tanka Society, brought tanka into the twentieth century. This traditional mood poem opened up to the currents of modern social and political life.

SEE ALSO *haiku, mono no aware, monostitch, renga.*

tapinosis Name-calling. *Tapinosis* is the use of degrading language to debase or belittle a person or thing. In *The Art of English Poesie* (1589), George Puttenham called it "the Abasser": "But if ye abase your thing or matter by ignorance or errour in the choise of your word, then it is by vicious maner of speach called *Tapinosis.*" *Tapinosis* is a form of vulgar insult, of putting a curse on someone, which is one of the time-honored strategies of poetic contests, from the Scottish *flyting* to the African American game of playing the dozens. John Synge dedicated his poem "The Curse" (1907) "To a sister of an enemy of the author's who disapproved of 'The Playboy' ":

Lord, confound this surly sister,
Blight her brow with blotch and blister,
Cramp her larynx, lung and liver,
In her guts a galling give her.
Let her live to earn her dinners
In Mountjoy with seedy sinners:
Lord, this judgment quickly bring,
And I'm your servant, J. M. Synge.

SEE ALSO *the dozens, flyting, meiosis, poetic contest, rhetoric.*

taste Aesthetic discernment. It took some four centuries for the metaphorical transfer from the physical sense of taste to an abstract quality of judgment, capitalized as *Taste,* which became an important critical and philosophical term in eighteenth-century aesthetics. Joseph Addison defined it in his *Spectator* papers on Taste (1712) as "that faculty of the soul which discerns the beauties of an author with pleasure, and the imperfections with dislike." He also spoke of "Rules . . . how we may acquire that fine Taste of Writing, which is so much talked of among the Polite World." Raymond Williams points out that taste had become equivalent to discrimination. "The word taste," James Barry explained in a lecture on design, "means . . . that quick discerning faculty or power of the mind, by which we accurately distinguish the good, bad, or indifferent" (1784).

Eighteenth-century philosophers raised a wide variety of questions about taste and its relationship to beauty and sublimity. Is taste purely subjective? Can it be intersubjective? Is it limited to a single individual or group in one period of time? Is it a natural quality, something innate, or a matter of cultivation, something acquired? Is it an independent faculty? Is it culturally specific or in any way cross-cultural? Can it be changed? How can we account for differences of taste? Are there universal canons of taste? David Hume sought the grounds for "a *Standard of Taste;* a rule, by which the various sentiments of men may be reconciled; at least, a decision, afforded, confirming one sentiment, and condemning another" (1757). Immanuel Kant treated taste as subjective but universal, since it is a response to the formal features of a work of art rather than to its content. "*Taste* is the ability to judge an object, or a way of presenting it, by means of a liking or a disliking *devoid of all interest,*" he asserts in *Critique of Judgment* (1790). "The object of such a liking is called *beautiful.*"

The late eighteenth-century philosophical concept of taste was compromised by its association with cultivation, good manners, as in the difference between the tasteful and the tasteless, which is one of the reasons Wordsworth attacked its superficiality in his 1800 *Preface to Lyrical Ballads,* where he mentions those "who will converse with us as gravely about a *taste* for Poetry, as they express it, as if it were a thing as indifferent as a taste for rope-dancing, or Frotiniac or Sherry." Wordsworth recognizes that taste is

> a metaphor, taken from a *passive* sense of the human body, and transferred to things which are in their essence *not* passive — to intellectual *acts* and *operations*. . . . But the profound and the exquisite in feeling, the lofty and universal in thought and imagination . . . are neither of them, accurately speaking, objects of a faculty which could ever without a sinking in the spirit of Nations have been designated by the metaphor — *Taste.* And why? Because without the exertion of a co-operating *power* in the mind of the Reader, there can be no adequate sympathy with either of these emotions: without this auxiliary impulse elevated or profound passion cannot exist.

Taste was renewed in the late nineteenth century as an important concept for those who opposed utilitarian notions of art. It was applied to aesthetic values. But the idea of taste was tainted by moral overtones and, as Raymond Williams argues, it "cannot now be separated from the idea of the consumer . . . and responses to art and literature . . . have been profoundly affected . . . by the assumption that the viewer, spectator or reader is a *consumer,* exercising and subsequently showing his taste."

SEE ALSO *Aestheticisism, sensibility, the sublime.*

tautogram Greek: *tauto gramma,* "same letter." A line of verse, a sequence of words or sentence in which every word begins with the same letter. In poetry, it is an alliterative sound poem, usually for comic purposes. In 1546, Johannes Leo Placentius, a Dominican friar and poet from Liège writing under the pseudonym Publius Porcius, published a poem called *Pugna Porco-*

rum ("The Battle of the Pigs") that consists of 253 hexameters in which every word begins with the letter *p*. Its beginning pops off the page:

> Plaudite Porcelli Porcorum pigra propago.
> Progreditur, plures Porci pinguedine pleni.

In our era, the Oulipo writers have enthusiastically experimented with tautograms.

SEE ALSO *alliteration, macaronic, Oulipo, sound poetry, tongue twister.*

tenor and vehicle, see *metaphor.*

tension As a critical term, *tension* generally refers to the equilibrium achieved in a poem by balancing opposed tendencies, such as the literal and the metaphorical or the concrete and the abstract. In his essay "Tension in Poetry," (1938), Allen Tate derived a special meaning of "tension" by "lopping the prefixes off the logical terms *ex*tension and *in*tension," and suggested that "the meaning of poetry is its 'tension,' the full organized body of all the extension and intension that we can find in it." Tate exhibited a New Critical preference for a poetry that embodies a dramatic interplay of opposing ideas.

SEE ALSO *New Criticism.*

tenson, tenzone, tencon A type of debate poem developed by the Provençal poets in the twelfth century. The *tenson,* which was called the *tenso* in Old Occitan, was a verbal exchange, an argument, a contest between two poets. The invective, which was intense, was sometimes feigned. A poet could also use the *tenson* to oppose an imaginary adversary. It was called a *torneijamens* when there were more than two disputants. The *tenson* could take any metrical form, though the respondent was often challenged to reply in the same meter and rhyme scheme used by the challenger. It is the forerunner of the Scottish *flyting.*

The *tenson* later developed or specialized into the subgenre of the *partimen* (or *joc partit*), which eliminated the personal element. One poet proposed two hypothetical situations. The second poet chose one position and the initiator chose the other. The structure matched. The wandering troubadours carried the *tenson* to Italy and Sicily, where the *tenzoni* was commonly practiced by the poets of the *dolce stil novo.* Adrienne Martin points out that in the Middle Ages the *tenson* adopted the new metrical scheme of the sonnet and, indeed, three of the sonneteers from the Sicilian Court of Frederick wrote the first *tensons* in sonnet form: Giacomo da Lentino, Piero delle Vigne, and Jacopo Mostacci. The subject was courtly love. Dante Alighieri and his one-time friend Forese Donati engaged in the earliest extant sonnet *tenson* ("Tenzone"), which consists of six rancorous and insulting sonnets traded back and forth between 1293 and 1296.

SEE ALSO *cobla, courtly love, débat, dolce stil novo, flyting, poetic contest, sonnet, troubadour.*

tercet A verse unit of three lines. The tercet was historically defined as three lines containing rhyme, but most contemporary poets and critics use it as the name for any three-line stanza, with or without rhyme. It is a synonym for *triad* or *triplet,* a word that is becoming antiquated.

There are many kinds of three-line stanzas. One thinks of three lines ending with the same rhyme word, as in this lovely stanza from Robert Herrick's "Upon Julia's Clothes" (1648):

> Whenas in silks my Julia goes,
> Then, then, methinks, how sweetly flows
> That liquefaction of her clothes.

The interlocking three-line stanzas of terza rima are called tercets, as are the three-line stanzas in the villanelle. The ancient Hawaiian creation chant *The Kumulipo,* composed and transmitted through oral traditions, unfolds in triads and so do many liturgical forms, such as the Kyrie prayer. William Carlos Williams exploited the tercet as a kind of descending staircase in many of his best poems, such as "To Elsie" (1923) and "Asphodel, That Greeny Flower" (1955). The tercet has never been as widely employed as the couplet and the quatrain, but it seems distinctive because each stanza has a beginning, middle, and end. The number three has always had magical significance.

SEE ALSO *terza rima, variable foot, villanelle.*

terza rima A verse form of interlocking three-line stanzas rhyming *aba, bcb, cdc,* etc. The terza rima form was invented by Dante Alighieri for the *Commedia* (*The Divine Comedy,* ca. 1304–1321), using the hendecasyllabic (eleven-syllable) line common to Italian poetry. In *De vulgari eloquentia* ("On eloquence in the vernacular," 1304–1307?), Dante called rhyme *concatenatio* ("beautiful linkage"), and the triple rhymes beautifully link together the stanzas. Rhyming the first and third lines gives each tercet a sense of temporary closure; rhyming the second line with the first and last lines of the next stanza generates a strong feeling of propulsion. The effect of this chain-rhyme is both open-ended and conclusive, like moving through a series of interpenetrating rooms or going down a set of winding stairs: you are always traveling forward while looking back.

Chaucer introduced terza rima into English in the fourteenth century with his poem "A Complaint to His Lady." Sir Thomas Wyatt's three *Satires* (1536) are the first sustained use of terza rima in our language. Shelley's "The Triumph of Life" (1824) is the finest English poem ever written in the form. The first eight lines capture its spiraling motion:

Swift as a spirit hastening to his task
Of glory and of good, the Sun sprang forth
Rejoicing in his splendor, and the mask

Of darkness fell from the awakened Earth—
The smokeless altars of the mountain snows
Flamed above crimson clouds, and at the birth

Of light, the Ocean's orison arose,
To which the birds tempered their matin lay.

Shelley also uses a terza rima sonnet for the five individual sections that comprise "Ode to the West Wind" (1819). The title poem of Randall Jarrell's *The Lost World* (1965) is a virtuoso piece of terza rima in three parts, Proust in plain American. Robert Pinsky capably uses slant rhymes to create what he calls "a plausible terza rima in a readable English" in his translation of Dante's *Inferno* (1994).

SEE ALSO *hendecasyllabics, tercet.*

tetrameter, see "accentual syllabic meter" in *meter.*

tétramètre, see *alexandrine.*

textual criticism The task of evaluating the authority of the words and the punctuation of a text. The goal is the restoration of an original or archetypal text, a "critical edition." The earliest textual critics sought to preserve the works of antiquity. Textual criticism is an act of recovery. Paul Maas defines the basic problem in *Textual Criticism* (1958):

> We have no autograph manuscripts of the Greek and Roman classical writers and no copies which have been collated with the originals; the manuscripts we possess derive from the originals through an unknown number of intermediate copies, and are consequently of questionable trustworthiness. The business of textual criticism is to produce a text as close as possible to the original (*constitutio textus*).

The textual critic relies on both external evidence (outside witnesses) and internal evidence (evidence that comes from the text itself). Ever since the nineteenth century, textual critics have sought to establish guidelines or canons of textual criticism, thus defining a methodology. G. Thomas Tanselle argues that the textual critic inevitably exercises critical judgment in the establishment of literary texts. Textual criticism, which is integral to the activity of reading, becomes inseparable from literary criticism.

Each text is a particular embodiment of a given poem. "What we ought to see," Jerome McGann states, "is that 'text' is the linguistic state of the 'poem's' existence. No poem can exist outside of a textual state any more than a human being can exist outside of a human biological organism. But just as a person is not identical to a particular body, so neither is a poem equal to its text." Think, for example, of the experience of reading Emily Dickinson's poems. What a difference there is between her original volcanic punctuation and the normalized punctuation imposed by her first editors. Or think of the many differences between the two major editions of Wordsworth's *The Prelude,* one from 1805–1806, the other from 1850, or the crucial differences between the many editions of Walt Whitman's *Leaves of Grass,* most significantly the 1855 and the so-called deathbed edition of 1891–1892.

SEE ALSO *variorum.*

texture Modern poetry criticism has borrowed the term *texture* from the plastic arts. Texture tends to refer to the surface qualities of a work of art, as opposed to its general design, and to the concrete particulars of a poem, as opposed to its abstract ideas. In prosody, texture refers to the physical effects of sound, in poetics to the tangible details inscribed in a poem. John Crowe Ransom made the term one of the cornerstones of his New Critical attempt to differentiate the incarnate poem from a prose statement. In "Criticism as Pure Speculation" (1941), Ransom advocates a "structural understanding of poetry" and divides a poem into two parts: "a central logic or situation," a so-called logical core, and a "local texture," which he characterizes as "excursions into particularity." The local texture gives a "sense of the real density and contingency of the world." For Ransom, then, a poem is "a logical structure having a local texture," and the "intent of the good critic becomes therefore to examine and define the poem with respect to its structure and its texture."

SEE ALSO *New Criticism, structure.*

than-bauk A Burmese form, the *than-bauk* is a witty or epigrammatic three-line poem. Each line has four syllables. The poem rhymes on the fourth syllable of the first line, the third syllable of the second line, and the second syllable of the third line. This so-called climbing rhyme is characteristic of Burmese verse.

SEE ALSO *lin-ga, tercet, ya-du.*

theme A summary statement about a work, a condensation or salient paraphrase of its main line of thought or feeling. A theme, a generalized meaning, may be explicit or indirect. Thus Wordsworth identifies the theme of his autobiographical poem, *The Prelude* (1805, 1850), in the subtitle *Growth of a Poet's Mind.* Milton names the theme of his epic, *Paradise Lost* (1667), in book 1: "to justify the ways of God to men." We infer that jealousy is the theme of *Othello* (ca. 1603).

The concept of theme originated in classical rhetoric as the subject around which an orator set out to construct a speech. The idea of a proposed subject migrated to religion and by the Middle Ages had become a scriptural text that served as the basis for a sermon. In literature, theme became the idea, the topic or subject matter, the *topoi,* on which a poet based a poem. In interpreting a medieval poem, Curtius suggests, "we must ask, not on what 'experience' it was based, but what theme the poet set himself to treat." Theme was initially identified by the orator or author, but it followed that the listener or reader could identify and abstract a theme from a given work. In literary criticism, *theme* was a didactic term used synonymously with the "moral" or "message" of a work. In twentieth-century formalist literary criticism, such as New Criticism, theme was divorced from the idea of authorial intention, the moral of a work, and grounded in close reading, in the particulars of a work of art. Criticism also borrowed from music the idea of theme as a principle of composition, which we recognize when critics speak of "theme and variations." Kenneth Koch's hilarious take-off on William Carlos Williams's "This is Just to Say" (1934) is called "Variations on a Theme by Williams" (1962).

SEE ALSO *didactic poetry, invention, New Criticism, paraphrase, topos.*

threnody, see *elegy.*

tlamatine In Náhuatl, the language of the Aztec world, one key word for poet was *tlamatine,* meaning "the one who knows," or "he who knows something." Poets were considered "sages of the word," who meditated on human enigmas and explored the beyond, the realm of the gods. The Aztec poets of the fourteenth and fifteenth centuries, who were perhaps the first known poets of the Americas, had all been instructed in the *calmecac,* or priestly schools, where, as Miguel León-Portilla puts it, "they had mastered the science of the calendar, the divine wisdom, the books of the annals, the ancient songs, and the discourses." Their indigenous texts were painted in what are now lost pictoglyphic codices. These were later recited to ethnographer-friars, who in turn transcribed them in Roman letters. The "ancient word" of the Náhuatl texts was preserved in a few sixteenth-century manuscripts. My favorite poet from this period is Ayocuan Cuetzpaltzin, who lived in the second half of the fifteenth century in what is now Puebla. He seems to have been a *teohua,* or priest, a "White Eagle." He was a seeker after heights who recognized, "Friendship is a shower of precious flowers" and "Earth is the region of the fleeting moment." From a lapidary statement in a poem sometimes called "Let the Earth Remain Forever," I have an image of him walking and chanting his songs on ancient roads. The Aztec poets had a keen sense of transience and sang often of *cahuitl,* "that which leaves us."

tone An elusive poetic concept, tone is generally taken to indicate a writer or speaker's sense of his situation, sometimes imagined. The tone is all in the inflection, how a thing is said, or seems to be said. The literary term *tone* is borrowed from the expression *tone of voice* and thus implies something spoken aloud. "Whenever a poem makes us conscious of someone speaking, tone is a relevant conception," Hugh Kenner states. The reader establishes a tone, a complex of attitudes toward a subject, by determining how a speaker takes himself, and, more complicatedly, how the poet takes his speaker. This includes determining a speaker's attitude toward her subject (what she is addressing) as well as toward her audience (whom she is addressing). In oral poetry, the listener responds to the intonations of spoken words. In written poetry, spoken intonations must be inferred by readers, who hear the tones with an inner ear. The tonal range is vast and sometimes difficult to determine — is it aggrieved, beseeching, curious, determined, elevated, furious, grim, happy, ironic, or many of these things at once? A poem often shifts and develops a variety of shadings in the course of its movement from beginning to end.

Tone has been a key concept in modern critical discourse. I. A. Richards characterized tone in *Practical Criticism* (1929) as a literary speaker's "attitude to his listener" and argued that tone reflects "his sense of how he stands towards those he is addressing." The New Critics made tone one of their central analytic devices and focused on the discrepant tones of ambiguity, paradox, and irony. The literary theorist Mikhail Bakhtin argued that tone or intonation is "oriented *in two directions:* with respect to the listener as ally or witness and with respect to the object of the utterance as the third, living participant whom the intonation scolds or caresses, denigrates or magnifies."

In modern poetry, the idea of tone of voice was especially crucial for Robert Frost, who said, "It's tone I'm in love with; that's what poetry is, tone." He argued that sentences can hold our attention only when they are dramatic: "All that can save them is the speaking tone of voice somehow entangled in the words and fastened to the page for the ear of the imagination."

SEE ALSO *ambiguity, drama, irony, New Criticism, paradox.*

tone color The timbre or auditory quality of a speech sound, a singing voice, or a musical instrument. Neither the German *Klangfarbe* (tone color) nor John Tyndall's proposed equivalent *clang-tint* ever caught on in English. Sydney Lanier adapted the term from music to describe specific sonic qualities in poetry in such works as *The Science of English Verse* (1880) and *Shakespeare and His Forerunners* (1902), where he explains: "Tone-colour . . . results from the fact that all the tones ordinarily heard are composite. Just as a ray of white light is composed of the three coloured rays united, so each tone we ordinarily hear — whether a tone of speech, such as a word, or a tone of a musical instrument — is composed of subordinate tones in combination with a chief tone called the fundamental tone. These subordinate tones are called 'upper partial' tones, or sometimes 'harmonics.' Now you can easily imagine in a general way that if the ingredients of such a composite tone be changed, the tone itself will be changed in some way. It is changed, and the change is one of tone-colour."

SEE ALSO *sound poetry*.

tongue twister A tongue twister is something tricky to repeat aloud, a phrase or sentence to tangle up the speaker. What makes it tricky is the repetition, usually of consonant sounds that are difficult for the mouth to make. Tongue twisters have been found in almost every language, which suggests that we need these fictive verbal expressions, these noninstrumental uses of language. Tongue twisters are passed on for generations by word of mouth and playfully draw attention to the features of language itself, the way something is said. Many playfully combine alliteration and rhyme; some are whole poems. Here is one, which is sometimes called "The Drunken Sailor":

> Amidst the mists and colder frosts,
> With barest wrists and stoutest boasts,
> He thrusts his fists against the posts
> And still insists he sees the ghosts.

In the nineteenth century, tongue twisters were at times classified as "charms" (J. O. Halliwell-Phillips, *The Nursery Rhymes of England*, 1886). The *Grammatica Linguæ Anglicane* (1674) lists "Peter Piper," which many people still know from childhood, as one of the ten tongue twisters that "are said to be certain cures for the hiccup if repeated in one breath":

Peter Piper picked a peck of pickled peppers;
Did Peter Piper pick a peck of pickled peppers?
If Peter Piper picked a peck of pickled peppers,
Where's the peck of pickled peppers Peter Piper picked?

SEE ALSO *charm, counting-out rhymes, nursery rhymes, tautogram.*

topographical poetry Samuel Johnson defined *topographical poetry* as "*local poetry,* of which the fundamental subject is some particular landscape . . . with the addition . . . of historical retrospection or incidental meditation." John Denham's "Cooper's Hill" (1642) brought the genre into vogue in English poetry for more than two centuries. Topographical poetry, which commences with a poet on a hill overlooking a river, "aims chiefly at describing *specifically named actual localities,*" as R. A. Aubin puts it in his standard history of the genre (1936). It re-creates a landscape or a generalized prospect ("something presented to the eye; a scene"), which is why C. V. Deane called it "prospect poetry." The "I" locates itself through the "eye." One of the peaks of topographical poetry is William Wordsworth's "Lines Composed a few miles above Tintern Abbey, on revisiting the banks of the Wye during a tour, July 13, 1798," which he composed on a four-day walk with his sister from Tintern to Bristol. He composed the last twenty lines as they walked down the hill from Clifton. The poem has caused a controversy in Wordsworth circles, since the poet must have been aware of, but did not acknowledge, the homeless beggars and vagrants camping in the abbey. He ignores the poor. The poem is perhaps more about the landscape of memory than the landscape of Wye.

The archaic term *chorography* (Greek: "writing about countries"), which suggests writing about regions or nations, is sometimes used interchangeably with *topographical poetry.* William Camden's Latin work *Britannia* (1586), the first county-by-county topographical survey of the entire British Isles, characterizes itself as a *Chorographica descriptio,* or chorographic poem. The Earl of Rochester wrote a mock topographical poem, "A Ramble in St. James Park" (1672), which brings together the beauty of the park with the depraved acts that people commit within it:

Poor pensive lover, in this place
Would frig upon his mother's face;
Whence rows of mandrakes tall did rise

Whose lewd tops fucked the very skies.
Each imitative branch does twine
In some loved fold of Aretine,
And nightly now beneath their shade
Are buggeries, rapes, and incests made.

Gary Snyder and Wendell Berry are both contemporary topographical American poets, since they cherish, describe, and ruminate about particular landscapes close to home. They create a poetics of the local. Charles Wright's southern landscape poems are also topographical. In contemporary poetry, the genre is sometimes relabeled "site-specific poetry," as in "site-specific art work," which consists of art made for a particular place.

SEE ALSO *nature poetry.*

topos, topoi (pl) Derived from the Greek word for *place,* short for *commonplace,* a topos is a literary passage or expression that becomes a convention in subsequent literature. In *Latin Literature and the European Middle Ages* (1948), Ernst Robert Curtius took the idea of rhetorical commonplaces, standardized methods for constructing and treating arguments, and adapted it to literary concerns, so that a topos becomes a typical "intellectual theme suitable for development and modification." Topics are a stockroom of motifs, themes, and ideas. One topos would be "affected modesty," which medieval poets sometimes expressed as "trepidation before the matter at hand"; another would be the "inexpressibility topos," an emphasis upon the speaker's inability to cope with a subject ("What virtues are thine, if I could, I would gladly set forth," Fortunatus declares, "But little wit cannot relate great things"). Some writers treat the world as a stage, others consider it a book, but both are taking up traditional topics, or topoi.

SEE ALSO *convention, theme.*

tornados, see *envoi.*

touchstone A touchstone is first of all a hard black stone, such as basalt or jasper, formerly used to test the quality of gold or silver. It is possible to compare the streak left on the stone by one of these metals with that of a standard alloy. Matthew Arnold introduced the word into literary criticism in "The Study of Poetry" (1880). He picked extremely short but distinctive passages to represent what is highest in poetry — as a benchmark, a standard of comparison, a method of evaluation, a corrective:

> There can be no more useful help for discovering what poetry belongs to the class of the truly excellent. . . . than to have always in one's mind lines and expressions of the great masters, and to apply them as a touchstone to other poetry. . . . If we have any tact we shall find them . . . an infallible touchstone for detecting the presence or absence of high poetic quality, and also the degree of this quality, in all other poetry which we may place beside them.

Arnold's beautiful but arbitrary touchstones are passages of one to four lines from Homer (eighth century B.C.E.), Dante (1265–1321), Shakespeare (1564–1616), and Milton (1608–1674). "In la sua volontade è nostra pace," Dante writes in the *Paradiso* (ca. 1315–1321, 111): "In His will is our peace." The Miltonic touchstone, which comes from *Paradise Lost* (1667, part 4), is the loss of Ceres to her daughter Proserpine, " . . . which cost Ceres all that pain / To seek her through the world."

Arnold's idea of the touchstone is outmoded in our relativistic, postmodern age. What may be considered a touchstone is up for grabs — who decides, for example, what constitutes a touchstone — poets, critics, scholars, general readers? The term would perhaps seem less dated if we think of every reader as having his or her own touchstones, passages of such enduring beauty that one wouldn't want to live without them. But that subjective notion of the touchstone undermines Arnold's idea of the common benchmark, the standard alloy.

tradition A handing down or handing over. Tradition suggests a consciousness of the past. The concept of tradition implies that we do not have our meaning entirely unto ourselves — rather, we are in relationship to what has come before us. Francis Bacon spoke of "the expressing or transferring our knowledge to others, which I will term by the general name of tradition or delivery" (1605). Tradition is not just a passive accumulation of all previous works; it is an active process of selection, of losses and gains, of renewals. Poets, readers, critics, and editors are all part of the process. Something from the past — a body of work, a style or convention, a set of beliefs — is excluded or lost; something else is chosen, renewed, and passed on. It would be more accurate to speak of traditions rather than tradition, since there are many different lines of descent, many separate inheritances. The idea that there is a single trajectory, one literary tradition that comprises the whole history of poetry, is a fantasy.

Tradition, in one sense, relates to culture and society. We speak of traditional cultures, which are bound to the established ways of the past. One type of poem, such as the traditional ballad, is handed down from one generation to another. A tradition in poetry may refer to a specific form, as when we speak of the tradition of the sonnet, or a line of inheritance, as when we speak of the romantic tradition or the neoclassical tradition. The concept of tradition has sometimes been equated with an idea of respect, duty, and ceremony, as in *Richard II* (ca. 1595):

> Throw away Respect, Tradition, Forme
> And Ceremonious Dutie . . .

Traditionalism takes on a conservative bent and makes an ideology out of doing things as others have done them before us. It defines itself by an adherence to previous doctrines, preordained values. It opposes what is progressive or modern.

T. S. Eliot was largely responsible for bringing the concept of tradition into modern poetry. In "Tradition and the Individual Talent" (1919), he argues that for the individual writer with a historical sense, "the whole of the literature of Europe from Homer and within it the whole of the literature of his own country has a simultaneous existence and composes a simultaneous order." For Eliot, the "existing monuments form an ideal order among themselves, which is modified by the introduction of the new (the really new) work of art among them." This leads him to the formulation that "art never improves, but that the material of art is never quite the same." Eliot posits a cultural unity, "the mind of Europe," which has an almost spiritual authority over the individual. But there is no singular mind of Europe or timeless European tradition. Some critics find it comforting to dream of an ideal realm, a total library, which includes all the oral and written works ever created. Tradition consists of selections from that library.

SEE ALSO *canon, impersonality*.

tragedy The word *tragedy* means, in Greek, "goat-song." Tragedy originated in ritual hymns sung during the sacrifice of a goat at Dionysian festivals. Goats were sacred to the god Dionysus, who made them his chosen victims (Euripides, *The Bacchae,* 405 B.C.E.). Sacrifice was a process of identification, and the goat was the embodiment of the god. The speaking/dancing chorus performed poems devoted to Dionysus, and, according to Aristotle, Greek drama grew out of these choral rites. Tragedy, which Aristotle considered the supreme form of poetry, developed as an interaction between a semi-detached speaker and the rest of the chorus. In time the choral drama — the true relations were between the actor and the chorus — loosened the connection to Dionysus, and the choral element was discarded. Greek tragedy was chanted, sung, and danced in verse, a heightened verbal mode, which George Steiner calls "the prime divider between the world of high tragedy and that of ordinary existence." The thirty-two plays that survive by Aeschylus (525–456 B.C.E.), Sophocles (496?–406 B.C.E.), and Euripides (480?–406 B.C.E.), which revolve around Fate, Necessity, and the nature of the gods, are the foundational achievement of European drama.

In the *Poetics* (350 B.C.E., 4 C.E.), Aristotle defined tragedy:

> Tragedy, then, is the imitation of an action that is serious and also, as having magnitude, complete in itself; in language with pleasurable accessories, each kind brought in separately in the parts of the work; in a dramatic not in a narrative form; with incidents arousing pity and fear, wherewith to accomplish its catharsis of such emotions.

Aristotle identified three elements of the tragic plot: *anagnorisis* or recognition, *peripeteia* or surprising reversal, and *pathos,* which he characterizes as "that act involving destruction or pain." The tragic hero is brought down by *hamartia,* his tragic flaw. Aristotle considered the response of an audience, its sense of "pity and fear," essential to tragedy.

Tragedies end badly; comedies end well. Tragedy is high, serious, dignified. Greek tragedy dealt with elevated figures in performance and referred exclusively to drama, or characters in action, as opposed to the epic, a poem narrated by a solo performer, a singer of tales. By the Middle Ages the term had generalized to refer to the pattern of a narrative. Diomedes characterized it in the fourth century as "the narrative of heroic (or semi-divine) characters in adversity." Tragedy thus formulates a dramatic story, the narrative of a fall. Chaucer defines its characteristic movement in the prologue to "The Monk's Tale" (ca. 1387–1400):

> Tragedie is to seyn a certeyn storie,
> As olde bokes maken us memorie,
> Of him that stoode in greet prosperitee
> And is y-fallen out of heigh degree
> Into miserie, and endeth wrecchedly.

The Renaissance brought the idea of tragedy back to theater. There is a sense of fatal necessity, of destiny worked out in dramatic tragedies. Something has been set in motion that cannot be stopped. Thomas Kyd's *The Spanish Tragedy* (1592), which looks back to the Senecan drama, inaugurated the bloodthirsty Elizabethan and Jacobean genre of the revenge tragedy, in which a leading character struggles to avenge the murder of a loved one. Some of these great "tragedies of blood" in which a wronged man sets out to do a terrible thing for a perfectly good reason: William Shakespeare's *Hamlet* (1603), *The Revenger's Tragedy* (published anonymously in 1607), Cyrill Tourneur's *The Atheist's Tragedy* (1611), John Webster's *The Duchess of Malfi* (1612), and John Ford's *'Tis Pity She's a Whore* (1633).

There was an effort in the eighteenth century to apply the formula of classical tragedy to the domestic interior. George Lillo (1693–1739) in England, Gotthold Ephraim Lessing (1729–1781) in Germany, and Louis-Sébastien Mercier (1740–1814) in France all contributed to the genre known as domestic tragedy or tragédie bourgeoise.

One of the major offshoots of tragedy is the hybrid genre of tragicomedy. It typically contains comic elements but tells a story that is inherently tragic. Pierre Corneille's enormously popular *Le Cid* (1636), which is based on the legend of El Cid, exemplifies this type of drama. It sparked a heated polemic (the Querelle du Cid) over the way it defied the classical unities.

SEE ALSO *Apollonian/Dionysian, catharsis, chorus, comedy, pathos, tragicomedy.*

tragicomedy Plautus (ca. 254–ca. 184 B.C.E.) coined the word *tragicocomoedia* to denote a play in which gods and mortals, masters and slaves, reverse traditional roles. Here is the passage from his play *Amphitruo* (ca. 206–186 B.C.E.):

Mercury. What's that? Are you disappointed
To find it's a tragedy? Well, I can easily change it.
I'm a god, after all, I can easily make it a comedy,
And never alter a line. Is that what'd like? . . .
But I was forgetting — stupid of me — of course,
Being a god, I know quite well what you'd like,
I know exactly what's in your minds. Very well.
I'll meet you half-way, and make it a *tragicomedy*.

Ever since, the hybrid genre of the tragicomedy has incorporated elements of both tragedy and comedy, as in Shakespeare's *Troilus and Cressida* (1602). Modern tragicomedy tends to be used interchangeably with absurdist drama, as in the work of Harold Pinter, where laughter is treated as the only remaining response to existence.

SEE ALSO *comedy, tragedy*.

translation The word *translation* derives from the Latin *translatio,* which in turn comes from *trans-* and *fero,* meaning "to carry across" or "to bring across." It is the transfer of meaning from one language to another. Strictly speaking, total translation is impossible, since languages differ and each language carries its own complex of linguistic resources, historical and social values. This is especially true in poetry, the maximal of language. It is axiomatic that in a poem there is no exact equivalent for the valences of sound, the intonations and sequences of words, the rhythm of separate lines, the weight of accruing stanzas, the totality of musical effects. That's why its untranslatability has been one of the defining features of poetry. Coleridge coined the word *untranslatableness.* Robert Frost famously said, "Poetry is what gets lost in translation." An Italian pun captures the idea: *traduttore/traditore,* translator/traitor.

Yet translation is also a necessity, the only way of bridging the barriers of language. It brings the world to our doorstep. For who among us can read in the original the Hebrew Bible and the Homeric epics, Horace, Dante, and Petrarch, Rumi and the medieval Arabic poets, the poems of Li Po and Tu Fu, Shakespeare and Whitman, Góngora, Bashō, Tagore, Pushkin? Translation, our humanistic conscience, makes it possible to make these poets part of our lives. George Steiner quotes Goethe's letter to Carlyle — "Say what one will of its inadequacy, translation remains one of the most important, worthwhile concerns in the totality of world affairs" — and adds: "Without it we would live in arrogant parishes bordered by silence." In 1611, the translators of the King James Bible employed biblical cadences, which they had so eloquently translated, to make the case for translation:

> Translation it is that openeth the window, to let in the light; that breaketh the shell, that we may eat the kernel; that putteth aside the curtain, that we may look into the most holy place; that removeth the cover of the well, that we may come by the water, even as Jacob rolle away the stone from the mouth of the well, by which means the flocks of Laban were watered. Indeed without translation into the vulgar tongue, the unlearned are but like children at Jacob's well (which was deep) without a bucket or something to draw with or as that person mentioned by Esau, to whom when a sealed book was delivered, with this motion, "Read this, I Pray thee," he was faith to make this answer, "I cannot, for it is sealed." . . .

There is a sliding scale in translating poetry from the strictest literalism to the freest adaptation. The literalists argue that the only faithful translation is an interlinear trot or a prose paraphrase. This is Vladimir Nabokov's position: "The clumsiest literal translation is a thousand times more useful than the prettiest paraphrase." The argument against the strict trot is that it can serve as only an auxiliary to a poem, while losing the poem itself, or at least what is most crucial about it. It is a useful but distant pointer. It never gives us a direct experience.

Another freer mode of translating poetry involves imitation (from the Latin, *imitatio*), the art of modeling, the act of following a prototypical source, an acknowledgment of precedence. John Dryden characterized the art of imitation as a kinship between authors in his *Preface to Fables* (1700). Here an imitation takes on the force of a refashioning of a previous poem. Dryden explains: "In the way of imitation, the translator not only varies from the words and sense, but forsakes them as he sees occasion; and, taking only some general hints from the original, runs diversions upon the groundwork." An imitation is different than a literal rendition. It takes greater license and moves in more ambiguous literary space. It is interpenetrated by its source. The tradition of imitation expands in our time to Robert Lowell's controversial *Imitations* (1961) and Stephen Berg's *The Steel Cricket: Versions*

1959–1997 (1997). Lowell confessed that he had been reckless with the literal meaning of poems, but labored hard to get the right tone. When an imitation succeeds, it accomplishes something closer to a fusion of two poetic selves. Thus Berg takes the final line from the German poet Ernst Stadler's 1914 poem "Der Spruch," or "The Saying," "*Mensch, werde wesentlich!*" ("Man, become substantial!"), and renders it: "STOP BEING A GHOST!"

Imitation as Lowell and Berg practice it widens out into a greater departure from the original, an adaptation. Michael Hamburger points out: "Imitation in classical practice was the taking-over and renewal of past conventions and kinds — as the Romans took over and renewed Greek models, generations of later poets took over and renewed the Latin and Greek. What mattered in that was not the individuality of the poets imitated, but the perpetuation of exemplars, conventions, and kinds." The idea originated with Horace (65–8 B.C.E.), who wrote in his *Odes* (23–13 B.C.E., 4.2) that it would be disastrous to imitate the sublime power of Pindar, whose music was like a rushing torrent "that boils and roars and overflows its banks," rushing down "the mountain-side of song." He compared Pindar to a great swan conquering the air by long rapturous flights, and compared himself to the humble bee, modestly and painstakingly gathering honey. This helps to account for the difference between the Pindaric ode and the Horatian ode. Seneca the Younger (ca. 4 B.C.E.–65 C.E.) picked up the Horatian image of the bee as a figure for the author. The bee, he suggests in Epistle 84, first samples various texts by earlier writers, and then "so blend[s] those several flavors into one delicious compound" that the final honey "is clearly a different thing from that whence it came." This freestanding adaptation, a kind of criticism and appreciation, is the mode of modern works such as Ezra Pound's *Homage to Sextus Propertius* (1917–1934) and Christopher Logue's accounts of Homer (*War Music,* 1997; *All Day Permanent Red,* 2003; *Cold Calls,* 2005). The translation of poetry inevitably strives to re-create a totality that can never be fully recovered. But something else emerges. Joseph Brodsky reformulated Frost's position: "Poetry is what is gained in translation."

SEE ALSO *heresy of paraphrase, imitation, ode, untranslatableness.*

trenta sei John Ciardi invented the *trenta sei* ("thirty-six" in Italian) in 1985. It consists of six six-line stanzas rhyming *ababcc.* The first stanza establishes the opening lines of each subsequent stanza: thus, the second line of the poem becomes the first line of the second stanza, the third line becomes the first line of the third stanza, and so on until the end. Ciardi's "A Trenta-Sei of the Pleasure We Take in the Early Death of Keats" was the last poem he completed before his death (*Echoes: Poems Left Behind,* 1989). The poet-physician John Stone fittingly composed a memorial poem, "A Trenta-Sei for John Ciardi (1916–1986)" (1987).

triadic line A line of Hebrew verse that contains three parallel units or half-lines, which are called *versets,* as in 2 Samuel (22:9), when the Lord descends to do battle: "Smoke came out of his nostrils, / fire from his mouth consumed, / coals glowed round him." William Carlos Williams's use of what he called a variable foot is sometimes called a three-ply or triadic line because it unfolds in three descending parts.

SEE ALSO *tercet, variable foot, verset.*

tribach, see *foot.*

trimeter, see "accentual syllabic meter" in *meter.*

trimètre, see *alexandrine.*

triolet From the French, "little trio." An eight-line poem with two rhymes and two refrain lines, *ABaAabAB* (the capital *A*s and *B*s represent the repeated lines). Here is W. E. Henley's light self-describing triolet from the late nineteenth century:

> Easy is the triolet,
> If you really learn to make it!
> Once a neat refrain you get,
> Easy is the triolet.
> As you see! — I pay my debt
> With another rhyme. Deuce take it,
> Easy is the triolet,
> If you really learn to make it!

An intricate, playful, and melodious form, the triolet was originally a medieval French verse form, which dates to the thirteenth century and comes from the same family as the rondeau. The first triolets in English were prayers written by Patrick Carey, a seventeenth-century Benedictine monk. Robert Bridges reintroduced the form into English in the late nineteenth century. Edmund Gosse said that "nothing can be more ingeniously mischievous, more playfully sly, than this tiny trill of epigrammatic melody, turning so simply on its own innocent axis" ("A Plea for Certain Exotic Forms of Verse," 1877).

The triolet has a strict formality. The first two lines establish the subject. The repetition of the fourth line creates a moment of lyric intensity. The fifth and sixth lines take on a sudden air of freedom and tend to expand the subject matter. The final lines tightly knit the conclusion. A key feature of the triolet is how the poet plays with the repeated lines to change the meaning as the poem proceeds.

French poets have tended to stick to eight-syllable lines (octosyllables), but poets in English have tended to rely on more open-ended line lengths and meters. Some contemporary poets, such as Barbara Howes and Dana Gioia, have employed triolet stanzas in longer poems. A good anthology of triolets would include poems by Alphonse Daudet, Stéphane Mallarmé, Arthur Rimbaud, Austin Dobson, Arthur Symons, Wendy Cope, and Sandra McPherson. Here is Thomas Hardy's double triolet "The Coquette, and After" (1901):

For long the cruel wish I knew
That your free heart should ache for me
While mine should bear no ache for you;
For long — the cruel wish! — I knew
How men can feel, and craved to view
My triumph — and fated not to be
For long! . . . The cruel wish I knew
That your free heart should ache for me!

At last one pays the penalty —
The woman — women always do.
My farce, I found, was tragedy
At last! — One pays the penalty
With interest, when one, fancy-free,
Learns love, learns shame . . . Of sinners two

At last one pays the penalty —
The woman — women always do!

SEE ALSO *octosyllabic verse, rondeau.*

triple meter (1) Any poetic measure consisting of three units, such as anapestic and dactylic feet. The distinctive 1–2–3 movement spaces the stresses out fairly evenly and the insistent rhythm now seems mostly suitable for light verse. (2) Any larger unit consisting of three feet or measures, such as the *tripody,* a Greek quantitative measure that treats three metrical feet as a single unit.

SEE ALSO *anapest, dactyl, light verse, meter.*

triple rhyme, see *rhyme.*

triplet, see *tercet.*

tripody, see *triple meter.*

triversen stanza, see *variable foot.*

trobar clus, trobar leu There was a controversy in troubadour circles between two different kinds of poetry: *trobar clus* ("closed" or "hermetic poetry") and *trobar leu* ("open" or "easy poetry"). One manner is knotted, oblique, and difficult; the other is light, smooth, and accessible. One is directed to a coterie audience; the other to a wider group. The *trobar clus* enabled the poet to conceal his message from one audience while making it available to another. It also influenced a later manner called *trobar ric* ("rich" or "elaborate" poetry). There is a parallel aesthetic difference in the Renaissance between the "aureate" (or "golden") and the "drab" poets, those who preferred elaboration and those who embraced the plain style.

SEE ALSO *aureate, courtly love, drab and golden, obscurity, the plain style, troubadour.*

trochee A metrical foot of two syllables, the first stressed, the second unstressed, as in the word *lúcky.* The trochee starts with a downbeat, as in the word *póĕt.* There are two thus trochees (a *di-trochee*) in the title of Hugh Mac-

Diarmid's autobiography *Lucky Poet* (1943). Longfellow's "Song of Hiawatha" (1855) is a celebrated example of trochaic meter, an insistent rhythm that encourages chanting:

> Should you ask me, whence these stories?
> Whence these legends and traditions,
> With the odors of the forest,
> With the dew and damp of meadows,
> With the curling smoke of wigwams,
> With the rushing of great rivers,
> With their frequent repetitions,
> And their wild reverberations,
> As of thunder in the mountains?

Longfellow was inspired by the national epic of Finland, the *Kalevala*, compiled in the nineteenth century, which was created in what amounts to trochaic tetrameter. Finnish is essentially a trochaic language, since the stress falls on the first syllable of the word and then all the other syllables trail after.

Since the sixteenth century the trochee, the opposite of the iamb, has been mostly employed to provide emphasis, substitution, and variation in iambic lines, as in John Milton's companion poems "L'Allegro" and "Il Penseroso" (both 1645). The trochee is the most common substitution for the first foot of an iambic line, as in Shakespeare's sonnet, "They that have power to hurt and will do none" (no. 94, 1609). It is the foot of reversal.

SEE ALSO *foot, iamb, iambic pentameter, meter.*

Troilus stanza, see *rhyme royal.*

trope A figure of speech. A trope provides a way of extending the meaning of words beyond the literal. *Turn* is an older English word for trope, and tropes have the capacity to turn, to change and deepen our sense of words and things. They can radically alter our sense of language and experience, and thus of ourselves. It's commonly said that figurative language — saying one thing and also meaning another — is an important resource for poetry, but in truth it is much more than that because it is at the heart of poetic thinking.

The master tropes, which include metaphor, simile, and synecdoche, have been considered and taught for at least twenty-five centuries. Metaphor, the most crucial and widely employed type of trope, creates a radical likeness, an imaginary identity, between different things, as when Dickinson says, " 'Hope' is the thing with feathers." A simile is an explicit comparison between two different things, using the word *as* or *like.* Wordsworth remembers, "I wandered lonely as a cloud." Synecdoche, a form of metonymy, substitutes the name of one thing with something else closely associated with it, as when we say "the heart" and mean "the emotions" ("be quiet, heart!" Paul Goodman cries out when he sees "the Lordly Hudson"). The Roman rhetorician Quintilian described synecdoche as "letting us understand the plural from the singular, the whole from a part, a genus from the species, something following from something preceding; and *vice versa*" (*Institutes,* IX, ca. 95 C.E.). Christopher Marlowe employs a synecdoche in *Doctor Faustus* (1604) when he asks

> Was this the face that launched a thousand ships
> And burnt the topless towers of Ilium?

The Russian poet Andrey Bely used both simile and metaphor when he informed the younger Marina Tsvetaeva, "A poet has to be condemned to poetry like a wolf to his howling, but you're a bird that keeps on singing." Tropes depend on a collaborative interpretive process between writer and reader. They rely on personal impressions and interpretations that readers discover and experience for themselves.

The word *trope* took on a special meaning in the Middle Ages when it came to refer to a phrase, sentence, verse, or strophe inserted into the liturgy. These verbal amplifications of passages in the authorized liturgy ornament, enforce, and enlarge the text. The elaboration of the Kyrie eleison (Lord, have mercy) is a notable early example: "Kyrie / magnae Deus potentiae, / liberator hominis, / transgressoris mandati, / eleison." The most well known of all, the *quem quaeritis trope,* the Introit of the Easter Mass, developed into resurrection plays, medieval liturgical and pageant drama.

SEE ALSO *figures of speech, metaphor, metonymy, personification, rhetoric, simile.*

troubadour The troubadours (their name derives from the Provençal word *trobar,* meaning both "to find" and "to invent") were poets who traveled from one court to another and flourished in southern France, northern Italy, and Spain between 1100 and 1350. Their language was Provençal, or the *langue d'oc.* They are akin to trouvères (court poets who thrived in northern France at the same time) and minnesingers (wandering lyricists who flourished in Germany between the twelfth and fourteenth centuries). They are also related to, though more elite than, jongleurs (itinerant minstrels, jugglers, and acrobats who entertained at the courts of medieval France and Norman England).

"Song again did not awake until the troubadour viol aroused it," Ezra Pound declared in *The Spirit of Romance* (1910). There are some 450 troubadours known by name. The first troubadour whose work has survived was William IX, Duke of Aquitaine, also known in Occitan as Guilhèm de Peitieus and in French as Guillaume de Poitiers (1071–1127). Peter Dronke suggests that his eleven "songs represent not the beginnings of a tradition but summits of achievement in that tradition." Bernart de Ventadorn (ca. 1130–1200), the acknowledged master of the *canso,* or love song, established the classical form of courtly love poetry ("With joy I begin the verse / And with joy bring it to a close"). Bertran de Born (ca. 1140–1215) was the recognized master of the *sirventes,* or political song. Dante portrays him in the *Inferno* (1304–1309) as one of the sowers of discord, holding up his severed head, like a lantern. Women troubadours were called *trobairitz,* the first female composers of secular music in the Western tradition.

The twelfth-century troubadour Arnaut Daniel, the inventor of the sestina, was praised by Dante as *il miglior fabbro* (the finer craftsman), a dedicatory phrase that T. S. Eliot famously borrowed for "The Waste Land" (1922). Dante has him introduce himself in *Purgatorio* (1308–1312, 26): "I am Arnaut, who weeps and goes on his way singing." He was transforming Arnaut's own signature lines:

> I am Arnaut, who gathers the wind
> And rides the ox to hunt the hare
> And swims against the tide.

Petrarch called him "The Grand Master of Love," and Ezra Pound deemed him the greatest poet who ever lived.

The troubadours wrote amorous poems of stunning technical virtuosity. Their field was the lyric; they did not write narrative poems. They composed in two competing styles: *trobar leu* (the plain or open style) and *trobar clus* (the hermetic or deliberately intricate style). Their creations were largely responsible for the phenomenon of courtly love. There is a great tension in their work between the poet/lover's allegiance to his lady and his allegiance to God. The troubadours, a deep source of the European lyric, have been called "the inventors of modern verse."

SEE ALSO *aubade, canso, courtly love, jongleur, minnesinger, sestina, sirventes, trobar clus, trouvère.*

trouvère Akin to the medieval troubadours, the trouvères were court poets who thrived in northern and central France during the twelfth and thirteenth centuries and wrote in *langue d'oïl,* which became the French language. They were aristocratic poet-composers. The first known trouvère was Chrétien de Troyes, remembered for his five Arthurian romances. The most famous was Thibaut de Champagne, who became king of Navarre. Sixty-six of his charmed songs survive. Many trouvères were knights, such as Gace Brulé. The repertoire of the trouvères was much like the troubadours. They excelled in the *grande chant* or *grande chanson courtoise* (courtly love songs) and also composed chansons de geste (songs of heroic deeds). Together, the troubadours and the trouvères created one of the greatest repertoires of love songs.

SEE ALSO *chansons de geste, chivalric romance, courtly love, troubadour.*

truncation, also called ***catalexsis*** The omission of a final syllable or syllables in a metrical line of verse. A line that lacks one syllable is called catalectic. A normal line of poetry (i.e., a line that has the full number of syllables) is acatalectic. A line foreshortened by more than one syllable is called brachycatalectic. A line with one syllable too many, thus going "beyond the last metrical foot," is called hypercatalectic ("To be or not to be, that is the question"). The term *initial truncation* is also used to describe a line that omits the first syllable (*acephalous*). All of these are used for variation and effect. Here are two stanzas from Shakespeare's octosyllabic poem "The Phoenix and the Turtle" (1601). Every line in the first stanza is acatalectic; every line in the second stanza is catalectic, pointedly truncated. The truncation seems to enact the feeling of reason being puzzled and confounded.

Reason, in itself confounded,
Saw division grow together;
To themselves yet either neither,
Simple were so well compounded,

That it cried, "How true a twain
Seemeth this concordant one!
Love hath reason, reason none,
If what parts can so remain."

SEE ALSO *acephalous.*

tumbling verse King James VI of Scotland coined this phrase in his treatise on verse, *Reulis and Cautelis* (Rules and Cautions, 1585). It refers to a four-stress loosely anapestic accentual verse. James contrasts tumbling verse to "flowing" or smooth verse, which suggests that tumbling verse is rougher and more irregular, like doggerel. He also called it *rouncefallis,* connected it to the dueling form of *flyting,* and gives an alliterative example from Montgomerie's "Flyting," which dates to the early 1580s:

Fetching fude for to feid it fast furth of the Farie.

Tumbling verse has roots in Anglo-Saxon alliterative meter. Thomas Tusser's popular *Some of the Five Hundred Points of Good Husbandry* (1557, 1573) is a well-known extended example. The term also applies to the type of verse that John Skelton invented known as Skeltonics.

SEE ALSO *doggerel, flyting, meter, Skeltonics.*

tz'u The Chinese word *tz'u* originally meant "words to be sung." *Tz'u* poetry was first written and performed by prostitutes in singing houses and later became the primary lyric mode of the Sung Dynasty (960–1279). The form flourished in part because it retained the freshness of its vernacular roots. As Julia Landau puts it: "The singing girls brought the music, the themes, the language, and probably the inspiration; the scholars, their refinement, intelligence and skill."

The *Ch'u Tz'u* or *Songs of the South* (third century B.C.E.–second century C.E.) is one of the two anthologies that mark the beginnings of the Chinese poetry tradition. *Tz'u* served as an alternative to *shih* poetry, which traced its origins to the Confucian classic, the *Shih Ching* or *Book of Songs* (tenth to sixth centuries B.C.E.). In *tz'u* poetry, the music at first drove the form — there were roughtly eight hundred different tunes — and the words followed. Its themes were initially light, gradually more serious. Traditional *tz'u* poetry stuck to the subjects of love and longing, but another type, considered heroic, widened the scope of the form. The poet Su Shih is generally credited (and blamed) for turning a folk into a literary, a sung into a written form. He added all kinds of material — personal, daily — and imported some of the subject matter of *shih* poetry, such as social commentary and political protest. The form moved away from music, and the original tunes became codified as meters. A musical skill had become a literary mode.

SEE ALSO *shih*.

ubi sunt The succinct Latin phrase *ubi sunt* ("where are they?") is used as the opening line or refrain in a telling number of Medieval Latin poems. The phrase encapsulates the poignant disappearance of beloved people and things. Poets used the motif to catalog the names of those dead and gone, meditating on the fragility of beauty and the transitory nature of life. François Villon's "Ballade des dames du temps jadis" (1450) is the greatest medieval example. Its well-known refrain line

> Mais où sont les neiges d'antan?

was rendered into English by Dante Gabriel Rossetti as

> But where are the snows of yester-year?

in his translation of "The Ballad of Dead Ladies" (1870). The *ubi sunt* theme — the perennial question *where are they now?* — recurs in such American poems as those in Edgar Lee Masters's *Spoon River Anthology* (1915) and Robert Hayden's "Elegies for Paradise Valley" (1978).

SEE ALSO *mono no aware.*

'Udhrī poetry 'Udhrī poetry is elegiac love poetry or poetry of unrequited love. This type of lovesick pre-Islamic poetry is named after two poets of the tribe of Yemeni Banu 'Udhra, 'Urwa ibn Hizām and Jamīl ibn Ma'mar, who wrote of their undying devotion to their beloveds, and supposedly died of love. The most famous of 'Udhrī poets, Qays ibn al-Mulawwah, became known by the epithet *Majnūn Layla,* "Mad for Laylā." The 'Udhrī poets and their inspirations — Majnūn and Laylā, Urwa and 'Afrā,' his paternal cousin, Jamil and Buthayna, Kuthayyir and 'Azza — were transformed into legendary, widely circulated romantic stories of doomed lovers. The three conventions of love poetry are devotion to a single woman, chastity, and faithfulness unto death. The Sufi poets developed the feelings of 'Udhrī poetry into a religious devotion to the beloved. The tradition of martyred, unattainable love was also developed into religious verse by medieval Arabic-Islamic and Hebrew poets.

SEE ALSO *the beloved, courtly love, ghazal, qasida.*

Ultraism, Ultraísmo (Spanish) The Argentine poet and fabulist Jorge Luis Borges was the creative spark of this avant-garde group of Spanish and Latin American writers, who sought to sever literature from the past. "We have cut the umbilical cord," the new Ultraists declared in 1918. Borges, who was joined in Spain by Geraldo Diego, Federico García Lorca, Guillermo de Torre, José Ortega y Gasset, and others, carried news of the movement across the ocean, where it initiated the avant-garde in Argentina, who called themselves the Florida Group after a street in Buenos Aires. The Ultraístas placed their faith in creation for its own sake. "This is the aesthetics of Ultra," the group claimed in the "Ultraist Manifesto" (1921):

> It wants to create: that is, to impose so far unsuspected ways of seeing on the universe. It demands from each poet a fresh view of things, clear of any ancestral stigmas; a fragrant vision, as if the world were arising like dawn in front of our eyes. And to conquer this vision, it is essential to cast away every aspect of the past.

The Ultraists exalted metaphor as the primordial element of poetry and banished "useless middle sentences, linking particles and adjectives." They invented a kind of elliptical poetry and vowed to avoid anything ornamental, circumstantial, confessional, preachy, or vague. And they determined to synthesize two or more images into one, widening its suggestiveness. Metaphor excited them, as Borges put it, "because of its algebraic way of bringing distances together."

SEE ALSO *Creationism, elliptical poetry, metaphor.*

ultra-talk, see *talk poem.*

unanimisme Around 1908, the writer Jules Romains founded this French literary movement, which was based on Walt Whitman's ideal of universal brotherhood. *Unanimisme* started out when a few enthusiastic young French intellectuals lived together in L'Abbaye, a residence at Creteil near Paris, and thus became known as the Abbaye Group (Groupe de L'Abbaye, 1906–1908). *Unanimisme* emphasized "the cult of life, of teeming nature and the fertile city," the transcendental power of group emotion and the collective consciousness. The unanimist theory of prosody was outlined in Georges Duhamel and Charles Vildrac's "Notes on Poetic Technique" (1910) and Romain and Georges Chennevière's "Little Treatise on Versification" (1923). The group proselytized for *poésie immédiate,* a direct, anti-symbolist poetry written in a clear, rhythmic, unadorned language. Whitman's free-verse rhythms were the method of transport for poets to overcome their isolation and merge with the transcendental.

SEE ALSO *free verse, vers libre.*

the uncanny The uncanny has to do with the mysterious or strange, with experiences that are weird or ghostly, possibly supernatural. It is a warp in time, a crisis in normalcy. *Webster's Dictionary* defines the adjective *uncanny:* "1) Having or seeming to have a supernatural or inexplicable basis; beyond the ordinary or normal; extraordinary; 2) Mysterious; frightening, as by superstitious dread; uncomfortably strange." Sigmund Freud's foundational 1919 essay, *"Das Umheimliche"* ("The Uncanny"), which claims that the uncanny is concerned with "the theory of qualities of feeling," teaches us how to see ourselves as split beings, how to look for what is most foreign in ourselves. "We are all haunted houses," the poet H. D. wrote in her *Tribute to Freud* (1956).

The word *uncanny* dates back to eighteenth-century Scotland. The *Oxford English Dictionary* cites Robert Fergusson's "An Eclogue. To the Memory of DR. WILLIAM WILKIE, late Professor of Natural Philosophy in the University of St. Andrews" (*Poems,* 1773) as the earliest instance of the word *uncanny.* The poem is a dialogue between two shepherds, Geordie and Davie, who are mourning the death of a third shepherd, named Wily. Davie says:

> They tell me, Geordie, he had sic a gift,
> That scarce a starnie blinkit frae the lift,
> But he would some auld warld name for't find,
> As gart him keep it freshly in his mind:
> For this some ca'd him an uncanny wight;
> The clash gaed round, "he had the second sight;"
> A tale that never fail'd to be the pride
> Of grannies spinnin' at the ingle-side.

The uncanny reminds us of the resistant strangeness of literature itself. Emily Dickinson recognizes the power of the uncanny when she writes in a letter: "Nature is a Haunted House—but Art—a House that tries to be haunted."

SEE ALSO *psychoanalytic criticism, the sublime.*

understatement, see *litotes, meiosis.*

unity Latin: "oneness, sameness." The idea that a work of art is self-contained and coherent, the parts are interdependent, and each part relates to the whole. Nothing can be taken away, nothing added. The crucial but contentious idea of artistic unity has a long philosophical history that runs from Plato (427?–347? B.C.E.) to Derrida (1930–2004). In the *Phaedrus,* Plato had Socrates argue that every composition should resemble a living organism. In the *Poetics* (350 B.C.E.), Aristotle expanded on this idea and argued that tragedy and epic should have a kind of "oneness." Each work should have a unity of action that is whole and complete. Homer "made the *Odyssey,* and likewise the *Iliad,* to center round an action that in our sense of the word is one," he says.

> As therefore, in the other imitative arts, the imitation is one when the object imitated is one, so the plot, being an imitation of an action, must imitate one action and that a whole, the structural union of the parts being such that, if any one of them is displaced or removed, the whole will be disjointed and disturbed. For a thing whose presence or absences makes no visible difference, is not an organic part of the whole.

Aristotle also argues that the epic "will thus resemble a living organism in all its unity, and produce the pleasure proper to it." In his *Ars Poetica* (ca. 19–18 B.C.E.), Horace denounced poets and painters who joined unharmonious parts together and followed Aristotle with a notion of unity: "In short, create what you wish, as long as it is a single harmonious whole."

Until the eighteenth century, most theories of literary unity dealt with drama and, occasionally, epic. Unity concerned formal rules, methods of plot construction. The French neoclassical writers expanded and rigidified Aristotle's "unity of action" into the so-called *Three Unities* (action, place, and time), which were commended by writers from John Dryden (1631–1700) to T. S. Eliot (1888–1965), and yet never quite caught on in English, mostly because Shakespeare (1564–1616), our standard-bearer, so frequently defied the norms. The romantic poets and critics expanded the idea of artistic unity to apply to lyric and shorter narrative poetry. They spoke of unity of feeling, unity created by the poet's mind in the act of creation, unity that grew organically from within a work, unity forged by the shaping and reconciling powers of the imagination. W. B. Yeats (1865–1939) was continually chiding himself to "hammer your thoughts into unity," obsessed by his own fragmented thinking, and seeking an elusive, even impossible unity of being. The discontinuities and fissures of modernism — think of "Hugh Selwyn Mauberley" (1920) or "The Waste Land" (1922) — forced critics to think about unity in wider and more various ways. Many different types of twentieth-century literary criticism — archetypal criticism, New Criticism — depend on an expanded idea of artistic unity, more open to ambiguity, paradox, and contradiction, a reconciliation of discordant elements and parts.

Postmodern Continental theorists have mounted a sustained critique against the idea of unity as a postulated whole. Michel Foucault made the case against the repressive structures of continuity and unity in our thinking. Jacques Derrida turned the assault on unity into one of the fundamentals of deconstruction, which challenges the idea of structure as an organic whole, a fiction that limits the field of "freeplay." Derrida replaced structural closure or unity with a vision of unlimited textual freedom. Paul De Man leveled his attack against Anglo-American aesthetics, especially the New Critical idea, adapted from Coleridge, that a poem has a formal unity analogous to a living organism. By pushing the interpretive process as far as they did, De Man contended, the New Critics "exploded" the metaphor and thereby confirmed "the absence of the unity [they] had postulated." If unity can ever be resurrected as a desirable or necessary feature of poetry, the argument must take into account these suspicious critiques, demonstrating that the open-endedness of poetic language can be part of its radical coherence.

SEE ALSO *ambiguity, archetype, deconstruction, imagination, imitation, New Criticism, organic form, paradox, postmodernism.*

universality The loose and baggy idea of universality, of poetry that appeals to all worldwide, has a long contentious history and a limited usefulness. Yet it keeps cropping up, like the equally controversial and old-fashioned idea of our common humanity. One problem with the notion of universality is that it is used in such a wide variety of ways. In *Literary Criticism: A Short History* (1970), Wimsatt and Brooks distinguish nine distinct meanings of the term in the neoclassical era. The concept of universality migrated to literary criticism from philosophy, which distinguishes universals (abstract propositions and relations) from particulars (concrete objects that exemplify them). In literature, the "universal" has inevitably been associated with the "general" and the "abstract" and placed in opposition to the "concrete" and the "particular." These terms, which Hegel tried to reconcile with the idea of the concrete universal, are dialectical and complementary.

Sheldon Zitner explains that "cultural moments of conformity and consolidation like the neoclassical emphasize universals in discussions of both the form and aim of literature, and moments of skepticism and iconoclasm like the romantic period or our own ignore them." We are relativists. Yet he also recognizes that the romantics, who rejected aesthetic universals, also believed in a universal human nature. Thus Wordsworth wrote in 1800: "The Poet binds together by passion and knowledge the vast empire of human society, as it is spread over the whole earth." Goethe told Eckermann in 1827: "I am more and more convinced that poetry is the universal possession of mankind." In "The Poet and Time" (1932), the Russian poet Marina Tsvetaeva defined a universal work as "one which, translated into another language and another age, translated into the language of another age — least of all then — loses nothing. Having given everything to its own age and land, it gives everything once again to all lands and all ages. Having revealed its own place and age, up to the furthest bounds, it boundlessly reveals all that is not-place, not-age: for all ages."

There is no longer any cultural consensus. All centuries have had their cataclysms, but the harrowing historical realities of the twentieth and twenty-first centuries especially seemed to call into question the idea of universal standards of behavior and common values. "They don't want any philosopher-kings in England," Louis MacNeice wrote on the precipice of World War II, "There ain't no universals in this man's town" (*Autumn Journal,* 1938). The idea of universality, of the general over the particular, seems to deny or at least repress the historical conditions under which poetry is written, its locality, how it is created at a specific time in a specific place by specific people. Feminist and minority critics have also argued that canons of universality are Eurocentric and exclusive; naive at best. It may no longer be possible or even desirable to believe the Enlightenment idea that the One is the All, or that human nature is unchanging, or that, as Longinus contended in *On the Sublime* (100 C.E.): "lofty and true greatness in art pleases all men in all ages." Yet we continue to need some idea of shared humanity. And poetry itself, however different its aims and ends, is a universal of culture.

SEE ALSO *concrete universal, Enlightenment, neoclassicism, postmodernism, romanticism, translation, Weltliteratur.*

untranslatableness Samuel Taylor Coleridge writes in *Biographia Literaria* (XXII, 1817): "In poetry, in which every line, every phrase, may pass the ordeal of deliberation and deliberate choice, it is possible, and barely possible, to attain that *ultimatum* which I have ventured to propose as the infallible test of a blameless style; namely; its *untranslatableness* in words of the same language without injury to the meaning."

Untranslatableness (or what we might call untranslatability) is Coleridge's primary requirement for poetic style. The meaning of a word includes all the associations around it. No linguistic substitutions or synonyms will do. He suggests that in the ideal poem nothing can be altered, how the thing is said is inseparable from what is being said, and all the parts must be integrated into the whole. Verbal precision — the right naming — is all.

SEE ALSO *heresy of paraphrase, translation.*

Uranians Between the 1880s and 1930, there was a small, clandestine group of poets writing in English on homosexual themes. In his book *Greek Love* (1964), J. Z. Eglinton (Walter Breen) called them "The Calamites: A Victorian Paidophilic Poetaster Clique." In 1970, the British bibliographer and antiquarian book dealer Timothy d'Arch Smith took the term *Uranians,* which had been used as a designation for homosexuals in general, and specifically applied it to this loosely affiliated literary group of gay poets, which included Lord Alfred Douglas, William Johnson Cory, John Addington Symonds, and a dozen or so others. These formally conservative poets sentimentalized adolescent boys and appealed to the history of ancient Greece to revive the notion of *paiderastia,* "love of boys," which Symonds called *l'amour de l'impossible* (1882). Uranian poetry played a role in the upper-class homosexual subcultures of the Victorian era. In *The Great War and Modern Memory* (1975), Paul Fussell makes the case that the homoerotic representations of the Uranians provided an essential model for the war poets of World War I.

uta, see *tanka.*

utaawase A Japanese poetry match. A nineteenth-century Japanese-English dictionary defines *utaawase* as "to cause or let sing," as in the phrase *hito ni utaawase kiku,* "to get another to sing that we may hear." Dividing into two groups, poets were assigned fixed topics (*dai*) and competed before judges. The earliest extant formal *utaawase* is the *Zaiminbukyōke* of 804. The *utaawase* was at first a frivolity, but later became a serious occasion that enabled poets to demonstrate their technical virtuosity. There were a set number of rounds in the typical medieval poetry match. Each round consisted of two poems on the same topic, which were pitted against each other, and then rated as winners (*kachi*), losers (*make*), or draws (*ji*). The poems were formal (*hare no uta*) and the topics were handed out well in advance for such major competitions as *Roppyakuban Utawaase,* or "Poetry Contest in 600 Rounds" (1193), and the *Sengohyakuban Utaawase,* or "Poetry Contest in 1,500 Rounds" (1201).

The *jikaawase,* or personal poetry competition, which developed in the twelfth century, was a poetry match against oneself. The poet would select a topic and then compose one or two rounds of poems, pitting them against each other for comparison. The poet-priest Saigyō' compiled two such sequences: *Poetry Contest at the Mimosuso River* (1187) and *Poetry Contest at the Miya River* (1189).

SEE ALSO *poetic contests, tanka, waka, yūgen.*

ut pictura poesis Horace coined the Latin formula *ut pictura poesis* ("as in painting, so in poetry") in his *Ars Poetica* (ca. 19–18 B.C.E.) to suggest that painting and poetry are parallel arts. But the principle of associating poetry and painting operated for centuries before him. Plato asserted in the *Republic* (ca. 380 B.C.E.): "The poet is like a painter." Aristotle refers to painting five times in the *Poetics,* 350 B.C.E. ("It is the same in painting.") And in "De gloria Atheniensium" (*Moralia,* first century), Plutarch attributed the statement to Simonides of Ceos (ca. 556–467 B.C.E.): "Painting is mute poetry, and poetry a speaking picture." Laurence Binyon claimed that "a precisely identical saying is proverbial among the Chinese."

Horace's motto was fiercely debated over the centuries. It established a primary kinship between the arts — Tertullian said, "There is no art which is not either the mother or a very close kinsman of another art" — and raised the question of literary pictorialism. Jean Hagstrum points out that Simonides's statement came to England in 1586 through Hoby's translation of Coignet called *Politique Discourses:* "For as Simonides saide: Painting is a dumme Poesie, and a Poesie is a speaking picture; & the actions which the Painters set out with visible coulours and figures the Poets recken with words, as though they had been perfourmed." So, too, the sixteenth-century Portuguese poet Luis de Comoëns characterized painting as "muda poesia," and the polymath Leonardo Da Vinci (1452–1519) declared:

> Painting is poetry which is seen and not heard, and poetry is a painting which is heard but not seen. These two arts (you may call them both either poetry or painting) have here interchanged the senses by which they penetrate to the intellect.

Horace's almost offhanded dictum, which he never explained, was repeated so often that it became one of the keystones of Renaissance criticism. Charles-Alphonse de Fresnoy's 1665 poem *"De Arte Graphica"* ("The Art of Painting"), a treatise that he worked on for twenty-five years, was modeled on Horace's *Ars Poetica.* It was translated into English in the mid-eighteenth century and had a great vogue, especially the lines: "*Ut pictura poesis erit similisque poesi / Sit pictura*" ("A poem will be like a picture, and let a picture be similar to a poem").

The strong linkage between the verbal and visual arts began to fray in the eighteenth century. Edmund Burke vigorously attacked the connection in "A

Philosophical Inquiry into the Origin of Our Ideas of the Sublime and the Beautiful" (1757):

> So little does poetry depend for its effect on the power of raising sensible images, that I am convinced it would lose a very considerable part of its *energy*, if this were the result of all necessary description. Because that union of affecting words, which is the most powerful of all poetical instruments, would frequently lose its force, along with its propriety and consistency if the sensible images were always excited.

Gotthold Lessing also made a revisionary statement in *Laocoön* (1766) by distinguishing clearly between visual and verbal art. It was no longer axiomatic that poetry should be pictorial. The use of painting to illuminate poetry virtually disappeared during the romantic era. Music and poetry were increasingly allied as sister arts. As an analogy for poetry, painting, a spatial art, was in effect replaced by music, a temporal one.

SEE ALSO *ekphrasis, imagism, picturesque.*

vakh The earliest form of Kashmiri poetry, *vakh* is a Sanskrit word that means "speech," "talk," "saying." It is solely practiced by the Shaiva school of poets, whose songs glow with devotional fervor. The mystical poems of Lal Ded or Lalla (1320–1384), who was first a poet and then a Shaiva saint, are the earliest compositions in the Kasmiri language. They are known as *Lal Vakhs* and have the status of beloved maxims and proverbs. Coleman Barks brings Lalla into English in *Naked Song* (1992).

variable foot William Carlos Williams (1883–1963) coined this term to explain the three-step line that he developed in his later work. Williams claimed that the traditional fixed foot of English prosody needed to be altered to represent idiomatic American speech rhythms. He was seeking metrical relativity, a more intuitive cadence based on speech. The variable foot, he said, "rejects the standard of the conventionally fixed foot and suggests that measure varies with the idiom by which it is employed and the tonality of the individual poem. Thus, as in speech, the prosodic pattern is evaluated by criteria of effectiveness and expressiveness rather than mechanical syllable counts. The verse of genuine poetry can never be 'free,' but free verse, interpreted in terms of the variable foot, removes many artificial obstacles between the poet and the fulfillment of the laws of his design."

There is a productive tension between discipline and freedom in Williams's use of the variable foot, which, as Hugh Kenner says, "seems like a rubber inch." Williams especially favored the *triversen* stanza, which consists of three lines that comprise a complete sentence. Each third of the sentence is a line. Each step is located further from the left margin and lower down on the page. "Each segment of a triadic cluster is a foot," Denise Levertov contends, "and each has the same *duration.*" Williams was transforming the rhetorical *tricolon* — a sentence with three clearly defined parts (*cola*) of equal length — into a new American measure. Here are six illustrative lines from "Asphodel, That Greeny Flower" (1955):

> Of asphodel, that greeny flower
>   like a buttercup
>   upon its branching stem —
> save that it's green and wooden —
>   I come, my sweet,
>   to sing to you!

SEE ALSO *free verse, measure, tercet, triadic line, vers libre.*

variorum A work that collates all the known variants of a text. The Latin term *variorum* ("of the various") derives from the longer phrase *edito cum notis variorum,* "an edition with notes of various editors." A variorum edition was originally a text that included annotations from a variety of editors, critics, and commentators. It is now considered a work that presents a suggested text, as definitive as possible, with various readings from different successive editions. It often includes the editor's notes as well as conjectural emendations proposed by previous editors.

SEE ALSO *textual criticism.*

vatic The word *vatic,* which means "inspired with the power of prophecy," derives from the Latin term *vates* ("prophet"). From earliest times, prophecy has been connected to rhythmical speech. The poet has often been considered a visionary, a divinely inspired seer, a *vates.* There may have been a caste of *vates* among the Celts, or so the first-century geographer Strabo thought:

> . . . there are generally three divisions of men especially reverenced, the Bards, the Vates, and the Druids. The Bards composed and chanted hymns; the Vates occupied themselves with the sacrifices and the study of nature; while the Druids joined to the study of nature that of moral philosophy.

The vatic impulse is signaled in poetry whenever a poet speaks in a prophetic voice beyond the social realm. He is a vehicle — as when Shelley calls out to the west wind, "Be thou, Spirit fierce, / My spirit! Be thou me, impetuous one!" ("Ode to the West Wind," 1819) or D. H. Lawrence testifies, "Not I, not I, but the wind that blows through me!" ("Song of a Man Who Has Come Through," 1917).

SEE ALSO *afflatus, bard, fili, inspiration, verset, vision.*

vehicle, see "tenor and vehicle" in *metaphor.*

Venus and Adonis stanza, see *sestet.*

verbless poetry Poems without verbs. On one hand, the verbless poem can create a static quality, a sense of the arrested moment, which is why it has appealed to poets who write haiku and other types of imagist poems. For example, Ezra Pound's defining imagist poem, "In a Station of the Metro," consists of fourteen words without a verb. It juxtaposes two images without a comment, suggesting rather than stating the relationship, and in the process freezes a moment in time. Here is the version that first appeared in *Poetry* (April 1913):

> The apparition   of these faces   in the crowd   :
> Petals   on a wet, black   bough   .

On the other hand, the verbless construction can give, as the linguist Otto Jespersen points out in "The Role of the Verb" (1911), "a very definite impression of motion." That's why verbless constructions especially appealed to the futurists, such as F. T. Marinetti (1876–1944), who eliminated verbs in order to create a sense of telegraphic communication in a furiously changing world.

Both verbless modes, the static and the dynamic, have been employed in Russian literature, which has an unusually strong tradition of verbless poetry. On the epiphanic side: two of the most well-known lyrics by the Parnassian Afansii Fet are verbless poems, "Storm in the evening sky . . ." (1842) and "Whispers, timid breathing . . ." (1850), which are impressionistic word pictures, stopped moments. On the hyperkinetic side: the Russian imaginists (1918–1925) created a sense of dynamism in verbless poems that consisted of long strings of startling images and metaphors.

SEE ALSO *epiphany, futurism, haiku, Imaginism, imagism.*

verisimilitude The doctrine that poetry should appear "lifelike" or "real." The term *verisimilitude* derives from the Latin words *verum,* meaning truth, and *similis,* meaning similar. Literature should thus resemble the truth. Improbabilities should be disguised; what one hears or reads should be believable. The critical principle originates in Aristotle's idea of mimesis or imitation of nature (*Poetics,* 350 B.C.E.). In "How to Study Poetry" ("Die audiendis poetis," ca. early 80s C.E.), Plutarch suggested that poetry brings pleasure when its fictions bear the semblance of truth. Verisimilitude, which became an important concept (*vraisemblance*) in seventeenth- and eighteenth-century French drama, is itself a convention that suggests a relation not so much with reality as with what people consider reality. "We speak of a work's verisimilitude insofar as the work tries to convince us it conforms to reality and not to its own laws," Tzvetan Todorov argues. "In other words, verisimilitude is the mask which is assumed by the laws of the text and which we are meant to take for a relation with reality."

SEE ALSO *feigning, imitation, mimesis, willing suspension of disbelief.*

vers, see *chanso.*

vers de société "Society verse." The French term applies to a fashionable type of light verse that deals with the frivolities of upper-class social life. It was said, for example, that the Abbé de Chaulieu (1639–1720) wrote verses—graceful trifles—only for his friends. Some early twentieth-century American critics preferred William Cowper's eighteenth-century term *familiar verse* for this kind of easy, buoyant, debonair lyric. In eighteenth-century England, Matthew Prior tossed off various types of *vers de société* in *Poems on Several Occasions* (1709) and so did Alexander Pope in his "Minor Verse: 1700–1717." In the nineteenth century, Lord Byron's "Letter to Mr. Hodgson Written on Board the Lisbon Packet" ("Huzza! Hudson, we are going") qualifies as a sophisticated frippery. W. H. Auden said of Winthrop Mackworth Praed (1802–1839) that "his serious poems are as trivial as his *vers de société* are profound." Here is the characteristic final stanza of Praed's "A Letter of Advice" (1844):

Don't listen to tales of his bounty,
    Don't hear what they say of his birth,
Don't look at his seat in the county,
    Don't calculate what he is worth;
But give him a theme to write verse on,
    And see if he turns out his toe;
If he's only an excellent person, —
    My own Araminta, say "No!"

John Betjeman playfully carried the *vers de société* into twentieth-century English poetry. Philip Larkin mocks the tradition he employs in his satirical "Vers de Société" (1971).

SEE ALSO *Anacreontic, light verse.*

verse A metrical composition. The word *verse* is traditionally thought to derive from the Latin *versus,* meaning a "line," "row," or "furrow." The metaphor of "plough" for "write" thus dates to antiquity. *Verse* may alternately derive from the Latin *vertere,* "to turn." Verse is metrical writing. The poet disturbs language, arranging words into lines, into rows, turning them over, turning them toward each other, shaping them into patterns. Metrical writing is a way of charging sound, of energizing syllables and marking words, of rhythmically marking time. Such formal writing is markedly and perhaps even metaphysically different from prose. "Verse," Sir Philip Sidney wrote, "being in its selfe sweete and orderly, and being best for memory, the only handle of knowledge, it must be in jest that any man can speak against it."

Verse has been generally distinguished from prose ("Prose proceeds, verse reverses," Richard Howard says), but it has also sometimes been differentiated from poetry. Thus Sidney also spoke of verse as

> being but an ornament and no cause to poetry, since there have been many most excellent poets that never versified, and now swarm many versifiers that need never answer to the name of poets. . . . It is not rhyming and versing that maketh a poet — no more than a long gown maketh an advocate, who though he pleaded in armour should be an advocate and no soldier.

In his key treatise, "The Defense of Poetry" (ca. 1582), Sidney was intent on distinguishing genuine poetry from its facsimile, true poets from mere dabblers, necessary words from ornamental ones, and yet it always gives me a minor jolt when poets use the term *verse* in a negative or somewhat derogatory way. It is not the fault of verse, of metrical composition, that it has been misused. The poet is a maker, and verse is a demanding art of its own. The formal deliverance of poetry gives it ceremonial authority, a way of inhabiting and marking us. Sidney also acknowledged that "the senate of poets hath chosen verse as their fittest raiment." Joseph Brodsky asserts, "The one who writes a poem writes it above all because verse writing is an extraordinary accelerator of consciousness, of thinking, of comprehending the universe."

The term *verse* is also used to refer to a single line of poetry, or to a single stanza, especially of a hymn or song.

SEE ALSO *line, meter, prosody.*

verse drama, see *drama.*

verse epistle, see *letter poem.*

verse essay A short expository composition in verse. The word *essay* derives from the French *essayer,* "to try" or "to attempt." Michel de Montaigne essentially invented the essay form in *Essais* (1580). Francis Bacon's *Essays* (1597) brought the short prose discourse into English. Consequently, the verse essay, which was once directed to a general audience, brought some of the didactic sweep and discursive power of the essay to lyric poetry. It is self-consciously rhetorical. Alexander Pope adopted the essayistic stance for his two poems in heroic couplets, "An Essay on Criticism" (1711) and "An Essay on Man" (1733–1734), which seeks to "vindicate the ways of God to man." There weren't many advocates for the verse essay after the eighteenth century, but the blurring of genres between lyric poetry and expository prose has interested contemporary poets. Karl Shapiro took up the mantle for his discussion of poetics, *Essay on Rime* (1945). The language poet Charles Bernstein prefaces his book *My Way: Speeches and Poems* (1999) with the questions: "What is the difference between poetry and prose, verse and essays? Is it possible that a poem can extend the argument of an essay or that an essay can extend the prosody of a poem?"

SEE ALSO *didactic poetry, discursive, Enlightenment, neoclassicism, rhetoric.*

verse novel A novel in poetry. A hybrid form, the verse novel filters the devices of fiction through the medium of poetry. There are antecedents for the novelization of poetry in long narrative poems, in epics, chronicles, and romances, but the verse novel itself, as a distinct nineteenth-century genre, is different than the long poem that tells a story because it appropriates the discourse and language, the stylistic features of the novel as a protean form. Alexander Pushkin's *Eugene Onegin* (1831) established the verse novel as a new type of poem in chapters and a new kind of novel in stanzas. Adam Mickiewicz's twelve-book verse novel *Pan Tadeusz* (1834), which recreates his Lithuanian childhood, stands at the top of nineteenth-century Polish literature. In English literature, the verse novel took different forms in the 1850s and '60s in Elizabeth Barrett Browning's fictional autobiography, *Aurora Leigh* (1856); in Arthur Clough's epistolary fiction, *Amours de Voyage* (1857); in George Meredith's sequence of sixteen-line sonnets, *Modern Love* (1962); and in Robert Browning's series of dramatic monologues, *The Ring and the Book* (1868–1869). Unlike the Victorians, the modernist poets showed little interest in the verse novel, but contemporary poets have used it to gain for poetry some of the sweep and sensibility of prose fiction. My shortlist of contemporary self-described novels in verse includes Les Murray's *Fredy Neptune* (1998), Anne Carson's *Autobiography of Red* (1998), Vikram Seth's *The Golden Gate* (1999), Brad Leithauser's *Darlington's Fall* (2002), and Alice Notley's *Culture of One* (2011).

SEE ALSO *epic, narrative poetry, Onegin stanza, romance.*

verse paragraph The verse paragraph is a self-contained unit of lines, a type of paragraph in verse. It is irregular in length and tends to be used in longer narrative and dramatic poems, often in blank verse. The word *stanza* was once reserved for units of equal length. A stanzaic poem was symmetrical and a poem in verse paragraphs was asymmetrical. Thus Matthew Arnold's poem "The Scholar-Gypsy" (1853) consists of stanzas while his poem "Dover Beach" (1867) consists of verse paragraphs. John Milton used the verse paragraph so powerfully that it is virtually synonymous with *Para-*

dise Lost (1667). Robert Frost wonderfully managed "the sound of sentences" in the verse paragraphs of the long narrative poems in *North of Boston* (1914). Since the 1960s, the word *stanza* has been increasingly used to name both regular and irregular units within a poem. To understand the formal organization of a poem, it is still necessary to distinguish symmetrical stanzas and asymmetrical paragraphs, but the term *verse paragraph* is rapidly becoming antiquated.

SEE ALSO *stanza, stichic, strophe.*

verset A short verse, especially from a sacred book, as in the Song of Songs and the psalms. It also refers to a form based on such biblical models. The *verset* is one of two or three subunits that comprise a line of Hebrew poetry. Each *verset* contains a minimum of two and a maximum of ten syllables. The first line of the Psalm 1 has three parallel members or *versets:* "Blessed *is* the man that walketh not in the counsel of the ungodly / nor standeth in the way of sinners, / nor sitteth in the seat of the scornful." This tripartite structure, a *tricolon,* is used sparingly. The prevalent pattern in Hebrew poetry contains two parallel *versets,* as in the second line of the Psalm 1: "But his delight *is* in the law of the LORD; / and in his law doth he meditate day and night." Each half of the line is also referred to as a *bicolon* or hemistich.

The strength of the *verset* is how the shorter units build up into long lines and surging rhythms that rise above and beyond speech. The long lines (two or three *versets*) help to create the feeling of prophecy and fit the outsize sentiments of the Hebrew Bible. The emotional power of the *versets* is enforced by the use of anaphora and other types of repetition, by the dynamic structures of parallelism and the sound devices of alliteration and assonance.

The *versets* anticipate free verse in the wide sweep of their emotional expression. The form was first adapted for religious and mystical texts. Over the centuries it has been periodically redeployed to create a prophetic feeling. Paul Claudel's quasi-biblical mixture of long-lined free verse and prose is called the *verset claudélien.* The *verset* is also a structural device in the German poetry of Friedrich Hölderlin (1770–1843), the Polish poetry of Adam Mickiewicz (1798–1855), the French poetry of Arthur Rimbaud (1854–1891), and the English poetry of D. H. Lawrence (1885–1930). It has been used in vatic American poetry from Walt Whitman (1819–1892) to Allen Ginsberg (1926–1997).

SEE ALSO *alliteration, anaphora, assonance, free verse, hemistich, parallelism, stichic, vatic, verse paragraph, vision.*

versicle This liturgical term can mean (1) a short sentence said or sung antiphonally (that is, in a call-and-response pattern); (2) a small verse; (3) a single verse of the psalms or Bible; (4) a short or lone metrical line.

versification The term *versification* has three meanings: (1) the making of verses; (2) the internal features, especially the metrical structure or style, of verse; (3) taking something that has been composed in prose and turning it into verse.

SEE ALSO *prosody, verse.*

versi sciolti In Italian poetry, unrhymed eleven-syllable lines are called *versi sciolti.* A passage was called a *selva* or *versi sciolti* when it mixed an eleven-syllable line (*endecasyllabi*) with a seven-syllable line (*settanari*) without any regular pattern or rhyme scheme. This makes it equivalent to the Spanish *silva. Versi sciolti* was popular with Italian poets of the sixteenth century and frequently used in opera and cantata texts. Henry Howard, Earl of Surrey, was steeped in Italian poetry and probably took the *versi sciloti* as a model for his translation into blank verse of Virgil's *Aeneid* (1540). It was thus a forerunner to English blank verse.

SEE ALSO *blank verse, hendecasyllabics, silva.*

vers libre French: "free verse." Vers libre was a radical innovation of French poetry dating to the 1870s, when the classically ordered language of traditional poetry began to break down. One strong impulse of vers libre was to rupture strictly prescribed metrical patterns and rules, especially to break the stranglehold of the conventional twelve-syllable alexandrine verse line that dominated French poetry from the mid-seventeenth century onward. In the poetry of Paul Verlaine and Tristan Corbière, Arthur Rimbaud and especially Jules Laforgue (one of the first to translate Walt Whitman into French), a symmetrical prosody gives way to the irregular surges and pauses of a new rhythm. The poets who investigated vers libre sought a fresh, emergent, asymmetrical lineation, a verbal music suited to a distinct subject matter. The dream of vers libre: that every poem would have its own originary music ideally suited to its subject. The use of free verse in American poetry predated the use of free verse in French literature, and yet the French practice of vers libre, especially the work of Laforgue, had terrific impact on the modernists T. S. Eliot, Ezra Pound, D. H. Lawrence, William Carlos Williams, and others, and thus greatly influenced the development of free verse in English in the early twentieth century.

SEE ALSO *alexandrine, free verse, prose poem.*

vers romantique, see *alexandrine.*

versus recurrentes, see *palindrome.*

Verticalism, Vertigralism In 1928, Eugene Jolas, an internationally minded Swiss poet and the editor of the modernist journal *transitions,* founded a movement he called Verticalism. He later renamed it Vertigralism, a word that seemed to combine the sensation of vertigo, the dream of upward movement, and the ideal of an integral or integrated vision. He was the primary author of the manifesto "Poetry Is Vertical" (March 1932), which was signed by Hans Arp, Samuel Beckett, and James J. Sweeney, among others. It consisted of ten points and begins: "In a world ruled by the hypnosis of positivism, we proclaim the autonomy of the poetic vision, the hegemony of the inner life over the outer life." The idea was that poetry could triumph over the temporal narratives of a "horizontal age." It would create a hermetic language to reach both downward and upward:

> The transcendental "I" with its multiple stratifications reaching back millions of years is related to the entire history of mankind, past and present, and is brought to the surface with the hallucinatory irruption of images in the dream, the daydream, the mystic-gnostic trance, and even the psychiatric condition.

This short-lived "movement" — part romantic Surrealism, part Jungian psychology — sought a pure poetry, a "revolution of the word," a new vertical mythology. It was a form of what Dickran Tashijian terms "skyscraper primitivism." "From the return to the earth, the land, the rooted life, to the perception of the Eiffel Tower," Mary Anne Caws writes, "style rises up like a shout."

SEE ALSO *modernism, Surrealism.*

viator The Canadian poet Robin Skelton (1925–1997) invented this form, which he named after the Latin word for *traveler.* It consists of any stanzaic poem in which the first line of the first stanza becomes the second line of the second stanza and so on until the poem ends with the line with which it began. The first line travels through the poem. In the double *viator,* which consists of half a dozen six-line stanzas, the first and last lines migrate in opposite directions. The first line of the first stanza becomes the second one of the second and so forth, while the last line of the sixth stanza becomes the penultimate line of the fifth stanza and so forth. The rhyme scheme of the first two stanzas (*ababab bababa*) is repeated three times.

Victorian period Poetry played a dynamic role in the eight decades spanning Queen Victoria's long reign in England (1837–1901), when Great Britain was the most powerful nation on earth. The *Oxford English Dictionary* records Edmund Clarence Stedman's *Victorian Poets* (1875) as the first instance of the adjective *Victorian.* The initial sense of the noun is "a person, especially an author, who lived in the reign of Queen Victoria."

The period should have begun with the second generation of romantic poets — Byron, Keats, and Shelley — all of whom died too young. Instead, it begins with the poetry of Thomas Lovell Beddoes and Alfred Tennyson; it includes Emily Brontë, Walter Savage Landor, Elizabeth Barrett Browning and Robert Browning, Lewis Carroll and Edward Lear, Dante Gabriel Rossetti and Christina Rossetti, Matthew Arnold, William Morris, George Meredith, Gerard Manley Hopkins, and Robert Louis Stevenson; and it concludes with Thomas Hardy, A. E. Housman, and the early poetry of W. B. Yeats, who sounded the death knell of Victorianism when he declared that "Victorianism had been defeated" in his introduction to *The Oxford Book of Modern Verse, 1892–1935* (1936):

> The revolt against Victorianism meant to the young poet a revolt against irrelevant descriptions of nature, the scientific and moral dis-

> cursiveness of *In Memoriam* — "When he should have been broken-hearted," said Verlaine, "he had many reminiscences" — the political eloquence of Swinburne, the psychological curiosity of Browning, and the poetical diction of everybody.

The modernist poets — Yeats, Eliot, Pound — devalued the Victorian poetic tradition, and it took decades to recover these major and minor poets, the Victorian achievement. One thinks especially of the Victorian genius for verbal flares and fireworks, for what Walt Whitman termed "the finest verbalism" ("A Word About Tennyson," 1892). The Victorians had a special gift for nonsense verse that, as Christopher Ricks puts it, "outdoes in its speed of consummated enterprise even the precedent of the Augustan mock-heroic." And Browning and Tennyson invented the dramatic monologue and inaugurated what George MacBeth calls "the great age of fiction in English poetry. In the course of it, the ways in which narrative could be used for poetic purposes were developed and exploited more widely and ingeniously than ever before or since." The Victorian poets wrote in an era of tremendous change — the Terror after the French Revolution, the fallout from the Industrial Revolution — and responded to the radical dualities of the age. As Charles Dickens recognized, "It was the best of times, it was the worst of times."

SEE ALSO *dramatic monologue, nonsense poetry.*

Village of the Poets, see *epic.*

villancico From the late fifteenth to the eighteenth century, the *villancico* (or *vilancete* in Portuguese) was a common poetic and musical form known throughout the Iberian Peninsula and Latin America. The poems are carols, songs of religious joy, similar to other European kinds of folk songs. The form evolved from the songs of *villanos,* or peasants, in Muslim Spain. The fifteenth-century Spanish *villancico* was sung in the vernacular and associated with rural themes. The Latin American *villancico* especially drew on different local dialects. For example, the *negro* or *negrillo villancicos* imitated African speech patterns and incorporated onomatopoeic African phrases and sounds. The poetic form had *coplas* (stanzas) and an *estribillo* (refrain) in various combinations. Devotional *villancicos* became popular in the sixteenth century. By the seventeenth century, *villancicos* had become sequences of compositions sung in churches on religious feast days. The form was considered *arte menor* (minor art). Sor Juana Inés de la Cruz (1651–1695) composed twelve complete sets of *villancicos.* Since the nineteenth century, the term has meant "Christmas carol" in Spanish.

SEE ALSO *canciones, carol, copla, estribillo.*

villanelle A French form codified in the sixteenth century, the villanelle has its roots in Italian folk song and was originally associated with pastoral verse (the name derives from *villa,* a "farm" or "country house"). It consists of nineteen lines divided into six stanzas — five tercets and one quatrain. The first and third lines become the refrain lines of alternate stanzas and the final two lines of the poem. They rhyme throughout, as do the middle lines of each stanza. The entire poem then builds around two repeated lines and turns on two rhymes. Here is the schema:

A1 (refrain)
b
A2 (refrain)

a
b
A1 (refrain)

a
b
A2 (refrain)

a
b
A1 (refrain)

a
b
A2 (refrain)

a
b
A1 (refrain)
A2 (refrain)

The villanelle entered English poetry in the nineteenth century as a form of light verse (there are pleasurable examples by Andrew Lang, Oscar Wilde, W. E. Henley, and others), but it has had a more majestic life in the twentieth century. Many modern and contemporary poets have intuited how the compulsive returns of the villanelle could be suited both to a poetry of loss ("The art of losing isn't hard to master," Elizabeth Bishop wryly acknowledges in "One Art," 1976) as well as to a poetry speaking up against loss ("Do not go gentle into that good night," Dylan Thomas insists, 1951). My gathering of modern American villanelles would include Theodore Roethke ("The Waking," 1953), Weldon Kees ("Five Villanelles," 1947), Sylvia Plath ("Mad Girl's Love Song," 1951), James Merrill ("The World and the Child," 1962), Richard Hugo ("The Freaks at Spurgin Road Field," 1975), Howard Nemerov ("Equations of a Villanelle," 1975), Donald Justice ("In Memory of the Unknown Poet, Robert Boardman Vaughn," 1987), Mark Strand ("Two de Chiricos," 1998), Marilyn Hacker ("Villanelle," 1974), Michael Ryan ("Milk the Mouse," 1989), Deborah Digges ("The Rockettes," 1989), and William Olsen ("Hereafter," 1996). Here is Edwin Arlington Robinson's "The House on the Hill" (1894):

They are all gone away,
    The House is shut and still,
There is nothing more to say.

Through broken walls and gray
    The winds blow bleak and shrill:
They are all gone away.

Nor is there one to-day
    To speak them good or ill:
There is nothing more to say.

Why is it then we stray
    Around the sunken sill?
They are all gone away,

And our poor fancy-play
    For them is wasted skill:
There is nothing more to say.

There is ruin and decay
    In the House on the Hill:
They are all gone away,
There is nothing more to say.

SEE ALSO *refrain.*

virelay, vereli Also called *chanson baladée.* The name suggests that the virelay is a song (*lai*) that turns or twists (*virer*). Along with the ballade and the rondeau, it was one of the three fixed forms that predominated in French poetry and song in the fourteenth and fifteenth centuries. It may have originated as a dance or it may have come from Arabic songs that were transmitted by the troubadours in the twelfth century.

The virelay had a simple musical structure, but there were so many variations and options that it is now difficult to define. One common version begins with a refrain. This is followed by a four-line stanza; the first two lines of the quatrain have a repeated musical line different from the refrain. The next two lines repeat the refrain. The initial refrain is then sung again. The alternating stanzas usually repeat for two more stanzas. Some of the great practitioners were Guillaume de Machaut (ca. 1300–1377), Jean Froissart (ca. 1337–ca. 1405), Christine de Pisan (1367–ca. 1430), and Eustace Deschamps (1340–1406), who defined the virelay in *Arte de Dictier* (1392), the first treatise on French versification.

A virelay with only one stanza was called a *bergerette.* The Italian *balata* and the Spanish *cantiga* follow the same form. The virelay was severed from music in the fifteenth century and virtually died out at the beginning of the sixteenth century. It never caught on in English. There is a virelay sometimes attributed to Richard Beauchamp, Earl of Warwick (1382–1439), which begins "I cannot half the woo compleyne / That dothe my woful hert streyne / With bisy thought and grevous payne . . ." Thomas Percy printed a "Balet," or virelay, which he attributed to Anthony Woodville, second Earl Rivers (ca. 1440–1483), in *Reliques of Ancient English Poetry* (1765).

SEE ALSO *ballade, formes fixes, lai, rondeau.*

virgule A diagonal mark (/). In poetry, the slash is used to mark either foot divisions within a line of verse or a line ending.

SEE ALSO *scansion.*

vision, visionary poetry One definition of *vision* is the ability to see, the visual faculty. This relates to the poetry of perception, how one visualizes and describes things. It is commonly called descriptive poetry, an exacting art. "The greatest thing a human soul does in this world is to *see* something, and tell what it *saw* in a plain way," John Ruskin declared in *Modern Painters* (1843). "Hundreds of people can talk for one who can think, but thousands can think for one who can see. To see clearly is poetry, prophecy, and religion — all in one."

Another definition of *vision* is "the work of imagination." This relates to poetry that goes beyond sight, seeing not with but through the eye, dramatizing the spiritual quest or realization. It is commonly called visionary poetry because it provides insight into the unexpected nature of reality, how things truly are or might be. "Vision, or imagination, is a representation of what actually exists really, and unchangeably," William Blake reports in "A Vision of the Last Judgment" (1810). Visionary poetry is prophetic or mystical poetry, the heightened consciousness of the book of Isaiah, of Saint John of the Cross's "Dark Night" (ca. 1578) and "Spiritual Canticle" (ca. 1578), of Dante's *Divine Comedy* (1308–1321), of Christopher Smart's *Jubilate Agno* (1759–1763) and Blake's *The Marriage of Heaven and Hell* (1790–1793), of Allen Ginsberg's 1959 "Howl" ("I saw the best minds of my generation . . ."). Wordsworth remembers the ecstatic or transcendental moments that he elsewhere calls "spots of time": "Thence did I drink the visionary power / And deem not profitless those fleeting moods / Of shadowy exultation" (*The Prelude*, 1805, 1850). Hart Crane announces his vocation: "And so it was I entered the broken world / To trace the visionary company of love" ("The Broken Tower," 1932).

English poetry began with a vision, the holy trance of a seventh-century illiterate herdsman called Caedmon, who stands as the initial Anglo-Saxon or Old English poet of record, the first to compose Christian poetry in his own language. The story goes that Caedmon invariably fled when it was his turn to sing during a merry social feast. He was ashamed he never had any songs to contribute. One night a voice came to Caedmon in a dream and commanded him to sing about the beginning of created things. "Thereupon," as Bede tells in his *Ecclesiastical History* (731), "Caedmon began to sing verses which he had never heard before in praise of God the creator."

SEE ALSO *descriptive poetry, dream vision, epiphany, imagination, inspiration, vatic, verset.*

voice The human voice — the sound produced by the vocal organs, our ability to produce such sounds — is the instrument of poetry. Poetry is made out of sound. It comes out of silence and ends in silence. It emerges from the body. The range of the human voice is great — from the lowest murmur to the loudest shout, from chanting to singing. Human beings are speaking animals and we speak because we are not alone. Speech is social, language is collective. The first poetry is oral poetry, the artful use of language, which is spoken, chanted, or sung aloud. It is sound that draws attention to itself, going beyond speech. Voice is an active, physical thing in oral poetry. That voice can speak directly (the poet speaks in his own voice) or indirectly (the poet speaks as someone else), but it must be sounded, realized. It needs a speaker and a listener, a performer and an audience. It is a bodily creation that thrives in live connection.

Voice is found in both speaking and writing, but the very nature of voice in written poetry must be metaphorical, it cannot be literal. The material qualities and acoustic range of voice (its tone, timbre, volume, and register) can only be invoked and inscribed. "The desire for live voice dwells in all poets," Paul Zumthor writes in *Oral Poetry* (1990), "but it is in exile in writing." The written poem appeals to the inner ear, the practice of aural reading. "And strangely on the silence broke / The silent-speaking words," Tennyson writes in *In Memoriam* (1849). Every speaker requires a listener, every voice needs an ear, and the printed voice must imagine that listener, its addressee, because it is a communicative act between two people who are not physically present to each other. It therefore textualizes its voice, which is represented in language, recalled through sound. Garrett Stewart calls the complicated act of responding to the written poem "reading voices," a zone of evocalization. When you recite a poem aloud, however, it is no longer disenfranchised from vocalized sound because your own voice becomes its instrument, the mechanism, by which it comes alive. The poem voices itself through you.

Critics speak of "the voice" in a poem to mean its characteristic sound, style, manner, and tone, its implied attitude. To speak of "a poet's voice" then becomes a metaphor for his or her distinctive way of speaking.

SEE ALSO *oral poetry, song, sound poetry.*

visual poetry, see *concrete poetry.*

volta, volte, see *sonnet.*

vorticism Vorticism (1914–1915) was a short-lived collective of writers, painters, and sculptors living in and around London. Wyndham Lewis (1882–1957), who designated himself the Enemy, the Outsider, was the combative founder of this avant-garde movement, which was influenced by the dynamism of Italian futurism and stood for nonrepresentational values in art. Vorticism shouted out its commitment to process in art. The magazine *Blast* provided a forum of assault. Ezra Pound named vorticism and treated it as a successor to imagism. The emblem of *Blast* was a cone and a wire. The idea is traceable to Pound's figure of words as electrified cones, charged with "the power of tradition, of centuries of race consciousness, of agreement, of association" (1912). Pound was activating the image, setting it in motion, and thus defined the vortex as the "point of maximum energy" that also "represents, in mechanics, the greatest efficiency" (1914). He was aiming for a system of energies with a still center. "The image is not an idea," he declared. "It is a radiant node or cluster; it is what I can, and must perforce, call a VORTEX, from which, and through which, and into which, ideas are constantly rushing. In decency one can only call it a VORTEX. And from this necessity came the name 'vorticism' " (1916). Vorticism was powerfully expressed in Lewis's explosive geometric abstractions in painting, in Henri Gaudier-Brzeska's rough-hewn sculptures, and in Pound's kinetic poems of the teens and early twenties.

SEE ALSO *avant-garde, futurism, imagism, modernism.*

vowel rhyme, see *assonance.*

vraisemblance, see *verisimilitude.*

vuelta, see *zéjel.*

waka The Japanese use *waka* to refer to all serious poetry written in Japanese from the earliest literate times. It references poetry as a native possession of Japan. In contrast to popular or religious songs, *waka* refers to the forms of court poetry, such as the tanka. *Waka* is also sometimes used in modern times as a synonym for tanka, in which case it refers to a traditional verse form consisting of five phrases with a syllable pattern of 5–7–5–7–7. A comic *waka* is called a *kyōka.*

Japanese poetry is syllabic, and all traditional forms of Japanese poetry involve five- and seven-syllable lines. Some scholars think the model derives from Chinese poetry; others speculate that the alternating line lengths suited archaic patterns of singing. But no one knows precisely why this syllabic pattern defines traditional Japanese poetry.

Kakekotoba is a "pivot-word," a type of wordplay crucial to *waka.* Pivot-words use sounds that mean two things at once by different parsings. A *makurakotoba,* or "pillow-word," modifies the words it follows in various and sometimes ambiguous ways. Pillow-words amplify. Japanese poetry employs these rhetorical resources to create its sense of a wide expanse released through a compact form. There are two basic terms in Japanese poetics. *Kotoba* refers to the materials of poetry and includes such things as syntax and prosody, diction and imagery, quality of sound and phrasing. *Kokoro* refers to the spirit and feeling, the heart of poetry. Thus *kokoro naki* is poetry without "heart," *kokoro ari* is poetry with a conviction of feeling.

Ki No Tsurayuki's preface to the *Kokinshū* (ca. 905) expresses his belief in the naturalness and human feeling at the heart of Japanese poetry:

> The poetry of Japan has its roots in the human heart and flourishes in the countless leaves of words. Because human beings possess interest of so many kinds, it is in poetry that they give expression to the meditations of their hearts in terms of the sights appearing before their eyes and the sounds coming to their ears. Hearing the warbler sing among the blossoms and the frog in his fresh waters — is there any living being not given to song? It is poetry which, without exertion, moves heaven and earth, stirs the feelings of gods and spirits invisible to the eye, softens the relations between men and women, calms the hearts of fierce warriors.

SEE ALSO *chōka, mono no aware, tanka.*

waka, wakoki (pl) The Hausa Muslim women of northern Nigeria use the word *waka* ("chanted poem") to refer to either a poem or a song, whether oral or written. For men, there are differences between written (*wakar baki*) and oral (*wakar rubutu*) poems, but for women they are virtually the same. The oral and written traditions cohabit easily together, and the poems are performed by both professionals and nonprofessionals. As Barbara Mack explains in *Muslim Women Sing: Hausa Popular Song* (2004), "Chanted verse pervades both men's and women's cultural experience, ranging from devotional expression of Qur'anic verses to the bawdiest of entertainment songs."

wasf, see *descriptive poetry.*

wedding songs, see *epithalamium.*

wedge verse, see *Rhopalic verse.*

Weltliteratur Looking out from the cultural center of Weimar, Johann Wolfgang von Goethe introduced the concept of *Weltliteratur,* or "World Literature." The German poet and classicist Christoph Martin Wieland appears to have coined the term in undated notes to his translation of Horace's letters. Whereas Wieland used it to refer to the world literature of antiquity, Goethe widened it to designate an epochal concert, the emerging literature of all nations and peoples. As he told Eckermann on January 31, 1827: "National literature at present means little; the epoch of world literature is imminent, and we should all assist its early advent." As a writer, Goethe was receptive to foreign influences, and his own work includes pseudo-Persian poetry, Shakespearian dramas, Pindaric odes, and Roman elegies. For most nineteenth-century writers and philosophers, *Weltliteratur* primarily designated "European literature," but it has subsequently had a more generous life designating literatures from around the world. It does not consist of "great books" and "canonic literature," but global literature of all types and kinds, oral and written. In *"Die Weltliteratur"* (2007), Milan Kundera makes an impassioned plea for considering national literatures as part of one world literature.

SEE ALSO *translation, universality.*

Weltschmerz A German word (from *Welt,* "world," and *Schmerz,* "pain") for world weariness, a vague, aching melancholy sometimes associated with romantic poetry. Wilfred Alfred Braun describes it as that "peculiar phase of lyric feeling which has characterized German literature, often in a more or less epidemic form, since the days of *Werther*" (*Types of Weltschmerz in German Poetry,* 1905). He focuses on the melancholy of Friedrich Hölderlin (1770–1843), Nikolaus Lenau (1802–1850), and Heinrich Heine (1797–1856) as "three progressive stages of Weltschmerz viewed as a psychological process."

SEE ALSO *romanticism, Sturm und Drang.*

wheel, see *bob and wheel.*

willing suspension of disbelief What would ordinarily seem incredible is temporarily accepted as believable. The willing suspension of disbelief refers to a reader or an audience's capacious ability to suspend judgment and respond to an unusual fiction — a poem, a play, a novel. Samuel Taylor Coleridge coined the phrase in chapter 14 of *Biographia Literararia* (1817):

> In this idea originated the plan of the "Lyrical Ballads," in which it was agreed, that my endeavours should be directed to persons and characters supernatural, or at least romantic; yet so as to transfer from our inward nature a human interest and a semblance of truth sufficient to procure for these shadows of imagination that willing suspension of disbelief for the moment, which constitutes poetic faith.

Coleridge enlarged his point about poetic faith in an 1816 letter:

> Images and Thoughts possess a power in and of themselves, independent of that act of the Judgement or Understanding by which we affirm or deny the existence of a reality correspondent to them. Such is the ordinary state of the mind in Dreams. It is not strictly accurate to say, that we believe our dreams to be actual while we are dreaming. We neither believe or disbelieve it — with the will the comparing power is suspended, and without the comparing power any act of Judgement, whether affirmation or denial, is impossible. The Forms and Thoughts act merely by their own inherent power . . . Add to this voluntary Lending of the Will to this suspension of one of its own operations . . . and you have the true Theory of Stage Illusion . . .

SEE ALSO *convention, drama.*

wine poetry The medieval Arabic poets had a lively genre of wine poetry called *khamriyyat,* which derived from the social institution of wine parties among Andalusian Muslims. The Abassid wine poem had numerous thematic possibilities. Poets spoke of the need for wine and the joys of drunkenness; they invited and implored others to join them; they provided lush descriptions of wine's color, texture, and provenance; they described the places where drinking is most enjoyed (in taverns, palaces, and gardens, along rivers); they praised their friends who drank with them, fellow partakers; they praised cup-bearers and responded to fault-finders; they celebrated wine's power to overcome grief. The Abbasid poet Abu Nuwas (d. ca. 814) is well known for taking the wine poem, which had been only an occasional element in the classical Arabic ode (*qasida*), and boisterously enlarging it. In the eleventh century, the medieval Hebrew poets adopted the conventions of the Arabic wine poem (Shmuel HaNagid, "Have You Heard How I Helped the Wise"; Moshe Ibn Ezra, "Bring Me a Cup").

Drunkeness is frequently compared to ecstatic union in sacred poetry all over the world. Mystic poets are often "drunk" with God. This motif is especially powerful in Sufi poetry, where wine-drinking is a common metaphor for spiritual intoxication. Jalāl al-Dīn Rūmī writes (#216): "Bring wine, for

I am suffering crop sickness from the vintage; / God has seized me, and I am thus held fast."

SEE ALSO *ghazal, qasida.*

wisdom literature The ancient Near East had an elastic genre of literature and a wide corpus of works known as wisdom literature, much of it poetry. These works of embodied knowledge deal with ethical and religious topics, with moral precepts, and with the nature of divinity. The book of Proverbs, which treats wisdom as something teachable in language, is the central biblical example of ancient Near Eastern wisdom literature. Some early Christian writers simply called it "Wisdom," and it was referred to in the Roman Missal as a "Book of Wisdom."

> A wise man will hear, and will increase learning; and a man
> of understanding shall attain unto wise counsels:
> To understand a proverb and the interpretation; the words of the wise,
> and their dark sayings. (Proverbs 1:5–6)

Wisdom literature includes the book of Job, Ecclesiastes, and the Song of Songs as well as books of Apocrypha known as *Wisdom of Solomon* and *Ben Sira* or *Ecclesiasticus.*

Biblical scholars coined the term *wisdom literature* as a genre for works embodying *hokmah,* or "wisdom." The term was subsequently adapted to other ancient Near Eastern works, such as the Mesopotamian corpus of wisdom texts, which seek to teach the art of leading a successful life in harmony with the divine. It is generally recognized that Proverbs 22:17–24:22 (the "Words of the Wise") borrows from the ancient Egyptian *Instruction of Amenemope* (ca. 1100 B.C.E.), which belongs to the primary didactic literary genre of *sebayt,* or "instruction," and derives from the royal court. Admonitions, a subcategory of wisdom texts, were used to warn against social and moral evils. The word for wisdom in Sumerian is *nam-kù-zu,* which means "pure, sacred knowledge." This sacred knowledge, embodied in proverbs, fables, instructions, disputations, and dialogues, was passed on by master scribes to their pupils through such "rhetorical collections" or "scribal training literature" as *The Instructions of Shuruppak* (ca. 2500 B.C.E.), the most significant piece of Sumerian wisdom literature. It is a carefully constructed collection of poetic instructions on the proper way to live. The Akkadian word for sacred knowledge is *nēmequ,* which appears in the most well-known work of Babylonian wisdom literature: "Let me praise the Lord of Wisdom" (late second millennium B.C.E.). There are two main types of Babylonian wisdom literature. One contains practical advice on how to live, what to do. These are frequently addressed to "my son." The other type reflects more generally on human experiences.

SEE ALSO *didactic poetry, gnome, proverbs.*

wit The ability to make quick, clever connections with verbal deftness, to perceive the likeness in unlike things, relating incongruities and thus awakening the intelligence. *Wit* is a term with a long critical history. In his treatise on *Rhetoric* (ca. 335–330 B.C.E.), Aristotle treated *asteia* (wit) as the ability to make apt comparisons as well as a form of "well-bred insolence." Classical rhetoricians generally used it to mean "cleverness" or "ingenuity." The Latin writers termed it *urbane dicta* (clever or witty sayings). To the Renaissance, the word meant "intelligence" or "wisdom." During the seventeenth century, wit was associated with the metaphysical poetry of John Donne and others, and identified with the ability to create startling, far-fetched figures of speech. "Tell me, O tell, what kind of thing is *Wit,* / Thou who *Master* art of it," Abraham Cowley writes in his witty "Ode of Wit" (1656). Reacting against the metaphysical mode, Dr. Johnson attacked Cowley for "heterogeneous ideas . . . yoked by violence together," a criticism that would later become a descriptive compliment.

Once viewed as an essential feature of poetry, wit was defined by the philosopher John Locke as "the Assemblage of Ideas, and putting those together with quickness and variety." John Dryden characterized it as "sharpness of conceit," thereby emphasizing the shared self-consciousness between the poet and the reader. In "An Essay on Criticism" (1711), Alexander Pope famously contrasted "true wit," guided by judgment, with mere fanciful writing:

> True Wit is Nature to advantage dressed,
> What oft was thought, but ne'er so well expressed.

Rebelling against the association of wit with reason and common sense, the romantic poets employed the concept of imagination to designate the ability to invent and perceive relations. Wit was degraded to a form of levity, from which it has never entirely recovered. In rediscovering the metaphysical poets, T. S. Eliot revived the concept of wit, which he described in an essay on Andrew Marvell as a "tough reasonableness beneath the slight lyric grace."

The meaning of *wit* should come full cycle. From Anne Bradstreet to May Swenson, James Merrill, William Matthews, and Billy Collins, there have always been American poets who have understood that ingenuity is not opposed to, but can serve, feeling in poetry.

SEE ALSO *conceit, imagination, metaphysical poets.*

witness of poetry, poetry of witness Poetry of testimony. In the early 1990s, Carolyn Forché transformed the Polish poet Czeslaw Milosz's phrase *the witness of poetry* (taken from the book of the same name, 1983) into "the poetry of witness." Her anthology *Against Forgetting: Twentieth-Century Poetry of Witness* (1993) gathers together the work of 145 poets "who endured conditions of historical and social extremity during the twentieth century—through exile, state censorship, political censorship, house arrest, torture, imprisonment, military occupation, warfare, and assignation. Many poets did not survive, but their works remain with us as poetic witness to the dark times in which they lived." Poetry, an act of the imagination, is subject to historical forces, but it also talks back to history. The idea of witnessing should be widened to go beyond the documentary response to events. "I am the man . . . I suffered . . . I was there," Walt Whitman declared. A broad imaginative sympathy was part of his lived experience.

In 1944, the Hungarian poet Miklós Radnóti wrote four harrowing "Postcard" poems in the midst of a forced march westward across Hungary. Radnóti was one of twenty-two prisoners murdered and tossed into a collective grave. After the war, his widow had his body exhumed and these poems were found in his field jacket, written in pencil in a small Serbian exercise book. Thus his poems nearly literally rise up from a mass grave. They inscribe a suffering unimaginably intense, a consciousness of death nearly unbearable. They are purposefully entitled "Postcards." Here the informality of the postcard (dashed off, superficial) is belied by the scrupulousness with which

Radnóti describes and re-creates the scene of his impending death. The postcard is a message directed to another person. It has a particular reader in mind, but its openness also suggests that it can be read by anyone. Thus the poem in the guise of a postcard is a testimony back to life, a signal that Radnóti had pushed back the silence long enough to embody a final experience. His poems of witness display the classical brevity and poise of an Orphic art that comes back from the underworld to give testimony.

word square, see *acrostic.*

wordless poetry Poetry without words. Wordless poetry defies the conventional idea that poetry is exclusively a linguistic entity, something that takes place in words. It is a paradoxical concept, since poetry is often viewed as inseparable from language. Christian Morgenstern's poem *"Fisches Nachtgesang"* ("Nightsong of the Fish," 1905) replaces words with the long and short scheme of quantitative poetry. It consists of symbolic marks. Man Ray created a sound poem, "Lautgedict" (1924), in which he canceled the words of a printed poem with a felt-tipped pen, making a crossed-out poem. The instrumental poetry of tribal cultures, such as drum poetry, relies on musical sounds rather than words. Zen poetry is a spiritual poetry that seeks to leave words behind and transcend language.

SEE ALSO *drum poetry, oral poetry, sound poetry, Zen poetry.*

work song The song to accompany work is an oral phenomenon, an ancient, fluid, rhythmic, and utilitarian form of verse. The work song increases labor efficiency by setting a steady pace for a group, timing its strokes. Tomb inscriptions from Egypt (ca. 2600 B.C.E.) include work songs for shepherds, fishermen, and chairmen. There are songs of the well-diggers in Numbers (21:17–18). In ancient Greece, there were songs for making rope and drawing water (fountain songs), for stamping barley and treading grapes, for spinning wool and herding sheep. The earliest French lyrics, called *chanson de toile* and dating from the twelfth century, were short poems to accompany needlework and tapestry weaving. It has been plausibly theorized that the rhythm of Anglo-Saxon poetry was based on the slow pull and push of the oar, whereas the Irish tradition developed a rhythm based on the pounding of hammer and anvil. If so, then English verse, which has a qualitative meter, has its origins in the physical action of work. Whenever the rhythm of certain tasks has become set — sowing, reaping, threshing, washing clothes, milking cows, rowing, hauling and pulling down sail, etc. — then there are accompanying work songs that preserve those rhythms.

African traditional poetry includes songs to accompany such occupations as canoe paddling, milling of rice, marching, and nursing children. The call-and-response pattern of these songs, the interplay between a leader and a chorus (*dokpwe* in Dahomey), carried over to the New World in the form of field hollers and other songs improvised by people forced into slavery, in the lyrics of woodcutters and fishermen, of rural and prison road gangs. In the African American work song, a leader provides a strong rhythmic cue with two or three bars, which are then answered in the ejaculatory word or words of moving workers. The rhythmic interaction makes both poetry and music a participatory activity. The West African pattern also influenced the agricultural songs of Trinidad (*gayap*) and Haiti (*combite*).

A wide variety of Japanese folk songs (*min-yo*) apply to work. The verse forms are based on syllable patterns, rather than meter and rhyme, as in other kinds of Japanese poetry. The repertoire includes earth-pounding songs, sung by communal groups working on roads, pile-driving, and other kinds of hard pounding (*dotsuki-uta* or *jitsuki-uta*), stone-hauling songs (*ishi-hiki-uta*), horse-driving songs (*umakata-bushi*), songs of fishermen and boatmen (*funa-uta*), loom songs (*hata-ori-uta*), songs of lumbermen, which include songs for hauling logs (*kobiki-uta*) and songs for sawyers (*kiyari-uta*), and various specialized songs for agricultural workers in the fields, rice paddies, tea plantations.

Some folklorists have persuasively argued that the work song actually challenges the nature of work by changing the mindset of the workers. The singer supplies a beat and relieves the tedium, transposing the space, creating a different relationship to time. The rhythm of the words — the work that poetry does — actively restructures time. It induces a kind of ritualistic hypnosis, a rhythmic ecstasy.

SEE ALSO *chanson de toile, folk song, oral poetry, rhythm, sea shanties.*

wrenched accent, wrenched rhyme At times the requirements of metrical stress prevail over the natural accent of a word or words. The rhythms of folk songs, for example, do not always correspond to speech rhythms. Folksingers seem to find wrenched accents quite "natural" in performing ballads, as in this stanza from "Sir Patric Spens," which changes the emphasis on the word *máster* to *mastér:*

Late late yestreen I saw the new moone,
  Wi the auld moone in hir arme,
And I feir, I feir, my deir master,
  That we will cum to harme.

A rhyme that depends on a wrenched accent is called a wrenched rhyme. It rhymes a stressed with unstressed syllable, as in the tenth stanza of the anonymous ballad "Mary Hamilton," which wrenches together the words *sae* and *free* so that they rhyme with the word *ladie:*

When she cam down the Cannongate,
  The Cannongate sae free,
Many a ladie lookd oer her window,
  Weeping for this ladie.

SEE ALSO *accent, folk song, meter, prosody, rhyme, scansion.*

ya-du A short Burmese lyric, the *ya-du* generally deals with a romantic or moody feeling, which is evoked by the changing seasons. It is frequently addressed to a lover or wife. Each stanza consists of five lines. The first four lines have four syllables each, but the fifth line lengthens to five, seven, nine, or eleven syllables. The rhymes follow a complex pattern of movement. The rhyme lands on the fourth syllable of the first line, the third syllable of the second line, and the second syllable of the fourth line. The third line ends with a syllable rhyming with the third and second syllables of the following two lines. The fourth line ends with a word that rhymes with the last syllable of the stanza. Not surprisingly, there are typically three or fewer stanzas in this highly codified form.

SEE ALSO *lin-ga, than-dauk.*

the Young Ones (Di Yunge) In America, three young Yiddish poets, all immigrants — Mani Leib, H. Leivick, and Moyshe Leyb Halpern — rejected the revolutionary political aspirations of Yiddish literature and founded a modernist movement that advocated art for its own sake. They published a journal, *Yungnt* (Youth), in 1907–1908, and thus developed their name, Di Yunge. The group, which was primarily active between 1907 and 1925, also included the poets Joseph Rolnik, Reuven Iceland, and Zisha Landau, the leading proponent of art freed from politics, propaganda, moralizing. The poet and translator Yehoash (the pseudonym of Solomon Bloomgarten), the first to translate European and American poetry into Yiddish, anticipated the cosmopolitan interests of this wildly energetic group.

The Young Ones rejected the radical political engagements of other Yiddish groups, such as Di Linke (the Leftist Writers) and the sweatshop poets, and sought to emancipate poetry instead, freeing it to treat romantic mysteries and modern urban life. Their forms were traditional and they were exceeded by the even more modernist group, the Introspectivists. The perennial battle between social engagement and aesthetic values takes vivid shape in modern Yiddish poetry.

SEE ALSO *the Introspectivists, the sweatshop poets.*

Young Vienna (Jung-Wien) Sensuality and despair characterize the poems, plays, and stories — the Aesthetic sensibility and Decadent spirit — of the Young Vienna group, who gathered in the Café Griendsteidl in Vienna in the 1890s. The term *Die Jungen* ("The Young Ones") was first used in politics in the 1870s to apply to a group of young rebels against the Austrian liberal establishment, and then spread to literature as *Jung-Wien.* The writers were well aware of Vienna as the crucible of psychoanalysis.

The Young Vienna group was championed by the critic and playwright Hermann Bahr, who praised their "romanticism of the nerves" (1894). Peter Altenberg's motto for his journal *Kunst* expressed the spirit of the group: "Art is art and life is life, but to live life artistically: that is the art of life." Two of its key writers are Arthur Schnitzler and Hugo von Hofmannsthal. Carl Schorske explains their situation in *Fin-de-Siècle Vienna* (1980): "Hofmannsthal and Schnitzler both faced the same problem: the dissolution of the classical liberal view of man in the crucible of Austria's modern politics. Both affirmed as fact the emergence of psychological man from the wreckage of the old culture." Hofmannsthal declared that the work of modern poets "stands under the decree of necessity, as though they were all building on a pyramid, the monstrous residence of a dead king or an unborn god."

SEE ALSO *Aestheticism, decadence, fin de siècle, Jugendstil.*

Young Vilna (Yung Vilne) This talented, short-lived group of progressive Yiddish poets in the early 1930s took their name from the Lithuanian city in which they worked and tried to live. The group was inspired by the poet Moishe Kulback, who glorified earthiness, and included Hirsh Glik,

Shmerke Kathsherginski, who would become a significant anthologist-historian, Chaim Grade, and Abraham Sutzkever, who would go on to become one of the great twentieth-century Yiddish poets. The life these poets knew in "the Jerusalem of Lithuania," one of the most vibrant centers of European Jewish life, was destroyed when the Germans marched into the city, which was then part of Russia, and set out to extinguish Jewish life. More than seventy thousand Jews of Vilna were murdered in the Ponary Forest, the terrifying symbol of the annihilation of Jewish life. Some twenty thousand Jews were crammed into two ghettos, where they were persecuted by Germans and Lithuanians, until both ghettos were liquidated in September 1943. Most of the Young Vilna poets joined the strong partisan group operating in the forests outside Vilna ("We were dreamers, we had to be soldiers," Sutzkever writes). Glik's song "Zog Nisht Keynmol" ("Song of the Partisans"), which he wrote in the Vilna Ghetto in May 1943, was taken up by Jewish partisans and, after the war, spread to Jewish communities around the world. Sutzkever's poem "The Lead Plates at the Rom Press," which was also written in the Vilna Ghetto in 1943, tells about the plan to melt down the lead plates from a great printing house to form crude bullets:

> Letter by melting letter the lead,
> Liquified bullets, gleamed with thoughts:
> A verse from Babylon, a verse from Poland,
> Seething, flowing into the one mold.
> *(tr. Neal Kozodoy)*

Ruth Wisse points out, "Chaim Grade and Abraham Sutzkever, who miraculously survived the war, seem to represent between them the two poles of contemporary Yiddish writing. Grade carries with him the burden and promise of the religious tradition. . . . Sutzkever belongs to the cosmopolitan brotherhood of art."

yüeh-fu Chinese: "music bureau." Folk songs and imitations of folk songs. The oldest anthology of Chinese poetry, the *Shih Ching* or Chinese *Book of Songs* (tenth to sixth century B.C.E.), traditionally thought to have been compiled by Confucius, is filled with folk songs and poems in the folk song style. The Chinese poetic tradition flows from this source, which valued clarity and wisdom. In 120 B.C.E., Emperor Wu of the Han dynasty (Liu Ch'e), who ruled from 140 to 87 B.C.E. and declared Confucianism the official creed of the state, expanded the *yü-fueh,* or Music Bureau, into a large bureaucracy employing over eight hundred people. Its function was to collect folk songs and ballads from the countryside, as had been done in antiquity. It was also to create poems and songs for ceremonial occasions, rites and sacrifices. Collectively, these folk songs and pseudo-folk songs, which date from the Han period, became known as *yüeh-fu.* Some of these early ballads use irregular line lengths; others rely on five-character or seven-character lines, which makes them formally indistinguishable from the lyric *shih.* The spirit of social protest that animated the early ballads appealed to many later poets, who used the setting of the Han era to comment on contemporary events. Pao Chao (?–466), the master of the *yueh-fu* ballad style during the Six Dynasties period (220–589), often took the persona of an aging, embittered ex-military man to express his disappointment about his own life. The old ballad themes would spring to life again in the T'ang dynasty (616–907). It is estimated that about one-sixth of Li Po's approximately one thousand poems are written in the *yüeh-fu* style. The poet speaks in the voice of a hunter, a peasant girl, a soldier on border patrol. Two of his finest poems, which entered modern poetry in 1915 through Ezra Pound's adaptations as "The River-Merchant's Wife: A Letter" and "The Jewel Stairs' Grievance," are *yüeh-fu.*

SEE ALSO *shih.*

yūgen This elusive Japanese term suggests mystery, subtlety, and depth. There is no exact equivalent in English for the deep aesthetic ideal of elegance and grace. *Yūgen* was originally a Buddhist term that referred to the dark or obscure meanings of the Buddhist Sutras. It means "difficult" or "obscure" in Ki no Yoshimochi's classical Chinese preface to the imperial anthology *Kokinshū* (ca. 905). The term *yūgen* was later applied to poetry and the other arts. It has had a bewildering number of critical interpretations over the centuries. The poet and nobleman Shunzei (1114–1204) was the first to advocate *yūgen* as a major poetic ideal. As he said in the Jūzenshi postscript to the Jichin Oshō Jikaawase, the poetry contest that he judged in 1198 or so:

> In general, a poem need not always attempt clever conceits nor present its ideas fully and systematically. Yet when it is recited, whether it

> is simply read aloud or is formally intoned, there must be something about it which resounds with allure (*en*) and with profundity (*yūgen*).

The term *yūgen* evolved over time to suggest an elusive kind of beauty. It was the aesthetic ideal of the No drama, the masked dance-drama of medieval Japan, which was perfected by Zeami (1363–1443), who believed the actor must develop a poetic sensibility, elegant and suggestive. Robert Brower and Earl Miner point out that despite the critical, historical, and semantic vicissitudes of the term, "the core of yūgen remained the ideal of an artistic effort both mysterious and ineffable, of a subtle, complex tone achieved by emphasizing the unspoken connotations of words and the implications of a poetic situation." As a Zen concept, *yūgen* suggests the paring down of things to their essence. The symbol for *yūgen* is a swan with a flower in its bill. It is a poetic ideal of intensity and restraint, something mysterious and strange.

LeRoi and Hetti Jones took the title *Yugen* ("profound mystery") for their magazine that ran for eight issues between 1958 and 1962.

SEE ALSO *Beats, No play, renga, utaawase, waka, Zen poetry.*

zaum, zaoum The Russian futurists Aleksei Kruchenykh (1886–1968) and Velimir Khlebnikov (1885–1922) were exponents of *zaum,* a coined word that means something like "trans-rational" or "beyond-sense." Trans-rational language (*zaumnyj jazyk* or *zaum*) refers to a kind of sound poetry, a disruptive poetic language that focused on the materiality of words. "It was a language of new words based on Slavic roots and the sounds indicated by individual letters of the alphabet," the translator Paul Schmidt explains. Khlebnikov especially loved puns and palindromes, neologisms, obsessive wordplay, and the magical language of shamans. He found eerie wisdom in separate linguistic sounds, such as *sh, m,* and *v.* He believed that universal truths are secreted in "the self-some word" (*samovitoe slovo*), the sheer materiality of language, and he sought to access them through spells and incantations, magic words, folk etymologies, archaic sounds. The impulse was to test the relationship between sound and sense, to distort language, and to wrench words from their habitual meanings.

The Russian futurists wanted to create an extreme poetic language, a primal speech, a mode of poetic thinking that could transcend common sense and the restrictive features of rational intellect. "If we think of the soul as split between the government of intellect and a stormy population of feelings," Khlebnikov wrote in his essay "On Poetry" (1919), "then incantations and beyonsense language are appeals over the head of the government straight to the population of feelings, a direct cry to the predawn of the soul . . ."

The Russian formalists, especially the literary scholar Viktor Shklovsky and the linguist Roman Jakobson, who wrote *zaum* poetry under the pseudonym Aljagrov, wondered whether or not all poetry aspired to become "trans-sense poetry." Jakobson is explicit in "The New Russian Poetry" (1919): "Poetic language strives, as to its limit, toward the phonetic word, or more exactly, inasmuch as the corresponding set is present, toward the euphonic word, toward trans-sense speech."

SEE ALSO *chants, futurism, palindrome, primitivism, pun, Russian formalism, shaman, sound poetry, spells.*

zéjel A Spanish poetic form, which is called *zajal* in Arabic and *zadjal* in French. The *zéjel* begins with an introductory stanza, a brief initial *estribillo* (refrain) that presents the theme of the poem. This is followed by a tercet, which is called a *mudanza* (i.e., a changing verse, from *mudar,* "to move or change") with a single rhyme (*monorrimo*). The *mudanza,* which at times also had internal rhymes, is followed by the repetition of one or more lines, a *vuelta* — the word means "turn" or "return" — rhyming with the initial stanza. The final line of the *estribillo* and that of the *vuelta* were sometimes shorter than the other lines. It is typically written in eight-syllable lines. The simplest and most common rhyme scheme is *aa, bbba, ccca, ddda,* and so forth.

The *zéjel* most likely was invented by the Hispano-Muslim poet Mucaddam ben Muafa, who was born in Cabra (Córdoba) in the mid-ninth century and died around 902. No *zéjels* by Mucaddam survive, but the invention of the form was reported by Aben Bassám de Santarem in 1109 and Aben Jaldún de Túnez in the fourteenth century. The *zéjel* thus has Arabic origins.

The troubadours picked up the *zéjel* form in the eleventh and twelfth centuries after crossing into Spain, and it was adopted early on by Macabru (fl. 1129–1150) and his patron, William IX, Duke of Aquitaine (1071–1150). The form is several centuries older than the French virelay and the Italian *lauda,* which have similar essential traits, and it most likely served as a model for these quintessential European forms.

The *zéjel* is closely related to the Arabic form *muwashshah.* The major difference is that the *zéjel* is written in vernacular Spanish and the *muwashshah* is written in classical Arabic, though the secular *muwashshah* typically closes with an envoi or closing couplet, which is usually written out in the Arabic or romance vernacular (*kharja*). Both forms are closely associated with music. Indeed, the word *zéjel* means *bailada,* which comes from the word *bailar,* to sway back and forth, to dance.

Both the *zéjel* and the *muwashshah* were cultivated by Arabic and Jewish poets and musicians in medieval Andalusia. The *zéjel* especially thrived in the thirteenth century, but over the centuries, many poets have continued to create *zéjels* among the Arabic peoples of the Mediterranean. As Tomas Narvarro reports in *Métrica Española* (1956), "The writer Aben Said, who died in 1274, said that more zéjels [by Aben Guzmán] were remembered and sung in Baghdad than in the Andalusian cities. The tradition is still alive in the Arab countries; in Tunisia the name *canto granadino* reflects the Spanish origin of the zéjel."

SEE ALSO *estribillo, lauda, muwashshah, octosyllabic verse, troubadour, virelay.*

Zen poetry Zen poetry tries to communicate the ineffable — the world of No-thing — through suggestion. The Japanese word *Zen* (or *Chan* in Chinese) literally means meditation, which Zen Buddhists believe is the Way of *satori* ("awakening"), the path to enlightenment. Zen originated in India and spread to China in the sixth century and then to Japan in the eighth century. Zen Chinese monks began to write poetry as an extension of their meditative practices. Zen poetry has no single formal property, though the Zen Chinese poets wrote quatrains with lines of equal length, and the seventeenth-century master Matsuo Bashō turned haiku into the quintessential Zen art. Zen can be written in any language, though no language is adequate to express its truths, since there is, in essence, no room in Zen for letters or words. The eighteenth-century Zen monk Ryokan states categorically:

> Who says my poems are poems?
> My poems are not poems.
> When you know that my poems are not poems,
> Then we can speak of poetry!
> *(tr. John Stevens)*

There is something helpless in Zen poetry, which tries to express the inexpressible, the realm of the absolute, primordial nothingness that cannot be named. Yet no Zen master poet doubts that this nothingness is present. The poet Jim Haba once said to me that there is poetry without words — a Zen observation. Wallace Stevens finds a Zen moment of stillness at the end of his poem "The Snow Man" (1921) when he recognizes a moment for the listener who, "nothing himself, beholds / Nothing that is not there and the nothing that is."

SEE ALSO *haiku, yūgen.*

ženske pesme, lirske pesme Serbian: "women's songs." A catch-all designation for the women's songs and poetry of the South Slavic tradition. The *junačke pesme* ("men's songs") and *narodne pesme* ("people's songs") were long heroic narratives, which belonged to the domain of epic. The *ženske pesme* were short lyric poems that dealt with such subjects as romance, love, marriage, and death. They were performed either by individuals or groups of women, often on ritual occasions. One of the oddities of the generic distinction is a crossover phenomenon: "men's songs" were sometimes sung by women and "women's songs" were sometimes sung by men. This suggests that in Serbia, whoever actually performs the song, the lyric is considered a "female" genre, the epic a "male" genre.

SEE ALSO *epic, lyric, oral poetry.*

zeugma A figure of speech that derives from the Greek word meaning "yoke." It describes the use of a single word, usually a verb or adjective, to apply to two or more nouns, when the sense is appropriate to only one of them, or appropriate in different ways. It is thus a pairing of two unlike things, a yoking together. It works by incongruity.

Alexander Pope uses a *zeugma* for comic effect in canto 3 of *The Rape of the Lock* (1712–1714) where he matches the verb *take* both to *counsel* and to *tea* to describe Queen Anne at Kensington Palace:

> Here thou, great Anna! whom three realms obey,
> Dost sometimes counsel take — and sometimes Tea.

SEE ALSO *metaphor, rhetoric.*

Credits

Excerpt from *Sir Gawain and the Green Knight: A New Verse Translation,* translated by Simon Armitage, copyright © 2007 by Simon Armitage. Used by permission of W. W. Norton and Company, Inc., and Faber and Faber, Ltd. All rights reserved.

"Yearning for the Emperor Tenji" by Princess Nukada, from *Japanese Love Poems: Selections from the Manyoshu,* edited by Evan Bates, copyright © 2005 by Dover Publications. Reprinted with the permission of Dover Publications, Inc. All rights reserved.

"Rondeau Redoublé" from *Making Cocoa for Kingsley Amis* by Wendy Cope, copyright © 1986 by Wendy Cope. Reprinted with the permission of Faber and Faber Ltd. All rights reserved.

Excerpt from "The Flyting of Dunbar and Kennedy," glossed by John Corbett, from *Language and Scottish Literature,* copyright © 1997. Reprinted by permission of the author and Edinburgh University Press.

Excerpt from "The brain is wider than the sky" [J 632 / F 598] by Emily Dickinson. Reprinted by permission of the publishers and the Trustees of Amherst College from *The Poems of Emily Dickinson,* Thomas H. Johnson, ed., Cambridge, Massachusetts: The Belknap Press of Harvard University Press, copyright © 1951, 1955, 1979, 1983 by the President and Fellows of Harvard College.

Russell Edson, "A Performance at Hog Theater" from *The Tunnel: Selected Poems of Russell Edson,* copyright © 1973 by Russell Edson. Reprinted with the permission of the Permissions Company, Inc., on behalf of Oberlin College Press. www.oberlin.edu/ocpress.

"Ghazal," reprinted from *The Rebel's Silhouette: Selected Poems, Revised Edition* by Faiz Ahmed Faiz, translated by Agha Shahid Ali, copyright © 1995 by Agha Shahid Ali. Published by the University of Massachusetts Press. All rights reserved. Reproduced with permission of Oxford University Press India © Oxford University Press. Unauthorized copying is strictly prohibited.

Excerpt from the 1999 edition of *The White Goddess* by Robert Graves, copyright © 1948, 1952 by Robert Graves, copyright © 1997 by The Trustees of the Robert Graves Trust. Reprinted with permission of Carcanet Press Limited, and United Agents on behalf of: The Trustees of the Robert Graves Copyright Trust. All rights reserved.

Linda Gregg, "Classicism" from *All of It Singing: New and Selected Poems,* copyright © 1981, 1991, 2006 by Linda Gregg. Reprinted with the permission of the Permissions Company, Inc., on behalf of Graywolf Press. www.graywolfpress.org.

Landay, "When sisters sit together, they always praise their brothers./When brothers sit together, they sell their sisters to others" from *I Am the Beggar of the World: Landays from Contemporary Afghanistan,* translated and presented by Eliza Griswold, copyright © 2014 by Eliza Griswold. Reprinted by permission of Farrar, Straus and Giroux, LLC.

"To Poetry" © Edward Hirsch, reprinted by permission of Edward Hirsch. "To Poetry" first appeared in the *Chronicle of Higher Education* "Monday's Poem" feature, edited by Lisa Russ Spaar. Also appeared in *PN Review,* Issue #209.

"Wongòl" by Pyè Banbou (Ernst Mirville), translated by Jack Hirschman and Boadiba, from *Open Gate: An Anthology of Haitian Creole Poetry,* edited by Paul Laraque and Jack Hirschman, copyright © 2001 by the authors; translation copyright © by Jack Hirschman and Boadiba. Reprinted by permission of Northwestern University Press/Curbstone Press. All rights reserved.

Excerpt from *Rhyme's Reason: A Guide to English Verse* by John Hollander, copyright © 1981, 1989, 2000 by John Hollander. Reprinted with the permission of Yale University Press. All rights reserved.

"Arnaut Daniel's 'Canzone: Of the Trades and Love,'" translated by Ezra Pound, from *Translations,* copyright © 1963 by Ezra Pound. Reprinted by permission of New Directions Publishing Corporation.

"The Monk's Tale" from *The Canterbury Tales* by Geoffrey Chaucer and translated by Burton Raffel, translation and notes copyright © 2008 by Burton Raffel. Used by permission of Modern Library, an imprint of Random House, a division of Random House LLC. All rights reserved.

"Praise of Dependent Origination" by Je Tsongkhapa, translated by Geshe Ngawang Samten and Gyaltsen Namdol. Reprinted with the permission of Vice Chancellor Geshe Ngawang Samten and the Central University of Tibetan Studies, Varanasi. All rights reserved.

"Epistle for John Guthrie" by Sydney Goodsir Smith, from *Collected Poems,* copyright © 1975, 2010 by Calder Publications. Reprinted by permission of Alma Books Ltd. All rights reserved.

Excerpt from *The Poems of J. V. Cunningham,* edited by Timothy Steele, copyright © 1942, 1947, 1950, 1957, 1960, 1964, 1965, 1967, 1971, 1973, 1983, 1988, 1997 by Jessie Cunningham. This material is used by permission of Ohio University Press. www.ohioswallow.com.

Ryōkan, ["Who says my poems are poems?"] from *Dewdrops on a Lotus Leaf: Zen Poems of Ryōkan,* translated by John Stevens, copyright © 1993 by John Stevens. Reprinted by arrangement with the Permissions Company, Inc., on behalf of Shambhala Publications Inc., Boston, Massachusetts. www.shambhala.com.

"The Lead Plates at the Rom Press" by Abraham Sutzkever, translated by Neal Kozodoy, from *The Penguin Book of Modern Yiddish Verse* by Irving Howe, Ruth R. Wisse, and Khone Shmeruk, copyright © 1987 by Irving Howe, Ruth R. Wisse, and Khone Shmeruk. Used by permission of Viking Penguin, a division of Penguin Group (USA) LLC.

"The Mystery" by Amergin, translated by Lewis Turco, from *The New Book of Forms* by Lewis Turco, copyright © 1986 by the University Press of New England, Lebanon New Hampshire. Reprinted with permission.

Reetika Vazirani, "Lullaby" from *World Hotel,* copyright © 2002 by Reetika Vazirani. Reprinted with the permission of the Permissions Company, Inc., on behalf of Copper Canyon Press. www.coppercanyonpress.org.

"Rondeau" from *Walking to Sleep: New Poems and Translations* by Richard Wilbur, copyright © 1968, renewed 1996 by Richard Wilbur. Reprinted by permission of Houghton Mifflin Harcourt Publishing Company. All rights reserved.

"Asphodel, That Greeny Flower" by William Carlos Williams, from *The Collected Poems: Volume II, 1939–1962,* copyright © 1944 by William Carlos Williams. Reprinted by permission of New Directions Publishing Corp.

"To a Poor Old Woman" by William Carlos Williams, from *The Collected Poems: Volume I, 1909–1939,* copyright © 1938 by New Directions Publishing Corp. Reprinted by permission of New Directions Publishing Corp.

Index

Index